Lecture Notes in Computer Science 717
Edited by G. Goos and J. Hartmanis

Ian Sommerville   Manfred Paul (Eds.)

Software Engineering – ESEC '93

4th European Software Engineering Conference
Garmisch-Partenkirchen, Germany
September 13-17, 1993
Proceedings

Springer-Verlag
Berlin Heidelberg New York
London Paris Tokyo
Hong Kong Barcelona
Budapest

Series Editors

Gerhard Goos
Universität Karlsruhe
Postfach 69 80
Vincenz-Priessnitz-Straße 1
D-76131 Karlsruhe, Germany

Juris Hartmanis
Cornell University
Department of Computer Science
4130 Upson Hall
Ithaca, NY 14853, USA

Volume Editors

Ian Sommerville
Computing Department, Lancaster University
Lancaster LA1 4YR, UK

Manfred Paul
Institut für Informatik, Technische Universität München
Orleansstr. 34, D-81667 München, Germany

CR Subject Classification (1991): D.2-3, C.3, K.6

ISBN 3-540-57209-0 Springer-Verlag Berlin Heidelberg New York
ISBN 0-387-57209-0 Springer-Verlag New York Berlin Heidelberg

Printed in Germany

Typesetting: Camera-ready by authors
Printing and binding: Druckhaus Beltz, Hemsbach/Bergstr.
45/3140-543210 - Printed on acid-free paper

Foreword

Twenty-five years ago, the first of two NATO workshops to discuss the software crisis was held at Garmisch-Partenkirchen. From these workshops, the discipline of software engineering was born. Now, the fourth European Software Engineering Conference returns to Garmisch to celebrate this 25th anniversary and to look forward to the next 25 years.

More than 135 papers were submitted to ESEC'93 out of which the 27 papers in these Proceedings were accepted. Papers were submitted from most European countries, from the US, Canada, Japan and other Asian countries. Quality was the principal selection criterion for selected papers but the Programme Committee also wanted to ensure that the papers presented included both advanced academic research and the industrial use of software engineering technology.

We have therefore a mixture of themes. Some, such as Software Engineering and CSCW, are forward looking and anticipate future developments; others, such as Systems Engineering, are more concerned with the reports of practical industrial applications. Some sessions, such as that on Software Reuse, reflect the fact that some of the concerns first raised in 1968 remain unsolved problems. The increasing importance of requirements engineering is reflected by the inclusion of two sessions on this topic. The long-term research objectives of understanding the software process and the development of effective environmental support are also covered here.

The submitted papers are complemented by presentations from distinguished invited speakers from Europe and North America. Invited papers cover real-time systems, software measurement and metrics, and industrial software engineering practice. We are particularly pleased to welcome our introductory speakers Professors F.L. Bauer and J. Buxton who played a large part in 1968 and 1969 workshops and who have made a major contribution to the development of software engineering.

The organisation of a major conference is impossible without a great deal of help and support. We are grateful to the members of the Programme Committee and to other reviewers for their time. Pere Botella and Johannes Siedersleben the Tutorial and the Tools Fair organisers have made an important contribution to the success of ESEC'93. Particular thanks also to Jacqui Forsyth at Lancaster University and to Uta Weber at the Technical University of Munich who provided invaluable help with the technical and the local organisation.

European work in software engineering is now comparable with the best in the world and in some fields, such as the use of formal methods, it is generally recognised that European work is pre-eminent. We believe that this series of ESEC conferences, first established in 1987, has contributed to this and we are confident that ESEC'93 will continue the high standard of its predecessors.

July 1993

Ian Sommerville
Manfred Paul

Program Committee

Program Chair

Ian Sommerville, Lancaster University (UK)

General Chair

Manfred Paul, Technische Universität München (Germany)

Tutorial Chair

Pere Botella, Universitat Politecnica Catalunya (Spain)

Tools Fair Chair

Johannes Siedersleben, sd &m (Germany)

Members

D. Barstow (France)
J. Bishop (South Africa)
D. Bjørner (Denmark)
P. Botella (Spain)
M. Broy (Germany)
J. Buxton (UK)
R. Conradi (Norway)
B. Dömölki (Hungary)
A. Endres (Germany)
J. Estublier (France)
C. Fernstrom (France)
A. Fuggetta (Italy)
F. Gallo (Italy)
J. Gorski (Poland)
W. Hesse (Germany)
P. Hruschka (Germany)
G. Kaiser (USA)
M. Lacroix (Belgium)
B. Lang (France)
K. Löhr (Germany)
B. Lennartson (Sweden)
N. Madhavji (Canada)
C. Montangero (Italy)
P. Navrat (Czechoslovakia)
G. Oddy (UK)
H. Obbink (Netherlands)
H.D. Rombach (Germany)
E. Rothauser (Switzerland)
A. Schultz (Austria)
M. Tedd (UK)
E. Tyugu (Estonia)
A.O. Ward (UK)
R.C. Welland (UK)
J. Winkler (Germany)

Reviewers

Z. Banaszak
D. Barstow
W. Bartsch
N. Belkhatir
R. Bentley
J. Bishop
D. Bjørner
G. Blair
L. Blair
P. Bochmann
P. Botella
A. Bradley
M. Broy
X. Burgues
J. Buxton
S. Chobot
R. Conradi
G. Dean
A. Dix
B. Dömölki
H. Ehler
A. Endres
J. Estublier
C. Facchi
C. Fernstrom
P. Forbrig
M. Fuchs
A. Fuggetta
F. Gallo
J. Gorski
T. Gritzner
R. Grosu
J. Handke
W. Hesse
P. Hruschka
H. Hussmann
Y. Ismailov
G. Kaiser
M. Lacroix
B. Lang
K. Löhr
F. Long
B. Lennartson
H. Loeper
N. Madhavji
A. McGettrick
C. Montangero
P. Navrat
D. Nazareth
H. Obbink
H. Oberguelle
G. Oddy
A. Olive
F. Orevas
M. Paul
J. Rowlands
G. Riedewald
T. Rodden
H.D. Rombach
E. Rothauser
K. Sandahl
T. Schafer
A. Schultz
E. Sharkawi
J. Sistac
O. Slavkova
I. Sommerville
K. Spiers
A. Spillner
R. Steinbruggen
K. Stoelen
M. Tedd
E. Tyugu
B. Uologh
T. Uustalu
A.O. Ward
R.C. Welland
J.Winkler

Table of Contents

Invited Papers

Requirements Specification 1

Requirements Specification 2

Environments 1

Environments 2

Systems Engineering 1

Systems Engineering 2

Distributed Software Engineering

Real-Time Systems

Software Engineering and CSCW

Software Reuse

Software Process

Formal Aspects of Software Engineering

On the Decline of Classical Programming

Professor J.N. Buxton

Chairman, Buxton-Douglas Ltd
Chairman, Room Underwriting Systems Ltd
Professor of Information Technology, King's College

Abstract. The paper puts forward the view that we are in a period of fundamental change in the nature of the I.T. business, in that the driving pressures are shifting from the supplier side to the applications user side. In part this is a long-term consequence of the unbundling of software pricing (discussed at the NATO conferences 25 years ago), and in part the consequence of the recent spectacular reductions in hardware costs. The paper discusses the consequences for business, education and research and it indicates the danger of rediscovering the problem of the "software crisis", but at a new level of programming by the applications owners.

1 Introduction

In this paper I shall put forward the view that we are in a period of far-reaching and fundamental change in the practice of Information Technology. This has been a gradual though accelerating process during the 1980s and some of its effects are now becoming apparent in the changes in the structure and activities of industry. The change involves more than a development of maturity after some 40 years since the first use of computers - a central aspect is the increasing shift to the design of computing systems by non-specialists in IT and indeed by those with little interest in the technology per se. The driving pressure on IT development is shifting from the supply side to the user side.

Necessary precursors for this change to come about have been, firstly the unbundling of software prices from associated hardware and secondly, the spectacular drop in hardware costs over the years. This revolution in electronics has given us the PC level of equipment at prices accessible to individuals. In part also the change is based on the development of new programming concepts which are nearer to the application field and which give the user direct access to the services of the machine

In my view a useful and helpful analogy can be drawn with the development of the motor car industry. In the first era before, say 1914, cars were expensive, their operation required the services of specialist engineers, they were far from reliable and their possession was a mark of status and prestige. The "owner-driver" was a wealthy eccentric or hobbyist. All this was changed in the 1920s by the advent of the Model T Ford in the USA and of the Austin 7 in the UK. The car went from being a status symbol for the privileged and the domain of experts to a necessity for ordinary life. Costs became highly competitive and user-friendly standardised interfaces were a necessity for survival in the market. The crucial steps in this transition were an order of magnitude reduction in cost of the hardware and improvements in reliability and usability which made the car simple enough for a non-engineer to learn to use.

In the case of IT, the introduction of spreadsheet systems provides a good example of the advent of technology which made the computer accessible to owners of problems in an application field. These systems are "programmed", but in the language of the accountant and without the services of professional computer programmers. Their use has transformed computing practice.

However, this new wave of applications which are programmed by the application owners has brought its own problems. In essence the activity involved is still programming - though in a very high level language - and in the longer term the critical issue is still that known as "maintenance". All is well while applications are small and personal, but when they become large, complex and even integral to the conduct of the business, and then the author leaves, we have real problems.
There is an urgent requirement to bring to this new field of user-programmed PC applications the same principles of good software engineering as those we need in the more classical programming field. Even with spreadsheet applications and the like, we need to develop well-engineered solutions, well documented and capable of enhancements and maintenance for the full working life of the requirement, by people other than the original author.

In this paper we look first in somewhat more detail at the general features of this new era. Then we turn to an analysis of some specific developments in computer programming and the role of the "professional programmer". Finally, we embark on some speculation as to the future of programming support environments and of research in the field.

2 The transition to the new era

The climate of the first era in computing was set above all by supply side dominance and in particular by the cost of hardware. The early field of technical applications was quickly overtaken by DP applications which became the principal area of use. In general terms, computing was taken on board as a new and expensive technology which would at some time in the future be of great importance. Companies bought computers to reserve their future positions and in the short term there was a passive acceptance of their unreliability, lack of real cost benefits and user-hostile interfaces.

As hardware costs began to fall dramatically in the 1970s and beyond, software began to be seen as the dominant cost and also the major problem. We can quote a few global estimates which have been widely circulated.

- in typical corporate applications, software costs are some 3x hardware costs;
- some 70% of systems cost is in "maintenance" - ie in repair and in enhancement of the software;
- in the US DoD, some 80% of delivered software becomes "shelfware" and is never put into use;
- the Japanese produced a national projected estimate of the need for programmers which suggested that in Japan alone, some 970,000 were needed by the year 2000.

These and many other observations combine to suggest that in aggregate terms, a scarce resource in programming skill is being utilised to a large extent ineffectively, in building expensive software which is of limited utility. This became generally known as the "software crisis".

In the 1980s a view was widely adopted that the software problem could best be addressed by a transformation of the industry, seen then as craft-intensive with inadequate basis in scientific theory or in engineering practice, into a more soundly based and capital-intensive industry. This was to be brought about by the introduction of better methods and by investment in the use of software tools -hence the research into CASE tools, IPSEs, software factories, formal methods and so on, all combined under the general title of "software engineering research".

This period of development, when hardware costs became less significant than software, was one when the supply side dominance of the market continued; though the dominant supply technology was now that of software development.

It is the central thesis of this paper that we are now undergoing a fundamental shift in the nature of the business: dominance of the supply side is now in effect superseded. On the hardware side, the major engine of change has been the development of the PC into the versatile and inexpensive professional workstation, together with the software to enable the user to make effective and direct use of the remarkable level of available computational power. The combination of the modern PC together with networking and with software packages for wordprocessing, spreadsheets, databases and so on has transformed the appearance of computing and has created a new and powerful user community throughout industry and commerce.

A further driving force for change in the current economic climate especially, is the growing realisation of the poor results in cost-benefit terms from much current IT use.

A recent report by the consultants A.T. Kearney states that 89% of British firms do not use technology successfully, and the greatest waste is in computing administration systems.

In other areas of industry the use of IT is an integral and necessary part of the business, where computers have been in use for decades and form integral components of products or production processes, eg in aerospace, banking and the process industries. Here also a process of change is going on, though less spectacular and clear-cut in nature. The process is that of gradual acquisition, by industries where IT is a necessary part of the business, of their own IT skilled personnel. In earlier days such companies relied heavily on the skills of their hardware suppliers to install their systems and on the systems/software consultants to carry out their requirements analysis and systems design. The result was the phenomenon of "locking-in" to a specific set of hardware and to the continuing services for maintenance of a specific systems house.

The rise of in-house skills, together with the spectacular development of a highly competitive market in hardware components means that users are less content now to be locked in. The pressure for open systems supply is now widespread and hardware suppliers are responding to it. Systems houses begin to see their future business as being increasingly as experts in "systems integration", ie in helping users to configure their systems from the best components available regardless of supplier. Users now expect to be able to run their selected packages or their own bespoke systems on new hardware platforms. So, to sell new hardware one must both offer transparent support to old systems and also give freedom for the user to add more software and to combine with hardware from other vendors.

The consequences in the service industry of systems, IT consultancy and software houses is also beginning to be considerable. Variations are wide, for instance between countries, but there seems to be evidence for a drift from traditional areas such as bespoke systems, with continuing supplier maintenance, towards software products which are parameterisable, user enhanceable or indeed programmable, in a sense which we discuss later, by the user.

3 Models of computer programming

The traditional model of software development was that of a multi-stage process often illustrated by a "waterfall model". Firstly, the analysis of user requirements was done by dialogue between the user and the systems analyst. The analyst then specified the system and designed the data structures and algorithms required for the solution. The results included documentation in flow charts, data layouts and so on. In the third stage, the "coding" was done by a real programmer in assembly code at or close to the level of the hardware machine.

The first great breakthrough in improvement of the process, was the development of high level languages in the late 1950s. The adoption of HLLS such as FORTRAN, Cobol and their successors took many years but led to an order of magnitude increase in productivity of the technical staff. In effect the analyst could now programme directly from the level of algorithms and data structures. The grades of systems analyst and programmer tended to merge and the domain of the "real programmer" or machine level expert is mainly now in the specialisms of operating systems or resource critical applications design.

Despite the productivity gains of high level language use, both per se in speeding up coding and indirectly in enabling increased populations to learn to "program" without having to understand detailed machine architecture, nevertheless the "software bottleneck" problem remained endemic in the 1970s and 80s.

There was an increasing strain on the scarce technical staff resource of people - now usually called "software engineers" - who are capable of thinking in IT terms of data structures and algorithms and who can transform a user requirement into an IT solution. The resource continues to be scarce because:

a) under this model of the process, the step of translation of requirements into the design of algorithms is still essential;

b) the increasing numbers of existing systems in use need "maintenance" - ie they must evolve with changing requirements, and they can only be maintained by software engineers.

There is limited scope for training more programmers. Though some largely untapped labour pools exist, it may well be that most of those with the ability to think in algorithms are already in the IT profession. Current directions of development in the area of capital-intensive software factories represent a response to the increase of demand for software skills together with the scarcity of engineers able to respond to the demand. The rationale for this response is that in other branches of engineering capital investment in the production line together with more rational approaches to the process have transformed industries from craft status with substantial success. We will suggest below that this strategy perhaps now looks somewhat outdated and overtaken by events. Indeed, one could take the view that it is based on a false analogy in that building software is a design issue; production is already largely automated by use of a programming language and compiler.

4 The next breakthrough

The development of the spreadsheet is the archetypical example of a next-generation approach. The approach is to automate the closed language of a specific application domain together with a generic algorithm for "solutions" of problems expressed in that domain - with the spreadsheet, the language is that of the rows and columns of figures familiar to accountants, together with arithmetical relationships amongst them, and the system ensures these always balance. So, the user designs and maintains his own "program" expressed directly in the language of the application domain and the intermediate step of designing problem-specific IT algorithmic solutions goes away. When combined with hardware cheap enough for all to afford, the result is a real order of magnitude change in computer use.

The spreadsheet can be regarded as an extreme position on a spectrum of computing systems. At the other end is the classical single applications system, designed and built by IT professionals to meet a user requirement. In between are more flexible approaches which in essence involve reuse of existing software intended to be of wider use than one application - for example, parameterisable systems or systems built around reusable kernels. Such approaches are now the norm for building customised systems where the new design and coding is performed by the IT engineer.

Returning to the real breakthrough area, typified by the spreadsheet, in which IT professionals are not involved as intermediaries in specific applications, we can cite other areas where closed domains have been automated and the user expresses his own problems in domain-specific forms. Wordprocessing is perhaps the widest used example. Text processing in the desk-top publishing area is not far behind. There are further example systems in engineering design and in architecture and other fields.

We maintain that any field in which real IT knowledge is essential to build a computer application is not an example in this class. It is interesting as an intermediate case to consider the currently fashionable issue of "object-orientedness" and to enquire as to whether or not this constitutes a breakthrough. The concepts of classes of objects with sets and attributes were invented as a means of representing real world entities such as machines and vehicles in the field of discrete event simulations in O.R; an early example of the entity - attribute-set model can be found in [2].

The further and important step of the concept of class inheritance was added by Dahl and Nygaard in SIMULA 67. Though objects, attributes, sets and inheritance provide powerful modelling tools for describing, in language close to the users terms, the entities in a problem domain, their rules of behaviour still have to be expressed in algorithmic terms and so object-based applications still need IT designers.

Another major area in which a good case can be made for maintaining that the programming approach of the new era has already arrived is that of DP applications, using 4th generation languages and database construction and enquiry languages. The advance of 4th generation languages has gradually weakened the grip of traditional Cobol programming in the DP field; and this has gone largely unobserved by more technical groups and in particular by academic computer scientists. As an example of the shift to a higher level style of application language domain programming, however, the 4th generation language area is still to some extent an intermediate case as IT knowledge is still essential to construct applications.

We do not propose to go on to consider further points on this spectrum of computer applications such as hypertext, building and vehicle structure design systems etc - suffice it to say that we think the point made that there is indeed a spectrum of a wide and important range of applications where the generation of IT solutions involves less than fully professional IT knowledge and indeed, at the spread sheet and word processing end, needs very limited IT skills.

Conclusions

A centrally important consequence of these developments concerns the projected demand for increased numbers of SW Engineers. A decade ago the rate of demand was increasing steadily and implausible predictions as to the eventual size of the programming population were made. this apparent demand has been eroded as the perceived need to develop ever more specific applications programs has been replaced in many areas by the use of domain-specific packages and user-programmable software. The quasi-potential increase in numbers has occurred: but it is in numbers of problem owners programming their own solutions directly rather than in numbers of software engineers acting as intermediaries between the problem owners and their computers.

As a corollary to this development, the market for new equipment suitable for direct use by problem owners has increased very substantially in order to provide the owners with direct access to their own machines. Sales of PCs and work stations now exceed by orders of magnitude in numbers the sales of main frames, and the PC business is now probably dominant over the mainframe business in financial measures.

Meanwhile, the need for bespoke software systems has not gone away in all application areas. There are many application domains not yet served by user-programmable packages. In particular in the high technology industries the need for large and highly application-specific software, for use in products or in production continues to grow and to be crucial to business success and even to survival.

I think we have not yet taken on board the consequences of this changed pattern of demand for software engineers in, for example, the education system. It may well be that current provisions for training engineers at the higher professional levels will turn out to be of the right order of magnitude, though at present one can only guess as statistics are not yet available. It is reasonably clear, however, that we will need to train large sections, if not most of the population in simple levels of computer familiarisation to aid them in access to the application specific systems they will need.

A further area of interest in speculating on the consequence of these recent changes is that of the development of PSEs, integrated toolsets and methods for support of software production. These were put forward during the 1980s as the essential technical way ahead in turning software production into a capital intensive industry, thereby solving the problem of the projected shortage of software engineers. If the above analysis is correct then the problem for which PSEs were perceived as the solution has in substantial measure gone away. Incidentally the development of PSEs to date has not proceeded as rapidly as was hoped - after some twelve years since the publication of "Stoneman", [3] one sees very few real examples of fully integrated toolsets, though there are very useful CASE tools on the market.

A more promising line of development in support systems and toolsets would now seem to be in the support of flexible and rapidly configurable CASE toolsets to offer support closely aligned to local needs within an organisation which is capable of rapid adaptation as businesses change. We need to pay more attention to the engineering process and to the central requirement for flexibility in that process to meet changing demand.

The need for support systems, and indeed for a more systematic approach to building software, clearly is still a fundamental part of the business. The custom built systems to be supported now include not only the high-tech areas discussed above but also the relatively new and unexplored field of software package production. In this context we include classical parametrisable packages and also the new product ranges of user programmable systems, spreadsheets, user driven database systems and so on. The producers of these systems compete in a market place which demands high quality, fast response to client wishes, low price (which depends on high volume sales) and the market is not unaffected by the dictates of fashion. Here is an area where the concept of the "software factory" really has relevance, but it may require a different sort of factory from those envisaged in earlier years.

Let us now turn to the consequences for research in the IT field. The changes we face now are due primarily to the development, in a few areas, of domain-specific ways of enabling the problem owner to utilise computers in implementing solutions to problems, expressed to the system directly by the user without the intermediate steps of algorithmic solution and bespoke programming. Urgent questions arise as to whether other areas can be found amenable to such approaches - this perhaps is the prerogative of the IT entrepreneur rather than the academic. A proper question for research however is to determine what can be said at a more generic level about domain-specific high level programming. What if any, are its general characteristics, what hypotheses can one make and what theories might be discovered to bring order to this area?

Again and at the level of engineering development, the area of construction of large bespoke systems will continue - both for high-tech fields and in the production of package software product lines - but these areas are also not immune from the need for much deeper involvement of their "users" - albeit technically very aware and competent users - in ensuring that such systems really meet their requirements and can be modified in step with changes to those requirements. We have here a major and relatively unexplored area for software engineering research: how do we build systems which can be maintained, modified and enhanced by their users? Some current work, notably concerned with study of the software process, is already moving in this direction.

Perhaps the most important conclusion, however, is the realisation that the level of success which we have achieved in the new area of very high level domain specific programming techniques has itself opened up a whole new area of emerging problems. Even programming a spreadsheet is still programming in the sense that an IT system is designed and built to fulfil a business purpose which will inevitably evolve and change in time. The spreadsheet model will need to be developed and maintained, and it will tend to grow both increasingly complex and increasingly essential to the business. In a word, we are about to embark on a rediscovery of all the problems of the software crisis - but at a new level of programming.

It is clear that application domain programming by users is still subject to the ailments of classical amateur programming. We observe that unwieldy, opaque and non-maintainable systems could now be even easier to produce than with classical programming. Our most urgent requirement is to bring some grasp of the elements of software engineering to this application world. We need to see the design of these systems carried out by effective engineering techniques and recorded in accessible documentation, so that such systems can be maintained and enhanced into the future. The requirements to bring this about, for instance on the educational system at all levels, are formidable indeed.

References

1. Malcolm, R., private comm., 1991
2. Buxton, J.N. and Laski, J., "Control and Simulation Language", Computer J. vol 5 no.3 (1962)
3. Buxton, J.N., "Requirements for an Ada Programming Support Environment", Department of Defence, 1980

Computers are not Omnipotent

David Harel

Department of Applied Mathematics and Computer Science
The Weizmann Institute of Science, Rehovot 76100, Israel

Abstract. In a cover article in April, 1984, TIME magazine quoted the editor of a software magazine as saying:

> "Put the right kind of software into a computer and it will do whatever you want it to. There may be limits on what you can do with the machines themselves, but there are no limits on what you can do with the software."

In the talk we shall disprove this contention outright, by exhibiting a wide array of results obtained by mathematicians and computer scientists during the last 60 years. Since the results point to inherent limitations of any kind of computing device, even with unlimited resources, they have interesting philosophical implications concerning our own limitations as entities with finite mass.

Technically, we shall discuss problems that are noncomputable, as well as ones which are computable in principle but are provably intractable as far as the amount of time and memory they require. We shall discuss the famous class of NP-complete problems, jigsaw puzzles, the travelling salesman problem, timetables and scheduling, and zero-knowledge cryptographic protocols. We shall also relate these "hard" results to the "softer" ideas of heuristics and artificial intelligence, and point out their relevance to software engineering.

Real-Time Systems: A Survey of Approaches to Formal Specification and Verification*

Carlo Ghezzi, Miguel Felder, Carlo Bellettini

Politecnico di Milano, Dipartimento di Elettronica e Informazione
P.za L. da Vinci 32, 20133 Milan, Italy

Abstract. This paper reviews past work done by our group in the area of formal specification for reactive, real-time systems. Different approaches are discussed, emphasizing their ability to verify formal specifications and systematically derive test cases for the implementation. The specification languages reviewed here are TB nets (a specification formalism belonging to the class of high-level Petri nets) and TRIO (a real-time temporal logic language).
Keywords and phrases Real-time systems, formal specification, requirement capture, Petri nets, high-level Petri nets, real-time temporal logic, analysis, testing, test-case generation.

1 Introduction

Real-time computer systems are increasingly used in the practical world. Moreover, they often constitute the kernel part of critical applications — such as aircraft avionics, nuclear power plant control, and patient monitoring — where the effect of failures can have serious effects or even unacceptable costs. These systems are generally characterized by complex interactions with the environment in which they operate and strict timing constraints to be met. They are real-time, since their behavior and their correctness depend on time: the effect of producing certain results too early or too late, with respect to the expected response time, may result in an error.

Existing semi-formal methods supporting specification, design, verification and validation of real-time systems ([16, 30, 15]) provide very limited support to high-quality software in the above domains. First, they often address only one or a limited set of the phases of the application development. Second, their semantics is informally defined, and therefore they provide no or partial support to analysis and execution. Most existing formal methods, on the other hand, are difficult to use, often lack facilities for handling real-time and for structuring large specifications, and provide limited tool support.

In the past, our group has been working in the area of formal specifications for reactive, real-time systems, with the goal of:

* This material is based upon work supported by the Esprit project IPTES, and by the Progetto Finalizzato Sistemi Informatici e Calcolo Parallelo (CNR).

- **Understanding different specification paradigms.** Our belief is that "the" correct approach to the problem does not exist. Rather, we will eventually need to integrate different approaches in a specification support environment. In our work, we pursued research in two complementary directions: specifications based on an operational approach (namely, Petri nets) and specifications based on a descriptive approach (namely, real-time temporal logic).
- **Supporting verification of formal specification.** Requirements capture for a new application is a highly critical activity, which can have a far-reaching impact on the quality of the product. Requirements errors are often discovered very late, when the system has been delivered to the final user and is operational in the target environment. At this point, however, not only the cost of (part of) the development effort would be wasted, but also the cost of failures would bear on the cost of the application. Our goal has therefore been to ensure that specifications are verified before proceeding to implementation, so that errors are not inadvertently transferred from requirement specification down through the whole development cycle. In this paper, we use the term "verification" as an umbrella concept that captures all forms of assessment of a specification[2]. In particular, we will discuss two complementary forms of verification: static verification (which includes a whole range of possibilities, from static semantic checking to all forms of mathematical proofs) and dynamic verification (i.e., testing). We also discuss symbolic execution, which is somehow in the middle between the two approaches.
- **Supporting the specification activity through an integrated set of tools.** Formal methods are intrinsically more supportive of mechanical manipulation than informal methods. Tools may in fact be based on both the syntax (e.g., syntax-directed editing tools) and the semantics (e.g., semantic checkers) of the formalism. Tool support is essential to promote the use of formal methods among users.
- **Enhancing usability of the formalism.** Formal methods are very often based on languages that non-mathematicians find difficult to read and write. The syntax of the language is often awkward; no graphical description facilities are provided; no modularization and abstraction mechanisms are available to structure large specifications; and no application-specific concepts can be added to the language. Tool support is a first step towards improving usability, but more is needed. In the work done by our group, a layered approach was followed. The start point is a concise, clean, and mathematically defined notation. Other linguistic layers were then defined on top of the kernel in order to provide more expressive, user-oriented notations. Structuring mechanisms were also provided to allow specifications to be modularized according to the principles of abstraction and information hiding. In the case of the Petri net approach, we also defined a way to

[2] Note that other authors distinguish between verification and validation. Others distinguish between verification, intended as formal verification, and testing.

make the specification notation extensible, by providing a definitional device (based on graph grammars) through which new graphical specification notations may be added.

- **Supporting subsequent development steps (design, implementation, testing, etc.).** There are approaches where the formal specification is transformed into an implementation through predefined and partially automated transformation steps. In the work done by our group, this aspect has not been investigated so far. Work has been done in the derivation of test cases from the specification; such test cases can be used to verify an implementation.

This paper provides a comprehensive view of the work done by our group in the two aforementioned research directions. The discussion is mainly based on a survey of previously published work; most notably, [10, 11, 12, 14] for the Petri net based approach, and [13, 7, 21, 24] for the real-time logic based approach.

The paper is structured as follows. Section 2 surveys TB nets and their verification methods. TB nets are a class of high-level Petri nets. Their definition is provided in Section 2.1. Section 2.2 deals with CABERNET, an environment designed to support net-based specification and verification of real-time systems. Section 2.3 focuses on the verification facilities provided by CABERNET to support timing analysis, while Section 2.4 focuses on structuring mechanisms. Section 3 surveys the real-time logic language TRIO, its verification, and its support to implementation verification. In particular, the language is presented in Section 3.1. TRIO's formal semantics is discussed in Section 3.2. Section 3.3 deals with different kinds of TRIO verification and shows how the specification can provide support for implementation verification. Section 3.4 discusses how TRIO can support formal verification. Finally, Section 4 draws some conclusions and outlines future work. Section 3.5 outlines the extensions proposed to include structuring mechanisms in a real-time logic.

2 TB Nets: an operational specification language

Time Basic nets (TB nets) ([11]) are an extension of Petri nets ([31]). TB nets have been introduced in [11]. In this paper, we introduce them rather informally by using a slightly different notation than in [11].

2.1 The language

In TB nets, each token is associated with a *timestamp*, representing the time at which the token has been created by a firing. Each transition is associated with a *time-function*, which describes the relation between the timestamps of the tokens removed by a firing and the timestamps of the tokens produced by the firing.

Definition 1 (TB nets). A TB net is a 6-tuple $< P, T, \Theta; F, tf, m_0 >$ where

1. P, T, and F are, respectively, the sets of places, transitions, and arcs of a net. Given a transition t, the preset of t, i.e., the set of places connected with t by an arc entering t, is denoted by ${}^\bullet t$; the postset of t, i.e., the set of places connected with t by an arc exiting t, is denoted by $t^\bullet$.
2. Θ is a numeric set, whose elements are the timestamps that can be associated with the tokens. The timestamp of a token represents the time at which it has been created. For instance, Θ can be the set of natural numbers, or the set of non-negative real numbers. In the following, we assume $\Theta = \mathbb{R}^+$ (the set of non-negative real numbers; i.e., time is assumed to be continuous).
3. tf is a function that associates a function tf_t (called time-function) with each transition t. Let en denote a tuple of tokens, one for each place in the preset of transition t. Function tf_t associates with each tuple en a set of values θ ($\theta \subseteq \Theta$), such that each value in θ is not less than the maximum of the timestamps associated with the tokens belonging to tuple en. $\theta = tf_t(en)$ represents the set of possible times at which transition t can fire, if enabled by tuple en. When transition t fires, the firing time of t under tuple en is arbitraryly chosen among the set of values θ. The chosen firing time is the value of the timestamps of *all* the produced tokens.
4. m_0, the *initial marking*, is a function associating a (finite) multiset of tokens with each place. In general, we use function m to denote a generic marking of nets, i.e., $m(p)$ denotes the multiset of tokens associated with place p by marking m.

The set T is partitioned into two sets ST and WT, the set of *Strong Transitions* and *Weak Transitions*, respectively. If a transition belongs to ST, then, if it is enabled, it *must* fire within its maximum firing time, as defined by function tf, unless it is disabled by some other firing. Instead, if a transition in WT fires, it fires if it is enabled and before its maximum firing time has expired (i.e., a weak transition *can* fire, but it is not forced to fire). Actually the initial marking m_0 of a TB net must ensure that there exists no enabling $< en, t >$, with $t \in TS$, such that the maximum firing time of t under tuple en is less than the maximum of the timestamps associated with the tokens in m_0.

In [11] a deeper discussion is presented where the two kinds of transitions lead to the definition of different semantics for the TB nets. The first class is there referred to as *Strong Time Semantics* while the other is referred to as *Weak Time Semantics*. In [11] it is shown how Weak Time Semantics is closer to the original semantics of Petri nets, while the other is closer to the intuitive notion of time evolution.

In order to define the rule by which new markings of the net may be generated, starting from the initial marking m_0, we need to define the concepts of *enabling tuple*, *enabling*, *firing time*, and *enabling time*.

Definition 2 (Enabling tuple, enabling, firing time, enabling time). Given a transition t and a marking m, let en be a tuple of tokens, one for each input place of transition t, the transition t can fire at a time instant τ under tuple en if and only if :

1. $\tau \in tf_t(en)$;
2. τ is greater than or equal to the time associated with any other token in the marking;
3. τ is not greater than the maximum firing time of every other strong transition enabled in the marking

If $tf_t(en)$ is empty, there exists no time instant at which transition t can fire under tuple en; i.e., transition t is not enabled under tuple en. If $tf_t(en)$ is not empty, en is said to be an *enabling tuple* for transition t and the pair $x =< en, t >$ is said to be an *enabling*. The triple $y =< en, t, \tau >$ where $< en, t >$ is an enabling, $\tau \in tf_t(en)$, and t can fire at instant τ under tuple en is said to be a *firing*. τ is said to be the *firing time*. We refer to the maximum among the timestamps associated with tuple en as the *enabling time* of the enabling $< en, t >$.

The dynamic evolution of the net (its semantics) is defined by means of firing occurrences, which ultimately produce firing sequences.

Definition 3 (Occurrence of a firing in a marking). Given a marking m and a firing $y =< en, t, \tau >$ such that en is contained in m, and t can fire at instant τ under tuple en, the firing occurrence of y in m produces a new marking m', that can be obtained from m by removing the tokens of the enabling tuple en from the places of ${}^\bullet t$, and producing a new token with timestamp τ in each of the places of $t^\bullet$. If x is a firing that produces marking m' from m we write $m[x > m'$.

Figure 1 shows a fragment of a TB net. Places $P2$ and $P3$ are marked with a token whose timestamp is 0. The timestamp associated to the token in place $P1$ is 1. Transitions $T2$ and $T3$ are strong; transition $T1$ is weak.

Function tf_{T1} states that transition $T1$ can fire at a time between the maximum time of the timestamps of the tokens in the place $P1$ and $P2$, and 5 time units after the value of the timestamp of token in $P2$. Transition $T1$ is weak and so it is possible that it does not fire also if the transition is enabled. In the example, this transition is enabled and the possible firing time is any value in [1,5].

Function tf_{T2} states that transition $T2$ can fire at a time between 8 time units after the maximum time of the timestamps of the tokens in the place $P1$ and $P2$, and 10 time units after the value of the timestamp of token in $P2$. In the example, this transition is enabled and the possible firing time is any value in [9,10].

Function tf_{T3} states that transition $T3$ can fire at a time between 3 and 15 time units after the value of the timestamp of token in $P3$. In the example, this transition is enabled and the possible firing time is any value in [3,10]. In fact, it cannot fire at a time greater than 10 unless transition T2 fires before (within 10).

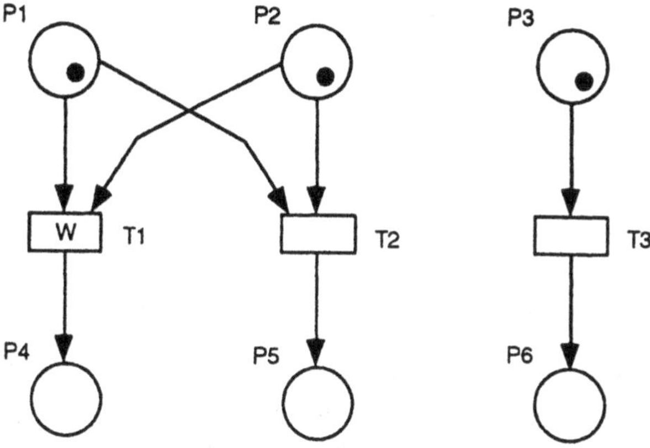

$tf_{T1}(P1, P2) = \{\tau \mid max(P1, P2) \leq \tau \leq P2 + 5\}$
$tf_{T2}(P1, P2) = \{\tau \mid max(P1, P2) + 8 \leq \tau \leq P2 + 10\}$
$tf_{T3}(P3) = \{\tau \mid P3 + 3 \leq \tau \leq P3 + 15\}$
$m(P1) = \{1\};\ m(P2) = \{0\};\ m(P3) = \{0\}$

Fig. 1. A Simple TB net.

2.2 An introduction to the CABERNET environment

CABERNET ([29]) is an environment designed to support specification and verification of real-time systems based on high-level Petri nets[3].

CABERNET provides editing facilities to describe nets and execution facilities to animate them. By executing the net, it is possible to test a specification to detect specification errors. CABERNET provides different facilities to control execution, such as:

Execution mode: It is possible to execute a net with respect to the temporal constraints or as a pure net; i.e., ignoring timing information attached to both tokens and transitions.

Step mode: The user can direct the interpreter to proceed in single step mode, i.e., the interpreter waits for a command after each firing or each phase of a firing (e.g., identification and choice of the enabling, evaluation of the action, etc.).

Enabling choice: If required the user can select the enabling to fire. In the other case this is chosen nondeterministically.

Firing time choice: Once an enabling is chosen for firing, the firing time can be chosen according to different options:

---

[3] The acronym stands for Computer-Aided software engineering environment Based on ER NETs. ER nets are the kernel formalism of the environment. ER nets are Petri nets augmented with features to describe data, functionality, and control ([11]). TB nets are a timed formalism which is defined on top of ER nets.

Random: The firing time is chosen randomly in the set of possible firing times of the enabling.

Lowest/Highest: The lowest (respectively, highest) firing time for the enabling is chosen.

User choice: The user is prompted to choose one among the possible firing times.

CABERNET provides facilities for analyzing nets. In particular, it supports certain kind of verification of timing requirements, as we will show in Section 2.3. Finally, one of the goals of CABERNET is to support customization of the specification notation by means of a tool, called Meta-editor. The Meta-editor allows new graphical notations to be added to the environment, by defining not only their syntax, but also their semantics in terms of translation to the underlying kernel notation (ER nets).

In this way, the specification environment is open and extensible. User-oriented and application-oriented interfaces can be formally defined, and specifications written in the newly defined notations can be formally manipulated. We developed examples of this approach, such as the definition of Statecharts in terms of ER nets. The definition of the mapping between the external graphical language and the kernel notation is formally specified by means of graph grammars ([27]).

2.3 Verification of TB nets

The importance of executing formal specifications to validate requirements has been advocated, among others, by [19]. By executing formal specifications and observing the behavior of the specified system, one can check whether specifications capture the intended functional requirements or not. In other words, by executing requirements, we perform testing in the early phase of the development process. Although testing cannot prove the absence of errors, it is especially valuable as a mechanism for validating functional requirements.

The previous description of CABERNET shows how the available execution facilities provide some basic support to specification testing. In this section, we discuss two other forms of verification provided by CABERNET, which support verification of timing properties.

Symbolic execution. Symbolic execution is a well-known technique for analyzing sequential programs. It can be applied with different goals, such as verifying correctness of a particular path for all the input data which cause the execution of a particular path, synthesizing test data for a path.

In [4], symbolic execution is extended to deal with concurrent programs. In [12] symbolic execution is proposed as a method for analyzing a subset of TB nets, while [23] applies this proposal for validation of concurrent ADA^{TM} programs. Let us now briefly introduce the mechanism for symbolically execute a TB net.

Let us suppose that the tokens of the initial marking contain symbolic values for the timestamps. Let C (*Constraint*) be a boolean expression initialized by the user to describe the initial constraint on the timestamps. C is used to record the assumptions made on the timestamps and therefore plays the role of the Path Condition in the sequential case. Let ES (*Execution Sequence*) be a data structure recording a firing sequence. The pair $< C, ES >$ fully characterizes a symbolic execution. Below we describe a symbolic execution algorithm using $< C, ES >$.

At each transition firing, the symbolic interpreter incrementally update C, ES and the current symbolic marking m. The whole execution is based on the symbolic initial marking; that is, every symbolic value of the token timestamp is an expression derived from a sequence of elaborations starting from the symbolic values of the initial marking. The symbolic execution algorithm is decomposed in six steps. The algorithm is described below with reference to the example of Figure 1:

Step 0 : Initialization

The initial marking m_0 is defined by providing symbolic values for the timestamps of the tokens initially stored in the places, and by providing an initial constraint (C) on such timestamps. ES is initialized to NIL.

In the example, we can assume a symbolic marking in which places $P2$ and $P3$ contain a token whose associated timestamp τ_0 can assume any value between 0 and 10, and place $P1$ contains a token whose associated timestamp τ_1 can assume any value greater than τ_0 and less than $\tau_0 + 15$. Thus, the initial constraint is:

$C_0 = 0 \leq \tau_0 \leq 10 \ \wedge \ \tau_1 \geq \tau_0 \ \wedge \ \tau_1 \leq \tau_0 + 15$

Step 1 : Identification of the set of enabled transitions in the current marking

For each transition t potentially enabled by a tuple en (i.e., there is at least a token in each place of its preset), evaluate if there is some time value $\tau_{new} \in tf_t(en)$ that satisfies C and τ_{new} is greater than or equal to the last symbolic firing time and is less than the maximum firing time of any other enabled strong transition.

In the example the three transitions are all enabled. For instance, $T3$ is enabled because the expression that results by the conjunction of the following inequalities is satisfiable :

- C_0 (i.e., the previous constraint)
- $\tau_0 + 3 \leq \tau_{new} \leq \tau_0 + 15$ (i.e., $\tau_{new} \in tf_{T2}(en)$)
- $\tau_{new} \geq \tau_1$ (i.e., there is no other timestamp in the net that is greater than τ_{new})
- $\tau_{new} \leq \tau_0 + 10 \ \vee \ \tau_0 + 10 < \tau_1 \ \vee \ \tau_1 + 8 > \tau_0 + 10$ (i.e., either the firing is less than the maximum firing time of the other strong transition, or the other strong transition is not enabled.)

Step 2 : Selection of the enabling to fire

An *enabling* $< t, enab >$ of those found at the step 1 can be selected nondeterministically or according to the user's interaction.

Step 3 : Update of C

C is updated with the (possibly simplified) constraint built in the step 1 for the chosen enabling. If there is only one possible symbolic value of τ_{new} that satisfies the constraint, it is possible to substitute the variable τ_{new} with the symbolic expression. In most of cases, it is necessary to build a new symbolic value for the new variable.

In the example, if transition $T3$ is chosen, the new C will be:

$0 \leq \tau_0 \leq 10 \ \wedge \ \tau_0 \leq \tau_1 \leq \tau_0 + 15 \ \wedge \ \tau_0 + 3 \leq \tau_2 \leq \tau_0 + 15 \ \wedge$
$\tau_2 \geq \tau_1 \ \wedge \ (\tau_2 \leq \tau_0 + 10 \ \vee \ \tau_0 + 2 < \tau_1)$

Step 4 : Transition firing and marking update

Transition t of the enabling selected at step 2 is fired, i.e., the enabling tuple *enab* is removed from the places of $^\bullet t$ and new tokens are inserted into places of $t^\bullet$, bound to a symbolic expression that represents the possible firing times, or to a new symbolic value, as shown above.

In the example, the new marking will consists of a token (τ_0) in the place $P1$, a token (τ_1) in the place $P2$ and a token (τ_2) in the place $P6$.

Step 5 : Update of ES

Finally, ES should also be updated:

$ES_{new} := append(< t, enab >, ES_{old})$

Timing analysis. Reachability analysis is traditionally understood as finite enumeration of reachable states of some finite state model ([33]). It has been extended, however, to cope with infinite state models. This is the case of conventional Petri nets that can have an unbounded number of tokens in some places. In the case of infinite state models, analysis procedures have been derived, where states are grouped in (possibly infinite) sets and reachability analysis is then applied to such sets.

The techniques used for reachability analysis of (unbounded) Petri nets cannot be applied to the analysis of TB nets, since they group together the markings that differ only in the number of tokens in the marked places. In the case of TB nets, markings differ also in the timestamps associated with the tokens. For example, the number of states (markings) reachable in the TB net of Figure 1 by the firing of transition $T3$ is infinite, because the timestamp associated to the token in place $P6$ can be any real value in the interval $[3, 10]$.

[14] presents a technique for reachability analysis of TB nets, where each reachable state is symbolic, and represents a (possibly infinite) set of states of the TB net. That is, the technique is based on the symbolic execution presented in Section 2.3. In the general case, the analysis produces an infinite tree. However, [14] shows that the number of tree nodes to be examined for proving an interesting set of temporal properties is finite. Such properties may be classified in two sets: *bounded invariance* and *bounded response*.

A *bounded invariance* (or *timed safety*) property states an invariant property that must hold until a certain lower bound for time is reached. A *bounded response* (or *timed liveness*) property specifies that a certain property eventually holds, before an upper bound for time is reached.

The technique builds a *symbolic time reachability tree* (TRT). A node of the tree represents a symbolic state. A symbolic state is composed by the constraint C (specified as before) and a symbolic marking. A symbolic marking is a function μ from places to multisets of symbolic values. The symbolic values represent sets of numeric values for the timestamps associated with tokens in the marked places. An arc of the tree represents the symbolic firing of a transition. Starting from the root of the tree, which represents the initial symbolic marking, the tree is built by using rules similar to those of symbolic execution.

The TRT of the net in Figure 1 is shown in Figure 2. Nodes are graphically represented by two symbols: circles and squares. A circle indicates that it is possible that no transition is enabled in that symbolic state. For example, if the value of the token in $P1$ is greater than $\tau_0 + 10$ in the state $S3$ there is no transition enabled. The arcs are labeled with the name of the respective firing transition. Any set of values satisfying the constraint C associated to a node represents a feasible firing time schedule of the net up to the transition leading to such a node.

In the CABERNET environment, the procedure sketched above is implemented by a tool for specification analysis called MERLOT ([1]). MERLOT allows the user to prove bounded response and bounded invariance properties of the specified system. More specifically, the tool allows one to prove the following properties:

Occurrence of events (firings) or of special states (markings). Properties can assert either that there exists at least one execution of the system where some states or events are reached or that all possible executions reach these events or states within a given time limit. Example states in the example are those characterized by a token in the place $P1$ and a token in the place $P5$.

Sequence of events and states. Properties can assert some precedence constraints between different states and events. For example, that the firing of $T3$ is followed by a firing of $T1$.

Time of occurrence of events. Properties can assert some constraints on the firing time. For example that the firing time of the transition $T3$ is greater of the firing time of $T2$ plus a constant.

Any logical combination of the previous properties can also be expressed as a property to be proved.

2.4 Abstractions and hierarchies

Net-based specifications suffer from the lack of adequate structuring mechanisms. In practice, specifications may become hard to read and understand, and verification procedures may become very inefficient, as the size of the net reaches certain bounds. In particular, reachability analysis suffers from the state explosion problem.

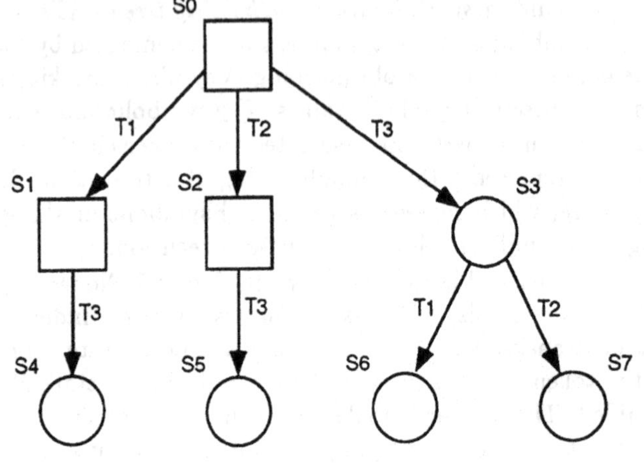

S0: $C_0 := \tau_0 \geq 0 \ \wedge \ \tau_0 \leq 10 \ \wedge \ \tau_1 \geq \tau_0 \ \wedge \ \tau_1 \leq \tau_0 + 15$
Marking:= $\mu(P3) = \{\tau_0\}$; $\mu(P2) = \{\tau_0\}$; $\mu(P1) = \{\tau_1\}$
S1: $C_1 := C_0 \ \wedge \ \tau_2 \leq \tau_0 + 5 \ \wedge \ \tau_2 \geq \tau_0 \ \wedge \ \tau_2 \geq \tau_1$
Marking:= $\mu(P4) = \{\tau_2\}$; $\mu(P3) = \{\tau_0\}$
S2: $C_2 := C_0 \ \wedge \ \tau_3 \geq \tau_1 + 8 \ \wedge \ \tau_3 \leq \tau_0 + 10$
Marking:= $\mu(P5) = \{\tau_3\}$; $\mu(P3) = \{\tau_0\}$
S3: $C_3 := C_0 \ \wedge \ \tau_4 \leq \tau_0 + 15 \ \wedge \ \tau_4 \geq \tau_1 \ \wedge \ \tau_4 \geq \tau_0 + 3 \ \wedge \ (\tau_1 > \tau_0 + 2 \ \vee \tau_4 \leq \tau_0 + 10)$
Marking:= $\mu(P6) = \{\tau_4\}$; $\mu(P2) = \{\tau_0\}$; $\mu(P1) = \{\tau_1\}$
S4: $C_4 := C_1 \ \wedge \ \tau_5 \geq \tau_0 + 3 \ \wedge \ \tau_5 \leq \tau_0 + 15 \ \wedge \ \tau_5 \geq \tau_2$
Marking:= $\mu(P6) = \{\tau_5\}$; $\mu(P4) = \{\tau_2\}$
S5: $C_5 := C_2 \ \wedge \ \tau_6 \geq \tau_0 + 3 \ \wedge \ \tau_6 \leq \tau_0 + 15 \ \wedge \ \tau_6 \geq \tau_3$
Marking:= $\mu(P6) = \{\tau_6\}$; $\mu(P5) = \{\tau_3\}$
S6: $C_6 := C_3 \ \wedge \ \tau_7 \leq \tau_0 + 5 \ \wedge \ \tau_7 \geq \tau_4$
Marking:= $\mu(P6) = \{\tau_4\}$; $\mu(P4) = \{\tau_7\}$
S7: $C_7 := C_3 \ \wedge \ \tau_8 \geq \tau_1 + 8 \ \wedge \ \tau_8 \leq \tau_0 + 10 \ \wedge \ \tau_8 \geq \tau_4$
Marking:= $\mu(P6) = \{\tau_4\}$; $\mu(P5) = \{\tau_8\}$

Fig. 2. The TRT of the TB net of Figure 1.

We addressed these issues by allowing nets to be defined in a hierarchical, top-down manner, where one specification level implements a more abstract level. We defined what it means that a TB net I is a correct implementation of a TB net S. Intuitively, I is an implementation of S if I adds details (i.e., transitions, arcs, and places) and possibly restricts the set of behaviors that are possible at the S level. If I is a correct implementation, then if certain properties have been proved to hold for the specification, they also hold for the implementation. This result is important since it allows properties to be proved for a net of limited size, and then extended to a net of larger size, under certain assumptions on the relationship between the two nets. Furthermore, a number of constructive rules have been defined through which a specification may be refined into a correct implementation. If these rules are followed, it is not necessary to prove the correctness of the implementation relation a-posteriori, since it is guaranteed to hold a-priori. These results are formally presented in [5].

As we mentioned, large net-based specifications are quite difficult to understand. Hierarchical definition helps, but does not solve the problem. Although nets are a graphical formalism, specifications are written according to mathematical abstractions, not using user and application-oriented concepts. Moreover, the specification language is defined once for all; it is not tailorable or adaptable to the needs of the specifier. On the other hand, it would be useful to provide a specification formalism that can be customized to match the specific needs of a specifier. It would also be useful to provide a notation that uses graphical concepts that are familiar to the user, so that requirements verification can be done more effectively. For example, in a control system for a hydraulic plant, user-oriented graphical abstractions may include valves that can be open or close, pipes, etc. This issue has considered by CABERNET, which allows a Meta-user to formally define new language layers on top of the underlying kernel formalism, using the Meta-editor mentioned in Section 2.2.

3 TRIO: a descriptive specification language

TRIO is a first-order temporal logic language for executable specification of real-time systems. The language deals with time in a quantitative way by providing a metric to indicate distance in time between events and length of time intervals.

A major goal of TRIO is *executability of specifications*. This means that TRIO formulas can be automatically checked for satisfiability or validity ([7]). When a formula specifying a given property of a system is interpreted, a *model* thereof is generated. Of course, since TRIO contains first-order theories, executability is undecidable in the general case. However, an analysis procedure on finite domains can be performed algorithmically by using the Tableaux Method ([32]), which provides an abstract interpreter of the language. The tableaux method is a widely used technique in temporal logic to constructively verify the satisfiability of a formula and to derive implementations from models of specification formulas ([22]). Although TRIO specifications are often stated by assuming an underlying infinite structure, such analysis may increase the confidence in the correctness of the specifications in much the same way as testing a program may increase the confidence in its reliability. That is, by examining the system behavior on finite domains, the user may infer the behavior on infinite domains. Such a generalization, however, cannot be proven, and can only be performed under the user's responsibility.

3.1 The TRIO language

The purpose of the following brief presentation of the TRIO language is to make the paper self-contained, *not* to provide a complete discussion of its features and its practical use. A complete description can be found in [25], [13], and [24].

TRIO is a first-order logic language, augmented with temporal operators that allow the specifier to express properties whose truth value may change over time. The meaning of a TRIO formula is not absolute, but is given with respect to a current time instant which is left implicit in the formula, in much the same way as in temporal logic.

Syntax: the temporal operators. The alphabet of the TRIO language includes sets of names for variables, functions, and predicates, and a fixed set of basic operator symbols. Variables are divided into *time dependent* (TD) variables, whose value may change with time, and *time independent* (TI) variables, whose value is intended to be invariant with time. Every variable name x has an associated *type* or *domain*, which is the set of values the variable may assume. A distinguished domain, required to be numeric, is called the *Temporal Domain*. Every function name has an associated arity $n \geq 0$ (when $n=0$ the function is called a *constant*), and the indication of a type for every component of the domain and for the range. Similarly, every predicate name is associated with the number and type of its arguments. Like variables, predicates are divided into time dependent and time independent ones: time independent predicates always represent the same relation, while a time dependent predicates correspond to a possibly distinct relation at every time instant[4]. The predicates $<$, $\leq$, $=$, and all other usual predicates on numbers, are assumed to be time independent, so that the associated relational operations are applicable the Temporal Domain. Also, addition and subtraction are assumed to be total functions, with the usual properties, applicable to elements of the temporal domain. Symbols are divided into propositional symbols ($\wedge$ and $\neg$), the quantifier $\forall$, and a temporal operator symbol *Dist*.

The syntax of TRIO defines terms in the usual inductive way: every variable is a term, and every n-ary function applied to n terms is a term itself. A *formula* is inductively defined by the following clauses:

1. Every n-ary predicate applied to n terms of the appropriate types is a formula (atomic formula).
2. If A and B are formulas, $\neg A$ and $A \wedge B$ are formulas.
3. If A is a formula and x is a time independent variable, $\forall x A$ is a formula.
4. If A is a formula and t is a term of the temporal type, then $Dist(A, t)$ is a formula[5].

The formula $Dist(A, t)$ intuitively means that A holds at an instant laying t time units in the future (if $t > 0$) or in the past (if $t < 0$) with respect to the current time value, which is left implicit in the formula.

Abbreviations for the propositional operators $\vee$, $\rightarrow$, *true*, *false*, $\leftrightarrow$, and for the derived existential quantifier $\exists$ are defined as usual. A large number of

[4] In principle, functions may also be divided into time independent and time dependent, but this feature is not essential and for simplicity it is not introduced here.

[5] We are introducing minor modifications with respect to the original TRIO definition in [13].

derived temporal operators may be defined by means of quantification over TI variables in the temporal argument of *Dist*. These derived operators include all the operators of classical linear temporal logic. We mention, among others, the following ones

$$
\begin{array}{ll}
Futr(A,t) & \stackrel{\text{def}}{=} t > 0 \wedge Dist(A,t) \\
Past(A,t) & \stackrel{\text{def}}{=} t > 0 \wedge Dist(A,-t) \\
AlwF(A) & \stackrel{\text{def}}{=} \forall t(t > 0 \rightarrow Futr(A,t)) \\
AlwP(A) & \stackrel{\text{def}}{=} \forall t(t > 0 \rightarrow Past(A,t)). \\
Always(A) & \stackrel{\text{def}}{=} AlwP(A) \wedge A \wedge AlwF(A) \\
SomF(A) & \stackrel{\text{def}}{=} \neg AlwF(\neg A) \\
SomP(A) & \stackrel{\text{def}}{=} \neg AlwP(\neg A) \\
Sometimes(A) & \stackrel{\text{def}}{=} SomP(A) \vee A \vee SomF(A) \\
Lasts(A,t) & \stackrel{\text{def}}{=} \forall t'(0 < t' < t \rightarrow Futr(A,t')) \\
Lasted(A,t) & \stackrel{\text{def}}{=} \forall t'(0 < t' < t \rightarrow Past(A,t')) \\
Since(A_1,A_2) & \stackrel{\text{def}}{=} \exists t(t > 0 \wedge Past(A_2,t) \wedge Lasted(A_1,t)) \\
Since_w(A_1,A_2) & \stackrel{\text{def}}{=} AlwP(A_1) \vee Since(A_1,A_2)
\end{array}
$$

Futr(A,t) means that A will be true in the future, t units from now (*Past(A,t)* has the same meaning but respect to the past); *AlwF(A)* means that A will hold in all future time instants, while *AlwP* has the same meaning with respect to the past; *Always(A)* means that A holds in every time instant of the temporal domain; *SomF(A)* means that A will take place sometimes in the future, and *SomP* has the same meaning in the past; *Sometimes(A)* means that A takes place sometimes in the past, now or in the future; *Lasts(A, t)* means that A will be true in the next t time units; *Lasted(A, t)* means that A was true in the last t time units; $Since(A_1,A_2)$ means that A_2 took place sometimes in the past, and A_1 held since then; $Since_w(A_1,A_2)$ defines the *weak* version of Since, which does not require A_2 to actually take place.

A *TRIO specification* is a closed TRIO formula. Only closed TRIO formulas are considered, since it is well known that in formulas expressing some kind of system property all variables are quantified, although sometimes implicitly.

Example 1. A transmission line receives messages at one end and transmits them unchanged to the other end with a fixed delay. The time-dependent predicate *in(m)* means that a message m enters the line at the current time (left implicit); the predicate *out(m)* means that the same message m exits from the other end. The TRIO formula

$$Always(in(m) \rightarrow Futr(out(m),5))$$

means that everytime a message m arrives a given time, then 5 time units later the same message m is emitted, i.e., the message does not get lost. The formula

$$Always(\forall m(out(m) \rightarrow Past(in(m),5)))$$

means that no spurious messages are generated.

Example 2. Let *higherLevel* and *safetyLevel* be two significant temperature values for the security of a chemical plant. Let *temp* be a time dependent variable representing the present system temperature. If *lightSignal* and *soundAlarm* are two different alarms in the control system, the formulas

$$Always(lightSignal(on) \leftrightarrow temp \geq higherLevel)$$

$$Always(soundAlarm(on) \leftrightarrow temp \geq safetyLeve)$$

mean that the light alarm must be on if and only if the temperature reaches *higherLevel*, and the sound alarm must be activated if and only if the temperature reaches the *safetyLevel*. The fact that a security action must be taken whenever the pressure value exceeds a fixed threshold is expressed by the following formula

$$Always(pressure \geq valveTolerance \rightarrow$$
$$Futr(Lasts(openGauge, k_1.pressure), k_2 \; / \; temp))$$

This formula specifies the gauge remains open for a duration that is proportional to the pressure, while the activation must be delayed by an interval inversely proportional to the current temperature.

3.2 TRIO's semantics

The concepts of satisfiability and validity of a TRIO formula with respect to suitable interpretations can be defined in much the same way as in classical first-order logic. A model-theoretic semantics for TRIO is based on the concept of temporal structure ([25]), from which one can derive the notion of evaluation function, that assigns to every TRIO formula a truth value for every time instant in the time domain.

A *interpretation structure* S assigns evaluation domains to variables, and values of the appropriate type to variable, function and predicate names occurring in formulas of the language. In particular, it associates a *temporal domain*, denoted by T, to temporal terms.

Traditional definitions of model-theoretic semantics introduce a meaning function S_i that assigns a value of appropriate type to terms and a truth value to formulas for every instant i of the time domain. A specification formula F is said to be *temporally satisfiable* for a given interpretation structure if there exists a time instant $i \in T$ for which $S_i(F) = true$. F is said to be *temporally valid* in the given interpretation iff $S_i(F) = true$ for every $i \in T$; it is *valid* if it is temporally valid in every syntactically adequate interpretation. An interpretation such that F is temporally satisfiable for it is called a *model* of F.

The definition of function S_i is however more complex when formulas are evaluated in a finite (time) domain. [24] introduces a model-parametric semantics that imposes restrictions on the evaluability of a formula at a time instant with reference to a given structure. A formula is considered not evaluable with respect to a given time instant if its evaluation at that time cannot be done without referencing a time point outside the time domain. In addition, the set of values that can be assigned to the quantified variables of a formula must be adequately restricted to subsets of their types in order to prevent from exiting the time domain when evaluating the formula.

3.3 Verification of TRIO specifications

A TRIO specification can be used to model a reactive, real-time system because the physical and structural components of the modeled system have a logical counterpart in the constituents of the temporal structure. Physical components of the systems and immutable relations among them are represented by individual constants and time independent predicates; temporary relations and events are represented by time dependent predicates; values and measures of physical quantities that are subject to change are represented by time dependent variables. Functions can be used to describe some predefined and fixed operations of the specified system, and time independent variables are used as placeholders to express, through the use of quantifiers, existential and universal properties of the specified system. Thus, one model of a TRIO specification intuitively corresponds to one possible evolution (*history*) of the specified system, that satisfies the requirements expressed by the specification formula. A history can be specified as follows:

Definition 4 (Event, history). An event is a pair $< L, i >$, where

- L is a literal
- i is a time instant, belonging to the time domain.

A history is a set of events that temporally satisfies a TRIO specification.

For instance, referring to Example 1 in Section 3.1, the pair $< in, 1 >$ describes the event of receiving a message at time 1; the pair $< \neg out, 1 >$ describes that no message is sent at time 1. Figure 3 illustrates 3 histories for that example.

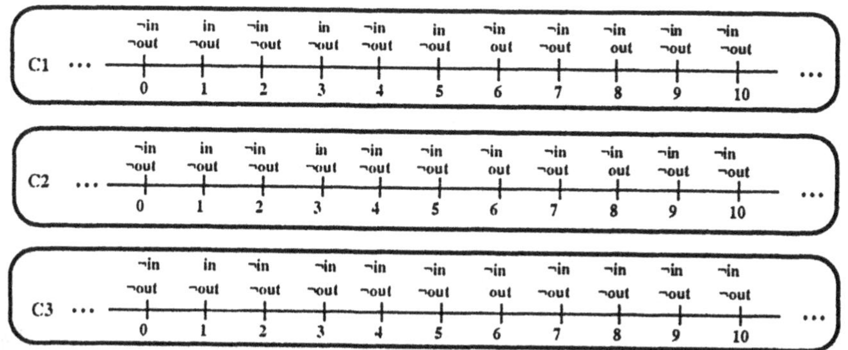

Fig. 3. Three executions for the line of example 1 in Section 3.1

Requirements validation. In order to validate requirements expressed as a TRIO specification, one may try to prove the satisfiability of the formula by constructing a model for it. In this view, some parts of the temporal structure to be constructed are assumed to be known, namely the temporal domain T, the domains for variables, and the interpretation of time independent predicates, which describe the static configuration of the specified system. Given a system specification as a TRIO formula and the static part of a structure adequate to its evaluation, the construction of the remaining parts of the structure determines the dynamic evolution of the modelled system: the events that take place and the values assumed by the relevant quantities.

If the interpretation domains for variables and the temporal domain T are all finite, the satisfiability of a TRIO formula is a decidable problem and effective algorithms to solve it can be defined. [7] presents an algorithm which, under the hypothesis of finite domains, determines the satisfiability of a TRIO specification (i.e., a closed TRIO formula) using a constructive method.

The main steps of the algorithm for verifying satisfiability are schematically shown in Figure 4. The specification formula is associated with a time value t that indicates the instant where it is assumed to hold; then a decomposition process is performed which transforms a formula into a set of simpler formulas, associated with possibly different instants, whose conjunction is equivalent to it. The decomposition uses well known (and intuitive) properties of the propositional operators, and treats universal (respectively existential) quantifications as generalized conjunctions (respectively disjunctions); it ends when each set of the subformulas, called a *tableau*, contains only literals. Every tableau that does not contain any contradiction (i.e., a literal and its negation) provides a compact representation of a model for the original formula, and thus constitutes a constructive proof of its satisfiability. Since each leaf tableau generated by the algorithm for verifying satisfiability corresponds to a history of the specified system, i.e., a temporal evolution of the system, this algorithm is called *history generator* (i.e., an interpreter that receives as input a TRIO formula and produces as result a set of histories that are compatible with such a formula).

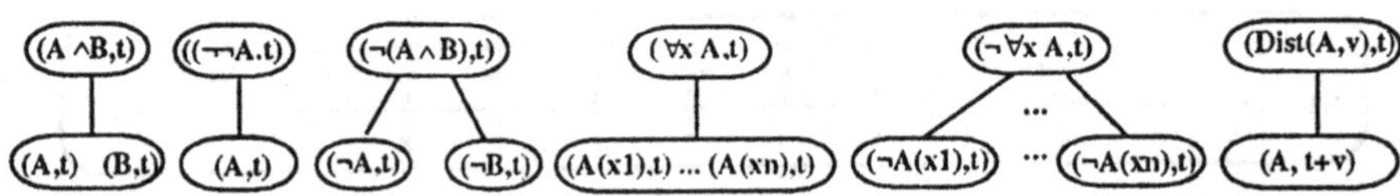

Fig. 4. Pictorial description of the decomposition of formulas by the tableaux algorithm.

Figure 5 shows part of the tableaux tree generated by a history generator for the formula Always(pressure $\geq$ valveTolerance $\rightarrow$ Futr (Lasts (openGauge, k_1.pressure), k_2 / temp)). It is shown for a generic time value i ranging from the minimum value of the time domain to the maximum. Since both leaves do not include contradictions, both represent models of the formula. Please notice that, for graphic reasons we omit the consonants in the predicate and variable names.

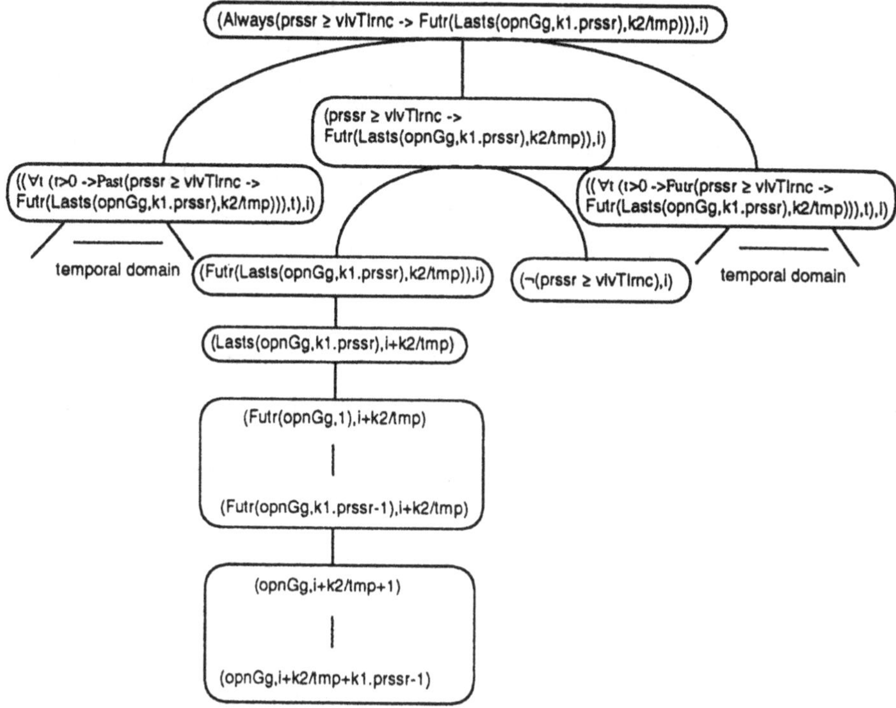

Fig. 5. The tableaux generated by the histories generator for the formula: Always(prssr $\geq$ vlvTlrnc $\rightarrow$ Futr (Lasts(opnGg,k_1.prssr), k_2 / tmp)).

The study of the complexity of the above algorithm, discussed in [7], shows that it is exponential in the number of existential quantifications, with the cardinality of the domains of the quantified TI variables appearing as the base of the exponential, while it is hyperexponential with respect to the number of universal quantifications, with the cardinality of the domain of the quantified variables appearing as the exponent.

Specification testing. Executability of TRIO formulas is also provided at lower levels of generality: the tableaux algorithm can be adapted to verify that a given temporal evolution of the system (a history) is compatible with the specification. This operation is called *history checking*, since it is analogous to what is called model checking, in the literature regarding branching-time temporal logic ([2]). Model checking refers to the operation of verifying whether a given state graph, or state automaton implementing a system, is a model of the specification formula. Hence it is equivalent to proving that every possible execution of the automaton satisfies the formula. Instead, in a linear time logic like TRIO, history checking refers to only *one* possible evolution of the system. That is, a history checker is an interpreter that receives as input a TRIO formula and a history and states whether the history is compatible with the given formula. As we already said, history checking is implemented through a specialization of the tableaux algorithm, whose main steps are shown in Figure 6. Now each tableau includes only *one* formula associated with a time instant at which it must be evaluated. An and/or tree is built and the literals obtained in the leaf nodes are checked against the history.

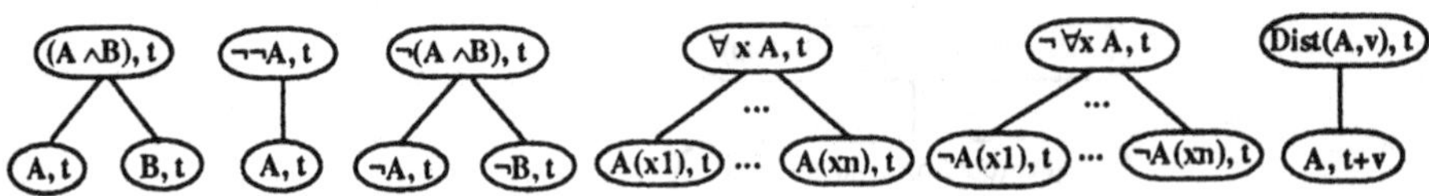

Fig. 6. Pictorial description of the decomposition of formulas by the history checker.

Complexity of the history checking algorithm has been shown to be exponential with respect to the dimension of the formula ([7]), i.e., the number of its quantifications and binary operators. It should however be noticed that the cardinality of the domains of the quantified variables appears now as the base of the exponential, not as the exponent (like in the more general algorithm for deciding satisfiability of formulas). In other words, for a given formula, the complexity of the history checking algorithm is a polynomial function of the cardinality of the evaluation domains. This result might be considered discouraging; however we point out that the dimension of the formula is usually relatively small with respect to the cardinality of the evaluation domains, so that, in the total complexity of checking the specification formula, the exponential factor has a limited influence with respect to the polynomial one. This was confirmed by experimental use of the prototype in cases of practical interest ([3]).

The history checking algorithm was the basis for the design and implementation of a prototype tool for specification testing. A set of facts representing a possible system evolution is *tested* with reference to a formula describing all the desired system behaviors. A history is represented by a set of time dependent ground literals, by the time independent predicates and functions which constitute the frame, and by the values for the time dependent variables.

The tool admits the possibility that the set of ground literals included in the history does not cover all possible instants of the temporal domain or all the argument values. In that case the user may choose to evaluate the formula under the closed world assumption or not. If the closed world assumption holds then the history is complete by definition because all the events not reported in the history are implicitly considered as false. Thus, the tool checks whether a formula is evaluable and then if it is satisfied by the history. Instead, whenever the closed world assumption does not hold, the checker is also able to recognize whether the history does not provide sufficient information to assign a truth value to the formula. In this case the formula is evaluated with respect to a

Using specifications to verify implementations. [21] proposes a method and a tool for the derivation of functional test cases for real-time systems, starting from a specification given in TRIO. [21] defines the notion of test cases adequate to performing functional testing of real-time systems specified in TRIO, and shows how the history generator and history checker can be effectively used, both to generate test cases and to support the testing activity itself.

A history (or a model) of a TRIO formula can be interpreted as a test case, since it represents an evolution trace of the modelled system and hence it can be compared with an actual execution of the system. In this view, the two mentioned interpreters (i.e. the algorithm for verifying satisfiability and the history checker) can become the core of a tool that allows to systematically generate test cases for the specified system and validate its responses to the provided stimuli. By this way, not only possible *stimuli* (i.e., system inputs) are generated from system specifications to test the system under verification, but also system *reactions* (i.e., outputs) are provided to check whether the system behavior really complies with the desired properties, thus solving the oracle problem ([18]) (i.e., given the inputs determine the expected outputs).

The TRIO language, unfortunately does not distinguish input events (data or commands introduced into the system) from output events (data or signals generated by the system). During the testing activity, however, it is essential to understand which events flow from the external environment to the system, and which flow from the system to the external environment. The solution adopted by the TRIO test case generator does not perform automatically such a classification, but solves the problem through interaction with the user. The user partitions predicate names of the specification formula into input, output, and input/output predicates.

Since each leaf tableau generated by the algorithm for verifying satisfiability corresponds to a history of the specified system, it is clear that the algorithm may generate, for some specification formulas, a very large number of histories, much more than those needed for performing an effective testing. [21] proposes some criteria to cope with such kind of complexity. When the complexity is high, the tool requires the user interaction to select the criteria it must follow or to use the history checker to check if the set of facts generated up to that moment satisfies the formula (i.e., it is a history).

3.4 Property proving

This section surveys the axiomatic definition of TRIO presented in [6]. Following the axiomatization, one can prove properties of TRIO specifications. The proof cannot be performed in a purely mechanical fashion, but requires human interaction in the general case.

Since TRIO allows almost any kind of interpretation domains to be used in specifications, any axiom system for it should include a first order theory for all three-value logic ([22]) which includes a third, "unknown" value.

of the used domains (say, real numbers for temporal domain, integers for some variables, booleans for others, etc.). Thus the final axiomatization depends on the selected domain. Following the same approach as adopted in a variety of temporal logics ([28, 20, 17]), all the valid formula of the chosen domains are implicitly assumed to hold as additional axioms in the TRIO's axiomatization.

TRIO's axioms are given below. For convenience they are partitioned into *general axioms*, which are shared with any first-order theory with equality, and *temporal axioms*, which are peculiar of the language. A universal axiom schema is added at the end of both class.

Let $\alpha, \beta, \omega, \ldots$ denote any TRIO formula; let s, v, u ...denote any term of a generic domain, whereas t, t1, t2, ...denote any term of temporal type; let x, y, ...denote any variable and c any constant.

General axioms These, in turn, are split into first-order predicate axioms and into equality axioms as shown below.

First order axioms

1. All instances of propositional calculus tautologies
2. $\forall x\ \alpha \rightarrow \alpha^x_s$ where s is a term substitutable for x in α [6] ([22])
3. $\forall x\ (\alpha \rightarrow \beta) \rightarrow (\forall x\ \alpha \rightarrow \forall x\ \beta)$
4. $\alpha \rightarrow \forall x\ \alpha$ if x is not free in α

Equality axioms

5. $s = s$, for any term s
6. $u = s \rightarrow (\alpha \rightarrow \alpha')$ where u and s are terms, α' is obtained from α by substituting zero or more occurrences of u in α by s.

Temporal axioms

7. $Dist(\alpha, 0) \leftrightarrow \alpha$
8. $Dist(\alpha, t1 + t2) \leftrightarrow Dist(Dist(\alpha, t1), t2)$
9. $Dist(\alpha \rightarrow \beta, t) \leftrightarrow (Dist(\alpha, t) \rightarrow Dist(\beta, t))$
10. $Dist(\neg\alpha, t) \leftrightarrow \neg Dist(\alpha, t)$
11. $\alpha \rightarrow Alw(\alpha)$ if α is time independent

Generalization For each formula ω in the above list 1 through 11, all formulas of the kind $Alw(\omega)$, and all their applications of universal quantifications (generalizations) are TRIO axioms.

There is a single rule of inference, namely Modus Ponens (MP). By using classical Hoare's notation, it is denoted as

$$\frac{\Gamma \vdash \alpha, \Gamma \vdash \alpha \rightarrow \beta}{\Gamma \vdash \beta}$$

Axioms 7 through 10 describe the essential properties of the basic temporal operator Dist: when in the formula $Dist(\alpha, t)$ the temporal argument t is 0 then the other argument, α, is asserted at the current instant; furthermore, nested applications of the operator compose additively, according to the properties of the temporal domain, and the operator is transparent with respect to propositional operators of its non-temporal argument. Axiom 11 simply states the time

[6] As usual, α^x_s denotes the result of substituting any free occurrence of x in α by s.

invariance of time independent formulas (those which do not contain any time dependent predicate or temporal operator): if the formula is true *now* then it is true at any time instant of the temporal domain (the converse is trivially true, and in fact the corresponding formula, $Alw(\alpha) \rightarrow \alpha$, is a theorem whose proof is immediate).

TRIO's axiomatization provides also the counterpart of well-known metatheorems[7] which hold for the most widely accepted axiomatizations of first-order logic, namely the Generalization theorem (GEN), the Deduction theorem (DED) and the Existential Instantiation theorem (EI). Similarly, since TRIO's axiomatization includes a standard first-order part, all the derived inference rules usually employed for first-order logic ([22]) are also valid in TRIO. Moreover, the axiomatization provides some useful temporal metatheorems:

Temporal Translation Theorem (TT)
This metatheorem asserts that if a formula α can be proved under a given set of assumptions that hold at the present time instant and all these assumptions hold at a different time instant, then it can be proved that α holds at that time instant too. The metatheorem is formalized as follows.

$$\text{if } \Gamma \vdash \alpha \text{ then } \{Dist(\gamma, t) | \gamma \in \Gamma\} \vdash Dist(\alpha, t)$$

Temporal Generalization Theorem (TG)
This metatheorem is an extension to the preceding result. It states that if the set of assumptions on which the proof of a property is based is true in every instant of the temporal domain, then the proven formula is also always true. Formally,

if $\Gamma \vdash \alpha$ and every formula of Γ is of the type $Alw(\gamma)$ or is time independent, then $\Gamma \vdash Alw(\alpha)$.

An important corollary of TG is obtained by taking $\Gamma = \emptyset$. In this case TG reduces to: if $\vdash \alpha$ then $\vdash Alw(\alpha)$. This corresponds to the intuitive fact that if property α is derived without making any assumption about the current time instant, then α holds at every time instant. Another consequence of TG is that any theorem τ of first-order logic is not only inherited as such in TRIO, but its temporal generalization, $Alw(\tau)$ is also a theorem. For instance, $Alw(\alpha(t) \rightarrow \exists z\ \alpha(z))$ holds by the fact that $\alpha(t) \rightarrow \exists z\ \alpha(z)$ is a theorem in any first-order logic.

3.5 Towards more usable real-time logic languages

TRIO is a quite terse language. It is an excellent notation for mathematically reasoning about specifications, but it is difficult to use in practice. Specifiers and readers have no ways of mastering the complexity of large specifications; no application-specific abstractions are provided to support end-users in the verification of a specification. Following the spirit of what was done for net-based

[7] Metatheorems are properties of the axiomatization. Instead, theorems are derived from deductions using the axiomatization.

specifications, TRIO is viewed as the semantic kernel notation of a specification environment, not as the notation used in practice. Other language layers have therefore been defined on top of TRIO.

TRIO+ ([26]) is an object-oriented extension of TRIO. TRIO+ allows the partition of the universe of objects into classes, the inheritance of relations among classes, and provides mechanisms such as inheritance and genericity to support reuse of specification modules and their top-down, incremental development. Moreover, an expressive graphic representation of classes in terms of boxes, arrows, and connections is defined. Such a representation allows depiction of class instances and their components, information exchanges, and logical equivalences among (parts of) objects.

ASTRAL ([8, 9]) is another linguistic layer defined on top of TRIO. ASTRAL views a real-time system under specification as a collection of abstract machines. Abstract machines may communicate with one another via exported variables. They may also interact with the external environment, which may cause state transitions to occur. ASTRAL is formally defined by means of a translation scheme into TRIO. The TRIO "code" generated by the translation may then be manipulated by the available TRIO tools. In particular, it is possible to test a specification by history checking.

4 The Dual Language Approach

An increasing interest is recently arising on the so-called dual-language approach, in order to support a complete formalization of specifications and the corresponding analysis [28]. In a dual language approach two entities are distinguished: a set of properties one wishes to verify and the system (or system part) about which these properties are to be verified. The dual language approach requires both entities to be formally described: the properties are described using an assertional (descriptive) language and the system is described using a model-based (operational) language. In this way properties are formally stated and can be formally proved. [6] proposed a dual language method where properties are expressed in terms of TRIO and the systems are modeled by means of TB nets. One may view TRIO as the language in which abstract properties and requirements are formally stated, while TB nets are used to model a more concrete operational description of an abstract implementation.

The basic idea of the method proposed in [6] consists of an axiomatization of the behavior of timed Petri nets in terms of TRIO axioms and proof rules, in the same style as Hoare's rules are provided for Pascal-like programs. Then, net properties, such as marking and firing conditions, are expressed as TRIO formulas and their validity is proved using the axiomatization presented in Section 3.4. The method supports the verification of properties of any kind of nets, whereas existing mechanical methods only apply to restricted subclasses and do not scale up to more general cases, where they become undecidable. [6] also provides examples of application of the method in the proof of non-trivial properties of classical benchmarks for the analysis of concurrent and real-time systems, such as an elevator system and a real-time version of the dining philosophers problem. For example, in the case of the elevator system, given some assumptions, it is possible to prove that if a person calls the elevator in certain circumstances, it will arrive within the next Δ time units; or, if a person pushes a button to close the elevator's doors and a person tries to enter the elevator while its doors are closing, the doors reopen.

5 Conclusions

In this paper, we surveyed the work done by our group in the area of specification and verification of reactive, real-time systems. Research is still active in the areas we reviewed here. For example, complete formal treatment of the graphical language extensions in CABERNET is still under scrutiny. In the case of TRIO, work is presently addressing further issues of higher-level language layers defined on top of the kernel (such as the cited TRIO+ and ASTRAL) and interlevel translation schemes, the problem of handling different time granularities in a specification, and others. The dual language approach is under further investigation, and will probably lead to an integration of the present environments supporting the two specification styles, nets and real-time logic in a single comprehensive environment.

Acknowledgements

The work we survey in this paper is the result of the work of many individuals over the past five years. The results we present could have never been achieved without their insights and enthusiasm. In particular, we wish to thank Dino Mandrioli, for his contributions to the whole research field, Mauro Pezzé for his contributions to CABERNET, Angelo Morzenti for his contributions to TRIO, Dick Kemmerer and Alberto Coen for their contributions to ASTRAL, Sandro Morasca for his contributions to CABERNET and test case generation from TRIO specifications, Pierluigi San Pietro for his contributions to TRIO+. Several generations of students contributed to the design of the current prototype environments.

References

1. Bellettini, C., Felder, M., Pezzè, M.: MERLOT: A tool for analysis of real-time specifications. Proceedings of the 7th International Workshop on Software Specifications and Design, Los Angeles, California, 1993. (to appear)
2. Clarke, C., Emerson, E., Sistla, S.: Automatic verification of finite-state concurrent systems using temporal logic specifications. ACM-Transactions on Programming Languages and Systems, Vol. 8, No. 2, April 1986.

3. Coen, A., Morzenti, A., Sciuto, D.: Specification and verification of hardware systems using the temporal logic language TRIO. In *Computer hardware description languages and their application*, Borrione, D. and Waxman, R., IFIP, North-Holland, Marseille, France, April 1991, pp.43–62.
4. Dillon, L.K., Avrunin, G.S., Wileden, J.C.: Constrained expressions: Toward broad applicability of analysis methods for distributed software systems. ACM-Transactions on Programming Languages and Systems, Vol. 10, No. 3, pp. 374–402, July 1988.
5. Felder, M., Ghezzi, C., Pezzè M.: Analyzing refinements of state based specifications: the case of TB nets. Proceedings of International Symposium on Software Testing and Analysis 1993, Cambridge, Massachusetts. (to appear)
6. Felder, M., Mandrioli, D., Morzenti, A.: Proving properties of real-time systems through logical Specifications and Petri Nets Models. IEEE-Transactions on Software Engineering (to appear). *Also in Tech-Report 91-072, Dip. di Elettronica-Politecnico di Milano, December 1991.*
7. Felder, M., Morzenti, A.: Specification testing for real-time systems by history checking in TRIO. Proceedings of the 14th International Conference on Software Engineering, Melbourne, Australia, May 1992.
8. Ghezzi, C., Kemmerer, R.A.: ASTRAL: An assertion language for specifying real-time systems. Proceedings of the 3rd European Software Engineering Conference, Milano, Italy, October 1991.
9. Ghezzi, C., Kemmerer, R.A.: Executing formal specifications: the ASTRAL to TRIO translation approach. TAV'91, Symposium on Testing, Analysis and Verification, Victoria, Canada, October 1991.
10. Ghezzi, C., Mandrioli, D., Morasca, S., Pezzè, M.: A general way to put time in Petri nets. Proceedings of the 4th International Workshop on Software Specifications and Design, Monterey, California, April 3-4, 1987.
11. Ghezzi, C., Mandrioli, D., Morasca, S., Pezzè, M.: A unified high-level Petri net formalism for time-critical systems. IEEE Transactions on Software Engineering, Vol. 17, No. 2, February 1991.
12. Ghezzi, C., Mandrioli, D., Morasca, S., Pezzè, M.: Symbolic execution of concurrent programs using Petri nets. Computer Languages, April 1989.
13. Ghezzi, C., Mandrioli, D., Morzenti, A.: TRIO: A logic language for executable specifications of real-time systems. Journal of Systems and Software, June 1990.
14. Ghezzi, C., Morasca, S., Pezzè, M.: Timing analysis of time basic nets". *submitted for publication*
15. Gomaa, H.: Software development of real-time systems. Communications of the ACM, Vol. 29, No. 7, July 1986.
16. Hatley, D.J., Pirbai, I.A.: *Strategies for Real-Time System Specification*. Dorset House, 1988.
17. Henzinger, T., Manna, Z., Pnueli, A.: Temporal proof methodologies for real time systems. Proceedings of the 18th ACM Symposium on Principles of Programming Languages, pp. 353–366, 1991.
18. Howden, W.E.: *Functional Program Testing & Analysis*. Mc Graw Hill, 1987.
19. Kemmerer, R.A.: Testing software specifications to detect design errors. IEEE Transactions on Software Engineering, Vol. 11, No. 1, January 1985.
20. Koymans, R.: Specifying Message Passing and Time-Critical Systems with Temporal Logic. PhD Thesis, Eindhoven University of Technology, 1989.

21. Mandrioli, D., Morzenti, A. and Morasca, S.: Functional test case generation for real-time sytems. Proceedings of 3rd International Working Conference on Dependable Computing for Critical Applications, IFIP, 1992 pp.13–26.
22. Mendelson, E.: *Introduction to mathematical logic.* Van Nostrand Reinold Company, New York, 1963.
23. Morasca, S. and Pezzè, M.: Validation of concurrent Ada programs using symbolic execution. Proceedings of the 2nd European Software Engineering Conference, LNCS 387, pages 469–486. Springer-Verlag, 1989.
24. Morzenti, A., Mandrioli, D., Ghezzi, C.: A model parametric real-time logic. ACM Transactions on Programming Languages and Systems, Vol. 14, No. 4, pp. 521–573, October, 1982.
25. Morzenti, A.: The Specification of Real-Time Systems: Proposal of a Logic Formalism. PhD Thesis, Dipartimento di Elettronica, Politecnico di Milano, 1989.
26. Morzenti, A., San Pietro, P.: An object oriented logic language for modular system specification. Proceedings of the European Conference on Object Oriented Programming '91, LNCS 512, Springer Verlag, July 1991.
27. Nagl, M.: A tutorial and bibliography survey on graph grammars. LNCS 166, Springer Verlag, 1985.
28. Ostrof, J.: *Temporal Logic For Real-Time Systems.* Research Studies Press LTD., Advanced Software Development Series, Taunton, Somerset, England, 1989.
29. Pezzè, M. and Ghezzi, C.: Cabernet: a customizable environment for the specification and analysis of realtime systems. *submitted for publication,* 1993.
30. Quirk, W.J.: *Verification and Validation of Real-Time Software.* Springer Verlag, Berlin, 1985.
31. Reisig, W.: *Petri Nets: an Introduction.* Springer Verlag, 1985.
32. Smullian, R.M.: *First Order Logic.* Springer Verlag, Berlin, 1968.
33. Taylor, R.: A general-purpose algorithm for analyzing concurrent programs. Communications of the ACM, Vol. 26, No.5, pp. 362–376, May 1983.

Software Engineering in Business and Academia: How Wide is the Gap?

Ernst Denert
sd&m GmbH
Technical University of Munich

Nothing is more practical than good theory.

Introduction

What does the abbreviation CSP stand for? Ask a computer scientist and he'll probably answer with Hoares' "Cooperating Sequential Processes." A data-processing specialist, on the other hand, might refer to "Cross Software Product," the allegedly strategic programming language in the framework of AD/Cycle from IBM. Neither of the two will probably know what the other is talking about. While this certainly isn't a representative test, it does provide a good example of the gap between the two worlds of business and science.

Someone like me, constantly on the move between these two worlds, can only view this schism with exasperation. It's not just a matter of changing from one language to another — at least that involves a certain element of challenge. No, what's depressing is how many good ideas from computer science meet with a lack of understanding among businessmen and, by the opposite token, how little scientists know and care about the real-world needs and problems of the businessmen.

In this paper I attempt to provide a description of the dilemma — avowedly subjective, undoubtedly incomplete, sometimes perhaps exaggerated. Be that as it may, my real aim is to provoke discussion. I can offer no solutions. I can only request that we take note of the gap and do our best to cross the borders that divides us whenever and wherever possible.

Since my opinions here are based on personal observations rather than scientifically verifiable studies, I owe the reader a few words about my own background. My attachment to computer science goes back to my work as an assistant at the Technical University in Berlin (1971-76) and later found expression in regular publications (not least in the book *Software Engineering*) and my teaching activities at the Munich Technical University (1986 to the present). Since 1976 I've predominantly been involved in business (Softlab, sd&m), where I'm mainly concerned with the development of software for *business information systems.*

This systems category claims — and I'm convinced of this even though I don't have any concrete numbers at hand — more than half of the effort that flows into software developments, perhaps as much as two-thirds or even three-quarters. And it's precisely in this area that the gap between science and business is especially large; it's probably smaller, by comparison, in systems software or technical applications.

In order to describe the gap I've picked out several areas: programming languages, operating and database systems, methods, and software engineering tools. All these examples underline the respective emphases of the two interests, their differences and the few common characteristics.

Programming Languages

The importance of programming languages is often overestimated by the scientists and underestimated by the practitioners[1]; the latter consider operating systems, transaction monitors, and database systems more important. Many scientists often don't (like to) recognize that their favorite languages (once Algol, then Pascal, today Modula, Eiffel, Lisp, Prolog ...) play virtually no role at all in practice. Meanwhile, they tend to have only scorn for the most widespread language, Cobol, although its bad reputation is only partly due to any real technical problems.

It would probably be a better idea to direct this scorn against other languages, particularly so-called languages of the fourth generation ("4GL"-examples include Natural, CSP) and against the type of programming imposed by certain CASE tools. The 4GLs are certainly quite useful — otherwise they wouldn't be so successful — in that they allow close interconnection of the programming language with the database system, the terminal, the transaction monitor, the data dictionary, and so on; in short, they offer an integrated programming environment. As a rule, however, they aren't very suited to good software engineering. They're too strongly influenced by the idea that it's only a matter of writing a few programs that merely transport data back and forth between screen and database. The scientific concept of modularity — propagated by Parnas over twenty years ago — is alien to them, as can be seen from their miserable subroutine mechanisms. I call such languages "call-hostile" in contrast to the "call-friendly" languages such as C, where the writing of subroutines is simple and calling them efficient. Modularity may be normal in call-friendly languages, but it's terra incognita for call-hostile languages. So it would definitely be worth the scientists' while to develop and distribute a good 4GL for software engineering rather than another 3GL with even more elegant linguistic constructs. For their part, the practitioners have to comprehend that information systems are more than a series of simple data-transport programs, and that certain computer-science

[1]For the sake of brevity, I'll simply write "scientists" when I mean academically oriented computer scientists, and "practitioners" for the software developers or data-processing engineers involved in practical business (who of course may have a computer science education).

concepts, such as modularity, would be useful in their design work and are continuing to gain in importance.

The decision in favor of a *programming language in practice* depends less on its linguistic quality than on its integration in the system environment (database, screen, etc.), the development tools (such as debuggers), and above all non-technical aspects such as availability and market penetration. Moreover it's worth noting that data-processing organizations rarely change their programming languages. Too great are the worries: the costs might be too high, the team could be overwhelmed, existing software could be endangered. So the scientists also have to learn to design good information systems with existing languages, whether it be Cobol, PL/1, or Natural, and not just to dream of programming in Modula, Eiffel, or some other beautiful language.

Apropos *Eiffel*: a beautiful, object-oriented language, well-known (and also widely used?) in the computer science world. What a great deed it would be to declare and make Eiffel *the* language in AD/Cycle (which would of course require a lot of work: integration with DB2, CICS, OS/2 and its presentation manager, etc.). But IBM evidently has neither the ideas nor the courage and the strength. Bertrand Meyer, the father of Eiffel, and several other scientists prefer to design language elements for parallel programming needed by (almost) no one in practice. So we'll probably have to go on suffering with CSP and other miscreations of software engineering.

For a time I placed my hopes in *Ada*, a fine language with "built-in" modularity. As the offspring of the US Department of Defense one expected that it would at least prove useful in practice. Unfortunately this hope was in vain: at least as far as business information systems are concerned, Ada doesn't play a role in Germany and probably not much of one in the US either. What a pity; Ada could have really become a bridge over the gap between science and business.

That leaves *C*, and increasingly *C++*, as the only remaining links between the two worlds — languages that are not (yet) being used for mainframe applications, but which have taken on great practical importance in Unix and client/server applications. Still, though, they are not satisfying because C and C++ are not aesthetically appealing languages; Eiffel, for example, is much better. Perhaps it has to do with the fact that C doesn't come from scientific language-designers, but was cobbled together in practice.

The bottom line on programming languages is a depressing one: in summary, there are *no well-designed languages available for practical use* (presumably also because many decision-makers don't recognize the significance of programming languages). Science, meanwhile, doesn't address the problem because it has all the good languages it wants and shows little interest in applying these to practical use. The only consolation for me is the thought that it's still possible to do good programming with a bad language and vice versa.

Operating Systems, Transaction Monitors

Unix connects both worlds. Unix isn't just an operating system; it also encompasses the programming language C, tools (lex, yacc, awk, make, m4 ...), and since recently also basic software for graphic user interfaces (X Windows, Motif). Unix was born in industry, albeit in an institution very close to research (Bell Laboratories), and quickly found many friends at universities and institutes; now their workstations are impossible to imagine without it. As a platform of business information systems, Unix still doesn't have a large share in business, but it's growing. Unix is especially useful for applications with small numbers of users (a couple of dozens), as with an production planning system in a factory, for example.

The big applications, however, cannot (yet?) be handled with Unix — applications with hundreds and thousands of dialogue users and enormous batch runs of the type operated by banks, insurance companies, airlines, tourism companies, and others. The accounts in a bank can't be managed on a network of decentral Unix servers and workstations (I'd probably close my account there just to be on the safe side), and writing up the monthly bills for 1.5 million members of the German Auto Club is a batch several hours long, not a dialogue application with a graphic interface. It's tasks like these that need *mainframes*, their operating systems (MVS, BS2000), and transaction monitors (CICS, IMS-TM, UTM). Sadly, the universities really have a blind spot in this area. It may be that these systems aren't very useful for research, but they should come up in teaching. It's a disgrace that scarcely a single computer science graduate today knows what a transaction monitor is! Do the professors know? One result of this blind spot is that young computer scientists virtually consider workstations and computers to be the same thing (the way that laymen now equate "computer" and "PC"). For the software engineer, whose training I see as one of the tasks of our universities, this is simply not acceptable.

Databases

Databases are the foundation of every business information system. The nineteen-eighties saw the ascendance of *relational systems*, and with them a concept that has a theoretical basis in the mathematics of relations, a positive factor that ought to be recognized by practitioners and which is not inhibited by the fact that relational theory was developed in proximity to practice, namely by Codd in an IBM research laboratory. The first prototype of a relational database system (System R) was also developed there, later evolving into DB2.

The relational data base management systems (DBMS) thus connect science and business, especially the ones that are Unix-oriented (Oracle, Ingres, Informix, etc.). In the area of business information systems, however, non-relational DBMS are (still) widely used (IMS, Adabas, UDS), a fact scarcely noticed by the universities; that can be endured.

What depresses me far more is the extent to which *computer scientists* continue to "*think in terms of main memory*" (with the exception of database people, naturally). This is shown by the basic course offerings in computer science, where algorithms work almost exclusively in main memory while background memories or DBMS scarcely come up at all. Even more serious, though, is my observation that many books about software engineering discuss databases little or not at all. Software engineering without databases — unthinkable in the broad field of business information systems! This abstinence can also be found in many of the new publications about object-oriented techniques, whose authors shouldn't try to excuse themselves with talk about persistent objects and object-oriented DBMS. First, it will be some time before such approaches reach maturity and become widely distributed; and second, we will continue to use relational DBMS anyway, simply because their data structure is suited to many problems.

One hobbyhorse of computer scientists is *distributed databases*, and a great deal of research and development has gone into this area. This interest has also been caused by data-processing decision-makers demanding that new DBMS should be distributed and handle the two-phase-commit-protocol even if they'll never use these capabilities. And what for? I still haven't encountered an application that could be reasonably performed with a distributed database. But it remains an entertaining playground for researchers and developers, albeit an expensive one for DBMS manufacturers.

Methods

The central methodological question with business information systems is: *How do you specify* them? And in such a way that you can move as smoothly as possible from the specification to its realization? Science gives no answer to the problem, and until recently it didn't even deal with the subject.

In practice people have tended to muddle through. They've used various ad hoc means of representation to describe what an information system is supposed to do — or sometimes simply started programming away, in which case the code ultimately became the (only) description. Organizations that found this approach a little too coarse turned to a different answer: *Structured Analysis* (SA). Published by Tom DeMarco in 1979, this method is based on two concepts: functional decomposition (top-down decomposition) and data flow diagrams. The latter reflect the simple fact that functions have inputs and outputs and are interconnected through them. Other forms of representation had already used similar approaches; they included SADT (Structured Analysis and Design Technique) from Doug Ross (1977) and HIPO (Hierarchical Input Processing Output) from IBM. Structured Analysis became truly popular only once CASE tools on PCs with graphic monitors enabled the many data flow diagrams to be drawn electronically. That was fun and looked professional. No one seemed disturbed by SA's method-related deficiencies (which is why it received so little attention earlier). This is demonstrated by the almost complete lack of theoretical works about this "method." The scientific community just isn't interested — correctly so, in my opinion.

The manufacturers of CASE have added a third component to SA (along with functional decomposition and data flow diagrams): *entity/relationship data modelling*. This method, introduced by Chen in 1976 as a process for designing relational data structures, is a rare case of luck, for it's both theoretically well-grounded (due to the relational mathematics upon which it's based) and proven in practice. Even more — it's been accepted without objections across the world. A scientific concept has proven itself in practical use in less than ten years.

I wish I could say the same of *object-oriented methods*. It has the potential to give us all a good instruction in method in all phases of software development, and it's been doing just that for quite a while: the first oo programming language, Simula 67, is as old as Software Engineering, and the concepts for modularization by means of data abstraction (i.e. to a certain extent oo design) were published by Parnas back in 1972. Not only is there a lot of practical experience with this approach, but it also has a strong theoretical basis, consisting of the many works, roughly since 1975, about the formal specification of abstract data types. High-level conferences (such as OOPSLA) provide a prominent forum for these scientific fundaments.

Such knowledge has so far had little effect on the practice of business information systems. This is not only due to the fact that people working in this field prefer SA, but also because the scientists have not explained how to specify such systems. Instead they've preferred to develop the umpteenth language for specifying stacks, queues, sets, bags, and similar trifles; they've gotten stuck in "specification-in-the-small."

Now that's changing. For the past few years there have been first attempts toward the *oo specification* of business information systems, by gurus such as Coad/Yourdon and James Martin and practitioners such as Rumbaugh et al. Ferstl and Sinz, professors of economic computer science, have also contributed, and our own work could be included as well. We won't have to wait long for the theoretical foundation — it's already on the way. But we should also warn against the panaceas sometimes yearned for by managers. The euphoria over CASE and its relative SA has just passed: it's time to look at object-orientation more matter-of-factly.

Computer science has plenty of useful and at the same time theoretically well-founded methods for practical use. Especially noteworthy, aside from E/R models and oo methods, is Dijkstra's *structured programming* and the theorem of Böhm-Jacopini (1966) on which it is based and according to which programming can be done without goto.

The theory of *automata and formal languages* continues to supply practical concepts for the creation of all types of models; interaction diagrams for the specification of dialogue control are one example.

But watch out: scientists tend to look for problems for their favorite theories instead of new solutions to given tasks. Petri nets seem to me an example: they've existed for thirty years, and scientists are still looking for suitable problems, at least in software engineering. And what about graph grammars, category theory, and correctness proofs? Of course we need basic research in computer science, and it shouldn't have to justify itself relentlessly with some kind of applicability; but that's not what we're talking about here. The subject here is research in software engineering, which, in my opinion, must have practical relevance. One area that comes to mind is that of *testing*. Horribly neglected in both science and business, it continues to await the development of effective methods and tools.

Practitioners want guidelines, procedural rules, rules of thumb, all as simple as possible, handy, tool-supported. They tend to be suspicious of talking about a method's theoretical foundations, while practical experience, on the other hand, means everything to them, even if a method's basis is intellectually thin. My own suspicions are immediately wakened by guidelines and rules that, sometimes even using tools, elaborately detail the procedures and results of development — watch out for counterproductive *software bureaucracy*! Instead, qualified developers should be encouraged to solve practical problems creatively with theoretically well-grounded methods.

Tools

One concept has dominated this subject in the past five years: *CASE*. CASE was spurred on in 1989 by the announcement of AD/Cycle and then, in 1992, reined in by the withdrawal of the IBM repository. Users have become uncertain, the initial euphoria has given way to sobriety, and the boom is over. This is no wonder and perfectly in order.

For the producers of CASE have raised a claim that they couldn't fulfill. The methods implemented in their tool systems can't be as comprehensive and consistent as they claim. At least not at the moment, presumably not in this millenium, probably never. And they will definitely never make it if they continue to neglect computer science and software engineering. One source of hope is the object-oriented mode, for it will have a massive influence on CASE, for example by incorporating modularity as an important principle that plays virtually no role at all in CASE today. The scientists could and should give up their reluctance towards CASE and contribute to a new emphasis on software engineering — in a word, to make present-day CAse into a real CASE.

The Gurus

The influence of several "gurus" was and remains huge: Tom DeMarco, Ed Yourdon, Larry Constantine, James Martin and a few others have shaped the world of software engineering, especially as far as CASE is concerned. Which side do they belong to, business or science? I don't think either one. They're first-class writers who have published a number of widely noted books (James Martin around eighty of them) and hold worldwide commercial congresses and seminars that are well-received by practitioners and strongly influence decision-makers. They're the theoreticians of software engineering because they don't report about their own practical project experience (which is many years behind them, if any). Still, that doesn't make them scientists. They rarely refer to scientific works; Parnas on modularization, for example, has scarcely affected them. The result of all this is superficial ideas, "tried out" in seminars where they're then fed to the practitioners and additionally implemented in CASE tools. (Once again there's a company designing a completely new CASE system according to James Martin's newest book *Object-oriented Analysis and Design.*)

Although they're scientists, the gurus naturally live in the business world. It should view their messages much more critically than before, though, while paying more attention to solid ideas and being more cautious of gimmickry. Here science can and should help.

Literature

Who reads (or doesn't read) what? The two worlds of science and business are especially far apart in their reading. As far as I can see, the practitioners tend to read little specialized literature (I don't include the German *Computerwoche* and *Online*), and there are virtually no computer science libraries in the companies, aside from some manufacturers and a few software houses. The events and publications of the German Gesellschaft für Informatik (GI) play a modest — and hopefully growing — role.

Which scientific publications can be recommended to practitioners? Definitely not *IEEE Transactions on Software Engineering*; they've become so mathematically formal that they could almost be an organ of theoretical computer science. Nor does the situation look much better with the new *acm Transactions on Software Engineering*. The specialized publications *Software Engineering Notes* (acm) and *Softwaretechnik-Trends* (GI) are good at up-to-date publication of less theoretical developments, but not always of the best quality.

Worthy of a strong recommendation to practitioners (and also scientists) is *IEEE Software*, as well as *Datamation* and *Software Magazine* (the latter not as specialized literature, but rather as a supplement to *Computerwoche* and *Online*). Noteworthy though expensive magazines are Ed Yourdon's *American Programmer* and Bob

Glass' *The Software Practitioner*, equally inspiring both for scientists and practitioners.

Scientists have to publish (or perish!), while practitioners rarely do. And so it will remain. Still, scientists in the field of software engineering ought to devote more of their efforts to achieving useful practical results and communicating them to the practitioners, rather than simply promoting the scholarly circuit of paper flow. And the practitioners should more frequently show the courage to publish their knowledge and experiences, even if this requires some additional work, doesn't bring in extra money, doesn't directly promote one's career. This also requires some encouragement from management.

Education

Computer science education at universities and colleges is generally good; I don't share the complaints habitual among practitioners. Certainly there are some improvements I would like to see. The coursework of every computer science student who wants to become a software engineer should include creating a large chunk of software, at least 5000 lines of code — and that preferably as part of a project team, so that the student doesn't only learn how to solve a technical problem, but also the connected social problems of human communication. This will prove most effective when the programming case applies to some less familiar side subject, for the developer of business information systems has to have the will and the ability to deal with an unknown area of application (it doesn't matter what kind, except that I don't count mathematics). This would also allow the linkage of two themes that should receive more attention in the educational process: requirements specification and testing.

Special system knowledge is less important than the ability to acquire it quickly if necessary. I'm not among those who demand that universities teach Cobol (which is merely one representative of a whole range of practically oriented languages and systems). What I do expect, though, is that the computer science students learn enough special knowledge (I've already bemoaned the lack of knowledge about transaction monitors) in order to arrive at informed judgement. And they shouldn't approach such areas in practice with the fastidious attitude that I often encounter and which is a result of the beautiful new world of technology depicted in glowing terms at university. Above all else, his studies should give the future software engineer the attitude that his primary task is to find the best possible solution to a given application problem with existing technologies that aren't necessarily the most up-to-date (and often for good reason).

Communications and Management

Good team spirit is more important for the success of a software project than any technology. For this reason management must constantly do its best to provide the conditions for a good working climate. Such a climate can only come about within the team itself, with everyone contributing; the better communications and understanding, the better the climate.

Good communications are also important in order to pass on project results to the outside world (management, users, customers). Of course, communication skills are also vital in advance, in order to get the necessary information. The ability to ask questions is crucial; indeed, one must be able to find out answers to questions that haven't even been asked. All this is self-evident. And yet I constantly encounter managers who don't create conditions for job enjoyment — not because they don't want to, but because they don't know how. On the other hand, university professors emphasize technology (this is their area, after all) and neglect to train their students in basic communication skills, whether this be because they do not see this as their job or because circumstances interfere. But good abilities in communication and management are vital in practice, so vital, that they should receive much more attention in computer-science education.

Summary

There's a wide gap between software engineering in science and business — a gap expressed in problems, interests, and language. This is a pity, since here as in other engineering disciplines practitioners should seek the help of theory and not view it as an alien world. Certainly there are some links between the worlds, such as Unix and E/R modelling, but they remain few. In order to improve this state of affairs, both sides have to move toward each other, find common interests, exchange information, listen to each other, work together. How often do people really ask others about their concerns and then listen to the answer instead of talking about their own affairs?

The practitioners must make the effort to understand the ideas of the scientists and to apply them for their own purposes. It's worth it; all the most valuable innovations have followed this direction. Contrarily, the scientists must recognize, understand, and take into account the genuine practical needs of the software engineers. Only then can scientific works be done that are practically useful and not just a further development of favorite theories whose relation to practical work is mentioned only in the introductions of publications.

The most important thing is to change sides frequently; far more people should become border-crossers. Professors for software engineering should have experience with business projects. This is far better than doing a Habilitation (post doctoral thesis), which in my opinion can even be detrimental insofar as it prevents widespread practical experience. And how about a sabbatical with a German company rather than in sunny California? Practitioners, in turn, should go to the universities and do some teaching. What manager will give a green light for that and what university will request it?

This report should provoke disagreement or trigger arguments through its undoubtedly controversial, perhaps even provocative statements. That, in any case, is my intention.

Software Faults in Evolving a Large, Real-Time System: a Case Study

Dewayne E. Perry and Carol S. Stieg

[1] AT&T Bell Laboratories, 600 Mountain Avenue, Murray Hill, NJ 07974 USA
[2] AT&T Bell Laboratories, 263 Shuman Blvd, Naperville, NJ 60566 USA

Abstract. We report the results of a survey about the software faults encountered during the testing phases in evolving a large real-time system. The survey was done in two parts: the first part surveyed all the faults that were reported and characterized them in terms of general categories; the second part resurveyed in depth the faults found in the design and coding phases. For the first part, we describe describe the questionaire, report the general faults found, and characterize the requirements, design and coding faults by the testing phases in which they were found and by the time they were found during the testing interval. For the second part, we describe the questionaire used to survey the design and coding faults, report the faults that occurred, how difficult they were to find and fix, what their underlying causes were (that is, what their corresponding errors were), and what means might have prevented them from occurring. We then characterize the results in terms of interface and implementation faults.

1 Introduction

It is surprising that so few software fault studies have appeared in the software engineering literature, especially since monitoring our mistakes is one of the fundamental means by which we improve our process and product. This is particularly true for the development of large systems. In preceding work [13, 14], Perry and Evangelist reported the prevalence of interface faults as a major factor in the development and evolution of a large real-time system (68% of the faults). One of the main purposes of that software fault study was to indicate the importance of tools (such as the Inscape Environment [16]) that manage interfaces and the dependencies on those interfaces.

Prior to this work, Endres [7], Schneidewind and Hoffman [19], and Glass [8] reported on various fault analyses of software development, but did not delineate interface faults as a specific category. Thayer, Lipow and Nelson [21] and Bowen [5] provide extensive categorization of faults, but with a relatively narrow view of interface faults. Basili and Perricone [2] offer the most comprehensive study of problems encountered in the development phase of a medium-scale system, reporting data on the fault, the number of components affected, the type of the fault, and the effort required to correct the fault. Interface faults were the largest class of faults (39% of the faults).

We make two important contributions in this case study. First, we present software fault data on evolutionary development [16], not on initial development as previous studies have done. Second, we use a novel approach in which we emphasize the cost of the finding (i.e., reproducing) and fixing faults and the means of preventing them.

In section 2, we provide the background for the study, describing the system in general terms, and the methodology employed in evolving the system. In section 3, we describe our experimental strategy and the approach we used in conducting the survey. In section 4, we report the overall Modification Request (MR) survey, providing first a summary of the questionnaire, then a summary of the results, and finally some conclusions. In section 5, we present the design and coding fault survey, providing first a summary of the questionnaire, then a discussion of the analysis, and finally a summary relating the results to interface faults. In section 6, we present conclusions and recommendations.

2 Background

The system discussed in this paper is a very large [3] scale, distributed, real-time system written in the C programming language in a Unix-based, multiple machine, multiple location environment.

The organizational structure is typical with respect to AT&T projects for systems of this size and for the number of people in each organization. Not surprisingly, different organizations are responsible for various parts of the system development: requirements specification; architecture, design, coding and capability testing; system and system stability testing; and alpha testing.

The process of development is also typical with respect to AT&T projects of this size. Systems Engineers prepare informal and structured documents defining the requirements for the changes to be made to the system. Designers prepare informal design documents that are subjected to formal reviews by three to fifteen peers depending on the size of the unit under consideration. The design is then broken into design units for low level design and coding. The products of this last phase are subjected both to formal code reviews by three to five reviewers and to low level unit testing. As components become available, integration and system testing is performed until the system is completely integrated.

The release considered here is a "non-initial" release —one that can be viewed as an arbitrary point in the evolution of this class of systems. Because of the size of the system, the system evolution process consists of multiple, concurrent releases —that is, while the release dates are sequential, a number of releases proceed concurrently in differing phases. This concurrency accentuates the inter-release dependencies and their associated problems. The magnitude of the changes (approximately 15-20% new code for each release) and the general make-up of the changes (bug-fixes, improvements, and new functionality, etc.) are generally uniform across releases. It is because of these two facts that we

[3] By "very large", we mean a system of 1,000,000 NCSL or more [4]. AT&T has a wide variety of such very large systems.

consider this study to provide a representative sample in the life of the project. This relative uniformity of releases contrasts with Lehman and Belady [11] where releases alternated between adding new functionality and fixing existing problems.

Faults discovered during testing phases are reported and monitored by a modification request (MR) tracking system (such as for example, CMS [18]). Access to source files for modification is possible only through the tracking system. Thus all source change activity is automatically tracked by the system. This activity includes not only repairs but enhancements and new functionality as well. It should be kept in mind, however, that this fault tracking activity occurs only during the testing and released phases of the project, not during the architecture, design and coding phases. Problems encountered during these earlier phases are resolved informally without being tracked by the MR system.

3 Survey Strategy

The goal of this study was to gain insight into the current process of system evolution by concentrating on a representative release of a particular system. The approach we used is that of surveying, by means of prepared questionnaires, those who "owned" the MR at the time it was closed. We conducted two studies: first, we surveyed the complete set of faults; second, we resurveyed the largest set of faults (i.e., the design and coding faults) in more depth.

It was mandated by management that the survey be non-intrusive, anonymous and strictly voluntary. The questionaire was created by the authors working with a group of developers involved in the study. It was reviewed by an independent group of developers who were also part of the subject development. What we were not able to do was to validate any of the results [3] and hence cannot assess the accuracy of the resulting data.

68% of the questionaires were returned in both parts of the study. In each case, the sample size was very large —sufficiently large to justify the precision that we use in the remainder of the paper. While there might be some questions about the representativeness of the responses, we know of no factors that would skew the results significantly [1].

4 Overall Survey

There were three specific purposes in the initial, overall survey:

- to determine what kinds of general problems (which we report here) and what kinds of specific application problems (which we do not report because of their lack of generality) were found during the preparation of this release;
- to determine how the problem was found (that is, in which testing phase);
- to determine when the problem was found.

In the discussion that follows, we first present a summary of the questionnaire, summarize our results, and draw some conclusions.

4.1 Questionnaire

The first survey questionnaire has two main components: the determination of the fault reported in the MR and the testing phase in which the fault was found. In determining the fault, two aspects were of importance: first, the development phase in which the fault was introduced, and second, the particular type of the fault. Since the particular type of fault reported at this stage of the survey tended to be application or methodology specific, we have emphasized the phase-origin nature of the fault categorization. The general fault categories are as follows:

- *Previous* —residual problems left over from previous releases;
- *Requirements* —problems originating during the requirements specification phase of development;
- *Design* —problems originating during the architectural and design phases of development;
- *Coding* —problems originating during the coding phases of development;
- *Testing Environment* —problems originating in the construction or provision of the testing environment (for example, faults in the system configuration, static data, etc);
- *Testing* —problems in testing (for example, pilot faults, etc);
- *Duplicates* —problems that have already been reported;
- *No problems* —problems due to misunderstandings about interfaces, functionality, etc., on the part of the user;
- *Other* —various problems that do not fit neatly in the preceding categories such as hardware problems, etc.

The other main component of the survey concerned the phase of testing that uncovered the fault. The following are the different testing phases.

- *Capability Test* (CT) —testing isolated portions of the system to ensure proper capabilities of that portion.
- *System Test* (ST) —testing the entire system to ensure proper execution of the system as a whole in the laboratory environment.
- *System Stability Test* (SS) —testing with simulated load conditions in the laboratory environment for extended periods of time.
- *Alpha Test* (AT) —live use of the release in a friendly user environment.
- *Released* (RE) —live use. However, in this study, this data refers not to this release, but the previous release. Our expectation is that this provides a projection of the fault results for this release.

The time interval during which the faults were found (that is, when the MRs were initiated) was retrieved from database of the MR tracking system.

Ideally, the testing phases occur sequentially. In practice, however, due to the size and complexity of the system, various phases overlap. The overlap is due to several specific factors. First, various parts of the system are modified in parallel. This means that the various parts of the system are in different states at any one time. Second, the iterative nature of evolution results in recycling back through previous phases for various parts of the system. Third, various testing phases are begun as early as possible, even though it is known that that component may be incomplete.

Looked at in one way, testing proceeds in a hierarchical manner: testing is begun with various pieces, then subsystems and finally integrating those larger parts into the complete system. It is a judgment call as to when different parts of the system move from one phase to the next determined primarily by the percentage of capabilities incorporated and the number of tests executed. Looked at in a slightly different way, testing proceeds by increasing the system's size and complexity, while at the same time increasing its load and stress.

4.2 Results

We present the summary of each fault category and discuss some of the main issues that stem from these results. Next we summarize the requirements, design and coding faults first as found by testing phase and then as found by time interval.

Table 1. Summary of Responses

MR Categories	Proportion
Previous	4.0%
Requirements	4.9%
Design	10.6%
Coding	18.2%
Testing Environment	19.1%
Testing	5.7%
Duplicates	13.9%
No problems	15.9%
Other	7.8%

Responses. Table 1 summarizes the frequency of the MRs by category. "Previous" problems are those which existed in precious releases but only surfaced in the current release. They indicate the difficulty in finding some faults and the difficulty in achieving comprehensive test coverage. The MRs representing the earlier part of the development or evolution process (that is, those representing requirements, design and coding) are the most significant, accounting for approximately 33.7% of the MRs.

The next most significant subset of MRs were those that concern testing (the testing environment and testing categories) —24.8% of the MRs. It is not surprising that a significant number of problems are encountered in testing a large and complex real-time system where conditions have to be simulated to represent the "real-world" in a laboratory environment. First, the testing environment itself is a large and complex system that must be tested. Second, as the real-time system evolves, so must the laboratory test environment evolve.

"Duplicate" and "No Problem" MRs are another significant subset of the data —28.9%. Historically, they have been considered to be part of the overhead. The

Fig. 1. Fault Categories found by Testing Phase

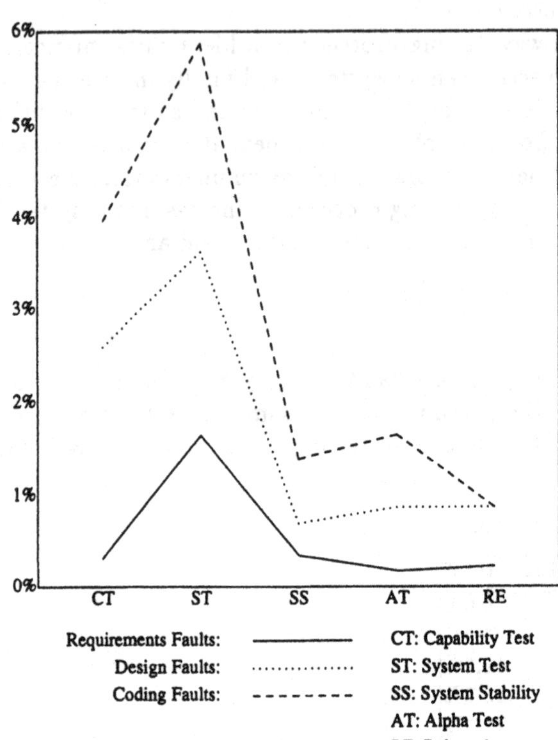

"duplicate" MRs are in large part due to the inherent concurrency of activities in a large-scale project and, as such, are difficult to eliminate.

Results by Testing Phase and Time. We focus on the early part of the software process because that is where the most MRs occur and, accordingly, where close attention should yield the most results. For this reason, we present the requirements, design and coding faults distributed by testing phase.

For the requirements, design and coding fault categories, Figure 1 shows the percentage of MRs found during each testing phase. There are two important observations. First, system test (ST) was the source of most of the MRs in each category; capability testing (CT) was the next largest source. Second, all testing phases found MRs of each fault category.

We note that there are two reasons why design and requirements faults continue to be found throughout the entire testing process. First, requirements often change during the long development interval represented here. Second, informal requirement and design documents lack precision and completeness (a general problem in the current state-of-practice rather than a project-specific problem).

The data present in figure 2 represents the same MRs as in figure 1, but displayed according to when they were found during the testing interval. The

Fig. 2. Fault Categories found over Time

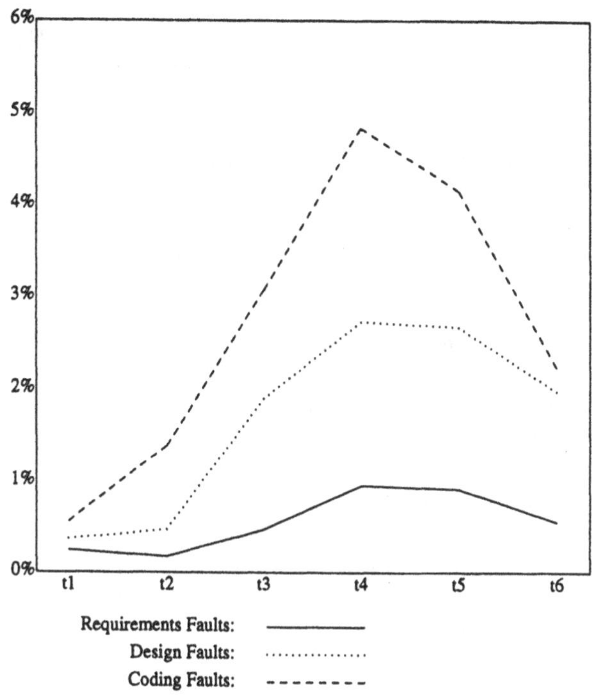

time values here are fixed (and relatively long) intervals. From the shape of the data, it is clear that System Testing overlaps interval t4.

For the requirements, design and coding fault categories over time, Figure 2 shows that all fault types peaked at time t4, and held through time t5, except for the coding faults which decreased. The two figures are different because there is non-trivial mapping between testing phase and calendar time.

4.3 Summary

The following general observations may be drawn from this general survey of the problems encountered in evolving a very large real-time system:

- all faults occurred throughout all the testing phases, and
- the majority of faults were found late in the testing interval.

These observations are limited by the fact that the tracking of MRs is primarily a testing activity. It would be extremely useful to observe the kinds and frequencies of faults that exists in the earlier phases of the project. Moreover, it would be beneficial to incorporate ways of detecting requirements and design faults into the existing development process.

5 Design/Code Fault Survey

As a result of the general survey, we decided to resurvey the design and coding MRs in depth. The following were the goals we wanted to achieve in this part of the study:

- determine the kinds of faults that occurred in design and coding;
- determine the difficulty both in finding or reproducing these faults and in fixing them;
- determine the underlying causes of the faults; and
- determine how the faults might have been prevented.

There were two reasons for choosing this part of the general set of MRs. First, it seemed to be exceedingly difficult to separate the two kinds of faults. Second, catching these kinds of faults earlier in the process would provide a significant reduction in overall fault cost —that is, the cost of finding faults before system integration is significantly less than finding them in the laboratory testing environment. Our internal cost data is consistent with Boehm's [4]. Thus, gaining insight into these problems will yield significant and cost beneficial results.

In the three subsections that follow, we summarize the survey questionnaire, present the results of our analysis, and summarize our findings with regard to interface and implementation faults.

5.1 Questionnaire

For every MR, we asked for the following information: the actual fault, the difficulty of finding and fixing the fault, the underlying cause, the best means of either preventing or avoiding the problem, and their level of confidence in their responses.

Fault Types. For this fault, consider the following 22 possible types and select the one that most closely applies to the cause of this MR.

1. *Language pitfalls* —e.g., the use of "=" instead of "= =".
2. *Protocol* —violated rules about interprocess communication.
3. *Low-level logic* —e.g., loop termination problems, pointer initialization, etc.
4. *CMS complexity* —e.g., due to change management system complexity.
5. *Internal functionality* —either inadequate functionality or changes and/or additions were needed to existing functionality within the module or subsystem.
6. *External functionality* —either inadequate functionality or changes and/or additions were needed to existing functionality outside the module or subsystem.
7. *Primitives misused* —the design or code depended on primitives which were not *used* correctly.

8. *Primitives unsupported* —the design or code depended on primitives that were not adequately developed (that is, the primitives did not work correctly).
9. *Change coordination* —either did not know about previous changes or depended on concurrent changes.
10. *Interface complexity* —interfaces were badly structured or incomprehensible.
11. *Design/Code complexity* —the implementation was badly structured or incomprehensible.
12. *Error handling* —incorrect handling of, or recovery from, exceptions.
13. *Race conditions* —incorrect coordination in the sharing of data.
14. *Performance* —e.g., real-time constraints, resource access, or response time constraints.
15. *Resource allocation* —incorrect resource allocation and deallocation.
16. *Dynamic data design* —incorrect design of dynamic data resources or structures.
17. *Dynamic data use* —incorrect *use* of dynamic data structures (for example, initialization, maintaining constraints, etc.).
18. *Static data design* —incorrect design of static data structures (for example, their location, partitioning, redundancy, etc.).
19. *Unknown Interactions* —unknowingly involved other functionality or parts of the system.
20. *Unexpected dependencies* —unexpected interactions or dependencies on other parts of the system.
21. *Concurrent work* —unexpected dependencies on concurrent work in other releases.
22. *Other* —describe the fault.

Ease of Finding or Reproducing the Fault. The MR in question is to be ranked according to how difficult it was to reproduce the failure and locate the fault.

1. *Easy* —could produce at will.
2. *Moderate* —happened some of the time (intermittent).
3. *Difficult* —needed theories to figure out how to reproduce the error.
4. *Very Difficult* —exceedingly hard to reproduce.

Ease of Fixing the Fault. For each MR, how much time was needed to design and code the fix, document and test it. [4]

1. *Easy* —less than one day
2. *Moderate* —1 to 5 days
3. *Difficult* —6 to 30 days
4. *Very difficult* —greater than 30 days

[4] Note that what would be an easy fix in a single programmer system takes considerably more time in a large, multi-person project with a complex laboratory test environment.

Underlying Causes. Because the fault may be only a symptom, provide what you regard to be the underlying root cause for each problem.

1. *None given* —no underlying causes given.
2. *Incomplete/omitted requirements* —the source of the fault stemmed from either incomplete or unstated requirements.
3. *Ambiguous requirements* —the requirements were (informally) stated, but they were open to more than one interpretation. The interpretation selected was evidently incorrect.
4. *Incomplete/omitted design* —the source of the fault stemmed from either incomplete or unstated design specifications.
5. *Ambiguous design* —the design was (informally) given, but was open to more than one interpretation. The interpretation selected was evidently incorrect.
6. *Earlier incorrect fix* —the fault was induced by an earlier incorrect fix (that is, the fault was not the result of new development).
7. *Lack of knowledge* —there was something that I needed to know, but did not know that I needed to know it.
8. *Incorrect modification* —I suspected that the solution was incorrect, but could not determine how to correctly solve the problem.
9. *Submitted under duress* —the solution was submitted under duress, knowing that it was incorrect (generally due to schedule pressure, etc).
10. *Other* —describe the underlying cause.

Means of Prevention. For this fault, consider possible ways to prevent or avoid it and select the most useful or appropriate choice for preventing or avoiding the fault.

1. *Formal requirements* —use precise, unambiguous requirements (or design) in a formal notation (which may be either graphical or textual).
2. *Requirements/Design templates* —provide more specific requirements (or design) document templates.
3. *Formal interface specifications* —use a formal notation for describing the module interfaces.
4. *Training* —provide discussions, training seminars, and formal courses.
5. *Application walk-throughs* —determine, informally, the interactions among the various application specific processes and data objects.
6. *Expert person/documentation* —provide an "expert" person or clear documentation when needed.
7. *Design/code currency* —keep design documents up to date with code changes.
8. *Guideline enforcement* —enforce code inspections guidelines and the use of static analysis tools such as lint.
9. *Better test planning* —provide better test planning and/or execution (for example, automatic regression testing).
10. *Others* —describe the means of prevention.

Confidence Levels. Confidence levels requested of the respondents were: *very high, high, moderate, low* and *very low* . We discarded the small number of responses (6%) that had a confidence level of either low or very low.

5.2 Analysis

Table 2. Chi-Square Analysis Summary

Variables	Degrees of Freedom	Total Chi-Square	p
Find, Fix	6	51.489	.0001
Fault, Find	63	174.269	.0001
Fault, Fix	63	204.252	.0001
Cause, Find	27	94.493	.0001
Cause, Fix	27	55.232	.0011
Fault, Cause	189	403.136	.0001
Prevention, Find	27	41.021	.041
Prevention, Fix	27	97.886	.0001
Fault, Prevention	189	492.826	.0001
Cause, Prevention	81	641.417	.0001

To understand the relationships between the faults, the effort to find and fix them, their underlying causes, and their means of prevention, the results of the survey were cross tabulated and then subjected to chi-square analysis. Table 2 provides a summary of the chi-square analysis.

To identify relationships, we tested against the hypothesis that each member of pairs were independent of each other. To establish whether any relationship existed we used the Chi-Square test [20]. Table 2 provides the results of that test. The numbers show that the relationships are statistically significant at the level indicated by the value of p. Note that that in all cases the relationships are statistically significant.

The relationship between the means of prevention and the ease of finding the fault coming closest to being independent (because $p = .041$; if p had been .05 or greater, we would say they were independent). The relationship between the means of prevention and the underlying causes is the most significantly interdependent (because the total chi-square is so large).

In earlier work, Perry and Evangelist [13,14] received comments about the cost of faults —specifically, were the interface faults the easy ones or the hards ones. It is with these questions in mind that we included the questions about the effort to find and fix the faults. We have devised simple weighting measures for finding and fixing faults that are meant to be indicative rather than definitive. These measures are intended to support a relative, not absolute, comparison of the faults with each other.

To estimate the effort to find a fault, we determine the weight by multiplying the proportion of observed values for each fault by 1, 2, 3 and 4 for each effort category, respectively, and sum the results. For example, if a fault was easy to find in 66% of the cases, moderate in 23%, difficult in 11%, and very difficult in

1%, the weight is 146 = (66 * 1) + (23 * 2) + (10 * 3) + (1 * 4). The higher the weight, the more effort required to find the fault.

To estimate the effort to fix a fault, we determine the weight by multiplying the proportion of observed values for each fault by 1, 3, 15, and 30. We chose these values because they are a reasonable approximation to the average length of time to fix each set of faults. Using the same proportions as above, the corresponding fix weight would be 315 = (66 * 1) + (23 * 3) + (10 * 15) + (1 * 30).

To compute the effort-adjusted frequencies of each fault, we multiply the number of occurrences of each fault by its weight and divide by the total weighted number of occurrences.

We first consider the difficulty of finding and fixing the faults. We then discuss the faults and the cost of finding and fixing them. Next we consider the underlying causes and the means of prevention, correlate the faults and their effort measures with underlying causes and means of prevention, and then correlate underlying causes and means of prevention. Finally, we divide the faults into interface and implementation categories and compare them in terms of difficulty to find and fix, their underlying causes and their means of prevention.

Finding and Fixing Faults. 91% of the faults were easy to moderate to find; 78% took less than 5 days to fix. In general, the easier to find faults were easier to fix; the more difficult to find faults were more difficult to fix as well. There were more faults that were easy to find and took less than one day to fix than were expected by the chi-square analysis. Interestingly, there were fewer than expected easy to find faults that took 6 to 30 days to fix.

Table 3. Summary of Find/Fix Effort

Find/Fix Effort	$\leq$ 5 Days	$\geq$ 6 Days
easy/moderate	72.5%	18.4%
difficult/very difficult	5.9%	3.2%

While the coordinates of the effort to find and fix the faults are not comparable, we note that the above relationship between them is suggestive. Moreover, it seems counter to the common wisdom that says "once you have found the problem, it is easy to fix it". There is a significant number of "easy/moderate to find" faults that require a relatively long time to fix.

Faults. Table 4 shows the fault types of the MRs as ordered by their frequency in the survey independent of any other factors. We also show the effort weights,the effort ranks, and the weight-adjusted frequencies for finding and fixing these faults.

The first 5 fault categories account for 60% of the observed faults. That "internal functionality" is the leading fault by such a large margin is somewhat surprising; that "interface complexity" is such a significant problem is not surprising at all. However, that the first five faults are leading faults is consistent with the nature of the evolution of the system. Adding significant amounts of

Table 4. Faults Ordered by Frequency

Fault Description		Observed	Find Weight	Find Rank	Find Adj'd	Fix Weight	Fix Rank	Fix Adj'd
5	internal functionality	25.0%	134	14	23.4%	414	13	18.7%
10	interface complexity	11.4%	145	11	11.6%	607	10	12.6%
20	unexpected dependencies	8.0%	124	19	7.2%	786	4	11.3%
3	low-level logic	7.9%	132	15	7.3%	245	17	3.5%
11	design/code complexity	7.7%	164	3	8.8%	904	3	12.6%
22	other	5.8%	131	16	5.5%	499	12	5.4%
9	change coordination	4.9%	150	10	5.1%	394	14	3.5%
21	concurrent work	4.4%	131	16	4.0%	661	9	5.2%
13	race conditions	4.3%	209	1	6.3%	709	7	5.5%
6	external functionality	3.6%	139	13	3.5%	682	8	4.4%
1	language pitfalls	3.5%	141	12	3.3%	244	18	1.5%
12	error handling	3.3%	163	4	3.7%	717	6	4.3%
7	primitive's misuse	2.4%	120	20	2.0%	520	11	2.2%
17	dynamic data use	2.1%	158	6	2.3%	392	15	1.5%
15	resource allocation	1.5%	161	5	1.7%	1326	2	3.6%
18	static data design	1.0%	100	21	.7%	200	19	.4%
14	performance	.9%	199	2	1.3%	1402	1	2.3%
19	unknown interactions	.7%	157	7	.8%	785	5	1.0%
8	primitives unsupported	.6%	151	9	.6%	200	19	.2%
2	protocol	.4%	125	18	.2%	250	16	.2%
4	CMS complexity	.3%	100	21	.2%	166	21	.1%
16	dynamic data design	.3%	157	7	.3%	166	21	.1%

new functionality to a system easily accounts for problems with "internal functionality", "low-level logic" and "external functionality".

The fact that the system is a very large, complicated real-time system easily accounts for the fact that there are problems with "interface complexity", "unexpected dependencies" and design/code complexity", "change coordination" and "concurrent work".

C has well-known "language pitfalls" that account for the rank of that fault in the middle of the set. Similarly, "race conditions" are a reasonably significant problem because of the lack of suitable language facilities in C.

That "performance" faults are a relatively insignificant is probably due to the fact that this is not an early release of the system. Their first ranking fix weight is consistent with our intuition that they are extremely difficult to fix.

Finding and Fixing Faults. We find the weighted ordering here affirms our intuition of how difficult these faults might be to find. Typically, performance faults and race conditions are very difficult to isolate and reproduce. We would expect that "code complexity" and "error handling" faults would also be difficult to find and reproduce.

When we inspect the chi-square test for faults and find effort, we notice that "internal functionality", "unexpected dependencies" and "other" tended to be easier to find than expected. "Code complexity" and "performance" tended to be harder to find than expected. There tended to be more significant deviations where the sample population was larger.

Adjusting the frequency by the effort to find the faults results in only a slight shift in the ordering of the faults. "Internal functionality", "code complexity", and "race conditions" change slightly more than the rest of the faults.

Adjusting the frequency by the effort to fix the fault causes some interesting shifts in the ordering of the faults. "Language pitfalls", "low-level logic", and "internal functionality" drop significantly in their relative importance. This coincides with one's intuition about these kinds of faults —i.e., they are easy to fix. "Design/code complexity", "resource allocation", and "unexpected dependencies" rise significantly in their relative importance; "interface complexity", "race conditions", and "performance" rise but not significantly so.

The top four faults account for 55% of the effort expended to fix all the faults and 51% of the effort to find them, but represent 52% of the faults by observed frequency. Collectively, they are somewhat harder to fix than rest of the faults and slightly easier to find. We again note that while the two scales are not strictly comparable, the comparison is an interesting one none-the-less.

When we inspect the chi-square test for faults and find effort, we notice that "language pitfalls", and "low-level logic" took fewer days to fix than expected. "Interface complexity" and "internal functionality" took 1 to 30 days more often than expected, while "design/code complexity" and "unexpected dependencies" took longer to fix (that is, 6 to over 30 days) than expected. These deviations reenforce our weighted assessment of the effort to fix the faults.

Underlying Causes. Table 5 shows the underlying causes of the MRs as ordered by their frequency in the survey independent of any other factors, the effort weights, effort ranks, and effort-adjusted frequencies for finding and fixing the faults with these underlying causes.

Table 5. Underlying causes of Faults

Cause	Description	Observed	Find Weight	Find Rank	Find Adj'd	Fix Weight	Fix Rank	Fix Adj'd
4	incomplete/omitted design	25.2%	139	8	24.6%	653	3	29.7%
1	none given	20.5%	150	2	21.5%	412	10	15.2%
7	lack of knowledge	17.8%	135	9	16.8%	525	8	16.8%
5	ambiguous design	9.8%	141	6	9.6%	464	9	8.1%
6	earlier incorrect fix	7.3%	147	4	7.5%	544	7	7.1%
9	submitted under duress	6.8%	158	1	7.5%	564	6	6.9%
2	incomplete/omitted req's	5.4%	143	5	5.4%	698	2	6.8%
10	other	4.1%	148	3	4.2%	640	4	4.7%
3	ambiguous requirements	2.0%	140	7	2.9%	940	1	3.4%
8	incorrect modification	1.1%	109	10	.8%	588	5	1.3%

Weighting the underlying causes by the effort to find or reproduce the faults for which these are the underlying causes produces almost no change in either the ordering or in the relative proportion of the underlying causes.

With respect to the relative difficulty in finding the faults associated with the underlying causes, the resulting ordering is particularly non-intuitive: the MRs with no underlying cause are the second most difficult to find; those submitted under duress are the most difficult to find.

Weighting the underlying causes by the effort to fix the faults represented by the underlying causes yields a few shifts in the proportion of effort: "incomplete/omitted design" increased significantly, "unclear requirements" and "incomplete/omitted requirements" increased less significantly; "none" decreased significantly, "unclear design" and "other" decreased less significantly. However, the relative ordering of the various underlying causes is approximately the same.

The relative weighting of the effort to fix these kinds of underlying causes seems to coincide with one's intuition very nicely.

When we inspect the chi-square test for fix effort and underlying causes, we notice faults caused by "none given" tended to take less time to fix than expected, while faults caused by "incomplete/omitted design" and "submitted under duress" tended to take more time to fix than expected.

The high proportion of "none given" as an underlying cause requires some explanation. One of the reasons for this is that faults such as "language pitfalls", "low-level logic", "race conditions" and "change coordination" tend to be both the fault and the underlying cause (7.8% —or 33% of the in the "none given" underlying cause category). In addition, one could easily imagine that some of the faults such as "interface complexity" and "design/code complexity" could also be considered both the fault and the underlying cause (3.3% —or 16% of the faults in the "none given" underlying cause category). On the other hand, we were surprised that no cause was given for a substantial part of the "internal functionality" faults (3.7% —or 18% of the faults in the "none given" category). One would expect there to be some underlying cause for that particular fault.

Means of Prevention. Table 6 shows the suggested means of prevention of the faults as ordered by their occurrence independent of any other factors, the effort weights, effort ranks, and effort-adjusted frequencies for finding and fixing the faults to which these means of prevention are applicable. We note that the various means of prevention are by no means independent or non-overlapping. Moreover, the means selected may well reflect a particular approach of the responder in selecting one means over another (for example, see the discussion below about formal versus informal means of prevention).

It is interesting to note that the application-specific means of prevention ("application walk-throughs") is considered the most effective means of prevention. This selection of application walk-throughs as the most useful means of error prevention appears to confirm the observation of Curtis, Krasner and Iscoe [6] that a thin spread of application knowledge is one of the most significant problem in building large systems.

Further it is worth noting that informal means of prevention rank higher than formal ones. On the one hand, this may reflect the general bias in the United States against formal methods. On the other hand, the informal means are a non-technical solution to providing the information that may be supplied by the formal representations (and which provide a more technical solution with higher

Table 6. Means of Error Prevention

Means	Description	Observed	Find Weight	Find Rank	Find Adj'd	Fix Weight	Fix Rank	Fix Adj'd
5	appl'n walk-throughs	24.5%	140	8	24.0%	438	8	18.9%
6	expert person/doc'n	15.7%	145	2	15.9%	706	3	19.6%
8	guideline enforcement	13.3%	154	1	14.3%	389	10	9.1%
2	req's/design templates	10.0%	129	10	9.1%	654	5	11.6%
9	better test planning	9.9%	145	2	10.1%	401	9	7.0%
1	formal requirements	8.8%	144	6	8.8%	740	2	11.4%
3	formal interface spec's	7.2%	142	7	7.1%	680	4	8.6%
10	other	6.9%	145	2	7.0%	517	6	8.7%
4	training	2.2%	145	2	2.2%	1016	1	3.9%
7	design/code currency	1.5%	140	8	1.5%	460	7	1.2%

adoption costs).

The level of effort to find the faults for which these are the means of prevention does not change the order found in the table above, with the exception of "requirements/design templates" which seems to apply to the easier to find faults and "better test planning" which seems to apply more to somewhat harder to find faults.

When we inspect the chi-square test for find effort and means of prevention, we notice that the relationship between finding faults and preventing them is the most independent of the relationships discussed here. "Application walk-throughs" applied to faults that were marginally easier to find than expected, while "guideline enforcement" applied to faults that were less easy to find than expected.

When we inspect the chi-square test for fix effort and means of prevention, it is interesting to note that the faults considered to be prevented by training are the hardest to fix. Formal methods also apply to classes of faults that take a long time to fix.

Effort-adjusting the frequency by fix effort yields a few shifts in proportion: "application walk-throughs", "guideline enforcement" and "better test planning" decreased in proportion; "expert person/documentation" and "formal requirements" increased in proportion, "formal interface specifications" and "other" less so. As a result, the ordering changes slightly to faults 6, 5, 2, 1, 8, 10, 3, 9, 4, 7: "expert person/documentation" and " formal requirements" are weighted significantly higher; "requirements/design templates", "formal interface specifications", "training", and "other" are less significantly higher.

When we inspect the chi-square test for faults and means of prevention, we notice that faults prevented by "application walk-throughs", "guideline enforcement", and "other" tended to take fewer days to fix than expected, while faults prevented by "formal requirements", requirements/design templates" and "expert person/documentation" took longer to fix than expected.

Underlying Causes and Means of Prevention. It is interesting to note that in the chi-square test for underlying causes and means of prevention there are a significant number of deviations (that is, there is a wider variance between the actual values and the expected values in correlating underlying causes and means of prevention) and that there does not appear to be much statistical structure. This indicates that there are strong dependencies between the underlying causes and their means of prevention. Intuitively, this type of relationship is just what we would expect.

5.3 Interface Faults versus Implementation Faults

The definition of an interface fault that we use here is that of Basili and Perricone [2] and Perry and Evangelist [13, 14]: interface faults are "those that are associated with structures existing outside the module's local environment but which the module used". Using this definition, we roughly characterize "language pitfalls" (1), "low-level logic" (3), "internal functionality" (5), "design/code complexity" (11), "performance" (14), and "other" (22) as implementation faults. The remainder are considered interface faults. We say "roughly" because there are some cases where the implementation categories may contain some interface problems —e.g., some of the "design/code complexity" faults were considered preventable by formal interface specifications.

Table 7. Interface/Implementation Fault Comparison

	Interface	Implementation
frequency	49%	51%
find weighted	50%	50%
fix weighted	56%	44%

Interface faults occur with slightly less frequency than implementation faults, but require about the same effort to find them and more effort to fix them.

In table 8, we compare interface and implementation faults with respect to their underlying causes. Underlying causes "other", "ambiguous requirements", "none given", "earlier incorrect fix" and "ambiguous design" tended to be the underlying causes more for implementation faults than for interface faults. Underlying causes "incomplete/omitted requirements", "incorrect modification" and "submitted under duress" tended to be the causes more for interface faults than for implementation faults.

We note that underlying causes that involved ambiguity tended to result more in implementation faults than in interface faults, while underlying causes involving incompleteness or omission of information tended to result more in interface faults than in implementation faults.

In table 9, we compare interface and implementation faults with respect to the means of prevention. Not surprisingly "formal requirements" and formal interface requirements" were more applicable to interface faults than to implementation faults. "Training", "expert person/documentation" and "guideline enforcement" were considered more applicable to implementation faults than to interface faults.

Table 8. Interface/Implementation Faults and Underlying Causes

	Interface 49%	Implementation 51%
1 none given	45.2%	54.8%
2 incomplete/omitted requirements	79.6%	20.4%
3 ambiguous requirements	44.5%	55.5%
4 incomplete/omitted design	50.8%	49.2%
5 ambiguous design	47.0%	53.0%
6 earlier incorrect fix	45.1%	54.9%
7 lack of knowledge	49.2%	50.8%
8 incorrect modification	54.5%	45.5%
9 submitted under duress	63.1%	36.9%
10 other	39.1%	60.1%

Table 9. Interface/Implementation Faults and Means of Prevention

	Interface 49%	Implementation 51%
1 formal requirements	64.8%	35.2%
2 requirements/design templates	51.5%	48.5%
3 formal interface specifications	73.6%	26.4%
4 training	36.4%	63.6%
5 application walk-troughs	48.0%	52.0%
6 expert person/documentation	44.3%	55.7%
7 design/code currency	46.7%	53.3%
8 guideline enforcement	33.1%	66.9%
9 better test planning	48.0%	52.0%
10 others	49.3%	50.7%

6 Conclusions

We have observed a large number of interesting facts about faults, the cost of finding and fixing them, their underlying causes and means of prevention. We offer the following general conclusions from these observations.

- The evolution of large, complex software systems involves a large overhead: approximately 51% of the MRs in the initial survey represented production faults, while 49% represented overhead faults(such as "duplicate" MRs, "no problem" MRs, and MRs on the system test environment).
- Interface faults were roughly 49% of the entire set of design and coding faults and were harder to fix than the implementation faults. Not surprisingly, formal requirements and formal interface specifications were suggested as significant means of preventing interface faults.
- Lack of information tended to dominate the underlying causes and knowledge intensive activities tended to dominate the means of prevention. Clearly, discovery (and rediscovery) are significant in the evolution of a very large real-time system.
- Relatively few problems would be solved by "better" programming languages (e.g., language pitfalls and race-conditions account for less than 8% of the faults). Technology that helps manage complexity and dependencies would

be much more useful (e.g., internal functionality, interface complexity, unexpected dependencies, low-level logic, and design/code complexity account for 60% of the faults).

The system reported here was developed and evolved using the current "best practice" techniques and tools with well-qualified practitioners. Because of this fact, we feel that this development is generalizable to other large-scale, real-time systems. With this in mind, we offer the following recommendations to improve the current "best practice".

- Obtain fault data throughout the entire development/evolution cycle (not just in the testing cycle) and use it monitor the progress of the evolution process [9].
- Incorporate the non-technological, people-intensive means of prevention into the current process. As our survey has shown, this will yield benefits for the majority of the faults reported here.
- Introduce facilities to increase the precision and completeness of requirements [10,22], architecture and design documents [17] and to manage complexity and dependencies [15]. This will yield benefits for those faults that were generally harder to fix and will help to detect the requirements, architecture and design problems earlier in the life-cycle.

Acknowledgements David Rosik contributed significantly to the general MR survey; Steve Bruun produced the cross-tabulated statistical analysis for the design/code survey and contributed, along with Carolyn Larson, Julie Federico, H. C. Wei and Tony Lenard, to the analysis of the design/code survey; Clive Loader increased our understanding of the chi-square analysis; and Larry Votta helped refine and improve our presentation. We especially thank Marjory P. Yuhas and Lew G. Anderson for their unflagging support of this work. And finally, we thank all those that participated in the survey.

References

1. Basili, Victor R., Hutchens, David H.: An Empirical Study of a Syntactic Complexity Family IEEE Transactions on Software Engineering SE-9:6 (November 1983) 664-672
2. Basili, Victor R., Perricone, Barry T.: Software Errors and Complexity: an Empirical Investigation. Communications of the ACM 27:1 (January 1984) 42-52
3. Basili, Victor R., Weiss, David M.: A Methodology for Collecting Valid Software Engineering Data. IEEE Transactions on Software Engineering SE-10:6 (November 1984) 728-738
4. Boehm, Barry W.: Software Engineering Economics. Englewood Cliffs: Prentice-Hall, 1981
5. Bowen John B.: Standard Error Classification to Support Software Reliability Assessment. AFIPS Conference Proceedings, 1980 National Computer Conference (1980) 697-705

6. Curtis, Bill, Krasner, Herb, Iscoe, Neil: A Field Study of the Software Design Process for Large Systems. Communications of the ACM 31:11 (November 1988) 1268-1287
7. Endres, Albert: An Analysis of Errors and Their Causes in System Programs. IEEE Transactions on Software Engineering SE-1:2 (June 1975) 140-149
8. Glass, Robert L.: Persistent Software Errors. IEEE Transactions on Software Engineering SE-7:2 (March 1981) 162-168
9. Humphrey, Watts S.: Managing the Software Process. Reading, Mass: Addison-Wesley, 1989.
10. Kelly, Van E., Nonnenmann, Uwe: Inferring Formal Software Specifications from Episodic Descriptions. Proceedings of AAAI 87. Sixth National Conference on Artificial Intelligence (13-17 July 1987) Seattle WA, 127-132
11. Lehman, M. M., Belady, L. A.: Program Evolution. Processes of Software Change. London: Academic Press, 1985
12. Ostrand, Thomas J., Weyuker, Elaine J.: Collecting and Categorizing Software Error Data in an Industrial Environment. The Journal of Systems and Software 4 (1984) 289-300
13. Perry, Dewayne E., Evangelist, W. Michael: An Empirical Study of Software Interface Errors. Proceedings of the International Symposium on New Directions in Computing, IEEE Computer Society (August 1985) Trondheim, Norway, 32-38
14. Perry, Dewayne E., Evangelist, W. Michael: An Empirical Study of Software Interface Faults —An Update. Proceedings of the Twentieth Annual Hawaii International Conference on Systems Sciences (January 1987) Volume II 113-126
15. Perry, Dewayne E.: The Inscape Environment. Proceedings of the 11th International Conference on Software Engineering, (15-18 May 1989) Pittsburgh PA, 2-12
16. Perry, Dewayne E.: Industrial Strength Software Development Environments. Proceedings of IFIPS Congress '89 —11th World Computer Congress (August 28 - September 1, 1989) San Francisco CA
17. Perry, Dewayne E., Wolf, Alexander L.: Foundations for the Study of Software Architecture. ACM SIGSOFT Software Engineering Notes 17:4 (October 1992) 40-52
18. Rowland, B. R., Anderson, R. E., McCabe, P. S.: The 3B20D Processor & DMERT Operating System: Software Development System. The Bell System Technical Journal 62:1 part 2 (January 1983) 275-290.
19. Schneidewind, N. F., Hoffman, Heinz-Michael: An Experiment in Software Error Data Collection and Analysis", IEEE Transactions on Software Engineering SE-5:3 (May 1979) 276-286
20. Siegel, Sidney, and Castellan, Jr., N. John: Nonparametric Statistics for the Behavioral Sciences. Second Edition. New York: McGraw-Hill, 1988
21. Thayer, Thomas A., Lipow, Myron, Nelson, Eldred C.: Software Reliability - A Study of Large Project Reality. TRW Series of Software Technology, Volume 2. North-Holland, 1978.
22. Zave, Pamela, Jackson, Daniel: Practical Specification Techniques for Control-Oriented Systems. Proceedings of IFIPS Congress '89 —11th World Computer Congress (August 28 - September 1, 1989) San Francisco CA

The Experience Factory and its Relationship to Other Improvement Paradigms

Victor R. Basili

Institute for Advanced Computer Studies
Department of Computer Science
University of Maryland

Abstract. This paper describes the Quality Improvement Paradigm and the Experience Factory Organization as mechanisms for improving software development. It compares the approach with other improvement paradigms.

1. Introduction

The concepts of quality improvement have permeated many businesses. It is clear that the nineties will be the quality era for software and there is a growing need to develop or adapt quality improvement approaches to the software business. Thus we must understand software as an artifact and software as a business.

Any successful business requires a combination of technical and managerial solutions. It requires that we understand the processes and products of the business, i.e., that we know the business. It requires that we define our business needs and the means to achieve them, i.e., we must define our process and product qualities. We need to define closed loop processes so that we can feedback information for project control. We need to evaluate every aspect of the business, so we must analyze our successes and failures. We must learn from our experiences, i.e., each project should provide information that allows us to do business better the next time. We must build competencies in our areas of business by packaging our successful experiences for reuse and then we must reuse our successful experiences or our competencies as the way we do business.

Since the business we are dealing with is software, we must understand the nature of software and software development. The software discipline is evolutionary and experimental; it is a laboratory science. Software is development not production. The technologies of the discipline are human based. There is a lack of models that allow us to reason about the process and the product. All software is not the same; process is a variable, goals are variable, etc. Packaged, reusable, experiences require additional resources in the form of organization, processes, people, etc.

2. Experience Factory /Quality Improvement Paradigm

The Experience Factory /Quality Improvement Paradigm [Ba85a], [Ba89], [BaRo87], [BaRo88] aims at addressing the issues of quality improvement in the software business by providing a mechanism for continuous improvement through the e xperimentation, packaging and reuse of experiences based upon a business's needs. The approach has been evolving since 1976 based upon lessons learned in the SEL [BaCaMc92].

The basis for the approach is the Quality Improvement Paradigm which consists of six fundamental steps:

Characterize the current project and its environment with respect to models and metrics.

Set the quantifiable goals for successful project performance and improvement.

Choose the appropriate process model and supporting methods and tools for this project.

Execute the processes, construct the products, collect and validate the prescribed data, and analyze it to provide real-time feedback for corrective action.

Analyze the data to evaluate the current practices, determine problems, record findings, and make recommendations for future project improvements.

Package the experience in the form of updated and refined models and other forms of structured knowledge gained from this and prior projects and save it in an experience base to be reused on future projects.

Although it is difficult to describe the Quality Improvement Paradigm in great detail here, we will provide a little more insight into the six steps.

Characterizing the Project and Environment. Based upon a set of models of what we know about our business we need to classify the current project with respect to a variety of characteristics, distinguish the relevant project environment for the current project, and find the class of projects with similar characteristics and goals. This provides a context for goal definition, reusable experiences and objects, process selection, evaluation and comparison, and prediction. There are a large variety of project characteristics and environmental factors that need to be modeled and base lined. They include various

- people factors, such as the number of people, level of expertise, group organization, problem experience,
- process experience,etc.; problem factors, such as the application domain, newness to state of the art, susceptibility to change, problem constraints, etc.,
- process factors, such as the life cycle model, methods, techniques, tools, programming language, other notations, etc.,
- product factors, such as deliverables, system size, required qualities, e.g., reliability, portability, etc., and
- resource factors, such as target and development machines, calendar time, budget, existing software, etc.

Setting Measurable Goals. We need to establish goals for the processes and products. These goals should be measurable, driven by models of the business. During this step, the measurement data is also defined. There are a variety of mechanisms for defining measurable goals: Quality Function Deployment Approach (QFD) [KoAk83], the Goal/Question/Metric Paradigm (GQM) [WeBa85], and the Software Quality Metrics Approach (SQM) [McRiWa77].

Goals may be defined for any object, for a variety of reasons, with respect to various models of quality, from various points of view, relative to a particular environment. For example, goals should be defined from a variety of points of view: user, customer, project manager, corporation, etc.

Choosing the Process Models. We need to be able to choose a generic process model appropriate to the specific context, environment, project characteristics, and goals established for the project at hand, as well as any goals established for the organization, e.g., experimentation with various processes or other experience objects. This implies we need to understand under what conditions various processes are effective. All processes must be defined to be measurable and defined in terms of the goals they must satisfy. The concept of defining goals for processes will be made clearer in later chapters.

Once we have chosen a particular process model, we must tailor it to the project and choose the specific integrated set of sub-processess, such as methods and techniques, appropriate for the project. In practice, the selection of processes is iterative with the redefinifion of goals and even some environmental and project characteristics. It is important that the process model resulting from these first three steps be integrated in terms of its context, goals and sub-processes. The real goal is to have a set of processes that will help the developer satisfy the goals set for the project in the given environment. This may sometimes require that we manipulate all three sets of variables to assure this consistency.

Executing the Processes. The development process must support the access and reuse of packaged experience of all kinds. One the other hand it needs to be supported by various types of analysis, some done in close to real time for feedback for corrective action. To support this analysis, data needs to be collected from the project. But this data collection must be integrated into the processes, not be an add on, e.g. defect classification forms can be part of the configuration control mechanism. Processes must be defined to be measurable to begin with, e.g., design inspections can be defined so that we keep track of the various activities, the effort expended in those activities, such as peer reading, and the effects of those activities, such as the number and types of defects found. This allows us to measure such things as domain conformance and assures that the processes are well defined and can evolve.

Support activities, such as data validation, education and training in the models and metrics and data forms are also important. Automation is necessary to support mechanical tasks and deal with the large amounts of data and information needed for analysis. It should be noted however, that most of the data cannot be automatically collected. This is because the more interesting and insightful data tends to require human intervention.

The kinds of data collected include:

- resource data such as effort by activity, phase, type of personnel, computer time, and calendar
  time;
- change and defect data, such as changes and defects by various classification schemes,
- process data such as process definition, process conformance, and domain understanding;
- product data such as
  - product characteristics, both
  - logical, e.g., application domain, function, and

- physical, e.g. size, structure, and

- use and context information, e.g., who will be using the product and how will they be using it so we can build operational profiles.

Analyzing the Data. Based upon the goals, we interpret the data that have been collected. We can use these data to characterize and understand, so we can answer questions like "What project characteristics affect the choice of processes, methods and techniques?" and "Which phase is typically the greatest source of errors?" We can use the data to evaluate and analyze to answer questions like "What is the statement coverage of the acceptance test plan?" and "Does the Cleanroom Process reduce the rework effort?" We can use the data to predict and control to answer questions like "Given a set of project characteristics, what is the expected cost and reliability, based upon our history?" and "Given the specific characteristics of all the modules in the system, which modules are most likely to have defects so I can concentrate the reading or testing effort on them?" We can use the data to motivate and improve so we can answer questions such as "For what classes of errors is a particular technique most effective?" and "What are the best combination of approaches to use for a project with a continually evolving set of requirements based upon our organization's experience?"

Packaging the models. We need to define and refine models of all forms of experiences, e.g., resource models, such as baselines, change and defect models, product models, process definitions and models, method and technique evaluations, products and product parts, quality models, and lessons learned. These can appear in a variety of forms, e.g., we can have mathematical models, informal relationships, histograms, algorithms and procedures, based upon our experience with their application in similar projects, so they may be reused in future projects.

The six steps of the Quality Improvement Paradigm can be combined in various ways to provide different views into the activities. First note that there are two feedback loops, a project feedback loop that takes place in the execution phase and an organizational feedback loop that takes place after a project is completed and changes the organization's understanding of the world between the packaging of what was learned form the last project and the characterization and base lining of the environment for the new project. It should be noted that there are numerous other loops visible at lower levels of instantiation, but these high level loops are the most important from an organizational structure point of view.

One high level organizational view of the paradigm is that we must understand (Characterize), assess (Set goals, Choose processes, Execute processes, Analyze data) and package (Package experience). Another view is to plan for a project (Characterize, Set goals, Choose processes), develop it (Execute processes), and then learn from the experience (Analyze data and Package experience).

2.1 The Experience Factory Organization

To support the Improvement Paradigm, an organizational structure called the Experience Factory Organization was developed [Ba89]. It recognizes the fact that improving the software process and product requires the continual accumulation of evaluated experiences (learning), in a form that can be effectively understood and modified (experience models), stored in a repository of integrated experience models (experience base), that can be accessed/modified to meet the needs of the current project (reuse).

Systematic learning requires support for recording, off-line generalizing,tailoring, formalizing and synthesizing of experience. The off-line requirement is based upon the fact that reuse requires separate resources to create reusable objects. Packaging and modeling useful experience requires a variety of models and formal notations that are tailorable, extendible, understandable, flexible and accessible.

An effective experience base must contain accessible and integrated set of models that capture the local experiences. Systematic reuse requires support for using existing experience and on-line generalizing or tailoring of candidate experience.

This combination of ingredients requires an organizational structure that supports: (1) a software evolution model that supports reuse, (2) processes for learning, packaging, and storing experience, and (3) the integration of these two sets of activities. It requires separate logical or physical organizations with different focuses/priorities, process models, expertise requirements.

We divide the activities into two separate logical or physical organizations (Figure 1): the Project

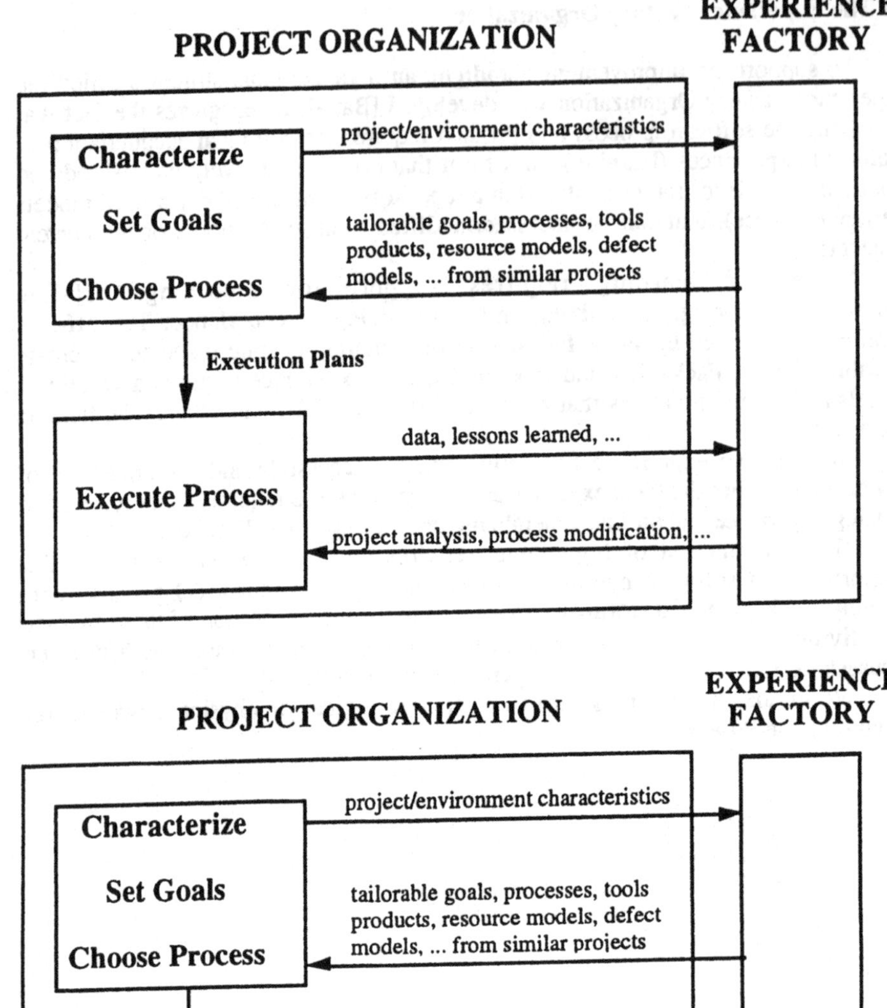

PROJECT ORGANIZATION
EXPERIENCE FACTORY
Characterize
Set Goals
Choose Process
project/environment characteristics
tailorable goals, processes, tools products, resource models, defect models, ... from similar projects
Execution Plans
Execute Process
data, lessons learned, ...
project analysis, process modification, ...

Figure 1. EXPERIENCE FACTORY ORGANIZATION

Organization whose focus/priority is delivery, supported by packaged reusable experiences, and an Experience Factory whose focus is to support project developments by analyzing and synthesizing all kinds of experience, acting as a repository for such experience, and supplying that experience to various projects on demand.

The Experience Factory packages experience by building informal, formal or schematized, and productized models and measures of various software processes, products, and other forms of knowledge via people, documents, and automated support.

As shown in Figure 1, the steps of the Improvement Paradigm are assigned various roles in the two organizational structures. In the Project Organization, the project management characterizes the project, sets the measurable goals and gets support from the Experience Factory to develop an executable process model, tailored to the project at hand. It then executes the processes, providing information to the experience factory which offers feedback on status, improvements, and risks. On the other hand the Experience Factory views the project as a source of information and data for model building. It analyzes what it gets and provides feedback to the project for real time project control. It also analyzes the data to build reusable experience models, stores them in an experience base, and provides support for projects based upon these packaged models.

The Experience Factory deals with reuse of all kinds of knowledge and experience. But what makes us think we can be successful with reuse this time, when we have not been so successful in the past? Part of the reason is that we are not talking about reuse of just code in isolation but the reuse of all kinds of experience and context for that experience. The Experience Factory recognizes and provides support for the fact that experience requires the appropriate context definition for it to be reusable and it needs to be identified and analyzed for its reuse potential. It recognizes that experience cannot always be reused as is, it needs to be tailored and it needs to be packaged to make it easy to reuse. In the past, reuse of experience has been too informal, not supported by the organization. It has to be fully incorporated into the development or maintenance process models. Another major issue is that a project's focus is delivery, not reuse, i.e., reuse cannot be a byproduct of software development. It requires a separate organization to support the packaging and reuse of local experience.

The Experience Factory really represents a paradigm shift from current software development thinking. It separates the types of activities that need to be performed by assigning them to different organizations, recognizing that they truly represent different processes and focuses. Project personnel are primarily responsible for the planning and development activities (Project Organization) and a separate organization (Experience Factory) is primarily responsible for the learning and technology transfer activities. In the Project Organization, we focus on problem solving. The processes we perform to solve a problem consist of the decomposition of a problem in to simpler ones, instantiation of higher level solutions into lower level detail, the design and implementation of various solution processes, and activities such as validation and verification. In the Experience Factory, we focus on understanding solutions and packaging experience for reuse. The processes we perform are the unification of difference solutions and re-definition of the problem, generalization and formalization of solutions in order to abstract them and make them easy to access and modify, an analysis synthesis process where we understand and abstract, and various experimentation activities so we can learn. These sets of activities are totally different.

2.2 Examples of Packaged Experience in the SEL

The Software Engineering Laboratory (SEL) has been in existence since 1976 and is a consortium of three organizations: NASA/Goddard Space Flight Center, the University of Maryland, and Computer Sciences Corporation [Mc85],[BaCaMc92]. When it was established, its goals were to (1) understand the software process in a production environment, (2) determine the impact of available technologies, and (3) infuse identified/refined methods back into the development process. The approach has been to identify technologies with potential, apply and extract detailed data in a production environment (experiments), and measure the impact (cost, reliability, quality,..).

Over the years we have learned a great deal and packaged all kinds of experience. We have built

- resource models and baselines, e.g., local cost models, resource allocation models,
- change and defect models and baselines, e.g., defect prediction models, types of defects
  expected for the application,
- product models and baselines, e.g., actual vs. expected product size, library access, over time,
- process definitions and models, e.g., process models for Cleanroom, Ada waterfall model,
- method and technique models and evaluations, e.g., best method for finding interface faults,
- products and product models, e.g., Ada generics for simulation of satellite orbits,
- a variety of quality models, e.g., reliability models, defect slippage models, ease of change models, and
- a library of lessons learned, e.g., risks associated with an Ada development.

We have used a variety of forms for packaged experience. There are

- equations defining the relationship between variables, e.g.

Effort = 1.48*KSLOC.98,

Number of Runs = 108 + 150*KSLOC,

- histograms or pie charts of raw or analyzed data, e.g.,

Classes of Faults: 30% data, 24% interface, 16% control, 15% initialization, 15% computation,

- graphs defining ranges of "normal" ,e.g., graphs of size growth over time with confidence levels,
- specific lessons learned associated with project types, phases, activities, e.g., reading by stepwise abstraction is most effective for finding interface faults, or in the form of risks or recommendations, e.g., definition of a unit for unit test in Ada needs to be carefully defined, and
- models or algorithms specifying the processes, methods, or techniques, e.g., an SADT diagram defining Design Inspections with the reading technique a variable dependent upon the focus and reader perspective.

These models are used on new projects to help management control development [Va87] and provide the organization with a basis for improvement based upon experimentation with new methods. It is an example of the Experience Factory/Quality Improvement Paradigm (EF/Quality Improvement Paradigm) in practice.

How does the EF/Quality Improvement Paradigm approach work in practice? You begin by getting a commitment. You then define the organizational structure and the associated processes. This means collecting data to establish baselines, e.g., defects and resources, that are process and product independent and measuring your strengths and weaknesses to provide a business focus and goals for improvement, and establish product quality baselines. Using this information about your business, you select and experiment with methods and techniques to improve your processes based upon your product quality needs and evaluate your improvement based upon existing resource and defect baselines. You can define and tailor better and measurable processes, based upon the experience and knowledge gained within your own environment. You must measure for process conformance and domain understanding to make sure that your results are valid. In this way, you begin to understand the relationship between some process characteristics and product qualities and are able to manipulate some processes to achieve those product characteristics. As you change your processes you will establish new baselines and learn where the next place for improvement might be.

3. Other Improvement Paradigms

Aside from the Experience Factory /Quality Improvement Paradigm, there has been a variety of organizational frameworks proposed to improve quality for various businesses. The ones discussed here include:

Plan-Do-Check-Act is a quality improvement process based upon a feedback cycle for optimizing a single process model/production line. Total Quality Management represents a management approach to long term success through customer satisfaction based on the participation of all members of an organization. The SEI Capability Maturity Model is a staged process improvement based upon assessment with regard to a set of key process areas until you reach a level 5 which represents a continuous process improvement. Lean (Software) Development represents a principle supporting the concentration of the production on "value added" activities and the elimination or reduction of "not value added" activities. In what follows, we will try to define these concepts in a little more detail to distinguish and compare them.

3.1 Plan-Do-Check-Act Cycle (PDCA)

The approach is based upon work by W. A. Shewart [Sh31] and was made popular by W. E. Deming [De86]. The goal of this approach is to optimize and improve a single process model / production line. It uses such techniques as feedback loops and statistical quality control to experiment with methods for improvement and build predictive models of the product.

PLAN → DO → CHECK → ACT →

If a family of Processes (P) produces a family of Products (X) then the approach yields a series of versions of product X (each meant to be an improvement of X), produced by a series of modifications (improvements) to the processes P,

P0, P1, P2, ..., Pn -----------> X0, X1, X2, ..., Xn

where Pi, represents an improvement over Pi-1 and Xi has better quality than Xi-1.

The basic procedure involves four basic steps:

Plan: Develop a plan for effective improvement, e.g., quality measurement criteria are set up as targets and methods for achieving the quality criteria are established.

Do: The plan is carried out, preferably on a small scale, i.e., the product is produced by complying with development standards and quality guidelines.

Check: The effects of the plan are observed; at each stage of development, the product is checked against the individual quality criteria set up in the Plan phase.

Act: The results are studied to determine what was learned and what can be predicted, e.g., corrective action is taken based upon problem reports.

3.2 Total Quality Management (TQM)

The term TQM was coined by the Naval Air Systems Command in 1985 to describe its Japanese style management approach to quality improvement [Fe90]. The goal of TQM is to generate institutional commitment to success through customer satisfaction. The approaches to achieving TQM vary greatly in practice so to provide some basis for comparison, we offer the approach being applied at Hughes. Hughes uses such techniques as Quality Function Deployment (QFD), design of experiments (DOE), and statistical process control (SPC), to improve the product through the process.

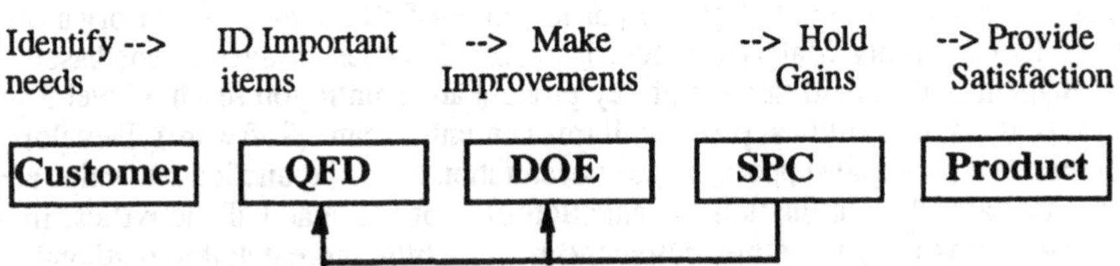

The approach has similar characteristics to the PDCA approach. If Process (P) --> Product (X) then the approach yields

P0, P1, P2, ..., Pn -----------> X0, X1, X2, ..., Xn

where Pi, represents an improvement over Pi-1 and Xi provides better customer satisfaction than Xi-1.

3.3 SEI Capability Maturity Model (CMM)

The approach is based upon organizational and quality management maturity models developed by R. Likert [Li67] and P. Crosby [Cr80], respectively. A software maturity model was developed by Ron Radice, et. al. [RaHaMuPh85] while he was at IBM. It was made popular by Watts Humphrey [Hu89] at the SEI. The goal of the approach is to achieve a level 5 maturity rating, i.e.,continuous process improvement via defect prevention, technology innovation, and process change management.

As part of the approach, a 5 level process maturity model is defined. A maturity level is defined based on repeated assessment of an organization's capability in key process areas. Thus for example at the lowest level, the focus is on heroes or good people who can rescue a project, at the second level, the focus is on good project management, at the third level, the focus is on good engineering process, etc. Improvement is achieved by action plans for poorly assessed processes.

Thus, if a Process (P) is level i then modify the process based upon the the key processes of the model until the process model is at level i+1.

Level	Focus
5 Optimizing	Continuous Process Improvement
4 Managed	Product & Process Quality
3 Defined	Engineering Process
2 Repeatable	Project Management
1 Initial	Heros

The SEI has developed a Process Improvement Cycle to support the movement through process levels. Basically is consists of the following activities:

- Initialize
  - Establish sponsorship
  - Create vision and strategy
  - Establish improvement structure
- For each Maturity level:
  - Characterize current practice in terms of key process areas
  - Assessment recommendations
  - Revise strategy (generate action plans and prioritorize key process areas)
  - For each key process area:
    - Establish process action teams
    - Implement tactical plan, define processes, plan and execute pilot(s), plan and execute
    - Institutionalize
    - Document and analyze lessons
    - Revise organizational approach

3.4 Lean Software Development

The approach is based upon Lean Enterprise Management, a philosophy that has been used to improve factory output. Womack, et. al. [WoJoRo90], have written a book on the application of lean enterprises in the automotive industry. The goal is to build software using the minimal set of activities needed, eliminating non essential steps, i.e., tailoring the process to the product needs. The approach uses such concepts as technology management, human centered management, decentral organization, quality management, supplier and customer integration, and internationalization/regionalization.

Given the characteristics for product V, select the appropriate mix of sub-processes pi, qj, rk, ... to satisfy the goals for V, yielding a minimal tailored process PV which is composed of pi, qj, rk, ...

Process (PV) ----------> Product (V)

The notation PV is used to imply that the process is dependent on the product characteristics.

3.5 Quality Improvement Paradigm

As stated above, this approach has evolved over 17 years based upon lessons learned in the SEL [Ba85a], [Ba89], [BaRo87], [BaRo88], [BaCaMc92]. Its goal is to build a continually improving organization based upon its evolving goals and an assessment of its status relative to those goals. The approach uses internal assessment against the organizations own goals and status (rather than process areas) and such techniques as GQM, model building, qualitative/quantitative analysis to improve the product through the process.

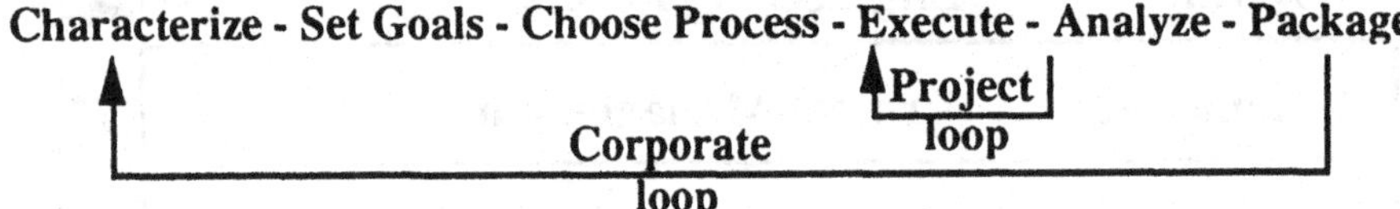

If Processes (PX, QY, RZ, ...) ---> Products (X, Y, Z, ...) and we want to build V, then based upon an understanding of the relationship between PX, QY, RZ, ... and X, Y, Z, ... and goals for V we select the appropriate mix of processes pi, qj, rk, ... (i.e., we use experience from different projects) to satisfy the goals for V, yielding a tailored

Process (PV) ---> Product (V)

4. A Comparison of the Improvement Paradigms

The Quality Improvement Paradigm / Experience Factory Organization is similar to the Plan-Do-Check-Act paradigm in that it is evolutionary, based upon feedback loops, and learns from experiments. It is different in the sense that the Plan-Do-Check-Act paradigm is based upon production, i.e., it attempts to optimize a single process model/production line. In development, we rarely replicate the same thing twice. In production, we can collect a sufficient set of data based upon continual repetition of the same process to develop quantitative models of the process that will allow us to evaluate and predict quite accurately the effects of the single process model. We can use statistical quality control approaches. This is not possible for development, i.e. we must learn form one process about another, so our models are less rigorous and more abstract. Development processes are also more human based. This again affects the building, use, and accuracy of the types of models we can build.

The Quality Improvement Paradigm approach is compatible with TQM in that it can cover goals that are customer satisfaction driven and it is based upon the philosophy that quality is everyone's job. That is, everyone is part of the technology infusion process. Someone can be on the project team on one project and experimenting team on another. All the project personnel play the major role in the feedback mechanism. If they are not using the technology right it can be because they don't understand it , e.g., it wasn't taught right, it doesn't fit/interface with other project activities, it needs to be tailored, or it simply doesn't work. You need the user to tell you how to change it. This is consistent with the Quality Improvement Paradigm philosophy that no method is "packaged" that hasn't been tried (applied, analyzed, tailored).

The Quality Improvement Paradigm/EF organization is different from the SEI CMM approach, in that you pull yourself up from the top rather than pushing up from the bottom. At step 1 you start with a level 5 style organization even though you do not yet have level 5 process capabilities. That is, you are driven by an understanding of your business, your product and process problems, your business goals, your experience with methods, etc. You learn from your business, not from an external model of process. You make process improvements based upon an understanding of the relationship between process and product in your organization. Technology infusion is motivated by the local problems, so people are more willing to try something new.

But what does a level 5 organization really mean? It is an organization that can manipulate process to achieve various product characteristics. This requires that we have a process and an organizational structure to help us: understand our processes and products, measure and model the project and the organization, define and tailor process and product qualities explicitly, understand the relationship between process and product qualities, feed back information for project control, experiment with methods and techniques, evaluate our successes and failures, learn from our experiences, package successful experiences, and reuse successful experiences. This is compatible with the Quality Improvement Paradigm/EF organization.

Quality Improvement Paradigm is not incompatible with the SEI CMM model in that you can still use key process assessments to evaluate where you stand (along with your internal goals, needs, etc.). However, using the Quality Improvement Paradigm, the chances are you will move up the maturity scale faster. You will have more experience early on operating within an improvement organization structure, and you can demonstrate product improvement benefits early.

The Quality Improvement Paradigm approach is most similar to the concepts of Lean Software Development in that it is based upon the ideas of tailoring a set of processes to meet particular problem/product under development. The goal is to generate an optimum set of processes, based upon models of the business and our experience about the relationship between process characteristics and product characteristics.

5. Conclusion

Some important characteristics of the EF/Quality Improvement Paradigm process is that it is iterative, you should converge over time so don't be overly concerned with perfecting any step on the first pass. However, the better your initial guess at the baselines the quicker you will converge. No method is "packaged" that hasn't been tried (applied, analyzed, tailored). Everyone is part of the technology infusion process. Someone can be on the project team on one project and experimenting team on another. Project personnel play the major role in the feedback mechanism. We need to learn from them about the effective use of technology. If they are not using the technology right it can be because they don't understand it or it wasn't taught right, it doesn't fit/interface with other project activities, it needs to be tailored, or it doesn't work and you need the user to tell you how to change it. Technology infusion is motivated by the local problems, so people are more willing to try something new. And, it is important to evaluate process conformance and domain understanding or you have very little basis for understanding and assessment.

The integration of the Improvement Paradigm, the Goal/Question/Metric Paradigm, and the Experience Factory Organization provides a framework for software engineering development, maintenance, and research. It takes advantage of the experimental nature of software engineering. Based upon our experience in the SEL and other organizations, it helps us understand how software is built and where the problems are, define and formalize effective models of process and product, evaluate the process and the product in the right context, predict and control process and product qualities, package and reuse successful experiences, and feed back experience to current and future projects. It can be applied today and evolve with technology.

The approach provides a framework for defining quality operationally relative to the project and the organization, justification for selecting and tailoring the appropriate methods and tools for the project and the organization, a mechanism for evaluating the quality of the process and the product relative to the specific project goals, and a mechanism for improving the organization's ability to develop quality systems productively. The approach is being adopted by several organizations to varying degrees, e.g., Motorola, but it is not a simple solution and it requires long term commitment by top level management.

In summary, the Quality Improvement Paradigm approach provides for a separation of concerns/focus in differentiating between problem solving and experience modeling/packaging. It offers a support for learning and reuse and a means of formalizing and integrating management and development technologies. It allows for the generation of a tangible corporate asset: an experience base of software competencies. It offers a Lean Software Development approach compatible with TQM while providing a level 5 CMM organizational structure. It links focused research with development. Best of all you can start small, evolve and expand, e.g., focus on a homogeneous set of projects or a particular set of packages and build from there.

References

[Ba85a]
V. R. Basili, "Quantitative Evaluation of Software Engineering Methodology," Proc. of the First Pan Pacific Computer Conference, Melbourne, Australia, September 1985 [also available as Technical Report, TR-1519, Dept. of Computer Science, University of Maryland, College Park, July 1985].

[Ba89]
V. R. Basili, "Software Development: A Paradigm for the Future", Proceedings, 13th Annual International Computer Software & Applications Conference (COMPSAC), Keynote Address, Orlando, FL, September 1989

[BaRo87]
V. R. Basili, H. D. Rombach, "Tailoring the Software Process to Project Goals and Environments," Proc. of the Ninth International Conference on Software Engineering, Monterey, CA, March 30 - April 2, 1987, pp. 345-357.

[BaRo88]
V. R. Basili, H. D. Rombach "The TAME Project: Towards Improvement-Oriented Software Environments," IEEE Transactions on Software Engineering, vol. SE-14, no. 6, June 1988, pp. 758-773.

[BaCaMc92]
V. R. Basili, G. Caldiera, F. McGarry, R. Pajerski, G. Page, S. Waligora, "The Software Engineering Laboratory - an Operational Software Experience Factory", International Conference on Software Engineering, May, 1992, pp. 370-381.

[Cr80]
Philip B. Crosby, "Quality is free : the Art of Making Quality Certain," New American Library,
New York, 1980.

[De86]
W. Edwards Deming,"Out of the Crisis," MIT Center for Advanced Engineering Study, MIT Press, Cambridge MA, 1986.

[Fe90]
Armand V. Feigenbaum, "Total Quality Control", fortieth anniversary edition, McGraw Hill, NY, 1991.

[Hu89]
Humphrey, Watts S., "Managing the software process," SEI series in software engineering, Addison-Wesley, Reading, Mass., 1989.

[KoAk83]
M. Kogure, Y. Akao, "Quality Function Deployment and CWQC in Japan," Quality Progress, October 1983, pp.25-29.

[Li67]
Rensis Likert, "The human organization: its Management and Value, " McGraw Hill, New York, 1967.

[McRiWa77]
J. A. McCall, P. K. Richards, G. F. Walters, "Factors in Software Quality," RADC TR-77-369, 1977.

[Mc85]
F. E. McGarry, "Recent SEL Studies," Proceedings of the Tenth Annual Software Engineering Workshop, NASA Goddard Space Flight Center, December 1985.

[Sh31]
Walter A. Shewhart, "Economic control of quality of manufactured product," D. Van Nostrand Company, Inc., New York, 1931.

[RaHaMuPh85]
Ron Radice, A. J. Harding, P. E. Munnis, and R. W. Phillips, "A programming process study," IBM Systems Journal, vol.24, no. 2, 1985.

[Va87]
J. D. Valett, "The Dynamic Management Information Tool (DYNAMITE):Analysis of the Prototype, Requirements and Operational Scenarios," M.Sc. Thesis, University of Maryland, 1987.

[WeBa85]
D. M. Weiss, V. R. Basili, "Evaluating Software Development by Analysis of Changes: Some Data from the Software Engineering Laboratory," IEEE Transactions on Software Engineering, vol. SE-11, no. 2, February 1985, pp. 157-168.

[WoJoRo90]
James P. Womack, Daniel T. Jones, Daniel Roos, "The machine that changed the world : based on the Massachusetts Institute of Technology 5-million dollar 5-year study on the future of the automobile," Rawson Associates, New York, 1990.

Inconsistency Handling in Multi-Perspective Specifications

A. Finkelstein D. Gabbay A. Hunter J. Kramer B. Nuseibeh

Department of Computing
Imperial College of Science, Technology and Medicine
180 Queen's Gate, London, SW7 2BZ, UK
Email: {acwf, dg, abh, jk, ban}@doc.ic.ac.uk

Abstract. The development of most large and complex systems necessarily involves many people - each with their own perspectives on the system defined by their knowledge, responsibilities, and commitments. To address this we have advocated distributed development of specifications from multiple perspectives. However, this leads to problems of identifying and handling inconsistencies between such perspectives. Maintaining absolute consistency is not always possible. Often this is not even desirable since this can unnecessarily constrain the development process, and can lead to the loss of important information. Indeed since the real-world forces us to work with inconsistencies, we should formalise some of the usually informal or extra-logical ways of responding to them. This is not necessarily done by eradicating inconsistencies but rather by supplying logical rules specifying how we should act on them. To achieve this, we combine two lines of existing research: the ViewPoints framework for perspective development, interaction and organisation, and a logic-based approach to inconsistency handling. This paper presents our technique for inconsistency handling in the ViewPoints framework by using simple examples.

1 Introduction

The development of most large and complex systems necessarily involves many people - each with their own perspectives on the system defined by their knowledge, responsibilities, and commitments. Inevitably, the different perspectives of those involved in the process intersect - giving rise to the possibility of inconsistency between perspectives and to a need for co-ordination. These intersections, however, are far from obvious because the knowledge from each perspective is expressed in different ways. Furthermore, because development may be carried out concurrently by those involved, different perspectives may be at different stages of elaboration and may be subject to different development strategies.

The problem of co-ordinating these different perspectives is partly 'organisational' and partly 'technical'. The organisational aspect requires that support is provided for ordering activities, interacting by passing information and resolving conflicts. The main technical aspect centres around the consistency relationship between these perspectives, given as partial specifications. Indeed checking consistency between perspectives and the handling of inconsistency creates many interesting and difficult research problems.

We do not believe that it is possible, in general, to maintain absolute consistency between perspectives at all times. Indeed, it is often not even desirable to enforce consistency, particularly when this constrains the specification unnecessarily or entails loss of design freedom by enforcing an early resolution [21]. Thus, there is a requirement for some form of inconsistency handling techniques in which inconsistency is tolerated and used to trigger further actions [15, 16].

In section 2 we provide a brief background to the ViewPoints framework, and in section 3 we provide an overview of inconsistency handling in this setting. In the subsequent sections, we illustrate and discuss the identification and handling of inconsistency using simple specification examples.

2 Background to the ViewPoints Framework

The integration of methods, notations and tools has generally been addressed by the use of a common data model, usually supported by a common, centralised database [33, 1]. This has some advantages in providing a uniform basis for consistency checking. Multiple views can still be supported by the provision of mappings to and from the data model. However, we believe that the general use of centralised data repositories is a mistake for the long term. General data models are difficult to design and tend to be even more difficult to modify and extend when new tools are to be integrated [34, 29]. This is analogous to the search for some universal formalism. Therefore, although the approaches based on common data models have enabled us to make good progress in the provision of current CASE tools, we believe that such data models are too tightly integrated. Such inherent logical centralisation will be one of the major restrictions in the provision of tools that integrate more methods and notations, cover a larger part of the life-cycle and support use by large teams of software engineers.

To address this we have developed a novel framework that supports the use of multiple distributed perspectives in software and systems development [11, 13]. The primary building blocks used in this framework are "ViewPoints" (Fig. 1), combining the notion of a "participant" in the development process, and the idea of a "view" or "perspective" that the participant maintains. A ViewPoint template is a ViewPoint in which only the representation style and work plan have been elaborated. A ViewPoint is thus created by instantiating a template, thereby producing a ViewPoint specification for a particular domain.

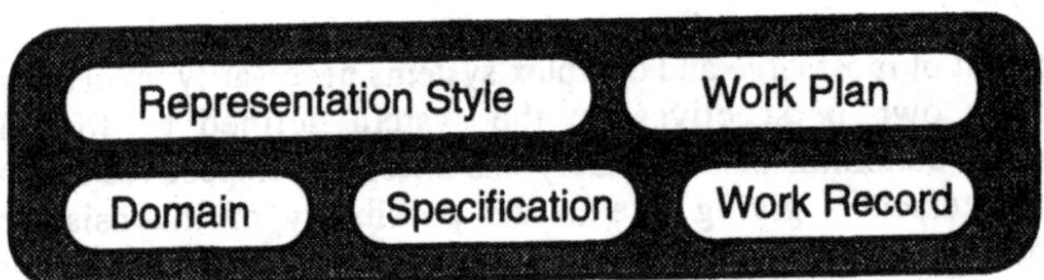

Fig. 1. A ViewPoint encapsulates representation, development and specification knowledge in its five "slots". The representation style defines the notation deployed by the ViewPoint. The work plan describes the development actions, strategy and process used by the ViewPoint. The specification slot delineates the ViewPoint's domain in the chosen representation style, while the work record contains a development history of the specification.

The framework has been implemented [25] to allow the construction of partial specifications in a variety of formalisms. A work record of the development, including the development history and rationale for each specification, is also recorded. A typical systems engineering project would deploy a number of ViewPoints described and developed using a variety of different languages. ViewPoints are bound together by inter-ViewPoint relations that specify dependencies and mappings between system components (Fig. 2). It is intended that ViewPoints be managed by maintaining local consistency within each ViewPoint and partial consistency between different ViewPoints.

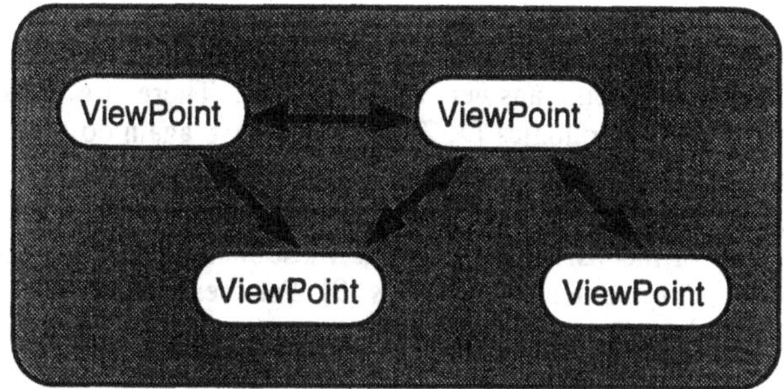

Fig. 2. A system specification in the ViewPoints framework is a configuration or collection of ViewPoints integrated together by one-to-one inter-ViewPoint rules. We can layer configurations of ViewPoints to reduce problems of scale [20], and use hypertext-like tools to navigate around large ViewPoint networks [18].

Thus, in contrast to the traditional approaches, the ViewPoints approach to specification development is inherently distributed. ViewPoints are loosely coupled, locally managed and potentially distributed objects, with integration achieved via one-to-one inter-ViewPoint relationships defined as inter-ViewPoint rules in the work plans of templates from which the ViewPoints are instantiated [26].

One of the drawbacks of distributed development and specifications is the problem of consistency. It is generally more difficult to check and maintain consistency in a distributed environment. Furthermore, we believe that we should re-examine our attitude to consistency, and make more provision for inconsistency. Inconsistency is inevitable as part of the development process. Forcing consistency tends to restrict the development process and stifle novelty and invention. Hence, consistency should only be checked between particular parts or views of a design or specification and at particular stages rather than enforced as a matter of course. Addressing the problems of inconsistency raises many questions including: What exactly does consistency checking across multiple partial specifications mean? When should consistency be checked? How do we handle inconsistency?

3 Inconsistency Handling in the ViewPoints Framework

Given that inconsistency is often viewed as a logical concept, we believe that it is appropriate that inconsistency handling should be based on logic. The problem of inconsistency handling in the ViewPoints framework can then be viewed as being equivalent to inconsistency handling in distributed logical databases. For this we need to define rewrites from specification information, and inter-ViewPoint information, in a ViewPoint to a set of logical formulae. However, before describing how we rewrite, identify and handle inconsistency in this kind of data, we briefly discuss the general problems of inconsistency in logic. We use this as a means of motivating our approach.

Classical logic, and intuitionistic logic, take the view that anything follows from an inconsistency. Effectively, when an inconsistency occurs in a database, it becomes unusable. This has prompted the logic community to study such logics as relevant [2] and paraconsistent logics [8] that allow reasoning with inconsistent information. These isolate inconsistency by various means, but do not offer strategies for dealing with the inconsistency. Therefore there still remains the question of what do we do when we have two contradictory items of information in a database. Do we choose one of them? How do we make the choice? Do we leave them in and find a way "around" them?

Other logics, such as certain non-monotonic logics (for a review see [6]), resolve some forms of inconsistency, but do not allow the representation of certain forms of inconsistent data, or give no answer when present. There are also attempts at paraconsistent non-monotonic logics [7, 28, 32], but these again do not answer all the questions of handling inconsistency.

The logic programming and deductive database communities have focused on alternative approaches to issues of inconsistencies in data. These include integrity constraints (for example [31]) and truth maintenance systems [9]. For these, any attempt to introduce inconsistency in the database causes rejection of input, or amendment of the database. Therefore these also do not constitute solutions for the ViewPoints framework since neither allow us to represent and reason with inconsistent information nor allow us to formalise the desired actions that should result from inconsistency.

These approaches constitute a significant shortfall in the ability required to handle inconsistency in formal knowledge representation. In [15, 16] an attempt was made to shift the view of inconsistency from being necessarily "bad" to being acceptable, or even desirable, if we know how to deal with it. Moreover, when handling inconsistencies in a database, it is advantageous to analyse them within the larger context of the environment of the database and its use. When viewed locally, an inconsistency may seem undesirable, but within the larger environment surrounding the data, an inconsistency could be desirable and useful, if we know appropriate actions to handle it. Dealing with inconsistencies is not necessarily done by restoring consistency but by supplying rules telling one how to act when the inconsistency arises.

To appreciate our view we need to formally consider both the data in the database, and the use of the database in the environment. The latter is usually not formalised, though for many database applications there are informal procedures, or conventions, that are assumed by the user. If we formalise the link between the database and the environment, it allows us to handle inconsistency in data in terms of these procedures and conventions. Furthermore, it also allows us to consider the inconsistencies resulting from contradictions between the data and the use of the data. For example, it is not uncommon for inconsistencies to occur in accounting systems. Consider the use of credit cards in a department store, where an inconsistency may occur on some account. In this case the store may take one of a series of actions such as writing off the amount owed, or leaving the discrepancies indefinitely, or invoking legal action. Another example is in government tax databases where inconsistencies in a taxpayer's records are "desirable" (at least from the tax inspectors point of view!), and are used to invoke an investigation of that taxpayer.

In our approach we capture in a logical language the link between the data and the usage of the data. In particular we analyse inconsistencies in terms of a pair of logical formulae (D, E) where D is a database of logical formulae representing some of the information in one or more ViewPoints, and E is a logical representation of some of the implicit assumptions and integrity constraints used in controlling and co-ordinating the use of a set of ViewPoints. We can view E as the environment in which the database operates and should include some information on inter-ViewPoint relations. We further assume that for the purposes of this paper the information expressed in E is consistent - that is, we use E as the reference against which consistency is checked. Using (D, E) we undertake partial or full consistency checking, and attempt to elucidate the "sources" of inconsistency in the database.

We handle inconsistencies in (D, E), by adopting a meta-language approach that captures the required actions to be undertaken when discovering an inconsistency, where the choice of actions is dependent on the larger context. Using a meta-language allows handling of a database in an environment by encoding rules of the form:

INCONSISTENCY IN (D, E) SYSTEM implies ACTION IN (D, E) SYSTEM

These rules may be physically distributed among the various ViewPoints under development, and invoked by the ViewPoint that initiates the consistency checking. Some of the actions in these rules may make explicit internal database actions such as invoking a truth maintenance system, while others may require external actions such as 'seek further information from the user' or invoke external tools. To support this formalisation of data handling, we need to consider the nature of the external and internal actions that result from inconsistencies in the context of multi-author specifications - in particular for the ViewPoints framework.

Fig. 3 schematically summarises the stages of rewriting, identification, and handling of inconsistency when checking two ViewPoints in the framework. To check the consistency of specifications in two ViewPoints, partial specification knowledge in each is translated into classical logic. Together with the inter-ViewPoint rules in each ViewPoint - which are also translated into logic - inconsistencies between the two ViewPoints may be identified. Meta-level rules are then invoked which prescribe how to act on the identified inconsistencies.

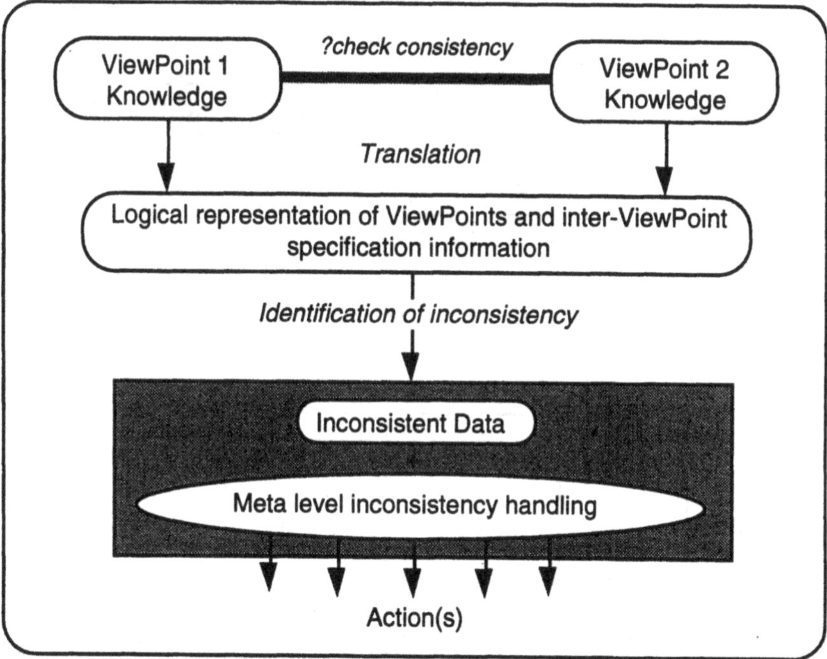

Fig. 3. Inter-ViewPoint communication and inconsistency handling in the ViewPoints framework. Selected ViewPoint knowledge in each of the communicating ViewPoints is translated into logical formulae and used to detect and identify inconsistencies. The meta-level rules may then be used to act upon these inconsistencies.

Note that we are *not* claiming that classical logic is a universal formalism into which any two representations may be translated. Rather, we argue that for any two partial specifications *a* common logical representation may be found and used to detect and identify inconsistencies.

4 A Simple Example

To demonstrate our approach, we will use a simplified library example specified using a subset of the formalisms deployed by the requirements analysis method CORE [24]. The two formalisms we use are what we call agent hierarchies (Fig. 4) and action tables (Fig. 5a, b, c). An agent hierarchy decomposes a problem domain into information processing entities or roles called "agents"[1]. Agents may be "direct", if they process information, or "indirect", if they only generate or receive information without processing it. For each direct agent in the hierarchy, we construct an action table showing the actions performed by that agent, the input data required for the actions to occur and the output data produced by those actions. The destination and source agents to and from which the data flows are also shown (action tables may thus be regarded as a standard form of data flow diagrams). An arc drawn between two lines in an action diagram indicates the conjunction of the two terms preceding the joining lines.

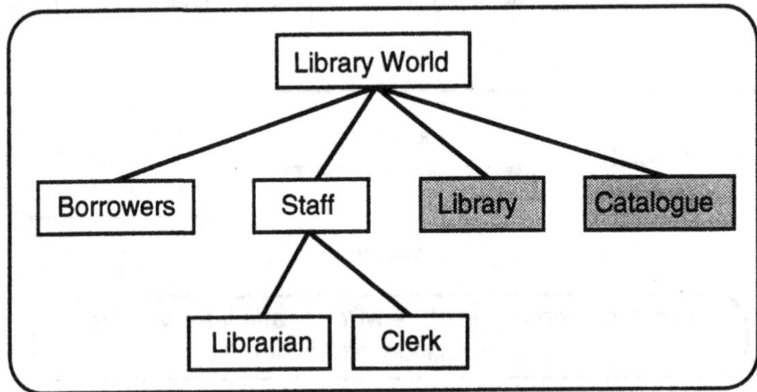

Fig. 4. An agent hierarchy decomposing the library problem domain into its constituent agents. Shaded boxes indicate indirect agents which require no further decomposition or analysis.

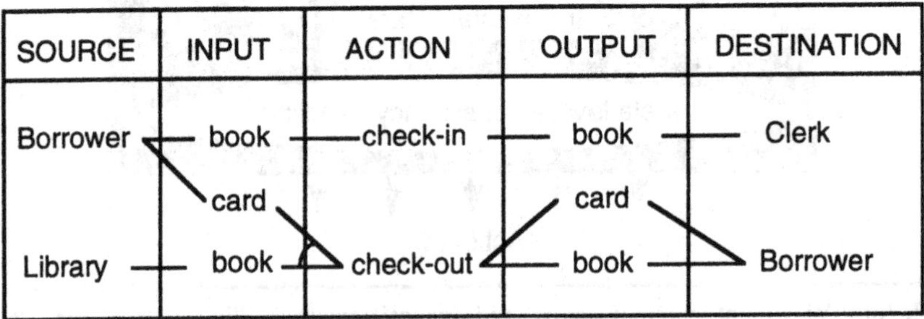

Fig. 5a. An action table elaborating the agent "Borrower". In ViewPoints terminology, the action table is part of a ViewPoint specification where the ViewPoint domain is "Borrower".

1 CORE uses the term "viewpoint" as part of its terminology, so we have renamed it "agent" to avoid the clash in nomenclature.

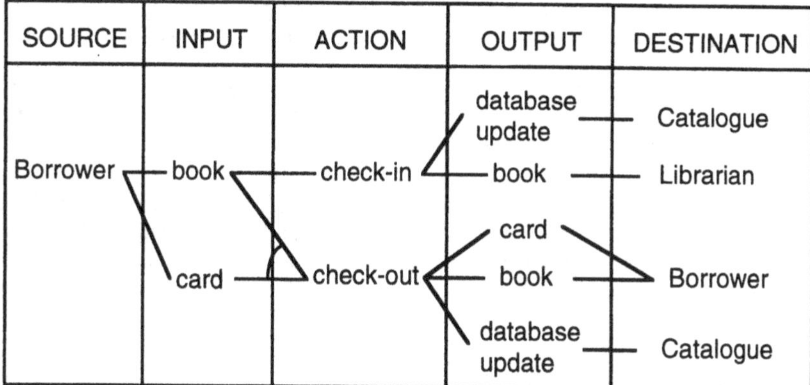

Fig. 5b. An action table elaborating the agent "Clerk". In ViewPoints terminology, the action table is part of a ViewPoint specification where the ViewPoint domain is "Clerk".

SOURCE	INPUT	ACTION	OUTPUT	DESTINATION
Clerk ——	book ——	shelve ——	book ——	Library

Fig. 5c. An action table elaborating the agent "Librarian". In ViewPoints terminology, the action table is part of a ViewPoint specification where the ViewPoint domain is "Librarian".

In ViewPoints terminology, figures 4 and 5 are contained in the specification slots of the different ViewPoints of the overall system specification. Thus, the specification shown in Fig. 5c for example, would appear in the ViewPoint outlined schematically in Fig. 6. Note that the domain of the ViewPoint is "Librarian" which indicates the delineation of the action table in the specification slot.

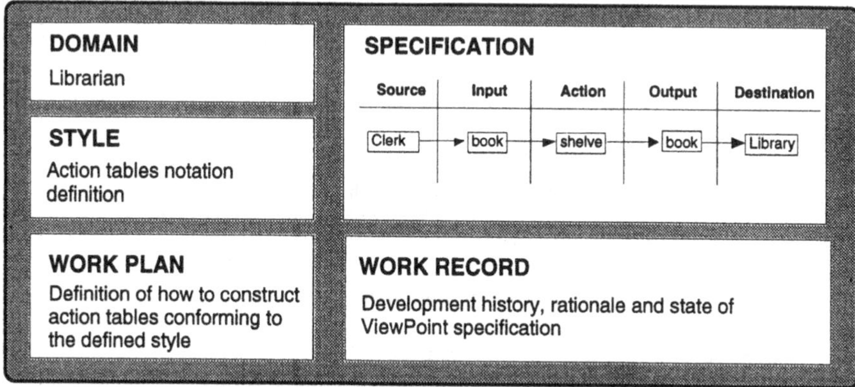

Fig. 6. A schematic outline of a ViewPoint containing the specification shown in Fig. 5c.

The agent hierarchy and action table formalisms are related in a number of ways (as specified by the CORE method designer). Two such relations are described informally by the follwing rules.

Rule 1 (between an agent hierarchy and actions tables): Any "source" or "destination" in an action table, must appear as a leaf agent in the agent hierarchy.

Rule 2 (between action tables): The output (Z) produced by an action table for an agent (X) to a destination (Y), must be consumed as an input (Z) from a source (X) by the action table for the original destination (Y).

We stress that both the library example and the formalisms used to describe it have been greatly simplified to illustrate our consistency handling mechanism. The library world in fact involves many more transactions and may require richer formalisms to describe it. This can be done by defining the desired formalism in the appropriate ViewPoint style slot.

5 Identification of Inconsistency

To undertake a partial consistency check between two or more ViewPoints, we form a logical database (D, E), where D contains formulae representing the partial specifications in these ViewPoints, and E contains formulae representing environmental information such as the definitions for the inter-ViewPoint relations. For the remainder of this paper we assume the language for (D, E) is first-order classical logic.

We start by looking at the action tables in Fig. 5. For these we consider the pre-conditions and post-conditions to an action. We use the function pre(X, Y) to denote X is a source and Y is a 'conjunction' of inputs that are consumed by some action. Similarly, post(Y, X) denotes that X is the destination of the 'conjunction' of outputs, Y, produced by some action. Now we denote the part of the action table associated with an action B as follows:

table(A, P, B, Q)

where, A is an agent name (the ViewPoint domain),
P is a 'conjunction' of pre-conditions for action B, and
Q is a 'conjunction' of post-conditions for action B.

Note that for this definition we are using 'conjunction' as a function symbol within first-order classical logic.

We can now represent each table in Fig. 5 using the above predicates. First we consider the information in Fig. 5a.

(1) table(borrower, pre(borrower, book), check_in, post(book, clerk)).
(2) table(borrower, pre(borrower, card) & pre(library, book), check_out, post(book&card, borrower)).

Similarly, we represent the information in Fig. 5b as,

(3) table(clerk, pre(borrower, book), check_in, post(database_update, catalogue) & post(book, library)).
(4) table(clerk, pre(borrower, book&card), check_out, post(book&card, borrower) & post(database_update, catalogue)).

Finally we represent the information in Fig. 5c as,

(5) table(library, pre(clerk, book), shelve, post(book, library)).

Obviously there are many ways we could present the information in figures 5a-5c in logic. However, it is straightforward to define a rewrite that can take any such table and return logical facts of the above form. We can also capture the inter-ViewPoint relations in classical logic. So rule 2 (between action tables) is represented by,

(6) for all A, B_i, C_i [[table(A, _, _, post(C_1, B_1) & .. & post(C_m, B_m))]
$\rightarrow$ there exist E_j, F_j such that [table(B_i, pre(E_1, F_1) & .. & pre(E_n, F_n), _, _)
and $A = E_j$ and $C_i = F_j$]]
where $1 \leq i \leq m$ and $1 \leq j \leq n$

where the underscore symbol '_' denotes that we are not interested in this part of the argument for this rule, and that it can be instantiated without restriction.

The formulae (1) - (5) are elements in D, and the formula (6) is an element in E. Since we have represented the information in D as a set of classical logic facts, we can use the Closed World Assumption [30] to capture the facts that do not hold in each ViewPoint specification. The Closed World Assumption (CWA) essentially captures the notion that if a fact A is not a member of a list of facts then ¬A (not A) holds. So for example, using the CWA with the borrower domain we can say that the following arbitrary formula does not hold,

(7) table(borrower, pre(borrower, book), check_in, post(card, clerk)).

In other words we can infer the following,

(8) ¬table(borrower, pre(borrower, book), check_in, post(card, clerk)).

Using this assumption we can identify ViewPoints that are inadequately specified. We show this for the relation between the borrower and the clerk. Suppose that formula (3) was not represented, then by the CWA we would have the following,

(9) ¬table(clerk, pre(borrower, book), check_in,
post(database_update, catalogue) & post(book, library)).

Using a classical logic theorem prover with the CWA, we can easily show that (D, E) is inconsistent and that the formulae (1), (6) and (9) cause the inconsistency - since (1) and (6) give,

¬table(clerk, pre(borrower, book), check_in, X, Y)

where X and Y can be instantiated with any term in the language, whereas the CWA gives,

table(clerk, pre(borrower, book), check_in, X, Y)

for any terms X, Y in the language.We address the handling of this situation in section 6.

In a similar fashion, we can represent the agent hierarchy by the following set of logical facts,

(10) tree(library_world, borrower)
(11) tree(library_world, staff)
(12) tree(library_world, library)
(13) tree(library_world, catalogue)
(14) tree(staff, librarian)
(15) tree(staff, clerk)

with the first argument to the predicate 'tree' representing a parent in the agent hierarchy, and the second argument representing its child. To these facts we add the axioms of reflexivity, transitivity, anti-symmetry, up-linearity, and leaf. Recall that,

(up-linearity) for all X, Y, Z, [tree(X, Z) and tree(Y, Z) → tree(X, Y) or tree(Y, X)]

(leaf) for all X, Y [tree(X, Y) and ¬(there exists a Z such that tree(Y, Z)) → leaf(Y)]

These axioms then allow us to capture the appropriate reasoning with the hierarchy so that from (11), (15) and the transitivity axiom for example we can infer the following,

(16) tree(library_world, clerk).

Another inter-ViewPoint relation (rule 1 between ViewPoints deploying different formalisms) is captured as follows,

(17) for all A_i [[table(_, pre(A_1, _) & .. & pre(A_m, _), _, _)]
→ there exists X such that [leaf(X) and X = A_i]]
where $1 \leq i \leq m$

(18) for all B_i [[table(_, post(_, B_1) & .. & post(_, B_m))]
→ there exists X such that [leaf(X) and X = B_i]]
where $1 \leq i \leq m$

As before, formulae (10) - (15) plus the axioms of reflexivity, transitivity, antisymmetry, leaf and up-linearity are elements in D, while (17) and (18) are elements in E. Remember that we are assuming that rules 1 and 2, expressed in logic as (6), (17) and (18) above, are correctly defined by the method designer.

Now suppose that formula (3) had not been inserted in the relevant ViewPoint, and again using the CWA together with a classical logic theorem prover, we can see how insufficient information in (D, E) leads to inconsistency.

We now turn our attention to the situation where we have too much information in a pair of partial specifications. Suppose in ViewPoint 1, we have the following information,

(19) reference_book(childrens_dictionary)
(20) for all X, reference_book(X) → ¬lendable(X)

and suppose in ViewPoint 2, we have the following information,

(21) childrens_book(childrens_dictionary)
(22) for all X, childrens_book(X) → lendable(X)

Taking the formulae in (19) - (22) as elements in D, we have an inconsistency in (D, E) resulting from too much information. Such a situation is common in developing specifications, though the causes are diverse. We address the handling of this situation in the next section.

To summarise, in this section we have advocated the use of classical logic together with the CWA to provide a systematic and well-understood way of finding inconsistency in specifications. It will not be possible to provide a universal and meaningful rewrite from any software engineering formalism into classical logic. However, for partial consistency checking it is often possible to compare some of the specification information, plus other information such as inter-ViewPoint relations, for two, or maybe more, ViewPoints.

6 Acting on Inconsistency

For the meta-level inconsistency handling we use an action-based meta-language [16] based on linear-time temporal logic. We use a first-order form where we allow quantification over formulae (Note that we are not using a second-order logic - rather we are treating object-level formulae as objects in the semantic domain of the meta-level.). Furthermore, we use the usual interpretation over the natural numbers - each number denotes a point in time. Using this interpretation we can define operators such as LAST^n and NEXT^n where LAST^n A holds at time t if A holds at t-n, and NEXT^n A holds at time t if A holds at t+n.

Using temporal logic, we can specify how the databases should evolve over time. In this way, we can view the meta-level handling of inconsistent ViewPoint specifications in terms of satisfying temporal logic specifications. So if during the course of a consistency check between two ViewPoints an inconsistency is identified, then one or more of the meta-level action rules will be fired. Furthermore, since we use temporal logic, we can record how we have handled the ViewPoints in the past.

The meta-level axioms specify how to act according to the context of the inconsistency. This context will include the history behind the inconsistent data being put into the ViewPoint specification - as recorded in the ViewPoint work record - and the history of previous actions to handle the inconsistency. The meta-level axioms will also include implicit and explicit background information on the nature of certain kinds of inconsistencies, and how to deal with them.

To illustrate the use of actions at the meta-level, we now return to the examples introduced in section 5. For handling the inconsistency resulting from formulae (1), (6) and (9), a simplified solution would be to incorporate the kind of meta-level axiom (23) into our framework. For this we provide the following informal definitions of the key predicates

- data(vp1, Δ_1) holds if the formulae in the database Δ_1 are a logical rewrite of selected information in ViewPoint vp1.
- union(Δ_1, Δ_2) $\vdash$ false holds if the union of the databases Δ_1 and Δ_2 implies inconsistency.
- inconsistency_source(union(Δ_1, Δ_2), S) holds if S is a minimal inconsistent subset of the union of Δ_1 and Δ_2.
- likely_spelling_problem(S) holds if the cause of the inconsistency is likely to result from typographical errors in S. Since we are using a temporal language at the meta-

level, we can also include conditions in our rule that we haven't checked this problem at previous points S in time. This means that our history affects our actions.

- tell_user("is there a spell problem?", S) if the message together with the data in S is outputted to the user. In software process modelling terminology, this is equivalent to a tool invocation say, such as a spell-checker or other tool [12].

Essentially, this rule captures the action that if S is the source of the inconsistency and that the likely reason that S is inconsistent is a typographical error, then we tell the user of the problem. We assume that the user can usually deal with this kind of problem once informed. However, we should include further meta-level axioms that provide alternative actions, in case the user cannot deal with the inconsistency on this basis. Indeed, it is likely that for handling inconsistency between different formalisms such as in (1), (6) and (9), there will be a variety of possible actions. This meta-level axiom also has the condition that this action is blocked if likely_spelling_problem(S) has been identified in either of the two previous two steps. This is to stop the same rule firing if the user wants to ignore the problem for a couple of steps.

(23) data(vp1, Δ_1) and data(vp2, Δ_2)
and union(Δ_1, Δ_2) $\vdash$ false
and inconsistency_source(union(Δ_1, Δ_2), S)
and likely_spelling_problem(S)
and $\neg$LAST^1 likely_spelling_problem(S)
and $\neg$LAST^2 likely_spelling_problem(S)
$\rightarrow$ NEXT tell_user("is there a spell problem?", S).

In a similar fashion, we can define appropriate meta-level axioms for handling the inconsistency resulting from formulae (9), (10), (17) and (18) in the above examples.

For handling the problem of too much information occurring in formulae, such as for example (18) - (21), a simplified solution would be to incorporate the kind of meta-level axiom (24) into our framework, where likely_conflict_between_specs_problem(Δ_1, Δ_2) holds if the inconsistency arises from just information in the specification. In other words this inconsistency does not arise because the method or tools have been used incorrectly, but rather, it arises from the incorrectly specifying system.

(24) data(vp1, Δ_1)
and data(vp2, Δ_2)
and union(Δ_1, Δ_2) $\vdash$ false
and likely_conflict_between_specs_problem(Δ_1, Δ_2)
$\rightarrow$ NEXT tell_user("is there a conflict between specifications?", (Δ_1, Δ_2)).

These definitions for the meta-level axioms have skipped over many difficult technical problems, including the general problems of decidability and complexity of such axioms, and the more specific problems of say defining the predicates "inconsistency_source", "likely_spelling_problem", and "likely_conflict_between_specs_problem". Also, we have skipped over the many ways that this approach builds on a variety of existing work by various authors in database updates, integrity constraints, database management systems and meta-level reasoning. Nevertheless, we have illustrated how a sufficiently rich meta-level logic can be used to formally capture intuitive ways of handling inconsistencies in our (D, E) databases. Moreover, such meta-level axioms may also be used to describe, guide and manage the multi-ViewPoint development process in this setting. The advantage over traditional approaches to process modelling [12] however, is that our technique allows very fine-grain modelling - at a level of granularity much closer to the representations deployed by the various ViewPoints [27].

7 Viability of Inconsistency Handling

Since the proposed system uses temporal logic, it is based on a well-developed theoretical basis. It is straightforward to show that this meta-level language inherits desirable properties of first-order until-since (US) temporal logic such as a complete and sound proof theory, and of semi-decidability. This temporal logic is sufficiently general for our purposes. Assuming that time corresponds to a linear sequence of natural numbers, we have all the usual temporal operators including $NEXT^n$, $LAST^n$, SOMETIME_IN_THE_FUTURE, SOMETIME_IN_THE_PAST, and ALWAYS. Similarly, if we assume time corresponds to a linear sequence of real numbers, we have many of these operators.

Furthermore for some sufficiently general subsets of US temporal logic there are viable model building algorithms, such that if the meta-level specification is consistent then the algorithm is guaranteed to find a model of the specification [4]. Using these properties we execute temporal logic specifications to generate a model [14]. This has led to the approach of Executable Temporal Logics - which have been implemented and applied in a variety of applications [5, 10, 22]. In the approach of executable temporal logics we view temporal logic specifications as programs. The model generated by executing the program is then the output from the program.

Though we have not yet implemented the described inconsistency handling for the ViewPoints framework, some of the components required have been implemented. Currently we have an implementation of the ViewPoints framework without the logic-based inconsistency handling technique described in this paper. Called *The Viewer* [25], it provides tool support for the construction of ViewPoint specifications in a variety of formalisms such as those in figures 4 and 5. Tool support for in-ViewPoint consistency checking is also provided. We also have an implementation of first-order executable temporal logic, and we have a first-order theorem prover for consistency checking [17]. We now need to implement the rewrites from the ViewPoints formalism to classical logic and to axiomatise meta-level actions for handling inconsistency.

Finally, in a distributed development setting, issues relating to inter-ViewPoint communication, co-ordination and synchronisation become even more significant. In [26], we proposed a preliminary model for such communication and investigated protocols and mechanisms for exchanging data between ViewPoints. However, the application of such protocols with the inconsistency handling techniques described here, is beyond the scope of this paper.

8 Discussion and Related Work

System specification from multiple perspectives using many different specification languages has become an area of considerable interest. Recent work by Zave & Jackson [37] proposes the composition of partial specifications as a *conjunction* of their assertions in a form of classical logic. A set of partial specifications is then consistent if and only if the conjunction of their assertions is satisfiable. Zave & Jackson's work complements our approach, but it does appear to differ in that they assume they can use classical logic as an underlying universal formalism. Also they do not consider the handling of inconsistent specifications.

Other authors have also considered multi-perspective or multi-language specifications, but again do not consider the *handling* of inconsistencies. In [36], specification level *interoperability* between specifications or programs written in different languages or running on different kinds of processors is described. The interoperability described relies on remote procedure calls and ways that interoperating programs manipulate shared typed data. The work serves as a basis for "the disciplined and orderly marshaling of interoperable components" to eradicate inconsistencies in the overall system specification or program. Wile [35] on the other hand uses a common syntactic framework defined in terms of grammars and *transformations* between these grammars. He highlights the difficulties of consistency checking in a multi-language framework, which suggests that, again, the handling of inconsistencies, once detected, has not been addressed in his work.

Traditionally, multiparadigm languages, which deploy a common multiparadigm *base language*, have been used to combine many partial program fragments [19], while more recently the use of a single, common *canonical representation* for integrating so-called "multi-view" systems has been proposed [23]. Both these approaches to integration do not support the notion of transient inconsistencies.

One approach that has addressed handling certain kinds of inconsistency is that of Balzer [3]. Here, the notion of relaxing constraints and tolerating inconsistencies is discussed, and a simple technique that allows inconsistencies to be managed and tolerated is presented. Inconsistent data is marked by guards ("pollution markers") that have two uses: (1) to identify the inconsistent data to code segments or human agents that may then help resolve the inconsistency, and (2) to screen the inconsistent data from other segments that are sensitive to the inconsistencies. Our approach goes a further by explicitly specifying the actions that may be performed in order to handle the inconsistencies.

In conclusion, the work presented in this paper outlines how we may address important issues of inconsistency handling in multi-perspective specifications. We have only sketched how this may be done. Nevertheless, in this process we have raised a series of new and important research questions.

Acknowledgements

We wish to thank the anonymous reviewers for their constructive comments. This work was partly funded by the CEC ESPRIT BRA project DRUMS II and the DTI Advanced Technology Programme (ATP) of the Eureka Software Factory (ESF).

References

1. A. Alderson (1991), "Meta-CASE technology", *Proc. of European Symposium on Software Development Environments and CASE Technology,* Königswinter, June 1991, LNCS 509, Endres & Weber (eds.), 81-91, Springer-Verlag.
2. A.R. Anderson & N.D. Belnap (1976), *The Logic of Entailment*, Princeton University Press.
3. B. Balzer (1991), "Tolerating Inconsistency", *Proc. of 13th International Conference on Software Engineering (ICSE-13),* 13-17th May 1991, Austin Texas, 158-165.
4. H. Barringer, M. Fisher, D. Gabbay, G. Gough & R. Owens (1989), "MetateM: A framework for programming in temporal logic", *REX Workshop on Stepwise Refinement of Distributed Systems,* LNCS 430, Springer-Verlag.

5. H. Barringer, M. Fisher, D. Gabbay & A. Hunter (1991), "Meta-reasoning in executable temporal logic", *Proc. of the 2nd International Conference on the Principles of Knowledge Representation and Reasoning,* 453-460, Morgan Kaufmann.
6. J. Bell (1990), "Non-monotonic reasoning, non-monotonic logics, and reasoning about change", *Artificial Intelligence Review,* 4, 79-108.
7. H. Blair & V. Subrahmanian (1989), "Paraconsistent logic programming", *Theoretical Computer Science,* 68, 135-154.
8. N.C. da Costa (1974), "On the theory of inconsistent formal systems", *Notre Dame Journal of Formal Logic,* 15, 497-510.
9. J. Doyle (1979), "A truth maintenance system", *Artificial Intelligence,* 12, 231-272.
10. M. Finger, P. McBrien & R. Owens (1991), "Databases and executable temporal logic", *Proc. of ESPRIT conference 1991.*
11. A. Finkelstein, J. Kramer & M. Goedicke (1990), "ViewPoint Oriented Software Development", *Proc. of International Workshop on Software Engineering and its Applications,* Toulouse, France, December 1990.
12. A. Finkelstein, J. Kramer & M. Hales (1992), "Process Modelling: a critical analysis", *Integrated Software Engineering with Reuse,* P. Walton & N. Maiden (eds.), Chapman and Hall and UNICOM, 137-148.
13. A. Finkelstein, J. Kramer, B. Nuseibeh, L. Finkelstein & M. Goedicke (1992), "ViewPoints: A Framework for Integrating Multiple Perspectives in System Development", *International Journal of Software Engineering and Knowledge Engineering,* 2(1):31-58, March 1992.
14. D. Gabbay (1989), "Declarative Past and Imperative Future: Executable temporal logic for interactive systems", *Proc. of Colloquium on Temporal Logic in Specification,* B. Banieqbal, H. Barringer & A. Pnueli (eds.), LNCS 398, Springer-Verlag.
15. D. Gabbay & A. Hunter (1991), "Making inconsistency respectable: Part 1", *Fundamentals of Artificial Intelligence Research,* Ph. Jorrand & J. Kelemen (eds.), LNCS 535, Springer-Verlag.
16. D. Gabbay & A. Hunter (1992), "Making inconsistency respectable: Part 2", *Technical report,* Department of Computing, Imperial College, London, 1992.
17. D. Gabbay & H. Ohlbach (1992), "Quantifier Elimination in Second Order Predicate Logic", *Proc. of the 3rd International Conference on the Principles of Knowledge Representation and Reasoning,* 453-460, Morgan Kaufmann.
18. P. Graubmann (1992), "The HyperView Tool Standard Methods", *REX Technical report REX-WP3-SIE-021-V1.0,* Siemens, Munich, Germany, January '92.
19. B. Hailpern (ed.) (1986) "Special issue on multiparadigm languages and environments", *IEEE Software,* 3(1):10-77, Special issue on multiparadigm languages and environments, January 1986.
20. J. Kramer & A. Finkelstein (1991), "A Configurable Framework for Method and Tool Integration", *Proc. of European Symposium on Software Development Environments and CASE Technology,* Königswinter, Germany, June 1991, LNCS 509, 233-257, Springer-Verlag.
21. J. Kramer (1991), "CASE Support for the Software Process: A Research Viewpoint", *Proc. of 3rd European Software Engineering Conference (ESEC 91),* Milan, Italy, October 1991, LNCS 550, A. van Lamsweerde (ed.), 499-503, Springer-Verlag.

22. J. Krogstie, P. McBrien, R. Owens & A. Selvit (1991), "Information systems development using a combination of process and rule-based approaches", *Proc. of the International Conference on Advanced Information Systems Engineering,* LNCS, Springer-Verlag.
23. S. Meyers & S.P. Reiss (1991) "A System for Multiparadigm Development of Software Systems", *Proc. of 6th International Workshop on Software Specification and Design,* Como, Italy, 202-209, 25-26th October 1991, IEEE CS Press.
24. G. Mullery (1985), "Acquisition - Environment", *Distributed Systems: Methods and Tools for Specification,* M. Paul & H. Siegert (eds.), LNCS 190, Springer-Verlag.
25. B. Nuseibeh & A. Finkelstein (1992), "ViewPoints: A Vehicle for Method and Tool Integration", *Proc. of Fifth International Workshop on CASE (CASE '92),* 6-10th July 1992, Montreal Canada, 50-60, IEEE CS Press.
26. B. Nuseibeh, J. Kramer & A. Finkelstein (1993), "Expressing the Relationships Between Multiple Views in Requirements Specification", (to appear in) *Proc. of International Conference on Software Engineering (ICSE-15),* Baltimore, Maryland, USA, 17-21st May 1993, IEEE CS Press.
27. B. Nuseibeh, A. Finkelstein & J. Kramer (1993), "Fine-Grain Process Modelling", *Technical report,* Department of Computing, Imperial College, London, 1993.
28. T. Pequeno & A. Buchsbaum (1991), "The logic of epistemic inconsistency", *Proc. of the 2nd International Conference on the Principles of Knowledge Representation and Reasoning,* 453-460, Morgan Kaufmann.
29. J. Pocock (1991), "VSF and its relationship to Open Systems and Standard Repositories", *Proc. of European Symposium on Software Development Environments and CASE Technology,* Königswinter, June 1991, LNCS 509, Endres & Weber (eds.), Springer-Verlag, 53-68.
30. R. Reiter (1978), "On Closed World Databases", *Logic & Databases,* H. Gallaire & J. Minker (eds.), Plenum Press.
31. F. Sadri & R. Kowalski (1986), "An application of general theorem proving to database integrity", *Technical report,* Department of Computing, Imperial College, London.
32. G. Wagner (1991), "Ex contradictione nihil sequitur", *Proc. of the 12th International Joint Conference on Artificial Intelligence,* Morgan Kaufmann.
33. A.I. Wasserman & P.A. Pircher (1987) "A Graphical, Extensible Integrated Environment for Software Development", *Proc. of 2nd Symposium on Practical Software Development Environments,* SIGPlan Notices, 22(1):131-142, January 1987, ACM Press.
34. A.I. Wasserman (1990) "Integration in Software Engineering Environments", *Proc. of International Workshop on Environments,* Chinon, France, September 1989, LNCS 457, F. Long (ed.), 137-149, Springer-Verlag, 1990.
35. D.S. Wile (1991) "Integrating syntaxes and their associated semantics", *USC/Information Sciences Institute Technical Report,* 1991.
36. J.C. Wileden, A.L. Wolf, W.R. Rosenblatt & P.L. Tarr (1991) "Specification-level interoperability", *Communications of the ACM,* 34(5):72-87, May 1991.
37. P. Zave & M. Jackson, "Conjunction as Composition", (to appear in) *Transactions on Software Engineering and Methodology,* ACM Press, 1993.

Requirements Engineering: An Integrated View of Representation, Process, and Domain*

Matthias Jarke, Klaus Pohl, Stephan Jacobs, [1]
Janis Bubenko, Petia Assenova, Peter Holm, Benkt Wangler,[2]
Colette Rolland, Veronique Plihon, Jean-Roch Schmitt,[3]
Alistair Sutcliffe, Sara Jones, Neil Maiden, David Till,[4]
Yannis Vassiliou, Panos Constantopoulos, Giorgios Spanoudakis[5]

Reuse, system integration, and interoperability create a growing need for capturing, representing, and using application-level information about software-intensive systems and their evolution. In ESPRIT Basic Research Project NATURE, we are developing an integrative approach to requirements management based on a three-dimensional framework which addresses formalism as well as cognitive and social aspects. This leads to a new requirements process model which integrates human freedoms through allowing relatively free decisions in given situations. Classes of situations and decisions are defined with respect to the three-dimensional framework through the integration of informal and formal representations, theories of domain modeling, and the explicit consideration of nonfunctional requirements in teamwork. Technical support is provided by a conceptual modeling environment with knowledge acquisition through interactive as well as reverse modeling, and with similarity-based querying.

1 Introduction

In software engineering, the requirements phase has traditionally been perceived as the fuzzy and somewhat dirty part in which a formal specification is gained from informal ideas. Everything prior to the formalization tends to be lost: in theory due to the inability to integrate informal information into the formal specification framework, in practice through burying requirements knowledge in bulky, practically unusable and unmaintainable documentation.

In contrast to this tradition stands the growing demand for "corporate ownership" of information technology. Organizations cannot take full advantage of information systems which they don´t understand and therefore don´t trust. The only way they can understand software systems is in application terms, i.e. from the requirements point of view. It is also from this perspective that they wish to evaluate software and to direct its change.

When presented to users, their managers, and other stakeholders, requirements information should adequately reflect the actual status and ongoing change of existing systems. Thus, consistent relationships between requirements information, system specification, and implementation must be maintained. In an ideal world, these relation–

* This work is supported in part by ESPRIT Basic Research Project 6353 (NATURE).
1 Informatik V, RWTH Aachen, Ahornstr. 55, 5100 Aachen, Germany
2 SISU-ISE, Isafjordsgatan 26, 1250 Kista, Sweden
3 Universite Paris 1, rue de al Sorbonne 17, 75231 Paris, France
4 Business Comp., City University, London ECIV OHB, UK
5 ICS-FORTH, Dedalou 36, 71110 Heraclion, Greece

ships would be created during initial development and continuously maintained. In the real world, there are lots of incomprehensible legacy systems; *reverse modeling* is therefore becoming a necessary if difficult complementary technique for requirements capture.

Such new ways to *capture* requirements information are only justified because there are also new *uses* of requirements information. In addition to the traditional forward design, there are:

- explicit and computer-supported *use of requirements*, especially non-functional ones, to drive design decisions in the systems development process;
- *reuse and shared maintenance of requirements models and processes* in the evolution of a system family or in the development of new applications;
- support of reuse and heterogeous system interoperability by standardized *reference models;*
- the *re-engineering* of systems and business processes based on requirements models.

All of these are no longer relevant only to information systems development. They also invade computer-integrated manufacturing, office systems, process control, and other areas where systems interact intensively with their environment.

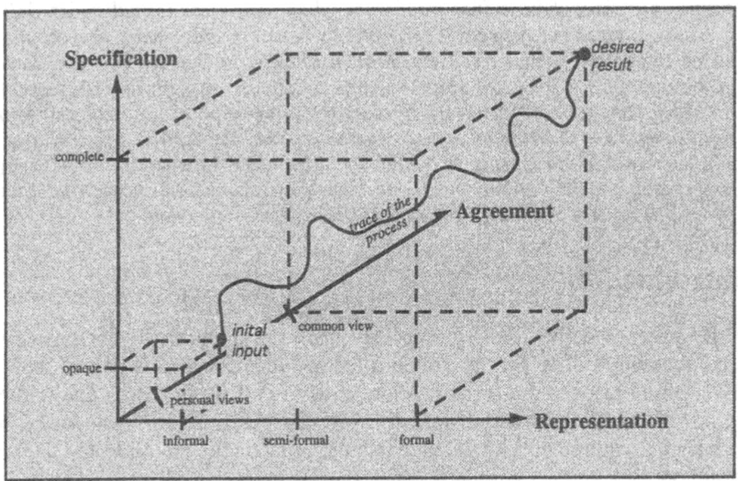

Fig. 1. The three dimensions of requirements engineering.

What does it take to capture, maintain and use requirements information? The NATURE framework [Pohl93] derives three dimensions (cf. figure 1) of interest from the major sources of problems in requirements engineering:

- As a basis for formal system development, requirements engineering moves along a *representational axis* typically from informal to more formal representations, ideally ending with a formal specification that can be transformed to executable code. Modeling and relating these representations is mostly a technical problem albeit one whose solution needs good knowledge of human-computer interaction.
- A second obvious goal is to end up with a complete system *specification*. We see this as orthogonal to the first problem: it is perfectly possible to hide poor understanding behind a lot of formalism, as well as to describe a very deep understanding in quite informal terms. Moves along this axis mostly face cognitive and psychological problems of requirements engineering.

- The third axis is concerned with the *agreement* reached on the current specification. Requirements engineering is understood here as a negotiation process which should lead towards at least sufficient agreement to start building a system. Hence this axis mainly deals with the social aspects of requirements engineering.

At the level of process execution, RE can be understood as a movement in this space which, in addition to the technical, cognitive, and social barriers, is also influenced by economical factors and the methods used. For example, the traditional requirements capture process starts near the origin with different personal views, little system understanding and a completely informal representation; it should end with agreement on a well-understood and formally described specification.

At the level of process definition and evaluation, we can evaluate particular methods or combinations thereof with respect to their contribution to overcoming the problems associated with each dimension.

This paper studies the impact of the views stated above on support for requirements information management. Section 2 argues that a requirements process model cannot be fully pre-planned but should take advantage of situations and human decisions. Section 3 presents, for each dimension in figure 1, partial answers NATURE has developed for the obvious question: what is a situation and what decision options and guidance do we have? Section 4 discusses the needs these models imply for representation and reasoning tools that create and search them. Section 5 sketches an extension of the well-known library example to illustrate the impact of our approach; a more detailed version of this example is found in the NATURE Initial Integration Report [JJP*92] on which this paper is based.

2 NATPROC: A Process Model Based on Situations and Decisions

According to [Dows87], process models can be classified in three categories. *Activity-oriented process models* [Royc70; Boeh88; HeEd90] come from an analogy with problem-solving and provide a frame for manual management of projects developed in linear fashion. This linear view is inadequate for methodologies which support backtracking, reuse of previous designs, and parallel engineering. *Product-oriented process models* [FKGo90; AHTo90] represent the development process through the evolution of the product. They are more synergetic with systemic methodologies that do not place constraints on the design process. They also allow design tracing in terms of the performed transformations and their resulting products. Finally, the *decision-oriented paradigm* integrates more deeply the semantics attached to evolutionary aspects. The notion of design decision facilitates under–standing of the designer's intention, and thus better reuse of its results [Pott89, RJG*91].

When considered from the viewpoint of requirements engineering, only the last of these approaches appears to be partially appropriate. It is difficult to impossible to write down a realistic state-transition diagram (to cite a popular activity-oriented model) that adequately describes what has to happen or actually happens in requirements engineering. But relying purely on the object history is also insufficient. Even the decision-based approaches offer only limited hints when and how to decide on what. The central idea of the NATPROC process model is therefore that it makes the notion of *situation* (in which to decide) explicit and relates it to the broader question of context handling.

Figure 2 gives an overview of the model. The basic building block of any process is modeled as a triple <*situation, decision, action*> [GrRo90]; a further component, *argument-types* underlying design decisions, is discussed later.

The triple associates the situation the requirements engineer has to deal with to one of the decisions he can take to solve the local problem and to one of the actions to be performed to apply the decision. The record of the selected triplets comprises a trace of the development. Situation perception can be based on activity status, product status, or just subjective impressions of the analyst.

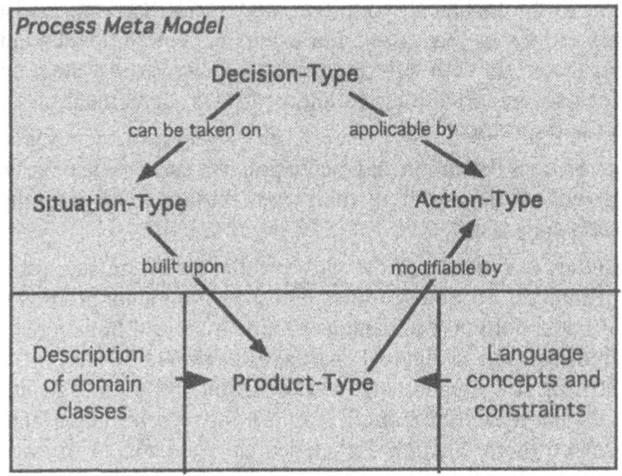

Fig. 2. The NATPROC requirements process meta model.

By refining the interrelated lattices of product, situation, decision, and action types, the NATURE process theory models software development activities at macro and micro levels of detail. Engineering activities deal with the RE artifacts (the specifications) and allow their creation, evolution, modification and deletion. Monitoring activities organise and order engineering activities, select the appropriate engineering activity for a certain situation, and allocate the necessary resources. Figure 3 shows a partial taxonomy of decision types.

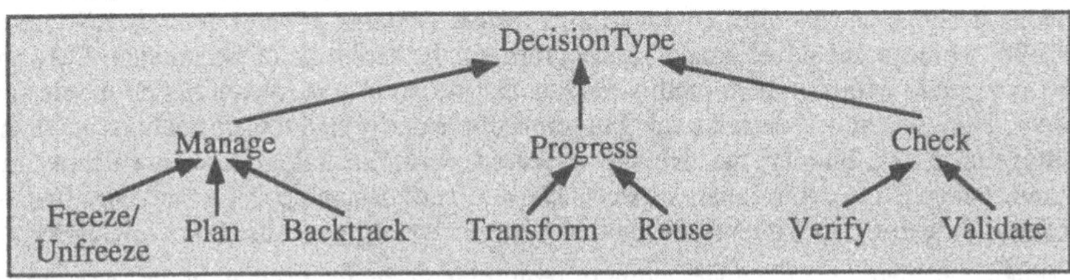

Fig. 3. Parts of a lattice of micro-level decision classes in NATPROC.

3 Support for Situation and Decision Modeling

Figure 2 simply says that a situation is defined on product information. This is a gross over-simplification. This section applies the three dimensions shown in figure 1 to elaborate contributions to the modeling of situations, actions and decisions made in NATURE.

3.1 The Specification Dimension: Domain Theory

The domain theory aims to describe the knowledge structures people develop, and ultimately remember, when they are investigating problems. Abstractions for various domains have been proposed as templates and mechanisms for analogical transfer of knowledge between domains belonging to the same class [GiHo83; Grei88].

The importance of domain knowledge has been recognised from two directions. First, cognitive studies of software engineering have demonstrated that experts use memory schema of domain knowledge to help construction of specifications [GuCu88; Guin90]. A model of domain abstraction appears to be necessary for retrieving application domain knowledge from memory, then understanding the implications of that knowledge in a new context. Studies of the matching problem [MaSu92; MaSu93] have demonstrated that software engineering domains can be described as abstract models and matched using a meta schema of goal related and structured domain knowledge. This approach synthesises concepts of templates, object-orientation and structure mapping theory [Gent83], which defines analogy as the matching of a structured set of propositions.

Second, there has been a progressive growth in semantic richness of specification languages to model domain concepts. The latter trend, manifest in languages such as TAXIS and Telos [Jark93], has culminated in the recognition of different *descriptive worlds* (figure 4), in which domain knowledge is necessary for effective system development. Making these worlds explicit does not only provide a certain degree of guidance in building a requirements model but also allows the association of non-functional goals with stake–holder groups in requirements teams.

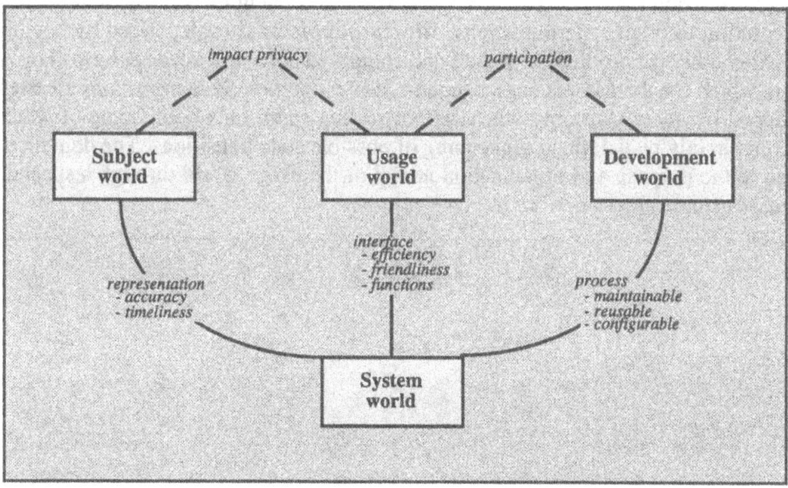

Fig. 4. Categories of domain models: the "worlds" of information systems.

The assumptions of the current theory [Maid92] are drawn from cognitive models of memory, in particular the hierarchical models of natural categories [Rosc91], hierarchical memory schemas [Ande90] and categories of dynamic memory [Scha82]. These assert in slightly different forms that human memory for several different types of knowledge (e.g. object, procedure, plan) is organised in an informal hierarchy of classes.

The domain theory recognises three broad knowledge areas, each related to a particular "world" and defined in a different model investigated in the project:

- domain model of the *subject world*, describing key state transitions and object structures in a software engineering domain. Generic domain models are similiar to the cliches proposed by [ReWa91];
- information systems model, describing computerised functions, design algorithms and their interaction with the domain (the *system world*). Knowledge reuse in the design space is tractable because mapping at the design level of abstraction have been effective in transformation programming [JJWS88]. The theory adds an intermediate level of abstraction linking designs to requirements through the concepts of system purpose;
- purpose model, defining goals of the domain and the required computer system; and organisation model, describing the business, its purpose, context and links to domains within the organisation [BNP*91], both related to the *usage world* of the system.

A fourth model defines the *development world*, statically by elaborating the three dimensions of figure 1, and dynamically by the NATPROC model.

Work so far has investigated the subject domain model and its links to the purpose and organisation models. The domain model consists of a meta-schema of domain knowledge, adapted from existing meta-schemata such as KAOS [DFLa91] and [Luba88], example-based analyses of software engineering analogies [MaSu92], and a set of domain abstractions modeled as classes and specialised by addition of further knowledge to describe different views on a single domain. Most software engineering domains can be ascribed to one of a tractably small set of domain classes.

The current domain meta schema (figure 5) focuses attention on structural objects and their evolution through state transitions. *Structural objects* are categorized by key objects and possibly other (first-order) properties and composed/decomposed, as described by *object structure* which can themselves have (second-order) properties. *State transitions* are triggered and stopped by *events* but only when certain *stative conditions* hold, some of which are also given directly by a defined sequencing of possible state transitions. The domain model is linked to the purpose and organization model of the usage world through a special kind of object structure called a *goal state*.

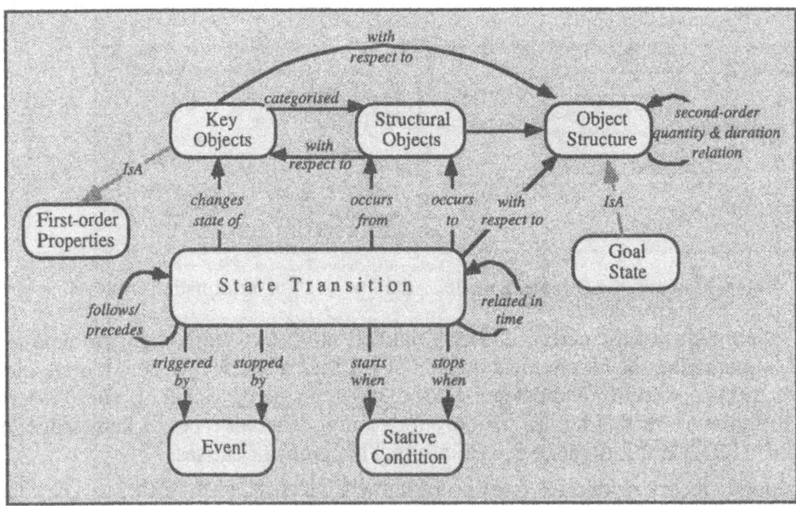

Fig. 5: Meta schema of domain model in which specific domain abstractions are defined.

3.2 The Representation Dimension: Integrating the Formal and Informal

Requirements can be represented using formal specification languages, semi-formal graphical methods or informal aids. Each of these representational forms has certain strengths and weaknesses, so a combination is necessary. This combination should be preserved throughout the software life-cycle rather than being defined away through a once-for-all formalization. Firstly, informal information provides an illustration which may be necessary for understanding formalism. Second, since any formalization implies an abstraction from the informal realities, certain revisions of the formalization may be incomprehensible without the ability of backtracking to informal statements.

To illustrate, consider a situation in a library model. Due to a new requirement (R27), the concept of book should be specialized. Figure 6 shows that there was an earlier decision *„No specialisation of book"*. Retrieving this information needs, in addition to the formal recording of the decision, the integration of informal and formal representations.

Semi-formal and informal languages allow the necessary freedom at the beginning of the acquisition process, but do not offer much support for reasoning about the requirements in a later stage. The use of knowledge representation languages as a backend to *semi-formal techniques* was proposed in [BGMy85]. Besides the advantages of formalization in terms of consistency and completeness checking, mapping support and validation assistance, they emphasize organizational principles such as aggregation (composability of requirements), generalization (avoiding redundancy by inheritance), and classification (meta-modeling). Meanwhile, several formalizations of specific semi-formal methods were proposed. Perhaps the best-known are Greenspan's formalization of SADT in RML [Gree84] and the formalization of an extended entity-relationship model in ERAE [Hage88]. Thus, the mapping between semi-formal representations and an underlying knowledge base is fairly well understood although few commercial CASE tools cover even the rather weak semantic checks for the standard methods [VJTr92].

The relationship between formal and informal representations is much less understood. In the NATURE prototype, we distinguish between static and dynamic aspects. *Statically*, a formal model can represent an informal object such as an image or a video clip as an uninterpreted node, described by some attributes which give an inkling about its content.

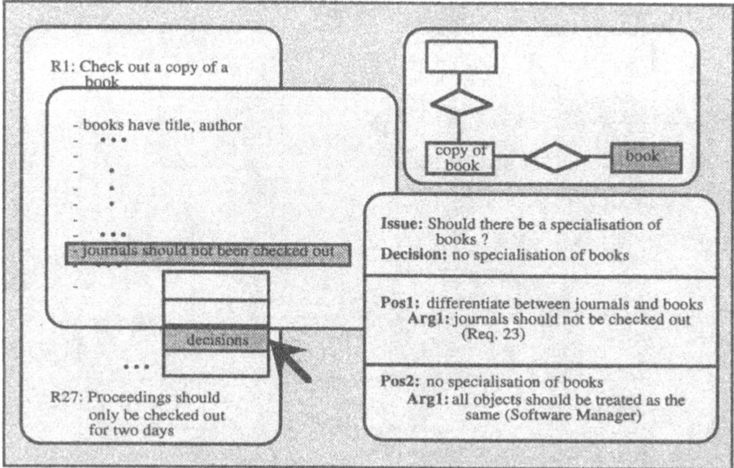

Fig. 6: The use of formal and informal knowledge during decision making.

Thus, the formal object can be considered as an access path to the informal object; this is a very familiar approach in software databases where the actual software is stored in files and the database contains a *description* of the software.Conversely, the informal object is a visualization, animation or illustration of the formal description.

Dynamically, we have to consider the two-way transition between formal and informal representations. In the creation process, the transition from informal to formal corresponds to knowledge acquisition, whereas the transition from formal to informal is associated with validation. The informal-to-formal transition corresponds to an abstraction process, the other direction to concretization and authoring. Since we lose information in abstraction, it is important to maintain the dynamic relationship between formal and informal object -- an aspect omitted in the original formalization may become important later on, possibly after a change in perspective or due to the revision of some design decision (cf. figure 6).

The NATURE environment focuses on the representation of these static and dynamic relationships in a concise and usable manner and in furthering the basic understanding of their roles in the requirements process. The integration of hypermedia and knowledge bases (e.g., [EhJa91, JoHa90]) seems to provide a suitable technological basis for this work.

3.3 The Agreement Dimension: Modeling Teams and Process Quality

Requirements engineering is not an activity conducted out of the blue. Before an RE team is established within an organization, some need for changing the existing world is always decided in a process such as rationalisation of perceived opportunities and threats, or political decision-making. The need for change is typically stated in a simple manner as a small set of basic requirements — the *vision* of the system [JaPo93]. A classical example is John F. Kennedy´s *"send a man to the moon before the end of the decade"*.

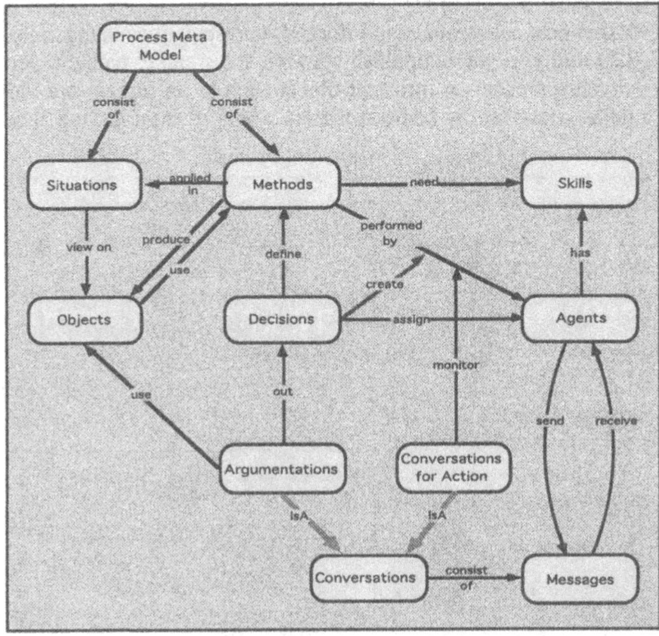

Fig. 7. Adding conversation-based teamwork support to the NATPROC model.

Gaining a requirements specification out of the vision is not an easy task. Within the world in which the vision has to be realized, many habits exist. Some of these habits are based on formally stated goals, policies, or competing visions. Others are just regularly observable phenomena for which no predefined structure or reasons are known.

Of course, the habits depend on the different contexts (worlds) people are in and the roles people in the requirements team own. Thus, and because of personal factors, they are often conflicting. Such conflicts can only be detected and resolved by communication within an interdiciplinary requirements engineering team.

Our proposition is that non-functional goals are expressed in such communications. Argumentation models such as Rittel´s IBIS or Toulmin´s Argumatics provide the formal framework for introducing non-functional requirements in this manner [CoBe88, HJRo91, RaDh92]. Taking a speech-act perspective [WiFl86], an extended NATPROC model organizes this cooperation in conversation structures. Decisions select among actions to be performed by agents (persons or machines) based on *conversations for argumentation*; figure 6 contains a partial trace following the IBIS model. Decisions do not only depend on the process situation, but also on the availability of agents with the necessary skills. Action performance is controlled through *conversations for action.*

These structures make conversations traceable and thus more understandable. Figure 7 shows how conversational modeling is integrated with the situation-decision-action model of section 2 [PoJa92]. Formally, this integration is achieved by linking conversations to objects and decisions, thus making them part of the working context (situation description along the agreement axis of figure 1).

4 Representation and Reasoning Tools

Technical support for the creation, management, and use of the models discussed in the previous sections must be based on a formal language which offers a rich spectrum of abstractional, constraint checking, and dynamic clustering facilities, and is sufficiently mature in terms of implementation so that substantial experiments can be made. In NATURE, we are using the language *Telos* [MBJK90] and its implementations *ConceptBase* [Jark92] and *SIB* [CJMV92].

4.1 Telos as a Requirements Modeling Language

The knowledge representation and reasoning mechanism has to be expressive enough to capture the essential specializations needed for representing domain knowledge and proccess dynamics adequately and concisely. Our modeling framework relies heavily on the kind of abstraction mechanisms offered by advanced semantic modeling, object-oriented databases, and knowledge representation languages, connected to semi-formal and informal information through the notions of view and structured hypertext, respectively.

Meta modeling is the most crucial requirement. Telos allows the association of predicative deduction rules and integrity constraints with meta classes, thus supporting semantic definition and consistency checking of multiple interacting metamodels. Thus, it cannot manage only a requirements model as an evolving knowledge base but also the meta models driving the process. Metamodels can be specialized to particular domains and methodologies. This provides the basis for integrating domain and process engineering theories into a knowledge representation framework for requirements engineering. Figure 8 shows the basic organization of the requirements information base and its integration of data and process information, essentially a semantic enrichment of the IRDS standard.

The full version of Telos implemented in ConceptBase appears to cover a large portion of the features to be expected from an extensible language for requirements modeling:

- full support for the abstraction principles of aggregation, generalization, and classification;
- no distinction between attributes and relationships -- attributes are first-class objects;
- full extensibility through the combination of meta–classing with deductive rules and integrity constraints;
- integration of temporal information about the evolution of the modeled worlds as well as about the history of the database content;
- data model that lends itself to hypertext-like switching between graphical and frame-oriented representations, fully compatible with semi-formal graphical techniques;
- client-server KBMS with support for teamwork in requirements modeling and process management which is itself based on appropriate meta models.

Considering the intended use of requirements models in capture, reuse, and re-engineering, several extensions to the present Telos version are needed, without giving up the advantages of formal semantics and automated reasoning support. These concern freedoms regarding the completeness and consistency of requirements models [Balz91, FeFi91], which are productive as a basis for finding out what are the real goals, what is important, etc., but also to support oversimplification of models to make them more understandable.

Telos has a formal semantics grounded in deductive database theory [Jeus92]. It offers predicative querying and update facilities similar to those in deductive relational databases, extended to the object-oriented framework. For requirements engineering, these fall short in at least two areas: the acquisition of requirements information from existing systems through *reverse engineering*; and the search in requirements databases where exact matching is highly improbable and therefore *similarity-based search* is necessary.

4.2 Reverse Modeling as a Knowledge Acquisition Facility

Reverse modeling (RM) concerns analysing components of existing computerised or manual systems in order to acquire knowledge of the application domain:

- *concept formation* during the initial requirements acquisition. This is particularly valuable in situations where the structure of the domain is large and complex;

IRDS	Product-Model		Process-Model
	Structure	Behavior	
Schema Description Layer	Definition of Product Type	Definition of BehaviorType	Definition of ProcessType
Schema Layer	Definition of Product-Models e.g., Entity-Type	Definition of Behavior-Models e.g., Activity-Type	Definition of Process Models, e.g., refine "Entity"
Data Layer	Definition of Products, e.g., Entity "Customer"	Definition of Behavior, e.g., Enter "Customer"	Trace of Process, e.g., refine "Person to Customer"
Production Layer	Application Data, e.g., Customer "Smith"	Application Data, e.g., Enter "Smith"	

Fig. 8: Meta modeling as a prerequisite for extensible requirements handling.

- *validation*: A conceptual schema for a new system can be compared to that of an existing system in order to check if it is reasonable and complete.
- *identification* of reusable components of existing systems and integration points when two systems are to be integrated.

The interest in RM has increased recently due to the large number of legacy systems presently in operation. Often, the exact understanding of the data and procedures in the existing systems has been lost after years of evolution, and reverse modelling is seen as a means to regain that understanding.

An example of reverse modelling is to extract a conceptual model out of examples of filled-in forms [TaWa90]. This technique could be used as a means for concept formation. It increases the role of the end user and decreases the role of the system analyst. Cost and time of requirements capture can be reduced considerably.

Another approach used within NATURE is to construct a conceptual model out of a relational DB schema [Kalm91]. First, relational schemas are transformed into a form appropriate for identifying object structures; certain cycles of inclusion dependencies are removed, and certain relation schemes are split. Second, the relational schema is mapped to a conceptual schema; each relation scheme gives rise to an object type, and the inclusion dependencies give rise to either attributes or generalisation constraints, depending on the structure of the keys in each relation scheme.

This transformation is not just a syntactic one but can be viewed as a knowledge acquisition process. It makes semantics hidden in application code and organisational assumptions explicit in an enriched representation. To get the needed information for the translation, we intend to use domain abstractions that provide suggestions for objects and relations which the data base gives rise to. An advantage of the method is that it makes clear what types of interactions with a user are needed to construct a conceptual schema.

4.3 Principles of Similarity-Based Search

In addition to classification-based retrieval of suitable domain abstractions (sec. 3.1), NATURE also investigates direct analogical reuse of requirements model instances through the definition of a quantitative similarity relation between desriptions of requirements.

The approach only assumes a fairly general conceptual modelling framework, namely the Telos language, but not any particular model for expressing requirements [Pern90]. This choice is motivated by our purpose to develop a rather generic model of similarity computation, applicable to any requirements description model. However, it restricts the final method to be applicable only to requirements specifications employing a certain degree of formality (structured descriptions as opposed to natural language specifications).

In the context of analogical retrieval, similarity is either used as a fine evaluator of source cases initially selected by some coarser search method [CoKj87], or to provide effective trial hints to the subsequent stage of mapping knowledge from source specifications to evolving ones. As a basis for prototypicality estimates [Tver77], similarity can be exploited in selecting prototypical instances of abstract specification models. Such prototypical instances are known to improve the ability of humans in comprehending abstractions, a prerequisite for successfully using them. Moreover, similarity estimates provide useful criteria for classification. Finally, similarity provides solutions to special problems in RE. For instance, parts of specifications which have been detected as sources of consistency violations can be replaced by similar parts, serving analogous roles in other specifications but not leading to the same contradictions.

Having as a final aim the formulation of a computational model of similarity, consistent with properties inherent to relevant kinds of human processing [Sjöb72, Tver77], the following principles have been identified:

- The principle of *ontological uniformity* says that similarity will be only computed at the same meta level of classification.
- The principle of only *partially uniform representation* implies that positive matching attempts are more relevant than discrimination attempts.
- The *normalization* principle requires that similarity must be defined as a monotonically decreasing function of a normalized distance measure.
- The principle of the *domain dominant schema* uses the requirements information base schema to identify key features salient for reuse.
- The principle of the *pragmatic utility subsumption* says that domain dominance subsumes other measures of salience.
- The principle of *classification optimality* defines the trade-off between type A and type B classification errors.

In a way consistent with these six principles, we are going to define similarity on the basis of an overall distance metric, aggregating partial measures of object distances. These partial distances correspond to the three abstractions along which requirements can be organized in Telos: classification, generalization and attribution [SpCo93].

Any elaboration of these concepts must take into account the trade-off between the quality of the final estimates and their computational cost for obtaining them. Moreover, it will be necessary to validate and calibrate the resulting method of estimating similarities between objects within the particular context of requirements engineering .

5 A Standard Example Revisited

To illustrate the interplay among the different NATURE models and tools, the NATURE demonstrator shows an extension of the standard requirements engineering and specification example of a *library system* [Wing90]. We sketch a small subset below.

Process model. Assume that a partial set of such requirements has been captured in a structure linking hypertext into the Telos language through static means and a recorded process history. At a certain point in the past, the existence of both books and proceedings led to a *situation* where the *decision* had to be made whether the same or different lending policies were to be adopted for the different subclasses. The team decided at that time to have a uniform policy, with the nonfunctional goal of a simple system (cf. figure 8). As a consequence, it did not formalize the distinction between books and proceedings (*action*).

Informal-formal integration / nonfunctional goals. Later on, it becomes known that the library will also contain journals which may not be lent for more than one day. The team now decides to create a generalization hierarchy of document types containing books and journals. Only the fact that the initial informal requirements in which both books and proceedings were mentioned reminds them to include proceedings as well in this hierarchy (they are nowhere present in the formal model!). In this situation, the process model can invoke a backtracking decision to revise also the original lending policy, for example, treating proceedings like journals rather than like books. The argument for that revision is that the original simplicity goal is no longer satisfiable anyway.

Similarity-based search. Assume the library system is to be developed by a software house with a large base of experience in similar systems. Through similarity-based search, the requirements model of a car rental system is found. Comparing the two models, the team decides to introduce borrower cards for identification and to distinguish different library users with different lending rights.

Reverse modeling. Suppose our library already has a simple and poorly documented relational database which describes the existing documents and their subject areas. In order to be able to reuse it as part of the new lending system, the team reverse-models it and tries to fit it together with the existing specification through view integration.

Domain abstraction. The team originally thought that the existing relational database would be sufficient for stock control. Comparison with a generic stock control domain abstraction -- triggered by informal critiques of the database -- shows, however, significant deficiencies (e.g., no handling of missing and damaged books) and leads to a completion of this part of the requirements model.

6 Summary and Conclusions

From a discussion of new sources and uses of requirements information, and from a three-dimensional framework derived from the major problems faced in the RE process, we arrived at a situation and decision-oriented process model, together with its characterization through domain theories and knowledge representation and management facilities.

The relationships between the different techniques presented here are summarized in figure 9 which shows how they contribute to the process of moving in the three-dimensional framework of figure 1; integration of formal and informal requirements, the formal model itself, and the modeling of nonfunctional requirements are all covered under the label of knowledge representation theory.

Initial prototype implementations of the models and tools presented in this paper exist or are in advanced stages of implementation. However, the framework has opened up a lot of questions for further research. Some of the more interesting ones include the study of the business and purpose models in domain theory, the design of advanced interactive capture tools using the theories, the development of process drivers and controllers based on the NATPROC model, and in particular the combination of reverse modeling and view integration for system integration or re-engineering.

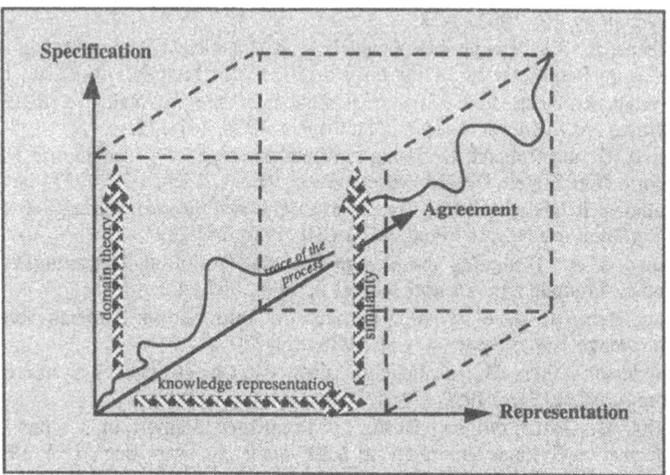

Fig. 9. Contributions of NATURE work to the requirements engineering tasks.

References

[AHTo90] Akman, V.; ten Hagen, P.J.W. and Tomiyama, T.: A Fundamental and Theoretical Framework for an Intelligent CAD System; Computer Aided Design 22, 6, 1990.

[Ande90] Anderson, J.R.: The Adaptive Character of Thought. Hillsdale, NJ: Erlbaum, 1990.

[Balz91] Balzer, R.: Tolerating Inconsistency; Proc. 13th ICSE, Austin 1991, 158-165.

[BiRi87] Biggerstaff, T. and Richter, C.: Reusability framework, assessment and directions; IEEE Software, March 1987.

[BGMy85] Borgida, A.; Greenspan, S.J. and Mylopoulos, J.: Knowledge Representation as the Basis for Requirements Specification; IEEE Computer, April 1985, 82-91.

[Boeh88] Boehm, B.W.: A Spiral Model of Software Development and Enhancement; IEEE Computer 21.

[BNP*91] Brian, P.M.; Niezette, M.; Pantatzis, D., Seltveit, A.H.; Sundin, U.; Theodolidis, B.; Tziallas, M.G. and Wohed, R.: A Rule Language to Capture and Model Business Policy Specifications; Proc. CAiSE 1991, Trondheim, Norway.

[CJMV92] Constantopoulos, P., Jarke, M.; Mylopoulos, J. and Vassiliou, Y.: Software Information Base: A server for reuse; ITHACA-Report, ICS-FORTH, Heraclion 1992.

[CoBe88] Conklin J. and Begeman M.L: A Hypertext Tool for Exploratory Policy Discussion; ACM Trans. Office Information Systems 6, 4, 1988, 140-151

[CoKj87] Cohen, P. and Kjeldsen, R.: Information Retrieval by Constrained Spreading Activation in Semantic Networks; Inf. Processing and Management, 23, 4, 1987.

[DFLa91] Dardenne, A.; Fickas, S. and van Lamsweerde, A.: Goal-Directed Concept Acquisition in Requirements Elicitation; Proc. 6th IEEE IWSSD, Como, Italy, 1991, 14-21.

[Dows87] Dowson, M.: Iteration in the Software Process; Proc. 9th ICSE, Monterey 1987.

[EhJa91] Eherer, S. and Jarke, M.: Knowledge Base Support for Hypermedia Co-Authoring; Proc. Database and Expert Systems Applications, Berlin, 1991, 465-470.

[FeFi91] Feather, M. and Fickas, S.: Coping with Requirements Freedom; Proc. Intl. Workshop Development of Intelligent Information Systems, Canada, 1991, 42-46.

[FKGo90] Finkelstein, A.; Kramer, J. and Goedicke, M.: Viewpoint-Oriented Software Development; Proc. Conf Le Génie Logiciel et ses Applications, 1990, 337-351.

[Gent83] Gentner, D.: Structure Mapping: a Theoretical Framework for Analogy; Cognitive Science 5, 1983, 121-152.

[GiHo83] Gick, M.L. and Holyoak, K.J.: Schema Induction and Analogical Transfer; Cognitive Psychology 15, 1983, 1-38.

[Gree84] Greenspan, S.J.: Requirements modeling: A Knowledge Representation Approach to Software Requirements Definition. Univ. Toronto, Tech.Report. CSRG 155, 1984.

[Grei88] Greiner, R.: Abstraction-based Analogical Inference, in Analogical Reasoning; D.H. Helman (ed.), Kluwer Academic Publishers, 1988, 147-170.

[GrRo90] Grosz, G. and Rolland, C.: Using Artificial Intelligence Techniques to Formalize the Information System Design Process; Proc. DEXA, Vienna 1990, 374-380.

[GuCu88] Guindon, R. and Curtis, B.: Control of Cognitive Processes During Software Design: What Tools are Needed? Proc. ACM-CHI, 1988, 263-269.

[Guin90] Guindon, R.: Designing the Design Process: Exploiting Opportunistic Thoughts; Human-Computer Interaction Journal 5, 1990, 305-344.

[Hage88] Hagelstein, J.: Declarative Approach to Information Systems Requirements; Knowledge Based Systems, 1, 4, 1988, 211-220.

[HeEd90] Henderson-Sellers, B., and Edwards, J.M.: The Object-Oriented Systems Life Cycle; Comm. ACM, Sept. 1990.

[HJRo91] Hahn, U.; Jarke, M. and Rose, T.: Teamwork Support in a Knowledge-Based Information Systems Environment; IEEE Trans. Software Eng., 17,5, 1991.

[JaPo93] Jarke, M. and Pohl, K.: Establishing Visions in Context: Towards a Model of Requirements Processes; Submitted for publication.

[Jark92] Jarke, M., ed.: ConceptBase V3.1 User Manual; Aachener Inf.Berichte 92-17, 1992.

[Jark93] Jarke, M., ed.: Database Application Engineering with DAIDA, Springer 1993.

[Jeus92] Jeusfeld, M.: Änderungskontrolle in Deduktiven Objektbanken; DISKI Volume 17, Bad Honnef, Germany: INFIX Publ. (Diss. Univ. Passau, in German)

[JJP*92] Jarke M., et.al.: NATURE: Initial Integration Report; RWTH-Aachen, 1992.

[JJWS88] Johnson, P.; Johnson, H.; Waddington, R. and Shouls, A.: Task-related Knowledge Structures: Analysis, Modelling and Application; Proc. HCI '88, Cambridge University Press, 1988, 35-61.

[JoHa90] Johnson L., Harris D.: The ARIES project; Proc. 5th KBSA, Liverpool, 121-131

[Kalm91] Kalman, K.: Implementation and Critique of an Algorithm which Maps a Relational Database to a Conceptual Model; Proc. CAiSE, Springer, 1991, 393-415.

[Luba88] Lubars, M.D.: A domain modeling representation; MCC Technical Report STP-366-88, Austin, Tx, Nov., 1988.

[Maid92] Maiden, N.: Analogical Specification Reuse during Requirements Analysis; Ph.D. Thesis, City Univ. London, 1992.

[MaSu92] Maiden, N. and Sutcliffe, A.: Exploiting Reusable Specifications through Analogy. Comm. ACM 35, 4, 1992, 55-64.

[MaSu93] Maiden, N. and Sutcliffe, A.: Requirements engineering by Example: An Empirical Study; Proc. Intl. Symp. Requirements Engineering, San Diego, 1993.

[MBJK90] Mylopoulos, J.; Borgida, A.; Jarke, M. and Koubarakis, M.: Telos: Representing Knowledge About Information Systems; ACM Trans. Inform. Systems 8, 4, 1990.

[Pern90] Pernici, B.: Objects with Roles; Proc. ACM COIS, Cambridge, Mass, 1990, 205215.

[Pohl93] Pohl, K.: The Three Dimensions of Requirements Engineering; Proc. of the CAiSE Conference, 8-11 June, Paris, Springer-Verlag, 1993.

[PoJa92] Pohl, K. and Jarke, M.: Quality Information Systems: Repository Support for Evolving Process Models; Aachener Informatik-Projekte 92-36.

[Pott89] Potts, C.: A Generic Model for Representing Design Methods; Proc. 11th Intl. Conf. Software Engineering, Pittsburgh, 1989.

[PTP*88] Punchello, P.P.; Torrigiani, P.; Pietri , F.; Burion, R.; Cardile, B. and Conit, M.: ASPIS: A Knowledge-Based CASE Environment; IEEE Software, March1988.

[RaDa92] Ramesh, B., Dhar, V.:Supporting Systems Development by Capturing Deliberations during Requirements Engineering; IEEE Trans. Software Eng. 18, 6, 498-510.

[ReWa91] Reubenstein, H.B. and Waters, R.C.:The Requirements Apprentice: Automated Assistance for Requirements Acquisition; IEEE TSE, March 1991, p. 226-240.

[RJG*91] Rose, T.; Jarke, M.; Gocek, M.; Maltzahn, C. and Nissen, H.: A Decision-Based Configuration Process Environment; Software Engineering Journal 6, 5, 1991.

[Rosc91] Rosch, E.: Prototype classification and logical classification; In Scholnick (ed.): New Trends in Conceptual Representation: Challenges to Piaget's Theory? LEA 1991

[Royc70] Royce, W.W.; Managing the Development of Large Software Systems; Proc. IEEE WESCON, 1970.

[Scha82] Schank , R.C.: Dynamic Memory: A Theory of Reminding and Learning in People and Computers; Cambridge University Press, 1982.

[Sjöb72] Sjöberg, L.: A Cognitive Theory of Similarity; Goteborg Psych. Rep. 2, 10, 1972.

[SpCo93] Spanoudakis, G. and Constantopoulos P.: Similarity For Analogical Software Reuse: A Conceptual Modelling Approach; Proc. CAiSE, Paris 1993.

[TaWa90] Talldal, B. and Wangler, B.: Extracting a Conceptual Model from Examples of Filled In Forms. In N. Prakash (ed.), Data Management: Current Trends; New Delhi: Tata McGraw-Hill, 1990, 327-358.

[Tver77] Tversky, A.: Features of Similarity; Psychological Review, 44(4), July 1977.

[VJTr92] Vessey, I., Järvenpaa, S.I. and Tractinsky, N.: Evaluation of Vendor Products: CASE Tools as Methodology Companions; Comm. ACM 35, 4, 1992, 90-105.

[WiFl86] Winograd, T. and Flores F.: Understanding Computers and Cognition: A New Foundation for Design; Ablex, Norwood, NJ, 1986.

[Wing90] Wing J.: A specifier's introduction to formal methods; IEEE Computer 23, 9, 8-26.

Making Changes to Formal Specifications: Requirements and an Example

David W. Bustard
Department of Computing Science, University of Ulster
Cromore Road, Coleraine, BT52 1SA
Northern Ireland
e-mail: dwb@uk.ac.ulster.ucvax

Adam C. Winstanley
Department of Computer Science
Queen's University, Belfast, BT7 1NN
Northern Ireland
e-mail: csg1486@uk.ac.qub.v2

Abstract. Formal methods have had little impact on software engineering practice, despite the fact that most software engineering practitioners readily acknowledge the potential benefits to be gained from the mathematical modelling involved. One reason is that existing modelling techniques tend not to address basic software engineering concerns. In particular, while considerable attention has been paid to the construction of formal models, less attractive maintenance issues have largely been ignored. The purpose of this paper is to clarify those issues and examine the underlying requirements for change support. The discussion is illustrated with a description of a change technique and tool developed for the formal notation LOTOS. This work is being undertaken as part of the SCAFFOLD project, which is concerned with providing broad support for the construction and analysis of formal specifications of concurrent systems. Most of the discussion is applicable to other process-oriented notations such as CCS and CSP.

1 Introduction

There are essentially two main ways to use formal models in software development, as summarised in Figure 1. In a *subsidiary support* role, a formal model (or models) helps to clarify requirements that are specified informally and provides a reference base for software design and implementation. In a *central construction* role, a formal model is refined in stages towards an implementation. Each refinement extends the preceding model by dropping down to some lower-level, less abstract description, which may bring in additional detail from the informal specification.

These two roles for formal models are quite distinct but the types of change involved in each case are similar. In both cases, a model is built initially and adjusted until it matches the corresponding informal description, which itself may be changed in the process. Refinement changes are obviously an important part of the central construction approach but similar changes are also made when a formal model in a subsidiary role is expanded to explore requirements in greater detail. Where the two approaches differ significantly is in the way that requirement changes are handled after models have been completed. In the subsidiary support case, such changes are no different from those made during initial model construction. However, in the central construction approach it is necessary to ripple changes through the refinement sequence. Even here, however, although the means of change may be different, the changed models can be evaluated in much the same way.

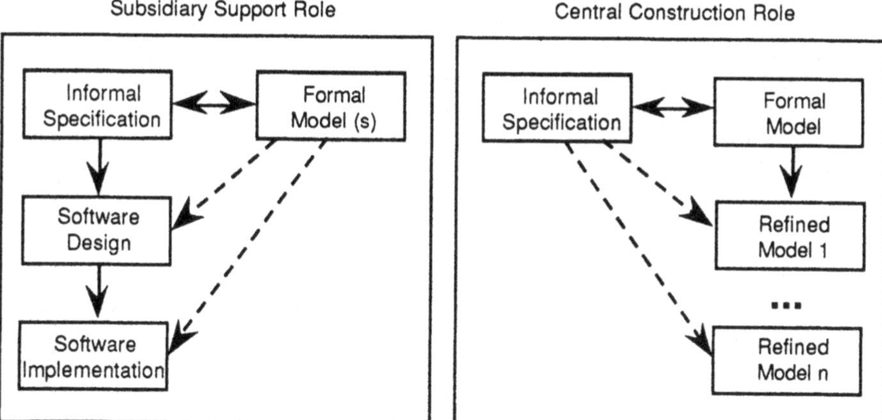

Figure 1. Roles of Formal Models in System Development

Very little research has been done on supporting change to formal system models. Some of the few examples of relevant work in this area include those contained in [1] and [2]. Indeed, it is often suggested [3, 4] that the term 'formal methods' is misleading because, as yet, users have been offered little more than formal notations. Clearly it is highly desirable to also have guidance on how such notations can be applied effectively in software production [5] and also to have tool support for the process involved [6]. This paper considers both issues with respect to making changes to formal models. More specifically, the paper concentrates on the basic question of how changes can be made to an individual formal model and how such a procedure might be supported. It can be assumed that change occurs under configuration management control [7]. This means that each formal model is an explicit configuration item, any changes made to it are agreed by a change control board, and a full change history is maintained. At this level, each change is made with respect to some particular version of the model - the *baseline*. The change is specified in advance and gives details of the requirement change. It may also include a definition of some of the necessary physical changes to the model, with remaining details recorded when the modified model is placed back under configuration control.

As a new model is developed it will go through a succession of intermediate, transient changes that are neither planned nor recorded. For all changes, however, the underlying steps involved are the same, namely: understand the need for change, implement it and evaluate the results. However, the precise means of change will vary considerably with the style of formal model used. The variety of styles [4] includes model-oriented specifications, algebraic specifications, modal logics and algebraic specifications. This paper considers just this last group which are typically used to specify concurrent systems. The particular language used is LOTOS [8, 9, 10] but much of what is said is also applicable to CCS [11] and CSP [12], the notations on which the behavioural component of LOTOS is based.

The next section gives a brief overview of LOTOS and illustrates its form and use with a simple example. This is then followed by a section that identifies how changes might be made to such models and a section that describes tool support that has been developed in the SCAFFOLD project [13].

2 LOTOS Specifications

LOTOS (Language of Temporal Specification) is used to define the behaviour of concurrent systems. Behaviour is described in terms of the significant events (or actions) in a system and the constraints on their order of occurrence. A LOTOS specification is structured as a hierarchy of communicating processes and the overall specification itself is also a process. As an example, consider the specification of a very simple automated bank teller (adapted from [14]). The teller accepts a cash card and PIN (Personal Identification Number) typed on a keypad and, if valid, returns £30; otherwise the transaction is rejected. In both cases the cash card is returned as the final action. For simplicity, it is assumed that there is sufficient money available in the account identified and in the teller machine itself.

From this description, the following events, representing communication between the teller and its user, can be identified: *AcceptCard*, *ReturnCard*, *RequestPIN*, *AcceptPIN*, *SupplyMoney* and *DisplayRejection*. In addition, there are internal teller events associated with the examination of the card and the PIN, and the subsequent actions taken: *IdentifyValidCard*, *IdentifyInvalidCard*, *IdentifyValidPIN*, *IdentifyInvalidPIN*. The behaviour of the teller can be described by the set of event sequences that can occur, namely:

1. a card is rejected because it cannot be read:
   AcceptCard; IdentifyInvalidCard; DisplayRejection; ReturnCard.
2. a transaction is rejected because the PIN is faulty:
   AcceptCard; IdentifyValidCard; RequestPIN; AcceptPIN; IdentifyInvalidPIN; DisplayRejection; ReturnCard.
3. a transaction is completed successfully:
   AcceptCard; IdentifyValidCard; RequestPIN; AcceptPIN; IdentifyValidPIN; SupplyMoney; ReturnCard.

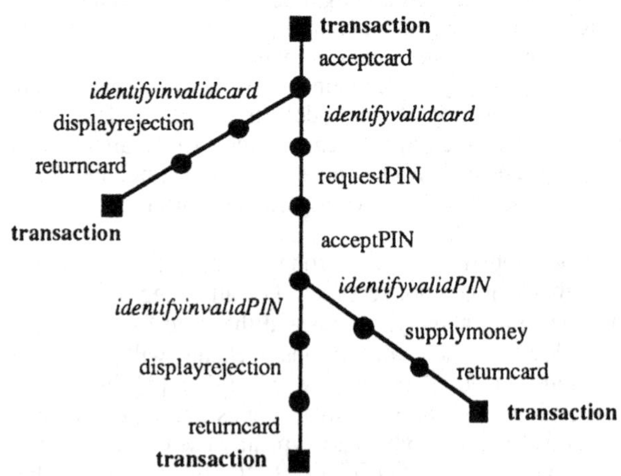

Figure 2. Action Tree for Teller Machine

As these sequences have common components it is more informative to combine then. Figure 2, for example, shows the permitted sequences in the form of an *action tree* [9]. The nodes in the tree represent unnamed system states and the arcs represent events. Each event is a transition from one system state to another. Branches indicate where there is a choice of event. Note that the repeated transaction behaviour has been suppressed. This is essential in cases where repetition occurs an unspecified number of times. A square leaf node, in general, represents a suppressed component. The elaboration of such a component is determined by locating an identically named node within the tree.

The corresponding LOTOS description might take the following form (the numbers have been added to aid the explanation given subsequently):

```
1.  specification teller [AcceptCard, ReturnCard, RequestPIN, AcceptPIN,
        SupplyMoney, DisplayRejection]: noexit
    behaviour
      transaction [AcceptCard, ReturnCard, RequestPIN, AcceptPIN, SupplyMoney,
        DisplayRejection]
      where
2.    process transaction [AcceptCard, ReturnCard, RequestPIN, AcceptPIN,
        SupplyMoney, DisplayRejection]: noexit :=
3.      hide IdentifyInvalidCard, IdentifyValidCard, IdentifyInvalidPIN,
        IdentifyValidPIN in
4.      (AcceptCard;
        ( IdentifyInvalidCard; DisplayRejection; ReturnCard; exit
5.      []
        IdentifyValidCard; RequestPIN; AcceptPIN;
        ( IdentifyInvalidPIN; DisplayRejection; ReturnCard; exit
6.      []
          IdentifyValidPIN; SupplyMoney; ReturnCard; exit)))
7.      >> transaction [AcceptCard, ReturnCard, RequestPIN, AcceptPIN, SupplyMoney,
        DisplayRejection]
      endproc
    endspec
```

The events that represent communication between the teller and the user are listed as specification parameters (1). The behaviour of the teller is described by a single process *transaction* (2) which takes all of the external events as parameters. Internal events are 'hidden' within the transaction process (3). The behaviour specified for transaction (4) follows the shape of the action tree in Figure 2. A choice expression defines a branch in the tree, from which one of several behaviours may follow (5,6). Once a particular sequence has been completed the transaction process is reinstantiated recursively (7) to indicate a return to the original teller state.

For larger specifications, and when refining a specification towards an implementation, it is usually desirable to structure a specification as a collection of interacting processes. For example, a LOTOS description of a card reader process might take the following form, indicating that the card reader repeatedly accepts and returns cards, distinguishing between cards that are valid and those that are not.

```
process cardreader [AcceptCard, ReturnCard, IdentifyValidCard, IdentifyInvalidCard]:
                                                                          noexit
  AcceptCard;
  (IdentifyValidCard; ReturnCard;
  cardreader [AcceptCard, ReturnCard, IdentifyValidCard, IdentifyInvalidCard])
  []
  (IdentifyInvalidCard; ReturnCard;
  cardreader [AcceptCard, ReturnCard, IdentifyValidCard, IdentifyInvalidCard])
endproc
```

The behaviour expression for the teller specification then becomes:

```
behaviour
  hide IdentifyValidCard, IdentifyInvalidCard in
  (transaction [AcceptCard, ReturnCard, RequestPIN, AcceptPIN, SupplyMoney,
                          DisplayRejection, IdentifyValidCard, IdentifyInvalidCard]
    | [AcceptCard, ReturnCard, IdentifyValidCard, IdentifyInvalidCard] |
  cardreader [AcceptCard, ReturnCard, IdentifyValidCard, IdentifyInvalidCard])
```

This indicates that the *transaction* and *cardreader* processes run in parallel and synchronise on the *AcceptCard, ReturnCard, IdentifyValidCard* and *IdentifyInvalidCard* events. Note that the declaration of the *IdentifyValidCard* and *IdentifyInvalidCard* events has been brought outside the *transaction* process.

This discussion presented so far has illustrated the form of a LOTOS specification and two alternative ways of describing the information it contains: (i) as a set of event sequences; and (ii) as an action tree. The order in which these representations have been presented also suggests a plausible means of using them in combination to help develop the LOTOS description, namely: define possible sequences, combine them in tree form and then build the LOTOS model to describe the resulting behaviour. Even if designers prefer to build LOTOS descriptions directly, the other representations are still of benefit in evaluating the LOTOS model produced. That is, they can be used as specifications of the model and verified automatically against the model. The same approach can be used when modifying a LOTOS specification. Details of how this approach has been implemented in practice are given in a later section. Before that, however, the next section takes a more detailed view of the general requirements for supporting change to formal models and the particular support needed for event-based models.

3 Change Requirements

The introduction described the basic process of model change in terms of three stages of activity: understanding the need for change, implementing the change and evaluating the change. This section considers the needs of each of these activities in turn and briefly identifies some of the existing tool support for LOTOS in this area.

3.1 Understanding the Need for Change

Understanding the need for change involves, in general, an investigation of the requirements for the system being modelled and an investigation of the existing model. To fix ideas, assume that in the case of the teller model it has been discovered that users are tending to pick up their money and leave without taking their card. It has therefore been decided that a card should be returned before the money is dispensed. This is the change requirement expressed informally. To produce a precise specification of the change it is then necessary to understand the model and describe the change in terms of modifications to the event sequences permitted.

At present, the most common way of examining a LOTOS model is through the use of a *simulator*, which effectively translates the model into an action tree and allows it to be explored. Typically, however, the tree is not presented in its entirety but is explored one event at a time. For each state in the tree the set of possible next events is computed, from which an observer then makes a selection. This allows the simulator to derive the next state. In this way, a trace of events representing one path down the action tree is built up step-by-step. A simulator only constructs those parts of the tree that are needed for this path. Examples of simulators include HIPPO, developed as part of the Esprit SEDOS (Software Environment for the Design of Open Distributed Systems) project [10]; SMILE, a development from HIPPO by the Esprit Lotosphere project [15] which is incorporated into LITE (Lotosphere Integrated Tool Environment) [16]; EXPOSE [17]; and the University of Ottowa LOTOS Toolset [18]. These simulators include various features to reduce the tedium of single step examination of the tree, such as an ability to use predefined sequences or to recognise when equivalent states have been encountered [15].

Examination of the teller specification indicates that the *SupplyMoney* and *ReturnCard* events need to be reversed, implying that the money is supplied only when the card has been retrieved. There are no existing tools that allow such a change to be specified any more formally than this, except perhaps in terms of the new event sequence that a revised model should permit. Of course, a satisfactory specification should also indicate that the old sequence is no longer acceptable, that all other sequences should remain unchanged and that no new sequences should be introduced. This is the same as defining the new tree.

3.2 Implementing the Change

Implementing change generally means editing the model. However, refinement, through the use of correctness preserving transformations, is possible for some types of change. This is the most difficult and least investigated aspect of LOTOS support. In fact, much work in his area has primarily been directed at transforming specifications into forms suitable for use in other tools (for example, verification tools that only act on subsets of LOTOS syntax) rather than for system development *per se*. ASDE (Advanced System Design Environment) [19] provides an interactive environment for defining transformations in a suitably extended version of LOTOS and for applying them to parts of LOTOS specifications. Application of a rule is performed by selecting its template and the behaviour expression (or part of one) to which it is to be applied. The system checks that the template contained in the rule matches the selected expression and that any conditions that are applicable are met. It then produces a new version of the specification as output.

The Lotosphere tool-set LITE [16] supports transformational refinement in three main ways:

1. the facilities provided by a structure editor allow the interactive transformation of parts of a specification using the analysis tools to ensure correctness;
2. the *bipartition of functionality* divides a process into two communicating sub-processes; and
3. *re-grouping of parallel processes* re-arranges the topology of processes - for example to allow for the separation of implementation concerns.

In general, however, most changes will require direct adjustment of the model.

3.3 Evaluating the Change

Evaluating a change means (i) verifying that the change has been implemented as intended; and (ii) validating that the requirement for change was appropriate, by comparing the new model with the real world. Verification will involve the comparison of the new model with either the existing model or a specification of the required behaviour of the new model.

Overall, there are four main reasons for changing a model:

1. a *corrective change*: to repair a mismatch between a model and the system it represents;
2. an *adaptive change*: to mirror actual changes to a system that have occurred or to define proposed changes;
3. a *refinement change*: to extend a model with lower level detail; and
4. a *presentation change*: to modify the appearance of a model; presentation changes typically include adjusting the layout of the model, rearranging the presentation order of components and adding comments.

The semantics of the model are changed in the first three cases but not the fourth. For example, the restructuring of the LOTOS teller model to include a cardreader process, as described earlier, is a presentation change and should not effect the behaviour of the model. This can be confirmed by exhaustive comparison of the action trees for the two specifications concerned. More precisely, this means proving that the new form is *strongly equivalent* [20] to the original, i.e. that the two specifications produce the same set of event traces and, in each state, offer the same events.

An example of a refinement change would be the introduction of further internal events such as one to represent a database enquiry to determine if a PIN number was registered. This change produces a description that is *observationally* or *weakly* equivalent to the original [20]. Again the correctness of the change involved can be verified automatically although this would not guarantee the preservation of the original order of internal events. Thus, the designer might also need to see how the new tree differs from the old to ensure that the new event has been located correctly. This might be achieved by displaying the trees and highlighting their differences. Such an approach would be the main technique when dealing with corrective and adaptive changes that modify the external behaviour of the model.

As mentioned earlier, another approach would be to specify a change fully in advance and then compare the new and specified models for strong equivalence. Again, however, a mechanism would be needed for reporting differences to help locate faults when a model has been modified incorrectly.

Two specifications can be compared for strong, weak and other equivalences using algorithms such as those presented in [21] and [22]. A substantial amount of memory is needed to hold an action tree for most practical specifications and this tends to limit the size of specification that can be handled. Such state limitations can be alleviated to some extent, however, by performing an equivalence comparison "on the fly" as the action tree is being constructed [23]. Aldébaran [24] verifies specifications with respect to several equivalences (strong, observational, and safety) using the Paige and Tarjan algorithm. It has also been used to prototype the "on the fly" algorithm [23]. Other verification tools include Squiggles [25], part of the SEDOS tool-set, and AUTO [26], which is now integrated as part of the LITE tool-set [16].

In summary, to facilitate change to formal models, in general, there appears to be a need to provide support for:

- the specification of a model prior to its construction
- the analysis of an existing model prior to its modification
- the specification of a model change
- the transformation of a model, preserving its semantics
- the verification that a new model meets its specification or is equivalent, in some

defined sense, to the model from which it has been derived

- the investigation of unexpected differences between models, because of a faulty change or faulty requirement.

The next section describes an approach to providing such support.

4 An Approach to Supporting Change for LOTOS Models

Tool design and development for LOTOS is being undertaken as part of the SCAFFOLD project (Support for the Construction and Animation of Formal Language Descriptions) [13]. Its broad concern is to investigate ways of making formal descriptions more accessible and thereby encourage the wider use of formal modelling as a standard software development technique. It is using LOTOS as a specific example notation. This section outlines some of the facilities that have been developed to support change to such models.

SCAFFOLD allows event-based descriptions of behaviour to be expressed in the three equivalent forms discussed in earlier sections: (i) a set of event sequences; (ii) an action tree; (iii) a LOTOS specification. The action tree is the common conceptual representation of these descriptions but from a development point of view the event sequences and action tree are there in support of LOTOS specification construction and modification. A tool has been developed that will input pairs of descriptions in any of these forms, compare them with respect to strong or weak equivalence and report any differences that are found. For convenience in this experimental work, trees are currently represented textually. For example, the tree for the teller specification, shown in Figure 2, would have the following form:

```
0  AcceptCard
1  | +i:IdentifyInvalidCard
2  | | DisplayRejection
3  | | | ReturnCard
4  | | | | i:exit  --> 0
5  | +i:IdentifyValidCard
6  | | RequestPIN
7  | | | AcceptPIN
8  | | | | +i:IdentifyInvalidPIN
9  | | | | | DisplayRejection
10 | | | | | | ReturnCard
11 | | | | | | | i:exit  --> 0
12 | | | | +i:IdentifyValidPIN
13 | | | | | SupplyMoney
14 | | | | | | ReturnCard
15 | | | | | | | i:exit  --> 0
```

The numbers down the left hand side identify the nodes in the tree. Sequences of events are indented successively to the right. Internal events have an 'i:' prefix. A '+' before an event indicates that it is at a fork in the tree. Other branches from the same fork can be determined by looking down the same column. Any subsequent indentation to the left indicates the end of a branch. Looping behaviour is marked by an arrow followed by the number of the node at the beginning of the loop.

Such trees can be constructed or modified directly using a text editor and can also be generated from a LOTOS model. The LOTOS analyser recognises simple tail recursion but other more complex forms of looping have to be identified and reported by the user. This is achieved interactively by generating the tree to some specified branch limit and then inviting the user to name any pairs of nodes between which loop connections should be made. Even with such adjustments, however, trees may be very large and so the option has been provided to prune them if necessary by indicating that further events exist along a branch but should be ignored. Where this is done the preceding event is followed by the marker '>>>'. Such partial trees can then only be used as a test of a LOTOS specification rather than a full verification.

When two equivalent representations are compared the analysis will simply confirm this equivalence. If they differ, two trees are generated to explain the difference. For example, in the case of the teller machine where the *SupplyMoney* and *ReturnCard* events were reversed, the following two trees would be produced on comparing the models:

```
Original Specification                          Modified Specification
0   AcceptCard                                  0  AcceptCard
1   | +i:IdentifyInvalidCard                    1  | +i:IdentifyInvalidCard
2   | | DisplayRejection                        2  | | DisplayRejection
3   | | | ReturnCard                            3  | | | ReturnCard
4   | | | | i:exit --> 0                        4  | | | | i:exit --> 0
5   | +i:IdentifyValidCard                      5  | +i:IdentifyValidCard
6   | | RequestPIN                              6  | | RequestPIN
7   | | | AcceptPIN                             7  | | | AcceptPIN
8   | | | | +i:IdentifyInvalidPIN               8  | | | | +i:IdentifyInvalidPIN
9   | | | | | DisplayRejection                  9  | | | | | DisplayRejection
10  | | | | | | ReturnCard                      10 | | | | | | ReturnCard
11  | | | | | | | i:exit --> 0                  11 | | | | | | | i:exit --> 0
12  | | | | +i:IdentifyValidPIN                 12 | | | | +i:IdentifyValidPIN
13  | | | | | SupplyMoney * >>>                 13 | | | | | ReturnCard * >>>
```

An asterisk in one tree indicates where it differs from the other tree. This has occurred at node 13 in both cases. The following '>>>' symbol shows that there are subsequent events on each branch that have been ignored. In general, there may be several such branches identified in this way.

The basic recursive algorithm for comparing two action trees T1 and T2 for strong equivalence is as follows:

```
function Equivalent action trees (T1, T2: action tree): Boolean;
  Determine sets of first level events(initials), I1 and I2, for action trees T1 and T2
  {Each event has a:  name (name)
                      current equivalence status (matched) - set initially to false;
                      reference to the subtree (if any) following that event (subtree) }
  for each event E1 in I1 do
    for each event E2 in I2 do
      if E1.name = E2.name then   (* event names match *)
        if Equivalent action trees (E1.subtree, E2.subtree) then
          begin E1.matched := true; E2.matched := true; end;

  Compress (E1.subtree); Compress (E2.subtree);
  Equivalent action trees := matched true for every event in I1 and I2
```

This algorithm is a modified version of the "on the fly" algorithm described by Fernandez and Mounier [23]. Versions to compare specifications for strong, safety and observational equivalence have been developed but only that for strong equivalence is described here. Whereas, in the interests of efficient use of memory, the original "on the fly" algorithm explicitly uses stacks, the SCAFFOLD comparison tool uses the calling mechanism of the recursive procedure to store the equivalence results for successor states during a depth-first exploration of the two action trees. Testing for strong equivalence between two specifications consists of comparing each event sequence and the choices offered by one specification with those of the other. At the end of the analysis, skeleton trees for each specification will have been constructed, subject to any truncation imposed. To save memory space, state information at each node is discarded as each node is checked. Equivalent states in the two trees are marked during the analysis and so any difference can be determined by performing a further traversal of the trees, examining each state in turn.

There are several ways in which the facilities provided might be used. It is possible, for example, to work mainly with the LOTOS descriptions and use the tree representations as an evaluation or debugging aid to help understand differences between two models. Alternatively, models might be built and modified by trying to define the desired event sequences, then define a matching action tree and finally build or modify a LOTOS description. These are two extreme approaches and there are many possibilities in between. The choice may well depend on the nature of the system described. If the tree is complex, for example, then it would be preferable to first build the LOTOS model and then examine the tree it produces (It may be useful to at least prepare a few expected event sequences as tests of the developed model). Thereafter, however, it is beneficial to save the tree, after dealing with looping behaviour, and have it available for editing when future modifications are required. This then would be a full specification of an intended change and make verification straightforward.

5 Conclusion

This paper has discussed the general issue of providing support for change to formal models. Requirements for such support were identified and an example of how that support might be realised discussed for the particular case of models expressed in LOTOS. Details of specific facilities developed within the SCAFFOLD project were also presented. This is a research area that has been given little attention generally and yet it is a fundamental concern for those who wish to see formal methods become an integral part of an acceptable software engineering process.

The ideas presented here will undoubtedly be refined as further experience is gained with the approach advocated. In addition, there are other aspects of the research and tool development work that need further investigation. In particular, it would be desirable to:

- provide hypertext links between the various representations to show how they interconnect; this is a particular difficulty because of the basic mismatch between the process-based structure of a LOTOS description and the flat behaviour tree;
- provide a graphical representation for an action tree;
- examine the approach with respect to other types of formal specification; of immediate concern is the incorporation of the data type component of LOTOS although the state explosion problems here are considerable; and
- examine how support might be provided for changes rippling through a refinement sequence.

This last issue is a particularly difficult problem. The strategy suggested would result in the need to manage evolving versions of a specification, each made up of a refinement sequence. Changes may be started at different points in each sequence depending on the level of concern so the resulting version network is relatively complex. Fortunately, such relationships can be handled with existing configuration management techniques and research in this area into merging versions of program modules may be adaptable for use with LOTOS descriptions and action trees. A more fundamental problem, however, is identifying user needs for refinement, since currently there are no well established refinement procedures for LOTOS.

In conclusion, the facilities developed so far through SCAFFOLD, and described in this paper, seem useful and the approach advocated promises to be a significant aid to improving the efficiency and effectiveness of formal process-based modelling.

Acknowledgements. The work described here was supported by SERC Grant GR/G 03700. Both authors have benefited from discussions with colleagues on the SCAFFOLD project at York University and British Aerospace, namely Michael Harrison, Roger Took, Dave Nuttall and Ji Song. Thanks are also extended to Mark Norris and Rodney Orr at British Telecom who were involved with the initial research that led to the SCAFFOLD project.

References

1. Kuhn, D.R.: A Technique for Analyzing the Effects of Changes in Formal Specifications, The Computer Journal, 35 (6), December 1992
2. de Vasconcelos, A.M.L. and McDermid, J.A.: Incremental processing of Z specifications, in Diaz,M. and Groz, R. (eds): Formal Description Techniques V (North-Holland, 1993)
3. Brinksma, E.: What is the Method in Formal Methods, in Parker, K. and Rose, G. (eds): Formal Description Techniques IV, (North-Holland, 1992)
4. Woodcock, J. and Loomes, M.: Software Engineering Mathematics (Pitman, 1988)
5. Bustard, D.W., Norris, M.T., Orr, R.A., Winstanley, A.C.: An Exercise in Formalising the Description of a Concurrent System, Software Practice & Experience, 22 (12), pp. 1069-1098, Dec. 1992
6. Patel, S., Orr, R.A., A.C., Norris, M.T. and Bustard, D.W.: Tools to Support Formal Methods, in Proceedings 11th International Conference on Software Engineering, Pittsburgh, USA, May 1989
7. Whitgift, D.: Methods and Tools for Software Configuration Management (Wiley, 1991)
8. ISO - Information Processing Systems - Open Systems Interconnection - LOTOS - A Formal Description Technique Based on the Temporal Ordering of Observational Behaviour, ISO 8807, 1989.
9. Bolognesi, T. and Brinksma, E.: Introduction to the ISO Specification Language LOTOS, Computer Networks and ISDN Systems, 1987, 14 (1), pp. 25-59, Jan. 1987.
10. van Eijk, P.H.J., Vissers, C.A. and Diaz, M.: The Formal Description Technique LOTOS (Elsevier, 1989)
11. Milner, R.: A Calculus of Communicating Systems, Lecture Notes in Computer Science, 9 (Springer-Verlag, 1980)
12. Hoare. C.A.R.: Communicating Sequential Processes (Prentice Hall International, 1985)

13. Bustard, D.W. & Harrison, M.D.: Animating Process-Oriented Specifications: Experiences & Lessons, Proc. IEE Colloquium on Automating Formal Methods for Computer Assisted Prototyping, London, January 1992
14. Alexander, H.: Structuring Dialogues Using CSP, in Harrison, M. & Thimbleby, H. (eds.): Formal Methods in Human-Computer Interaction (Cambridge University Press, 1991)
15. van Eijk, P.H.J. and Eertink, H.: Design of the LotosPhere symbolic LOTOS simulator, in Quemada, J., Mañas, J. and Vazquez, E. (eds): Formal Description Techniques III, (North-Holland, 1991)
16. van Eijk, P.H.J.: The Lotosphere Integrated Tool Environment Lite, in Parker, K. and Rose, G. (eds): Formal Description Techniques IV, North-Holland, 1992.
17. Winstanley A.C. & Bustard D.W.: EXPOSE: An Animation Tool for Process-Oriented Formal Descriptions, Software Engineering Journal, 6 (6), pp. 463-475, Nov. 1991
18. Logrippo, L.,: The University of Ottawa LOTOS Toolkit, in Parker, K. and Rose, G. (eds): Formal Description Techniques IV, (North-Holland, 1992)
19. León, G., Kloos, C.D., González, G., Ruz, M.A., Marchena, S., Santos, L. and Navarro, J.: ASDE: Design of a Transformational Environment for LOTOS, in Vuong, S.T. (ed.): Formal Description Techniques II (North-Holland, 1990)
20. Milner, R.: Communication and Concurrency (Prentice-Hall, 1989)
21. Paige, R. and Tarjan, R.E.: Three Partition Refinement Algorithms, SIAM J. COMPUT, 16, 1987.
22. Larsen, K.G. : Context-Dependent Bisimulation Between Processes, University of Edinburgh Technical Report CST-37-86, 1986.
23. Fernández, J. and Mounier, L.: Verifying Bisimulations on the Fly, in Quemada, J., Mañas, J. and Vazquez, E. (eds): Formal Description Techniques III, (North-Holland, 1991)
24. Fernández, J.C.: Aldébaran: A tool for the verification of communicating processes, Technical Report SPECTRE c14, LGI-IMAG,1989.
25. Bolognesi, T. , and Caneve, M.: Squiggles: A Tool for the Analysis of LOTOS Specifications, in Turner, K.J. (ed.): Formal Description Techniques (North-Holland, 1989)
26. Madelaine, E. and Vergamini, D.: Tools for Process Algebras, in Parker, K. and Rose, G. (eds): Formal Description Techniques IV, (North-Holland, 1992)

Formal Requirements Made Practical

J. Hagelstein, D. Roelants and P. Wodon
{hagelste,roelants,wodon}@sema.be

Sema Group Belgium
5, Place du Champ de Mars
B-1050 Brussels, Belgium

Abstract. This paper reports on the application of formal requirements engineering in an industrial context. We started from a logic-based specification language, and discovered a number of key ingredients that needed be added, for this approach to be accepted: the concept of agent as a means to structure large specifications, graphical notations whenever appropriate, compact textual notations for frequent patterns of behaviours, and methodological guidance for organising the process of requirements capture, analysis, and formalisation. The paper uses excerpts of an actual application to introduce the language and method.

1 Introduction

The use of a formal specification language turns out to be an appropriate answer to the stringent request for quality, in critical real-time control systems. This led us to try adapting a general-purpose formal requirements language named Glider to the specificities of both this application domain and the use in an industrial context. Glider is a property-oriented language, i.e. a language based on first-order logic [4], developed in the Icarus ESPRIT project. The derived language presented in this paper has been named Clyder.

The design of Clyder was influenced by the performance of actual industrial case studies, provided by development departments, and by contacts with technicians. Adaptations to Glider were felt necessary in the following domains.

- The first and maybe main problem has to do with the difficulty to specify behaviours with property-oriented specification languages, in particular cause-effect relationships. Without even considering the validation by customers, it is a fact that specifiers themselves have difficulties in handling their own specifications.
- Among the concepts specific to embedded control systems, that of *agent* plays a prominent role in structuring the understanding of an application. An agent is an active entity with a limited perception of its surroundings and with some responsibility for controlling it. Typical agents are devices, operators, and computer systems. A Clyder specification is presented agent by agent.

This work was partly funded by the Commission of the European Communities under the ESPRIT project ICARUS (P2537).

- Graphical notations are ideal to represent the structure of an application: the various agents, their communication, the other objects they perceive and control, the properties of these objects. Designers of formal languages are rarely interested in defining graphical notations, although there is no incompatibility between graphics and formality, as we experienced with the ERAE requirements language [6].
- A requirements language – be it formal or not – is of little help without a comprehensive methodology for using it. Collecting, analysing, and formalising requirements is a challenging task that needs be guided. The Clyder methodology, inspired by our past experience with ERAE [8], heavily relies on the concept of agent.

Of these lessons, the first one requires further discussion. Let us recall that property-oriented languages model an application by identifying types, functions and predicates, and describe its desired behaviours by means of assertions constraining the value of these functions and predicates at different times. Consider an application including a function 'salary' defined as follows.

$$\text{salary}: \text{Person} \times \text{Time} \rightarrow \text{Natural}$$

The assertion below states that '*salaries may only grow*'.

$$t_1 > t_2 \Rightarrow \text{salary}(p,t_1) \geq \text{salary}(p,t_2)$$

The ability to state such assertions is an advantage of property-oriented languages over operational specification languages, which describe changes in an algorithmic way. Assertions are similarly used to describe the cause-effect relationship between two phenomena, but here the result is less favourable to property-oriented languages. Consider the very simple example of events which increase the value of a counter by one within some delay D. The events are objects of type *Add* to which a function *time* can be applied. The counter is a function *counter* from time values to integers. The desired behaviour could be specified as follows.

$$\forall\ \text{add} \in \text{Add}$$
$$(\text{time(add)} = t \Rightarrow \exists t' \ \ (t \leq t' \leq t{+}D \wedge \text{counter}(t') = \text{counter}(t'{-}1) + 1))$$

However, on the basis of the assertion above, we are not entitled to assume that there is no change of counter in the absence of add events or that there is exactly one counter increase per event. This is the *frame problem*: it is not sufficient to require the needed changes; one must also exclude the undesired ones. Unfortunately, the needed additional assertions look artificial, are error-prone, and reduce the modularity of the specification [9].

In the present case, the assertion that must be added is far from obvious. We cannot simply say "if counter changes, then there must have been an add event before, within the delay D": this would allow any number of increases within this delay. We cannot say either "if counter changes, then it must have remained unchanged since the last add event": if two add events follow each other by less than D, it is admissible to have the two add events followed by two counter increases. The problem is most easily solved by adding an explicit relation between causes and effects, for example a function 'effect' from add event to counter increase events. It suffices to say that the function is one-one and that any counter increase follows the associated add event by less than D. The approach followed in Clyder is to predefine such a function and to provide shorthand for constraining it concisely. Another approach to circumventing the frame problem has been proposed in [9].

The rest of this paper discusses solutions to the above problems. Section 2 describes one of the case studies we handled and which we use for illustration purposes. Section 3 describes the Clyder language. Its semantics are given in Section 5 in the form of a rewriting towards Glider. Section 4 describes the methodology that has been followed during the case. Section 6 shortly compares the Clyder language and method with some other existing approaches.

2 A Case Study

This section sketches an application that was actually developed by our company, and that we use as illustration in the following sections. The required system must control the flow of ingots between a smelting furnace and a rolling mill: ingots arriving via rolling carpets are to be stored in a park, acting as a buffer, according to placement rules, and delivered later to a rolling mill according to a milling plan. The order of arrival is not that of the milling plan. Ingots are moved into and out of the park by a rolling bridge. All this equipment is as given. What is requested is a control system to ensure harmonious operations with a minimum of human intervention.

The two main requirements appeared to be: (1) when an ingot arrives, it must be automatically moved into the park to a position obeying the placement rules (maximum height for piles, no large ingot on top of a small one, etc); (2) when an ingot is requested at the rolling mill, one must be automatically moved according to the milling plan (the rolling mill requests a precise ordering of its inputs). Other requirements concern manual modes of operation, alarms of all kinds, user interfaces, priorities between operations, housekeeping, etc.

Practically, we had access to existing requirements documents, in French or English, and were given the necessary explanations or clarifications whenever the documents were unclear. Our aim was not to obtain a better requirements document (the system is already in operation) but to exercise formal constructs and accompanying methodology on reasonably sized actual cases.

This case illustrates some conspicuous characteristics of embedded real-time systems:

- a number of devices (*agents*) are working asynchronously but need synchronisation: bridges, cameras, rolling carpets, and their control, all run in *parallel*; some of them need be conceived, others are imposed and act as design constraints;
- cause-effect relationships are prominent, *actions* being triggered (*caused*) by *events*; for example, when an ingot arrives, it needs be parked;
- actions can be *interrupted*, e.g. by alarm conditions or by requests with higher priority;
- time constraints are often critical, although not in this particular case.

3 The Clyder Language

The Clyder language will be shortly presented in this section, with a stress on its characteristics contributing to industrial acceptance, but with no intent of completeness.

Clyder specifications consist of *declarations* and *behaviours*. Declarations identify objects, their properties and relationships : there are bridges, cameras, ingots; an ingot has an identifier and a position; a bridge can modify the position of an ingot, etc. Declarations are mainly described graphically. Behaviours specify in textual form the desired evolution of the system over time, essentially cause-effect relationships like "when an ingot arrives, it must be moved to the park".

3.1 Declarations

We distinguish in the application domain four kinds of "items"[1] :

- *agents* – lasting active things, sensitive to events and causing events; for instance bridges or cameras;
- *objects* – lasting passive things, like ingots;
- *events* – instantaneous phenomena, like the arrival of an ingot;
- *data*.

Clyder has four corresponding kinds of types. Some of these types may be restricted to only contain one element, because individuals like the agent 'Bridge' are common in process control applications. The same name is then used for the type and the only element in it.

Type declarations. Declarations may be given graphically, which is found important in practice : this provides a synthetic view from which it is easy to distinguish the overall structure of a system, allowing easy discovery of errors and omissions. The graphical declaration of a type is accompanied by a textual specification providing additional details.

The Clyder graphical notations are illustrated in the following figure. Agent types are introduced as rounded rectangles, whereas objects are normal rectangles. A simple box indicates a type with only one element, whereas double boxes indicate other types. Ovals introduce event types. Data types are only defined textually. The figure hence defines three agent types – Users, Operator and System – an object type – Ingots – and two event types – MoveIngot and ControlCmd. The type Operator and System contain only one element. The two names listed below ControlCmd indicate that this event type is partitioned into the sub-types Start and Stop. The other elements of the figure will be explained later.

[1] A better word is "object" but it is too much overloaded.

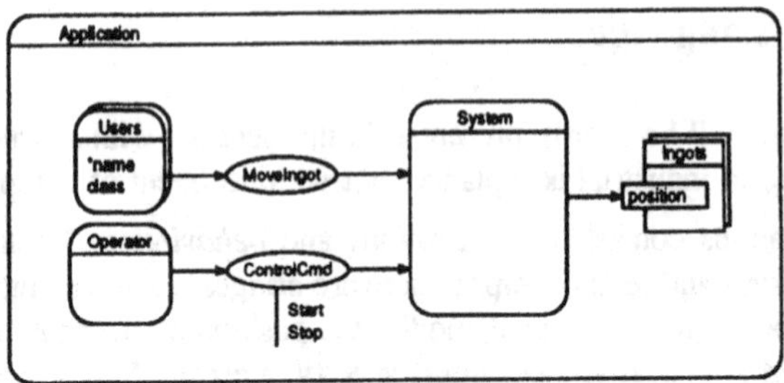

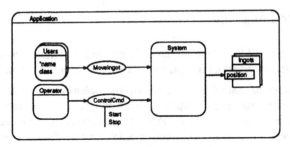

Fig 1: Graphical declarations in Clyder.

Objects and agents can be made of parts which also are objects and agents. The corresponding boxes are nested, as in Figure 1 where Application contains all other declarations.

Attributes. Attributes express properties of or relations between agents, objects and events. For example, the name of a user is an attribute of the agent type Users whose value is of data type String. Attributes are optionally indicated in the graphical form as a name inside the box corresponding to its first argument. The arity of the attribute is given textually. In the example above, 'name' and 'class' are specified separately as attributes of Users.

The value of an attribute may or not vary with time. A star ('*') preceding the name indicates time-independence.

Perception. One of the specificities of agents is that they perceive a limited part of their surroundings : only a limited set of types and attributes may be mentioned in the textual description of the agent behaviour. This set includes the internals of the agent, plus the external events and attributes that the agent is said to perceive. This perception is indicated graphically by linking the agent to an event type, or to an *visibility window* of an object or agent type. In the example above, the agent System perceives the event types MoveIngot and ControlCmd, as well as the attribute 'position' of Ingots. The perception may be in 'read-only' or 'read/write' mode, depending on the direction of the arrow. MoveIngot and ControlCmd are read-only, i.e. perceived; 'position' can be written, i.e. System may be responsible for modifying it.

Two agents A and B may thus communicate in a number of ways: A may cause events that B perceives, A may change an attribute of some object that B can read, or A may directly modify an attribute of B.

3.2 Behaviours

Graphical declarations introduce types, name attributes, and identify perceptions. This must be complemented by a textual part specifying the application behaviour, i.e. the desired evolution of the value of attributes over time and the desired occurrence of events. The textual specification is organised per type. For example, agent specifications have the following form.

```
agent[s] < type identifier >
  [ < clause > ] *
end
```

Four kinds of clauses may appear in such specifications: definition clauses, reaction clauses, spontaneous clauses, and invariant clauses. Object, event, and data type specifications are identical except that the keyword **agent** is replaced by **object[s]**, **event**, or **data**. Moreover, they may only contain definition and invariant clauses.

Definition clauses allow to give declarations textually. They are actually the only way to declare variables, data types, and the arity of attributes. They are an alternative to the graphical form for the other declarations.

Just as boxes are nested in graphics, textual type declarations may contain other type declarations. Most of the time, however, textual type declarations are large and it is more readable to avoid nesting them. Instead of declaring type T inside type T_1, one may equivalently declare type $T_1.T$ outside of the declaration of T_1.

Reaction clauses. Reaction clauses are central to the description of an agent behaviour. They are designed to specify frequent patterns of behaviours in a compact way. Their syntax is

```
when < change > :
  < action >
```

and their intended meaning is "when the change occurs, the action has to occur as well". A change specifies an event occurrence or the change of value of a time dependent attribute. An action specifies a set of changes, possibly non-deterministically. A predefined cause-effect function is assumed between causing changes and sets of caused changes. The reaction clause constrains this function in a compact and readable way. The semantic details are given in Section 5.

A single change takes one of the following two forms :

```
MoveBridge(pos)
position(ing) := Carpet
```

The first specifies the occurrence of an event of type MoveBridge, with the value 'pos' (a desired position) for the unique property attached to this event. The second form specifies a change of value of the attribute 'position', taking the value 'Carpet' for the domain object 'ing' (an ingot). (This is *not* an algorithmic assignment !)

The changes constituting an action may occur at different times, all following that of the causing change. An action may be specified by means of first order logic assertions, but Clyder also provides shorthands to handle situations which frequently occur in control systems.

It should be noted that the overall behaviour of an agent, as specified by its reaction clauses is not necessarily sequential. In other words, the agent may start reacting to an event during its reaction to another.

Actions. An action which is not a single change can be composed in parallel or in sequence. The action 'Act_1 & Act_2' denotes the free interleaving of the changes denoted by the actions Act_1 and Act_2, whereas the serial composition 'Act_1; Act_2' specifies that the changes denoted by Act_1 must precede those denoted by Act_2.

In the following example, the setting of blocked to false induces two changes without specifying their order. The symbol '^' denotes the agent in which this text occurs. It can also be written **self**.

```
when blocked(^) := false :
  status(^) := free &
  MovtPossibleAgain()
```

An action may be conditional : a list of pairs 'condition→action' denotes the action whose condition is true. If several conditions are true, all corresponding actions occur, in parallel. The condition **else** may be used as one of the conditions.

```
when MoveBridge(pos) :
  case not in-service(^) → OutOfService(),
     busy(^)             → BridgeBusy(),
     else                → MoveDone()
```

The following construct (keyword **some ... until**) specifies a non-deterministic set of changes ending when some condition is met : when the bridge moves, it undergoes a number of intermediate positions until the requested position is reached.

```
when MoveBridge(pos) :
  some position(^) := pos1 until position(^) = pos
```

Finally, a last frequent pattern of behaviour definitely calls for a shorthand, the *interruptibility* of an ongoing action by an event : the repositioning of a bridge can be interrupted and cancelled by an emergency event StopBridge. This is specified as follows :

```
when MoveBridge(pos) :
  some position(^) := pos1 until position(^) = pos
  interrupted by StopBridge
```

The interpretation is that the cause-effect function associates to the MoveBridge event, either a series of position changes until the desired position is reached, or any prefix of this series provided an event StopBridge follows.

An action can also be denoted be "free text", any sequence of characters between apostrophes. This is particularly useful when writing first drafts of specification :

```
when MoveBridge(pos) :
  'move the bridge to the desired position'
```

Spontaneous clauses. Some of the agents of interest are not simply reactive; they may also spontaneously perform changes. These changes are indicated in spontaneous clauses (key-word **spontaneously**). The action in a spontaneous clause may take place at any arbitrary moment. The format is:

```
spontaneously
  < action >
```

Invariants. Invariant clauses (keyword **invariant**) contain assertions that must be preserved. Actually, they reduce the non-determinism of the reactions. For example, the Bridge agent contains reaction clauses allowing for an undeterminate number of position changes; it also contains the following invariant which prevents it to move to an already occupied position :

> **invariant**
> **not** (**Exists** ing (ing $\notin$ carried-ingots(^) **or** position(ing) = position(^)))

4 The Clyder Methodology

4.1 Overview

The availability of methodological guidance is critical to the acceptance of an approach like Clyder. We tried to provide more guidance than the often encountered 'identify the objects in the application domain', common to many object-oriented specification methods. Actually, the Clyder methodology is based on the idea of *responsibility refinement* introduced in [5] for data processing systems, further elaborated in [3], and applied to control systems in [8]. It is also close to the concept of *composite system* introduced in [7].

The starting point is the observation that customers are not really interested in a new computer system, but in some improvement in their application. Therefore, requirements engineers should first identify and formalise the desired application behaviour. If a computer system is able to guarantee this behaviour, the work is done, but this is typically not the case. In the steel-factory example, a desired behaviour is that *incoming ingots are moved to the park according to placement rules.* A computer system cannot ensure this, as it does not perceive the arrival of ingots, nor can it move them to the park. The requirements engineer must then identify responsibilities which can be assigned to cooperating agents: the rolling carpet is made responsible for signaling the arrival of ingots, the bridge controller is responsible for moving ingots, and a control system synchronises the two. In the end, it is provable that the desired overall behaviour is implied by the various agent behaviours.

Following this idea, the requirements specification is elaborated in three stages : overall system specification, existing agents description, and new agents specification. These stages are described below.

4.2 Stage 1 : overall application specification

This stage identifies the behaviour that the customer wants to obtain in his environment. This behaviour is ensured by an agent – ParkingSystem in the example – perceiving changes in the environment and causing other changes in reaction. This system is a composite one formed by the sensors, machinery, the planned computer systems, etc., but this internal structure is not considered for the moment. The activities of this stage are organised into the steps described below.

Step 1: main inputs and outputs. This step identifies the main changes perceived (inputs) and controlled (outputs) by the agent ParkingSystem, like ingot arrivals or operator requests to move ingots. The agents causing the inputs or perceiving the outputs may be introduced, but this is optional as the information may be irrelevant. For example, the user command to move an ingot is an input event, which has a well-identified origin: the operator. The desired reaction is an ingot movement, modelled as a change of the property 'position' of some object of type 'Ingots'. The agents constituting the future system (devices, computer systems) are omitted for the moment.

This first step produces the graphical declaration below which names the events and objects, and possibly some object or event properties. The precise definition of these properties is left for a subsequent step.

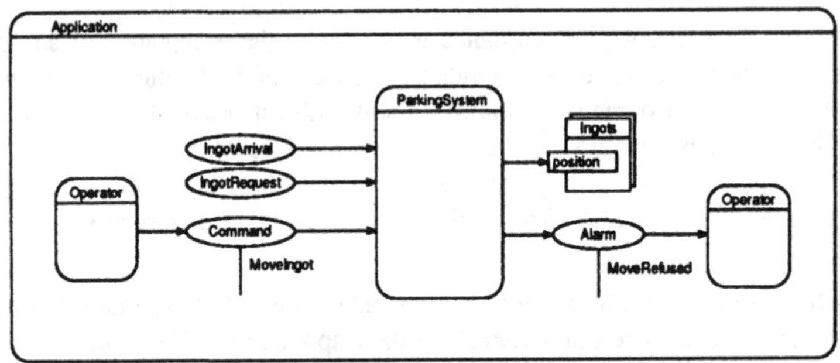

Fig 2: Main inputs and outputs of the ingot parking system.

A textual specification is also produced, which informally characterises the required reactions. Part of it is reproduced below.

```
agent Application.ParkingSystem
  when IngotArriva() :
    'If automatic mode, move ingot to pile according to the placement rule.'
  when MoveIngot() :
    'If automatic or semi-automatic mode: move the ingot as specified. If manual
    mode, move the ingot if possible; otherwise raise the MoveRefused alarm.'
end
```

Step 2: definition of additional properties. This step investigates the properties of the events, agents, and objects introduced in the first step. This has impact on both the graphical presentation, which includes the properties of objects and agents, and on the textual specification which is extended by declarations of event types, data types, and attributes.

For the present application, this step adds ingot properties, like identifier, size, weight, etc.; it identifies properties of the ParkingSystem, i.e. a working mode, a placement rule, and a milling plan; it introduces the data types WorkingMode and Position; etc. For example, the textual specification is extended, among others, by what follows.

```
agent Application.ParkingSystem
  attrib
    mode : ParkingSystem → WorkingMode
end

data WorkingMode = { manual, auto, semi-auto }
end
```

Step 3: additional input and output events. The initial list of events is now extended to include secondary objectives and housekeeping actions, according to a set of guidelines including among others the following ones:

- The properties of the system (e.g. 'mode') should be modified by some input event.
- Events to start and stop the system should be considered.
- Events to access the information stored in the system are often provided.
- Requests issued by a human operator should generally be acknowledged. At least, their failure must be notified.

These rules lead to introduce such input events as AddPlan for modifying the milling plan, ChangeMode for changing working mode, etc. As for the initial input and output events, the required reactions are informally stated and the properties of the new concepts are also formalised.

Step 4: constraints on properties. The various object and agent properties are now systematically reviewed. Two main categories of properties are considered for each of them: time-dependency and cardinality. For instance, the property 'position' of an ingot varies, but the property 'identifier' does not. An ingot has a unique identifier, and a given identifier applies to at most one ingot.

Other constraints of interest appear as assertions in invariant clauses. Various heuristics are available to guide their investigation.

Step 5: Input/output behaviour. This step formalises the informal reaction clauses collected during Steps 1 and 3. The outcome is illustrated below.

```
agent Application.ParkingSystem
  when IngotArrival() :
    /* If automatic mode, move ingot to pile according to rule. */
    case mode(^) = auto and position(ing) = Carpet
      → some position(ing) := pos1 until position(ing) = rule(ing)
    interrupted by ChangeMode() or Stop()
  /* Etc. */
end
```

The precise definition of the input/output behaviour is guided by a set of heuristics like the following ones:

- All events perceived by the agent should be reviewed to check that they trigger a reaction, or are at least referenced in a reaction.
- All properties should be reviewed to check whether they affect an action (e.g. appear in a conditional), or whether their change triggers a reaction, or is part of an action.
- Having done those checks, it must be true that
  - every input event triggers a reaction,
  - every input and every property of the agent either affects an action or triggers a reaction,
  - every property of the agent is affected by at least one action,
  - every output is affected by at least one action,
  - no input is affected by any action.
- Every action should be checked for its possible interruptibilities by every event or change of property. In particular, if the action contains a conditional, check whether the change of value of the test after it has passed may interrupt the action.

4.3 Stage 2 : existing agents overview

This stage investigates the various active entities (people, machines, sensors, etc) that can perceive and cause the events, or observe and control the objects identified in the first stage. These agents appear as sub-agents of the planned application. They are identified by systematically going through all inputs and outputs of the planned system, and seeing whether an existing agent can perceive or control them. Some inputs and outputs may be impossible to attach to any existing agent. This indicates that the next stage has to introduce new agents perceiving them.

The various existing agents are represented on the following figure.

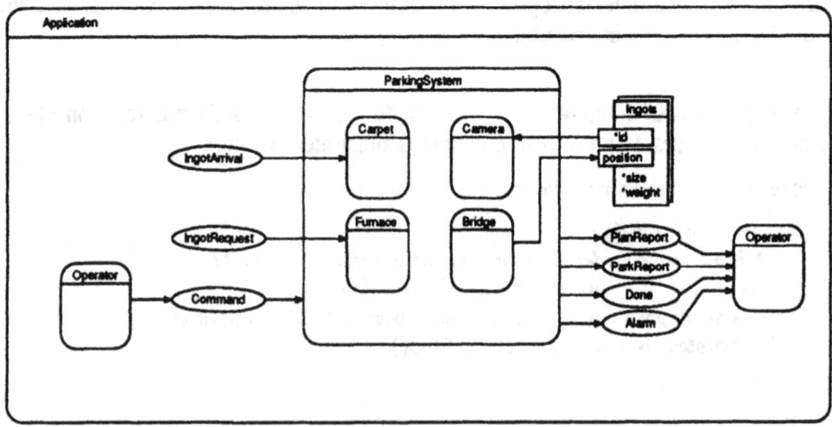

Fig 3: Existing agents in ParkingSystem.

These agents must be reviewed to identify their communication capabilities with other agents, their capacity to perceive and act upon objects, and the details of their behaviour. While doing so, the steps and heuristics given for stage 1 still apply and we do not detail them here. We only sketch the specification of the Bridge agent, which actually abstracts from a set of devices: a physical bridge, its local controller, and some micro-computer controlling it remotely. The graphical declaration of this agent is given below.

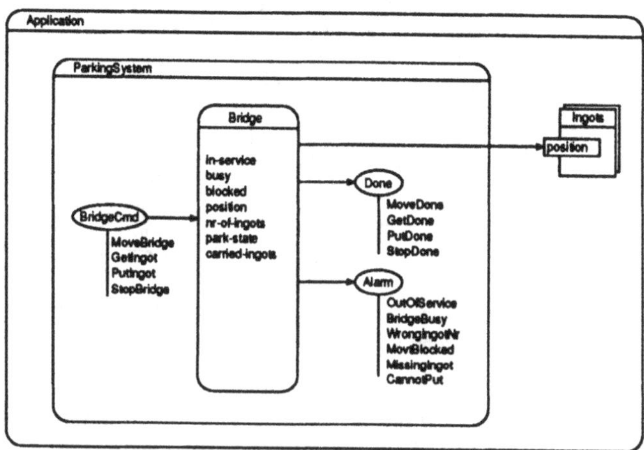

Fig 4: The bridge controller.

The details of the interface objects are given in the definition clause of the containing agent, i.e. ParkingSystem. The behaviour of the Bridge agent itself is partly specified below.

```
agent Application.ParkingSystem.Bridge
  when PutIngot() :
  case
    not in-service(^) → OutOfService(),
    busy(^)           → BridgeBusy(),
    else              → ( carried-ingots(^) := {} ; PutDone() )
    interrupted by
      StopBridge or in-service(^) := false
  spontaneously
    in-service(^) := false
end
```

4.4 Stage 3 : new agents specification

In the present case, only one agent needs be introduced, namely a computer-based control system. This agent is found by trying to 'fill the gap' between what ParkingSystem as a whole is supposed to do, and what the various agents constituting it can do in isolation.

The method suggests to first identify the communication capabilities of the controller with the various other agents. This is done in rough form in the following figure.

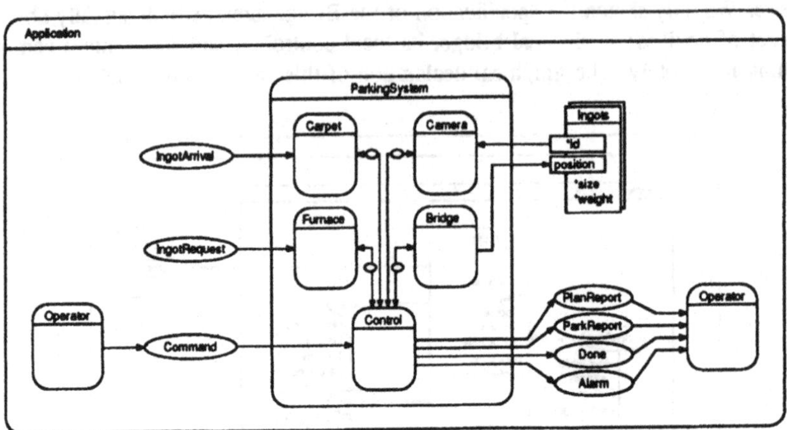

Fig 5: Control system in ParkingSystem.

Next, the specifier should follow the chains of consequences from the inputs of ParkingSystem to its outputs, and back from the outputs to the inputs. Proceeding forward, each input is perceived by specific agents which react in several possible ways. Other agents perceive these reactions and react in turn. Proceeding backward, any desired output can be obtained from one or several agents, as a reaction to certain triggers. The control system is supposed to process the information obtained by the agents perceiving the inputs, and to address requests to those controlling the outputs.

For example, the arrival of an ingot is perceived by the agent Carpet, which can signal it to the controller. To achieve the desired behaviour – parking this ingot – the controller must eventually ask the bridge to move the ingot, but before doing so it must do two things: identify the place to put the ingot, and ask the carpet to move the ingot somewhat further, where the bridge can take it. For identifying the destination position of the ingot, the controller needs know the characteristics of the ingot, which it can deduce from the ingot identifier. Hence, it must also ask the camera to read and communicate this identifier. Besides, it must react appropriately to any alarm or error condition.

In addition to these heuristics, most of those used in the earlier stages still apply. This finally leads to a specification, of which a very limited and simplified part is given below.

```
agent Application.ParkingSystem.Control

  when IngotAtCarpet() :
    ReadIdentifier()

  when IdIsRead(id) :
  case
    check(id) = OK → IngotToStopper(id),
    else → UnknownIngot
```

```
/* Etc. */
end
```

5 Semantics

This section provides an overview of the semantics of Clyder, in the form of its rewriting into Glider. Actually, the part of Glider used is only a multi-sorted first order logic, though it allows subsorting and has certain predefined types (Integer, Time, etc) and type constructors (Set, Seq, etc).

5.1 Rewriting declarations

The first-order counterpart of a Clyder specification always contains four disjoint predefined types, namely *Agent*, *Event*, *Object* and *Data*. Events have a predefined function 'time' assigning a unique time of occurrence to each event. Every explicit Clyder declaration generates a declaration of subtype in one of the four predefined types, all Clyder type names being replaced by their absolute form.

Each Clyder function or predicate has its obvious counterpart on the appropriate types. Time-dependent functions and predicates have an additional last argument of type Time. Cardinality information adds straightforward constraints to these definitions.

For each time-dependent function or predicate, there is an event type corresponding to its changes. If we have 'f: A → B', there is an event type 'Set_f', whose elements have two properties of type A and B. This allows to interpret 'f(a) := b' as an event of type Set_f with values a and b of its properties. Glider allows us to denote this event as 'Set_f(a,b)'. Assertions guarantee that the appropriate function change is simultaneous with the occurrence of such events.

The rewritten form of a Clyder specification also contains a number of predefined functions, namely *perceives*, *controls*, *spontaneous*, and *effect*, and a predefined predicate *partof*. These are constrained as follows:

- The function *perceives* maps each agent to the sets of events it perceives. These events are all those in the types declared locally to the agent type, linked to the agent type by a perception line, or perceived by any of its sub-agents. If a perception line links an agent type to a function in a visibility window, the agents in that type are said to perceive the change events associated to this function.
- The function *controls* maps each agent to the sets of events it controls, which is a subset of those it perceives. The controlled events must belong to the types declared locally to the agent type, linked to the agent type by an <u>outgoing</u> perception line, or controlled by any of its sub-agents.
- The function *spontaneous* maps each agent to the events it spontaneously causes, which must be controlled by the agent. For technical reasons, the codomain is a set of set of events, each set corresponding to a specific spontaneous clause.
- The function *effect* is the cause-effect function announced in Section 1. It takes an agent ag and an event ev as argument and maps them to the set of events that ev

cause under the responsibility of ag. The causing event must be perceived by the agent, whereas the caused events must be controlled by it.

- The predicate *partof* reflects the possible hierarchy of agents and objects. It induces some constraints on the arity of the sorts:
  - An object is *partof* exactly one other, except the top agent which is *partof* no other.
  - If an object or agent type A with one element is declared in a type B, this means, in fact, that there is exactly one object or agent of type A per element of type B. Hence, the type corresponding to A has the same number of elements as the one corresponding to B.

5.2 Rewriting behaviours

The clauses in the textual part of the specification actually generate constraints on the functions *effect*, *spontaneous* and *controls*.

Reaction clauses. Let the reaction clauses for some agent type A be '**when** $event_i$ $action_i$', for $i \in \{1, \ldots, n\}$[2]. These clauses constrain the *effect* function as follows:

$$\forall ag \in A\ \forall ev \in event_i\ \exists Ev \in Set(Event)$$
$$(effect(ag, ev) = Ev \wedge \mathcal{RW}(action_i, time(ev), Ev))$$

$$\forall ag \in A\ \forall ev \in perceives(ag)\ (ev \notin \bigcup_{i=1}^{n} event_i \Rightarrow effect(ag, ev) = \emptyset)$$

where $\mathcal{RW}(action, t, Ev)$ is an assertion defined below and stating that Ev is a set of events corresponding to $action$, and taking all place after time t. The assertion $\mathcal{RW}(a, t, Ev)$ is defined recursively below for the different kind of actions in Clyder.

- $\mathcal{RW}(event, t, Ev) \equiv \exists ev\ (Ev = \{ev\} \wedge t \leq time(ev) \wedge ev \in event)$
- $\mathcal{RW}((a_1, a_2), t, Ev)$
  $\equiv \exists Ev_1 \exists Ev_2\ (Ev = Ev_1 \cup Ev_2 \wedge \mathcal{RW}(a_1, t, Ev_1) \wedge \mathcal{RW}(a_2, t, Ev_2))$
- $\mathcal{RW}((a_1; a_2), t, Ev)$
  $\equiv \exists Ev_1 \exists Ev_2\ (Ev = Ev_1 \cup Ev_2 \wedge \mathcal{RW}(a_1, t, Ev_1) \wedge \mathcal{RW}(a_2, t_2, Ev_2)$
  $\wedge\ \forall ev_1 \in Ev_1\ \forall ev_2 \in Ev_2\ (time(ev_1) < time(ev_2)))$
- $\mathcal{RW}(c_1 \rightarrow a_1 \ldots c_n \rightarrow a_n\ else \rightarrow a_{n+1}, t, Ev)$
  $\equiv \exists t' \geq t\ ((\exists Ev_1 \ldots \exists Ev_n$
  $(Ev = Ev_1 \cup \ldots \cup Ev_n \wedge \bigvee_{i=1}^{n} c_i(t')$
  $\wedge \bigwedge_{i=1}^{n} ((c_i(t') \wedge \mathcal{RW}(a_i, t', Ev_i)) \vee (\neg c_i(t') \wedge Ev_i = \emptyset)))$
  $\vee (\bigwedge_{i=1}^{n} \neg c_i(t') \wedge \mathcal{RW}(a_{n+1}, t', Ev))))$
- $\mathcal{RW}(event$ **until** $cond, t, Ev)$
  $\equiv \forall ev \in Ev\ (ev \in event \wedge \exists t'\ (t \leq time(ev) \leq t' \wedge cond(t')))$
- $\mathcal{RW}(a$ **interrupted by** ev_1 or ... or $ev_k, t, Ev)$
  $\equiv \exists Ev' \in Set(Event)$
  $(\mathcal{RW}(a, t, Ev')$

[2]For the sake of simplicity, we suppose here that the $event_i$ are exclusive.

$$\wedge \forall ev \in Ev' \; (ev \in Ev \Leftrightarrow \forall ev' \in Event \; (t \leq time(ev') \leq time(ev) \\ \Rightarrow ev' \notin ev_1 \cup \ldots \cup ev_k)))$$

Spontaneous and invariant clauses. Let the spontaneous clauses for some agent type A be **spontaneously** $action_i$, for $i \in \{1, \ldots, n\}$. The *spontaneous* function is then constrained as follows:

$$\forall ag \in A \; \forall Ev \in spontaneous(ag) \; (\bigvee_{i=1}^{n} \mathcal{RW}(action_i, 0, Ev))$$

An invariant clause is trivially rewritten into the assertion it contains.

Frame assertions. Finally, the following two frame assertions ensure that the only happening events are the ones due to the spontaneous behaviour or to a reaction of some agent.

The first one prevents an agent to control other events than those specified in the spontaneous and reaction clauses, or the events being controled by its sub-agents.

$$\forall ag \in Agent \; (controls(ag) = \bigcup_{\{ag' | partof(ag', ag)\}} controls(ag') \\ \cup \bigcup_{Ev \in spontaneous(ag)} Ev \\ \cup \bigcup_{ev \in perceives(ag)} effect(ag, ev)).$$

The second assertion ensures that only events controlled by some agent may occur. If $A_1, \ldots, A_m$ are all agent types controlling an event type Ev, then each event in Ev must be output of at least one agent in $(A_1 \cup \ldots \cup A_m)$.

Note that these two assertions are independent of the behaviour part of the specification. They can be stated on the sole basis of the declarations.

6 Conclusion

We have endeavoured to test if it is possible to define and use a formal requirements language that is both theoretically well founded and practically manageable in an industrial environment for a given application area. This demonstration is well on its way: actual applications have been handled as examples, interest is raised in production departments, and a support environment has been developed. The latter is available on *Concerto*, a generic software engineering platform distributed by Sema Group, and includes graphical and textual editors, checkers, documentation generators, etc.

Raising the interest of developers required to pay attention to several critical issues. First, the concepts in the language must be natural for its users. This led us to introduce agents with limited perception, as well as language patterns, such as "when E, do A". Of course, the formal semantics of these concepts must be in accordance with their intuitive meaning. The problem of mastering the complexity of a large specification must also be addressed; we did it by means of graphical notations for displaying the hierarchies of agents and their interfaces. These notations allow to grasp at a glance the general structure of a system or any of its parts, with the details left out but provided elsewhere. Methodological guidelines have also been defined to help specifiers conduct their work.

This work can be shortly compared to a number of other approaches. The first and largest category is formed by the various informal methods targeted at control systems, like the real-time extensions of Structured Analysis [15,10]. Clyder shares with these the use of graphical notations and a methodology emphasising top-down system decomposition. With the more recent object-oriented analysis methods like [2,13] (to name only a few) it shares the concept of object, and a methodological emphasis on application domain modelling. But the Clyder approach exhibits strong differences with all these informal methods: formality of the language, declarative nature of the behaviour specification, analysis of chains of consequences to guide the decomposition, etc.

A number of other methods reach a higher level of rigour, without going however as far as a full formal semantics. Among these, JSD provides a graphical notation and an organisation in processes somewhat comparable to agents, but [1] relies on an algorithmic and sequential language for specifying behaviours, and lacks agent decomposition. GIST [11] is an older language, rather close to Clyder in spirit and intent. The agent concept is present, and behaviours are specified by combining reactions to events and invariants. GIST lacks however a graphical notation, the hierarchical organisation of agents in sub-agents, and a complete formal semantics.

Fully formal requirements engineering methods are not numerous, and generally do not provide such ingredients as graphical notations or an accompanying methodology. There are exceptions, though, and the ERAE method on which we worked earlier is one [6,8]. Compared to it, Clyder provides a number of improvements, the most notable being to admit agent types and not only individuals, to give semantics to the perception lines, to address the frame problem through a cause-effect relation, and to introduce the patterns for specifying behaviours, which were missing in ERAE. The Clyder language is also close to some other object-oriented formal languages, like OBLOG [12] or RML [14], which are however typically optimised for data processing systems rather than embedded control systems. For example, they miss the patterns for expressing typical real-time behaviours, that Clyder provides in its agent specifications.

References

1. J.R. Cameron. An overview of JSD. IEEE Transactions on Software Engineering, SE–12(2), February 1986.

2. P. Coad and E. Yourdon. Object-Oriented Design. Prentice Hall, 1991.

3. E. Dubois. Supporting an incremental elaboration of requirements for multi-agent systems. In Proceedings of International Working Conference on Cooperating Knowledge based Systems, pages 130–134, University of Keele (UK), 1990.

4. E. Dubois, Ph. Du Bois, A. Rifaut, and P. Wodon. The GLIDER manual. Deliverable of the ESPRIT project Icarus, 1991.

5. E. Dubois, J. Hagelstein, E. Lahou, F. Ponsaert, A. Rifaut, and F. Williams. The ERAE model: a case study. In T.W. Olle, H.G. Sol, and A.A. Verrijn-Stuart, editors, Information System Design Methodologies: Improving the Practice, North-Holland, 1986.

6. E. Dubois, J. Hagelstein, and A. Rifaut. Formal requirements engineering with ERAE. Philips Journal of Research, 43(3/4):393–414, 1988. (A revised version is available from the authors).

7. M.S. Feather. Language support for the specification and development of composite systems. ACM TOPLAS, 9(2):198–234, 1987.

8. J. Hagelstein, A. Rifaut, J. Vangeersdael, and M. Vauclair. The ERAE Language and Method. Manuscript M336, Philips Research Laboratory Brussels, 1990.

9. J. Hagelstein and D. Roelants. Reconciling operational and declarative specifications. In 4th Conference on Advanced Information Systems Engineering (CAISE·92), Manchester, May 1992.

10. D.J. Hatley and I.A. Pirbhai. Strategies for Real-Time System Specification. Dorset House Publishing Co., New York, NY, 1987.

11. N.M. Goldman R.M.Balzer and D.S. White. Operational specifications as the basis for rapid prototyping. ACM Software Engineering Notes, 7(5):3–16, 1982.

12. A. Sernadas, C. Sernadas, P. Gouveia, P. Resende, and J. Gouveia. Oblog: An Informal Introduction. Technical Report, INESC, 1991.

13. S. Shlaer and S.J. Mellor. Object-Oriented Systems Analysis: Modeling the World in Data. Prentice Hall, 1988.

14. A. Borgida S.J. Greenspan and J. Mylopoulos. A requirements modeling language and its logic. Information Systems, 11(1):9–23, 1986.

15. P.T. Ward and S.J. Mellor. Structured Development for Real-Time Systems. Yourdon Press, New York, 1985

Databases for Software Engineering Environments

—

The Goal has not yet been attained

Wolfgang Emmerich[1], Wilhelm Schäfer[1] and Jim Welsh[2]

[1] University of Dortmund, Informatik 10
D-44221 Dortmund, Germany
[2] University of Queensland, Dept. of Computer Science,
Queensland 4072, Australia

Abstract. We argue that, despite a substantial number of proposed and existing new database systems, a suitable database system for software development environments and especially process-centred environments does not yet exist. We do so by reviewing and refining the requirements for such systems in detail based on a number of examples. We then sketch a number of available and archetypical database systems and indicate why they do not meet these requirements.

1 Introduction

Software development environments (SDEs) include tools which support most of the software life-cycle phases, i.e. construction and analysis of the corresponding documents and document interdependencies. Sophisticated integrated environments enable the incremental, intertwined and syntax-directed development and maintenance of these documents such that errors are easily traced back through different documents and necessary changes are propagated across document boundaries to correct the errors (c.f., for example, [11, 9, 4]). Such environments should provide multi-user support[3], i.e. they should have flexible and adaptable mechanisms (often called "design transactions") to control access by a number of users to shared information. The construction of such environments and corresponding advanced design transaction mechanisms is an area of active research (c.f., for example, [2, 20, 22]). We call this latter kind of environment a process-centred environment (PSDE), because the provided multi-user support is or rather should be based on a well-defined development process, i.e. the definition of the users' responsibilities, their corresponding access rights, and the schedule of the activities to be carried out by them.

For any kind of environment, a large number of objects and corresponding relations on very different levels of granularity have to be stored and retrieved,

[3] As the people normally called software developers are the users of an SDE and this paper discusses only SDEs, we use the term user instead of developer hereafter.

and, in case of a process-centred environment, these objects must be manipulated under the control of an advanced transaction mechanism. An underlying database management system is thus a key component of a PSDE and if not chosen carefully, could become a major performance bottleneck when the PSDE is in use.

As early as 1987, Bernstein has argued that dedicated database systems for software engineering, specialised with respect to functionality and implementation, are necessary [3]. He, and others [22] argued that the functionality and efficiency of existing systems (in particular, relational systems) do not adequately support the construction of software engineering tools and environments. A number of systems, some of which differ radically from standard relational technology, have since been described in the literature and some are now available as commercial products.

In this paper we argue that, despite the substantial number of these new database systems, a suitable database system for SDEs, and especially PSDEs, does not yet exist. We are aware of the fact that we put very stringent requirements on those database systems as we require that the systems (1) allow to efficiently manipulate abstract syntax graph representations of documents and (2) provide advanced transaction mechanisms on those graphs to enable sophisticated multi-user support (c.f. section 3). Many existing commercial environments or tools resp. [13] and even PSDEs [15, 22] developed as research prototypes do not (yet) have those stringent requirements, because they handle documents as monolithic blocks. This, however, reduces significantly the possibility of checking and preserving inter-document consistency and thus provides no adequate support for incremental, intertwined development and maintenance of software documents. We even believe that partly due to missing appropriate database systems, the currently available environments lack appropriate functionality with respect to support of evolutionary software development. Thus, this paper adds an important viewpoint to the discussion about dedicated software engineering databases, because the other papers known to us have either never expressed such a stringent requirements list (like Bernstein) or have never discussed them in full detail (like [16]).

This paper reviews and refines, in sections 2 and 3, Bernstein's requirements based on our own experiences in building environments and tools. Section 4 then briefly reviews a number of available database systems, and sketches that these requirements are not met by them. It finally, sketches the ongoing work to remedy the situation.

2 Process centred Software Development Environments

Architecturally, a process centred software development environment consists of the following main components:

- a process engine that coordinates the work of developers involved in a project,

- a set of integrated, syntax-directed tools that allow developers to conveniently manipulate and analyse documents and to maintain consistency between related documents of different types, and
- an underlying database for software engineering (DBSE) which is capable of storing project information and documents.

2.1 The Process Engine

The process engine executes a formal description of a software process in order to coordinate the work of the users involved in a project. In more detail this covers the following issues.

Multi-User support The process engine determines for each user participating in a project a personal agenda that indicates on which documents he or she may perform particular actions. The contents of the agenda depend on

- the user's responsibilities in the project and
- the current state of the project.

The invocation of tools that enable a user to perform the actions contained in an agenda is controlled by the process engine via the agenda. In simple terms, the agenda acts as a menu from which the user selects his or her next activities.

In most projects a number of users work in parallel on different parts of the overall project activity. This means that changes to a user's agenda are not only necessary due to his or her own actions. They are also necessary when some other user changes the state of a document on which the first user's agenda depends. As each user usually works at a personal workstation, the agendas must be presented and updated in a distributed fashion. Likewise, the tools that are called via the agenda have to access documents in a distributed fashion.
To ensure orderly use of documents in parallel development activities, the process engine must also be able to create versions of documents, or sets of documents, to retrieve a particular version and to merge version branches of documents.

Efficiency The state of the project changes, when a new document is introduced or an existing document is deleted, when a document is declared to depend on some other document, when a document becomes complete or when it becomes incomplete due to a change in some other document it depends on. Although this list is incomplete, it already indicates that changes to project states occur frequently. All of them cause a recomputation of the agenda. As a user cannot perform any tasks while his or her agenda is being computed, the computation must be done efficiently.

Persistence and Integrity The process engine may need to be stopped from time to time. Therefore it must be able to store the state of the project persistently in order to prepare a restart. Even if it is stopped accidentally e.g. by a hardware or software failure, it must resume with a consistent project state. Moreover, such a failure must not result in a significant loss of project information. Thus we require that the process engine preserves integrity of any project information, i.e. it ensures that continuation of any operation is possible after any failure.

Change It has been widely recognised that software processes can not completely be defined in advance [17, 19]. The process being executed needs to be changed "on the fly" from time to time. For example, new users may participate in the project, responsibilities may be redefined, new types of documents may be introduced or new tools for manipulation of these documents may need to be integrated.

Reasoning capabilities As it might not always be clear to a user why a particular document is to undergo a particular action, the process engine should have the capability to explain this to the user. For instance, the process engine should be able to answer questions from a user like "What is the state of the specification of module m1?", "Who else is involved in the project?" or "What happens if I now code module m1?". The latter example indicates that the reasoning capabilities do not only explain how a particular project state was reached, i.e. the past (as in classical expert system reasoning) but that they also give insights about possible future consequences of a particular action.

2.2 Highly integrated syntax-directed tools

Syntax-direction The tools contained in a PSDE are used by users to edit, analyse and transform documents. To give as much support to users as possible, the tools should be directed towards the syntax of the languages in which documents are written. In particular, they should reduce the rate at which errors concerning the context-free syntax are introduced to documents.

Consistency preservation Besides dealing with errors concerning the context-free syntax, tools should also deal with errors concerning both the internal static semantics of documents and inter-document consistency constraints. The tools may allow temporary inconsistencies to be created both during input and as the result of edit operations, since document creation in a way which avoids such temporary inconsistencies is impractical in many cases.
Tools should also support users in removing inconsistencies. In particular, follow-on inconsistencies such as use of a non-existing import, could be removed on demand by change propagation, such as propagating the change that redefines the import to all places where it is used.
Finally, tools must allow the user to define additional semantic relationships during the course of a project. For instance, dependencies between the source-code, the test plans and the technical documentation on the level of identifier names (and corresponding section titles in the technical documentation) may only be defined in this way.

Persistence and Integrity Obviously, documents must be stored persistently because they must survive editing processes. Moreover, users require tools to operate as safely as possible, i.e. in case of a hardware or software failure they expect that the integrity of documents (their immediate usability by the same or other tools) will be preserved and that significant user effort will not be lost. Thus, we require the persistence to be achieved as follows: An interactive session with a tool of the PSDE consists of a sequence of user-actions like changing the type-identifier exported in a module or adding a parameter to a procedure. We require from tools that a user-action is persistent if and only if it is completed. Moreover, user-actions must be designed in a way that the integrity of a document is guaranteed whenever a user-action is completed. In case of a hardware or software failure we require that the tools should recover to the last completed user-action.

Backtracking When the consequences of user actions are persistent, users must have the ability to backtrack or "undo" such actions when mistakes are made. Thus, in addition to the document versions used for management purposes in a multi-user project, users may want to store intermediate revisions of a document so that they can revert to a previous revision if their subsequent modifications turn out to be ill-chosen.

Efficiency Very fast typists can type about 300 characters per minute. In this case, the time between successive keystrokes is about 200 milliseconds. Thus any response time of an editor below 200 milliseconds is non-critical, as users are never going to recognise them as delays.
Unlike secretaries, users do not type continuously. They frequently pause to think about what to do next. These thinking periods break the basic sequence of user transactions into a higher-level sequence of task-oriented transactions. If the non-trivial processing that a tool carries out is aligned with these natural breaks in user interaction, much higher response times may be acceptable.
In other circumstances, users may accept much higher response times, if they occur less frequently and can be justified by the complexity of the task concerned [24]. No user, for instance, would reject using a compiler just because it needs more than a second to compile a source.

3 Requirements for DBSEs

3.1 Persistent Document Representation

What is a document in the database? The common internal representation for syntax-directed tools such as syntax-directed editors, analysers, pretty-printers and compilers is a syntax-tree of some form. In practice, this abstract syntax-tree representation of documents is frequently generalised to an abstract syntax-graph representation for reasons such as efficient execution of documents, consistency preservation by tools, and user-defined relations within documents.

```
PROCEDURE InitWindowManager(y:<TypeIdentifier>);
VAR x:<TypeIdentifier>;
BEGIN
  WHILE <BooleanExpression> DO
    x:=Expression;
    <Assignment>
  END
END InitWindowManager;
```

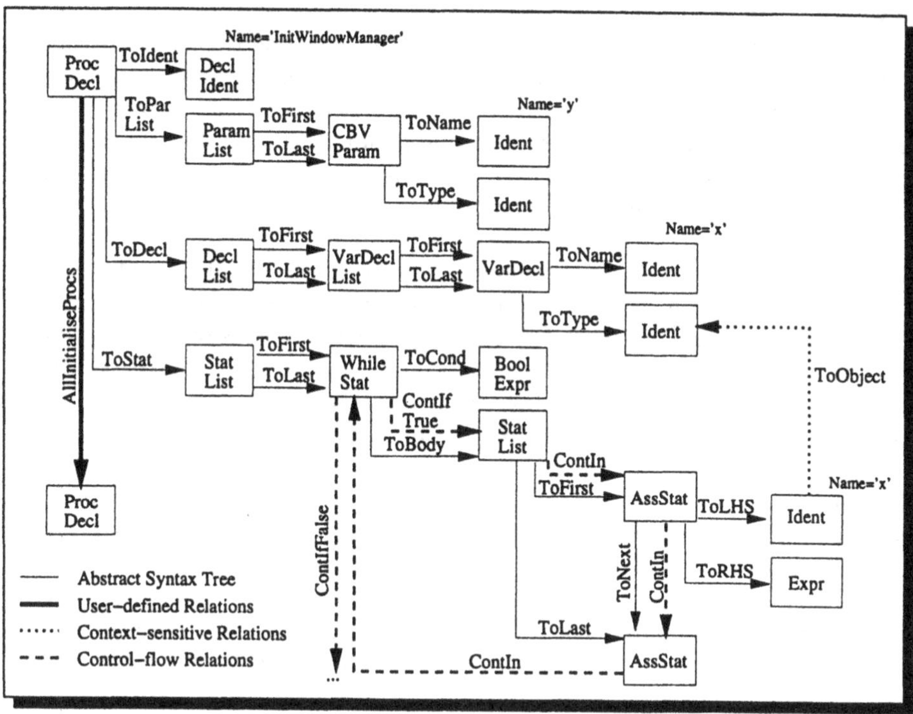

Fig. 1. Modula-2 external textual and internal graph representation

As an example of a small excerpt from an internal Modula-2 program representation c.f. Fig. 1 which will be used to explain further details in the following.

Consistency checking on a document can be done by attribute evaluations along parent/child paths in the document's attributed abstract syntax tree. The evaluation paths are computed at generation-time based on attribute dependencies. This approach, however, has proven to be quite inefficient even for static semantic checks of a single document, because of the long path-lengths involved. Techniques based on the introduction of additional, non-syntactic paths for more direct attribute propagation have been developed [14, 12]. Such non-syntactic paths are examples of context-sensitive relationships which connect syntacti-

cally disjoint parts of a document, and are used in both consistency checking and change propagation when the document is changed (c.f. the "····►" edge which connects declaration and use of an identifier in Fig. 1).
Most PSDEs offer test and execution of software documents by interpretation of the document syntax-tree. Such interpretation can be achieved purely in terms of an attributed syntax-tree itself but is very inefficient. For executable documents, therefore, the abstract syntax-tree representing the document is commonly enhanced by additional edges that indicate the control flow in order to enable more efficient interpretation (c.f. the "--►" edges exemplifying the control flow of a while statement in Fig. 1).
As noted in section 2.2, the user may also introduce additional user-defined relations between document parts for purposes of documentation, traceability, etc.. All such relationships must also be seen as edges in the abstract syntax graph that represents the document during manipulation, as illustrated by the "—►" edge labelled *AllInitialiseProcs* which connects all procedures which implement create/initialise operations.

How is it stored? Due to the requirements of persistence and integrity, a persistent representation of each document under manipulation must be updated as each user-action is finished. Typically a user-action affects only a very small portion of the document concerned, if any. Given that the representation under manipulation is an abstract syntax-graph, however, the update can easily become inefficient if, firstly, a complex-transformation between the graph and its persistent representation is required and, secondly, the persistent representation is such that large parts of it have to be rewritten each time, although not being modified. This would for instance be the case, if we had chosen to store the graph in a sequential operating system file which is updated at the end of each user-action.
Such inefficiency can be avoided completely if the persistent representation takes the form of an abstract syntax graph itself, with components and update operations that are one-to-one with those required by the tools concerned. To allow this approach, therefore, the DBSE must support the definition, access and incremental update of a graph structure of nodes and edges with associated labelling information. To preserve the integrity of the abstract syntax-graph, the DBSE must support atomic transactions, i.e., a transaction mechanism that allows us to group a sequence of update-operations such that they are either performed completely or not performed at all. To ensure that a tool can recover in case of a failure to the state of the last completed user-action, each completed DBSE transaction must be durable.

Inter-document relationships Context-sensitive relations and user-defined relations between document components, as discussed above, contribute to the need for an abstract syntax-graph representation of a software document. In practice, however, such relations are not confined to within individual documents – they frequently exist between components of distinct documents. As an example c.f. Fig. 2.

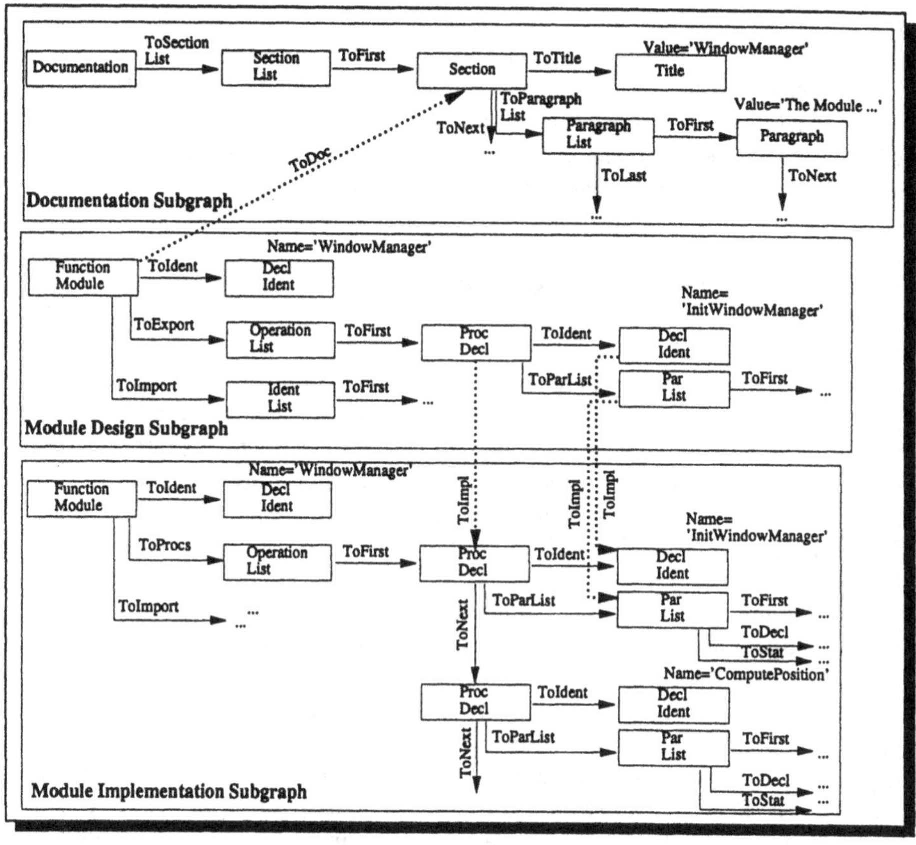

Fig. 2. Internal representation of Inter- and Intra-document Relations

The figure illustrates the connection of the previously shown source-code graph (Fig. 1) with the corresponding parts of a design document and the technical documentation respectively. Thus a module definition in the design document has inter-document relationships with the implementation of that module in the corresponding implementation document. Likewise, a paragraph in the technical documentation may be linked to the corresponding (formal) module definition in the design document, for traceability reasons.

To handle these inter-document relationships in a consistent way, the obvious strategy is to view the set of documents making up a project as a single project-wide graph. This approach, however, immediately reinforces our concern that the cost of updating its persistent representation should be independent of the overall size of the graph concerned, and requires that the DBSE must avoid imposing limits on the overall size of the graphs it can handle.

We note that this generalisation to a single project-wide graph does not necessarily undermine the concept of a document as a distinguishable representation component. If we distinguish between *aggregation* edges in the graph which express syntactic relationships, and *reference* edges, which arise from control, context-sensitive or user-defined relationships, then a document of the project is a subgraph whose node-set is the closure of nodes reachable by aggregation edges from a document node (i.e., a node not itself reachable in this way), together with all edges internal to the set[4]. The edges not included in this way are then necessarily the inter-document relationships inherent in the project.

3.2 Data Definition Language/Data Manipulation Language (DDL/DML)

The kinds of nodes and edges required to represent a project, and the attribute information associated with each, cannot be determined by the DBSE itself. It should be defined and controlled, however, by the DBSE in order to have different tools sharing a well-defined project-graph. The overall structure of the project's syntax-graph should therefore be defined in terms of the data definition language of the DBSE and be established and controlled by the DBSE's conceptual schema.

As a minimum, we require that the data definition language can express the different node types that occur within the graph, that it can express which edge-types may start from node types and to which node types they may lead, and that it can express which attributes are attached to node types. Such basic requirements are common to any graph storage.

In practice, the data definition language should be tailored to the syntax graphs that the DBSE is used to store. Structures that occur often in syntax-graphs are lists, sets and dictionaries of nodes that contain nodes of possibly different types. The data definition language should therefore offer means to express these common aggregations as conveniently as possible.

As argued previously, changes to the internal syntax-graph should become incrementally persistent. Therefore, edit operations performed by tools on documents have to be implemented in terms of operations modifying the internal syntax-graph. These operations should be established as part of the DBSE schema for mainly two reasons:

Encapsulation The structure definition of the project-graph should be encapsulated with operations which preserve the graph's integrity. They then provide a well-defined interface for accessing and modifying the graph. In order to enforce usage of this interface, the operations must become part of the DBSE schema.

Performance Executing graph accessing and modifying operations within the DBSE is more efficient than executing similar operations within tools as the number of nodes and edges that need to be transferred from the DBSE to tools via some network communication facility is reduced significantly.

[4] What we call a subgraph here, is comparable to the notion of a *composite entity* in PACT VMCS (cf. [23])

To establish graph-modifying operations as part of the DBSE schema, the DML must be powerful enough to express them. This means in particular, that the DBSE's DML must be capable of expressing creation and deletion of nodes and edges as well as assignment of attribute values. Moreover, the DML must be computationally complete, as alternatives and iterations are needed in graph-modifying operations for navigation purposes.

In addition, we noted in subsection 2.1 that the user may wish to query the project state via a reasoning component in the process engine. In practice, such queries may also arise from within the process engine itself, and from the process engineer who maintains the process governing any project.
The process engine needs to query the project's current syntax graph in order to extract information about the states of documents on which the engine must base its decisions. An example for such a query could be: select all program modules from the set of modules for which programmer p_1 is responsible that are incomplete but whose specifications are complete.
The process engineer may want to query the internal project graph in order to determine the project state.
The queries to be answered by the reasoning component are not known in advance, they have to be formulated in a process-related query language and must be translated by the reasoning component into a DBSE query. Likewise the queries the process engineer will use are not known a priori, i.e. at the time the PDSE is being built, so they cannot be precompiled. Thus, the DBSE must offer ad-hoc query facilities to be used by the process engine, and indirectly by the user and the process engineer.

3.3 Schema Updates

In section 2.1 we noted that the process being executed may have to be changed "on the fly". The DBSE must therefore enable the definition of new types of nodes and edges that are to be included in the internal syntax graph. Existing nodes and edges must not be affected by this kind of schema update.
Moreover, it is necessary that new types of edges can be added to existing types of nodes to allow the integration of nodes of newly defined types into an existing syntax graph. This implies that existing nodes whose types are modified by such a schema update can migrate from the old type to the modified one.

Consider as an example, the introduction of a new quality assurance procedure to be applied to all future documents as well as existing ones. The new procedure may require that the person who reviews a document writes a review report that is attached to the document. Furthermore his or her name is to be recorded as an attribute of the reviewed document. In this situation, the schema of the internal syntax graph needs to be modified: A new document type *review report* must be included and each reviewable document needs to have an additional node to record the document's reviewer and an additional edge to express its relationship to the review report.

3.4 Revisions and Versions

Given the overall representation of a project defined in section 3.1, the DBSE must support the creation and management of versions of those subgraphs that represent versionable document sets. In particular, it must enable its clients to derive a new version of a given subgraph, to maintain a version history for a subgraph, to remove a version of a given subgraph, and to select a current version from the version history. In doing so it must resolve between alternative duplication strategies, both within versions and for extra-version relations, preferably in a definable way.

Within versioned subgraphs the DBSE must resolve between fully lazy, fully eager and hybrid duplication strategies for the nodes and aggregation edges of the subgraph concerned. Fully lazy duplication gives maximum sharing of components, and hence minimum storage utilisation, but complicates the update process during user edits. Fully eager duplication avoids all such complications, but implies maximum storage utilisation. To meet the needs of all PSDE functions, a definable hybrid strategy between these two may have to be supported by the DBSE.

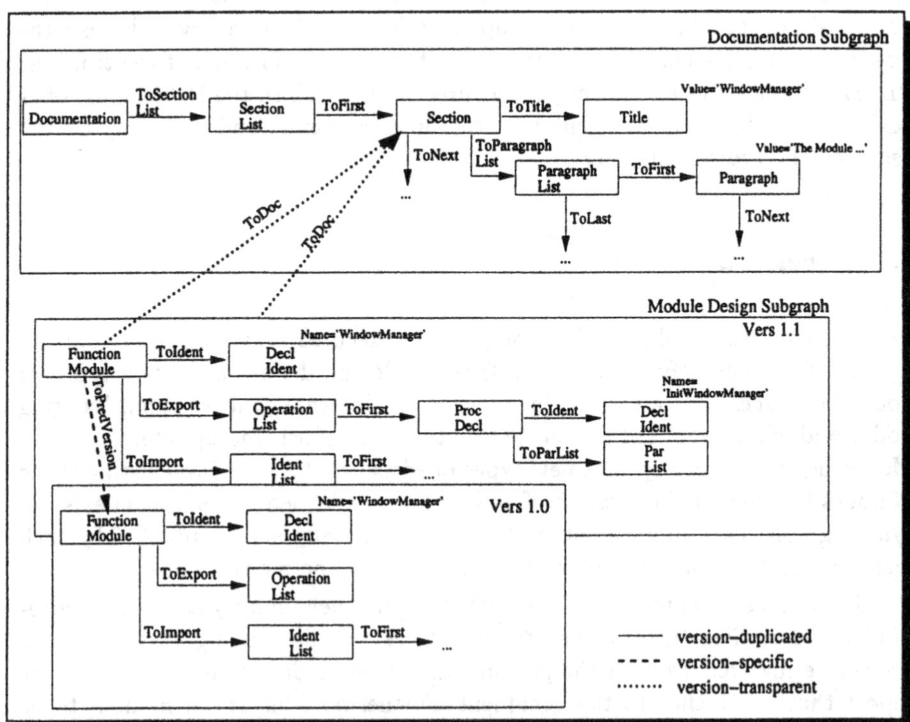

Fig. 3. Logical View of a Document under Version Control

The DBSE must also resolve between alternative strategies for handling both intra- and inter-document relationships (or reference edges). Within a document, reference edges will normally be treated (like aggregation edges) as *version-duplicated* (i.e., a new edge is automatically created for each version created). In particular circumstances, however, such edges may be seen as *version-specific* (and hence not duplicated when new versions are created). Relations between documents within a versioned document set (i.e. within a configuration) are treated similarly, i.e., they may be either version-duplicated or version-specific. Relations between a versioned document and a document outside the versioned set are also subject to the same basic choice, but version-duplication in this leads to a state which we call *version-transparent* since the same relation necessarily holds between all versions within the versioned set and the same (component of the) unversioned document. Again a definable hybrid strategy may be necessary for effective PSDE support.

Fig. 3 depicts the logical view of the module design graph being under version control. An additional (version-specific) edge *ToPredVers* is introduced that makes the version history explicit by leading for each document node to the document node of the predecessor version. An example of a version-transparent edge is the *ToDoc* edge connecting a function module node with the corresponding section title node in the documentation subgraph.

3.5 Access Rights and Adjustable Transaction Mechanisms

Requirements on the DBSE functionality which stem from the multi-user support of PSDEs, are the definition of access rights for particular documents and parts thereof and the definition of a variety of transaction mechanisms to control and enable parallel access to shared information by multiple users.

In more detail, to define access rights, the DBSE must be able to identify users and arbitrary many (probably nested) user groups. Secondly, the DBSE must allow to define and modify the ownership of subgraphs (which could even be a single node) at any time. Similarly, a subgraph may be accessed by several groups. Thus a subgraph needs to maintain its group memberships. Thirdly, the DBSE must allow to define and modify access rights for a subgraph individually for its owners and groups at any time. Finally, the DBSE must enforce that the defined access rights are respected by all its users[5].

Conventional transaction mechanisms which control parallel updates of the database have been proven to be too restrictive to be used in PSDEs because they could result in a rollback which deletes the effect of a possibly long-lasting human development effort, or they could block the execution of a certain activity for days or even weeks. Both situations are untolerable.

Consequently, advanced transaction mechanisms such as split/join transactions [21] or cooperating transactions [18] have been developed. Their common

[5] The kind of discretionary access control required here is similar to that provided by modern operating systems like e.g. UNIX. It differs in that a subgraph can have more than one group that may access it. Thus, we can express access rights in a more flexible way without introducing artificial user groups.

characteristics is that they relax one or more properties of conventional transaction mechanisms which are atomicity, consistency preservation, isolation and durability. For a detailed overview and critical evaluation of those mechanisms we refer to [2].

We argue, however, that none of them is powerful enough to be incorporated as the transaction mechanism into the database of a PSDE. As already argued in [20], only the process engine which knows the current state of an ongoing project, can decide whether and when to request a lock for a particular subgraph and how to react, if the lock is not granted. It also defines whether a transaction is executed in isolation or in a non-serialisable mode.

The requirements for the transaction mechanisms of a DBSE are that it offers the possibility to define and invoke either a serialisable transaction or a non-serialisable transaction which only guarantees atomicity and durability.

Atomicity and durability are needed to preserve the integrity of the project graph against hard/ or software failures as required in subsection 2.1 and 2.2 resp. Serialisability is needed, for example, when project state information and corresponding user agendas are updated (c.f. subsection 2.1). This information must not be invalidated by parallel updates as that could hinder the process engine from continuing its work or let the user perform unnecessary work. Fortunately, these updates are relatively short and do not involve any human interaction. Moreover, computation of a users' agenda only incorporates read access to project's state information such that it may be performed in an optimistic mode.

An example of a situation where transactions are either executed in a serialisable or non-serialisable mode depending on the project state is the following. During the very first development of a document, editing the document could and should be done in isolation until the document has evolved into a certain mature state, maybe a state where the document is released. During maintenance phase, a released document should be always consistent in itself as well as with respect to other documents. Thus a transaction which does change propagations due to error corrections should be executed immediately, even if affected documents are currently accessed by other transactions.

3.6 Distribution

Distribution of the project activities over a number of single-user workstations can be achieved in two ways. The first is to allow for a distributed access from the users' (client) workstations to a DBSE server. The second way would be to distribute transparently the syntax graph itself over various DBSEs that are locally accessible from user's workstations.

With the first approach, the server would surely become a performance bottleneck for the whole PSDE. Hence, this approach seems feasible only for small projects (say less then 10 users). It is, however, worth consideration, as many projects are either small projects or can be split into fairly independent subprojects that are small enough.

With the second approach, the process engine can arrange that those parts of the internal syntax graph that represent a particular document are locally accessible from the workstation of the responsible user[6]. The tools that operate on the syntax graph, however, should not need to know anything about the physical distribution of the syntax graph, i.e. the distribution must be transparent for them. It should rather be the responsibility of the DBSE to manage physical distribution.

3.7 DBSE Administration

As the contents of the DBSE might be the most important capital of software houses, issues of data security are very important. This involves two aspects: access to the database and the possibility of hardware crash recoveries.

The DBSE must be able to restrict the access to its objects such that non-authorised persons are excluded from any access. This means that the DBSE must be able to identify its users. Additionally, the DBSE must enforce authentication e.g. by assigning passwords to DBSE users such that it can assure that persons correspond to DBSE users.
For purposes of user management, the DBSE has to offer means to be used by a database administrator (DBA) in order to enter new users and groups to the DBSE, to change user informations like passwords, to remove users from the set of known users and groups from the set of known groups, and to change membership to groups.

Moreover, data stored in the DBSE must be protected from any hardware failures such as disk crashes. Therefore the DBSE has to offer means for dumping the contents of the DBSE to backup media like e.g. tapes. As the size of a project database may be too large to be completely backed up daily, the DBSE must allow for incremental backups. The DBA should not have to shut down the database in order to perform these incremental backups.

3.8 Views

As proposed in subsection 3.1, the project graph may contain a lot of redundant information – in Fig. 2 the nodes *Function*, *Module*, *DeclIdent*, *OperationList* and the edges *ToIdent* and *ToExport* are duplicated in the design and implementation subgraphs. Eliminating this duplication by sharing the aggregation subtrees concerned has the following advantages: (1) the conceptual schema is simplified (2) storage of the schema and corresponding data requires less space, and (3) consistency preservation especially across document boundaries becomes much easier. Such sharing cannot be contemplated, of course, if automatic consistency preservation between documents is inappropriate.

If subtree sharing is to be used, tools accessing the project graph need a view mechanism like that offered in many relational database systems, to maintain

[6] Though the document itself is locally accessible, there may still be inter-document relationships in the internal syntax graph, that lead to remote nodes.

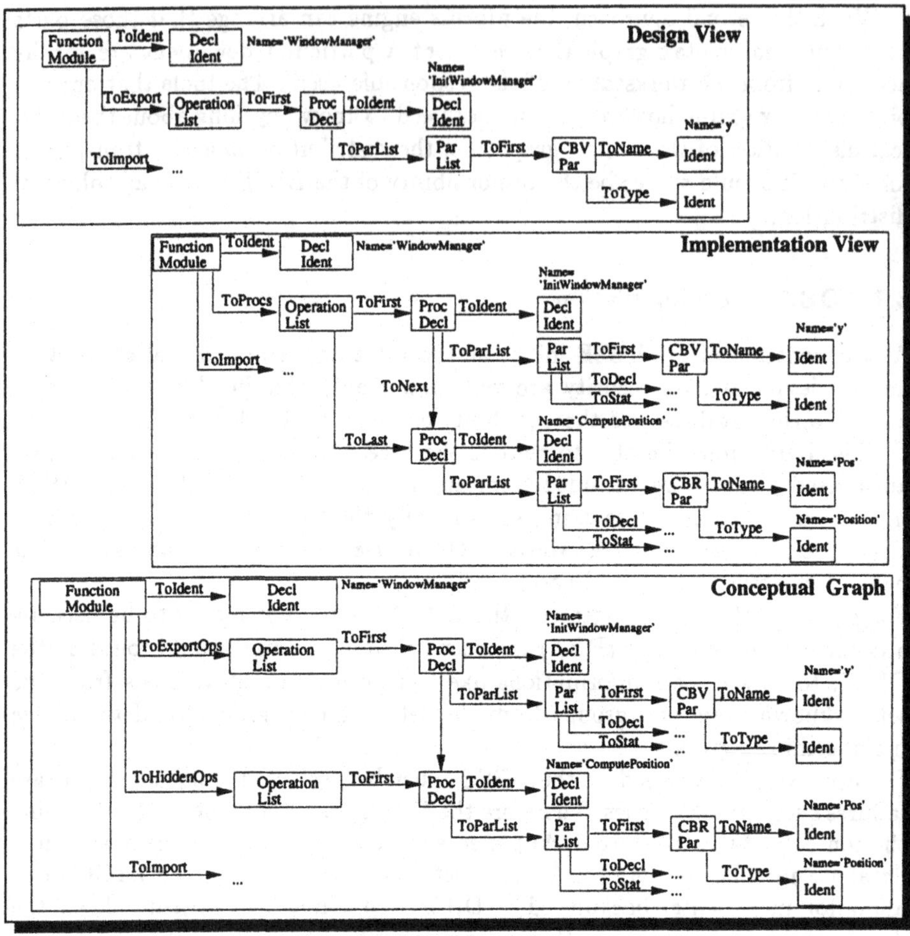

Fig. 4. Reducing Redundant Information with Views

appropriate separation of tool concerns and so allow separate tool development and maintenance.

Fig. 4 sketches how the redundancy which exists in Fig. 2 is reduced in a new schema. The schema will be accessed by the design editor and the implementation editor through two views. The figure depicts the conceptual project-graph together with the design and implementation view of this graph.
The **design view** of a function module node is declared to hide the *ToHiddenOps* edge defined in the conceptual schema as these operations shall not be seen at the module interface level. The design view also renames the *ToExportedOps* edge of a conceptual function module node to *ToExport*. Finally, the design view hides the *ToDecl* and *ToStat* edges defined for procedure declaration nodes in the conceptual schema from each procedure declaration node in the design view. Consequently, all node types reachable only from these edges in the conceptual schema are also hidden in the design view.

The **implementation view** of a function module declares the *ToProcs* edge to lead to a node of a virtual node type which is constructed by concatenation of the lists accessed via the *ToExportedOps* and *ToHiddenOps* edges of a function module in the conceptual schema. This allows us to have exported and hidden operations merged in one operation list of the implementation graph.

These tool-oriented views must be regarded as virtual structures since they are not actually stored in the DBSE, but updates on views by tools must propagate automatically to the underlying project graph.

Introduction of a view mechanism, however, has non-trivial consequences for the access control mechanisms required (since users see this access control as applying to document views) and for the versioning policy which the PDSE designer or the users may adopt. Detailed resolution of these issues is largely a matter of PSDE design and is thus beyond the scope of this paper. We note, however, that provision of such a view mechanism is clearly a requirement for effective PDSE design and implementation.

4 State-of-the-Art in DBMS Technology and Further Work

Relational DBMSs are inappropriate for storing project graphs, since (1) the data model can not express syntax graphs appropriately, (2) RDBMSs do not support versioning of document subgraphs and (3) RDBMSs can not be used to implement customised transaction schemes.
No structurally object-oriented DBMS meets all of our requirements. Those that are capable of efficiently managing project graphs, lack functionality w.r.t. views, versioning, access rights and adjustable transaction mechanisms, and distribution like GRAS [16]. Others that offer these functionalities are unable to manage the large collections of small objects as they occur in project graphs and are therefore inappropriate like e.g. PCTE [10] or Damokles [6]. Moreover, none of these systems enables encapsulation of nodes with operations, which we regard to be crucial.
For this reason we focus on ooDBMSs like GemStone [5] or O_2 [1] in the future. As general databases, they have not been designed to manipulate a particular granularity of objects. They provide powerful schema definition languages which particularly enable encapsulation, inheritance and polymorphism. Some have been proven to perform fast enough even while accessing document subgraphs from a remote host [7]. A more detailed investigation and reasoning about the non-appropriateness of existing RDBMSs and structurally object-oriented DBMSs is done in [8].

Currently, we are porting the Merlin PSDE to an ooDBMS and enhancing Merlin with syntax-directed tools which store their document subgraphs in this ooDBMS. Merlin is a research project (c.f. [20, 19]) at the University of Dortmund carried out in cooperation with STZ, a local software house. One result of Merlin is the prototype of a PSDE based on a rule based description of the software process.

The requirements discussed in this paper provide the foundation for the ESPRIT-III project GoodStep (General Object-Oriented Database for SofTware Engineering Processes) whose goal is to extend the ooDBMS O_2 to make it particularly suitable as a DBSE. The project will improve version management, add view definition capabilities and break up the transaction management to enable implementation of customised transaction schemes with the O_2 system.

Acknowledgements

We are indebted to the members of the Merlin project, namely G. Junkerman, C. Lücking, O. Neumann, B. Peuschel and S. Wolf, for a lot of fruitful discussions about PSDE architectures. We thank the participants of the GoodStep project for stimulating discussions, in particular, Prof. C. Ghezzi, Prof. R. Zicari, Dr. S. Abiteboul, Dr. P. Armenise, Dr. A. Coen. Last, but not least, we enjoyed working with Prof. U. Kelter, Dr. S. Dewal, F. Buddrus, D. Dong, H. Hormann, M. Kampmann, D. Platz, M. Roschewski and L. Schöpe on the experimental evaluation of existing database systems.
The joint work described here was done at University of Dortmund while J. Welsh was on study leave from University of Queensland. The authors are grateful to the German Ministry of Research and the Australian Department of Industry Trade and Commerce for enabling this cooperation.

References

1. F. Bancilhon, C. Delobel, and P. Kanellakis. *Building an Object-Oriented Database System: the Story of O_2*. Morgan Kaufmann, 1992.
2. N. S. Barghouti and G. E. Kaiser. Concurrency Control in Advanced Database Applications. *ACM Computing Surveys*, 23(3):269–317, 1991.
3. P. A. Bernstein. Database System Support for Software Engineering. In *Proc. of the 9th Int. Conf. on Software Engineering, Monterey, Cal.*, pages 166–178, 1987.
4. P. Borras, D. Clément, T. Despeyroux, J. Incerpi, G. Kahn, B. Lang, and V. Pascual. CENTAUR: the system. *ACM SIGSOFT Software Engineering Notes*, 13(5):14–24, 1988. Proc. of the ACM SIGSOFT/SIGPLAN Software Engineering Symposium on Practical Software Development Environments, Boston, Mass.
5. R. Bretl, D. Maier, A. Otis, J. Penney, B. Schuchardt, J. Stein, E. H. Williams, and M. Williams. The GemStone data management system. In W. Kim and F. H. Lochovsky, editors, *Object-Oriented Concepts, Databases and Applications*, pages 283–308. Addison-Wesley, 1989.
6. K. R. Dittrich, W. Gotthard, and P. C. Lockemann. Damokles – a database system for software engineering environments. In R. Conradi, T. M. Didriksen, and D. H. Wanvik, editors, *Proc. of an Int. Workshop on Advanced Programming Environments*, volume 244 of *Lecture Notes in Computer Science*, pages 353–371. Springer, 1986.
7. W. Emmerich and M. Kampmann. The Merlin OMS Benchmark – Definition, Implementations and Results. Technical Report 65, University of Dortmund, Dept. of Computer Science, Chair for Software Technology, 1992.

8. W. Emmerich, W. Schäfer, and J. Welsh. Databases for Software Engineering Environments — The Goal has not yet been attained. Technical Report 66, University of Dortmund, Dept. of Computer Science, Chair for Software Technology, 1992.
9. G. Engels, C. Lewerentz, M. Nagl, W. Schäfer, and A. Schürr. Building Integrated Software Development Environments — Part 1: Tool Specification. *ACM Transactions on Software Engineering and Methodology*, 1(2):135–167, 1992.
10. F. Gallo, R. Minot, and I. Thomas. The object management system of PCTE as a software engineering database management system. *ACM SIGPLAN NOTICES*, 22(1):12–15, 1987.
11. A. N. Habermann and D. Notkin. *Gandalf: Software Development Environments. IEEE Transactions on Software Engineering*, 12(12):1117–1127, 1986.
12. R. Hoover. *Incremental graph evaluation*. PhD thesis, Cornell University, Dept. of Computer Science, Ithaca, NY, 1987. Technical Report No. 87-836.
13. P. Hruschka. ProMod - in the age 5. In *Proc. of the* 1st *European Software Engineering Conference*, Strasbourg, Sept. 1987.
14. G. F. Johnson and C. N. Fisher. Non-syntactic attribute flow in language based editors. In *Proc. of the* 9th *Annual ACM Symposium on Principles of Programming Languages*, pages 185–195. ACM Press, 1982.
15. G. E. Kaiser, P. H. Feiler, and S. S. Popovich. Intelligent assistance for software development and maintenance. *IEEE Software*, pages 40–49, May 1988.
16. C. Lewerentz and A. Schürr. GRAS, a management system for graph-like documents. In *Proc. of the* 3rd *Int. Conf. on Data and Knowledge Bases*. Morgan Kaufmann, 1988.
17. N. H. Madhavji. Environment Evolution: The Prism Model of Changes. *IEEE Transactions on Software Engineering*, 18(5):380–392, 1992.
18. M. H. Nodine, A. H. Skarra, and S. B. Zdonik. Synchronization and Recovery in Cooperative Transactions. In *Implementing Persistent Object Bases – Principles and Practice – Proc. of the* 4th *Int. Workshop on Persistent Object Systems* , pages 329–342, 1991.
19. B. Peuschel and W. Schäfer. Concepts and Implementation of a Rule-based Process Engine. In *Proc. of the* 14th *Int. Conf. on Software Engineering, Melbourne, Australia*, pages 262–279. IEEE Computer Society Press, 1992.
20. B. Peuschel, W. Schäfer, and S. Wolf. A Knowledge-based Software Development Environment Supporting Cooperative Work. *International Journal for Software Engineering and Knowledge Engineering*, 2(1):79–106, 1992.
21. C. Pu, G. Kaiser, and N. Hutchinson. Split transactions for open-ended activites. In *Proc. of the* 14th *Int. Conf. on Very Large Databases*, pages 26–37. Morgan Kaufman, 1989.
22. R. N. Taylor, R. W. Selby, M. Young, F. C. Belz, L. A. Clarce, J. C. Wileden, L. Osterweil, and A. L. Wolf. Foundations of the Arcadia Environment Architecture. *ACM SIGSOFT Software Engineering Notes*, 13(5):1–13, 1988. Proc. of the 4th ACM SIGSOFT Symposium on Software Development Environments, Irvine, Cal.
23. Ian Thomas. Tool Integration in the Pact Environment. In *Proc. of the* 11th *Int. Conf. on Software Engineering, Pittsburg, Penn.*, pages 13–22. IEEE Computer Society Press, 1989.
24. J. Welsh, B. Broom, and D. Kiong. A Design Rational for a Language-based Editor. *Software — Practice and Experience*, 21(9):923–948, 1991.

A Regression Testing Database Model

Lulu Liu†, David J. Robson‡, Rod Ellis†

†School of Computer Science and Information Systems Engineering,
University of Westminster, 115 New Cavendish Street,
London W1M 8JS, U.K.

‡Centre for Software Maintenance, University of Durham,
Durham DH1 3LE, U.K.

Abstract. Regression testing involves revalidation of modified software. It is a major component of software maintenance, aimed at ensuring a correct and reliable maintenance activity. Recently proposed regression testing strategies have problems in their practical use because of the lack of management and control information about regression testing or maintenance activities. The need for a database to aid regression testing has been recognised. This paper presents a model of a regression testing database(RTD) which emphasises configuration management, traceability and change impact analysis of data used in regression testing. A prototype of the RTD, entitled SEMST, has been implemented on a Sun workstation to manage all versions of specifications, test cases and programs, as well as to control relationships between these components. SEMST is introduced in this paper.

1 Introduction

Regression testing is a testing process applied after a change to the program or to the specification, causing the program to be changed. It is commonly thought of as a major maintenance testing technique, although it can also involve retesting a *tested program* in the system development phase. The goal of regression testing is testing a changed program with a number of test cases so as to convince the maintainer that the program still performs correctly with respect to its functional specification(i.e., no new errors are introduced, and no unintended, side effects are caused by the change).

It has been realised that completely retesting the whole program which had a few changes is very expensive in terms of time and computational resources, while intuitively or randomly selecting test cases to rerun is unreliable. Hence, it is highly desirable to apply intelligent test case selection to retesting relevant areas of a changed program. Recent research in regression testing is mainly aimed at exploring a systematic approach to the test case reselection problem in order to support an economical revalidation process. There have been a number of such strategies developed[3] [4][11], and these are called *selective regression testing strategies*.

However, the application of these strategies has difficulties due to insufficient management information. Leung and White [5] indicated that current regression testing is based on three assumptions: (1) the test plan is high quality; (2) sufficient change information is obtained; and (3) the program is (regression) testable. In order to support regression testing, a database which can provide efficient management of the data and activities associated with regression testing has been found to be indispensable. Although a number of maintenance environments developed in recent years claimed their support for regression testing[2], they failed to elaborate the corresponding requirements. Therefore, the functionalities provided in these environments for regression testing were far from sufficient.

This paper is intended to present a database model for supporting regression testing. Compared to other issues on regression test support[5] [6], this paper is looking at all types of data involved in regression testing and addressing the management and control of these data and their relationships so as to help the selection of the test cases to rerun.

The paper contains 6 sections: section 2 describes the activities, data features and problems in regression testing in order to indicate our motivation for developing this database model; section 3 discusses requirements for the database together with an investigation of related work; section 4 introduces a prototype of the database, named SEMST[7][8], which has been implemented on Unix and RCS(A Revision Control System)[10] on a Sun Workstation at the Centre for Software Maintenance, University of Durham; section 5 discusses our experience with SEMST in terms of its advantages and limitations; and the final section contains a conclusion of the paper.

2 Regression Testing and Its Problems

In general, a regression testing process involves five essential activities: (1) identify the effects of changes; (2) select the test cases to test the affected regions; (3) execute the modified program based on the selected test cases; (4) ensure that the modified program still performs the intended behaviour specified in the (possibly modified) specification; and (5) update old test plan for the next regression testing process.

The first activity in regression testing is fundamental, which should be performed in a way that the testers first understand what changes have been made, and then analyse the impact of changes to recognise the affected regions by the changes. Most previous issues on supporting this activity [5] focused on studying the impact of changes within a program. However, the virtual effects of a change, particularly when the specification is changed, would apply to not only the program but also the specification and test cases. Therefore we think that after the affected regions(in the specification or program) have been recognised, the test cases associated with these affected regions should be identified as *affected test cases* by changes, when perform this activity.

The second activity is concerned with the selection of the test cases to rerun. It involves the generation of new test cases and the reselection of old test cases. In [5], the old test cases are divided into three classes. *Reusable test cases* are those which tested unmodified parts of the specification and their corresponding unmodified parts of the program. They remain valid after the modifications to the specification and program, and need not to be rerun. The test cases relevant to the modified parts (of the specification or program), which we refer to as the affected test cases, have two categories: those still valid are called *retestable test cases*, and should be rerun; while those which become irrelevant or out of date to the changed specification or program are called *obsolete test cases*, and should be removed from the test plan.

2.1 Problems in Regression Testing

Current regression testing strategies assume that a complete and high quality test plan is available [5]. However, in the actual system development, it is a difficult task as the test plan should be completed at an early stage of the system development, which requires an early understanding of what is going to be accomplished. The project plan is usually based on an imprecise or misunderstood specification of requirements.

Another problem with regression testing is concerned with the maintenance of test data. Regression test data components are of three kinds, namely ***specifications***, ***test cases*** and ***programs***. In the software life cycle, these components are usually enormous, stored in a variety of different files and data formats, and storage media. There are few methods provided to record the history of these data so that the testers generally have no knowledge about what changes have been made to these components and how these components have evolved in the software life cycle.

Furthermore, relationships between these components are usually poorly controlled so that the traceability over them and information about the effects of changes cannot be obtained. There are, in fact, very close and complex relationships (which are of the type many-to-many) existing between these components. The change to part of a component would affect the validity of the other components.

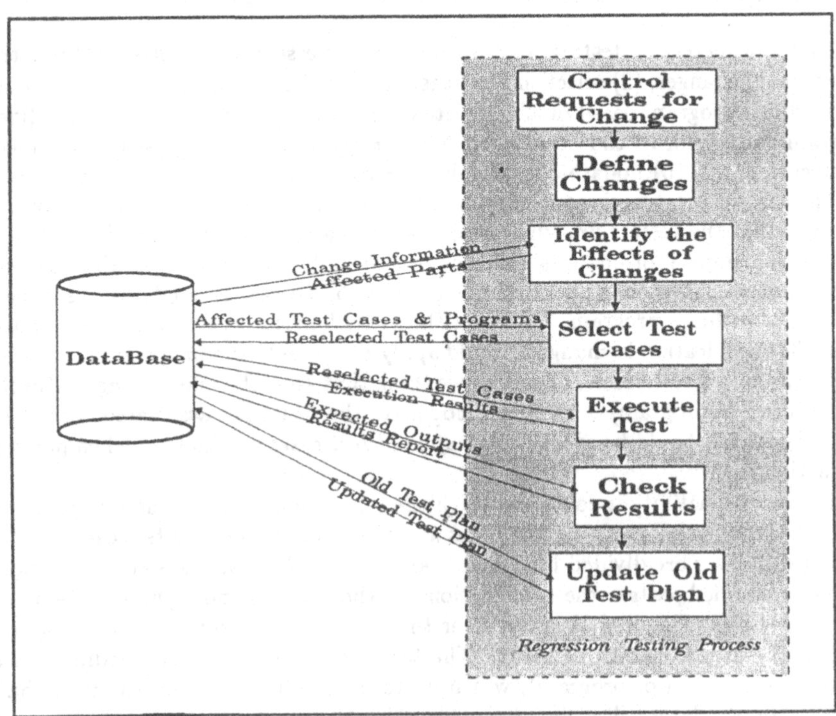

Figure1. A Regression Testing Support System Model

3 Requirements for a RTD

From the above discussions, it can be seen that to support regression testing, it is important to provide information about scope of the changes and to maintain the history of test data. In figure 1, a conceptual model of a RTD that supports the regression testing activities is illustrated. These activities should be supported by a set of tools, including a *change impact analyser, test case reselector, test executor* and a *test reporter.* A RTD should play a role of being as a central, common area allowing these tools to communicate with each other, and should be integrated into a maintenance environment.

3.1 RTD Objects

A RTD should be populated with data involved in regression testing: the specifications, test cases, and programs.

The specifications should be stored in a function-identifiable format to allow an easy obtaining of individual functions specified in the specifications. The programs in a RTD should be independent of languages and organised into a set of modules(i.e., procedures or functions). A module should be stored with its attributes (e.g., control flow and data flow information obtainable from a program static analyser). A test case generally consists of a set of input test data and a set of expected output data against the input data. In a RTD, it is useful if a test case can indicate its type(i.e., functional test case or structural test case).

All these objects should be typed, and an object type can be defined by a name.

3.2 RTD Mechanisms

First of all, the database should provide mechanisms to enable the storage, retrieval and update of the objects. The objects should be loaded into and stored in the RTD in line with the conceptual schema for representing these objects. The access to each of the objects should be allowed. It will be more efficient if the system has the ability to communicate with other life cycle tools(e.g., a test case generator and a static program analyser) so as to load the objects automatically.

Secondly, the system should provide configuration management of the data objects. As regression testing involves an analysis of all previous test cases and their relationships with specifications and programs, the configuration management mechanism, whose feature is to control the architecture and the state of system components in the life cycle, should be applied to these objects. Version control of these components is very useful as this will enable the understanding of details of changes to the components(e.g., what changes have been made). Other supports from this mechanism include defining a configuration[1] for a group of these components; baselining a set of these components; and controlling data security to prevent unexpected modification to the data.

[1] in the context of regression testing, a configuration can be defined to be a group of data consisting of specifications, test cases and programs, which are used together for performing one regression testing process. It can also be defined to be a set of test suits including test input data and the resulting outputs.

In addition, it is very important that the system should provide traceability over the objects. For doing this, relationships between the objects should be established. A relationship is a bi-directional association between two objects, it can also be regarded as a pair of mutually inverse links. In this context, we take a view that the overall data relationships in the life cycle are of two kinds, which we name *inner relationship* and *outer relationship.*

The inner relationship is to view the data relationships based on only a single type of object(e.g., a program) in the life cycle. It is focused on relationships between the components which make up only a single object(e.g., several subroutines that build up a program may have relationships with each other). Compared to the inner relationship, the outer relationship is concerned with the relationships between the life-cycle objects(e.g., links between specifications, test cases and programs). The outer relationship reflects relationships between the objects over the life cycle.

A RTD should be able to manage the above data relationships. Links should be created between objects in terms of the versions. All possible links between the objects(to reflect many-to-many relationship) should be considered, and more importantly, the validity of the system links should be ensured. This means that the system should be able to control the state of links to be up to date. Within the database, a sequence of links can make a path, and this path enables the tracking over the objects.

Another important activity that a RTD should support is the analysis of the effects of changes on the objects and their links. Because data objects in the life cycle have the inner and outer relationships with each other, when a change is made to an object component, the effects of the change could be on either innerly related components or outerly related components or both. Therefore, the analysis of such problems should involve two aspects, which we call *inner impact of change* and *outer impact of change.* Basically, the analysis of impact of change(including both of the aspects) should provide information about affected regions in the objects, so that after a component is modified, the affected parts in the whole system can be recognised, and the links between the object components created in the system can be adjusted with respect to the changes.

3.3 RTD Data Model

A data model defines the facilities for representing and handling information from a DBMS point of view. The data model underlying RDBMS is *relational model* (also called *record-oriented data model),* which, however, does not capture data semantic information to serve adequately as the data model underlying the conceptual schema of the RTD.

From the RTD's functionalities described above, the RTD's conceptual schema should be defined to represent the specifications, test cases and programs, as well as their relationships. These objects are usually in a large scale and can derive many types of entities(e.g., subroutines and paths), involving complex relationships with each other. So a RTD requires sophisticated data and linkage management.

It is believed that a richer set of capabilities for controlling data and the associated activities is vital to a regression testing support environment, and an Entity-Relation-Attribute data model is more appropriate for supporting the RTD data handling requirements.

3.4 Related Systems

Most of recently developed software development and maintenance environments are based on an *object management system*(OMS) that supports the entity-relationship-attribute model. OMSs are designed to support typed objects with inheritance and the links which bind several objects together to provide the required functionality. Configuration management and version control mechanisms are also included in OMSs. However, current OMSs provide little support for the traceability, which enables the tracking of effects of change on these data items and their relationships.

A number of *hypertext-based systems* have been developed to manage links between the life cycle documentation[1]. These systems are based on an entity-relation-like data model, and use graph concept to manage relationships between the data. Nodes are used to store data and relationships between the data are reflected by links(i.e., the edges in the graph). Traceability is provided in the way that it allows the traversing of the nodes and links. Unfortunately, current hypertext-based systems do not suggest the management of the effect of change on the system documents and the links. After a modification to some parts of the system documents, the state of linkage kept in these systems may not be valid. Furthermore, to provide a configuration management mechanism(e.g., version control) in current hypertext systems and to ensure the links are automatically controlled in terms of the document versions, more work is still needed.

A *ripple effect analyser* was introduced in a maintenance environment issue [2]. It supports identification of affected areas of software by change. However, the ripple effect analyser is only focused on code analysis. The change impact on other objects(e.g., test cases) in the life cycle was not considered.

ASSAY[6] is a tool for supporting regression testing. The main features of the system include configuration control of the tests and the ability to continue testing after a mismatch occurs. It is significant that ASSAY supports test case management and execution, but it does not support traceability and change impact analysis of test data.

4 SEMST – A Prototype of the RTD

In the following, we introduce a prototype version of the RTD, entitled SEMST, which supports the maintenance of all versions of specifications, test cases, and programs, together with their relationships. With SEMST, the data used in regression testing can be maintained in the most recent state, and when a change has been made to a part of specification or program, affected test cases by the change can be identified. The main concept of SEMST is shown in figure 2.

4.1 The Design of SEMST

The SEMST system has been designed to provide its functionalities through four major components: *system monitor, specification segment, program segment* and *test case segment*, which manipulate on the *SEMST database.*

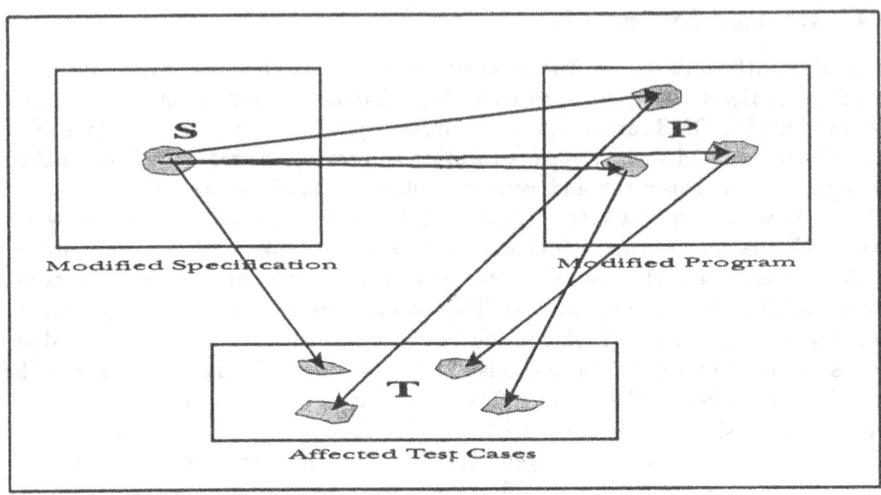

Figure 2. SEMST Concept

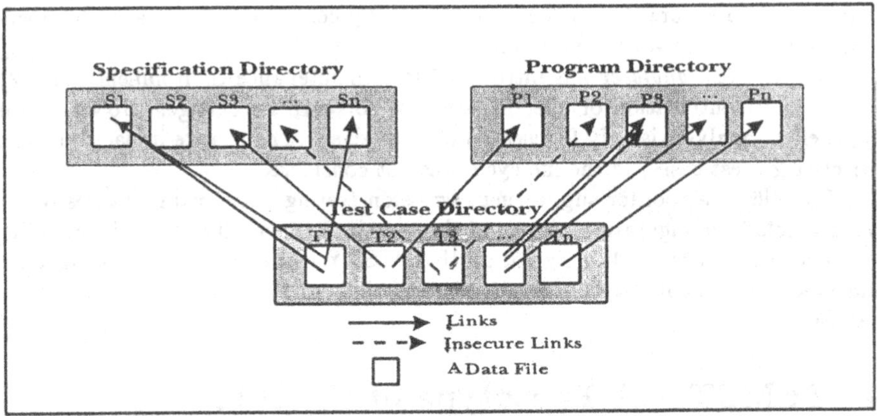

Figure 3. Internal Structure of the SEMST Database

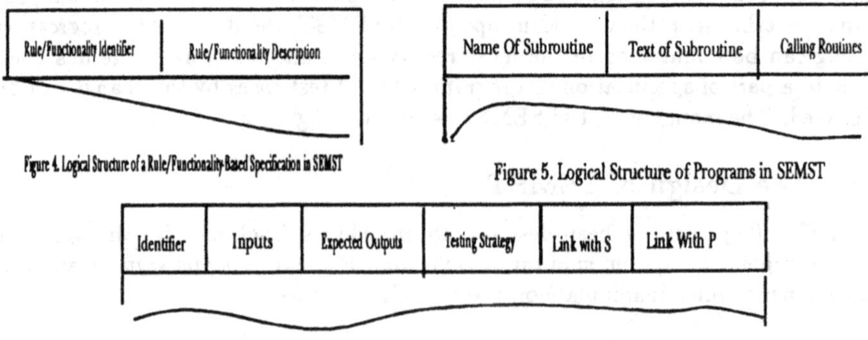

Figure 4. Logical Structure of a Rule/Functionality-Based Specification in SEMST

Figure 5. Logical Structure of Programs in SEMST

Figure 6. Logical Structure of a Test Case in SEMST

The system monitor acts as a main control program in the SEMST system, whose major functions include: analysing the user's commands; invoking the relevant subsystems; creating a new database(i.e., new directory) for a new user; and saving the systems information into the database before exiting the system.

The three segments mentioned above are the *subsystems* of SEMST, and each of them is functionally independent of the other. There are four general, functional areas associated with each segment, namely *input process, output process, data maintenance* and *linkage management.*

The SEMST database is designed as a central repository where the test data and the system information are stored, and shared by the subsystems. It is the common data area on which the independent subsystems are able to communicate with each other. The database structure is tailored to the Unix file system which is a hierarchical architecture. The database can be separated into a number of areas with respect to numbers of the users. Each user area contains three directories, namely *specification directory, test case directory* and *program directory*[see figure 3]. The data items stored in these three directories are all under RCS control.

4.2 Data Representation in SEMST

The SEMST database supports an Entity-Relation-Attributes data model. The objects in the database are the data files which are treated as entities with attributes and relationships.

The specifications supported by the SEMST prototype are those written in a style which is rule-based or functionality-based. The logical representation for such specifications is indicated in figure 4. A program in SEMST is supposed to be pre-processed by a program analyser, by which the subroutines constructed in the program and their calling relations are identified. A subroutine is logically represented by its *name*, its *text* and the names of *other routines* which call it(see figure 5). The test cases can usually be described in a variety of formats. In SEMST, a test case is represented by the description of *input data*, the description of *expected output* and the *testing strategy* on which the test case is based, shown in figure 6. There are also two additional areas associated with a test case, which store the pointers pointing to the parts of the program or specification that have relations with it.

At the lowest level, the system's data model and representation are implemented as a collection of directories with each data class mapped onto a Unix directory. An object, which is an instance of a data class, is then implemented as a file within the directory.

4.3 Data Maintenance in SEMST

The SEMST system provides a mechanism to load the data items into its database and store the data based on the logical representations described above. The procedure of loading data can be guided by the system.

RCS is employed by the SEMST system to support version control of the data in the database. Hence, any changes made to each data item are tracked, arising a new version for each changed item. Any version of a data file can be retrieved from the system by giving the version number. A retrieved file can be modified within the system.

A *release* is a software deliverable or an end product which may be baselined. SEMST supports releases, so for example the user can define all the latest versions of test cases used for testing a particular module to be a release.

In SEMST, data components are maintained with their links. The next section describe the linkage management in more detail.

4.4 Linkage Management in SEMST

The current SEMST system manages the links of test cases with the specifications and programs(see figure 3). When one of the objects has been modified, the system will provide the users with change information so that the items linking with this changed item should be given attention. In this situation, the state of the links between these objects in the system is defined to be *insecure*.

The links are controlled depending on an *identifier* associated with each item. SEMST requires that each test data item be given a distinct name as its identifier. There are four mechanisms to support this functionality:

Creating Links. The links are established when the test cases are entered into the SEMST database.

Enquiring Links. The users are allowed to make an enquiry about the current state of the links created between the data in the SEMST system.

Reporting Insecure Links. When a changed made to part of the specification or program, the links of the test cases with that part of the specification or program have become insecure. In order to keep the links between the data in the system up to date, SEMST provides a mechanism to control and manage these insecure links. By indicating the insecure links, the users can be made aware of the changed parts in the specification or program and of the change effects on other objects (i.e., the affected test cases by the change). The insecure links may become valid in SEMST after a modification to them.

Modifying Links. In order to support that the links created between the data components are controlled based on the data versions, SEMST provides a facility for modifying the links. The important purpose of this facility is to keep the state of the system data up to date. With this, the links of a changed item with other items are able to be adjusted to become relevant. This facility should apply to the insecure links identified in the system. Meanwhile, it can also be used to correct wrong links created previously.

5 Experience With SEMST

The SEMST prototype has been used to simulate the management of test data in a project development. Several outputs from the system can be seen from figures 7 and 8, where the specification is a rule-based specification, written in a Pascal-like language, and the test cases are functional test cases relevant to such a rule-based specification. These test data examples are from the test documents associated with part of a *Control System* project.

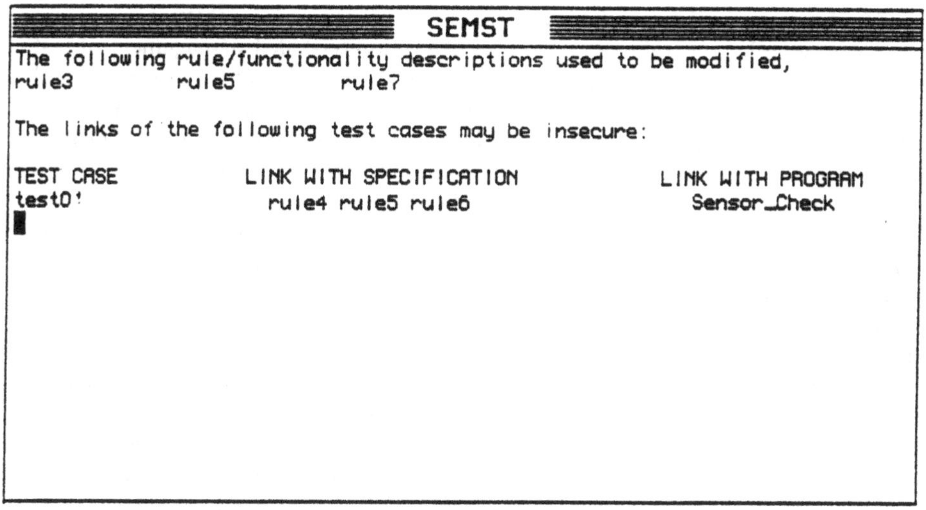

SEMST

The following rule/functionality descriptions used to be modified,
rule3 rule5 rule7

The links of the following test cases may be insecure:

TEST CASE	LINK WITH SPECIFICATION	LINK WITH PROGRAM
test01	rule4 rule5 rule6	Sensor_Check

Figure 7. An Example of the Links Checking in the Specification Segment

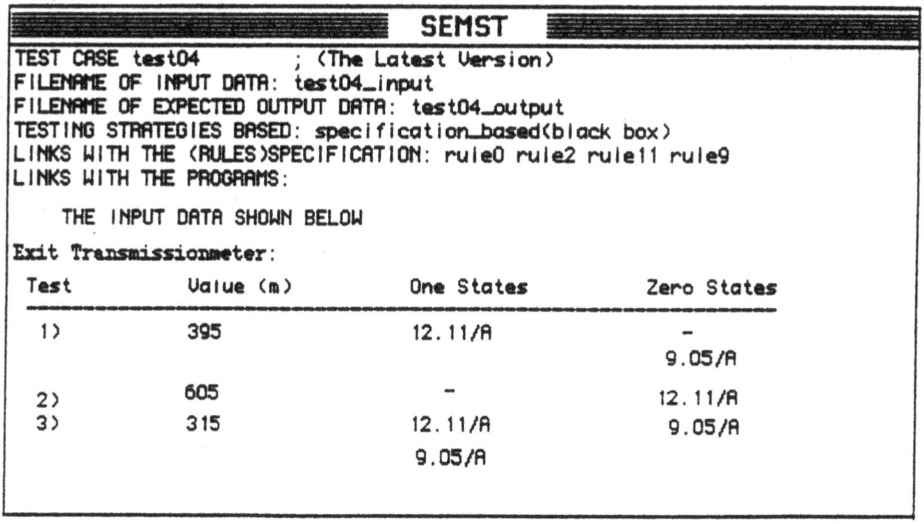

SEMST

TEST CASE test04 ; (The Latest Version)
FILENAME OF INPUT DATA: test04_input
FILENAME OF EXPECTED OUTPUT DATA: test04_output
TESTING STRATEGIES BASED: specification_based(black box)
LINKS WITH THE (RULES)SPECIFICATION: rule0 rule2 rule11 rule9
LINKS WITH THE PROGRAMS:

THE INPUT DATA SHOWN BELOW

Exit Transmissionmeter:

Test	Value (m)	One States	Zero States
1)	395	12.11/A	- 9.05/A
2)	605	-	12.11/A
3)	315	12.11/A 9.05/A	9.05/A

Figure 8. The Display of a Retrieved Test Case Record

The following is observed from our experience in using the prototype:

The system has provided a method for the computer-aided management of test data used in regression testing; all versions of the specifications, test cases and programs could be maintained, so that details of a change to these objects(e.g., when and what changes are made) could be recorded; a baseline for a set of objects could be defined; links between the objects could be created manually; traceability between the objects is allowed; the effect of changes on the objects and their links could be identified; and the state of the data items and their relationships could be controlled to be up to date. The significant contributions of the SEMST system to regression testing are that it helps to identify the insecure links resulting from the data modification, so that the affected test cases can be recognised; and it allows the modification of the links, so they may reflect the most recent system state.

The current SEMST concentrates on outer impact of change, the impact of a change on the objects across the life cycle. The support for identifying the inner impact of change in the system is weak. Some other shortcomings of the current system include: the configuration management mechanism provided in the system is only based on RCS, so it has the same limitations as RCS(e.g., inapplicable to non-text data); the linkage management mechanism in the system cannot control all possible links between the specifications, programs and test cases; no systematic validation approach is provided to ensure the correctness of the links created in the system; and links are not named, so the kind of relationships existing between the linked data is not clearly represented.

6 Conclusion

In this paper, a RTD model, used for regression testing, has been described together with an analysis of its requirements. The key concept addressed is the application of configuration management, traceability and identification of impact of changes to the data involved in regression testing. SEMST, a prototype of the RTD, has been presented to exhibit its features for helping regression testing. However, to fulfill the entire RTD requirements, many improvements on SEMST are needed. We believe that if the formal specifications can be accepted as the style of a specification, the efficiency reliability for controlling the relationships between specifications, test cases and program in SEMST would increase. We also believe that, in the future, a merging of SEMST with the mechanisms provided in the object management systems and hypertext systems would greatly strengthen the power of SEMST to support regression testing.

Acknowledgements

The work on developing the SEMST system was a part of an Esprit II project – REDO. Lulu Liu wishes to thank the University of Durham, Centre for Software Maintenance, for providing the grant and the facilities to work on this project. She also wishes to thank her current sponsor – University of Westminster, School of Computer Science and Information Systems Engineering, for its support.

References

[1] Bigelow, J., "Hypertext and CASE", In: IEEE Software, Vol. 5, No. 2, pp. 23-27, March, 1988.

[2] Collofello, James S. and Orn, M., "A Practical Software Maintenance Environment", In: Proceedings of IEEE Conference on Software Maintenance, pp. 45-51, Phoenix, Arizona, October, 1988.

[3] Fischer, K.F., Raji, F. and Chrusciki, A., "A Methodology for Re-Testing Modified Software", In: National Telecomms Conference Proceedings, pp. B6.3.1-6, Nov., 1981.

[4] Hartmann, J. and Robson, D.J., "Techniques for Selective Revalidation", In: IEEE Software, Vol. 7, No. 1, pp. 31-26, January, 1990.

[5] Leung, Hareton K.N. and White, Lee J., "A Study of Regression Testing", Technical Report, TR-88-15, Dept. of Computer Science, University of Alberta, Canada, Sept., 1988.

[6] Lewis, R., Beck, D. W., Hartmann, J. and Robson, D. J., "Assay – A Tool To Support Regression Testing", British Telecom Research Lab/Dept. of Computer Science, Durham, Technical Report, 1988.

[7] Liu, L., "A Support Environment for the Management of Software Testing", M.Sc Thesis, Dept. of Computer Science, University of Durham, 1992.

[8] Liu, L., Robson, D.J. and Ellis, R., "A Data Management System for Regression Testing", In: Proc. 1st International Conference on Software Quality Management, pp. 527-539, British Computer Society, Wessex Institute of Technology, Southsampton, March, 1993.

[9] Taylor, Richard N., Belz, Frank C., Clarke, Lori A., Osterweil, Leon, Selby, Richard W., Wileden, Jack C., Wolf, Alexander L., and Young, Michal, "Foundations For The Arcadia Environment Architecture", In: Proceedings of the Third ACM SIGSOFT/SIGLAN Software Engineering Symposium on Practical Development Environments, pp. 1-13, 1988.

[10] Tichy, Walter F., "An Introduction to the Revision Control System", In: Programmer's Supplementary Documents, Vol.1, 4.3 Berkely Software Distribution, Virtual VAX-11 Version, University of California, Berkeley, California, April, 1986.

[11] Yau, S. S. and Kishimoto Z., "A Method for Revalidating Modified Programs in the Maintenance Phase", In: IEEE COMPSAC 87 Int. Conf. Procs., pp.272-277, Tokyo, Japan, 1987.

Experiences with a Federated Environment Testbed

Alan W. Brown, Edwin J. Morris, & Paul F. Zarrella
Software Engineering Institute[1]
Carnegie Mellon University

Fred W. Long
University College of Wales, Aberystwyth

W. Michael Caldwell
U.S. Department of Defense

Abstract: In order to address the question, "What tool integrations are possible for third party tool users given the current state of Commercial Off The Shelf (COTS) tools and integration technology?", a set of tool integration experiments were undertaken. These experiments used existing COTS tool and integration technology to create a loosely integrated toolset supporting a simple process scenario. The experiments demonstrated that tool integration is possible by third party tool users with moderate effort. A set of lessons learned from the experiments is provided, along with potential future directions for this work.

1 Introduction

In assembling a Software Development Environment (SDE) from a collection of COTS tools, third party tool users must find ways to connect the tools such that they provide adequate support for their particular software development approach. This task must take place in the context of limited knowledge of the tools, no access to the source or internal structures of the tools, limited resources with which to perform and maintain the tool connections, and evolving understanding of the needs of the tool users. Such a context places severe restrictions on what can be attempted in terms of tool interconnection. Unfortunately, many organizations have already made significant investments in tools and technologies that are ultimately "disjoint".

On the other hand, COTS vendors are making claims of the "open", "flexible", and "integrated" nature of their products. The ability to connect their tools is viewed as an important marketing need by the vendors, and hence they advertise their services in this area. In addition, a number of "environment framework" technologies are appearing which claim to provide a set of common integration services. However, it is far from clear what can easily be

---

1. This work is sponsored by the U.S. Department of Defense. The views and conclusions are those of the authors and should not be interpreted as representing official policies, either expressed or implied, of the Software Engineering Institute, Carnegie Mellon University, the Department of Defense, or the U.S. Government.

accomplished using these services with current COTS tools, particularly when the tool connections are to be implemented by third party tool users and not the tool vendors themselves. It is also unrealistic to consider that the available vendor-supplied "point-to-point" integrations provide a sufficiently substantive framework within which to begin population of a software development environment.

In order to expand our own expertise in tool integration, and to answer the question "What tool integrations are possible for third party tool users given the current state of COTS tools and integration technology?", we have undertaken a set of experiments. These experiments involved the integration of a collection of common COTS tools with environment framework technologies in support of a typical development scenario.

The experiments are not unique: in fact, a number of larger scale efforts similar in approach are being undertaken elsewhere. However, many of these other efforts are proprietary and therefore the lessons learned are not generally available.

This paper reports on our integration experiments with COTS tools and integration frameworks. We believe that our experiments thus far demonstrate that:

- COTS tool integration is possible by third party integrators requiring a moderate amount of effort.
- COTS tool integration is far from straightforward, and a general, life cycle wide solution seems unlikely.
- the costs and benefits of COTS tool integration must be carefully defined before embarking on large scale COTS tool integration.
- a number of products are available that aid tool integration. They appear to be very promising.

These findings will be discussed in subsequent sections.

2 Motivation

The SEI has a long standing interest in the integration of tools into SDEs [Dart 87, Feiler 88, Wallnau 91, Brown 92]. The experiments discussed in this report compliment this earlier work and are motivated by the desire to:

1. Determine what types of third party tool integration are currently realistic.
2. Investigate the practicality of "Federated Environments" [Wallnau 91].
3. Exercise framework technologies in order to become more familiar with these capabilities.

4. Investigate the potential of combining control with data integration capabilities in support of a process scenario.

These motivations will be discussed in subsequent sections.

2.1 Third Party Tool Integration

Software engineering organizations employ a wide variety of tools in support of unique processes and methods. Tool support often includes COTS tools interacting with a number of locally produced ("home grown") tools. The practical software engineering environments produced by organizations which are primarily users of tools must integrate both COTS and home grown tools utilizing the limited resources and techniques normally available.

In order to accurately represent the sort of third party integration that is common in such commercial and government communities, we set a number of "ground rules" for our integration experiments. These ground rules include:

- The tool versions chosen were not to be constructed so as to take advantage of framework capabilities. We believe this reflects the reality of the present tool marketplace, with non-integrated existing tools and relatively unproven framework capabilities. Interestingly, while we were working on the tool integration, a version of a COTS tool (PROCASE SMARTsystem) which claimed to be integrated with a framework product (Hewlett Packard SoftBench) became available. Still, such tool and framework integrations are not common.
- No modifications could be made to source code of a COTS tool, even if source were available. A few organizations with which we have spoken have modified COTS tool source code. It is our contention, however, that only the largest organizations are able (often reluctantly) to accept the configuration and maintenance costs associated with modifying COTS tool source code. This ground rule does not preclude the use of the extensive tailoring facilities offered by many tools. In fact, such tailoring (often by updating start-up files, or building custom user interfaces) is encouraged as a way of taking maximum advantage of tool capabilities.
- The integration was driven by a simple process scenario. The process scenario aided us in two ways: it reflected a type of integration that organizations commonly want, and it provided a blueprint for integration decisions.
- The integration experiments represented a relatively low to moderate investment in resources beyond those already allocated for purchase of the various tools. In our experience, a large scale tool integration effort at an organizational level can quickly become prohibitively expensive and complex. Our approach was to attempt a less extensive level of integration that may be possible at a project level.

- We made use of tool-provided capabilities for developing the system wherever possible. Thus, for example, we used the SoftBench Encapsulator tools to build a browser capability for the Emeraude Portable Common Tool Environment 1.5 V12 (PCTE) [2]database.

2.2 Federated Environments

In assembling the COTS tools we have attempted to expand and validate the notion of a "federated environment" as described in earlier papers [Wallnau 91, Brown 92]. A federated environment views the facilities of an SDE as a set of services (figure 2-1).

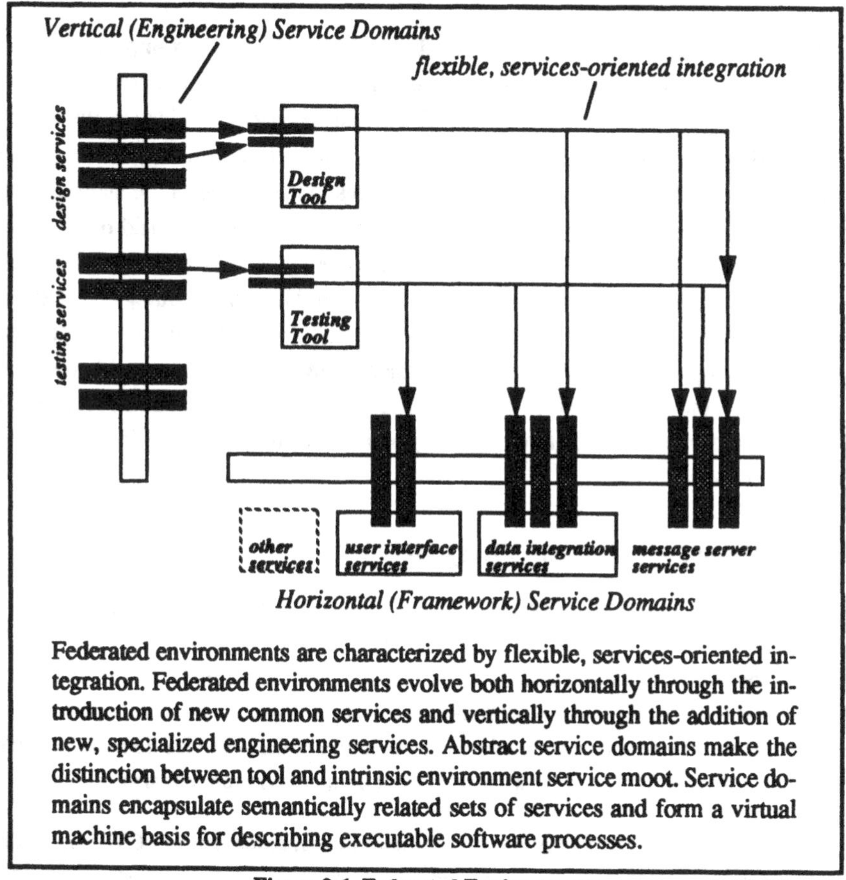

Federated environments are characterized by flexible, services-oriented integration. Federated environments evolve both horizontally through the introduction of new common services and vertically through the addition of new, specialized engineering services. Abstract service domains make the distinction between tool and intrinsic environment service moot. Service domains encapsulate semantically related sets of services and form a virtual machine basis for describing executable software processes.

Figure 2-1 Federated Environments

---

[2] For our experiments we used Emeraude PCTE 1.5 V12. This implementation supports a version of the PCTE interface specification that differs considerably from that endorsed by the European Computer Manufacturers Association (ECMA). Unfortunately, no implementation of ECMA PCTE is available. However, we believe that many of the lessons learned from our experiments with Emeraude PCTE 1.5 V12 are applicable to future ECMA PCTE implementations.

These services support some particular aspect of software development (e.g., design, coding, testing), or provide a framework capability (data integration, message server, user interface). Services are federated in the sense that they are essentially autonomous — a single service can be extended, replaced, or removed without unduly affecting the other services.

Clearly, there will be relationships between services as a consequence of a particular development scenario that is being supported. For example, the coding and testing services may interact when an error is detected in a piece of code. The exact nature of this interaction is a consequence of the particular development scenario, and should not be predefined within any of the services.

In our integration experiments, we viewed individual COTS tools as examples of Vertical Service providers and framework capabilities as examples of Horizontal Service providers. An immediate question to be addressed was whether the interfaces provided by the individual tools and frameworks could provide an initial but useful level of integration following the Federated model. A secondary but also critical question was whether the interfaces provided by different tools or frameworks of a particular service domain would be consistent enough to allow the relatively straightforward replacement of a tool/framework with another tool or framework of the same service domain. The problem of providing consistent interfaces between tools of the same type is being addressed by a number of groups, including CASE Communique, CASE Interoperability Alliance, and the ANSI technical committee X3H6, but tool conformance can be expected to lag far behind any standard developed. In the interim, experiments similar to the ones reported in this paper can provide an independent test of proposed interfaces.

2.3 Combining Control and Data Integration

Control integration (communication between tools in order to initiate, sequence, and terminate actions) and Data integration (sharing and interoperability of data across tools) are two forms of tool interaction that have received considerable attention [Thomas 91]. While strong support for Control or Data integration in isolation would no doubt facilitate tool integration, it is becoming apparent that the inter-operation of these service domains provides a potential for greater tool integration in support of a process driven scenario.

For instance, [Oquendo 89] identified the usefulness of an extension to PCTE supporting control integration. This extension allowed the association of "reactions" with PCTE "events". Reactions allowed user-specified processing following events such as access to the object base or PCTE process start-up and termination. [Oliver 91] discussed a re-implementation (or porting) of the SoftBench Broadcast Message Server (BMS) using the services provided by the PCTE implementation. In this implementation, the BMS actually runs as a PCTE process and uses the PCTE inter-process communication mechanism to communicate with other tools.

In our experiments, we were interested in the possibilities of a "loose" integration of the control integration capabilities of the BMS with the data integration capabilities of PCTE. In keeping with a third party strategy, a loose integration would require no changes to the source code of either framework, and would be accomplished using integration capabilities provided by PCTE and SoftBench BMS as much as possible.

2.4 Exercise Framework Technologies

A major goal for the SEI CASE Environments project is to improve our understanding of the current capabilities and limitations of framework technologies. Such technologies will eventually require major reworking of tools in order to take maximum advantage of their integration possibilities.

Of immediate interest was whether there was some advantage in utilizing environment framework technology today for integrating tools that are not designed to use framework capabilities. Such loose integration could potentially provide a degree of integrated process support while providing a useful mechanism to learn about the technologies. Experience with loose integrations may also simplify the eventual migration toward more tightly integrated tools and frameworks. A related interest involved the comparison of the short term costs and benefits of using control versus data integration framework capabilities to integrate today's tools.

Since framework technologies are so new and organizations have so little experience integrating tools into these frameworks, guidelines and conventions for tool-framework integration do not exist. Such guidelines and conventions will be at least as critical for consistent and successful SDE integration as similar rules are today when building tools to a specific operating system. We hope experiments exercising framework technology can begin to identify necessary guidelines and conventions.

Finally, it was expected that an exercise involving framework technologies could aid in the identification of the tool support that is necessary in order to make effective use of the technologies. Tools such as schema editors, database navigators, and screen painters are just now being conceived and developed.

3 A Federated Environment Testbed

To validate federated environment concepts, a testbed was assembled using COTS tools and framework products as examples of service providers. A process controller was built to provide a process service and to implement our test scenario. The services identified as necessary for our experiments are identified in figure 3-1. The federated environment testbed is discussed in subsequent sections.

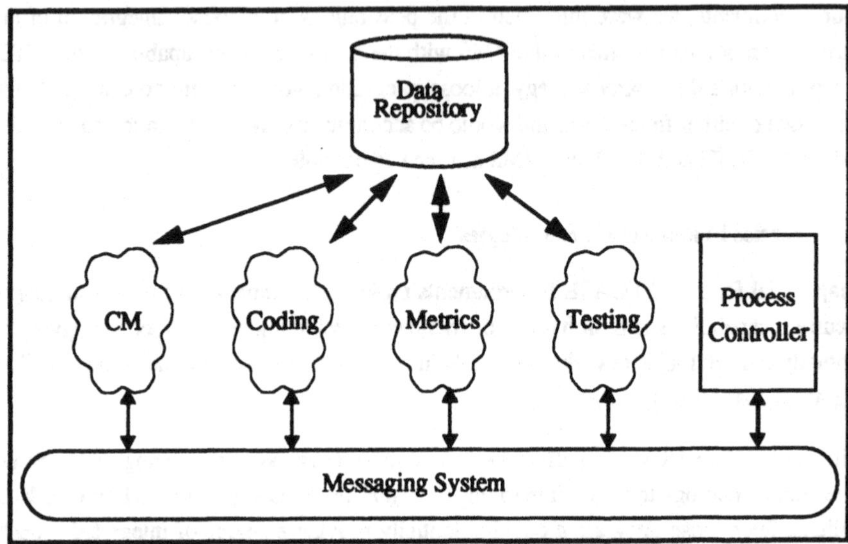

Figure 3-1 System Service Architecture

3.1 Scenario

The focus of the experiment was to highlight and examine the activities involved in integrating a variety of tools supporting the software development life cycle, initially concentrating on coding activities[3]. Therefore, in order to concentrate on the aspects of the integration itself (as opposed to the resulting functions of the integration), we developed a simple, single-purpose scenario for the integration experiment. This scenario represents the code and test cycle that is common to development and maintenance activities. Details of the scenario include:

- The starting point of the scenario requires that the source code is under configuration management (CM) control.
- A change to the source is to be made.
- The source module is checked out from CM.
- Check out initiates record keeping.
- Invocation of the coding tool initiates record keeping.

---

3. While our concentration in these experiments is on coding activities, we are aware of the importance of integrating front end analysis and design tools into an environment. Integration of such tools is a particularly challenging problem that we plan to address in subsequent experiments.

- The source is imported into the coding tool for modifications.
- The coding tool termination is trapped, and initiates source check-in to CM along with appropriate record keeping.
- Check-in initiates compiling, linking, and record keeping.
- The object image is checked into the CM.
- Completion of the compile initiates the activities of the testing tool and record keeping.
- The test data and results are checked into CM.
- Completion of testing initiates the metrics tool and record keeping.
- The metric data is checked into the CM tool.

When a new version of the source is checked into the CM tool, compilation, test data generation/execution, generation of metric data, and storing of information back into the CM tool are executed automatically due to messages sent via the message server. In order to implement the scenario within our resource/time limits however, a number of simplifying assumptions were made for the first phase of the experiments, including support for only a single source file, executable, and a single user.

3.2 Encapsulation

The HP Encapsulator is the tool integration facility of the HP SoftBench environment that allows a user to integrate existing tools into the SoftBench environment. The Encapsulator provides the capability to create a BMS message interface for control integration and a Motif user interface that is consistent with other tools in the SoftBench environment. The SoftBench Encapsulator Definition Language (EDL) was chosen for our encapsulations. Alternatively, encapsulations can be created using a C or C^{++} interface to the Encapsulator tool.

The encapsulation approach for a tool is driven by three factors: the type of interface to be provided, the nature of the tool to be encapsulated, and the features that are to be provided in the encapsulated version. Encapsulated tools can be placed into three general categories based upon their interface type and the nature of the underlying tool:

- Encapsulation of a tool with standard input/output and command-line interfaces (with or without modifying the application's source code).
- Encapsulations with no user interface.
- Encapsulations with an existing graphical user interface (requires source code modification).

Encapsulations of the first two categories can be constructed using EDL. Most encapsulations for the experiment fell into these two categories. The PROCASE SMARTsystem encapsulation is a combination of the last two categories. The underlying tool, SMARTsystem, provides a graphical user interface and some command-line options. To avoid modifications to source code, an encapsulation was built to provide a message interface making use of command line functionality, but with no graphical user interface.

The method used in developing encapsulations for the metrics and testing tools proved to be a good general strategy for encapsulating. First, a stand-alone tool with a graphical user interface that accessed the desired functionality of the underlying tool was constructed. This first step provides presentation integration (visual consistency across the tools) and improves the usability of the original tool. As part of this step the functionality may be extended by accessing other encapsulated tools through their message interface. An example of extending functionality by accessing other encapsulated tools can be seen in our access to the static analysis tool from the metrics tool.

Once the stand-alone tool exists, it is desirable to provide a message interface so that other tools may make use of the functionality of the encapsulated tool by deciding on the set of tool services that may be of interest to other tools.

3.3 Messaging Standards

The selection of messages that each tool would send and receive was driven by the functionality of the tool and guided by existing message standards. The message interface of a tool specifies the functionality available to other encapsulated tools. Decisions had to be made as to which interactive capabilities would be useful as non-interactive services.

Each tool that was encapsulated needed one or more "Request" messages to activate it, and at least one "Notify" message to report its completion. In some instances, "Failure" messages were created to report errors. Where SoftBench supplied tools were used, the message interface was already provided. For SCCS, the message interface was also provided via the SoftBench/SCCS integration that comes with SoftBench. For all other tools, including PROCASE SMARTsystem, metrics, Emeraude PCTE, and Software TestWorks, the message interfaces had to be defined. In these cases, the message interfaces were designed in a style consistent with that of existing SoftBench-supplied tool integrations.

3.4 Use of PCTE

In these experiments, PCTE was used primarily to define a repository in which to store tool artifacts, and to provide configuration and version control over those artifacts. Tools were not re-written to take advantage of PCTE services, nor was the structure of a tool's internal data modified or mapped onto PCTE. The data files from individual tools were stored directly as the contents of PCTE file objects. When a tool was to be started, a copy of the data in the PCTE file object was made available to the tool. When the processing of the tool was complete, a new PCTE object was created along with the appropriate links to other objects.

While few PCTE facilities were used in our experiments, the use of PCTE to maintain and relate tool data does provide a measure of traceability between the data (source, object, metrics, test data) and the potential for defining new tools to access the shared data.

To avoid forcing the encapsulation code to be aware of the object type and name in the PCTE Object Management System (OMS), a mapping scheme was developed which allowed the encapsulation code to derive the necessary PCTE OMS information based on a standard file naming convention. This resulted in a message interface to the PCTE encapsulation that supports the same messages as the SCCS and RCS encapsulations. Thus, the CM service can be implemented either by the SoftBench SCCS encapsulation or our PCTE CM encapsulation simply by changing a single entry in a start up file for the experiments. This approach illustrates the potential advantages of a common message standard within a service domain.

3.5 Tools

Before selection of tools to populate the development scenario could begin, several simplifying requirements were first determined. In order to be encapsulated (for integration with the SoftBench BMS, which was chosen as the messaging tool), the tools each had to supply a "command line" or standard input/output (UNIX "stdio") interface. Also, in order to minimize OMS schema requirements (for integration with PCTE, which was chosen as a repository), the tools had to involve a limited number of external files/objects.

According to the development scenario, the tools used would provide support for a "typical" software maintenance function. It was decided that to complete this scenario we would need to employ coding, metrics, testing, and CM tools, along with a message server, and a "process control" tool to control the execution scenario. The tools involved in the scenario would not communicate directly with each other, but only with/through the process controller. In order to utilize the capabilities of PCTE, a simple file transfer mechanism was developed between PCTE and the UNIX file system. Figure 3-2 identifies the tools and framework capabilities necessary to realize the architecture identified in figure 3-1.

Details of the specific tools selected include:

- The message server used would be the SoftBench BMS. As previously indicated, we were particularly interested in understanding the capabilities the BMS could provide.

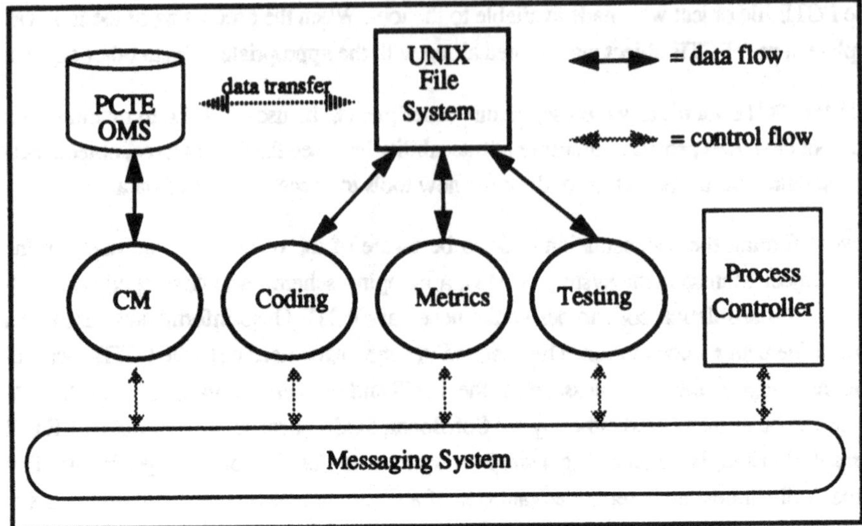

Figure 3-2 Tool and Framework Structure

- The CM tool would be developed in-house, as we did not have access to an existing CM tool that provided an interface to the PCTE OMS. We would use the existing functions built into the PCTE system to provide the fundamental object access facilities. The CM tool encapsulation would then provide the interface to these facilities of the PCTE system (through the Emeraude "esh" utility). The CM tool encapsulation would be driven via BMS request messages to check-in/check-out a particular object from/to the UNIX filesystem. It would then send notification of success/failure via a BMS message. To demonstrate the potential for replacing one instantiation of a service by another, an alternative implementation would use SCCS as a CM capability, with the file system serving as an OMS.

- For coding, we would use the PROCASE SMARTsystem[tm] code management/development system, and the existing "BUILD"/"EDIT" facilities available from SoftBench ("softbuild" and "softeditsrv", respectively). In our scenario, the SMARTsystem tool would be treated as a "black box". That is, we would import the source file into the system, and export back a (possibly) modified version. We were uninterested in the intervening events/functions of the tool. The SMARTsystem tool would be started through the encapsulation as the result of a specific request via BMS. SMARTsystem tool completion (upon user "Quit") would trigger the encapsulation to send a BMS notification message.

- The metrics tool would be developed as a "wrapper" around existing public domain utilities providing McCabe, Halstead, and KDSI metrics, and the SoftBench static analysis tool ("softstatic"). These utilities would be used without modification. The encapsulation would be driven via BMS requests for application of one of the specific metrics. Completion of the metrics operation would then be broadcast via a BMS notification message.

- The testing tool used would be the Software TestWorks[tm] "tdgen" utility from Software Research, Inc. This tool generates test cases that would then be used as test input without requiring any intermediate steps which were "obtrusive" to the scenario (e.g., source code instrumentation, special tool interfaces, complex results analysis). The encapsulation would be driven via BMS request messages to generate test cases (i.e. invoke "tdgen") or to perform test execution. Again, test success/failure would be communicated via a BMS notification message.
- The process control tool would be implemented in house to support our specific process scenario. This tool would provide a "master" user interface to allow testing and fine-tuning of the scenario via manual file check-in/check-out from the CM system, as well as interactive execution of the encapsulated tools that comprised the scenario. In addition, the scenario would be "hard coded" inside the process controller, acting much like a serialized shell script. In this automated mode of operation, the successful completion of one step of the scenario (as indicated by a BMS notification message from an encapsulated tool) would initiate the next step (via a BMS request message from the process controller to an encapsulated tool). The process controller would also maintain the state of the scenario via interaction with the CM tool. Prior to initiating each step of the scenario, the process controller would request check-out of any required objects. As each step was completed, the process controller would request check-in of any resulting objects.

3.6 Approach

The component tools of the experiment were first encapsulated (using the SoftBench Encapsulator) to provide a Motif user interface. The encapsulations were then used for interactive testing and verification purposes. After each supporting piece of the scenario was completed and verified, its message interface was constructed and tested via the SoftBench "MONITOR" facility. Finally, the "process controller" was developed using the SoftBench Encapsulator Definition Language (EDL) language that provided the interface to the component tool encapsulations (via the SoftBench BMS), and which implemented the development scenario. The SoftBench BMS serves as the backbone for the integration.

In parallel with the development of the tools/interfaces, the PCTE OMS schema was designed to support the development scenario. The schema was very closely tied to the scenario as objects and relationships were designed to exactly fit the intended process. Issues of object precedence (for check-in/check-out and linkage) were left to the process controller to coordinate. In order to verify the correct implementation/application of the schema, a general-purpose PCTE OMS "browser" utility was also developed at this time. This utility was used to facilitate traversal of the OMS, and to allow examination of the underlying objects and their attributes.

Since the PCTE-based CM system was being developed in-house, and as it relied upon prior completion of the demonstration schema, it ended up being the last component of the scenario to be completed. However, the CM system was fundamental to the development scenario. In order to check out the interfaces in the interim, the CM system was evolved incrementally. First, a simple UNIX shell script was developed to simulate the check-in/check-out functions of the CM system. The next step was to implement a message interface in order to utilize the SoftBench front-end to the UNIX SCCS version control functions ("softsccs"). This provided a "real" source control facility to the scenario. Finally, the PCTE-based CM system was implemented. Since the messaging format chosen was intentionally identical to that used by SoftBench for SCCS, the PCTE CM system was easily "plugged into" the scenario.

3.7 Effort Expended

The effort expended to complete the experiment was approximately 3 person months (distributed among 5 participants). This included the time spent on selection of tools, and familiarization with PCTE, SoftBench, and COTS tools, but did not include the "front-end" time spent developing the scenario. Prior to the start of the experiment, only one of the participants had any hands-on experience with SoftBench, and only two of the participants had any working knowledge of PCTE. Future efforts can build upon this experience and allow for quicker implementations of the basics of the tool integrations.

4 Lessons from the Experiments

Analyzing the results of our efforts in performing these experiments, we are able to describe a number of lessons from our work.

4.1 The Need for a Tool Builders' Kit

As tool integrators, we ourselves required tools to help us in our task, particularly as the tools with which we are dealing are large and complex. While the tool documentation is useful, it is clear that much more is needed.

1. *Examples, examples, examples.* For much of the work it was important to have examples of encapsulations from SoftBench, and examples of schemas and interface code for PCTE. These were essential in bringing novice users of both of these tools to the point where they could write their own encapsulations and schemas.
   This points to the need for a larger library of examples of both encapsu-

lations and schemas being maintained. For our work we relied on examples provided in the documentation of the tools, some example encapsulations provided with the SoftBench tool, and work by the SFINX project who produced examples and a tutorial introduction to the use of PCTE [Schiavoni 88].

2. *Utilities*. A number of small utilities were developed to help us in our integration work. The most significant of these were to help make PCTE more usable, and to help browse the PCTE OMS.
   The Emeraude PCTE command line interface is quite complex and not particularly intuitive to use. One of our first tasks was to use the SoftBench Encapsulator to develop a graphical front end to the PCTE shell. This provides a much simpler "point and click" interface to many of the most frequent PCTE commands.
   As an extension of this PCTE encapsulation, a browser for the PCTE OMS was developed. While a graphical style of display was investigated, the simplest approach was to extend the PCTE encapsulation to display a list of the names of objects at some point in the object graph. Users browse the OMS by navigating the object graph.[4]

3. *Schema definition tools*. Perhaps the greatest unfulfilled need was for a graphical schema definition tool for use with PCTE. There was significant effort in designing a schema, encoding it in the PCTE data definition language (DDL), testing it for correctness, populating it with instances of the object types, and evolving it as the integration requirements changed. Tools to help in some of these tasks would be essential in any larger scale experiment.

4.2 Situational Selection of Tools

A major tool in our integration work was the Encapsulator that comes with HP SoftBench. In our situation, we found this to be a simple, versatile tool that quickly allowed us to make tool interconnections and provide a graphical interface to command line tools. To relatively inexperienced users of windowing and message passing technology, Encapsulator was of significant assistance, particularly when contrasted with an alternative strategy using low level remote procedure call interfaces for tool interconnection and learning to program in the X-window system.

However, for organizations already familiar with other technology to build graphical user interfaces (GUI Building Tools) and possessing strong knowledge of C or C^{++} and message passing technology, Encapsulator would be of lesser value. The basic BMS capability could be used effectively without Encapsulator (and EDL). In fact, Hewlett Packard is now marketing BMS capabilities without the Encapsulator. This strategy of providing messaging services unbundled from support tools is also being followed by Sun (ToolTalk).

---

4. Details of this PCTE encapsulation will be specified in a subsequent paper.

4.3 Replacing Components

One of the design goals of the experiments was to investigate the notion of a federated environment consisting of service providers communicating through a control-oriented infrastructure. We would hope that providers of any one service are insulated as much as possible from changes in the provider of another service. This separation of SDE components would make the assembly, evolution, and maintenance of an SDE much more flexible.

1. *Service Providers.* The possibility of providing multiple service providers is demonstrated in the CM service area. Here, we have two different implementations of the service providing equivalent functionality. A choice is made at run-time as to which of the two tools actually responds to any CM messages simply by changing a single entry in a start up file.
   The reason that this flexibility is possible is that in any one service area an agreement is made on the exact syntax and semantics of the messages that are sent and received for that service. Without such an agreement the flexibility would be lost.

2. *Process Controller.* In theory the process controller contains all of the scenario-specific information for our experiments. For example, to support a different scenario we would hope that we would simply change the process controller and leave all other components of the testbed unchanged.
   In practice, however, this has proved to be more complex. For example, the schemas that have been implemented in PCTE directly support the particular scenario we followed. It would have been possible to have a much more abstract set of data definitions supporting many related scenarios, but not without losing much of the control and support that detailed data definition provides.

3. *Repository.* The use of PCTE as a repository provides a structured approach to storing objects and their interconnections. As we used few of the facilities provided by PCTE, another E-R-based repository could have been used. In this case it would be necessary to change a number of details in the CM implementation.

4. *Message Services.* The use of SoftBench as a message passing component could also (at least in principle) be replaced by an equivalent product such as Sun's ToolTalk or DEC's FUSE. As discussed in previous sections, the SoftBench utilities of the Encapsulator would have to be replaced by other technologies.

4.4 A "Loose Federation" of Framework Services

There has been much talk of the flexibility and utility of combining a control-oriented integration product such as SoftBench with a data-oriented integration product such as PCTE as the way forward for a comprehensive tool integration strategy. While this approach has been widely discussed in abstract terms, there have been few reported instances of implementations applying this strategy. Where it has been tried [Oliver 91], it has been a "tight federation" of the two approaches — SoftBench was re-implemented to take advantage of the message queue facilities of PCTE. While this is a suitable approach to architecting a new integration product, it is clearly not an approach that could be easily accomplished by a third party integrator. Hence, the approach we have taken can be described as a "loose federation" of the two approaches — neither SoftBench nor PCTE has been amended.

The lesson from our experiments is that a loose federation of control-oriented and data-oriented integration approaches is both feasible, and provides benefits to an end-user organization. In particular, a loose federation allows tools built for either SoftBench or PCTE to co-exist without having to change the tools. In comparison to a tight federation, we also have the advantage that we can move from one implementation of PCTE to another when new, higher performance implementations are made available. As the current implementation of SoftBench does not allow multiple users to share a single instance of the BMS, we also found that we could make use of PCTE as a controlled repository for data sharing that provides some of the necessary synchronization between users (through the permissions, locking, and transaction facilities offered by PCTE).

4.5 The Problems of Scaling Up

The integration work that we have carried out are experiments to examine what is currently possible as a third party integrator. There is no intention that these experiments be used as, or evolve into, a usable production system. However, for such a system to be built we would have to address a number of limitations with the experiments we carried out.

1. *Multi-user.* While the use of PCTE facilitates synchronization of simultaneous access to data by multiple users, this aspect of SDE use was not considered in detail as part of our experiments. The data locking implemented in both SCCS and PCTE would prevent attempts to simultaneously update a data item, but when the scenario is expanded to consider the complex interactions that take place in a large, multi-person project, there may a considerable burden on the development of the process controller code.

2. *More extensive scenario.* Expanding the scenario to cover more of a typical development life cycle would have a significant impact on the experiments. One particular problem would be the design and evolution of the necessary PCTE schema. The problems of developing a large schema for a software engineering application should not be under estimated [Penedo 91].

3. *Broader set of services.* Adding a broader set of services to the experiments (e.g., requirements tools and design tools) would naturally increase the complexity of the integration work. However, we have no reason to believe that this increased work would be out of proportion with the ef-

forts required for the existing tools. However, the process controller code may become significantly more complex when its coordination role is greatly expanded to deal with a larger number of tools.

4.6 Relationship of the Filestore to the OMS

Typical of most SDEs will be the use of a wide range of tools with very different architectures. In particular, some tools will be implemented to work directly with the filestore through the operating system interface, some tools will implement their own structured data repositories, and others will expect a structured data repository to exist within the SDE. Typical of this last category of tools will be those built to interface with the OMS of PCTE. As a result of this hybrid arrangement of data storage mechanisms, a number of problems came to light.

1. *Naming*. Within the UNIX filestore and the PCTE OMS there are different constraints and conventions concerning the naming of data items. While some of these are more annoying than substantial problems, the differences can lead to more complicated data processing logic in some programs, misunderstanding and confusion in some control logic, and subtle interference problems that are difficult to detect.
   One particular issue is the extent to which the different external data names are evident to end-users of the SDE. In some cases we found it unavoidable to make the users aware of the different naming syntaxes.

2. *When and where to transfer*. Due to maintaining information in different repositories, the issue of duplication and data transfer arose. For example, in order for the source code to be edited, compiled, and built we had to decide which tools should perform these tasks — SMARTsystem, SoftBench, and UNIX each have editors, compilers, and build tools. The overlap of functionality, and the different storage approaches maintained, led to interesting decisions about what data is moved from where and when to allow the tools to operate on it.

3. *Permissions*. Access to data is controlled in each of the tools. However, each can have its own approach to allocating and supporting permissions on the data. For example, PCTE has a notion of a registered PCTE user, while UNIX has its own notion of a registered user. It may seem a sensible approach to have the UNIX notion of a user correspond to actual project members ("alan", "fred", and so on), while PCTE users correspond to project roles ("administrator", "developer", and so on). However, when information is transferred from PCTE's OMS to the UNIX filestore, care has to be taken to ensure that user/group/world permissions are set up correctly. It is tempting (but clearly unacceptable) to make all data readable and writable by everyone!

4.7 Potential Inflexibility in the OMS

Even our limited experience with PCTE pointed out a potential for inflexibility in the OMS. In our experience (later verified by a PCTE expert), the data schema chosen tends to be closely related to the process being supported. The tight coupling of the process and the data schema increases the difficulty of changing either the process or the schema. It may also increase the difficulty of creating and modifying "generic" schemas.

It is probable that tight coupling of the process scenario and data schema are an intrinsic problem of integrated environments. This problem increases the need for tools to support rapid process modeling, process instrumentation, and schema generation.

5 Conclusions and Future Work

From our experiences, it is clear that some degree of COTS tool integration by third party integrators is possible using new framework products like SoftBench and PCTE. Integration is possible in support of relatively small, well defined tasks within the software life cycle.

However, COTS tool integration is not a straightforward task. While a degree of success can be had integrating a small number of tools into a tight scenario, it is likely that a more general, life cycle wide solution would exceed the means of most third party integrators. A more general environment to support the full software life cycle would most likely require extensive tool modification to make better use of the services provided by SoftBench and PCTE. In summary, we have concluded that:

- Loose integration of COTS tools is possible by third party integrators able to expend a moderate amount of effort. The relatively simple level of integration achieved required approximately three man months effort.
- Tight integration of existing tools to produce an environment that covers a large portion of the life cycle seems unlikely. Before life-cycle integration is achievable, modifications must be made to COTS tools in order to make tool data and processing more accessible to other tools.
- The costs and benefits of COTS tool integration must be carefully defined before embarking on large scale COTS tool integration. The experiments suggest that even small scale enhancements to the integrated toolset could be prohibitively expensive.
- A number of products are available that aid tool integration. They appear to be very promising. However, few organizations have experience with these products. Tool support and guidelines for use of framework products are lacking.

The CASE Environments project commands neither the resources nor the desire to develop a large scale environment. However, these experiments have provided a number of useful lessons and will likely be continued. A number of potential future directions for this work have been identified. These include:

1. *Add a design service.* A design service, represented by a tool such as Software through Pictures, Teamwork, or ObjectMaker would provide a commonly desired and more complete integration scenario. However, a design service would stress the integration scenario since representative tools have extensive and complex internal databases. Integrating a design tool might also require more extensive message passing to transmit information about the internal state of the tool while it is operating. It is also unclear whether common services to support a variety of design tools can be identified.

2. *Evaluate ToolTalk in place of SoftBench.* A number of technologies similar to SoftBench are available. ToolTalk, one such technology, is available as part of Sun OpenWindows 3.0. ToolTalk is a low cost product (assuming an organization is using OpenWindows 3.0, access to ToolTalk can be had for the cost of documentation) that claims to provide messaging between processes (a la SoftBench) as well as object oriented access to data. However, ToolTalk does not provide the support for user interface generation available via SoftBench's Encapsulator. ToolTalk also does not provide ready-made integrations to tools such as editors, compilers, and SCCS. These features were used heavily in our integration experiments. Nevertheless, It would be interesting to evaluate the additional capabilities provided by the object orientation and the potential impact of these capabilities on the service model.

3. *Investigate the potential for common schemas.* Before any serious, large scale integration can occur with PCTE, a number of common schemas must be developed toward which tool builders can aim their products. These schemas will allow for the interoperability of data within and across tool types. The presence of common schemas and tools built to utilize them will potentially allow for quicker and more complete integration of tools. An interesting activity entails investigation of how (and whether) common schemas can be developed that support a wider range of tool types and process scenarios.

4. *Construct a schema design front end from a tool supporting entity-relationship (ER) modeling.* The design and generation of even an extremely simple schema proved to be time consuming for naive users of PCTE. In order for third party integrators to efficiently design schemas to address their unique needs, better tool support for schema design is necessary. PCTE (both PCTE 1.5 and ECMA PCTE) schemas are in essence ER models of the database. A potential approach to creating better tool support for schema design involves extending the capabilities of current ER modeling tools to diagram PCTE schemas and generate the associated DDL. The resulting schema modeling and generation tool may simplify schema definition and potentially open PCTE to more users.

5. *Analyze other possibilities for the process controller*. The process controller used in the experiments made use of the SoftBench EDL language. However, in order to remove this dependance on SoftBench and potentially treat process control as an additional service, other process definition languages could be investigated. In the short term, a chosen process definition language may need to be compilable to languages like EDL. A related area of interest is the potential for moving from an early binding language (like EDL) to a later binding language. Early binding languages, while tending to be efficient, must make a large number of decisions early in the code generation process, and therefore tend to lead toward inflexible execution of the resulting system. Later binding languages, on the other hand, have the advantage of providing a greater degree of flexibility. Previous work at the SEI has found that inflexibility of process control has been a significant problem for earlier environment efforts. Ideally, some degree of flexibility of process control would be maintained up to the actual point of use of a specific system capability. A late binding process control language may assist in working toward the ideal situation.

6. *Analyze the CM service implications*. The experiments undertaken identified a number of potential problems with the use of PCTE as CM system in support of a federated approach to tool integration. A particularly difficult problem involved the determination of an appropriate transaction model. A potentially fruitful investigation would relate the experiences from our experiments with the CM service model under investigation in the CASE Environments project [Dart 92].

In related work, the SEI CASE Environments project is investigating the current industry best practice in integrating tools. A number of larger scale tool integration efforts have been identified, but a surprisingly small number have actually made their way into organizational use. The identification of best practices today and the complete requirements for an SDE in the future remain viable areas of study. By our experiments with current and emerging technology, we are attempting to assist in a small way with the transition of SDE technology into practice.

Acknowledgments

We are grateful for the excellent comments on previous drafts of this paper from Anthony Earl, Herm Fisher, Bob Ekman, and Marv Zelkowitz.

We would also like to thank our sponsor for continuing support of our work in configuration management and environment technology.

References

[Brown 91] Brown, Alan W. *A Critical Review of the Current State of IPSE Technology* (CMU/SEI-91-TR-29). Pittsburgh, Pa. Software Engineering Institute, Carnegie Mellon University. October 1991.

[Brown 92] Brown, Alan W. & Feiler, Peter H. *The Conceptual Basis for a Project Support Environment Services Reference Model.* (CMU/SEI-92-TR-2). Pittsburgh, Pa. Software Engineering Institute, Carnegie Mellon University. January 1992.

[Dart 92] Dart, Susan, *The Past, Present, and Future of Configuration Management* (CMU/SEI-92-TR-8). Pittsburgh, Pa. Software Engineering Institute, Carnegie Mellon University. July 1992.

[Dart 87] Dart, Susan; Ellison, Robert; Feiler, Peter; & Habermann, A. Nico. *Software Development Environments* (CMU/SEI-87-TR-24). Pittsburgh, Pa. Software Engineering Institute, Carnegie Mellon University. November 1987.

[Feiler 88] Feiler, Peter; Dart, Susan & Downey, Grace. *Evaluation of the Rational Environment.* (CMU/SEI-88-TR-15). Pittsburgh, Pa. Software Engineering Institute, Carnegie Mellon University. July 1988.

[Oliver 91] Oliver, Hugh. "Adding Control Integration to PCTE" pp. 69-80. in *Software Development Environments and CASE Technology, European Symposium, Königswinter, Germany, June 1991*, A. Endres and H. Weber, eds. Springer-Verlag, LNCS Vol. 509. 1991.

[Oquendo 89] Oquendo, Flavio; Zucker, Jean-Daniel; & Tassard, Guy; "Support for Software Tool Integration & Process-Centered Software Engineering Environments." *Third International Workshop on Software Engineering and its Applications Proceedings*. Toulouse, France. December 1990.

[Penedo 91] Penedo, M.H. & Shu, C. "Acquiring Experiences with the Modeling and Implementation of the Project Life Cycle Process: the PMDB Work". *Software Engineering Journal*, 6, 5. September 1991. 259-274.

[Schiavoni 88] Schiavoni, Luciano; Mancini, Marina; Bux, Giuseppe & Le Saint, Gilles. "A Comprehensive Introduction to the Portable Common Tool Environment". SFINX Consortium, ESPIRIT Project 1262 (1229). March 1988.

[Thomas 89] Thomas, Ian. "PCTE Interfaces: Supporting Tools in Software Engineering Environments." *IEEE Software*, 6, 6. Nov 1989. 15-23.

[Thomas 92] Thomas, Ian. & Nejmeh, Brian. A. "Definitions of Tool Integration for Environments." *IEEE Software*, 9, 2. Mar 1992. 29-35.

[Wallnau 91] Wallnau, Kurt. & Feiler, Peter. *Tool Integration and Environment Architectures* (CMU/SEI-91-TR-11). Pittsburgh, Pa. Software Engineering Institute, Carnegie Mellon University. May 1991.

Observations on Object Management Systems and Process Support in Environments

Ian Thomas

Software Design & Analysis Inc., 444 Castro St., Suite 400,
Mountain View, California 94041, USA
thomas@sda.com

Abstract. During the development of a schema design method for a data management system for a software engineering environment, we observed that we were making software process decisions at schema design time. The code of tools would embody aspects of the schema design, and hence the software process assumptions made at schema design time. If this observation is generally true, then we must either begin to develop new data management systems which do not force binding of software process decisions at schema design time, or recognize explicitly that designing a schema is designing, or at least constraining, a software process.

1 Introduction and Overview

It has been accepted for some time (at least in the software engineering community) that data management systems for software engineering environments (SEEs) have different requirements from other application domains for database technology. This has resulted in many proposals for data management systems.

More recently, there have been suggestions that we evolve from a data-centered view of environments to a process-centered view [SHY89]. This evolution raises the question of whether object management systems should be designed differently for process-based environments from the way in which they are designed for data-centered environments. Will object management systems for process-centered environments require new features?

Emmerich et al [EMME92] assert that "suitable databases for process-centered environments do not yet exist". Their arguments include a need for more flexible transaction models than are found in some of today's object management systems and a need for finer levels of granularity for the explicit data representation.

This paper hypothesizes one way in which object management systems should support process-based environments that is different from the reasons usually cited. The hypothesis was developed by looking at how one object management system, the PCTE OMS [ECMA90], is actually used. We then tested the hypothesis on another object management system, a commercially available object-oriented database (OODB).

We arrived at the hypothesis by developing a schema design method for the PCTE OMS. While we were doing schema design we observed that: we were making software process decisions at schema design time; and tool code depends on these process-related schema design decisions.Neither of these seem desirable dependencies, since we would like to be able to develop tools and schemas that can be used in a wide range of processes.

It also seemed that the reasons for these dependencies were not PCTE-specific. The chain of reasoning that leads to this conclusion is that most sophisticated SEE object management systems define units, for example, the collection of data that can be versioned together. Designing a schema involves making decisions that are imposed by the definition of units in the object management system, and these are process decisions. The code of the tools assimilates these process assumptions and depends on them. These characteristics seem to be typical of many of today's object management systems. In order to check that, we looked at the schema design process for an OODB.

Our results lead us to the hypothesis that today's object management systems force us to bind some process decisions too early, often at tool construction and/or schema design time, rather than at tool installation or process construction time.

This paper describe the analysis and evidence that lead to the development of this hypothesis. It describes how it was tested on an object-oriented database management system. It ends with a discussion of the consequences on SEE data management systems if this hypothesis is generally true.

2 Object Management Systems for SEEs Define Units

Data management systems for SEEs define units. A unit here is a collection of data identified as a conceptual entity in the Application Programmer's Interface (API) to the data management system, and supported by the operations of the API. For example, an API that provides a checkout operation for certain sorts of defined collections of instance data identifies that sort of collection as a unit of data which can be versioned.

There are different sorts of units (collections of instance data) that are commonly defined for SEE data management systems:

- identity:

  The unit of identity is the collection of data that has a single unique identification. This is similar to the concept of object identity in object-oriented databases, as described in the Object-Oriented Database Manifesto [ATKI89]. References to elements of the collection are with respect to its unique identification. When the unique identification becomes invalid (object deletion), references to all elements of the collection of data become invalid.

- locality:

  Data in large-scale SEEs is distributed. The unit of locality is the collection of data that is guaranteed to be physically located together (the data is always co-located, rather than as an accident of location). For an object management system, we could ask whether parts of the persistent state of an object can be located on distinct machines, or does the object management system require that all of the persistent state be on the same machine. Clearly, this definition needs to be refined for object management systems that support the notion of complex objects (objects constructed from other objects [ATKI89]).

- discretionary access control:

  Access to data in a SEE will depend on permissions given to individual users, user groups (fulfilling roles), and maybe program groups. The unit of discretionary access control is the collection of data that share the same access permissions in all cases, which may be different from the access permissions of other collections. For example, suppose an object management system defines the unit of discretionary access control to be an object together with all of its attributes. This means that a single object can not have two attributes for which the environment builder using the object management system wants to specify different access permissions.

  Some systems may also support type-level discretionary access controls. The PCTE OMS has a notion of usage modes for types in schemas [ECMA90], and Kelter [KELT92] has examined a generalization of this mechanism to use similar discretionary access control mechanisms for both objects and types.

- mandatory access control:

  In some environments there will be a need to support mandatory access controls on access to data (defined as the means of restricting access based on the sensitivity of the information contained in the objects). The unit of mandatory access control is the collection of data that share the same mandatory access permissions (which may be different from the mandatory access permissions of other collections).

- concurrency control:

  SEEs support multiple users and multiple processes (executing programs). The users and processes compete for data accesses. The unit of concurrency control is the collection of data that can be locked or otherwise protected against corruption by unmanaged and incompatible concurrent access. For example, if some of the attributes of an object are locked in a transaction, is it possible for another process to access other attributes of the same object?

  This definition focuses on locks held by executing programs (locks which cease to exist when the executing program ceases to exist). A similar definition for a unit can be produced for the notion of persistent locks.

- versioning:

  SEE data management systems must be able to create copies of collections of data each of which is a "version" of the same abstract object. An API may support an operation to create a new copy of such a collection. The unit of versioning is the collection of data for which it is possible to create a copy representing a new version. The new version preserves the internal structure and information (at least) of the original collection.

  This definition merges discussion of versioning and copying. In some systems it may be appropriate to separate these two things and to define a unit of versioning and a distinct unit of copying. For example, the checkout operation may be considered as the creation of a new mutable copy. The effect on the original varies from system to system, but may include making it immutable (stabilization).

When we analyze an object management system using these features, we usually try to identify the smallest definition of units (the smallest collection of data). In systems that support composition of data (for example complex objects) we need to know whether each element of the composite can have independent values for a property (for example, access permissions) or whether the property is defined once for the aggregate and hence, by implication, for all of its elements.

3 An Overview of Two Object Management Systems

We have based this work on two object management systems, the PCTE OMS and a commercially available object-oriented database system. We present a brief overview of each of these to support later discussion.

The PCTE OMS is based on the Entity-Relationship-Attribute model, with objects corresponding to entities, and binary relationships. Object types are organized into a directed, acyclic graph supporting multiple inheritance. A child type inherits the attributes defined on its parent types, and the relationships in which its parent types can participate. There is a pre-defined object type called file that is defined to have contents - a sequence of bytes whose internal structure is not managed by the PCTE OMS. File objects can have other attributes and relationships, and not all objects in PCTE are files or one of its subtypes. There is no direct support for association of user-defined operations with object types.

Relationships may be uni or bi-directional, a bi-directional relationship is a pair of mutually inverse links. Links may have attributes. A link type has characteristics, including its category, that define its semantics for PCTE version operations, transitive locking, etc. A link type may also have the stability property which makes the destination object of instances of the link type immutable (transitive stability makes the destination composite object immutable).

Type information is represented in a metabase that is part of the object base. As PCTE does not assume a global schema for the object base, type information is divided into Schema Definition Sets (SDSs) which are self-contained. Each PCTE process (executing program) has an associated working schema that defines which types in the object base are visible to the process. A working schema is a union of SDSs, created dynamically at process execution time. Each type in a SDS has an associated usage mode. The usage mode indicates the range of operations that are permissible on instances of that type when it is "viewed" through that SDS.

PCTE defines a notion of atomic and composite objects (broadly equivalent to the complex object in the OODB Manifesto). An atomic object is a collection of data with a unique object identifier. It contains the attributes of an object, the contents of the object (if any), the outgoing links of the object, and their attributes. A composite object with root atomic object R is defined as the transitive closure of links of category composition from R (with the internal links between the atomic objects of the transitive closure).

The object-oriented database supports applications written in C++. The data definition language (DDL) used to describe the database structures defines C++ objects, and relationships between C++ objects. The relationships have semantics beyond those that are found in object pointers in C++. Relationship semantics include properties that describe whether versioning, locking, and deletion operations propagate along the relationship. This is similar to the technique proposed by Rumbaugh [RUMB88]. This means that complex objects can be defined by the transitive closure of relationships that have the appropriate values for versioning, locking, and deletion properties.

A DDL description is used to generate a meta-base structure stored in the object base, and stubs that are linked to the application program. The semantics of the relationships are supported by interpretation of the metabase structures, so changes to those properties can be effected without recompiling the application.

Object storage is organized hierarchically. Objects are grouped into containers, containers are grouped into a database, databases are grouped into a federated database. Relationships between objects can cross container and database boundaries.

The table below illustrates the units for the two data management systems.

	PCTE Object Management System	**Object-Oriented Data Base**
identity	A PCTE atomic object	A C++ object, with its attributes
locality	A PCTE atomic object	A container (currently implemented for a database).
discretionary access control	A PCTE atomic object, though the set of its attributes, its contents (if any), the set of its links, and the set of their link attributes may have independent access permissions)	A database
mandatory access control	A PCTE atomic object	Not applicable
concurrency control	A PCTE atomic or composite object; outgoing links can be locked independently	A container; locking an object implies locking its container
versioning	A PCTE composite object	A complex object, with its attributes and internal relationships

4 Schema Design Involves Process Decisions

This section shows an example of how schema design for SEEs requires answers to software process questions by describing part of a schema design method for the PCTE OMS. The method is described more fully elsewhere [BREM92], in this section we focus on the influence of process assumptions on the schema design activity. The questions on process assumptions are raised by the definition of the units managed by the PCTE OMS.

4.1 An Overview of the Schema Design Method

Figure 1 shows an overview of the schema design method using a SADT-like formalism. It shows that the method has four phases:.

- conceptual design;

  This phase is similar to the conceptual design phase for other database applications such as is proposed by Batini *et al* [BATI92] or Teorey [TEOR90]. The phase produces data flow diagrams that identify processes and operations that will operate over data stores. For each data store, there will also be Entity-Relationship-Attribute schemas describing the contents of the data store (with additional constraints that cannot be expressed in the ERA model). The phase also produces a list of groups that perform the processes and operations, a number of representative instance diagrams of the data stores, and before and after instance diagrams for the processes and operations defined on a data store.

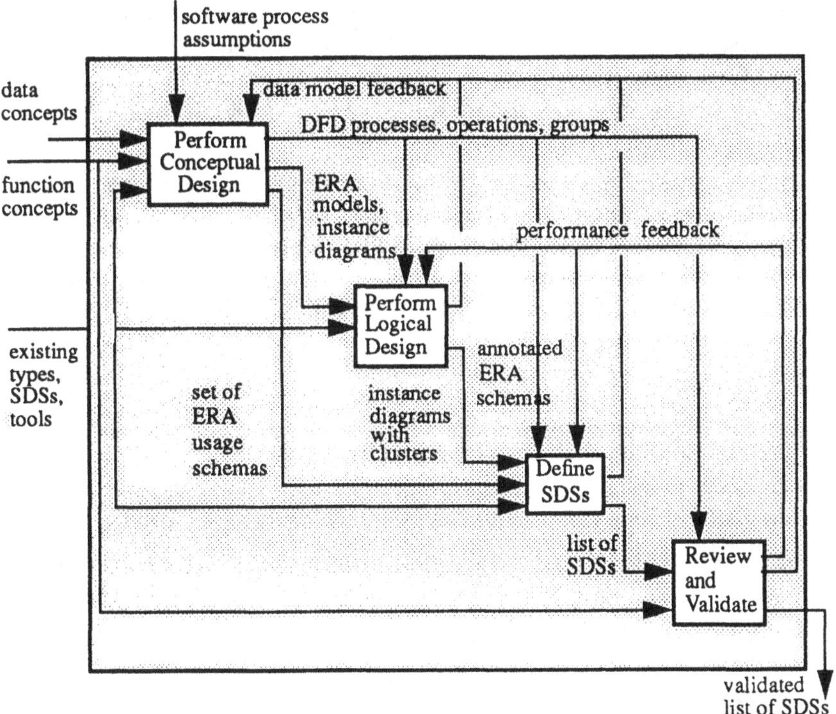

Fig. 1. An Overview of the Schema Design Method

Although the conceptual design phase is similar to the conceptual design phase for other database applications, there are some differences. The first is that we know that we are not doing schema design for a whole application in the sense that we are defining the schema for only some small part of the software process, not the whole process. This leads us into a slightly different definition (in the data flow diagrams) of the interfaces of the system we are modeling, and different questions that are asked about the interface. The second difference is that we place a great emphasis on the identification of different data stores. Since the processes and operations for one data store could be different from the processes and operations on another, even though they contain what seems to be identical information, the data stores could end up with different PCTE schemas. The third difference is a strong focus on identifying the groups that will perform processes and operations. These groups represent roles in the software process, and will eventually become discretionary access groups in the PCTE model. We need to know which groups perform which processes on which data stores so that we can manage the allocation of type information to different PCTE Schema Definition Sets (SDSs) with different access permissions (to take advantage of type-level access controls).

- logical design;

  This phase maps the ERA models developed in conceptual design into PCTE schemas. This means that the ERA schemas are refined and annotated with PCTE specific information. For example, in this phase we decide whether a relationship in the ERA model is to be represented as a PCTE link type or a PCTE relationship type, we decide on the categories of link types (which determine many aspects of their semantics), we decide on which of the predefined PCTE types is to be used for an attribute, etc. The result of this phase is an annotated ERA schema for each data store.

  It is during this phase that we see the greatest influence of software process assumptions on schema design (even though the assumptions were captured by the conceptual design phase). Because of the fact that the PCTE OMS supports certain process-related units, we are obliged to ask process-related questions during this phase, and the answers to these questions affect the schema. We discuss this in more detail in Section 4.2 "The Logical Design Phase.".

- definition of SDSs;

  This phase takes the annotated ERA schemas from the logical design phase and distributes this typing information into a number of PCTE Schema Definition Sets (SDSs). The results of the phase are a set of SDSs, with usage mode information for the types, access permissions required for the SDSs for users, user groups, and program groups.

  There are a number of factors that influence this distribution of typing information into SDSs: the usage modes that processes and operations require on the types, the access permissions that are appropriate for data accessed through a SDS, the availability of existing and standardized SDSs, etc.

- review and validation;

  This phase validates the whole collection of design choices made during the earlier parts of the design process. A key element of this validation is analysis of performance.

  In the design of the method, we have attempted to move review and validation questions into the phase where the decisions that most affect them are made. We have also tried to ensure that the answers to these questions are the right ones by designing a method that ensures the correct answers ("correct by construction" ideas).

4.2 The Logical Design Phase

The ERA models that are produced during the conceptual design phase show groupings of information into entities with attributes, and relationships between them (which may also have attributes). One of the first tasks in the logical design phase is to ensure that the groupings of information in the ERA models conform to the collections of data (units) that are supported by the PCTE OMS. This task will probably lead to a refinement of the ERA model.

The principal technique used in this ERA model refinement task is study of instance diagrams. The conceptual design phase produces instance diagrams conforming to the ERA model for a data store. It also produces before and after versions of these instance diagrams for processes and operations. We use these to identify boundaries around information in the instance diagrams. These boundaries define:

- clusters of information that are always versioned together, and may be versioned at different times from other clusters in the instance diagrams. We also identify dependencies between these versioning clusters of the sort: Cluster A can be versioned independently of Cluster B, but versioning of Cluster B always implies versioning of Cluster A.
- clusters of information that share common access permissions, and whose permissions may be different from the access permissions of other clusters. Again, we need to know something of the relationships between clusters, since if cluster B is part of cluster A, changing the access permissions on A may result in changes to the access permissions on Cluster B. We need to carry out two analyses on this subject, the first for discretionary access control, the second for mandatory access control.
- clusters of information that are always stabilized together, and may be stabilized at different times from other clusters. Once again, we need to analyze the dependencies between clusters to determine whether Cluster B can be stabilized independently of Cluster A, but that stabilization of Cluster A always implies stabilization of cluster B. Stabilization of objects in the PCTE OMS means that the objects become immutable.

  The order in which inter-related clusters become stabilized is also significant. The PCTE OMS prohibits the creation of certain sorts of relationships from stabilized (immutable) objects, as the relationships are considered to reflect semantically relevant changes to their origin objects.
- clusters of information that can be locked together, and may be locked while other clusters of data are locked by other PCTE activities. This analysis is more difficult than for the other cases, since it must consider which processes and operations may be simultaneously active (in pairs and groups), then consider the compatibility of lock modes for these processes and operations on clusters of objects.

  The above analysis is for the non-persistent locks that are supported by the PCTE activity mechanism.

Figure 2 shows an example of an ERA model and an instance diagram with versioning cluster boundaries drawn in. Single arrowheads represent cardinality one, double arrow heads represent cardinality many. It represents the following policy decisions on the part of the schema designer (obviously other policy decisions could have been chosen, this is just

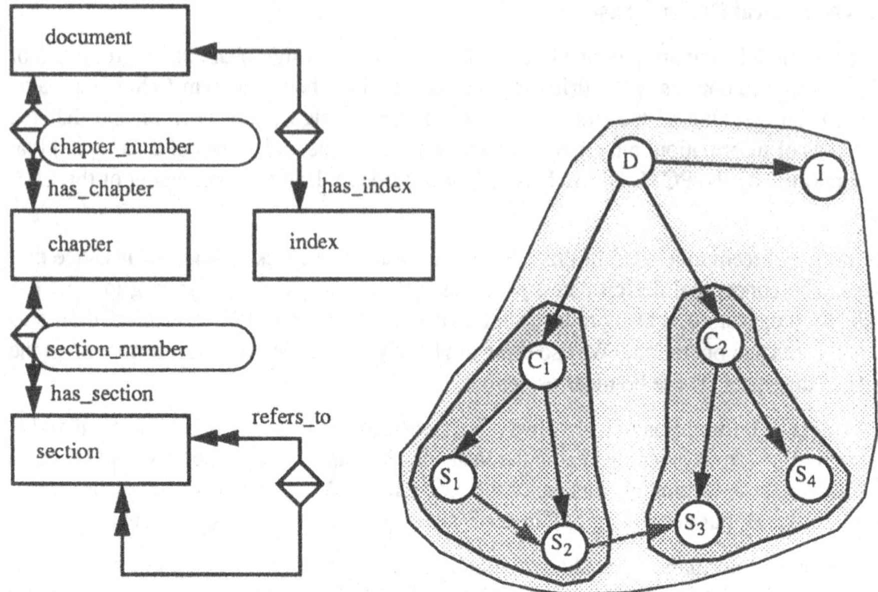

Fig. 2. An ERA Model and Instance Diagram with Versioning Cluster Boundaries

one example):

- versioning of a chapter makes a new version of all of the sections in it. Sections are not versioned independently of chapters;
- versioning of an index is not supported except as part of a new version of a document;
- versioning a document makes a new version of all of its chapters (and therefore their sections), as well as the index.

The purpose of cluster analysis is to make sure that the unit boundaries for the units identified in the schema to support our software process correspond to the unit boundaries for which there is support in PCTE.

There are two sorts of results of the cluster analysis:

- the cluster boundaries do not fall on unit boundaries supported by the PCTE OMS. This should lead to a refinement of the ERA model.

  An example of such a case, reported by James Kiso [KISO91], occurred during the development of PCTE-based tools to support program development and release. A PCTE schema was designed with an object type to represent a program source file. The source file object had two attributes, the text of the program source, and quality assurance metrics for the source text. The data conforming to this schema was intended to be used in the following way. The development team would develop the text of the program source and, at an appropriate time, make a stabilized version of the source of the system for release to the quality assurance team. The QA team is permitted to compute metrics for the source and assign these values to the quality assurance metrics attribute of the source object but is not allowed to change the source text. It became apparent very quickly that the original schema choice of putting the source_text and QA_metrics attributes on the same PCTE object was inappropriate. The reason is that the PCTE unit of stability is the PCTE object. It is not possible, therefore, to stabilize only one attribute of the object (the source_text) and not the other (the QA_metrics attribute). The units identified in the definition of the process did not correspond to the units supported by PCTE for the schema they had developed. Figure 3 shows how this situation would have appeared in a stability cluster diagram.

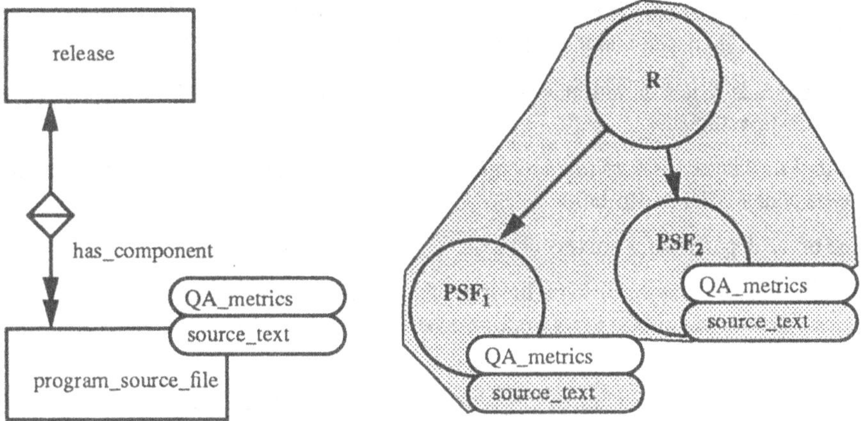

Fig. 3. Stabilization Clusters

- the cluster boundaries fall on the boundaries of units supported by PCTE. No schema refinement is necessary in this case. We use the cluster diagrams later in the logical design phase, however, since we will examine which links cross cluster boundaries, and which are always contained within cluster boundaries, to help establish the categories of PCTE link types.

4.3 Lessons from the Logical Design Phase

We can learn several lessons from the logical design method we have just described. We believe that the lessons have applicability beyond the schema design method for the PCTE OMS in particular.

The first lesson is that the logical design process will lead to schema refinement based on the units supported by the data management system which will be used. The original ERA model which was developed during the conceptual design phase to support the software process is refined.

The second lesson is that the questions that the schema designer needs to ask in order to make sure that the conceptual schema is well-suited to the support offered by the object management system can be legitimately called software process questions. In our method, we draw cluster boundaries around instance data to support answering the questions.

Much work on software process description concentrates on control of actions, and places less emphasis on information access and propagation models for the process descriptions. We have determined that certain sorts of boundaries are important for logical design, and these are determined by the units of the data management system. These data management system units are designed to support and reflect the information access and propagation requirements of software processes.

5 Tools Assimilate Process Assumptions

The tools (implementations of the processes and operations identified during the conceptual design phase) depend on the schema in a number of ways. Some of these are obvious:

- a tool reads/writes an attribute and assumes an attribute name and a particular value type to be returned;
- a tool navigates a link to find an object, and assumes a link name and the number and type of any link key attributes.

Some of the dependencies are less obvious:

- a tool creates an object using a link type that it calls T, and therefore assumes that the link type with that name in its working schema has either existence or composition category;
- a tool navigates along a link of link type T to find an object, and is dependent on having the NAVIGATE usage mode for that link type in its working schema.

These dependencies are built into the code of the tool itself. For the example of the source_text and the QA_metrics attributes, Figure 4 shows the original schema and a sec-

Fig. 4. Schema and Tool Code for Two Attributes on a Single Object Type

tion of tool code to access the QA_metrics attribute (the pathname's reference object "current_source" is assumed to point to an instance of a program_source_file object. Figure 5 shows the refined schema that takes the stability clusters into account by decomposing the original program_source_file object type into two object types. Instances of a program_-source_file object type can then be stabilized at different times from instances of the source_metrics object type. It shows how the tool's code differs from the first case.

It is clear that all tools embody process assumptions. Tools are built to support some activity in one (or preferably many) software processes. For example, a data flow diagram editor makes specific assumptions about the design activity in the software processes within which it will be used. We believe that the dependencies we are discussing here are different from process assumptions resulting from choices of particular engineering methods. We would like to separate the function offered by a tool from decisions about its concurrent use with other tools, which parts of its data we want to version independently, etc.

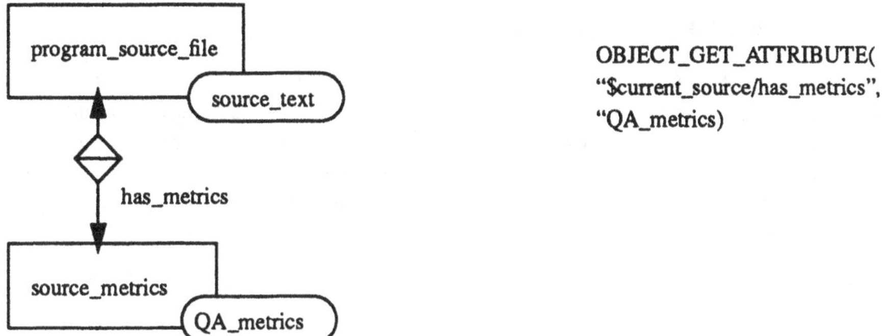

Fig. 5. Schema and Tool Code for Attributes on Two Distinct Object Types

Transparent version management has already received attention as a particular case of this separation of support for tool functionality from software process assumptions. Oquendo et al have defined transparent version management as "tools may execute, refer to objects in the object base, navigate around the object base, etc. without having to explicitly designate the versions of the objects and relationships they wish to follow" [OQUE89]. This paper extends the objectives of this definition. We want to minimize the impact on the schema of the definition of data that we might want to version so as to reduce the impact on tool code. A tool's dependence on process decisions on versioning is currently more subtle than just not representing versions explicitly in the schema

6 Tool Dependency on the Schema Properties is Undesirable

This dependency of a tool on a schema, through the way that its code to access data is written, is undesirable for several reasons:

- a tool writer would like his or her tool to be usable in many processes that have different policies on what is versioned, what is stabilized, which data can be concurrently accessed, etc.;
- a tool writer, and especially an environment assembler, would like the definition of those policies to be "late-bound". The policies should not need to be defined at tool construction time but at tool installation or process construction time;
- a process designer/manager for a software project would like to be able to change the sorts of policy decisions outlined above, preferably dynamically and for existing project data, but certainly without requiring changes to the code of the tool.

Intuitively, it seems reasonable to accept that, when we have a tool that supports data flow design and we wish to change it so that it supports object-oriented design, we will need to make changes to the code of the tool (or replace it). It seems less reasonable to have to make changes to the data flow design support tool when we change our policy on whether to permit concurrent access to parts of a data flow design.

7 A Hypothesis on SEE Object Management Systems

There have been a number of discussions on whether object management systems will need different characteristics as we move towards process-centered environments (see "Object Management Systems and Mechanisms" in [ISPW90], for example). One of the frequently stated requirements is that the object management system not contain any predefined process policies that would constrain the range of processes that it could support. There is an additional requirement that it should be possible to change the process after it has begin execution. Many of today's object management systems for SEEs support these requirements to a reasonable extent.

The hypothesis proposed in this paper is that today's object management systems require tool writers to make process decisions too early (at tool writing time), rather than providing facilities to delay those decisions until tool installation or process construction time.

8 Testing the Hypothesis on an Object-Oriented Database

The hypothesis was constructed on the basis of in-depth experience with, and knowledge of, the PCTE Object Management System, and with some knowledge of other SEE data management systems. In order to test the hypothesis, we have examined whether it holds for an object-oriented database.

The units supported by the object-oriented database have already been described in Section 3 "An Overview of Two Object Management Systems". The presence of three independent properties of a relationship type definition for locking, versioning, and deletion means that there are three different definitions of complex object, according to the operations being invoked on it.

The process of schema design involves analysis (similar to the conceptual design phase for our method). This is followed by the development of a class hierarchy. Relationship types are also defined, as are their properties: cardinality, uni or bi-directional, versioning, locking and deletion propagation. Software process decisions affect schema design in the following ways:

- what is to be versioned together (by deciding the value of the versioning propagation property for relationship types);
- what information is to be locked against concurrent access together. This decision affects two things, the locking propagation property of a relationship type, and the grouping of objects into containers (since locking an object involves locking its container);
- what information has the same access permissions. Logically related information that has different access permissions must be decomposed into two objects in different containers in different databases.

Tools written to use the database assimilate these assumptions. As the class hierarchy is refined and classes decomposed (because we cannot have versionable and shared (non-versionable) properties on the same object, for example), the tool code is different. When a class is decomposed into two related classes, the code to invoke operations on instances of the class will be different. This can be masked in a method, but only in certain cases. It is possible to make a limited number of schema changes without requiring changes to the tool code, as long as the new cluster boundaries fall on object boundaries (this is also the case for the PCTE OMS).

Schema design is influenced by process questions, e.g versioning, that decide properties of relationship types. Nevertheless, there is a separation between the type information for a relationship and some of the properties of the type. In some cases, the properties of a relationship type (for example, whether it propagates versioning operations) can be changed without requiring a change to tool code, or to data already in the object base. This useful capability stems from the way in which the relationship facility is supported, rather than the fact that the database is object-oriented.

A tool's code depends on the schema refinement carried out as a result of software process analysis. It also embodies other process assumptions. One example is that it is possible to give clustering hints to the OODB software when a new object is created. One hint suggests clustering the new object on the same page as another object - a pure performance hint with no relevance for process. The other requests the new object to be placed in a certain container. Because a container is also the unit of concurrency control, the latter is a case where an assumption about concurrent use of data is built into the tool.

The executable of a tool also depends on the schema as it is currently compiled with the tool. This is a technology issue, not a logical model issue, as a dynamic linking solution would avoid this difficulty.

9 Discussion/Conclusions

The usual requirement expressed for object management systems for process-centered environments is that the OMS support modeling of data for whatever process the tool or environment is intended to support. We believe that, for today's OMSs, this allows process decisions to influence the schemas. We believe that tools are built with these schema dependencies hard-coded into them, and that this is undesirable.We therefore need a stronger requirement. We have argued that we need object management systems that limit the influence of process decisions on the schema design process.

Not a single part of this argument or hypothesis depends on the "granularity", coarse or fine, of object level support. The argument is based on the fact that current object management systems define granules (units), they define the semantics of these granules by the support that they provide for them, and the definition of these granules forces process questions to be asked during the schema design process. The argument does not depend on the size of a granule.

If we accept the limitations of current object management systems outlined above, or if it is not possible to invent data management systems that circumvent them, then there are significant consequences for environment frameworks, tools and environments:

- The current plug-and-play objectives for tools in SEEs will succeed only if there is some detailed common agreement about the processes within which the tools will be used. Brown and McDermid [BROW92] have already warned of unrealistic expectations for what can be delivered simply by adoption of common environment framework services, and the need for additional integration agreements. If there are no agreements, this is likely to lead to disappointment about the extent to which it is possible to take tools and use them to support many different software processes;
- Defining standard schemas, a necessary condition to realize the integration benefits of SEE OMSs, implies defining some standard aspects of a process;
- Tool writers will need to make their process assumptions very clear so that it will be easier to tell whether tools can be integrated in the same environment.

If we want to remove the limitations of current object management systems, the next generation of OMS technology should allow late binding of software process decisions, though this will make it harder to develop tools since the tool writer can make fewer assumptions and must do more work to deal with error conditions.

We need OMSs so that process decisions are explicit; do not need to be known by tool writers, are late bound into tools (offering a very wide range of process choices); and do not require changes to tool code/executables when the process changes.

Does OO technology provide a way of solving this problem? The answer seems to be that it is not a sufficient condition. OO technology may support late binding, and therefore provide part of the answer. The classes and interface definitions of an OO schema provide an abstraction (or view) of underlying data representations, but they must be mapped to some data representation that is capable of supporting the locking, access permission, versioning, etc. model supported by the class definition model.

10 Acknowledgments

I would like to thank Christian Bremeau, Alan Brown, Brian Nejmeh, Bill Riddle, and Rick Spickelmier for helpful comments on earlier drafts of this paper.

11 References

[ATKI89] Atkinson M., Bancilhon F., DeWitt D., Dittrich K., Maier D., Zdonik S., "The Object-Oriented Database Manifesto", in Proceedings of the First Conference on Deductive and Object-Oriented Databases, Kyoto, Japan, December 1989.

[BATI92] Batini C., Ceri S., Navathe S.B., "Conceptual Database Design: An Entity-Relationship Approach", Benjamin/Cummings Publishing Co., Redwood City, California, USA, 1992.

[BREM92] Bremeau C., Thomas M.I., "A Schema Design Method for ECMA PCTE", submitted for publication.

[BROW92] Brown A.W., McDermid J.A., "Learning from IPSE's Mistakes", IEEE Software, March 1992.

[ECMA90] "Portable Common Tool Environment (PCTE): Abstract Specification", European Computer Manufacturers Association, December 1990.

[EMME92] Emmerich W., Schaefer W., Welsh J., "Suitable Databases for Process-Centered Environments do not yet Exist", in Software Process Technology, The Proceedings of the Second Workshop, EWSPT '92, Trondheim, Norway, September 1992, Springer-Verlag LNCS 635, Ed. J-C. Derniame.

[ISPW90] Proceedings of the Sixth International Software Process Workshop, Hakkodate, Japan, Oct. 1990, ed. T. Katayama, IEEE Computer Society Press.

[KELT92] Kelter U., "Type-Level Access Controls for Distributed Structurally Object-Oriented Database Systems", to appear in the Proceedings of the European Symposium on Research in Computer Security, Toulouse, France, Nov 23 - 25, 1992 (ESORICS-92).

[KISO91] Kiso J., "Schema Development for HyperWeb", Presentation to the North American PCTE User Group, December 1991.

[RUMB88] Rumbaugh J., "Controlling Propagation of Operations using Attributes on Relations", in Proceedings of OOPSLA '88, in SigPLAN Notices, Vol. 23, No. 11, November 1988.

[SHY89] Shy I., Taylor R.N., Osterweil L.J.,., "A Metaphor and a Conceptual Architecture for Software Development Environments", in Proceedings of the International Workshop on Environments, Chinon, France, September 1989, published as Springer-Verlag Lecture Notes in Computer Science No. 467, ed. Fred Long.

[TEOR90] Teorey T.J., "Database Modeling and Design: The Entity-Relationship Approach", Morgan Kaufman Publishers Inc., San Mateo, California, 1990.

[OQUE89] Oquendo F., Berrada K., Gallo F., Minot R., Thomas I., "Version Management in the Pact Integrated Software Engineering Environment", in Proceedings of the Second European Software Engineering Conference, Warwick, UK, September 1989.

Software Technology

for a Distributed Telecommunication System

Harald Eggers

SIEMENS AG, Public Switching Systems Division
D-8000 Munich 70, Germany

Abstract. Influenced by the progress in the Asynchronous Transfer Mode (ATM) and in high performance RISC processors, the development in telecommunications is recently moving towards distributed message based switching systems. The contribution describes the software technology required for a distributed telecommunication system which is currently being developed under Siemens' Vision O•N•E strategy (Optimized Network Evolution). The key elements of this technology are:

* Visible and efficient design units with standardized standalone interfaces which reduce development cost and time.

* Loosely coupled communication mechanisms so that changes in switch architecture or hardware technology and system upgrades can be performed without disturbing the system.

* A more reliable execution environment that restricts the consequences of software errors to small recoverable units thereby making the switching system more fault tolerant.

1 Introduction

To define the general requirements for current and future switching systems, it is neccessary to consider the interests of network operators and system suppliers.

The network operator purchases services that are then made available to his customers via the switching system. The following criteria are therefore of importance to him:

* Non-stop reliability which can be summed up as "Don't stop the calls and don't lose the money (Billings)"

* Competitive system prices

* Low maintenance costs

* Short lead times for new features from concept phase through to availability in the network

* Fast and simple upgrading to new features

The system supplier designs, markets and maintains the system. In doing so he must address both existing and future requirements, primarily:

* High performance system characteristics

* Competitive edge in the major development costs

* Low maintenance costs

* Lasting competitive edge in system features

The system requirements of both the network operator and the system supplier mainly concern qualitity and cost but also include performance and service competitivenes over a long period with an evolving system. These common goals must therefore be reflected already at the system design and development stage. Since qualitiy, cost, performance, and competitivenes of a telecommunication system are mainly determined by its software, the ability to meet the general requirements largely depends on the software. That is the reason that software technology is differentiating successful systems from the "not so successful".

For example, the supplier's requirement of attaining a competitive edge in basic development costs must be achieved by a combination of efficient hardware and software development. However, the dominant costs are in the software sector. These costs are due to the increasing amount and complexity of system and feature software. System development costs can be reduced by a software technology which provides the following:

* Support for design and execution environment for functional software service units that have standardized standalone interfaces.

* Enable reuse of these service units via the linking stage of software production.

In a similar way it can be shown that the network operator's requirement for non-stop reliability can best be met if

* the software of the system is divided into small functional failure units

* the software failure units can be isolated and independently recovered without affecting the execution of other software.

This enables defective equipment to be pinpointed more quickly and errors can be corrected without disturbing the overall system.

2 Technology Goals

To achieve the objectives set, it is necessary to extend the existing high-level programming languages, their corresponding support software, and their related operating systems. This mainly affects the four areas of structures, reusability, distribution and communication.

Structures

The quantity and intensity of language support for software structure with respect to dynamic and robustness attributes is increased. For example, the software structure known as a "Process" conventionally has a dynamic characteristic (task that can be activated, replicated, etc.). This concept is extended to enable processes to be grouped into a service or function providing structure, known as a Service Provision Unit - SPU. This structure is created by the designer.

It has as a group of processes a dynamic characteristic and can be executed by the operating system. It can also be relocated and replicated e.g. on different processing platforms. This structure is the fundamental software building block and the key element for reusability.

Reusability

The efficiency of the development process is increased. This is principally accomplished by providing the visibility of reusable system services and by making it possible to take advantage of a reusable system service wherever it is physically located in the system (location transparency). Furthermore several language features will reduce the complexity of software design by reducing the amount of system knowledge needed e.g. where and in what form functions and data are resident in the system.

Distribution

Provision of a distributed processing platform which can support the following capabilities:

- **Relocation:** Shifting a unit of software from one processing platform to another at build time, i.e. without changes in the design or the implementation only by changing the linking and production information.

- **Upgrade:** Replacing a unit of software on one or more processing platforms by a new version of this unit of software which may differ from the old one either by some corrected software errors or by an extended functionality.

- **Migration:** Shifting a unit of software from one processing platform to another at run time without service interruption.

Communication

New communication mechanisms are introduced which permit a more flexible, loosely coupled function distribution among the various processors in the system. These communication mechanisms enable the processors to operate as a network of distributed processing platforms. They are the keystones in the operating system to support reusability, software upgrades, and load distribution.

3 Technology Components

This section describes the software processing platform which is currently in development for next generation switching systems under Siemens' Vision O•N•E (Optimized Network Evolution) strategy. The platform is illustrated in figure 1 and figure 2 below. It provides an execution framework for a combination of software structure units with which the stated technological goals can be achieved. The top down hierarchy of the supported structural units is as follows:

* A processing platform contains one or more capsules.

* A capsule contains one or more Service Provision Units (SPU).

* A Service Provision Unit contains a mix of the CHILL elements processes, data, regions, and procedures all defined in modules. An SPU communicates with other SPUs **only** at operating system level.

* A Recovery Suite (RS) is any set of processes within one SPU which can be recovered (e.g. initialized) as an individual entity without disturbing the operation of other software.

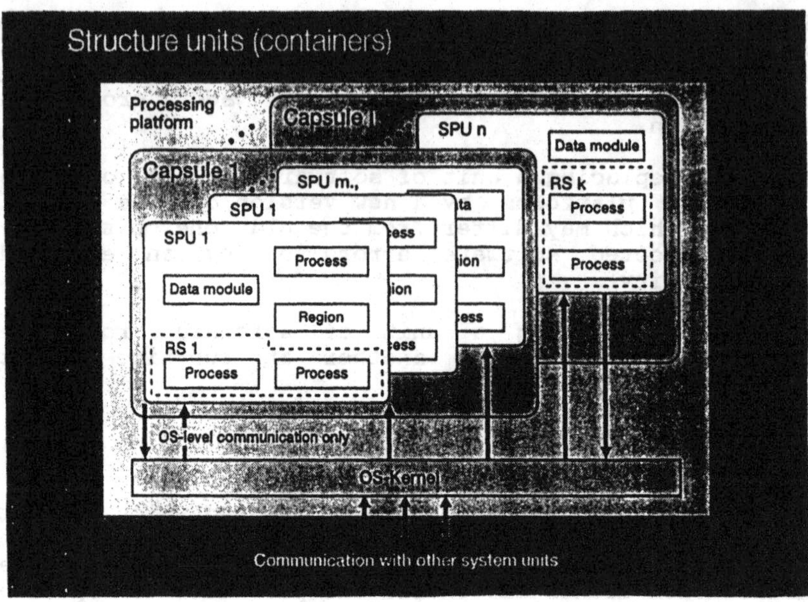

Fig. 1: Software Structure Units

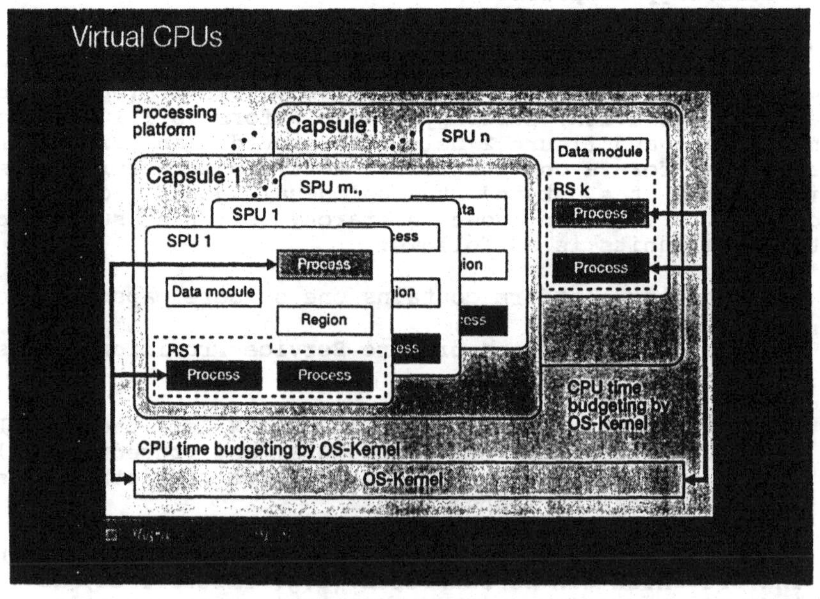

Fig. 2: Virtual CPUs

Figure 2 shows a processor containing one ore more virtual CPUs (VCPU). A virtual CPU is any set of processes to which is assigned a common CPU time budget, for example all processes which perform certain administration activities. As is shown, there is no hierarchical relationship between VCPUs and the other structure units.

A shell model for processing platforms with system and application software is shown in figure 3. The shell model provides a structuring of the software into several large layers, called shells. It enables a stepwise production of the software and large scale testing with a stepwise extended functionality according to the following hierarchy (bottom to top):

* Hardware
* Core Software: Boot program, hardware interface, error detection, etc.
* Kernel Software: Operating system, software error treatment, start up, etc.
* Basic Software: Recovery manager, enhancement manager, database, overload control, etc.
* System Software: Configuration, administration, etc.
* User Software: Call processing, protocol handlers e.g. CCS7.

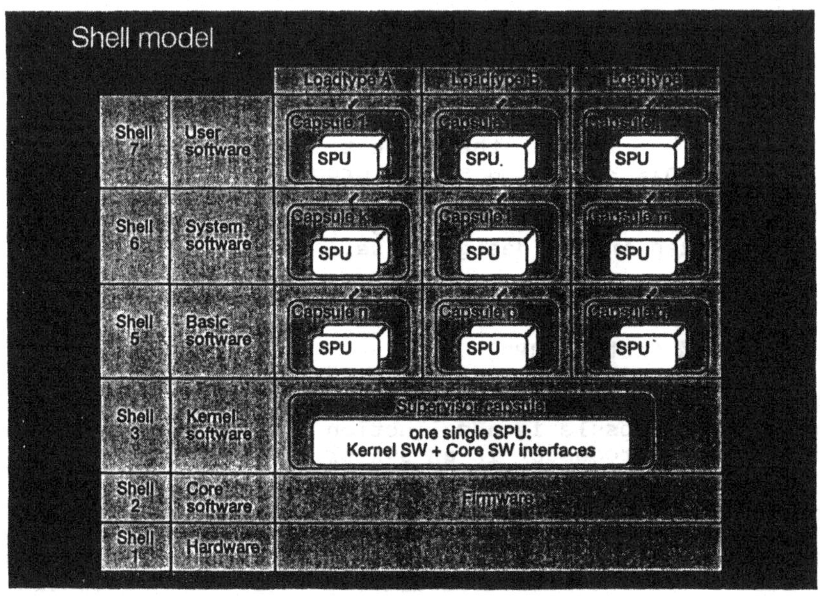

Fig. 3: Shell model for telecommunication software

Only the software running above Shell 2 is constructed from SPUs and is encapsulated. Shells 1 to 3 together constitute the processing platform. They provide the same user interface for every type of platform.

Design units SPU and Recovery Suite

The SPU is constructed of processes, modules, and regions (Fig. 1), and provides the designer with a larger and more functional container than a process currently allows. This therefore increases the functional relevance in design. The SPU hides the complexity of the system from the designer and enables the focus of work to be on design-specific problems.

The SPU enforces communication integrity since communication between the SPUs is performed only at operating system level. The service provided by a SPU is defined by its Published Interface (PIF). The PIF is the only aspect of the SPU which is externally visible, internal implementation details remain hidden. At build time the SPU can be relocated from one processing platform to another (see Fig. 4) or be replicated on several processing platforms (location and replication transparency). It is therefore the key element in reusability.

The SPU is compatible with object-oriented design and programming methods and will be extended to include objects and classes. Since the interfaces between SPUs are only loosely coupled, the operating system is able to execute both conventional SPUs and object-oriented SPUs in parallel.

The Recovery Suite provides the designer with a recovery unit which limits the effect of software errors. Generally this will be a single process but it can also be a set of processes within a SPU. The prevention of isolatable failures from causing system degradation will be emphasized in the design phase.

Capsule and virtual CPU

At build time, groups of SPUs are combined to form capsules. A capsule is a collection of SPUs which execute on the same processor in an own protected address space. To each capsule is allocated a subset of the total available processing resources (pool memory, timers). The engineering of a capsule is performed according the definition of SPUs which have related functions and therefore a related cumulative need of processing resources. Capsules are then assigned to processing platforms.

Due to these properties the capsule is the key structure enabling redistribution. A capsule can be introduced to the system or replaced by an upgraded version online - without any interruption to service. This system flexibility is enabled by the language system and monitored by the operating system.

The virtual CPU provides a CPU time budget for larger functional complexes like call processing, administration, and maintenance. This allows a collection of processes to be allocated a part of the available CPU time. There will be only a small number of VCPUs on a processing platform.

At design time each process is assigned to some process class which is related to one of the larger functional complexes in the system. At build time for each platform type, the contents of the virtual CPUs are defined by organizing the process classes into VCPUs and allocating the CPU time budget according to the load model of the given platform type.

Communication Mechanisms

The application software is structured as a collection of SPUs interacting as clients and servers. Since communication between SPUs is performed only at operating system level, the application can be distributed over several processors.

Service Provision Units can be replicated on several processing platforms or even a number of times within the same platform. As a consequence, there will normally be more than one SPU that can provide a specific service. Therefore a new system function - Service Addressing - is required to set up the communication between two SPUs at run time.

The SPU designer must publish the services which are provided by his SPU. This is achieved by the Published Interface (PIF). For each service provided by a SPU, there is a corresponding PIF which is exported by the SPU and explained in a service specification (brief description with syntax and semantics). PIFs are supervised by a PIF review bord and are made available to the designers by a PIF catalogue.

Whenever a SPU wants to establish communication with another SPU, it performs a call to the operating system where the requested Published Interface is specified by its name and additional criteria for the selection of the server SPU are transmitted. Possible selection criteria are

- own processing platform, i.e. least dynamic cost
- attributes that specify a well defined data partition
- explicit platform numbers or capsule numbers

The calling client SPU is then given a communication path which is used to communicate with the selected server SPU via Inter Process Communication (Fig. 4). This can happen either by sending messages (asynchronous communication) or by calling Remote Procedures (synchronous communication).

* **Sending messages:** The most important primitive of the asynchronous communication is CAST. CAST provides two kinds of communication with only one syntax: a local communication on the same processing platform and a remote communication to another platform. The CAST is location transparent, i.e. the sending process need not care whether his partner is running on the same or another processor.

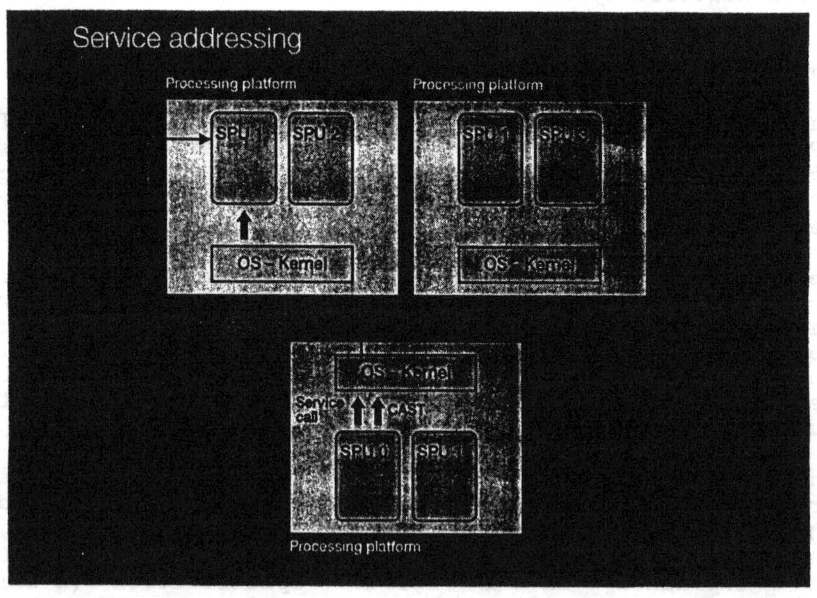

Fig. 4: Communication setup with Service Addressing

* **Remote procedure calls:** The remote procedure call performs a synchronous communication without restriction as to the location of the called procedure: The called procedure may be defined either on the same processor as the calling process or on a different processor (Fig. 5).

With these communication mechanisms it is possible to:

* Increase fault tolerance: If a processor is out of service, both messages and remote procedure calls can be forwarded to another processor by an additional call to the Service Addressing.

* Support load balancing: If a processing platform is overloaded, the surplus load can be redirected to another platform.

* Support upgrades: When replacing a capsule, messages and remote procedure calls can be forwarded to the SPUs in the new capsule with service addressing.

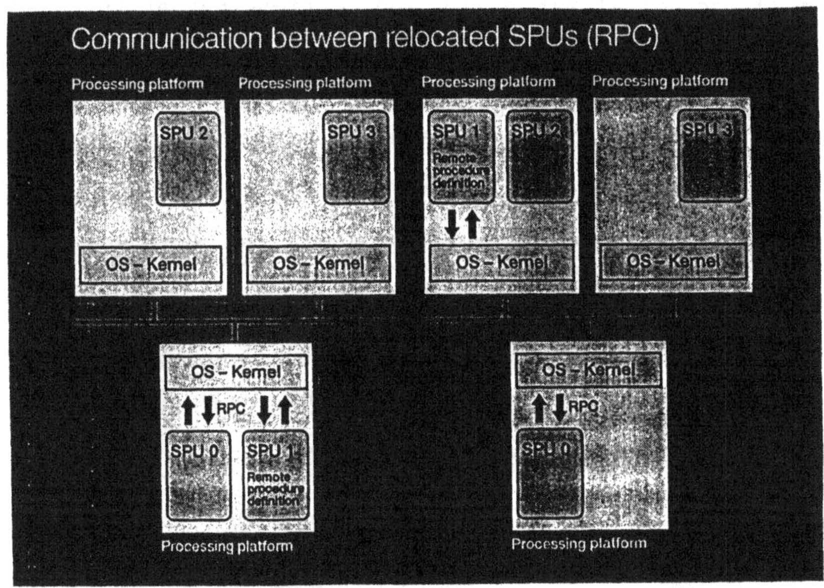

Fig. 5: Remote Procedure Call between two SPUs

4 Evolution Strategy for Existing Switching Systems

The software technology described in the previous section is not only applied to a completely new system like a broadband switch, it is also used to extend the currently existing narrowband systems. This evolution follows a well defined strategy:

* New platforms as in figure 1 are added to the system to provide specific features, e.g. protocol handling for CCS7.

* The language system and the operating system of the existing platforms are extended to support the new software structure elements and communication mechanisms.

* For the existing platforms the old software is embedded in one big Pseudo-SPU, which has the same interface properties as an SPU but is not location transparent. This software may be kept untouched or may be modified to use the new communication mechanisms to communicate with other processing platforms.

* New software is added to the existing platforms, which is designed and implemented in terms of SPUs. The major part of these SPUs is able to execute on both old and new processing platforms.

* A switching system extended in this way is not only used for normal narrowband applications but at the same time forms the basis for the construction of a new broadband switch.

An example for the evolution of an existing platform is shown in figure 6. Since the underlying hardware in this

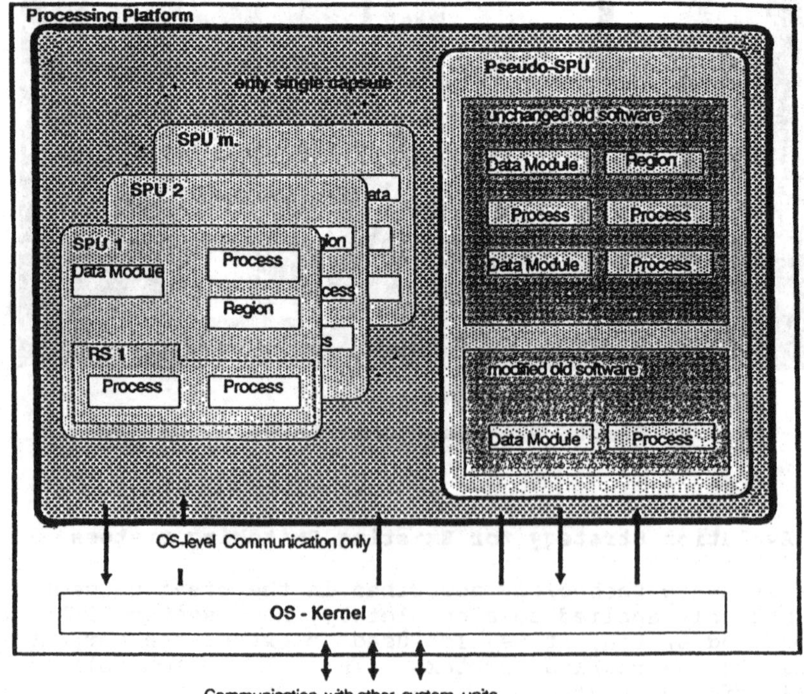

Fig. 6: Evolution of an existing processing platform

example is not equipped with a a paged memory management unit, the processing platform contains only one single capsule. The plattform carries an huge amount of old software, which is written in a higher programming language (CHILL) but is not yet structured with respect to the new design rules. This old software is surrounded by one big Pseudo-SPU.

When a new hardware platform is introduced in the system, it is often necessary to reuse software from an old processor. This old software must then execute on the new platform in parallel with software that has already been designed in terms of the new structures defined in the previous section.

This is again solved by embedding the old software in an own Pseudo-SPU, but in addition this software is encapsulated in an own capsule. With that technique the effects of errors in the old software are restricted to that particular capsule and have no influence on the execution of the new software.

5 Conclusions

The software technology sketched above provides a foundation for the design, execution, and evolution of telecommunications services in any kind of switch architecture. Furthermore, from the switch architecture point of view it enables decentralized networked software interaction. This technology therefore not only allows flexibility in the software domain but also in the choice of the hardware platforms and their logical and spatial configurations.

The new software technology will also influence the further development of intelligent networks (IN) as is shown with the following two examples.

The software structure unit SPU provides with its two basic attributes of function and interface a standalone system building block called via its PIF. This buildig block, once it exists, may be combined in diferent ways with other SPUs to provide new system services. This principle is also the base for the standardized software building blocks associated with current intelligent network standardization.

In addition, the Service Addressing function can be extended to create a global communication at network level (Global Title Translation). Because of the high transport capacity of the ATM this will enable to integrate the functionality of a Control Point into an ordinary broadband switch. As a consequence, the current hierarchical architecture of IN can be replaced by a flat broadband network architecture which supports the complete functionality of IN via a distributed technology similarly as described in this paper.

References

1. H.-E. Binder, B. Schaffer: Vision O•N•E - Optimized Network Evolution, telcom report international, Vol. XIV,12-19 (1991)
2. CCITT St.G. XI, Brown Document, Introduction to CHILL, the CCITT High Level Language
3. W. Sammer, H. Schwärzel: CHILL - Eine moderne Programmiersprache für die Systemtechnik, Berlin: Springer 1982
4. J.F.H. Winkler, G. Dießl: Object CHILL - An Object Oriented Language for Telecom Applications, Proc. of the XIV International Switching Symposium, 204-208, Yokohama 1992
5. Intelligent Network Realization and Evolution: CCITT Capability Set 1 and Beyond, Proc. of the XIV International Switching Symposium, 127-131, Yokohama 1992

Industrial Software Development - A Case Study

Ulf Cederling

Department of Mathematics, Statistics, and Computer Science
Växjö University
S-351 95 Växjö, Sweden

Abstract. To understand the software development process in practice and be able to transfer knowledge from large-scale software development projects to academic basic education as well as to other industrial software projects, it is necessary to gather experiences where those systems are built. This paper describes the development process of one particular Swedish company, NobelTech Systems AB, where they decided to design a system family of distributed solutions instead of specific systems to provide a platform for building similar systems over a long period of time.

1 Introduction

In recent years, more and more efforts have been made to increase the productivity of the software development process and to improve the quality of the final product. One key factor in improving productivity and quality is reusability. Previously, little effort has been spent on reusing software. However, with increased requirements on productivity and quality, reuse of existing program components has attracted system managers and developers to an ever increasing extent.

To get a better understanding of the development process for large complex software systems, it is necessary to gather experiences where such large-scale systems are built. It is not possible to study and analyse the problems related to the development of large systems in an isolated academic environment.

There has been relatively little interest in studying the practice of software engineering at industrial companies in Sweden. In other countries some work has been done, for example in the United States by David L. Parnas et al. [12, 13, 15, 16], and by Bill Curtis et al. [5, 6].

Other activities can be found among the programs of the Software Engineering Institute. One example of such a program is the Software Engineering Process Program led by Watts Humphrey [10, 11].

Furthermore, according to both Parnas et al. [15] and Zelkowitz et al. [18], there is a gap between software engineering principles as written about in books and conference papers and the actual practice of software engineering at many industrial and governmental laboratories. To narrow this gap, field studies must be performed in order to achieve better knowledge about the software engineering principles as they are used in practice.

The purpose of this paper is to describe the software development process at one particular Swedish company, NobelTech Systems AB. In December 1985, NobelTech signed two contracts with the Danish and the Swedish Navy respectively. This was the formal start of a program of projects collectively known as Ship System 2000 (SS2000). SS2000 is a family of integrated, distributed real-time systems controlling all aspects of a battle.

The feasibility study started in the early eighties. There were a lot of decisions to be taken by the management. Some of the issues were:

- Should existing applications be used or should the software be rewritten?
- Should the existing home-built software development environment be used or should a new one be bought externally?
- How could the productivity in developing software be raised?
- Could existing hardware technology be used or was it necessary to invest in a new generation?

Since SS2000 was intended to constitute a platform for new systems towards the end of the nineties, and as these kinds of applications have very long life cycles, the management made the strategic decision to go for a technology shift in both software and hardware. After preliminary evaluations of many technologies, NobelTech decided to evaluate Ada and the Rational Environment in a project.

At that time Ada was not an absolut requirement for either of the two customers, even though it was recommended. Actually, both systems were originally specified to use RTL/2 as the implementation language. As a result of the evaluation project, NobelTech concluded that the technology was robust enough to be used on the large-scale SS2000 program. NobelTech then renegotiated the contract with their SS2000 system customers to use Ada and the Rational Environment in the project.

It also became clear that it was necessary to abandon the minicomputer-based systems for an integrated, distributed solution. Earlier shipborne systems consisted of a number of autonomous systems connected through relatively low-bandwidth connections. The nodes of a SS2000 system are connected through a dual Ethernet Local Area Network. The node can contain several processors, so the operational software runs in an environment of loosely coupled processors. This approach gives a flexible system with the possibility to distribute load over all CPUs, and where for example functionality can be moved from one node to another in case of failure. Except for hardware redundancy, an integrated distributed system also offers operational advantages as well as simplified maintenance.

2 Software Development In Practice - NobelTech Systems AB

2.1 The Structure of the Software System

When NobelTech started the SS2000 program in December 1985, it was of vital interest to design a system family of distributed systems instead of two specific systems. They wanted to provide a platform for building similar systems over a long period of time. Reuse appeared here as a fundamental strategic principle.

Since the start of the SS2000 program, new ship systems have been ordered from the Finnish, Australian and New Zealand Navies. NobelTech has also begun to develop a new Swedish Air Defense System. In all these projects a rather high degree of reuse of the process model, design decisions, software architectures, documents, software components and people is expected, and it was essential to obtain a software structure from the beginning that contributed to reuse.

The software architecture can be viewed from several different aspects. Parnas [14] distinguishes between three software structures. These are the module structure, the uses structure, and the process structure.

The module structure is the result of a lot of important design decisions about what should constitute the parts, the modules, of the software architecture and the interfaces of those parts.

In the beginning of the SS2000 program, the software system was organized in a hierarchy including three different software component levels - Ada Unit, System Function, and Functional Area.

A System Function is a component defining a set of software that implements a logical collection of requirements. It encapsulates an object found during system analysis. A System Function consists of a number of Ada units. Since the number of System Functions and Ada units is rather large in the SS2000 project, about 200 respectively 2 000 at the moment, the uses structure becomes very complex. To handle the complexity of large software development and maintenance, a more implementation-oriented software component level was also needed. The Rational Environment provided such a level in the form of a mechanism called a Rational Subsystem. It forms the interface between a development team and an integration team.

A Rational Subsystem allows the developer to release subsystem implementations for use in testing independent of continued development of the subsystem. It consists of a collection of Ada units including information about exports, imports, and history, together with the Ada packages' specifications and bodies. The exports specifies the resources that are available for other subsystems and the imports consists of the names of the subsystems that the actual subsystem uses. In general a System Function cointains several Rational Subsystems.

The concept of System Functions was transfered to the SS2000 project from earlier projects. Based upon experiences from these projects, the components became rather small. Relatively early in the project, about a hundred System Functions were identified, each with its own Software Requirement Specification (SRS), Software Design Specification, and System Function Acceptance Test (SFAT) Specification.

Two people had primary responsibility for the definition of the System Functions. It is not unusual for only a few designers to define the software architecture. As Curtis et al. [6] point out, many projects have one or two key people holding the prime responsibility for designing the system. Their application domain knowledge was far superior to that of their development collegues, and they stood out here (as in other studies [2, 4]), as a scarce resource.

During the analysis phase of the SS2000 project, it became obvious that yet another software component level lying between Functional Area and System Function was needed. One reason for that was the need for an abstraction level that constituted a better amount of work assignment to a development team, compared to a System Function. Another reason was that the number of documents became too large to be manageable after a couple of years. Moreover, too much energy was being spent on the development of these documents.

From this context, the decision to introduce a more general component level, the System Function Group, was made. The purpose was to reduce the number of documents and to concentrate the development of documents to fewer individuals.

The customer's functional requirements were already clustered in so called Main Operational Function Groups (MOFGs) arrived at during analysis. These MOFGs represented the available functionality towards a customer, but they were not used as an internal project management instrument with their own requirement specifications.

New documents were introduced for System Function Groups, instead of SRS and SFAT on the System Function level. These new documents were System Function Group Requirement Specification, System Function Group Acceptance Test Specification, and System Function Group Design Description. The changes were accomplished despite resistance from those who had already written a Software Requirement Specification for a System Function.

A System Function Group is a component that fulfils a set of system requirements which are logically connected to some kind of object. System Function Groups are, like MOGFs, reflections of the functionality of the system.

The decision to introduce System Function Groups was important. This made it possible to distribute the software development responsibility to different development teams technologically as well as economically. A System Function was regarded as too small a component for that purpose. With a requirement specification for every System Function Group, it was also possible to get a closer relation to a function in the Product Specification.

Currently there are about 30 System Function Groups distributed over four functional areas:

- C3
- Weapon/Director
- Fundamentals
- MMI Manager

One System Function Group consists of up to 20 System Functions.

To increase the potential degree of reuse, System Functions are classified in different layers of dependencies, according to whether they are application specific or not. The purpose is to establish a system hierarchy where general purpose components do not depend on services from higher layers in order to attain as much reusability as possible. A set of tool-supported rules controls the dependencies.

The process structure consists of a number of Ada programs in execution on the available set of network nodes. Each CPU contains several Ada programs. The processes interact through the Inter-Program Communication facility (IPC2000), a part of the base system BS2000. Because of IPC2000, the modularization of the software will become independent of the distribution of the hardware and of how the program units are distributed on different nodes in execution time.

It is perhaps too early to draw any final conclusions about the design decisions made and their impact on reuse in the land-based Air Defense System. However, NobelTech has achieved a rather high degree of reuse, or perhaps commonality in software between projects, in the SS2000 program. About 60% of the software can be reused without modification and still more, about 20%, after modification when building new shipborne systems. For the land-based Air Defense System, NobelTech estimates a degree of reuse around 40-50%.

It is however evident that the hierarchical uses structure defined above, in the form of the layers of dependencies, is necessary in order to provide a reuseable and expandable system structure. Furthermore, the different software components levels provide means for managing complexity in the application area and facilitate the adaptation of the software modules to changing requirements from current customers as well as to new requirements from new customers.

2.2 The Software Life-Cycle Model

The software life-cycle model at NobelTech can be considered from the abstraction levels discussed in Section 2.1, and a work activity of the model is linked to one of the following classes:

- System Family
- System Function Group
- System Function
- System Product

The process can be described using two models, one containing the System Product level phases and the other the System Family phases. The latter stage covers the need for development of new software functionality in the form of System Function Groups and/or System Functions.

The organization of the process model in the SS2000 project, based on the software

component structure described in Section 2.1, provides an ability to manage complexity. Besides supporting decomposition of a problem area into smaller parts (which is necessary in order to analyse a complex problem area), the layered process model makes a clear distinction between specification, design, implementation, and integration.
It is obvious that both this approach and the choice of Ada as the programming language have shifted the work intensity from the coding phase to earlier phases of the life-cycle model.

Furthermore, in earlier projects integration of the components took place first when all components actually were developed. This was the effect of a too strict behaviour in relation to the waterfall model and it led to revelations of problems very late in the software development process, just before delivery.
The transition to Ada produced an opportunity to handle that problem. The division of an Ada software component in a specification and a body, makes it possible to use incremental integration. After specification of the components, the integration team can build a skeleton system to check the interfaces for consistency and successively further functionality is integrated into the system.

This way of adding more and more functionality to the components gradually is even more pronounced in the process model of the new Air Defense System project (see Section 3.1).

2.3 Methods

There are numerous, more or less well-defined methods in use today. However, hardly any method is suitable to use in development of all kinds of applications and there are only a few methods that pretend to cover the whole life-cycle of the software. Therefore, often a chain of methods must be constructed to support all the life-cycle phases.

NobelTech tried to combine Structured Analysis and Object-Oriented Design in the beginning of the SS2000 program. They had developed a Requirements Specification for the Swedish Navy 1983 and it was natural for them at that time to use a functional approach in the analysis phase.

NobelTech used a variant of Yourdon's structured analysis method, Structured Analysis for Real-Time Systems (SART) described by Ward and Mellor [17]. The purpose of SART is to describe the environement by identifying external events, and to build a logical system model responding to the required functionality. DeMarco [7], and Gane and Sarson [9] are among those who make a clear distinction between logical and physical models in order to separate system analysis from system design.

Ward and Mellor talk about an essential model and an implementation model instead of a logical and a physical model. The essential model consists of the two submodels:

- The Environmental Model
- The Behavioral Model

The Environmental Model describes the environment in which the system operates, i.e. the events that occur in the environement and the boundary between the system and the environment. The Behavioral Model describes the required behavior of the system.

In the first step in establishing these models, a Context Definition is created, in which the interfaces to the external systems are defined. NobelTech divided the functional requirements into so called Main Operational Function Groups (MOFGs). To define the interfaces to external systems, each MOFG was analysed together with representatives from the customer.

An analysis method must contain characteristics that facilitate for those involved in the development process, to use and understand the models that are produced. This was not the case in the SS2000 family of projects. The customer representatives had difficulties in interpreting the diagrams. In their opinion, the number of different symbols also was too large to become easy to handle.

Another problem was, that even if the interfaces to the hardware turned out to be fairly well-known, the other interfaces were very vague. Furthermore, the number of external events to which the system must have a planned response, was too large to become manageable.

The use of SART in the SS2000 project was of little success (as will be further discussed in Section 3.2) and they decided to establish a software architecture by hand, based upon a few designers experiences and application domain knowledge.

One important issue for NobelTech was to obtain reuseable and expandable software. Military systems of the kind produced in the SS2000 project tend to have a very long life-cycle. Therefore it was necessary to plan for system expandability. Those aspects had led NobelTech to adopt Object-Oriented Design (OOD), according to Grady Booch [1], as the design method.

The component structure was defined using this approach by identifying a hundred main design objects (System Functions). Today, there are about 200 System Functions, but those defined in this first stage have turned out to be very stable.

3 Conclusions

Development of large software systems has to undergo continous changes to keep up with the increasing complexity of the application areas. This complexity is also inherit by the software systems. As Brooks [2] points out, "The complexity of software is an essential property, not an accidental one. Hence, descriptions of a software entity that abstract away its complexity often abstract away its essence."

Therefore, it is neccesary to let the software development rely on an established process definition. It is however a rather slow process to obtain a high degree of maturity in the software development process. It may take a decade or two before an organization has reached the highest level of the maturity model as proposed by the Software Engineering Institute.

3.1 The Software Development Process

The software development approach at NobelTech shows many similarities to the approaches described in the open literature. Many of the software engineering principles discussed, for example by Parnas [13, 14], have also been taken into account. The information hiding principle is particularly widely utilized.

The life-cycle model is founded on the waterfall model, but a clear shift to a more abstraction-oriented development model is evident in the SS2000 project. This approach has resulted in more time spent on design and less on coding, integration and test, compared to earlier projects. The choice of Ada and the Rational Environment is, of course, also a contributing reason for that.

However, some opinions have been expressed, whether it is meaningful to have a life-cycle model that diverges from an established standard. In consequence of this discussion and the adaptation to DoD-STD-2167A amongst several developers of military systems, the life-cycle model used in the development of a new Swedish Air Defense System is more adjusted to this standard. This new model is also more release-oriented and the functionality is supplied to the system step by step. The last release constitutes the complete system.

Stepwise development with successive releases has been used before, but it is not until now that the process model so clearly indicates the use of incremental development with a release as result of every model cycle. This incremental development combines the advantages of exploratory programming with the management's need to control the progress in large-scale software development.
Plans and documents are produced in every system increment and the problems of continous changes which characterize exploratory programming are avoided here.

The model used in the SS2000 project may also be considered to be too complicated. In the new project a System Product is going to be developed, not a System Family. This can motivate a simplified life-cycle model compared to the former project. The case is not closed, however. Discussions are still going on as to how the land-based System Division is going to exploit this new product in the future. This may well lead to the incorporation of a family strategy here too.

Some organizational problems have been observed. The size of the SS2000 project (about 150 people, at peak time up to 250 people, have been involved in the software development process) implies that the project organization should be built-up at a rather slow speed. The number of people involved must be limitied in the initial stages of the project. Once the interfaces between the various software components have been specified and frozen, more people can be supplied to the project.

3.2 Methods

The use of SART in the SS2000 project was unsuccessful. Some of the reasons were the complexity of the problem area and the difficulty of using SART in such complex areas, and the lack of suitable tools supporting SART.

The method requires well-known system boundaries, which did not exist in the SS2000 program of projects. The number of stimuli from the environment was also too large to be manageable. Another experience was that it is hard to disregard the implementation model when establishing the essential model.
NobelTech's opinion is that SART can be used in the development of small systems, but not in large-scale development. By proceeding from the operative functions and modelling outside-in, the specifications of the hardware platform are discovered too late.

As mentioned in Section 2.3, the customer representatives also had difficulties apprehending the diagrams of SART. If the diagrams of a model have more informal symbols, similar to the graphical interfaces of today, it will be easier for customers to interpret the diagrams.

The work effort using SART was not totally wasted. The use of the method in the project gave the software developers an understanding of the problem area. This is indeed a fundamental property of an analysis method.

When the SS2000 project started, the access to CASE tools was rather limited. NobelTech used a tool called Promod running under VAX/VMS. This tool offered a tolerably useful Data Dictionary, but the graphical support was very poor.

After some years of the SS2000 project, the need of traceability between the Requirements Specification and underlying documents became obvious. The requirements were divided into requirements clauses and put into a Requirement Database. This database is handled with the help of a set of documentation tools, called EXCO.

Today, NobelTech uses Macintosh to draw Booch- and Buhr-diagrams. Rational's ROSE is under evaluation. Teamwork is used in other divisions of the company.

Most of the methods in use by the industry were originally developed in the 1970s. They are either process-driven like SA/SD and SART, or data-driven like ER and NIAM. An investigation by Floyd [8], shows that many of the well-known methods often tend to create problems instead of being a help in solving problems. One reason for that is that the methods are inexact in several ways and therefore not practically applicable. Another reason is that the methods are too labour-intensive. According to Yourdon [3], 90% of the software professionals are familiar with structured methods and 50% of their organizations have used them occasionally. However, only 10% use them actively.

One reason for the relatively limited interest in methods may be that it is hard to scale up a method for use in development of complex systems, compared to the simplicity and size of the examples used in the literature. Methods also seem to lack important features needed for large-scale development of software. Another reason has been the lack of computer-based support.

The opinion at NobelTech also seems to be that the knowledge of the application area and the experience accumulated by the software developers are the most valuable resources in a software development project.

In order to increase the understanding of the industrial software development process, further empirical studies have to be accomplished. They can give experiences valuable for developers of methods and CASE tools as well as for academic and post-academic education.

3.3 Software Reuse

Reuse is a corner-stone in NobelTech's software development strategy. A very important feature of a software reuse technique is abstraction. Parnas et al. [16] discuss abstractions from the principle of information hiding. They conclude that the use of abstractions always gives results that may be reused.
NobelTech has utilized the information hiding principle in their software development approach in many ways. Some examples are the separation of the Man-Machine Interface from the applications and the division of the software packages into a visible and a hidden part even before the introduction of Ada.

Other examples of abstractions are the division of software in the levels Functional Area, System Function Group, System Function, and Ada Unit and the classification of the System Functions in different layers of dependency to support future reuse.

However, reuse at the System Function Group level can cause problems in the future. The replacement of Software Requirement Specifications at the System Function level can lead to a Software Requirement Specification for a certain System Function Group that contains information about functionality packed in different System Functions completely independent of each other. Because of the common documentation, there is a risk that these System Functions cannot be separated in future systems, even if that would be desirable.

It has also already been discovered during the design work in the Air Defense System project, that certain rearrangements of System Functions between the System Function Groups have to be made with accompanying modifications to the documents.

Consequently, the development model has been extended to allow for arbitrarily deep component hierarchies. It has also been made more symmetric, since the same documentation principles now apply to any component, regardless of its place in the hierarchy.

3.4 Application Knowledge

One special abstraction problem during design is the process of abstracting the behaviour of the application. Even if information about the required behaviour is a part of the requirement specification, good application domain knowledge is needed to capture that information. Curtis et al. [5] found that superior software products always are designed by people with good application knowledge.

The experiences from NobelTech support this claim. The use of methods and CASE tools can never replace insufficient application knowledge.

However, as discussed in Section 2.1, there are several examples of projects where only a handful of developers are capable of doing design with respect to their degree of application knowledge. That was also the case in the SS2000 project.

This fact should worry the people responsible for a project, not only because of the strong dependency on those designers, but also because of good application knowledge at all levels in a project is of great importance for the product beeing developed. Varying degrees of application domain knowledge creates distances between the different members of the project. The transition of the knowledge that is embedded in a certain model representation, therefore runs the risk of being unsuccessful.

3.5 Future Work

In this paper an industrial approach to software development has been described. This approach comprises the establishment of a hierarchy of software components which hopefully will facilitate software reuse in future projects.

One project where software reuse from SS2000 is one fundamental presumption is the new Swedish Air Defense System project. In fact, reuse of software components, software development process model, and personnel having a thorough knowlegde of the SS2000 Family has affected the contract work from the beginning.

The next step of this project is to study and identify the mechanisms which contribute to or prevent software reuse. The purpose in the long term is to develop a conceptual framework for construction of reusable software. It is also essential to become aware of the functionality needed in CASE tools in order to give maximal support during development of reusable software.

References

1. G. Booch: Software Engineering with Ada. Benjamin/Cumming 1986
2. F. Brooks: No Silver Bullet, Essence and Accidents of Software Engineering. Information Processing '86, Elsevier Science Publishers B.V.
3. E. J. Chikofsky: Software Technology People Can Really Use. IEEE Software, March 1988

4. D. Christiansen: On Good Designers. IEEE Spectrum, May 1987

5 B. Curtis et al.: Empirical Studies of the Design Process: Papers for the Second Workshop on Empirical Studies of Programmers. MCC Technical Report Number STP-260-87

6. B. Curtis, H. Krasner, N. Iscoe: A Field Study of the Software Design Process for Large Systems. Communications of the ACM, Vol. 31 No. 11, November 1988

7. T. DeMarco: Structured Analysis and System Specification. Yourdon Press 1978

8. C. Floyd: A Comparative Evaluation of Systems Development Methods. Information System Design Methodologies: Improving the Practice. Elsevier Science Publishers B.V. 1986

9. C. Gane, T. Sarson: Structured Systems Analysis: Tools and Techniques. Prentice-Hall 1979

10. W. S. Humphrey, D. H. Kitson, T. G. Olson: Conducting SEI-Assisted Software Process Assessments. Technical Report CMU/SEI-89-TR-7

11. W. S. Humphrey, T. R. Snyder, R. R. Willis: Software Process Improvement at Hughes Aircraft. IEEE Software, July 1991

12. D. L. Parnas: Use of Abstract Interfaces in the Devlopment of Software for Embedded Computer Systems. NRL Report No. 8047, 1977

13. D. L. Parnas, K. L. Heninger, J. W. Kallander, J. E. Shore: Software Requirements for the A-7E Aircraft. NRL Memorandum Report 3876, 1978

14. D. L. Parnas: Software Engineering Principles. Infor Vol. 22, No. 4, November 1984

15. D. L. Parnas, P. C. Clements, D. M. Weiss: The Modular Structure of Complex Systems. Proceedings 7th International Conference on Software Engineering, 1984

16. D. L. Parnas, P. C. Clements, D. M. Weiss: Enhancing Reusability with Information Hiding. In T. J. Biggerstaff, A. J. Perlis (eds.): Software Reusability, Vol. I, Concepts and Models, ACM Press 1989

17. P. T. Ward, S. J. Mellor: Structured Development for Real-Time Systems. Yourdon Press 1985

18. M. V. Zelkowitz, R. T. Yeh, R. G. Hamlet, J. D. Gannon, V. R. Basili: Software Engineering Practices in the US and Japan. IEEE Computer Vol. 31, No. 11, June 1984

Quantitative Approach to Software Management : the aml [1] Method

Annie KUNTZMANN-COMBELLES

CORELIS Technologie, France

Abstract : The paper is describing the **aml** method to get started with metrication, a 12 steps supported approach. It ensures benefits for project planning and management, cost-effectiveness and match of quality objectives. The **aml** project is partly funded by the CEC and lead by practitioners in the European Software Industry.

The approach is adapted from the Goal-Question-Metric (GQM) method and achieves a well structured step by step guide to install metrics in any organisation. The background for each group of steps (phase) is described in the following sections and the main recommendations raised from the projects having run validation clearly pointed out.

The **aml** approach has already been selected by several European Companies such as ALCATEL, GEC Marconi, GEC Alsthom, EDF, Bull A.G. and ESA to act from metrics and to improve both the software process and the product quality.

1. INTRODUCTION

It is now common practice in business management to use quantitative methods in justifying and supporting decision-making. Considering Information Technology (IT) and Software Management, we can observe that quantitative approaches are generally absent.

---

[1] The **aml** project is sponsored by CEC DGXIII under the ESPRIT initiative. The following companies are participating to the project : GEC-Marconi Software Systems (UK), South bank polytechnic (UK), CORELIS Technologie (France), GEC Alsthom (France), Rheinisch-Westfälischer TÜV (Germany), Bull-AG (Germany), ALCATEL-ELIN (Austria), Ingenieria & Tecnologia de Sistemas (Spain), O. Group (Italy)

The Japanese began to apply measurement to software production in the mid 70's. By the 80's, they had the capability of distinguishing the creative aspects of software technology from software production that uses and generates re-usable components. Measurement is now a major factor in software quality and productivity improvement in Japan, and to a growing extent, in the USA.

ami is a collaborative ESPRIT project involving nine European centres of excellence with many year's experience in implementing measurement for software industry. The aim of the project is to make the European software industry aware of the benefits of using measurements. Furthermore it is to provide a practical and validated approach to installing and using quantitative approaches to control and improve software process. The ami approach has undergone extensive industrial trials across Europe and has the support of the European Space Agency. Now, an ami Handbook detailing the approach and incorporating feedback from those experiences, has been presented in several countries by the end of March 1992.

2. SUMMARY OF THE ami METHOD

The application of goal oriented measurement in an organisation requires a structured method. Each organisation must construct its own measurement framework. Which organisation, after all, would borrow the mission statement of another ?

The ami method implements four distinct activities - Assess, Analyse, Metricate, Improve :

Assess your project environment (with its objectives and problems) to define primary goals for measurement. Managers who initiate measurement must be involved in this activity.

Analyse the primary goals to derive sub-goals and the relevant metrics. This analysis is formalised as a goal tree with a corresponding set of questions to which these metrics are linked. The participants affected by the metrication goals (metrics promoter, project managers, quality engineers, etc.) will generally carry out this activity.

Metricate by implementing a measurement plan and process the collected primitive data into measurement data. The metrics promoter will write the measurement plan and co-ordinate its implementation.

Improve, as the participants affected by the goals start to use the measurement data and implement actions. Comparison of the measurement data with the goals and questions in the measurement plan will guide you towards achievement of your immediate project goals. When your measurements show that you have achieved a goal, you have improved enough to reassess your primary goals.

The relationship between the four activities are illustrated in the following diagram :

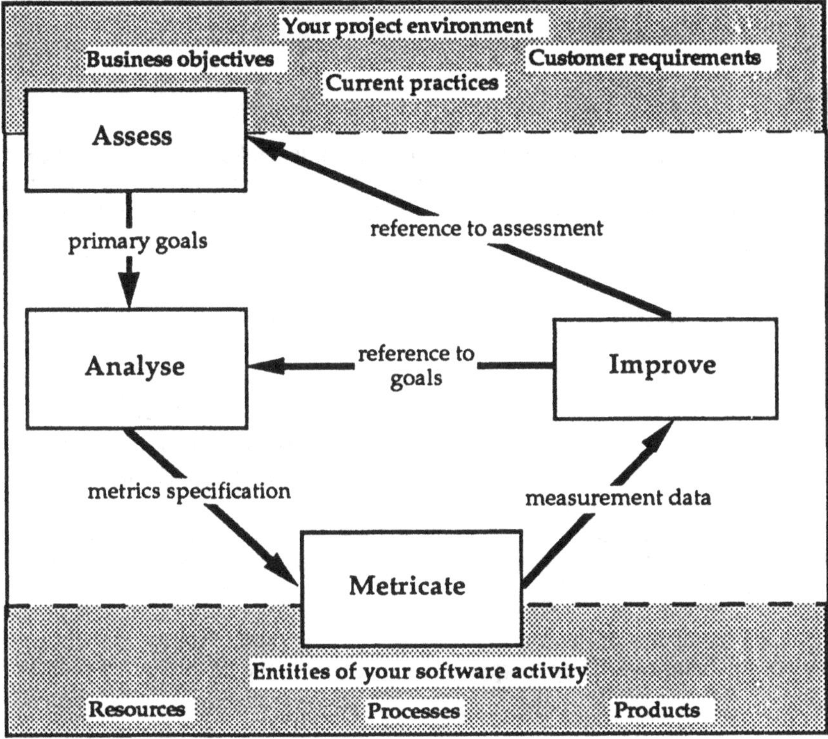

The method is a sequence of 12 steps with a series of support tools (guide-lines, templates and examples) to make it easy to use.

3. DEFINING THE PRIMARY GOALS

This phase is addressing how to assess the project environment in order to define and evaluate primary goals for subsequent metrication. These primary goals may be business driven or may evolve more directly from the project environment.

It is vital that the strategic decision to develop and implement a software measurement plan is taken by management. Management must also be fully involved in the examination of assessment data and in the definition of primary goals for metrication.

Areas of concern and problems in the way in which your organisation currently responds to business and customer needs must first be identified.

A procedure and model, such as the SEI Capability Maturity Model from the Software Engineering Institute of Carnegie-Mellon University, is helpful in the assessment process. Alternatively, a localised procedure for problem identification and analysis can be used.

Either of these methods enables you to produce a list of issues. These are then assessed to identify the key items to be tackled first, which in turn leads to the definition of the primary goals for metrication .

Your primary goals should always be checked against your assessment conclusions to confirm the link between the two questions.

3.1. Step 1 : Assessing the project environment

Assessment is the first step of the ami method. It is evident from experience that there is more than one procedure for assessing the environment of a company or a team. The conclusions of this assessment are used in the second step of the ami method as an aid to the definition of primary goals.

3.2. Step 2 : Defining primary goals for metrication

Two classes of goals exist :

Evaluation goals : these are expressed by the use of such verbs as evaluate, predict or monitor. Evaluation looks at the past, prediction looks at the future and monitoring looks at the present. For example : evaluate product quality, predict testing requirements, monitor test coverage,
Improvement goals : these are expressed by the use of such verbs as increase, reduce, achieve or maintain. For example : increase component reuse, reduce errors, achieve greater productivity, maintain quality.

The primary goals are defined according to the assessment results and the global strategy of the company. They fix quantitative targets to the development process.

3.3. Step 3 : Validating primary goals

A validation should be performed to ensure the consistency of primary goals :

• consistency between goals and your assessment conclusions,

• consistency between selected goals and time scales,

• consistency between goals and metrication budget.

4. DERIVING METRICS

The purpose of this phase is to break down the primary goals into more manageable sub-goals, and to clarify the measurement objectives of all the main participants in the measurement process.

Each primary goal is analysed and decomposed into sub-goals to create a goal tree. There is also a table of questions that document the thinking process of how each branch was derived. The final questions (at the end of each branch) are a specification for the metrics.

One of the main objectives of the breakdown is to set goals that correspond to domains of responsibility and to the decision making activity of teams or individuals. The measurement data that is collected will then support decision making and goal achievement.

A second objective for breakdown is to achieve greater precision in the primary goals. Once created, the goal tree is checked for consistency of sub-goals with primary goals and of goals with decision making.

4.1. Step 4 : From goals to sub-goals

The ami approach to goal-driven derivation of metrics is adapted from the Goal-Question-Metric (GQM) method. GQM was devised by Victor Basili at the University of Maryland in 1985 [BAS88] and further refined during his work with the NASA Goddard Space Centre.

The analysis of primary goals is achieved either by a series of interviews conducted by a metrics promoter (external or internal) in charge of the definition of the measurement plan, or by a simple analysis carried out by each person affected by the goals and co-ordinated by a working group.

4.2. Step 5 : Verifying the goal tree

The goal tree that results from analysis of the primary goal should be verified. This verification is carried out against :

- the global balance of the tree
- the internal consistency of the tree
- the external consistency of the tree

4.3. Step 6 : From sub-goals to metrics

Metrics derivation starts from the bottom of the goal tree. The questioning process is used to identify metrics. A question about a sub-goal acts as a specification for a metric. These questions are either the ones used to identify sub-goals because metrics are obviously implicit behind the question, or new ones necessary to describe sub-goals quantitatively.

5. IMPLEMENTING A MEASUREMENT PLAN

The results from activities described above are the starting point for writing the project's measurement plan. The plan is written by the metrics promoter and validated by those involved in the definition and derivation of goals.

From the metric's specification a complete definition of the metric and the analysis and collection procedures are produced. A metrics template is used to support this process.

The implementation of the plan should be monitored for effectiveness. The plan can be incorporated into project or department plans and be subjected to their review procedures. Regular feedback of metrics for analysis will also help validate and further motivate those involved. Syntheses of measurement data presented to management at regular intervals, say, every three months, also helps to keep higher management involved.

5.1. Step 7 : The Measurement Plan

This document is one of the first fruits of your investment in software measurement. In addition to being a plan for the collection of data, it is a record of your software development environment, your development process, the strengths and weaknesses of the environment and process, and a standard for communication between the participants in your metrication programme. Each metric is defined as follows :

Part A : Metric definition and analysis procedure.

A1. Name	Name of the metric and any known synonyms.
A2. Definition	Which attribute of which entities may be measured using this metric. Whether the metric is derived from the aggregation of primitive metrics (description of the calculation method) or directly measured.
A3. Goals	Why the metric is used. List of goals related to the metric. List of questions related to the metric (if any)
A4. Analysis procedure	How the metric is used. Preconditions for the interpretation of the metric (e.g. valid ranges of other metrics). Target trends of the metric values. Models or analysis techniques and tools to be used. Implicit assumptions (e.g. of the environment or models). Calibration procedures. Storage.
A5. Responsibilities	To whom the measurement data is available. Who will prepare the reports. Who will analyse the data
A6. Training Required	What training is required for application and/or interpretation of this metric.

Part B : Primitive data definition and collection procedure.

Note : If the metric is computed from several collected primitives, Part B is repeated for each.

B1. Name	Name of the primitive metric.
B2. Definition	Unambiguous description of the metric in terms of the projects environment (customisation).
B3. Collection Procedure	Description of the collection procedure. Data collection tool and form to be used. Time(s) in the life cycle when the data is collected. Verification procedure to be used with the data. Where data will be stored, its format and precision.
B4. Responsibilities	Who is responsible for collecting the data. Who is responsible for verifying the data. Who will enter the data into the database. Who has access to modify the data.

5.2. Step 8 : Implementing the plan

5.3. Step 9 : Verifying the data

It is vital to verify the data as it becomes available. The reasons are that it ensures that the data is as complete and correct as possible, at the only time when it is possible to make corrections and additions. Also the accuracy of the data collection process may be quantified (how many mistakes vs. how many measurements) and it provides important, motivating feedback to the data collectors.

6. EXPLOITING YOUR MEASURES

The analysis starts with an effective presentation of the measurement data. It is shared with those involved in the relevant goals.

Measurement data is then analysed. Analysis of data with goal oriented measurement is self referencing and fairly simple. For example, estimates use past data, error rates should tend to zero, progress should tend to 100%, and so on. However the analysis must always be done with careful reference to the context. There is no model that can be used to say "since the error rate has not fallen, it means that...". Analysing in context means obtaining the background information, involving project staff and comparing the measurement data with the goals and assumptions. This analysis will validate your metrics, and you will avoid using data blindly.

By relating data to goals you will be able to implement improvement actions or correct decisions that have been taken.

The analysis of data will immediately help in guiding actions. However a set of metrics should also help to ask more questions and derive new goals. For example, metrics of phase costs compared with errors should indicate possible leverage points and associated metrics. Goal oriented measurement is naturally iterative since the basic motivation of improved results and increased understanding is always present.

6.1. Step 10 : Presentation of the data

Software data often has too many undesirable properties for the successful application of traditional statistical analysis techniques. The main ones are :

- data is not numerous enough to validate correctly any model,
- the usual assumptions supporting the most widely used laws are not valid for software (i.e. gaussian distribution),

For these reasons, and according to ami paradigm, we will recommend graphical analysis for the robustness and user-friendliness.

6.2. Step 11 : Validating the metrics

For an objective validation we compare the measurement data with an expected trend or with an expected correlation to other data. In a subjective validation people who are involved in the process give an opinion as to whether the metric corresponds to the sub-goal.

6.3 Step 12 : relating data to goals

This last step of the aml method is leading to decisions for the future ; generally these decisions will result into modifications of the goals assigned : improvement or more detailed information i.e. sub-decomposition of the actual goals will be looked for.

Relating data to goals means a global analysis, most of the time a statistical analysis of the results compared to the sub-goals and goals selected for the metrics initiative. Warning signals might have appeared and corresponding corrective actions in the development process should be taken.

6.4 Strategies for improvement : going further

We have reached the last step in the aml method.

Having validated the metrics vs. the assumptions and/or models supporting them, they can be related, singly or in combination, to the goals of the measurement plan.

Software measurement is an iterative process - the more you collect, the better you know how to collect and what to collect.

One simple way to do this is to set up a permanent database and feed in data from every project involved in data collection. In this way, data is treated as a resource for the whole organisation, and more sophisticated data analysis and reporting facilities can be considered.

7. FEEDBACK FROM THE aml METHOD VALIDATION

The aml approach has been experimented by project partners and affiliated bodies on more than 18 projects over more than one year. The task consists into metrics initiative installed in the companies and/or departments at partners sites. Consultants who where acting as metrics promoters have reported about the main problems raised by the method . Extension of the approach to Corporate metrication programme has been evaluated too.

The project environments on which aml method was applied were diverse : real time embedded systems, clerical systems, software engineering tools and expert systems. The maturity of companies was also different ; this was resulting into various levels of metrics plans and types of primary goals.

The most difficulties encountered are related to the primary goals selection in order to match the assessment results and the decomposition into sub-goals. After analysis of these difficulties, some very basic recommendations can be written down :

Keep it simple

If the metrication programme is a new initiative tor you, don't try to draw a complex goal tree. Two levels of breakdown are sufficient. One or two primary goal is enough.

Think it through for yourself

Try to define your own metrics plan rather than using one from another company. Satisfaction will be greater because you address your own problems.

Consolidate your foundations first

Don't try to set primary goals too far above your present understanding and maturity level. It causes disappointment when analysing the benefits of measurement.

Get support and commitment

Don't start an extensive metrication programme if you don't have the commitment and support of the managers. Managers have to be convinced of the possible benefit they will get from the metrication programme prior to initialize it.

Write it down

Be aware of the relevance and importance of the questions in the goal breakdown and also in the metrics derivation. They must be written down.

Communicate

Use metrics that can be understood by all the participants and involve them as much as possible.

The **ami** bank of case studies is one of a number of supporting materials that help users derive maximum benefit. Off this bank we extracted two significant feedback that are presented in the next two paragraphs. Both are related to real projects applying the **ami** approach.

The first example is related to a huge switching system (over 1 million LOC) in which software represents about 80% of the development costs. development was managed in a distributed environment over four European sites. The main target of the metrication initiative was to get a better control of the development process and to derive subsequent indicators for the next generation of systems. As far as historical data were already existing when the **ami** initiative started, the method was slightly amended. The goals tree was the following one :

To improve and test activities for

the current release

To get a better resources estimation of the test phase	To apply a better testing strategy
To find out the most relevant indicators for test effort (unit and integration test) modules	To find out the most relevant indicators to detect error prone

Two kinds of metrics were collected :

- static product metrics

- a posteriori information for conducting the analysis which consists of process metrics extracted from the configuration management and subjective estimation done by designers. Demonstration of the adequacy of the selected metrics has been conducted : different test strategies are compared taking into consideration errors that are discovered. Almost all errors were detected while completely testing 70% of all modules. Another interesting figure states that the 20% most complex modules according to the metrics contain 50% of all errors. These results motivated the decision to use metrics on a periodical basis for monitoring the evolution of complexity of the software and support the choice of a testing strategy. As a benefit, a new product release can be envisaged on the market with a better quality level while the complexity is under control. Indirect benefits concern the bad psychological effect that might be observed : metrics were rather considered as a support for the daily life.

The second example concerns safety critical embedded system development. All the products and processes are closely monitored in terms of cost. The historical data are showing that the hardware-software integration phase of development is a very high proportion of the local cost. The metrics initiative has consequently been decided with a two fold target : get a better detailed knowledge of the present position and measure the impact of new tools such as analyser on the integration phase. The goals tree has been designed as follows :

Improve development process	*Measure new technology*
a) reduce present rework effort levels by 20%	a) monitor time utilisation during analyser testing
b) reduce the percentage of errors produced by 30%	b) measure number of code overall changes due to analyser usage
c) reduce the percentage of errors found after unit test by 20%	
d) improve the estimation of time to end of project.	

Selected metrics include : track of the number of modules integrated against the effort expended, track of how many defects were discovered as the integration stage of the life cycle progressed, list of how many of each defect type was being discovered, measurement of how many modifications were due to the analyser tool, track of the number of modules the analyser tested against the effort expended.

It was fount that the tool reported very few genuine errors for the amount of time expended on its use. The main benefits identified so far are :

- large numbers of software updates are being carried out late in the life cycle,

- modifications are arising from unexpected sources e.g. requirements and hardware changes late in the project,

- the analyser tool appears to give little benefit for the large amount of effort needed to use it.

Furthermore, almost all the companies who started measurement programmes reported positive results after 6 months ; the initiative forced people to analyse properly their understanding of the software development process and to determine realistic goals for control or improvement. Some of them were looking for ISO 9000 qualification and the **ami** approach helped them progressing in the right direction.

8. CONCLUSION

International reports point out that almost 80% of software projects fail because a lack of management and control ; technical difficulties represent only 15% of unsuccessful projects. 30% of budget overrun is the average of observed discrepancies. A deeper analysis shows that indicators should have been noticed in the early life of the project and actions taken to solve the difficulties. But a lack of visibility and quantitative information has resulted into financial and economical slippage.

We do believe that software measurement should be integrated into the software development process as a critical activity. Actions derived from a metrication initiative are usually cost effective ; if you understand the software process, you will identify the critical activities and how to get data about them. The next step should be improvement of the process through an optimisation of the effort to get a given quality for the final product. Metrication is iterative - the more you collect, the better you know how to collect, what to collect and how to act from this point.

Measurement that is used for both the control and improvement of software projects gives the following benefits :

Planning, managing and monitoring projects

Measurement enables increased visibility of the quality and progress of a project. Use of data improves predictions and evaluations. Goal orientation improves project co-ordination. Evolution of real effort with time against predictions is a good indicator of unstable process if a continuous slippage is observed.

Matching the software development process to business objectives

Better matching of the software development process to business objectives can lead to improved confidence between you and your customer, between business managers and project managers and between the Software Development Department and the rest of the organisation. Communications between people need quantitative information.

Implementing of quality and productivity improvement programmes

The problem of managing investment in software engineering activities is becoming increasingly important. Such investment may be in "preventive" activities such as use of methods, quality assurance, increased training and more testing, or in "productive" activities enabled by CASE tools and new technologies. Measurement helps you to justify, manage and evaluate such improvement programmes. Production unit -whatever it is- has to be carefully defined before any measurement.

Aiding sub-contracting

Installing a measurement programme to assess the work achieved by sub-contractors is one of the multiple perspective of the ami approach. Unfortunately, most of the companies who are massively using sub-contractors for software development are not often making a difference between their maturity capability levels ; financial considerations are supporting the selection. As a consequence, the resulting product does not reach the adequate quality level and/or delay is not matched.

Measurement is not necessary easy. To achieve full benefits, measurement must first be applied systematically according to a customised view of goal-oriented method and be supported by the whole hierarchy. On the other hand, a wide range of developers and engineers should participate and formalise their view of the high level goals for measurement. very active participation is recommended from both side ; feedback about decisions made after metrics observation and exploitation has to be given to participants. Individual behaviour will be changed by metrics initiative and hostility has to be avoided : metrics do not support individual judgement but collective process.

ACKNOWLEDGEMENTS

The author is expressing thanks to the whole ami consortium, to the CEC and to the editorial team who have supported the ami method development. All critics received have resulted into clarity and quality of the method.

BIBLIOGRAPHY

[ami 92] The ami handbook, version 3, December 1992

[ami 93] ami Case studies, Report, January 1993

[BAS88] *The TAME project : Towards improvement-oriented software environments*, V.R.Basili & D.Rombach, IEEE Trans Soft Eng 14(6), 1988, 758-773.

[BOEHM91] *Software Risk Management : Principles and Practices*, B.W.Boehm, IEEE Software, January, pp 32-41.

[CARD90] *Measuring Software Design Quality*, D.Card and R.Glass, Prentice Hall, 1990.

[FENTON91] *Software metrics : a rigourous approach*, N.Fenton, Chapman & Hall, 1991.

[GRADY87 *Software metrics: Establishing a Company-wide Program*, R.B.Grady and D.L.Caswell, Prentice Hall, 1987

[GRADY92] *Software metrics:* R.B.Grady, Prentice Hall, 1992

[HUMPHREYS89] *Managing the software process*, W.S.Humphreys, Addison Wesley, 1989.

[MATSUBARA91] *Project Management in Japan*, T.Matsubara, American Programmer, June 1991, pp 41-50.

[SEI87] *A method for assessing the software Engineering Capability of Contractors*, Technical Report, CMU/SEI-87-TR-23.

[SEI91] *Capability Maturity Model for Software*, Tech Report CMU/SEI-91-TR-24, Carnegie-Mellon University, 1991.

Preventative Software Engineering

Johannes Reichardt

Fachbereich Informatik, Fachhochschule Darmstadt
64295 Darmstadt, Germany

Abstract. This article is dedicated to the "individual" programmers whose personal style still too often dominates the software development. It analyses the design process in terms of interconnectivity, a collective term for the entirety of physical, logical and chronological relations within a software system. It uses two drastic but, nevertheless, realistic metaphors to more fully expose the underlying problems.

First, the increase of mainly undesigned interconnections through the construction process is presented by analogy to the increase of *entropy* of a natural system.

Second, principles for the effective management of the development process are advanced in an extended military metaphor as a form of warfare against interconnectivity. In particular, strategy and tactics are shown to address the primary design goals of flexibility and simplicity.

The rule of reduction-of-interconnectivity is promoted as the central design rule and the development process is characterised as a suitable application for *crisis handling* techniques.

1 Introduction

During the design and implementation of software, it can often be observed that, with the increase of the (time and space) complexity, by adding of lines of code, the degree of intricacy either stays constant or increases in value, but never decreases. This (entropic) behaviour may be due to the particular difficulties of software as a material in that its intricacy is not visible and defies control. As a consequence, there is a requirement for design and implementation methods which effectively contain the entropy of software.

Limitations of Computer Aided Software Engineering. A recent trend in Computer Aided Software Engineering has concentrated on the visualisation of development data and their interconnections in order to be able to cover seamlessly the entire software life cycle [1]. Such a solution calls for an ambitious step beyond the limited diagrammatic techniques of traditional CASE tools.

A major problem with the current CASE approach is that, whatever representation is chosen, no interconnections can be represented other than those explicitly designed. However, while designed interconnections cater for functionality, it is the undesigned interconnections which affect flexibility and simplicity and are thus chiefly responsible for the quality of the software.

The task of detection and visualisation of undesigned interconnections makes computer-aided software engineering closely related to expert systems. One conclusion is that CASE is as far from its objectives as expert systems are from theirs. In the meantime, the situation in software development still requires design and implementation support at a subsistence level.

The Difficulty of the Material Software. Compared to the materials of architecture and mechanical engineering, software knows very few limitations which could otherwise guide or delimit the construction process.

Consequently, software construction more than the physical sciences tends to promote undesigned effects at each construction step. Therefore, software design (much more than architecture and mechanical engineering) needs to be based on "negative formulas" [2], representing pessimistic assumptions.

Established Design Methodologies. Perhaps reflecting the critical nature of software development, most of the commonly agreed software design principles and rules are of a preventative nature. This is true of such established concepts as "information hiding", "design for change", "reduction of interconnectivity", "hierarchical design" and "modularisation". This is also true for the whole concept of object-oriented programming.

Moreover, all of the above concepts reflect the problems with undesigned interconnections in that they are just variations of the rule of "reduction of interconnectivity".

This suggests that reduction-of-interconnectivity can be considered as the quintessential objective of software engineering. However, this requires an extended view of that rule considering, in particular, the many facets of interconnectivity.

Basic Design Goals. It is tempting to reflect that essential design goals may be achieved only to the extent that interconnectivity is mastered. The primary goals that can be achieved by a reduction of interconnectivity are flexibility and simplicity. Flexibility can be considered as the opposite of interdependence, whereas simplicity is the opposite of confusion. Both interdependence and confusion are realisations of a high interconnectivity.

Flexibility and simplicity can be termed basic, as most of the recognised design goals are derivatives of one or both of them. A "modular" system is always the paragon of flexibility. "Portable", "adaptable", "extendable" or "subsettable" [3] implementations all incorporate a special form of flexibility. "Symmetrical", "orthogonal" or "complete" implementations are flexible in that they establish some sort of universality. "Reliability", "robustness", "faultlessness" and "maintainability" are secondary effects of both simplicity and flexibility. "Efficiency" is itself largely ensured by the use of simple constructions and by observing bounds of flexibility.

A Basic Methodology. Since the first goal (flexibility) determines what is to be implemented and the second one (simplicity) concerns how it is to be implemented, they can be seen as goals of, respectively, strategy and tactics.

Indeed, a fundamental tenet of this presentation is that the needs and principles of software construction can be considered in direct analogy with the role and implementation of military strategy and tactics. An "algebra of action" [13] is offered by the classical military authors which can be easily "beaten into ploughshares" (Isaiah 2:4). The principles already identified show a striking affinity to military ones. For instance, the universal rule above is just another formulation of Julius Caesar's "divide-et-impera". Taking into account the universal concern about software quality [5], it is reasonable to deal with it from the point of view of crisis-handling.

2 The Many Facets of Interconnectivity

The difficulty in coming to terms with interconnectivity is already evident from the fact that basic structural properties of programs such as halting or the equivalence to other programs are undecidable. How much less can it be expected that the detection of interdependency and confusion is an easy task? Nevertheless, even the mere awareness of interconnectivity is already an important step towards reducing the risks of its negative effects.

The Problem of Definition. Interconnectivity was defined in [4] as the "assumptions a module makes about its environment". This paper originated the design strategy of "reduction of interconnectivity" and recognised interconnectivity as something to be contained, rather than as a constructive element. However, the coupling of modules is only one of many possible forms of interconnectivity and, perhaps, not the critical one. The real problem is more subtle and relates to the less calculable way in which interconnectivity manifests itself.

A term which, perhaps, better describes this situation is "cohesion". In [6], cohesion is further classified into functional associations. The following classes are proposed in order of decreasing functional significance - sequential, communicatory, procedural, temporal, logical and coincidental. There is also a classification of containment for less functional associations. Indeed, it could even be argued that the nature of interconnectivity is such that it requires a holistic view. Certainly, regardless of what definitions exist, a preventative design must take all types of interconnection into account.

Beyond a Metric. In [8], over a hundred software complexity measures, collected from the literature, are discussed. All of them claim to express "psychological complexity" - the difficulty in designing, maintaining, changing and understanding software. However, the expression of software complexity in terms of a metric has not proved to be productive. "Conventional measures of software complexity have so far proved unsatisfactory, and many have unsound logical foundations" (Ejiogu in [8]). Indeed, "there is a lack of formalism and a lack of analytical tools in defining and for evaluating complexity measures" (Howatt and Baker in [8]) and "the situation in software complexity measurement is confusing and not satisfying for the user" [8].

Obviously, the many facets of interconnectivity can, as yet, neither be adequately represented by a metric nor modelled. Instead, interconnections require to be identified and designed in their respective concrete forms.

Multiple Dimensions. Interconnectivity has several dimensions and, at least, the physical, the logical and the chronological dimensions must be considered. For example, a simple kind of physical interconnections is the physical neighbourhood between lines of source code or between run-time data items in storage. A simple logical interconnection might be formed by identities between lines of source code or between the values of run-time operands. A chronological interconnection might be associated either with the distance between the execution of an operation and the appearance of its "side-effect", or between the implementation of a design decision and its proof in the course of a change.

Analysis and Synthesis. In any event, the design of interconnections is only the second stage of system design. The other, pre-requisite, stage is the determination of the atomic and independent parts of the system. These two stages correspond to the design phases of synthesis and analysis, respectively. During analysis, the key question is which elements belong together and which do not. This is always a question of finding common ground and determining differences. The former task is of a constructive nature while the latter is preventative.

Purpose and Motivation. As stated, a purposeful design always tends to join together that which belongs and, more importantly, separates that which does not. The degree of interconnectivity between system elements should be determined by their common purpose. In turn, the question of purpose raises the issue of motivation and it is easily seen that, with regard to the purpose of the system elements, interconnections in real systems are often unmotivated.

In general, motivation can be classified into "causa formalis", "causa materialis", "causa efficiens" and "causa finalis". This enumeration is said to be complete [9]. The first three causes clearly apply to any interconnection. They characterise implicitly what is defined below as "software entropy". Only the last one, however, "causa finalis", can help to conquer the system; an ideal system would have only finally motivated interconnections.

3 The Entropy of Software

Due to the particular difficulty of software as a material (causa materialis) and an optimistic way of coding (causa efficiens), each construction step is usually accompanied by undesigned effects. As an instance of the law of entropy, it can be observed that the absence of a systematic interest in the interconnectivity and its containment leads to an equally systematic increase of interdependency and confusion, striving unrelentingly to a state of maximal disorder. This phenomenon yields a strong motivation for the rule of reduction-of-interconnectivity.

Functionality and Interconnectivity. To model the design process in real and ideal terms, it is sufficient to consider the interests in functionality and interconnectivity (see Figure 1) as its driving forces. The model is based on the strong correlation between cognition and interests, which has been pointed out in [10].

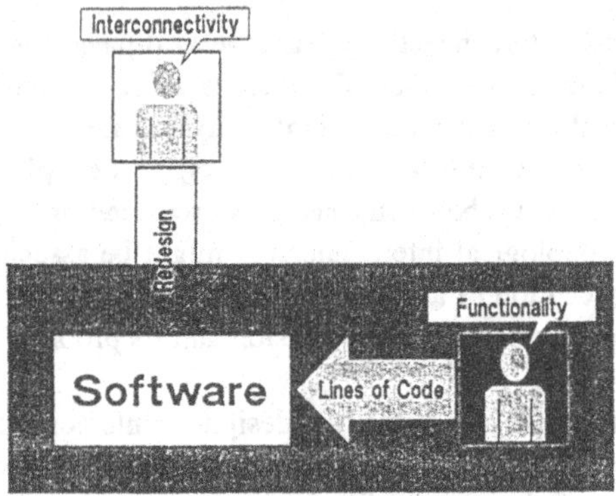

Fig. 1. Model of the Design Process

In this model, the "normal" design process assumes only the superficial interest in functionality. This is sometimes still defined in terms of productivity as "number of lines-of-code" or the criterion of "functioning". Not bound to a systematic interest in the interconnectivity of the software, it manifests itself essentially by functional expansion. Whereas this does not preclude sporadic measures beneficial to the interconnectivity of the system, the prospects for profits and losses connected to interconnectivity demand a systematic, unremitting and deep interest. This interest must be directed to tracing out interconnections and to implementing permanent corrections, while they are possible. This is why, in Figure 1, the normal design situation is shown as a closed system, that is, closed against ordering energy and left to its own resources.

Complexity and Intricacy. It is instructive to consider the second main theorem of thermodynamics [11] which states that, for any closed system in nature, a quantity exists which, at any change of state, either stays constant (with reversible processes) or increases in value (with irreversible processes). This quantity is referred to as the "entropy of the system".

By analogy, it can be observed during functional expansion in software design that the interconnectivity of a system increases monotonically. In other words, with the increase of the complexity of a system, the degree of intricacy either increases or stays constant (complexity, representing the number of steps or storage cells necessary for the computation and, necessarily, increasing during functional expansion, can be seen as a quantity of the system, whereas intricacy represents a qualitative property). Thus, interconnectivity can be considered as the "entropy of a software system", reflecting the degree of intricacy or disorder. A high value of entropy expresses a high degree of interdependency and confusion within the system, whereas a low value signifies flexibility and simplicity.

More than the Sum of its Parts. From thermodynamics, it is known that the entropy of a natural system is greater than the sum of entropies of its sub-systems. This means that, with regard to its interconnectivity, a system is more than the sum of its parts.

Looking at technical design from a logical or functional point of view, it is axiomatic that it should strive to ensure that the components of a system obey the principle of superposition, summing up hierarchically functional units [12]. This gives rise to interconnectivity increasing faster than functionality which, in turn, means that undesigned interconnections increase faster than designed interconnections. It follows that quality and cost oriented software design must be always a struggle against entropy.

Economy of Disorder. Another lesson which can be learned from the above inequality is that decomposing things (in a non-destructive manner) is always more difficult than composing them. The former is a problem of, comparatively, high interconnectivity. Therefore, any mistake in keeping system elements separate, is always less expensive than one introduced by an erroneous interconnection. The establishment of interconnections can be made even at a very late stage in design with much less effort than the late dissolution of early connections. Therefore, in any case of doubt, keeping system elements separate is a demand of economy.

4 An Algebra of Action

The analysis above suggests that software design can be based on one single rule - the rule of reduction-of-interconnectivity. However, since this rule is universal, it is not so easy to apply and use it. This agrees with the characterisation of military strategy in [13] that "everything is very simple in strategy, but not necessarily easy".

To develop a working understanding of that rule, it is necessary to discuss how design problems can be identified and categorised with a view to their prioritisation and resolution. The following approach relies mainly on the distinction between design strategy and design tactics.

Distributed and Local Problems. Strategic and tactical problems can be quantitatively characterised by the number of system locations involved and affected by the implementation. A strategic problem affects many locations and can thus be termed a "distributed problem". Tactical problems affect only a few locations and can be termed "local problems". The degree of interconnectivity inherent in a distributed or local problem corresponds to the number of locations involved in its implementation. In general, a strategic problem consists of many - often, replicated - tactical problems.

4.1 Design Strategy

The effect of a good strategy is characterised primarily by the absence of severe tactical problems. "It is simply the aim of a strategy to reduce struggling to a minimum ... The perfection of a strategy would even demand that a decision be achieved without severe struggle" [14]. Therefore, a strategy must stand the test on tactical level, in that any tactical problem encountered should be easily resolved.

A strategy has to define and assign the tactical tasks. Its job is the "arrangement of battles" [13] or, using a project management term, the "location of the solution" [7]. Thereby, it is much more important to avoid elementary mistakes than to demonstrate great sophistication. "The effects of a strategy do not appear as newly invented forms of action, which would instantly catch a person's eye, but manifest themselves in the auspicious final result of the whole. It is the right incidence of the silent suppositions, it is the noiseless harmony of the whole action, which is to be admired" [13]. Thus a successful strategy often turns out to be unspectacular, rather than brilliant. Brilliance, always seeking out difficulties, even contradicts the aim of prevention.

Management of Distributed Problems. The concern of a strategy is the identification and management of distributed problems. In its original sense, a strategy involves the study and application of laws determining the "total situation" (of war) [15], whereas tactics only consider "partial situations".

The total situation can never be expected to be visually conceivable. Instead, it is characterised by an immense number of interconnections between and among organisational groupings, geographic locations and chronological events. "As the characteristics of the total situation cannot be distinguished by means of the eyes, there is no alternative to intensive thinking" [15].

Analogously, the total situation of a software system can be characterised by the interconnections bridging physical, logical or chronological distances between causes and effects. Strategic interconnections are predominantly wide ones and are therefore latent or at least not evident.

The Precedence of Flexibility. The objective of a strategy is always directed towards the preservation and advance of flexibility. This is a necessary and sufficient condition for achieving superiority, equivalent forces assumed. "The quantitative superiority is the most general principle of victory" [13]. However, since quantity must be considered as a given magnitude, there is no alternative to "superiority on the crucial point" [13]. This, in turn, can only be achieved by a skilful game of dislocation, movement and concentration of forces - in effect, by the "concentration of strength against weakness" [14]. Flexibility in full measure is a pre-requisite - "the flexible deployment of forces is the main task of military command, and by no means an easy one" [15].

In other words, flexibility is not, as often represented in the software engineering literature, one of several strategic goals, each having perhaps equal rights. Rather, flexibility is the central goal from the point of view of true strategy.

Threats to Flexibility. Typically, the interconnections inherent in a distributed problem are irreversible. Such interconnections can severely jeopardise flexibility.

Therefore, the primary objectives of the identification and management of distributed problems must be based on methods for outflanking them. Any distributed problem must be examined with a view to its resolution or avoidance. Where a distributed problem can neither be outflanked nor reduced to local problems, highest vigilance - in terms of the interest in its interconnectivity - must be directed to its resolution.

Flexibility by Reduction of Interconnectivity. Following the fundamental rule of divide-et-impera, prevention of distributed problems amounts to a reduction of interconnectivity. This reduces distributed problems to local ones. It also affects the complexity and reduces the criticality of each part in the total performance of the whole. It implies that the scope of design decisions always tends to be limited and kept to a minimum. Universal decisions are to be avoided, according to the rule of "avoiding decisive battles" [13]. In general, the effect of universal interconnections is that "nothing works until everything works" [3].

Flexibility as a Principle of Organisation. Flexibility is a principle of organisation and it can never emerge without assistance. To prevent situations from getting out of control, a constant supply of energy is necessary.

Before implementation, this energy must be provided in the form of a permanent conceptual redesign. During implementation, the absence of a strategy leads to unforeseen tactical problems occurring from day to day. A mere tactician, even if brilliant, can succeed only in building up a increasingly interconnected system through ad-hoc measures. In the course of time, this converts originally local problems into distributed ones which are of increasing difficulty and which divert the efforts of the software development team from its proper task.

Lower Bounds of Interconnectivity. Modularity implies frictional losses between the modules. This is responsible for the trade-off between flexibility and efficiency. However, some of the criteria of modularisation tend to minimise those frictional losses. For instance, after modularisation, the need for intra-modular interaction should be essentially higher than that for inter-modular interaction. This means that modularity may itself contribute to the overall efficiency of the system, as long as things that belong together are being joined. Examples are the parallelling of algorithms, the divide-et-impera principle in the design of championship algorithms, the modularisation of communication networks and the clustering of data elements for efficient access.

Any modularisation that goes beyond the dictates of the purpose, however, is going to disjoin things which belong together. As simple examples of data access procedures demonstrate, the effect of over-modularisation can easily reduce performance by an order of magnitude. This cautionary note serves as a reminder to observe the lower bounds for the reduction of interconnectivity.

4.2 Design Tactics

Management of Local Problems. Evidently, a strategy tolerates tactical mistakes, since their effects are local and reversible. Nevertheless, there is a demand for tactical support with respect to the - local - processes of creating, changing, debugging, documenting, understanding and running a program under the constraints of time and resources.

The Precedence of Simplicity. It is obvious that human involvement with the processes of program development can best be supported by simplicity - starting with a simple algorithm and coding in a simple way. But what is "simple" and how is simplicity undermined?

Threats to Simplicity. Considering a confused program, there are three main sources of confusion. First, the program may contain code which reflects different levels of abstraction. This, however, is an error of strategy and should not occur after a good modularisation.

Second, a program normally allows, within limits, the permutation of source lines without affecting the underlying computation. This freedom often encourages and indulges the programmer's carelessness. A structured program requires neighbouring source lines to be interdependent with distant lines independent. This requirement is best met by a continuation of the strategy of "being local and not distributed" on the monolithic level. This decreases interconnectivity between and increases interconnectivity within the independent sections of the monolithic program.

Third, a program may contain both more operands and operations than necessary. That is, there may be operands highly interconnected in that they combine to play the role of one or more of the operands, essential to the problem's solution. The same is true for operations. The elimination of redundant operands and operations along with their interconnections again follows the stated strategy, aiming at decreased interconnectivity between and increased interconnectivity within the functional units of the program.

Simplicity by Reduction of Interconnectivity. A monolithic program can, therefore, be said to be "simple", if it

1) represents one level of abstraction and
2) exhibits a low degree of interconnectivity both between distant source lines and among operands and operations.

The first condition itself results from the - strategic - need for a reduction of interconnectivity.

Simplicity as a Principle of Organisation. As with flexibility, simplicity is a principle of organisation and, by the "law of increasing entropy", it can never emerge without assistance. To prevent chaotic situations from arising, a constant supply of energy is necessary and must be provided in the form of a permanent redesign. Redesign on a local level is not expensive. Moreover, the pay-off of the invested efforts will be realised later in the simplification of the processes of debugging, changing, documenting and understanding the program.

Upper Bounds of Interconnectivity. The different nature of constraints of time and resources for humans and machines gives rise to contradictory design requirements. In particular, since optimisation can be considered as the exploitation of logical and physical interconnections, the machine requirements would amount to an increase in the interconnectivity of operands and operations.

In a software system, it may be good policy to employ championship algorithms of, possibly, high inherent interconnectivity at certain places. However, as simplicity demands sophisticated, rather than simple minds, any other attempt at sophistication should be directed towards simplicity. On a local level, an order of magnitude in efficiency is less valuable than a corresponding improvement in clarity. This may be considered as an upper bound for the increase of interconnectivity within the functional units of the system and, in turn, as an upper bound for the tactical efforts in software design.

5 Summary

It has been argued that software design and implementation can be based on one single rule, namely the rule of reduction-of-interconnectivity.

Interconnectivity, including all kinds of physical, logical and chronological relations within a software system, is mainly determined by undesigned rather than designed interconnections. Whereas designed interconnections cater for functionality, it is the undesigned interconnections which affect flexibility and simplicity and are thus chiefly responsible for the quality of the software.

As an instance of the law of entropy, it can be observed that the absence of a systematic interest in the interconnectivity and its containment leads to an equally systematic increase of interdependency and confusion, leading unrelentingly to a state of maximal disorder.

This relationship is used to promote a methodology of "warfare against interconnectivity", based on true military principles. Design strategy and design tactics are differentiated by their respective goals of flexibility and simplicity. Both goals can be achieved by the application of the rule of reduction-of-interconnectivity in the large and in the small scale, respectively.

This approach conforms with many of the recognised design goals, principles and rules, permitting a consistent interpretation. Moreover, while it shares a common interest in the interconnectivity of software with recent CASE efforts, it points up the lack of concern for undesigned interconnections as a weakness of such systems.

6 Conclusion

Interconnectivity can be seen to be a central topic in the design and implementation of software. Form and content of software are essentially determined by interconnectivity and functionality. Thus, interconnectivity and functionality are topics worthy of equal importance in the study of software engineering.

Experience suggests that quality and productivity can be satisfied only to the extent that interconnectivity is mastered. This implies that there is need for a preventative engineering which aims at the containment of interconnectivity.

However, the detection of undesigned interconnections remains a practical problem for which neither formal methods nor CASE support are available. This may be a challenge for theory and CASE. On the other hand, it seems to be quite an ordinary task for the experience and intuition of an engineer. He needs only to be aware of it.

A more practical preventative engineering would totally relinquish conventional programming. The critical tasks would be dealt with by the compilation of standard solutions of determined intra- and inter-connectivity, leaving the software engineer with only the non-procedural specification tasks.

Acknowledgement

I am very grateful to Bill Hood, Pathways Programming Ltd., UK, for his active support and encouragement and for many critical and stimulating discussions. Moreover, that the text is readable is largely due to his editing.

References

1. Datapro Research Group: Introduction to Computer Aided Software Engineering. Datapro Reports on Software. McGraw-Hill 1990

2. H. Wedekind: Zur Entwurfsmethodologie von Systemen. Angewandte Informatik 1 (1972)

3. D.L. Parnas: Designing Software for Ease of Extension and Contraction. IEEE Transactions on Software Engineering, Vol SE-5, 2 (1979)

4. D.L. Parnas: Information Distribution Aspects of Design Methodology. Information Processing 71. North-Holland Publishing Company 1972

5. P.F. Elzer: Management von Softwareprojekten. Report on 2nd IFAC/IFIP Workshop 'Experience with the Management of Software Projects',Sarajevo 1988. Informatik-Spektrum 12 (1989)

6. E. Yourdon, L. Constantine: Structured Design. New York: Yourdon Press 1978

7. J. Schumann, M. Gerisch: Softwareentwurf. Köln: Verlagsgesellschaft Rudolf Müller 1986

8. H. Zuse: Software Complexity - Measures and Methods. Berlin: Walter de Gruyter 1991

9. Aristotle: Metaphysics. Oxford University Press 1992

10. J. Habermas: Erkenntnis und Interesse. Merkur: Deutsche Zeitschrift für europäisches Denken, Heft 213. Stuttgart 1965

11. M. Planck: Über den zweiten Hauptsatz der Mechanischen Wärmetheorie. München: Verlag Theodor Ackermann 1879

12. H.A. Simon: The Architecture of Complexity. Proc. of the American Philosophical Society, Vol. 106, No. 6 (Dec. 1962)

13. C.v. Clausewitz: Vom Kriege (On War). Stuttgart: Philip Reclam jun. 1980

14. B.H. Liddell Hart: Strategie. Wiesbaden: Rheinische Verlagsanstalt 1955

15. Mao Tsetung: Sechs Militärische Schriften (Six Military Treatises). Peking: Verlag für fremdsprachliche Literatur 1972

Distributed Information Systems: An Advanced Methodology

Alfred Aue, Michael Breu

European Methodology and Systems Center

Siemens Nixdorf Informationssysteme AG

Otto-Hahn Ring 6

8000 München 83

Abstract. Information systems ranging over wide areas show properties that must be carefully analysed and designed in order to meet the needs of the customers. Thus the development of such information systems is to be guided by software engineering methods that address problems like distribution of data and processes, communication aspects and fault tolerance.

This paper shows the basic modelling concepts and the development process employed by the BOS-Engineering Method to meet these requirements. The BOS-Engineering Method applies the concept of business transactions to specify behaviour in the early analysis phase. Appropriate abstraction levels are defined to reduce the complexity of specifying distribution issues.

The development of complex distributed information systems needs a rigorous life cycle model. The BOS-Engineering Method relaxes the waterfall life cycle model to allow controlled look ahead and feedback up and down the abstraction levels.

Keywords: Distributed Information Systems, Requirements Analysis, Requirements Engineering Method, Business Modelling, Development Process

1 Introduction

Developing distributed information systems in a systematic, cost-effective way is the challenge for the software engineering community during this decade. The technology for appropriate hardware and system software is available. But stringent methods for developing distributed information systems are not.

There is a rapidly increasing desire for information systems which range over wide areas. The common European market demands for systems allowing Europe wide exchange and administration of information, e.g. EURES (European employment information system) and EDIS (Electronic data interchange for the social domain). Trends towards common markets can also be observed on the Asian and the American continent.

Each of the information systems needed in this application area consists of a considerable number of cooperating data processing systems. Currently island solutions are connected by ad-hoc approaches. But methods are needed that support the comprehensive planning and construction of distributed information systems. An examination of well established systems engineering methods as Structured Analysis [Yourdon 89], SSADM [SSADM 90] or Merise [Tardieu et al. 89] reveals that all are targeted to the construction of centralized information systems. Neither takes into account distribution aspects like communication, locality of data and processes.

The work in [ABR 92] has shown that geographically distributed information systems have properties that must be addressed already on a high level of abstraction early in the development process. The requirement for fault tolerance, for example, makes the analysis and design of robustness and consistency inevitable.

The European Methodology & System Center - a joint initiative of the companies Bull, Olivetti and Siemens-Nixdorf - developed the BOS-Engineering Method to support the development of trans-european information systems. This paper presents the basic concepts of the BOS-Engineering Method that allows to model and develop geographically wide distributed information systems.

The BOS-Engineering Method roots in a harmonization and extension of the software engineering methods Merise/Omega from Bull, MOiS from Olivetti and GRAPES®/ Domino® from Siemens Nixdorf. It enhances these methods by additional concepts that capture distribution issues and track them through the levels of abstraction.

This paper introduces basic notions of distributed information systems engineering. It presents their use to describe information systems on appropriate levels of abstraction. Also a case is made for structuring the engineering process according to a relaxed waterfall model. The conclusion summarizes the contributions of the paper.

For illustration we use throughout the paper parts of a project in which the BOS-Engineering Method was used to model a car rental company with many rental stations. The main business of the company is to let cars. Car acquirement and sale were also covered by the project.

2 Concepts of the BOS-Engineering Method

The basis of every systems engineering method is the precise definition of the concepts the system analysts and designers have to deal with. The concepts of the BOS-Engineering Method are related to real world terms but are used throughout this paper with their defined meaning. We give here a short overview to make the presentation self-contained, a complete glossary can be found in [BBPU 92].

2.1 Information System

The BOS-Engineering Method considers an *information system* as a system that steers the execution of enterprise services and keeps track of services the enterprise relies on. Similar to Structured Analysis, SSADM and Merise, information systems are considered to do event processing. Interaction with an information system is achieved by the exchange of messages. An *event* is the sending or receipt of a message or a defined point in time. All activities in an information system are triggered by events.

A distributed information system is reactive in nature, i.e. it successively reacts to input stimuli issued by its environment (cf. [Pnueli 85]). It is not its goal to obtain a final result, but rather to maintain the interaction with the environment, e.g. the customers and car manufacturers related to the car rental company.

An information system describes a socio-technical organisation including automated and manual parts. The information systems, targeted at by the BOS-Engineering Method, are typically geographically distributed, i.e. they collect and provide information at numerous geographically separate locations which are not to be considered as one organizational unit.

2.2 Business Transaction

An adequate description of a reactive system must refer to its ongoing behaviour. The BOS-Engineering Method utilizes the concepts of business activities, actions and business transactions for this purpose.

A *business transaction* is a combination of logically connected *business activities*, e.g. the business transaction car rental consists of activities like reservation, car pick-up, car return and invoicing. An enterprise always performs various business transactions. Analysis and description of a business transaction is quite independent of the presence or absence of a computerized system. However, how it is performed may depend heavily on an information system.

Each business activity may be broken down into several lower level business activities. On a given level, there are causal dependencies among some business activities. This may mean that a given business activity must be preceded by certain other business activities, or must be performed before other business activities can be performed.

Actions are atomic business activities in the sense that during the execution of an action there are no intermediate states which are meaningful in the business area.

A business transaction is therefore defined by a finite set of causally related actions. Each business transaction is triggered and steered by a defined combination of events and executed by performing actions. This may include communication with the environment, e.g. the acknowledgement of a reservation, and depend on actions in other business transactions.

The main motivation for using business transactions for behaviour description is that they are an intuitive concept in business organization. They capture the units of understanding about the business of the business people. Thus there can be no objective criteria to judge which actions belong to a business transaction and which not. Business transactions have to be discovered in close correspondence with business people.

2.3 Information Resource

To document an information system in a systematic manner, the specification has to be structured. One type of structuring is the *organisational hierarchy* which shows the structure of the information system in terms of divisions, departments, locations etc. Equally important is the *conceptual hierarchy* which structures the responsibility for information, e.g. in the car rental system there are responsibility areas for information about cars, customers, booking etc.

An *information resource* encapsulates a part of the memorized information and the related actions this information can be manipulated with. In the BOS-Engineering Method the information resources are the building blocks for the conceptual hierarchy. In the car rental system, the car information resource is responsible for all information about cars. Its actions are register car, update car licence number, register car maintenance, car write off and car delete.

The business transactions together with the information resources provide a complete specification of the services of an information system. Especially in the case of geographically wide distributed information systems, the organizational structure needs to be described additionally. Although there seems to be a close relationship with object oriented analysis techniques as in [Coad 91], an information resource is rather related to the concept of "Sachbearbeiter" in [Denert 91]: An information resource does not necessarily correspond to a single entity in a data model, but may correspond to a collection of related entities together with the typical manipulations carried out on it.

A *data view* defines which entities an information resource is responsible for, and which entities it needs access to. It also defines the relationships between these entities.

2.4 Actor and Location

The building blocks of the organizational structure are the *actors*. At each geographical location individual actors are working that participate in the information system. The actors carry out the business activities in cooperation, i.e. they perform the business transactions. Each actor is uniquely assigned to a geographical *location*, i.e. to an organizational unit. The assignment of actors to locations is static. Change of the location, which an actor is assigned to, corresponds to a reorganisation of the business system.

The actors are supported (and in some rare cases replaced) by one or several *data-processing systems* (dp-systems), that steer and manipulate some of the information in the information system in electronic form. Thus a dp-system is an automated part of the information system. Typically a distributed information system contains several dp-systems.

A dp-system cooperates with other dp-systems, but may also run autonomously in case of communication failure by providing a degraded service and/or by buffering requests to other dp-systems. Typically, a dp-system is associated with one location, but may also serve other locations by remotely connected terminals or clients (client-server architecture, cf. [CD 88]).

3 Information System Models

These concepts are used to define the system model in the BOS-Engineering Method. The system model is an abstraction of a real world information system, may it already be existing or still planned. It documents all relevant facts and their relationships that are necessary to analyse, design and construct an information system. Additionally, it serves for the communication between different kinds of partners cooperating in a system development project.

This is reflected by two model views:

- The *business view* describes the management and business rules in the application area. It defines the information system inside the context of the enterprise. Manual and automated business activities are described by the same means. This view is mainly dedicated to the end user, but also defines the requirements for the technical view.
- The *technical view* describes the information system according to the needs of automated data processing. It gives the precise specification of the software and hardware components. The technical view must fulfil the requirements documented in the business view.

Each view splits into different levels of abstraction describing a submodel of the system model (see fig. 1). The top-most abstraction level in both views is the context model. It embeds the considered system into its context by defining its interface syntactically. In the business view the context model relates the information system to the whole enterprise and its business partners. In the technical view it embeds each dp-system into the considered information system and the network of other dp-systems. The internal levels give glass box descriptions on different levels of detail.

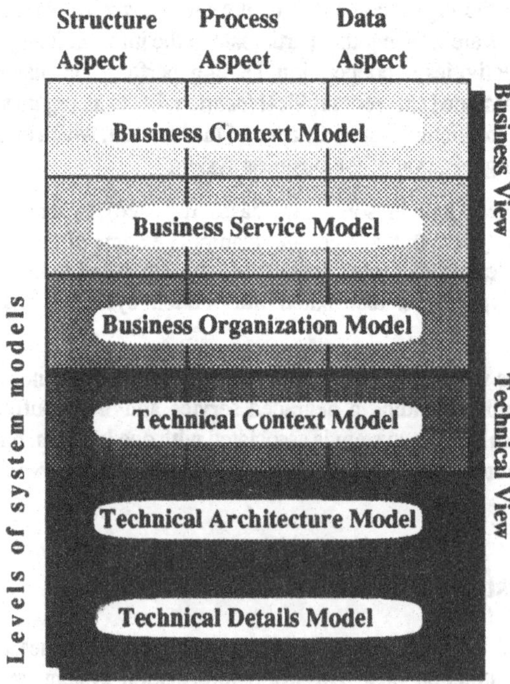

Fig. 1: Structure of the system model

Each level is described by

- its structure aspect, identifying the structure and relationship of the components of the system,
- the process aspect, documenting the behaviour and functionality of the components,
- the data aspect, documenting the information the components have to memorize or have to exchange with other components.

The following sections explain the upper four levels in more detail. These levels deal with distribution issues not covered by other methods. For a complete description of all levels see [BBPU 92].

3.1 Business Context Model

The business context model (for an example see fig. 2) defines the scope of the information system. It identifies the external partners, e.g. customer, that cooperate with the system and the messages, e.g. reservation, car delivery, it exchanges with them. Thus it shows the embedding of the information system in its context.

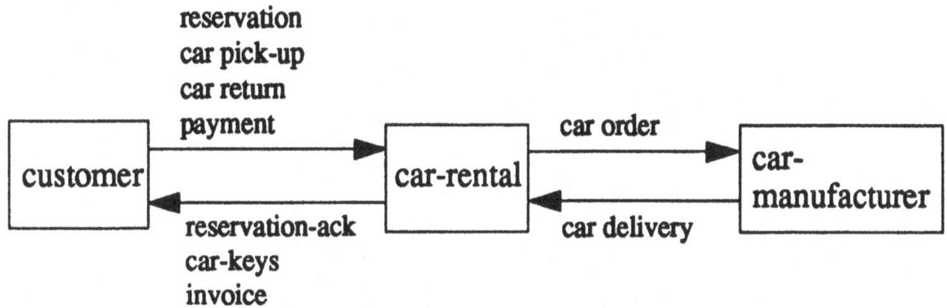

Fig. 2: Context Model of the *car rental information system*

This type of model is typical also for other methods like Structured Analysis, SSADM and SADT [RS 77].

3.2 Business Service Model

The business service model defines the conceptual structure and behaviour of the information system. It shows the underlying semantics of the business in terms of temporal distribution, i.e. causality and concurrency. Spatial distribution, i.e. the physical and organizational separation is described in the business organization model.

The business service model is built from an analysis of what has to be done in the part of the enterprise which is identified in the business context model. The business activities are not synonymous to computerized processes. The BOS-Engineering Method regards the specification of computerized processes as a matter of a different abstraction level.

Process Aspect

The processing aspect of the business service model contains a description of system behaviour and system functionality. Thus two perspectives of the processing aspect, the behaviour and the functionality, are distinguished (cf. [Olle et al. 91]). In distributed information systems the description of behaviour has to be given more emphasis as in conventional information systems because of their reactive nature and their inherent concurrency.

Behaviour Specification

The system behaviour, i.e. the semantics of the interface which is syntactically defined in the business context model, is specified directly by business transactions. Practical experience shows that we need to distinguish service transactions and support transactions (see fig. 3). It is important to note that only both types of business transactions together specify the behaviour of the system by a complete network of transactions.

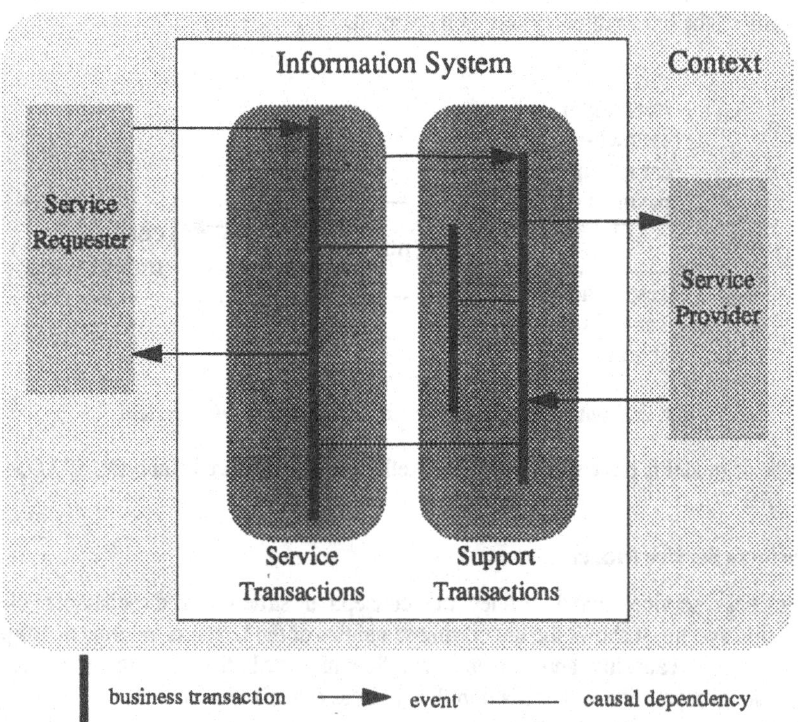

Fig. 3: Behaviour specification concepts

The causal dependencies of the business transactions complete the specification of the system behaviour. These causalities include exchange of information and synchronization. A causal dependency relates business activities in different business transactions, e.g. a business activity of one kind cannot happen until some other business activity has happened.

The *service transactions* are those business transactions which directly provide a service to the external partners (for an example see fig. 4), i.e. the semantic interface as seen by the service requesters. They are identified from the context model by choice of triggers. While direct causal dependencies of the service transactions can be shown, most of the causalities can only be expressed when including the support transactions.

Experience shows that in general the number of service transactions tends to be small, but the individual transactions tend to be complex.

The *support transactions* are those business transactions which are needed for the service transactions to provide the service. They include transactions that request services from external partners and purely internal transactions. The business transactions requesting services from external partners define the semantics of the external interface as seen by the service providers. The internal business transactions complete the behaviour specification. They make it possible to show the nature of all causal dependencies among business transactions as seen by the external partners.

An example of a support business transaction in the car- rental company is the internal car transfer between stations in order to resolve unbalanced demands for cars at certain stations.

System Functionality

The system functionality is described by the actions that make up the business transactions. The parameters and results of actions are specified. For each action the entities accessed and the mode of access (read or update) are recorded.

Each action is assigned to exactly one information resource. Each entity and each relationship must be assigned to the update responsibility of exactly one information resource data view. An entity or relationship may be used for enquiries in several data views. Thus the principles of data encapsulation and information hiding are used.

The concept of information resources thus naturally connects the processing and the data aspects early in the analysis process. This is the reason why the BOS-Engineering Method does not show the problems of incompatible data and process specifications which are inherent e.g. in Structured Analysis (cf. [Coad 91], [Ferstl et al. 91]).

Data Aspect

The data are described by data views which are assigned to information resources.

Traditionally, the business view of the system data is specified by a data model. The things to be modelled are that entities in the real world about which information must be held, and the relationships between those entities. The data model is represented by an E/R-diagram (cf. [Chen 76]) together with supporting descriptions of entities and relationships.

To avoid problems of complexity and comprehensibility of the representation the BOS-Engineering Method uses the concept of information resource data views for describing this information. All data views together make up an information model of the considered information system. Technically each data view is again represented by an E/R-diagrams plus supporting documentation.

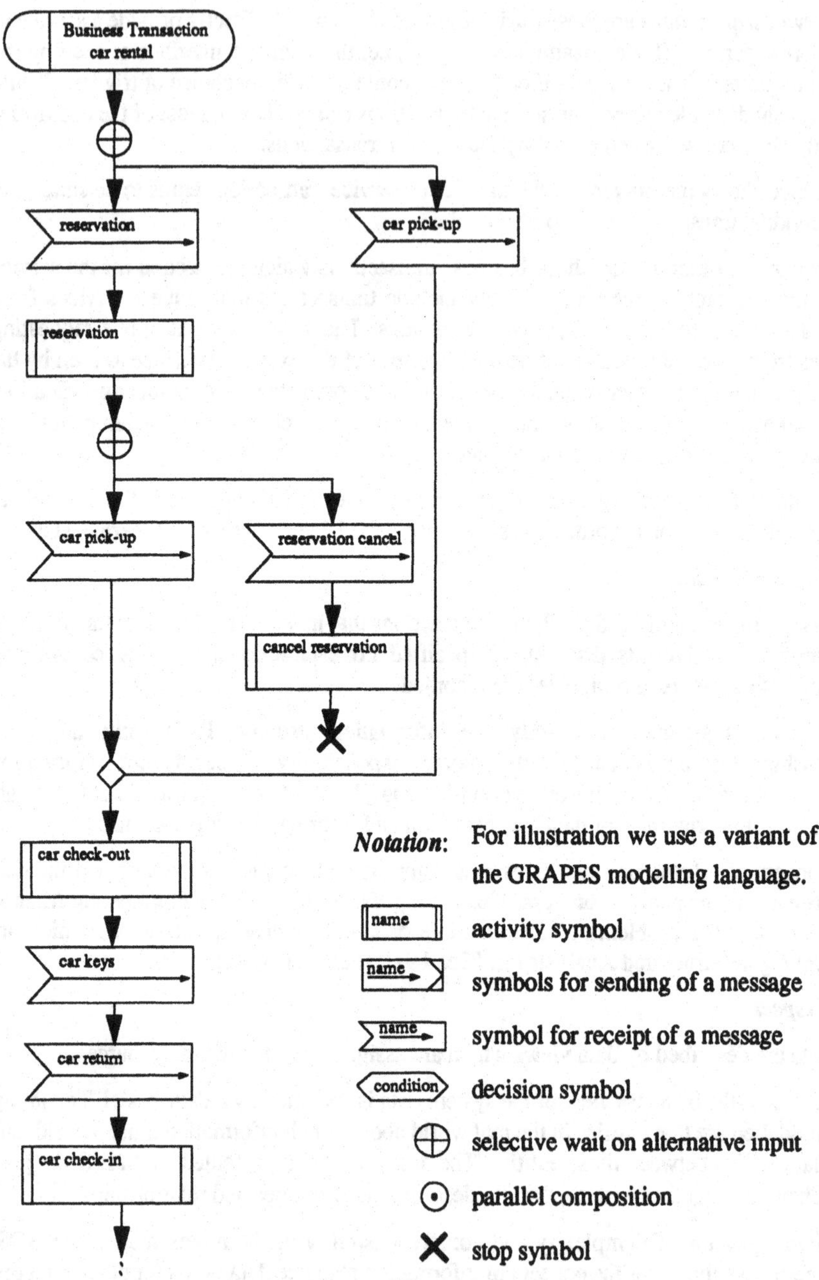

Fig. 4: A part of the *Car Rental Business Transaction*

Structure Aspect

The structure of the information system is described in the business service model by the conceptual hierarchy. No component or location structure is specified on this level of abstraction.[1]

The information resources are grouped into *information subjects* which correspond to business areas and sub-areas. Thus the conceptual hierarchy is built. The purpose of building this hierarchy is to structure the variety of information resources to larger units.

3.3 Business Organization Model

The purpose of the Business Organization Model is the mapping of the conceptual description of the business service level to the organizational and especially physical distribution structure of an enterprise.

Process Aspect

The execution of a business transaction in general spreads over several geographical locations and several actors. Thus the business activities, making up one business transaction, are carried out by different actors.

For each actor in the system his activities are documented, i.e. the process aspect of the business organization model shows the parts of the business transactions carried out by each actor (see e.g. fig. 5). The causal dependency between activities is now achieved by synchronization messages exchanged between actors within and across locations. Thus the process aspect of the business organization level is derived from the business transactions on the business service level by distributing them to different actors.

Although we do not distinguish between manual and automated activities in the business view, it is here, where we describe the degree of automatization: manual, interactive, or batch. This leads to the design of manual activities, dialogues and schedules for batch activities in the technical view.

Data Aspect

On the business organization level also the location of data usage is identified. This builds the base for the physical distribution of data on the technical levels. For each actor and each location the accessed data is documented in a dedicated data view. Each data view of an actor contains all the entities that are accessed by the actions contained in the fractions of the business transactions assigned to this actor. In other words, the data view of an actor is the union of the data views of the information resources he uses.

1. It is important not to confuse business transactions with system components or processes. When producing a component oriented specification (cf. [Weber 92]) we structure the system description according to the logical or physical structure of the system. When describing the system by a network of business transactions, we structure the system description according to our understanding of the business area, independently of the system structure.

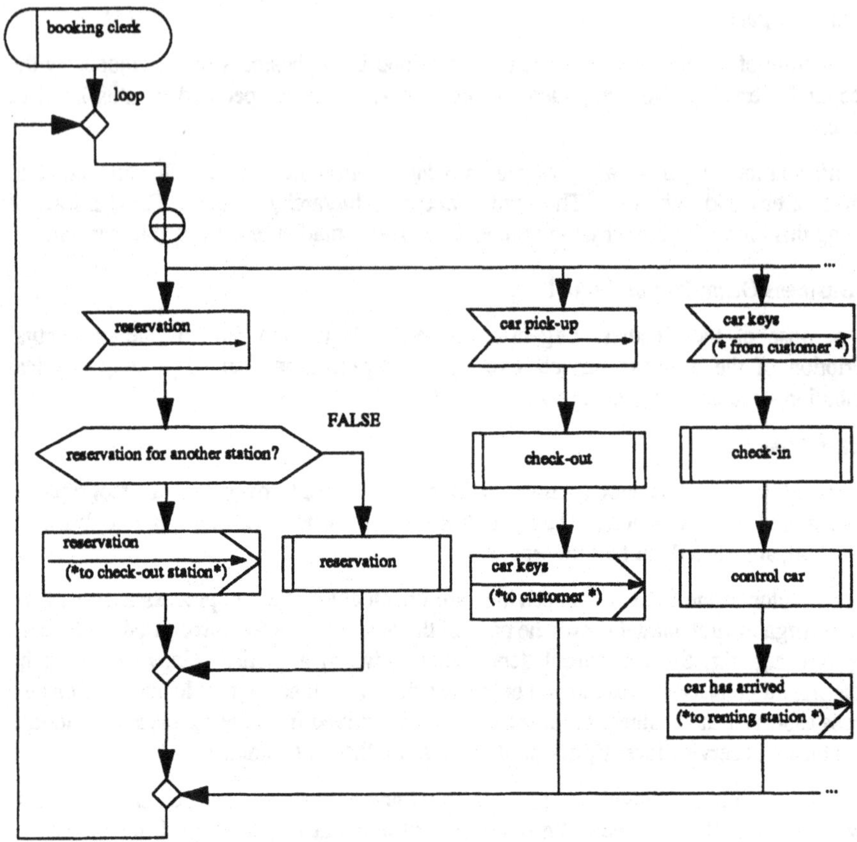

Fig. 5: Activities of the actor *booking clerk*

The data view of a location is the union of all data views of the actors operating in that location. Data views of different actors and locations naturally overlap, e.g. a car rental station needs access to the data shown in fig. 6.

As already explained, the business view uses the same techniques for describing manual and automated parts of the system. But we assign to each action in a business activity its degree of automation (manual, interactive, batch). Note that a business activity may be refined by several sets of actions with different degrees of automation.

Structure Aspect

In the business organisation model the system is described as a structure of cooperating actors achieving together the business transactions of the system. Actors are associated with locations representing the geographical units the information system is distributed to. Thus actors and locations represent the organizational hierarchy.

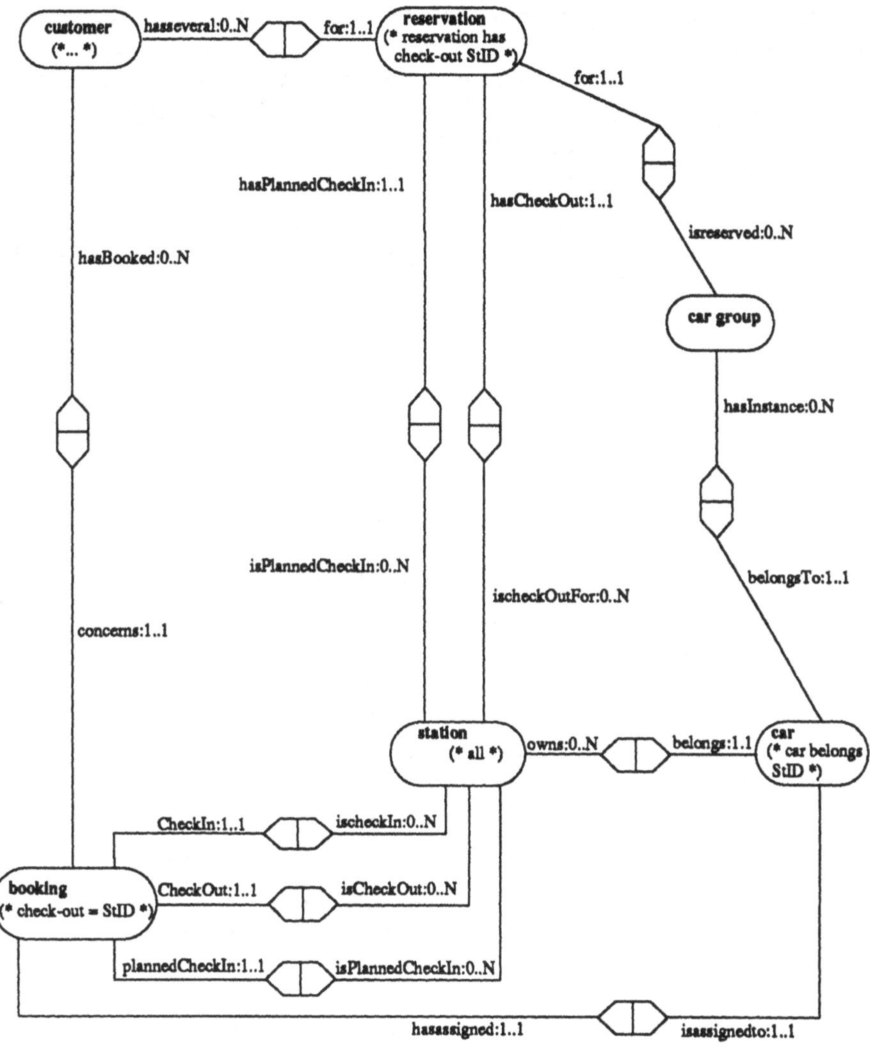

Fig. 6: Data view of *car rental station*

Since often a distributed information system consists of a huge number of locations it is not fruitful to show the interaction between all of them. It is better to investigate the different roles a location can play and show their communication.

In the car rental example a station is involved in four main fields of activity: Processing of reservations, renting of cars (check-out), processing of car returns (check-in) and internal transfers of cars between stations. The interaction of these location roles is illustrated by a location interaction diagram (see fig. 7). It shows the communication between different instances of locations, each playing only one role.

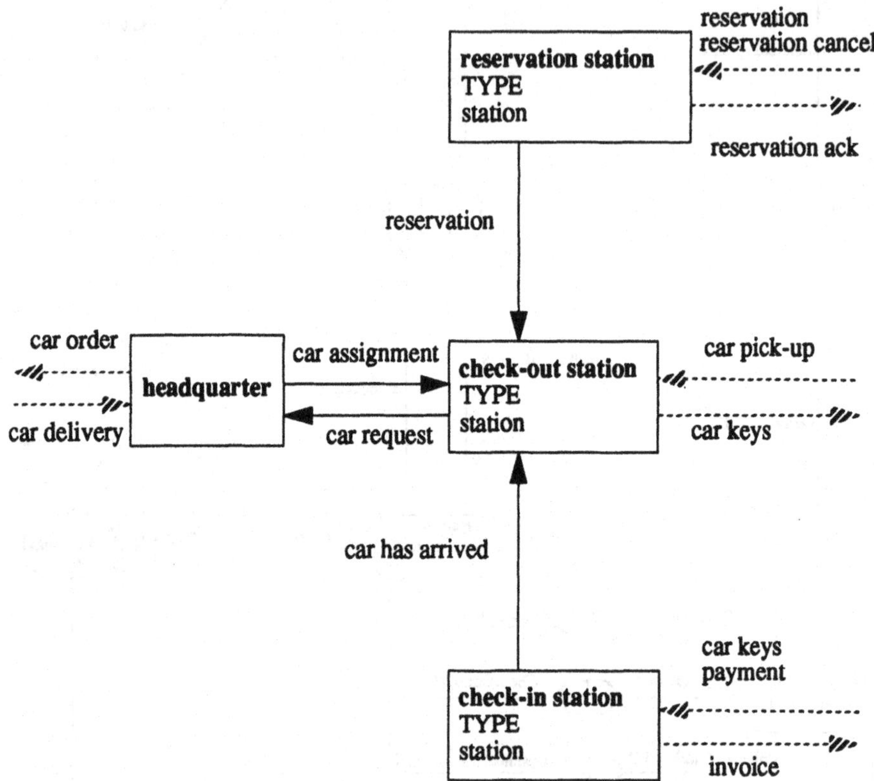

Fig. 7: Location interaction diagram for car rental station

3.4 Technical Context Model

The technical context model converts the business view into the technical view. It identifies the data-processing systems that cooperate to achieve the automated parts of the whole information system. Thus the context of a dp-system contains all the other dp-systems and the human actors using the dp-system. Additionally the precise distribution of data and processing to locations and actors is fixed (we do here not discuss fine grain distribution on multi-processors etc.). On the lower levels of the system model the distribution aspect only plays a minor role. There we concentrate on the description of each dp-system separately.

Structure Aspect

The structure aspect is given by the following two interface descriptions:

- *dp-system interface structure*: It defines the interfaces to the other dp-systems, i.e. the type and contents of the messages exchanged and/or communication protocols to be used. The main input for its definition is the location interaction diagram.
- *user dialogue structure*: It defines the principal functionality as seen from the human actors using the dp-system. The processing aspect of each actor of the business organization model is the main input for the definition of user dialogue structures (e.g. interaction diagrams cf. [Denert 91]).

The functionality of the application kernel is defined by the information resources needed to support the actors (humans and dp-systems). They lead to the definition of the process and the data aspect.

Process Aspect

The assignment of the information resources to the dp-systems is defined. The actions associated with the information resources are the main part of the application kernel. The precise design of the actions is done on the lower levels of abstraction.

Information resources are atomic units with respect to automation on a data-processing system, i.e. an information resource (its data and its actions) can only be automated as a whole.

Data Aspect

The location data views serve as a basis for the evaluation of different data distribution scenarios: Data only accessed by one location should naturally be stored locally. For data accessed at different locations the storage location must be decided explicitly.

The data base schema for each dp-system is defined. It represents in general a vertical and horizontal partitioning of the global information model perhaps with replication (cf. [BG 92]). If a distributed data base management system (DDBMS) is used, remote data is accessed in the same way as local data. Without a DDBMS remote access and consistency control must be done by explicit communication.

4 Information System Development Process

The information system development process in the BOS-Engineering Method follows a well defined development process, which is basically a relaxed version of the waterfall model (cf. [HE 90]). The main difference to the waterfall model is that at some points in the development draft documents may be part of a project deliverable. Another feature is that work products belonging to a deeper level of abstraction may cause feed back to earlier levels. So levels of abstraction are only loosely coupled with progression in development. In this section we shortly sketch the structure of the development process.

4.1 Phases, Stages

The development process consists of the requirements definition phase, the design phase and the implementation phase. Each phase decomposes into stages as shown in fig. 8.

Phase	Stage
Requirements Definition	*Preliminary Study* *Information System Requirements Specification* *Data-processing System Specification*
Design	*Information System Specification* *Data-processing System Specification*
Implementation	*Production and Qualification* *Installation of Information System*

Fig. 8: Phases and stages

The purpose of the *preliminary study*, which is the start of the requirements definition phase, is the analysis of the problems in the current information system and the elaboration of requirements and constraints for the new information system. It shows up options to overcome the problems and to fulfil the requirements and constraints.[1] The scope of the selected information system option is elaborated and validated in the *information system requirements specification*. The definition of the information system is developed further during the *data-processing requirements specification* in order to identify the appropriate data-processing systems.

The design phase begins with the *information system specification*. During this stage, the conceptual analysis and organizational design of the information system is completed, respecting influences of the selected data-processing systems. The system model is completed in the *data-processing system specification*. Thus after this stage the data-processing systems and the manual activities to be implemented are specified completely.

The implementation phase completes the development. The *production and qualification* stage comprises the coding, the testing and qualification of the data-processing systems. During the *installation of information system* stage, the data-processing systems are integrated and installed to establish the whole information system.

4.2 Milestones, Baselines

In the BOS-Engineering Method each phase terminates at a *baseline*. A baseline is a precisely specified set of products (documents and software) which are administrated together by the configuration management and which are a reliable basis for any further activities. The components of a baseline must only be modified with a formal change procedure. Thus at a baseline certain products go under the administration of change control. Baselines link the system development to change control.

1. It is project dependent what level of detail or abstraction is seeked. Not untypical is a bottom-up approach for the current system from technical details to the business concepts.

Each of the stages in the BOS-Engineering Method terminates at a *milestone*. A milestone is an important point in the course of the development process which can be scheduled and may be used for evaluating the progress of the development. At a milestone the work products developed so far are collected for project control, quality inspection and decision making. Thus milestones provide the link from system development to project management.

4.3 Progression through Abstraction Levels

Although structured in phases and stages the BOS-Engineering Method does not follow strictly the idea of a waterfall development. At any stage of the development process, several levels of the system model are considered in parallel (see fig. 9).

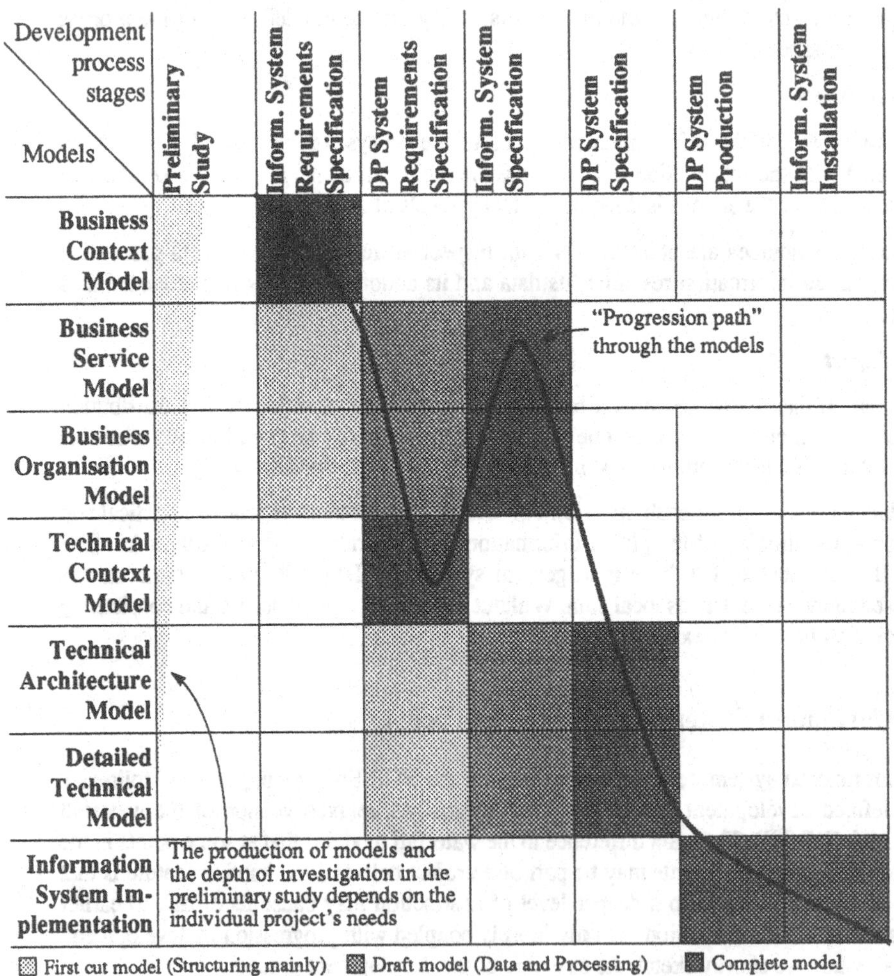

Fig. 9: Progression through the abstraction levels

There is a many to many mapping between milestones and abstraction levels. This allows for feedback and look ahead up and down the abstraction levels which is essential for judgment of risks and realizability of decisions which have to be taken at high levels of abstraction. This means e.g. that technical considerations may be used to refine the information system requirements specification.

The development process defines a sequence of decisions without imposing a sequence of development steps along the levels of the system model. To keep the development process manageable despite this relaxation of the waterfall model, the states through which each product passes have to be made explicit.

4.4 States of Products

The state of each product has two dimensions, the development state and the decision state. Thus the state of a product reflects how elaborated a product is and which management decisions it has gone through (see fig. 10).

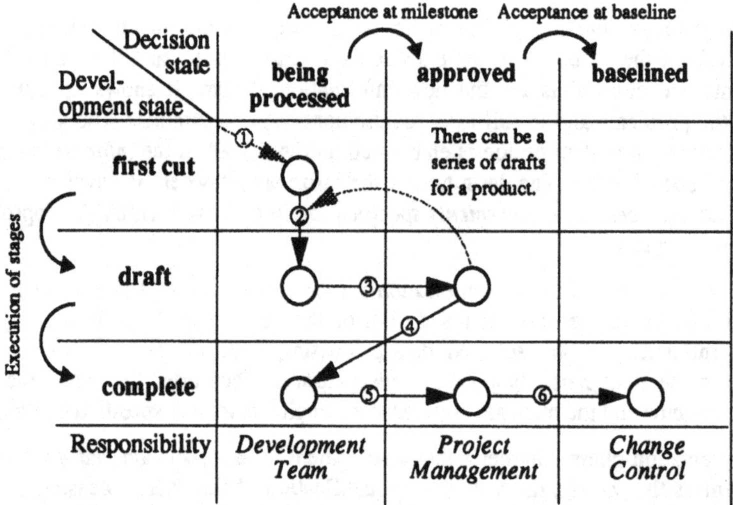

Transition between states

1. The life of a product starts as a first cut product produced by the development team which also has the responsibility for changes to the product.
2. Starting from the first cut product a draft is produced by the development team.
3. At milestones, draft products are examined by project management. In case of acceptance the product becomes an approved draft.
4. Starting from the approved draft a complete product - or the next draft defined for the product - is produced by the development team.
5. At milestones, complete products are examined by project management. In case of acceptance the product becomes an approved complete product.
6. At baselines, approved complete products go under change control. In this case they become baselined products.

Fig. 10: States of products

The development states are *first cut*, *draft* and *complete*. At *first cut* state, the content of the product is not yet well established. It just gives an outline of the product. A product with well established content which is still not complete is in *draft* state. Only products with well established and complete content are in *complete* state.

The decision states are *being processed*, *approved* and *baselined*. A product which is currently under development is in *being processed* state. A product reaches the approved state when the content of the product is considered stable but not yet definitive. The content might be changed if successive development discovers the need to do so. Changes to the product are under the control of the project management. The *approved* state is allowed for draft and complete products only. If a product is in state *baselined* its content is definite, i.e. all successive products have to be consistent with its content. The product can be changed through change control procedures only. This state is allowed for complete products only.

5 Conclusions

The systematic development of large-scale distributed information systems is still one of the major challenges in software engineering. The BOS-Engineering Method shows the way towards well-adapted methodologies which can help to cope with the enormous quantitative and qualitative complexity involved.

The main contributions are:

Specification of behaviour early in the analysis

Specification of behaviour in early analysis phases is only possible if the concepts used are appropriate for discussion with users. Business transactions are an intuitive concept in business organization. There are no objective criteria to judge which actions belong to a business transaction and which not. Business transactions have to be 'designed' in close correspondence with the business people. However, they are appropriate to capture their units of understanding of the business.

When modelling distributed information systems two important sets of facts have to be recorded corresponding to temporal and spatial distribution. The BOS-Engineering Method shows how to reduce the complexity of this task by separation into abstraction levels. The business service level describes the temporal distribution, i.e. facts about causality and concurrency. The business organization level adds facts about the spatial distribution, i.e. location information for data and processes.

Solve feedback problems in the waterfall model

The main problem of the waterfall lifecycle model is to handle feedback, i.e. changes of products of earlier phases. The BOS-Engineering Method shows how to solve this problem without raising project management problems inherent in spiral models (cf. [Boehm 86]).

Important is the separation of milestones and abstraction levels. This allows to "look ahead" for judgement of risks and realizability of decisions that have to be taken at high levels of abstraction, i.e. distribution of data and processing.

However, this separation is not enough. The collection of knowledge during analysis and design naturally proceeds in parallel at several abstraction levels. The products describing the separate levels depend on each other, i.e. they cannot be produced in one shot. To allow for a controllable engineering process in spite of this, the BOS-Engineering Method explicitly recognizes states of products which show how elaborate the descriptions of an abstraction level are and which decisions are based upon it.

Although we are close to a method for the development of distributed application systems which finds wide acceptance in the SSADM, MERISE, MOiS and GRAPES communities, further work has to be done towards adequate description formalisms including graphical representations that are able to support such an advanced methodology.

Acknowledgments: This paper relies heavily on the initial definition of the BOS-Engineering Method. We gratefully acknowledge the work of L. Barengo, M. Pfeiffer and J.-C. Utter who developed the BOS-Engineering Method.

References

[ABR 92] A. Aue, M. Breu, K. Robinson, Distributed Systems Guide, Feasibility Report, internal report by EMSC and CCTA 1992

[BBPU 92] L. Barengo, M. Breu, M. Pfeiffer, J.-C. Utter, Definition of the BOS-Method - A Method for Transeuropean Information Systems (Version 0), EMSC Report, München, Paris, Ivrea, 1992

[BG 92] D. Bell, J. Grimson, Distributed Database Systems, Addison-Wesley, 1992

[Boehm 86] B. W. Boehm, A Spiral Model of Software Development and Enhancement, ACM SEN, Vol. 11, No. 3, pp. 14-24, August 1986

[Chen 76] P. Chen, The Entity-Relationship Model - Toward a unified View of Data, ACM Trans. on Database Systems, Vol. 1, 1976

[Coad 91] P. Coad: Object Oriented Analysis; Englewood Cliffs 1991

[CD 88] G. Colouris, J. Dollimore, Distributed Systems: Concepts and Design, Wokingham, 1988

[De Marco 78] T. De Marco: Structured Analysis and System Specification; New York 1978

[Denert 91] E. Denert: Software Engineering, Springer Verlag, 1991

[Ferstl et al. 91] O. K. Ferstl, E. J. Sinz, Ein Vorgehensmodell zur Objektmodellierung betrieblicher Informationssysteme im Semantischen Objektmodell (SOM), Wirschaftsinformatik, Vol. 33, No. 6, 1991, pp. 477-491

[GRAPES 91] G. Held (ed.): GRAPES - Language Description; Munich 1991

[Held 91] G. Held (ed.): Informations- und Funktionsmodellierung mit GRAPES; Munich 1991

[HE 90] B. Henderson-Sellers, J. Edwards, The object oriented systems life cycle, Comm. ACM, Vol. 33, No. 9, September 1990, pp. 142-159

[Hopkins/Duschl 92]N. Hopkins, R. Duschl (eds.): The SSADM-GRAPES Comparison Study; Springer, Berlin, 1992

[Olle et al. 91] T. W. Olle, J. Hagelstein, I. G. Macdonald, C. Rolland, H. G. Sol, F. J. M. Van Assche, A. A: Verrijn-Stuart, Information System Methodologies: A Framework for Understanding, 2nd ed., Wokingham, 1991

[Peters 88] L. Peters: Advanced Structured Analysis and Design; 1988

[Pnueli 85] A. Pnueli, Applications of Temporal Logic to the Specification and Verification of Reactive Systems: A Survey of Current Trends, in: LNCS 224, Berlin Heidelberg NewYork, 1985, pp. 510-584

[RS 77] D. Ross, K. Schomann Jr., Structured Analysis for Requirements Definition, IEEE Trans. on SE, January 1988, pp. 6-15

[SSADM 90] CCTA: SSADM Version 4 Manuals; Norwich 1990

[Tardieu et al. 89]H. Tardieu, A. Rochefeld, R. Coletti, G. Panet, G. Vahée: La Méthode Merise (3 tomes); Paris 1989

[Weber 92] R. Weber, Eine Methodik für die formale Anforderungsspezifikation verteilter Systeme, Technische Universität München, Dissertation 1992

[Yourdon 89] E. Yourdon: Modern Structured Analysis; New Jersey 1989

Tractable Flow Analysis for Anomaly Detection in Distributed Programs

S.C. Cheung J. Kramer

Department of Computing,
Imperial College of Science, Technology and Medicine
180 Queen's Gate, London SW7 2BZ, UK.

Abstract. Each process in a distributed program or design can be modelled as a process flow graph, where nodes represent program statements and directed edges represent control flows. This paper describes a flow analysis method to detect unreachable statements by examining the control flows and communication patterns in a collection of process flow graphs. The method can analyse programs with loops, non-deterministic structures and synchronous communication using an algorithm with a quadratic complexity in terms of program size. The method follows an approach described by Reif and Smolka [9] but delivers a more accurate result in assessing the reachability of statements. The higher accuracy is achieved using three techniques: statement dependency, history sets and statement re-reachability. The method is illustrated by a pump control application for a mining environment. A prototype has been implemented and its performance is presented.

1. Introduction

There is a need for automatic analysis techniques to detect anomalous behaviour in distributed systems. Exhaustive analysis of the behaviour in terms of state space graphs is difficult due to the combinatorial state explostion problem, where the state space of a system can increase geometrically in terms of the system size [12]. To avoid this problem, more tractable but non-exhaustive techniques using flow analysis have been proposed [6, 9, 13].

In our analysis, a distributed application is made up of a system of sequential processes. Processes in the system *communicate synchronously* with each other by transmitting and receiving messages. A process sending a message needs to wait for the process receiving the message; and vice versa. We assume a pure message passing system where synchronous communications are the only way through which processes can interact with one another.

Flow analysis is a method to detect two classes of errors in distributed applications: *synchronisation errors* and *data-usage errors* [5]. Synchronisation errors, such as deadlock and starvation, are errors usually caused by communication anomalies. Data-usage errors are errors caused by misuse in data variables. They include errors of reading uninitialised variables or simultaneously updating a shared variable by parallel processes. In this paper, we are only concerned with the synchronisation errors.

Process *P*	Process *Q*	Process *R*
x, y: variables	x, y: variables	x, y: variables
p1 loop	*q1* loop	*r1* y = 0
p2 read x from file1	*q2* read x from file2	*r2* loop
p3 send x to channel a	*q3* send x to channel b	*r3* receive x from channel a
p4 receive y from channel d	*q4* receive y from channel e	*r4* y = func(x, y)
p5 if y > 0 then	*q5* send x - y to channel d	*r5* if y > 0 then
p6 send x*y to channel c	*q6* end loop	*r6* receive y to channel b
p7 end loop		*r7* else
		r8 send x to channel e
		r9 receive y from channel c
		r10 end loop

Fig. 1. A System *S* of Three Processes *P*, *Q* and *R*

For instance, consider a system *S* with three sequential processes *P*, *Q* and *R* whose behaviours are shown in Fig. 1. A flow analysis of system *S* using the method described in this paper, reveals that statements *p4*, *p5*, *p6* and *p7* of process *P*, statements *q4*, *q5* and *q6* of process *Q*, and statements *r8*, *r9* and *r10* of process *R* are never executed.

2. Related Work

Flow analysis of distributed systems has been studied by several researchers.

Kanellakis and Smolka proposed an algorithm to detect non-progress properties [3]. However, the algorithm is only polynomial under various assumptions, such as the interconnection of processes is a tree and that the processes are free of loops.

Peng and Purushothaman proposed a flow analysis technique for networks of two communicating finite state machines to detect non-progress properties [7]. The approach involves the construction of the network's product machine restricted to a network with two communicating processes. The work is extended in [8] to analyse a network of multiple processes but the complexity of the algorithm may grow exponentially with the number of processes.

Yang and Chung proposed a method to check the feasibility of a given linear execution path, based on several synchronisation rules [13]. However, the number of execution paths to be examined, increases exponentially with the number of non-deterministic structures.

Reif and Smolka refined their work [10] in [9]. In their paper [9], a linear algorithm is presented to detect unreachable statements and construct an event spanning graph for asynchronous communication systems. The algorithm does not give a sufficiently accurate result in the communication models where messages are removed from the channels after reception. Some statements identified as reachable by the algorithm may, in fact, be unreachable in the actual systems. A higher accuracy can be achieved with the method described in this paper with a small increase in computational cost.

Mercouroff proposed an approximate method to identify matching communication pairs based on their number of occurrences [6]. Lattices of arithmetic congruences are required to approximate the sets of event counters. However, there is a lack of detail in selecting the factor adjusting the sensitivity of analysis, constructing the lattices of arithmetic congruences, and analysis of the complexity.

Avrunin et. al. adopted an approach that approximates a concurrent system by a set of event inequalities [1]. The algorithm may produce "spurious" solutions that do not correspond to the behaviour of the concurrent system. Depending on individual cases, the computation of inequalities can suffer from exponential complexity. In addition, the approach provides little information about the anomaly when a set of inequalities is found to be inconsistent.

Generally, each method has its pros and cons. The compromises are usually made along three lines: how general is the method, how accurate is the result, and how tractable is the method. It is unlikely that there is a single method which can achieve all three goals simultaneously. In this paper, we describe a tractable method that is general enough for practical problems, and useful enough for a preliminary understanding of processes' behaviour. An approach similar to [9] is taken because of its generality and tractability. Although our method does not reveal all possible synchronisation errors in a system, it manages to identify a number of errors which cannot be easily spotted manually. It is a technique that one would employ to acquire an initial analysis of a design before submitting it to more sophisticated but computationally expensive analysis methods, such as state space graph construction or proposition provers.

Our method is general enough to analyse systems with arbitrarily loops and nested non-deterministic structures. The method adopts an approach similar to [9], but delivers a higher accuracy with a complexity quadratic in terms of program statements. The higher accuracy is achieved by cutting down spurious execution sequences using three techniques: statement dependency, history sets and statement re-reachability.

These techniques will be described respectively in sections 6, 7 and 8 along with three polynomial algorithms: A, B and C. Algorithm A, described in section 5, is an adaptation of Reif's algorithm in [9] for synchronous communication systems. The algorithm is used to compute the dependency among statements in section 6. Algorithm B is an algorithm achieving a more accurate result than A with the first two techniques: statement dependency and history sets. Algorithm C improves B with the third technique: statement re-reachability. These algorithms are illustrated by a pump controller example in section 9. A prototype based on algorithm C has been implemented and the performance is given in section 10.

3. The Flow Graph Model

The flow graph model presented below is adapted from [9] for synchronous communication. A formal description of a similar flow graph model can be found in [9].

The behaviour of a process can be described by a *process flow graph (PFG)*, where nodes represent statements and directed edges represent control flows. For example, process *P* in Fig. 1 can be described by a PFG in Fig. 2a. Flow graphs (sometimes known as flow charts) are commonly used in the design and analysis of sequential systems. They are usually extended to accommodate transmit and receive statements for distributed systems.

3.1. Descriptions

Nodes in a PFG can be classified into three types: internal, transmitting and receiving. Internal nodes are executed locally without a need for synchronisation while both transmitting and receiving nodes have to be executed synchronously with their complements in other processes. A node *n'* is said to be a *complement* of *n* if (i) they both share the same channel; and (ii) one of them is a transmitting node and the other is a receiving node. For example, in Fig. 2, node *a*! is a complement of *a*?, and vice versa.

In a PFG, an internal node is symbolised by a local name (e.g. *p* in Fig. 2a); a transmitting node is symbolised by a *channel name* followed by '!' (e.g. *a*! in Fig. 2a); and a receiving node is symbolised by a channel name followed by '?' (e.g. d? in Fig. 2a). A node is said to be a *child* (*parent*) of another node *n*, if it is a succeeding (preceding) neighbour of *n* in a PFG. For example, node *d*? is a child and *p* is a parent of *a*! in Fig. 2a.

A node in a PFG has to be *visited* before it is executed. Initially, only *start nodes*, marked by two concentric circles in PFGs, are visited. When a node is visited, the type of the node is examined. If the type is internal, the node is executed immediately. Otherwise, the node has to wait for a visit of its complement before it can be executed. When a node has been executed, one of its children in the PFG is chosen arbitrarily for the next visit. The process terminates when no child can be chosen. The process blocks when it is visiting a communicating node that can never be executed synchronously with a complement.

3.2. Definitions

A PFG G_i of a process P_i in a system is a tuple $< N_i, E_i, s_i >$, where N_i denotes the set of nodes, E_i denotes the set of directed edges, and s_i denotes the *start node*. There is a single thread of control in a PFG. An *execution sequence* is a sequence of nodes that have been executed by a process. The execution sequence must be a path in the associated PFG beginning at the *start node*. For example, "*p.a*!" is a sequence taken by process *P* to execute nodes *p* and *a*! in Fig. 2.

A node in a PFG is visited by means of an execution sequence. A node can only be visited by the current execution sequence if it is a child of the last element in the sequence. A node is said to be *reachable* by the current execution sequence if it can be visited and executed by the sequence; otherwise it is said to be *unreachable*. For example, in Fig. 2a, node *d*? cannot be visited by an execution sequence "*p*"; therefore it is unreachable by the sequence. However, *d*? can be visited by an sequence "*p.a*!". If it can then be executed upon the visit, we say that *d*? is reachable by "*p.a*!"; otherwise we say that *d*? is unreachable by "*p.a*!". If *d*? is unreachable by any execution sequence, it is said to be unreachable.

Conditional "*if-then-else*" statements from the original program are modelled as non-deterministic choices in the PFG. The data value held by the conditional or guarded variables are discarded in the model. This simplification is common to many synchronisation analysis techniques for distributed programs but has the disadvantage of allowing additional and spurious execution sequences [11]. Symbolic execution techniques can be used if data values are considered [14].

A node identified as unreachable in our method implies the corresponding statement can never be executed in the original program where the usual semantics of conditionals are considered. But a node identified as reachable in our method does not necessarily mean the corresponding statement can be executed in the original program. Hence, the results delivered are *conservative* in *unreachability* but *not conservative* in *reachability*.

3.3. Example

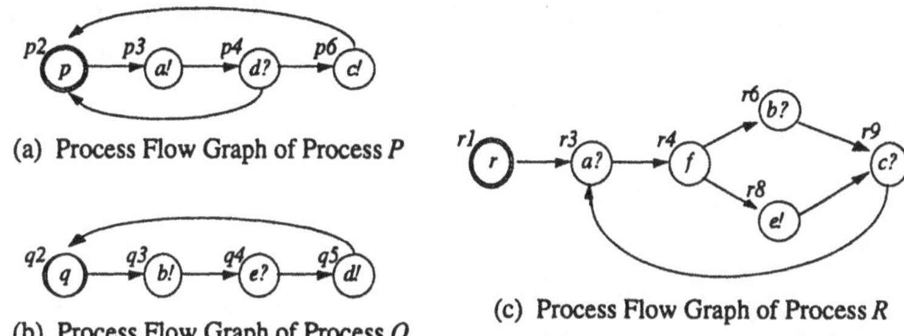

(a) Process Flow Graph of Process *P*

(b) Process Flow Graph of Process *Q*

(c) Process Flow Graph of Process *R*

Fig. 2. PFGs of Process P, Q and R

Fig. 2 shows the PFGs of process *P*, *Q* and *R* in Fig. 1. Corresponding statement labels in Fig. 1 are shown next to nodes in the PFGs. Some internal statements in the original programs are omitted to make the graph simpler. The *if* statement *p5* is modelled as a non-deterministic choice of two edges (*d*?,*p*) and (*d*?,*c*!). Similarly the *if-then-else* statement *r5* is modelled as a non-deterministic choice of two edges (*f*,*b*?) and (*f*,*e*!).

4. Renaming of Statements

For simplicity, the flow analysis algorithms presented in the paper assume uniqueness of synchronisation pairs, such that there is a unique complement for each communicating node in a collection of PFGs. For example, there is a unique complement *a*! in the system, which may synchronise with the node *a*? in Fig. 2. Under this assumption, a node is therefore unreachable if it can never be executed synchronously with its unique complement. This assumption imposes no restriction to the generality of the algorithms. This can be achieved by a simple renaming mechanism and introduction of non-deterministic structures.

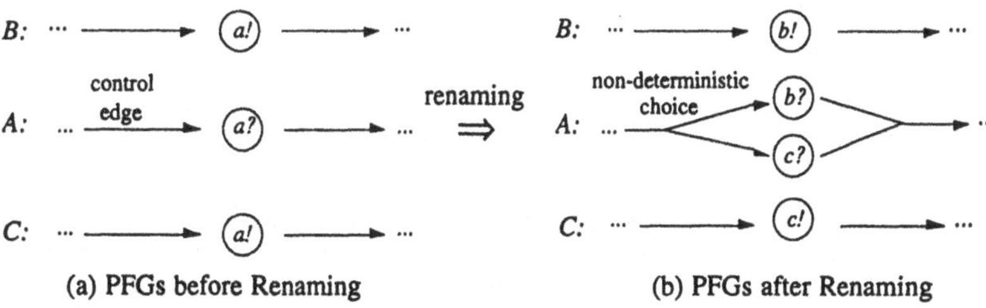

(a) PFGs before Renaming

(b) PFGs after Renaming

Fig. 3. Achieving Unique Synchronisation Pairs by Renaming

For example, a set *Chl* (say $\{b, c\}$) is generated when node *a*? is identified to have two complements in Fig. 3a. The statement *a*? in the original graph is then replaced by a non-deterministic structure of branches containing nodes *b*? and *c*? in Fig. 3b. The channel names of the complements are exclusively renamed to *b*! and *c*!.

```
while there is a node x in the system with more than one complement do
    let n be the number of complements
    generate a set Chl containing n unique channel names
    replace the node x by a non-deterministic structure of n branches, each of them containing a
        node, and the channel of each node is exclusively named by a name in Chl
    rename the channel name of each complement exclusively by a name in Chl
end while
```

5. Adaptation of Reif's Algorithm

A linear algorithm to detect unreachable nodes for asynchronous systems is given in [9]. The algorithm is adapted slightly in this section for synchronous systems. In the adapted algorithm, *RS* denotes a set of reachable nodes. A set of unreachable nodes *US* is given by subtracting *RS* from the set of nodes in the system.

5.1. Algorithm A

The algorithm works according to the following rules:

(i) All start nodes can be visited.
(ii) An internal node is reachable if it can be visited.
(iii) A communicating node is reachable if both the node and its complement can be visited.
(iv) Children of a reachable node can be visited.

5.2. An Implementation of Algorithm A

Let

G (=<*N*,*E*>) be an union of all PFGs in the system, where *N* is the set of nodes and *E* is the set of edges.
Q denote a queue of unprocessed reachable nodes
RS denote the set of reachable nodes
BS denote the set of visited communicating nodes waiting for the visit of their complements
n' denote the complement of node *n*

```
procedure initialise( G )
    empty sets Q, RS and BS
    for each n ∈ N do
        if n is a start node then
            block( n )
end initialise

procedure block( n )
   if n is an internal node then
      add n to RS and Q
   else if n' ∈ BS then
        remove n' from BS
        add both n and n' to RS and Q
   else
        add n to BS
end block
```

```
procedure alga( G )        /* main procedure */
    initialise( G )
    while Q ≠ Ø do
        choose and delete some n in Q
        for each child c of node n do
          if ( c ∉ BS ) and ( c ∉ RS ) then
             block( c )
    end while
    return RS
end alga
```

The *block* procedure checks to see if a node being visited is reachable[1]. The node is assumed reachable if (i) it is an internal node (e.g. node *p* in Fig. 2a) or (ii) its complement has been waiting for synchronous execution in set *BS*. The set *BS* contains transmitting and receiving nodes which are waiting for their complements. Newly reachable nodes are inserted to the processing queue *Q* for further processing. When a node in *Q* is processed, its children not having been visited are examined by the *block* procedure.

---

[1] The implementation assumes a closed system where transmitting or receiving nodes are blocked forever if they have no complement. A modification of the if-condition in procedure *block* can change the assumption to an open system.

The algorithm terminates when the processing queue Q is empty. The complexity of the algorithm is $O(|N|+|E|)$, where N is the set of nodes and E is the set of control edges in a system of PFGs. Upon termination, the algorithm delivers a reachable set RS. Nodes in set RS are potentially reachable in the sense that they may not be actually reachable in the original program. The unreachable set US of unreachable nodes is given by

$$US = N \setminus RS .$$

Nodes in set US are definitely unreachable in the sense that they must be unreachable in the original program. A correctness proof of Reif's original algorithm and analysis of the complexity can be found in [9].

The problem with this algorithm is the inaccuracy in detecting reachable nodes. For example in Fig. 2, although some nodes in the PFGs are actually unreachable, all of them are identified as reachable by the algorithm. This is because the rules on which the algorithm based, only provide necessary conditions but not sufficient conditions for reachability. This inaccuracy can be improved by our method with the use of the techniques described in sections 6, 7 and 8. Nevertheless, the algorithm is a useful tool to determine the node dependency in section 6 because of its simplicity and tractability.

6. Dependency

Algorithm A does not perform an exhaustive elaboration of execution sequences in a given system. It therefore invariably contains some spurious execution sequences which may not be exhibited by the actual system. These spurious execution sequences account for the inaccurate conclusions on the node reachability. A reduction in these spurious execution sequences results in a higher accuracy. The reduction can be achieved by working out the depend relations among nodes in the same PFG. Execution sequences with order of nodes violating the relations are spurious. Since each execution sequence is local to a PFG, only depend relations among nodes in the same PFG need to be considered.

6.1. Depend Relations

A node x is said to *depend on* y, written as xDy, if x is only reachable by execution sequences containing y. For example in Fig. 2c, node $a?$ cannot be executed unless r has been executed; and node f cannot be executed unless $a?$ has been executed. Suppose x and y are two nodes belonging to the same PFG. Therefore, $a?$ depends on r and f depends on $a?$.

For convenience, let us denote ξ_i as the set of all possible execution sequences taken by a process P_i, whose behaviour can be modelled as a PFG $<N_i, E_i, s_i>$; and let $\|\varepsilon\|$ be the set of nodes that has been traversed by an execution sequence $\varepsilon \in \xi_i$. The definition of depend relation can be given as:

$$\forall\, x, y \in N_i,\ xDy \stackrel{\text{def}}{=\!=} (\forall\, \varepsilon \in \xi_i, x \text{ is reachable by } \varepsilon \Rightarrow y \in \|\varepsilon\|)$$

For instance, node $a?$ is only reachable by execution sequences containing r; and node f is only reachable by execution sequences containing $a?$. Therefore, execution sequences described by a node order, which does not have any r before an $a?$, or does not have any $a?$ before an f, must be spurious. There are two properties of the depend relation:

The depend relation is *transitive* so that
for any three nodes a, b and c, $aDb \wedge bDc \Rightarrow aDc$.

A *symmetrical* depend relation between two nodes implies a synchronisation anomaly; i.e.
for any two nodes a and b, $aDb \wedge bDa \Rightarrow a$ is unreachable and b is unreachable.

6.2. Derivation of Dependency Set

Depend relations can be efficiently determined based on the unreachable sets provided by algorithm A. Suppose x and y are two nodes in a PFG and x is found to be unreachable when y is unreachable. Then x depends on y.

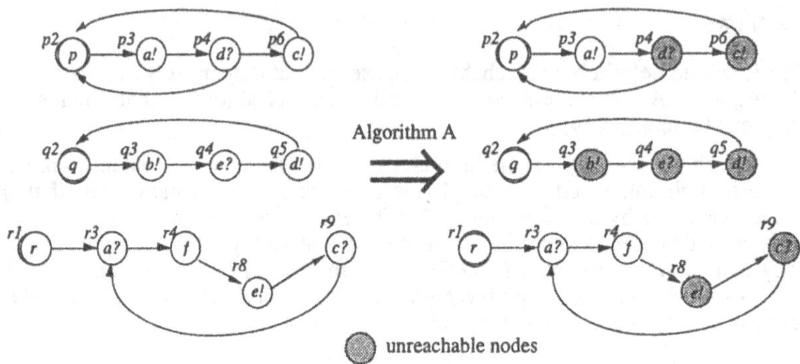

Fig. 4. Deriving Dependent Nodes by Algorithm A
(the bottom process started with statement *r1* is different from that in Fig. 2)

For instance, algorithm A reports an empty unreachable set for a system in Fig. 2. But it reports an unreachable set { *e*!, *c*? } when node *b*? is removed from the PFG of process *R* in Fig. 4. So, both nodes *e*! and *c*? depend on *b*?.

Suppose n is a node in a PFG $<N_i, E_i, s_i>$, and US_n (US_n') is the unreachable set given by algorithm A with (without) the presence of node n in the PFG. Let us denote a *dependency set* D_n as a set of nodes depending on n such that

$$D_n = (US_n' \setminus US_n) \cap N_i$$

Equating n to node *b*? in Fig. 2, we get

$$D_{b?} = (\{ d?, c!, b!, e?, d!, e!, c? \} \setminus \{\}) \cap \{ r, a?, f, b?, e!, c? \} = \{ e!, c? \} .$$

The dependency set D_n for a given node n can be determined by algorithm A in a complexity $O(|N|+|E|)$, where N is the set of nodes and E is the set of control edges. To obtain the dependency sets for each node in the system, we need to run the algorithm $|N|$ times. Hence, the dependency between every pairs of nodes in a system can be computed in a complexity $O(|N|(|N|+|E|))$. Section 10.2 shows the time taken by a prototype to work out the dependency for the example systems given in the paper.

6.3. Depend Relations and Spurious Execution sequences

The number of spurious execution sequences can be reduced by the depend relations. Execution sequences violating the depend relations must be spurious. For example, an execution sequence "*r.a?.f.e!*" (in Fig. 2c), which is considered legitimate by algorithm A, can be eliminated because it violates the relation that *e*! depends on *b*?. The execution sequence does not contain an occurrence of *b*? before an occurrence of *e*! in the sequence.

7. History Sets

To detect spurious execution sequences, all possible sequences are examined. However, an explicit elaboration of all possible sequences is computationally too expensive. Some kind of tradeoff is needed to keep the method tractable for non-trival systems. A compromise is to approximate the event histories by a set of nodes, and omit the ordering information (e.g.

node x occurs before node y). For example, an execution sequence "$r.a?.f.e!$" can be approximated by $\{r, a?, f, e!\}$. So, a single set of nodes can represent a number of execution sequences. The approximation essentially trades off the execution details for tractability.

7.1. Definition of History Sets

For every node n in a PFG $<N_i, E_i, s_i>$, it associates with a single history set, denoted as H_n. H_n is a minimal set with all nodes appearing in those execution sequences that may reach n.

$$H_n = \bigcup_j \{ s \mid s \in \| \varepsilon_j \| \bullet \varepsilon_j \in \xi_i \text{ and } n \text{ is reachable by } \varepsilon_j \}$$

An existence of node x in the history set H_n indicates n is reachable by some execution sequences containing x.

$$\forall x \in N_i, x \in H_n \Rightarrow \exists \varepsilon \in \xi \bullet (n \text{ is reachable by } \varepsilon \wedge x \in \|\varepsilon\|)$$

Suppose H_f is empty and node f is reachable by an execution sequence "$r.a?$" in Fig. 2c. The execution sequence is recorded by adding nodes r and $a?$ to set H_f and becomes $\{r, a?\}$. Now, from node f's point of view, existence of nodes r and $a?$ in the history set H_f indicates that it is reachable by execution sequences containing some elements in $\{r, a?\}$. The ordering information that r occurs before $a?$ is ignored. This approximation results in a big reduction in storage and computational efforts to keep the method tractable for practical problems.

7.2. Storage and Computation of History Sets

For all history set associated with the nodes in a PFG $<N_i, E_i, s_i>$, each of them contain at most $|N_i|$ elements. If the existence of a node in a history set is represented by a storage bit, the maximum requirements of memory (in bits) to store all history sets for nodes in the PFG $= |N_i|^2$. Therefore, a system of processes $\{ P_1, ..., P_r \}$ would require a maximum of M bits to store all history sets, where M equals

$$\sum_{i=1}^{r} |N_i|^2 \quad .$$

For example, a medium sized system of 64 PFGs each with 64 nodes, would require a maximum 32K bytes of memory to hold all history sets.

In addition, set computations concerning history sets can be efficiently performed by bitwise arithmetic supported in many imperative languages (e.g. C). For instance, merging two sets can be performed by a bitwise-OR operation between two integer variables representing the sets.

7.3. Reduction of Spurious Execution sequences

The number of spurious execution sequences can be reduced by using the techniques of dependency and history sets. Suppose n is a node and D_n^{-1} is the set of nodes on which n depends. The following propositions can be derived using the techniques of dependency and history sets [2].

Proposition 1: Suppose m is a reachable parent of a node n, and m occurs at the end of an execution sequence ε. *Node n is reachable by* ε *only if the set* $H_m \cup \{m\}$ *contains all the nodes on which n depends.*

The necessary condition for reachability in proposition 1 is not enforced by Algorithm A. A check of the necessary condition prevents a node reachable by *dependency violating* execution sequences. As a result, the number of spurious execution sequences is reduced and the accuracy is improved. These conditions, however, do not eliminate all spurious execution sequences because a history set is merely an approximation of the actual execution sequences.

Proposition 2: For any node n in a process flow graph,

$$H_n \subseteq \bigcup_m \{ s \mid s \in H_m \cup \{m\} \bullet m \textit{ is a reachable parent of } n \wedge D_n^{-1} \subseteq H_m \cup \{m\} \}$$

This proposition establishes an upper bound of the history set of a node based on those of its reachable parents. An upper bound of a history set is assumed in algorithm B (see rule (iv) in section 7.4). So, if the upper bound of a history set is empty then the actual history set must also be empty, which means n has not been reachable by any execution sequences.

7.4. Algorithm B

Algorithm B achieves a higher accuracy in reachability by extending the rules in algorithm A based on propositions 1 and 2.

(i) All start nodes can be visited.
(ii) An internal node is reachable if it can be visited.
(iii) A communicating node is reachable if both the node and its complement can be visited.
(iv) $H_n = \bigcup_m (H_m \cup \{m\})$, where node m is a reachable parent of node n and the set $H_m \cup \{m\}$ contains all the nodes on which n depends.
(v) A node n can be visited if H_n is non-empty.
(vi) All history sets are initially empty.

This set of rules can be reduced to that of algorithm A if

(a) we ignore the dependency information so that nodes do not depend on one another in (iv); and
(b) we also ignore the history set by replacing the set $\{m\}$ in (iv) with a set $\{\bullet\}$ which contains a token carrying no value.

An application of algorithm B on a system modelled in Fig. 2 reveals that nodes *d*? and *c*! in Fig. 2a, nodes *e*? and *d*! in Fig. 2b, and nodes *e*! and *c*? in Fig. 2c are unreachable(see Fig. 5). These nodes are reported reachable by algorithm A.

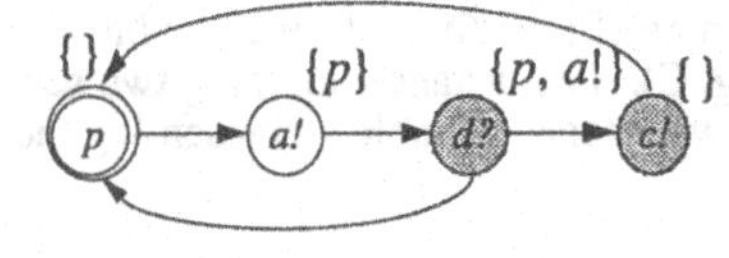

(a) Process Flow Graph of Process *P*

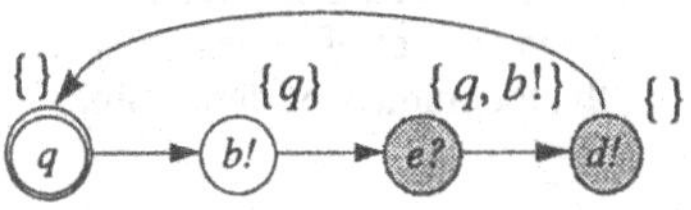

(b) Process Flow Graph of Process *Q*

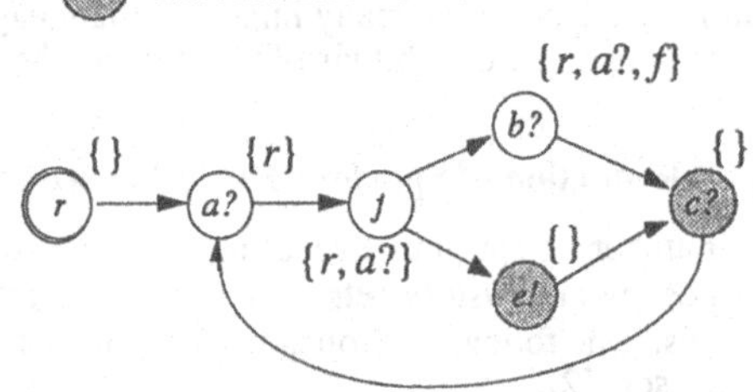

(c) Process Flow Graph of Process *R*

Fig. 5. Unreachable Nodes and States of History Sets upon the Termination of Algorithm B

7.5. An Implementation of Algorithm B

Denote

the complement of a node n as n';
the history set held by a node n as H_n;
the set of nodes depending on n as D_n and the set of nodes on which n depends as D_n^{-1};
Q as a queue holding unprocessed reachable nodes;
V as a set holding nodes which can be visited but not yet reachable;
R as a set holding reachable nodes;

```
procedure initialise( )
    empty Q, V, R and all history sets
    for each node n in the system do
        work out D_n and D_n^-1
    for each start node s in the system do
        visit( s, Ø )
end initialise

procedure execute( n )
    K = H_n ∪ {n}
    for each immediate child c of n do
        if ¬(K ⊆ H_c) and (D_c^-1 ⊆ K) then
            visit( c, K )
end execute

procedure visit( n, K )
    H_n = H_n ∪ K
    if (n ∉ R) and (n ∉ V) then
        block( n )
    else if (n ∈ R) then
        execute( n )
end visit

procedure block( n )
    if n is an internal node then
        add n to both R and Q
    else if n' ∉ V then
        add n to V
    else
        remove n' from V
        add n and n' to both R and Q
    end if
end block

procedure algc( )        /*  main procedure    */
    initialise( )
    while Q ≠ Ø do
        remove a node n from Q
        execute( n )
    end while
    report sets R
end algc
```

The *initialise* procedure initialises all history sets to empty (rule (vi)) and asserts that all start nodes can be visited (rule (i)). The *block* procedure examines the reachability of visited nodes according to rule (ii) and (iii). Nodes that have been newly found reachable are inserted to Q, and wait for further processing. The *execute* procedure visits the children of a node according to rule (iv). The procedure *visit* detects if there are any additional nodes that can be visited according to rule (v). The procedure also keeps an upper bound of the history set of a node and propagates the changes to children of the node. The algorithm terminates when no more nodes can become reachable, i.e. when Q is empty.

Suppose a process flow graph of a process P_i is given by a tuple $<N_i, E_i, s_i>$. Upon the termination of the algorithm, the following result is delivered:

$N_i \cap R$	gives the set of reachable nodes in process P_i
$N_i \setminus R$	gives the set of unreachable nodes in process P_i

The results delivered are conservative in unreachability but not conservative in reachability. A discussion of the limitations and comparisons with algorithms A and C will be given in section 9.

7.6. Complexity of Algorithm B

Suppose n is a node in a PFG $<N_i, E_i, s_i>$. Let us denote $\#visit_n$, $\#execute_n$ and $\#block_n$ as the number of times the procedures *visit*, *execute* and *block* are called with the parameter equals n. The *if-clause* in the procedure *execute* asserts

$$\#visit_n \le |N_i| \quad .$$

The first *if-clause* in procedure *visit* enforces that node n is at most blocked for once. This asserts

$$\#block_n \leq 1 \ .$$

The *execute* procedure can be called by the *algc* procedure and the *visit* procedure. Since n is put into the queue Q via the calling of the *block* procedure in the *visit* procedure, From this, it can be asserted

$$\#execute_n \leq \#visit_n \leq |N_i| \ .$$

Please note that set operations in the implementation can be achieved in constant time by a bitwise arithmetic operation supported in imperative languages. The computational effort for a node n is equal to the sum of the efforts taken by procedure *visit*, *block* and *execute* for a node n together with the efforts to evaluate the sets D_n and D_n^{-1}. Let us denote $depend_n$ as the computational effort to compute D_n and D_n^{-1}. The computational effort for a node n is given by

$\lambda|N_i| + depend_n$ (where λ is a small positive integer constant).

Therefore the computational effort of algorithm B is given by

$$\sum_{P_i} \lambda|N_i|^2 + \sum_n depend_n$$

$\leq O(|N|^2) + O(|N|(|N|+|E|))$ (where N and E stand for set of nodes and set of control flows in the system respectively)

Hence, the complexity of algorithm B is $O(|N|(|N|+|E|))$ which is dominated by the efforts to compute the dependency set for each node in the system.

8. Re-reachability

The accuracy of algorithm B can be further improved using a concept of re-reachability by checking whether nodes can be executed more than once. Consider a system S' consisting of three processes: U, V and W modelled as follows:

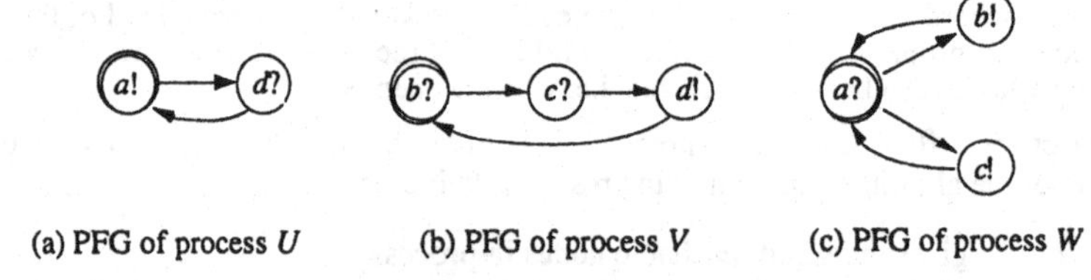

(a) PFG of process U (b) PFG of process V (c) PFG of process W

Fig. 6. PFGs of Processes U, V and W

In system S', nodes $c!$, $c?$, $d!$ and $d?$ are unreachable. This anomaly cannot be detected by an algorithm based on the rules in section 5.1 or 7.4. The accuracy of the algorithm can be improved with the knowledge that $a?$ can never be executed more than once. Using this additional information, the anomaly in system S' can be detected.

8.1. Definition of Re-reachability

A node n is *re-reachable* by an execution sequence ε if and only if it is reachable by ε and $||\varepsilon||$ contains n. A node n is *first reachable* by an execution sequence ε if and only if it is reachable by ε and $||\varepsilon||$ does not contain n.

$\forall\, n \in N_i, \varepsilon \in \xi_i,$

n is re-reachable by $\varepsilon \Leftrightarrow n$ is reachable by $\varepsilon \wedge n \in \|\varepsilon\|$

and

n is first reachable by $\varepsilon \Leftrightarrow n$ is reachable by $\varepsilon \wedge n \notin \|\varepsilon\|$

A reachable node is re-reachable if it is re-reachable by some ε; otherwise it is first reachable. A node has been *executed once* by an execution sequence ε if it appears once in ε. A node has been *executed more than once* by an execution sequence ε if it appears more than once in ε.

8.2. Further Reduction of Spurious Execution sequences

Spurious execution sequences can be further reduced using the technique of re-reachability. Assuming the notations in section 7.3, the following two propositions can be derived [2].

Proposition 3: Suppose m is a reachable parent of a node n, and m ONLY occurs at the end of an execution sequence ε. Node n is reachable by ε only if the set $(H_m \setminus D_m) \cup \{m\}$ *contains all the nodes on which n depends.*

Proposition 3 enforces a stricter necessary condition for reachability than that in proposition 1. Spurious execution sequences can be further eliminated based on a stricter necessary condition for those nodes whose parents only occur at the end of the sequences. This additional information is used in algorithm C to improve the accuracy of algorithm B.

Proposition 4: For any node n in a process flow graph,

$$H_n \subseteq \bigcup_m \{\, s \mid s \in (H_m \setminus D_m) \cup \{m\} \bullet m \text{ is a first reachable parent of } n \wedge D_n^{-1} \subseteq (H_m \setminus D_m) \cup \{m\} \,\} \cup \bigcup_m \{\, s \mid s \in H_m \cup \{m\} \bullet m \text{ is a re-reachable parent of } n \wedge D_n^{-1} \subseteq H_m \cup \{m\} \}.$$

Like proposition 2, proposition 4 allows us to establish an upper bound of a node's history set from its reachable parents. It enforces a tighter upper bound than that in proposition 2 with the additional information of re-reachability. An upper bound of a history set is assumed in algorithm C (see rule (iv) in section 8.3). Therefore, if the upper bound of a history set is empty then the actual history set must also be empty, which means n has never been visited by any execution sequences. By enforcing a tighter upper bound, it can disclose some empty history set which cannot be disclosed by proposition 2.

8.3. Algorithm C

The accuracy of algorithm B can be further improved using the following rules. The rules only allow a node to be visited by execution sequences which satisfy proposition 3.

(i) All start nodes can be visited.
(ii) An internal node is reachable (re-reachable) if it can be visited (re-visited).
(iii) A communicating node is reachable (re-reachable) if both the node and its complement can be visited (re-visited).
(iv) $H_n = \bigcup_m (K_m \cup \{m\})$, where node m is either
  (a) a first reachable parent of node n and the set $(H_m \setminus D_m) \cup \{m\}$ contains all the nodes on which n depends. In this case, $K_m = H_m \setminus D_m$; or
  (b) a re-reachable parent of node n and the set $H_m \cup \{m\}$ contains all the nodes on which n depends. In this case, $K_m = H_m$.
(v) A node n can be visited if H_n is non-empty.
(vi) A node n can be re-visited if $n \in H_n$.
(vii) All history sets are initially empty.

If the re-reachability information is ignored by setting D_m in the rules (iv) to Ø, Proposition 3 is reduced to Proposition 1, Proposition 4 is reduced to Proposition 2, and the set of rules in algorithm C is reduced to that of algorithm B.

An application of algorithm C on a system modelled in Fig. 6 reveals that node *d*? in Fig. 6a, nodes *c*? and *d*! in Fig. 6b, and node *c*! in Fig. 6c are unreachable (see Fig. 7). It further identifies that node *a*! in Fig. 6a, node *b*? in Fig. 6b, and nodes *a*? and *b*! in Fig. 6c are reachable but not re-reachable.

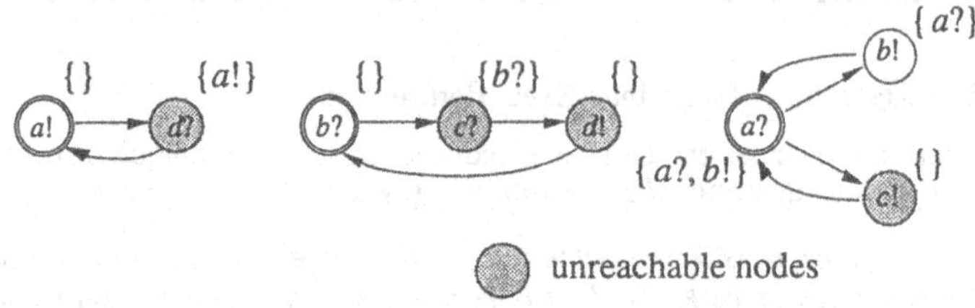

Fig. 7. Unreachable Nodes and States of History Sets upon the Termination of Algorithm C

Since node *a*? is not re-reachable, the element *b*! in the history set $H_a?$ is not passed onward to node *c*! which depends on node *b*!.

8.4. An Implementation of Algorithm C

Denote
- the complement of a node *n* as *n'*;
- the history set held by a node *n* as H_n;
- the set of nodes depending on *n* as D_n;
- the set of nodes on which *n* depends as D_n^{-1};
- *Q* as a queue holding unprocessed reachable and re-reachable nodes;
- *V* as a set holding nodes which can be visited but not yet reachable;
- *VV* as a set holding nodes which can be re-visited but not yet re-reachable;
- *R* as a set holding reachable nodes;
- *RR* as a set holding re-reachable nodes.

```
procedure initialise( )
    empty Q, V, VV, R, RR and all history sets
    for each node n in the system do
        work out D_n and D_n^-1
    for each start node s in the system do
        visit( s, Ø )
end initialise

procedure execute( n )
    if n ∈ RR then
        K = H_n ∪ {n}
    else
        K = ( H_n \ D_n ) ∪ {n}
    for each immediate child c of n do
        if ¬(K ⊆ H_c) and (D_c^-1 ⊆ K) then
            visit( c, K )
end execute

procedure algc( )      /* main procedure */
    initialise( )
    while Q ≠ Ø do
        remove a node n from Q
        execute( n )
    end while
    report sets R and RR
end algc

procedure block( n, VS, RS )
    if n is an internal node then
        add n to both RS and Q
    else if n' ∉ VS then
        add n to VS
    else
        remove n' from VS
        add n and n' to both RS and Q
    end if
end block

procedure visit( n , K )
    H_n = H_n ∪ K
    if (n ∈ H_n) and (n ∉ RR) and (n ∉ VV) then
        block( n, VV, RR )
    else if (n ∉ R) and (n ∉ V) then
        block( n, V, R )
    else if (n ∈ R) then
        execute( n )
end visit
```

The *initialise* procedure initialises all history sets to empty (rule (vii)) and asserts that all start nodes can be visited (rule (i)). The *block* procedure examines the reachability of visited nodes according to rule (ii) and (iii). Nodes that have been newly asserted reachable or re-reachable are inserted to Q, waiting to be executed. The *execute* procedure visits the children of a node according to rule (iv). The procedure *visit* detects if there are any additional nodes that can be visited or re-visited according to rule (v) and (vi). The procedure also keeps an upper bound of the history set of a node and propagates the changes to children of the node. The algorithm terminates when there no more nodes can become reachable or re-reachable; i.e. when Q is empty.

Suppose the PFG of a process P_i is given by a tuple $<N_i, E_i, s_i>$. Upon the termination of the algorithm, the following information is delivered:

$N_i \cap R$	gives the set of reachable nodes in process P_i
$N_i \setminus R$	gives the set of unreachable nodes in process P_i
$N_i \cap RR$	gives the set of re-reachable nodes in process P_i
$N_i \setminus RR$	gives the set of not re-reachable nodes in process P_i

8.5. Complexity

Algorithm C gives a more accurate result than that of algorithm B with the same complexity in $O(|N|(|N|+|E|))$ where N is the set of nodes and E is the set of edges in a system modelled as a collection of process flow graphs. The complexity of algorithm C can be analysed using similar steps of algorithm B as given in section 7.6. Like algorithm B, the computational effort of the algorithm C is dominated by the effort to evaluate the dependency sets for each node in the system. This domination is confirmed by the statistics of the prototypes given in section 10.2.

9. A Pump Control System - An Example

9.1. Introduction of the Pump System

As an example for flow analysis method, we present a simplified pump control application for mining environment [4].

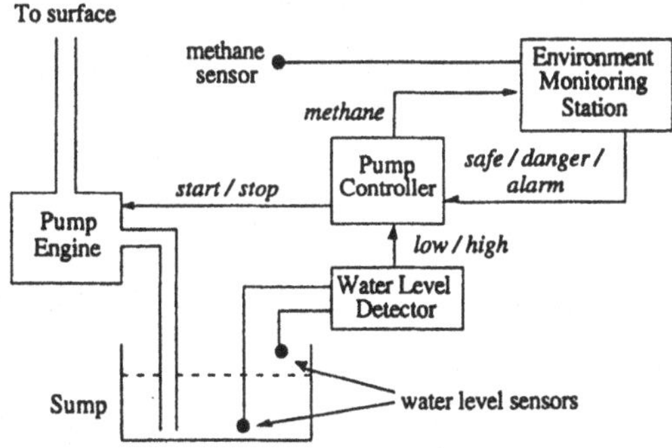

Fig. 8. Control of a Main Pump for Mine Drainage

Fig. 8 shows the schematic of a simplified pump installation. It is used to pump mine-water collected in a sump at shaft bottom to the surface. The pump runs automatically, controlled by water level as sensed by the high- and low-level detectors. Detection of high level causes the pump to run until low level is indicated. The pump is situated underground in a coal-mine, and so for safety reasons it must not be started or continue running when the level of methane in the atmosphere exceeds a preset safety limit. The pump controller gets information on methane level by communicating with a nearby environment monitoring station.

9.2. Flow Graphs of the Pump System

The system is composed of four sequential processes, namely pump controller, environment monitoring station, water level detector and pump engine.

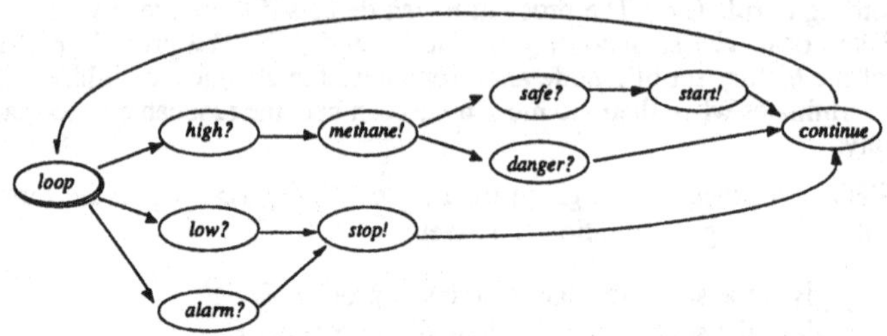

Fig. 9(a). Pump Controller

Fig. 9(a) describes the behaviour of a pump controller. When the pump controller is informed a high water level, it checks the methane level with the environment monitoring station. If the methane remains at a safe level, it starts the pump engine; otherwise it does nothing. If it is informed of a low water level or is warned of the alarming methane level, it stops the pump engine immediately.

The environment monitoring station in Fig. 9(b) upon request to check the methane level, it replies whether the methane level is safe or danger. The station also periodically checks the methane level and gives warning if the methane level is at an alarming level.

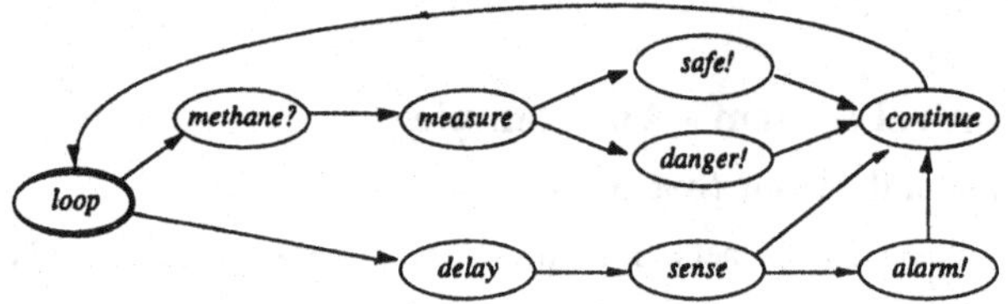

Fig. 9(b). Environment Monitoring Station

The water level detector in Fig. 9(c) notifies the pump controller if the water level is low or high. The pump engine in Fig. 9(d) accepts the command to start or stop the engine.

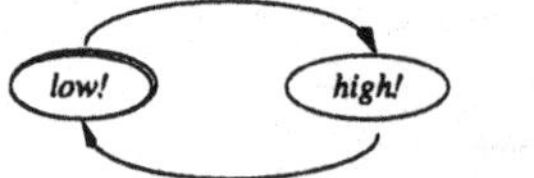

Fig. 9(c). Water Level Detector

Fig. 9(d). Pump Engine

9.3. Flow Analysis with Algorithm A

An application of the algorithm A fails to detect any unreachable nodes in the system. The unreachable set *US* given by the algorithm is empty.

9.4. Flow Analysis with Algorithm B and C

In this example, algorithm B gives the same results as algorithm C. The information of re-reachability, in this example, gives no further information to isolate more unreachable nodes. The dependency analysis derives a set of depend relations which includes (i) the *high*? node depends on *low*? node and (ii) *stop*! node depends on *high*? node in the PFG of Fig. 9(a).

To differentiate internal nodes with the same name, let us denote $node_{PC}$ and $node_{EMS}$ for nodes belonging to pump controller and environment monitoring station respectively for convenience. An application of the algorithm B or C on the example gives

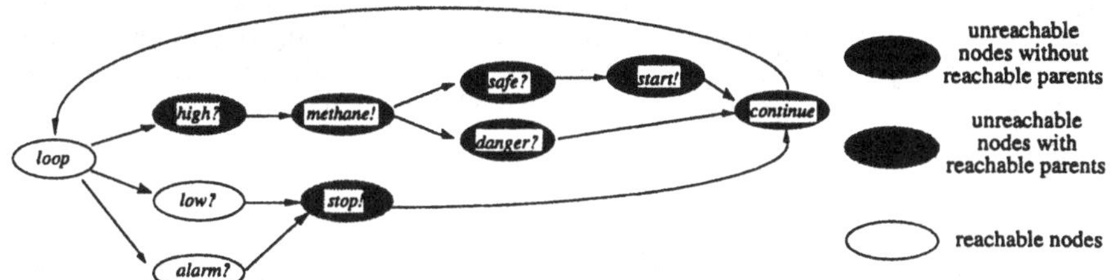

Fig. 10 PFG of the Pump Controller showing the Results of the Algorithm B & C

A set of unreachable nodes = { *high?*, *high!*, *methane?*, *methane!*, *safe?*, *safe!*, *danger?*, *danger!*, *start?*, *start!*, *stop?*, *stop!*, $continue_{PC}$, *measure* }

A set of reachable nodes = { *low?*, *low!*, *alarm?*, *alarm!*, $loop_{PC}$, $loop_{EMS}$, *delay*, *sense*, $continue_{EMS}$ }

A set of not re-reachable nodes = { *high?*, *high!*, *methane?*, *methane!*, *safe?*, *safe!*, *danger?*, *danger!*, *start?*, *start!*, *stop?*, *stop!*, $continue_{PC}$, *measure*, *low?*, *low!*, *alarm?*, *alarm!*, $loop_{PC}$ }

A set of re-reachable nodes = { $loop_{EMS}$, *delay*, *sense*, $continue_{EMS}$ }

Nodes in the set of unreachable nodes can never be executed by the actual system. Nodes in the set of reachable nodes may be executed by the actual system. Nodes in the set of not re-reachable nodes can never be executed more than once by the actual system. Nodes in the set of re-reachable nodes may be executed more than once by the actual system.

A designer can focus on those unreachable nodes which have reachable parents in the PFGs. These nodes identify the potential places at which the processes are likely to be block. Examples of these nodes in the PFG of the pump controller are slightly shaded in Fig. 10.

The results are confirmed by a prototype implementation of the algorithms on SUN IPX workstations. The performance of the prototype is given in section 10.1.

10. Analysis

10.1. Limitations of Algorithms A, B and C

Let RS_a, RS_b, RS_c, RS_r be the set of reachable nodes given by algorithm A, algorithm B, algorithm C and the real system respectively. Similarly, let US_a, US_b, US_c, US_r be the set of unreachable nodes given by algorithm A, algorithm B, algorithm C and the real system respectively. The sets can be related by the following equations:

$$RS_a \supseteq RS_b \supseteq RS_c \supseteq RS_r$$
$$US_a \subseteq US_b \subseteq US_c \subseteq US_r$$
$$RS_a \cup US_a = RS_b \cup US_b = RS_c \cup US_c = RS_r \cup US_r = \text{the set of nodes in the system}$$

The results in unreachability delivered by algorithm A, B, and C are conservative. A node identified as unreachable by our method implies the corresponding statement can never be executed in the original program where the usual semantics of conditionals are considered. The results in unreachability delivered by the algorithms are not conservative. A node identified as reachable by our method does not necessarily mean the corresponding statement can be executed in the original program. Algorithm B achieves a more accurate result than algorithm A by reducing spurious execution sequences using Proposition 1. With the use of Proposition 3, algorithm C cuts down the spurious execution sequences further based on the additional information on re-reachability.

Algorithm C also detects the set of nodes which can never be executed more than once by the system. Let RR_c and RR_r be the set of re-reachable nodes given by algorithm C and the real system respectively; and UR_c and UR_r be the set of not re-reachable nodes given by algorithm C and the real system respectively. They can be related by:

$RR_c \supseteq RR_r$
$UR_c \subseteq UR_r$
$RR_c \cup UR_c = RR_r \cup UR_r$ = the set of nodes in the system

10.2. Performance of the Prototypes

Algorithm A and algorithm C have been implemented on a SUN IPX workstation according to section 5.2 and 8.4 respectively. The following table gives the performance of the prototype for the examples given in this paper.

Examples	#nodes	Computational Time in milliseconds			Ratio =
		Dependency Evaluation	Algorithm A T_a	Algorithm C T_c	T_c / T_a
Fig. 2	14	2.6	0.23	2.8	12.2
Fig. 6	8	0.8	0.13	0.8	6.15
Fig. 9	23	8.5	0.42	8.6	20.5

Table 11 Prototype Performance

The columns give, respectively, the experiments performed, the number of nodes in each example, the time taken for algorithm A, the time taken for algorithm C, the time taken to evaluate the dependency based on algorithm A and the ratio between the time taken by algorithm C and algorithm A. All the experiments were run on a SUN IPX workstation with 16MB of memory; times given are in CPU milliseconds on that machine and include both user and system time. The CPU time is given by looping each experiment 10000 times and then divide the time by 10000.

The results show the time taken to derive the dependency among nodes in the system occupies approximately 99% of the total time taken by algorithm C. This confirms the complexity analysis that the complexity of algorithm C is dominated by the complexity of dependency derivation. The ratio between the time taken by algorithm C and that taken by algorithm A is roughly equal to the number of nodes in the example. This agrees with the difference in $O(|N|)$ between complexity of algorithm C and that of algorithm A, where N is the set of nodes in the PFGs modelling the program. The experiments confirm the computational tractability of algorithm C. It takes 8 seconds for algorithm C to analyse a dining philosopher system of 64 diners.

11. Conclusions and Future Work

In this paper, we have presented three flow analysis algorithms to detect synchronisation anomalies in a distributed program. All the three algorithms support distributed programs with arbitrarily number of loops and non-deterministic structures. Algorithm A is an adaptation of the algorithm proposed by Reif [9]. The accuracy of algorithm A is improved in algorithm B with the techniques of dependency and history sets. Algorithm C further improves the accuracy of algorithm B by considering re-reachability . The complexity of algorithm C is quadratic in terms of the statements in a program and its tractability is confirmed by the performance of a prototype given in section 10.2. Given the tractability of algorithm C, it can be readily applied to designs of practical applications for preliminary checks which help to increase the designers' confidence in the designs.

We intend to further improve the prototypes and perform more analysis using case studies. We are also extending the technique to handle dynamic communication, where communication structure is dynamic and channels may be passed as arguments. Data flow analysis techniques can be employed to derive all the potential communication structures of such systems.

Acknowledgement

The authors would like to acknowledge discussions with our colleagues in the Parallel and Distributed Systems Group during the formulation of these ideas. We gratefully acknowledge the Swiss Bank and the DTI (Grant Ref: IED 410/36/2) for their financial support. We would also like to express our thanks to the anonymous reviewers for their invaluable suggestions to improve the quality of the paper.

References

1. G.S. Avrunin, U.A. Buy, J.C. Corbett, et al.: Automated Analysis of Concurrent Systems with the Constrained Expression Toolset. *IEEE TOSE 17*, 11, 1204-1222.
2. S.C. Cheung and J. Kramer: Tractable Flow Analysis for Anomaly Detection in Distributed Programs, Technical Report, DOC 1993/3, March 1993.
3. P.C. Kanellakis and S.A. Smolka: On the Analysis of Cooperation and Antagonism in Networks of Communicating Processes. In Proc. *4th ACM Symposium on Principles of Distributed Computing*, Ontario, Canada, August 1985, pp. 23-38.
4. J. Kramer, J. Magee, M. Sloman, et al.: CONIC: an Integrated Approach to Distributed Computer Control Systems. *IEE Pròceedings, Part E 130*, 1 (January 1983), 1-10.
5. C.E. McDowell and D.P. Helmbold: Debugging Concurrent Programs. *ACM Computing Surveys 21*, 4, 593-623.
6. N. Mercouroff: An Algorithm for Analyzing Communicting Processes. In Proc. *Mathematical Foundation of Programming Semantics '91*, Pittsburgh, PA, March 1991, published in LNCS 598.
7. W. Peng and S. Purushothaman: Towards data flow analysis of communicating finite state machines. In Proc. *8th ACM Symposium on Principles of Distributed Computing*, August 1989.
8. W. Peng and S. Purushothaman: Data Flow Analysis of Communicating Finite State Machines. *ACM Transactions on Programming Languages and Systems 13*, 3, 399-432.
9. J. Reif and S. Smolka: Data Flow Analysis of Distributed Communicating Processes. *Internation Journal of Parallel Programming 19*, 1 (1990), 1-30.
10. J.H. Reif: Dataflow Analysis of Communicating Processes. In Proc. *6th ACM Symposium on Principles of Programming Languages*, June 1979, pp. 257-268.
11. K.C. Tai and C.Y. Din: Validation of Concurrency in Software Specification and Design. In Proc. *3rd International Workshop on Software Specification and Design*, London, UK, August 1985, pp. 223-227.
12. R.N. Taylor: Complexity of Analyzing the Synchonization Structure of Concurrent Programs. *Acta Informatica 19*, 57-84.
13. R.D. Yang and C.G. Chung: The Analysis of Infeasible Concurrent Paths of Concurrent Ada Programs. In Proc. *14th Annual International Computer Software and Applications Conference (COMPSAC 90)*, Chicago, Illinois, October 1990, pp. 424-429.
14. M. Young and R.N. Taylor: Combining Static Concurrency Analysis with Symbolic Execution. *IEEE Transactions on Software Engineering 14*, 10, 1499-1511.

A Pragmatic Task Design Approach Based on a Ward/Mellor Real-Time Structured Specification

J. Tuya, L. Sánchez, R. Zurita, J. A. Corrales

Universidad de Oviedo, Campus de Viesques,
Escuela Técnica Superior de Ingenieros Industriales
e Ingenieros Informáticos.
Área de Lenguajes y Sistemas Informáticos.
Carretera de Castiello, s/n. E-33394 GIJON/SPAIN

Abstract. This paper shows some details about the development of a distributed system for the control and supervision of all processes related to the coal feeding a thermal power station. Starting from a structured specification based on the Ward/Mellor methodology for real-time systems, a method for systematic design and implementation is built. The method can be automated in the future, and includes a series of guidelines, rules, procedures, reusable components and graphical representations to successfully derive the implementation from the structured specification.

1 Introduction *

Structured analysis and Design methodologies as Ward/Mellor [18] are suitable for the use in mixed real-time & data-base oriented applications because they are data-flow oriented (as in DeMarco Structured Analysis [9]) and event-driven oriented (they can express the behaviour of a system using state-transition diagrams: STD's or Petri Nets [14]).

Several extensions to Ward/Mellor methodology have been proposed for a better support to specify the behaviour of Real-Time Systems. Some of them by specifying timing characteristics [15], extending the graphical notation [4], associating a formal specification from the data-control flow diagrams [11], or adopting object-oriented point of view [10]. Also, tools for the execution of the structured specification [3], and checking [1] have been developped.

The main gap when a methodology and a CASE tool is used, is that the relationship from the specification to the implementation is weak or inexistent. A small change to a requirement causes a change in the specification and design documents and also in the source code. So, it would be useful to have a way to perform a systematic translation from the specification to source code.

---

* This work has been supported by the Patronato de Industrias Eléctricas (Spain) under project PIE-031/017, by the Compañía Eléctrica de Langreo (Spain) under project CEL-053, and by the Universidad de Oviedo (Spain) under project D3-029-90.

This paper describes how the Ward/Mellor methodology has been used in the development of an application that combines the use of a relational data-base and the control of a relatively high number of devices. From the structured specification, we design an architecture that, complemented with a selected set of components, will permit to derive an implementation directly from its specification, a task able to be automated in the future. A substantial change of the specification can be easyly implemented.

2 System Description

The goal of the ANAC system (ANálisis Automatizado y rápido de Carbones: Fast Automated Coal Analysis) is to control and supervise the life-cycle of the coal and vehicles transporting it in a thermal power station. The process starts when a lorry or train arrives at the plant and ends when the coal is stored for further use by the power station and factured to the supplier. The intermediate processes are relatively complicated because it is mandatory to pick a sample of the coal for each vehicle; in a brief instant the sample must be analyzed in order to reject the full vehicle if the coal quality is poor, previous to the unload.

Each accepted sample will suffer a complete set of different analysis, resulting a global quality factor (for individual samples or mixed samples) that will be the basis for invoicing. The analysis is a complicated process that involves a number of automated and supervised manual procedures for samples analysis and mixture, and it requires high degree of security: there must be impossible to connect the sample with the supplier (for unauthorized personnel only). Also the system includes several traffic lights, platform scales (gross weight, tare weight and reserve), a point for the coal unloading, and other devices.

The system is implemented in an ethernet network of VAX™ workstations, the serial input/output is made using ethernet terminal servers, and the digital and analog input/output using two networks of INTERBUS™ devices.

In the following we shall refer only to the first phase of the project. At the moment of write this paper, the system is coded, installed and partially operative. This phase includes all proceses until the storing of individual samples of coal. The second phase is under development.

3 Requirements Specification

The functional requirements expressed in a pair of documents from the customer, have been completed and refined using the Ward/Mellor structured methodology for Real-Time Systems. The CASE tool used was *Teamwork*™ [17]. Because the *Teamowrk* tool supports the Hatley/Pirbhai methodology [12], some of its representation conventions have been adapted to Ward/Mellor (for example, the use of ENABLE, DISABLE and TRIGGER flows). This tool has been used for civil and military projects ([2], [16]).

™ Teamwork is Trade-Mark of Cadre Technologies Inc.

A simplified context diagram for the essential model built can be shown in Fig. 1. Note that some of the terminators and the data and control flows have been removed.

Fig. 1. Context diagram for the essential model of the ANAC system

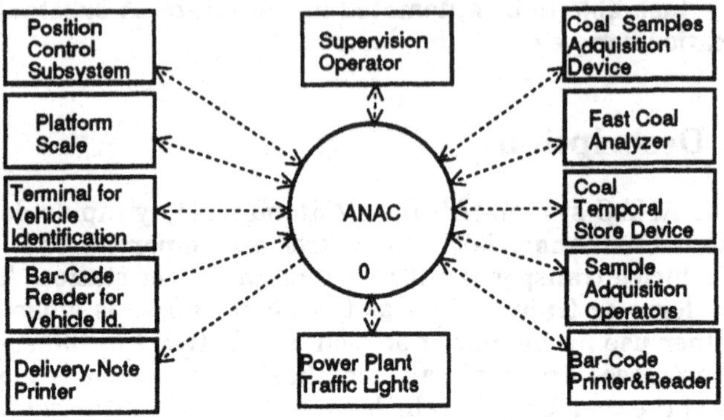

The first level diagram makes a partition of the system in three main processes:

- *Vehicle Process:* Control of the positioning in the platform scale, identification and authorization, weighting (gross and tare), delivery note, etc. There are four instances of this processs (one for each lorry platform scale and one for the unique wagon platform scale).

- *Coal Sample Process:* Control of the coal sample adquisition, fast analysis, authorization for unloading and sample labeling and storing. There are two instances of this process (one for lorry and other for wagon).

- *Supervision:* It includes on-line monitoring and the dialogs for the Supervision Operator (answers to exceptional situations, configuration changes, system startup and shutdown).

The resulting specification (for the first phase of the project) is an essential model having:

- 23 Data-Flow/Control-Flow Diagrams

- 20 State-Transition Diagrams (176 states and 306 transitions)

- 12 State-Event Matrices and Decision Tables

- 68 Primitive Process Specifications

- 398 Data Dictionary Entries

The data must be stored in a relational data-base using SQL, and the implementation must be made in FORTRAN under the VMS operating system.

Nevertheless, the most important requirements that have conditioned the design are the quality requirements. Table 1 summarizes the most important RADC quality factors ([13]) required for this project.

Table 1. Most important quality requirements

Factor	Comments
Integrity	Data connecting the samples of the coal with the supplier is confidential. These data can not become lost since high monetary damages can be produced
Usability	The system must be able to run without user intervention, but must be possible to monitor and to supervise it in a friendly fashion from a windowed screen based in the X-Window System
Flexibility	It is foreseeable that the same system will be installed in another power stations with variants in the behaviour and/or hardware environment; the changes made for it must be minimum. Also the system features must be configurable by the operator at run time
Reusability	This is a developer's requirement. The design must provide a set of criteria and software components in order to be reused in another project with similar characteristics (real-time distributed system, relational data-base, INTERBUS devices, VMS)
Interoperability	The produced data-base must be integrated with the corporative data-base of the power station

It is essential that the system will be distributed in several nodes in a ethernet local area network. Additionally, it is necessary to allow an easy reconfiguration of functions in each node, so that when a node crashes, another one will take its functions.

4 Architecture Design

Ward/Mellor methodology starts the design (implementation model) with processor modelling. Because of this system must be highly reconfigurable, a task must be able to run in different processors, so, this stage will be delayed up to run-time with our approach (a configuration file will decide for each task in what processor to run).

4.1 Development of a Kit of Canonical Task Types

A classification of several tasks in functional types must be made previously to the task selection and requirements allocation. Several classifications have been made in the literature: [5] and [8] diferentiates between eight canonical types of tasks (slave, server, scheduler, buffer, secretary, agent, transporter and user). In [7] thirteen task "idioms" are identified. In the proposed design we will define:

- *User:* Autonomous task that interacts directly with the user and other tasks.

- *Agent:* Autonomous task that performs the main functions allocated to the essential model. The agent tasks are directly derived from the essential model.
- *Secretary:* Provides services to an agent task and interacts with the hardware or a server task. The secretary tasks are derived from the expansion of the terminators present in the essential model. Usually it will be necessary to build a separate model for each terminator.
- *Server:* Some devices will require to build a server task for its control.
- *Transporter:* Its only purpose is to transport messages between some of the above tasks, for example message passing between different nodes.

The communication paths between these canonical task types are shown in Fig. 2.

Fig. 2. Canonical task types

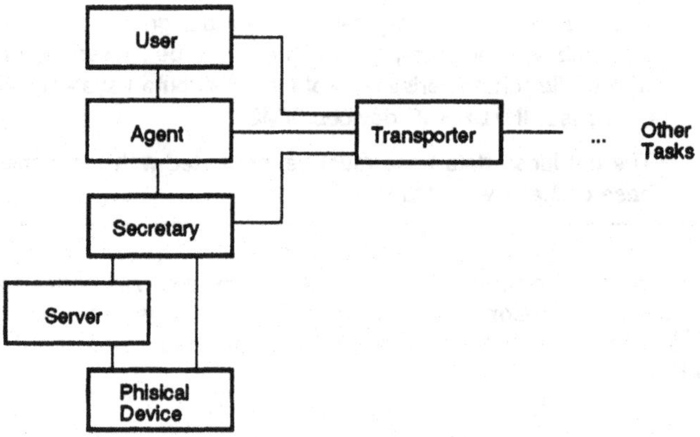

4.2 Task and Subtask Modelling

The problem of task modelling is that a high number of state transition diagrams which control the real-time system behaviour will derive in a too high number of tasks (consuming a high amount of operating system resources). To decrease the number of tasks it is necessary to reorganize the essential model and introduce a distorsion on it. The approach used is to do not distorsion any of the essential model and introduce the concept of task and subtask:

A task will be a program running under the control of an operating system (named process in Unix). A subtask will be a section of the task that implements one and only one STD present at the essential model, so a subtask is a single object with its own state and local data structures. The task is only a way to organize a set of subtasks in order to decrease the number of tasks that the operating system will manage. Obviously, an arbitrary grouping of subtasks into tasks will be undesirable, and some criteria (functional, geographical, priorities, etc.) must be used.

The first pass in task modelling will be to determine the agent task classes by grouping the processes present in the essential model. A task class will derive several tasks if there are multiple instances of the process.

Usually, additional models specifying the behaviour for the terminators are needed. These models will derive into other secretary task classes.

When all the models have been completed, the structure of tasks, subtasks and communication paths between them must be determined. This can be accomplished grafically using an entity relationship diagram. A sample of this diagram (using the Chen notation [6]) can be shown in Fig. 3 for a reduced and simplified part of the system, and it is explained below.

Fig. 3. Sample of a Task-Subtask relationship diagram

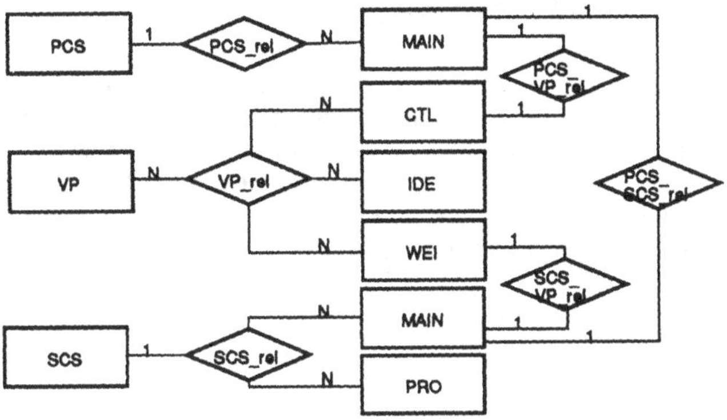

In the figure, the first column of entities (rectangles) represent the three task classes that will be considered. We shall have a task class for the vehicle process (VP) having three task instances (one for each platform: gross, tare and reserve), a secretary task class for the position control subsystem (PCS) with only one instance, and another secretary task class for the control of the scale itself (SCS). The names of each task are specified for each class:

```
VP  = VPG + VPT + VPR
PCS = PCS
SCS = SCS
```

The second column (in Fig. 3) represents the subtasks classes (a subtask class for each STD in the model). There will be several instances for each class. The cardinality and the names for each subtask are indicated by the relations (diamonds):

```
PCS_rel = PCS.MAING + PCS.MAINT + PCS.MAINR

VP_rel =
  [ VPG = VPG.CTL + VPG.IDE + VPG.WEI
  | VPT = VPT.CTL + VPT.IDE + VPT.WEI
  | VPR = VPR.CTL + VPR.IDE + VPR.WEI
  ]
```

The communication between subtasks is derived from the structure of the models. For example, each subtask of PCS comunicates with another subtask of VP, so that:

```
PCS_VP_rel =
  [ PCS.MAINB + VPG.CTL
  | PCS.MAINT + VPT.CTL
  | PCS.MAINR + VPR.CTL
  ]
```

Last relations detail the communication paths between subtasks. A more complete specification should include specific attributes, showing details about how the communication is made, for example, if the subtask must wait until the message is delivered or read, how long must be the awaiting period, or if some exception must be delivered.

4.3 Task Execution and Message Transport

In the most simplified design, each task will have a single queue to receive messages. When a task receives a message, it is passed to the subtask (it is said that this activates the subtask) via a simple procedure call. The subtask recognizes the event, executes a transition and goes to another state, returning the control to the caller. Then the task enters in a waiting state for another message. This mechanism is shown in Fig. 4

Fig. 4. Control abstraction for subtask activation

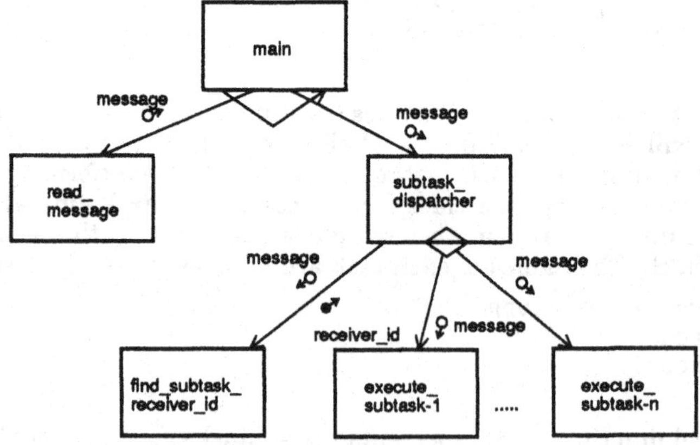

Each message must contain:

- Identification of the sender subtask
- Identification of the receiver subtask
- Identification of the event flow that is transmited
- Optionally transmitted data across the interface

All control and data flows going between subtasks are implemented as messages composed by the four fields enumerated above. Before sending a message, the source and destination identifiers must be built. These have a maximum of four fields.

- Node name
- Task name
- Subtask name
- Device name (when the message goes to a server)

The mailbox component (MB) implements the primitives used to sending and receiving messages (Fig. 5 shows a portion of it). When the destination node is the same that the local node, it puts the message into the corresponding task queue. If the node is different, the message is forwarded to a reusable task named NET. This is a transporter task that accepts messages and forward them across a network interface. The transport mechanism is fully transparent for the sender task. So, an easy reconfiguration of the node where a task executes can be made simply by changing the node component of the addresses.

Fig. 5. Mailbox component

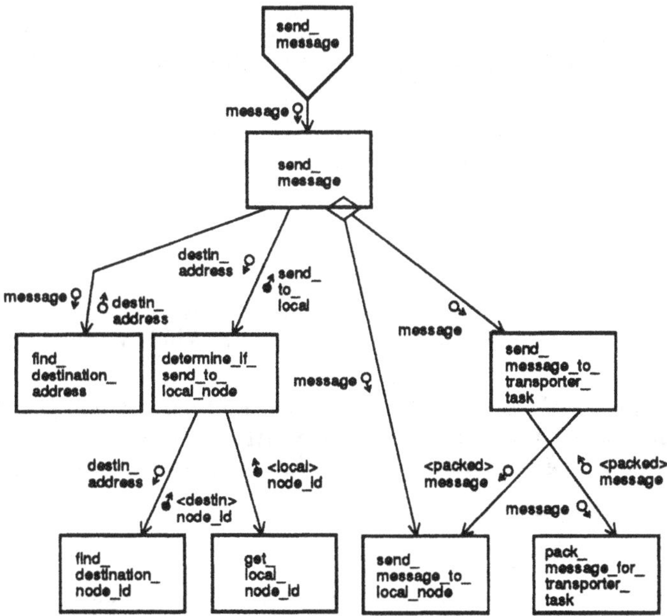

Each subtask must know the address of the receiver subtask. There can be three cases:

1. The outgoing flow must be received by the same subtask that have produced the ingoing flow: There is no problem because the address of the sender subtask is present into each message.
2. The outgoing flow must be received for another subtask: The address is predetermined using the relations of the task-subtask entity relationship diagram.
3. The outgoing flow must be received by a physical device (for example, sending some characters to a serial line): In this case we must use a specific module that implements the necessary source code.

In the models, an input operation from a physical device is represented by sending a control flow and awaiting in another state for the answer. The output flow is implemented as a module call. This module will install an interrupt service routine (in VMS called Asyncronous System Trap: AST) which will be delivered by the operating system at input completion. This interrupt routine will put the message and the data read in the subtask queue.

4.4 User Interface

The user interface function is accomplised by an user type task that will communicates with both agent and secretary tasks in order to centralize the on-line monitoring, configuration changes and responses to anomalous situations. Due to security reasons, this task must not be active all time, but only when an authorized operator gives his/her password. The information to be monitored and the requests for operator response are locally stored in each node in a special transporter task called monitor. When the operator logs in the system the user type task is activated, a message is sent to the monitor task on each node, and all monitor information is sent back to the user task and displayed in his/her screen.

The monitor task is another reusable task because it works with abstract objects (items to be monitored and requests to the operator), independently from the application.

5 Implementation

Due to customer specification, the coding was made in FORTRAN, using embedded SQL for data-base access and UIL for the X-Window based user interface.

The total volume of code is near a hundred thousand lines of source code (comments included). If it is meassured in KNCSS (thousand lines of noncomment source statements) then the total is 51 KNCSS distributed as is shown below:

- 16 for the agent tasks
- 6 for the secretary tasks
- 10 for server and transport tasks and other reusable components
- 13 for the user tasks (FORTRAN) plus 6 (UIL)

6 Review of the Design Process

6.1 Stages of the Development Process

In short, the stages of the method for a complete or partial system are:

1. Build the specification (essential model).
2. Build additional models for the terminators.
3. Build the task-subtask entity-relationship diagram and specify the names and relationships between tasks and subtasks.
4. Generate the source code for the above.
5. Complete the coding of the details not present in the models.
6. Compile and link all together.
7. Determine the node distribution for all tasks (this will generate a task configuration file which will be used to run the system).
8. Run and test the system in all nodes.

6.2 CASE Tool Requirements for an Automated Code Generation

The above method can be used to implement different systems with different structured specifications but, in order to have in the future an automatic translator from specification to source code, some additions must be made to the Ward/Mellor methodology:

- Support for mixed data and control flows: The Ward/Mellor methodology specifies clearly the separation between data and control. But because events have many times a data content associated to it, it is necessary to provide some way to associate them. The *Teamwork* tool provides mixed data and control flows specified in the data dictionary, but no graphical representation for them.
- Rigurous convention for the meaning of the right part of a transition. When the action consists in a trigger flow the following convention must be used: All incoming data flow to the bubble that receives the trigger plus the incoming control flow that has executed the transition must be packed into some data+control flow. For the output the rule is similar: All outgoing data flows from this bubble plus all outgoing control flows of the action part must be packed into one or several data+control flows (one for each control flow departing from the STD).
- Extended attributes for control and data stores, as a way to specify abstract data types as stack, queue, set, etc.
- A standard way to represent abstractions for counters and timers. We suggest a special control store capable to send and receive special control flows for the operations associated with them (for example, a timer could receive the cancel and set flows, and send the time-out flow).
- A way to build the task-subtask entity relationshp diagram and checking the correctness of the specification of the objects and their relations.

- Support for several models in a project, sharing common data-dictionary entries.

7 Lessons Learned and Conclusions

This project has served to experiment the use of structured specification techniques in a real medium-sized project and to derive a method that, adequately automated will allow to make fast implementation of real-time distributed systems. The method includes a series of guidelines, rules, procedures, reusable components and graphical representations to successfully derive the implementation from the structured specification. Some of the observations and lessons we learned include:

- The adoption of new techniques caused a high delay at early stages of the project, because the effect of the learning curve of the project staff. Otherwise, at last stages, the impact of a specification change is decreased, because there is an easy translation from the structured specification to the code.

- The structured specification is useful to be used in interviews with the client, but too hard for him. There are some risk of a misunderstanding the requirements if the client is not cooperative.

- The development and testing of a low-level component set was expensive. The benefits of the reuse will appear in the next project where this method will be used.

- The manual task of translating the structured specification to code is very time consumming, error prone and without any creativity. It is essential to automate it.

- In some cases, the device selection was not completed until the analysis was finished. So the development of an abstract set of operations (flows between the terminators and the bubbles in the essential model) was useful. The agent task (implementing the details of the behaviour of the system) could be translated into code and tested against the requirements. When the hardware was defined, the secretary task was built and there where no problems in the integration.

- Because the unique interface between tasks is the message system, it is very easy to make the test of individual tasks. The drivers and stubs for this test are very similar: a task that receives messages and presents them at a window, and another that sends messages. The testing problems are minimized.

References

1. Atlee, J., Gannon, J. (1991) *"State-Based Model Checking of Event-Driven System Requirements"*. In: ACM SIGSOFT Conference on Software for Critical Systems. December, pp. 16-28

2. Bartlett, P. F., Robinson, P. F, Hains, T. A., Simms, M. J. *"Use of Structured Methods for Real-Time Peripheral Firmware"*. In: Hewlett-Packard Journal, August 1989, pp. 79-86

3. Blumfoe, R., Hecht, A. (1988) *"Executing Real-Time Structured Analysis Specifications"*. In: ACM SIGSOFT Software Engineering Notes, Vol. 13, no. 13, July, pp. 32-40

4. Bruyn, W., Jensen, R. Keskar, D., Ward, P. (1988) *"ESML: An Extended Systems Modeling Language Based on the Data Flow Diagram"*. In: ACM SIGSOFT Software Engineering Notes Vol. 13, no. 1, January, pp. 58-67

5. Buhr, R. J. A. (1984) *"System Design with Ada"*. Prentice-Hall

6. Chen, Peter W. (1985) *"Principles of Database Design"*. In: Database Design Based on Entity and Relationship, Edited by S. Bing Yao, chapter 5. Prentice-Hall

7. Cherry, G. W. (1988) *"PAMELA-2: An Ada-Based Object-Oriented Design Method"*. Conference paper. Februry.

8. Chi, R., Lai, T. (1991) *"Ada Task Taxonomy Support for Concurrent Programming"*. In: ACM SIGSOFT Software Engineering Notes, Vol. 16, no. 1, pp. 73-91, January

9. DeMarco, T. (1979) *"Structured Analysis and System Specification"*. Prentice-Hall

10. Faulk, S., Brackett, J., Ward, P., Kirby, J. (1992) *"The Core Method for Real-Time Requirements"* In: IEEE Software, Set 1992, pp. 22-33

11. France, R. B. (1992) *"Semantically Extended Data Flow Diagrams: A Formal Specification Tool"*. In: IEEE Transactions on Software Engineering, Vol. 18, no. 4, April, pp. 329-346

12. Hatley, D. J. , Pirbhai, I. (1987) *"Strategies for Real Time System Specification"*. Dover Press, New York, N. Y.

13. McCall, J. A., Richards, P. K., Walters, G. F. (1977) *"Factors in Software Quality Assurance"*. RADC-TR-77-369 (Rome Air Development Center). November.

14. Miranda, E. L. (1989) *Specifying Control Transformations through Petri Nets"*. In: ACM SIGSOFT Software Engineering Notes, Vol. 14, no. 2, April, pp. 45-48

15. Peters, L. (1989) *"Timing Extensions to Structured Analysis for Real Time Sustems"*. In: ACM SIGSOFT, 5th International Workshop on Software Specification and Design, May 1989, pp. 83-89

16. Polack, A. J. (1990) *"Practical Applications of CASE Tools on DoD Projects"*. In: ACM SIGSOFT Software Engineering Notes, Vol. 15, no. 1, pp. 73-78, January

17. *"Teamwork Environment, Release 3.0.3"* (1989). Cadre Technologies, Inc.

18. Ward, P., Mellor, S. (1985) *"Structured Development for Real-Time Systems"*. Prentice-Hall

Integration of Structured Analysis and Timed Statecharts for Real-Time and Concurrency Specification

Michael von der Beeck

Technical University of Aachen, Lehrstuhl für Informatik III,
Ahornstr. 55, 52056 Aachen, Germany
e-mail: beeck@rwthi3.informatik.rwth-aachen.de

Abstract. SA-RT-IM (Structured Analysis with Real-Time extensions and Information Modelling) is a graphical requirements analysis method, combining well-known techniques like data flow diagrams, state transition diagrams, and the entity relationship model. Despite being widespread, SA-RT-IM suffers from considerable drawbacks: It does not always express concurrent control clearly, it lacks in specifying real-time constraints, and its syntax and semantics are defined incompletely and ambiguously. Our improvements shall remove these disadvantages: We use Timed Statecharts for the specification of concurrent and timed control processes, introduce additional control flow types and data flow attributes, use finite automata for defining precise semantics of data and control processes, and develop a table specifying the activation condition of a data process.

Keywords. Requirements Engineering, Structured Analysis, SA-RT-IM, Timed Statecharts, Concurrency, Timing Constraint, Real-Time System

1 Introduction

Structured Analysis [1, 2] is a widespread graphical requirements analysis method. For the sake of preciseness we only denote the original version with Structured Analysis (SA) and the version additionally extended by a control model [3, 4, 5] (based on finite automata) and an information model [6] (based on the entity relationship model) with SA-RT-IM.

Though SA-RT-IM is easy to learn, its application provides substantial difficulties:

- SA-RT-IM's control processes are defined by "conventional" finite automata with output (represented by state transition diagrams) which do not offer the optimal way for expressing concurrent control.
- SA-RT-IM insufficiently supports the specification of real-time aspects like preemption, delay, timeout, and interrupt.
- SA-RT-IM is no formal requirements method, but belongs to the large group of "formatted methods" [7] which are characterized by - and suffer from - loosely defined syntax and semantics. In contrast to them, formal methods are characterized by a mathematical basis and the usage of formal notations - what results in precise requirements.

  On the one hand it is necessary that a requirements analysis method is precisely de-

fined. On the other hand formal methods such as e.g. LOTOS [8], CCS [9], CSP [10], and VDM [11] are difficult to use, since they require rigorous usage of their detailed and complex mathematical formalism. This results in low acceptance degree of the latter. In contrast, SA-RT-IM is widely used in practice.
One solution is to combine the aspects of easy usage and preciseness as far as possible. SA-RT-IM fulfils the first aspect very well, but for the sake of preciseness some incomplete or ambiguous definitions have to be improved.

The following is an overview of our SA-RT-IM enhancements:

- Definition of control processes using Timed Statecharts [12, 13] for the specification of complex (timed and concurrent) control providing a clear view of concurrently active states and transitions
- Additional prompts *suspend*, *resume*, and *interrupt* besides the usual ones *activate* and *deactivate*
- Introduction of data flow attributes *overwrite-property* (with values *blocking* and *non-blocking*) and *read-property* (with values *consuming* and *non-consuming*)
- Usage of (enhanced) finite automata for the semantics definition of data processes and control processes
- Definition of the *data-existent table* determining the necessary input data flows for the activation of a data process (a subset of all of its input data flows)

2 Control Modelling

2.1 Control Processes

Control processes can control data processes by activating, deactivating, suspending, resuming, or interrupting them (section 2.2). The control is performed by finite automata with output (Mealy-automata, [14]), reacting on incoming events.

In the following the usage of enhanced finite automata for the specification of control processes will be explained. There we examine sequential and concurrent control.

Sequential Control. Sometimes finite automata contain a set of transitions with identical labels starting from a set of states, but all ending in a common state. This amount of transitions can be reduced, if Statechart's [15, 16, 17] hierarchical OR-states are used: An OR-state is active, if and only if exactly one of its substates is active. A transition leaving an OR-state replaces a set of transitions each of them leaving one of the substates. In figure 1 three transitions with label *c* leaving the states *A*, *B*, and *C* are represented by only one transition with label *c* leaving the OR-state *E*. Therefore we use OR-states for the definition of control processes.

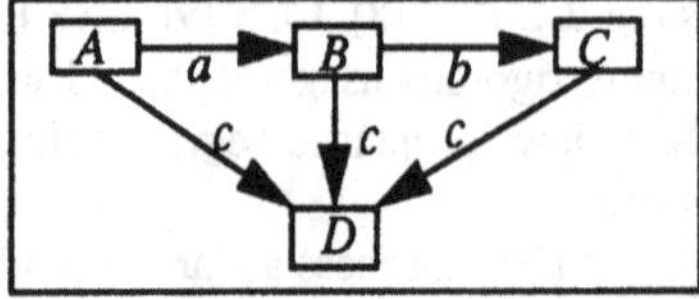

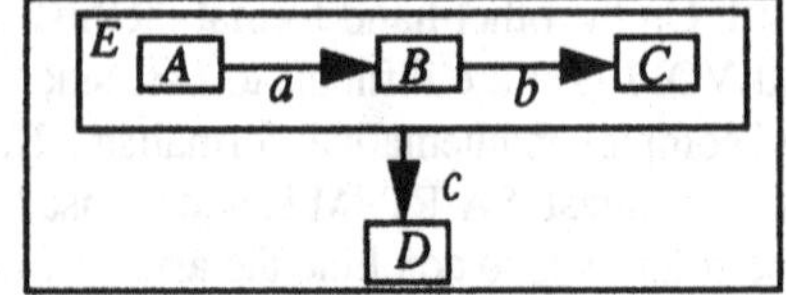

Fig. 1. Sequential control without/with an OR-state.

Concurrent Control. We compare three possibilities for the definition of control processes performing concurrent control: *N* concurrent data processes of a common data flow diagram have to be controlled *(N>1)*:

1. *N* finite automata[1] communicating via event flows are used, so that each automaton controls one data process.
2. Instead of *N* finite automata one equivalent product finite automaton is used, controlling all data processes. This is the common solution in SA-RT-IM.
3. An enhancement of finite automata allowing simultaneously active states and transitions is used to control all data processes. Examples of such techniques are Statecharts [15, 16, 17], Timed Statecharts [12, 13], Modechart [18], Argos [19], and HMS-machines [20].

   From the enhancements listed above[2] we have chosen Timed Statecharts - essentially an enhancement of Statecharts. This technique offers AND-states to express concurrency. Such an AND-state contains substates and is active (inactive), if and only if all of its substates are active (inactive).

One result of the comparison of the three possibilities to specify control processes is obvious: A product automaton (second possibility) leads to badly arranged state transition diagrams compared with both other possibilities, because it contains more states and more transitions and it does not reveal independent (concurrent) state change sequences.

Comparing the first possibility (several finite automata) with the third one (Statechart) is more subtle. Therefore we use the example of figure 2: Two data processes *D1* and *D2* are controlled by event flows *a, b,* and *c*. If for example substate *D* of the (complex) OR-state *G* is active and the external event *b* occurs, then the internal event *a* is generated and broadcasted, the action *act D2* is performed, and the active state changes from *D* to *E*. If the substate *A* of the OR-state *F* is active, the occurrence of the generated and broadcasted event *a* triggers the transition from state *A* to state *C*, so that the action *act D1* is performed. The actions *act D1* and *act D2* activate the data processes *D1* and *D2*.[3] The control processes

1. In this case usage of the term "Mealy automaton" instead of "finite automaton" would be more precise, since an output of events and actions has to be provided. But for the sake of simplicity we use the more customary term.
2. The other enhancements are briefly described in section 5.
3. As in [5, 6] - but in contrast to [3, 4] - we represent prompts like event flows graphically by arrows - starting at the control process and ending in the data process to be controlled.

C1, *C2*, and *C* in figure 2 are represented by hatched circles and the specification of each control process is given below the circle by a finite automaton (left side) or a Statechart (right side).

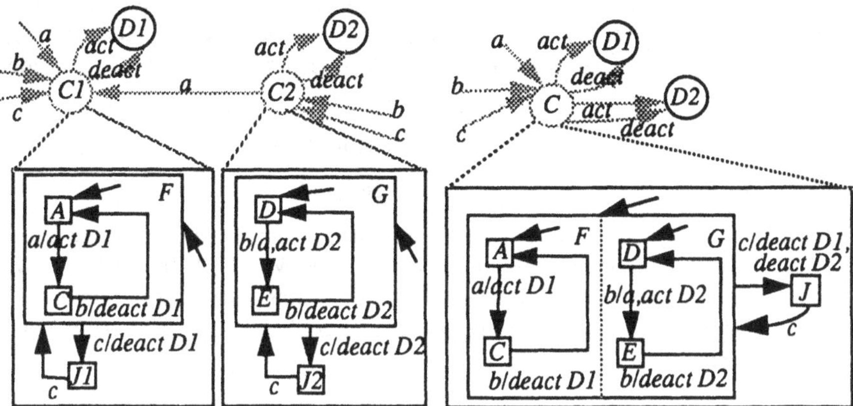

Fig. 2. Two finite automata (left) and a Statechart (right) specifying two/one control process(es)

In the first possibility (several finite automata) two states *J1* and *J2* are necessary, while in the third one (Statechart) the state *J* suffices. Besides the larger state number it is a disadvantage that the first solution does not express that *J1* and *J2* are always simultaneously active. But also the third solution (Statechart) has a disadvantage compared with the first one (several finite automata): The dependency between the communicating finite automata of control processes *C1* and *C2* is more obvious than the dependency between the AND-states *F* and *G* of the third solution due to the event flow *a* between the control processes.

Therefore we use AND-states according to the Statecharts notation. Additionally, we allow conventional (communicating) finite automata out of two reasons:

1. This is a notation many analysts are familiar with [3, 4, 5, 6].
2. This solution is needed anyway, if two control processes residing in different data flow diagrams have to communicate.

But we restrict data flow diagrams to have at most one control process symbol. This means that all finite automata which have to control data processes of the same data flow diagram are represented by the same control process. Since the finite automata of the common control process have to communicate, they are (graphically) connected by event-labelled arrows representing the sending of events from one automaton to another.

Timed Control Processes. Reactive systems [21] are characterized by being event-driven: They continuously have to react on external and internal events. Many models (e.g. Statecharts, Lustre [22]) specifying reactive systems follow Esterel's "synchrony hypothesis" [23] stating that the model immediately reacts on inputs without delay (i.e. time is not progressing in between).

If real-time systems have to be specified, an adequate notion of time has to be introduced in the modelling language being able to express timing constraints.

Therefore we adopt Esterel's synchrony hypothesis only partially: Besides the usual untimed transitions of "conventional" Statecharts[4] we follow the proposal of Timed Statecharts additionally using timed transitions:[5] A timed transition is associated with a time interval specifying a lower and an upper bound of the period while the transition must be continuously enabled before it is executed. Hence, situations can be modelled in which the reaction on an incoming event takes place after a time delay. The formal syntax of a transition label is as follows:

- *e[c]/a* (untimed transition)
- *([c] for I) /a* (timed transition)

Hereby the trigger *e* is a conjunction of events or negated events, *c* is a condition, *a* is a sequence of actions and generated events, and *I* is a time interval $\{l, u\}$, specifying a lower bound *l* and an upper bound *u* on the duration for which the transition must be continuously enabled before it is taken. (If $l=u$, then an exact duration is given). All transition label components are optional.

Timed transitions work synchronously, i.e. they are executed simultaneously. Time can progress only by an amount on which all transitions agree, i.e. the amount must not cause any enabled transition *T* to be continuously enabled for more than *u* time units without being taken, if *u* is the upper bound of *T's* time interval. On the contrary, untimed transitions (taking zero time) are executed asynchronously: Concurrency is modelled by interleaving.

It is sometimes claimed that the interleaving model of computation is inappropriate for real-time specification and instead of this maximal parallelism [26] should be used. But in [27] it is proven that the interleaving model of timed transition systems - used for Timed Statecharts' semantics definition - can express the following characteristic features of real-time systems: delay, timeout, and preemption.

We present simple examples of Timed Statecharts modelling these features:

- *delay*
  A process has to perform an action for a given period (specified by lower and upper bounds), before it starts with a second action. This is modelled as follows: The process resides in state *S1* - performing the first action - for at least *l* and for at most *u* time units. Then it changes to *S2* to start the second action.

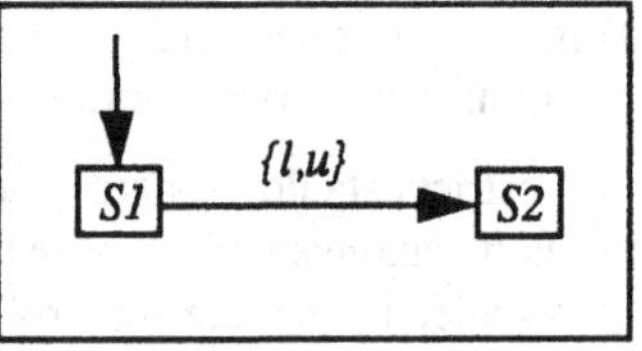

4. In [24] it is shown, why "conventional" Statecharts are insufficient for expressing real-time aspects.
5. The combination of timed and untimed transitions for modelling real-time features is also used in timed automata [25].

- *timeout*

  A process checks, whether the external event *e* takes place within time *t*. When residing in state *S1* for a shorter period than *t* time units, the process will immediately change to state *S2*, if *e* occurs. If *e* does not occur in the period of *t* time units, the process will change to state *S3*. (*{t,t}* is an abbreviation for *([true] for {t,t})*).

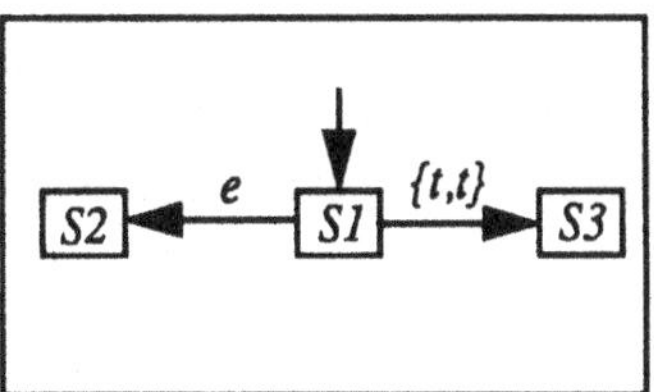

- *preemption*

  A process shall perform an action *A* until a first step of a second action *B* can be taken, so that the rest of action *A* will be discarded and action *B* will executed until it terminates. In the example action *A* is composed of all subactions which are performed in the state *S4*, while the first step of action *B* is given by the state change from *S4* to *S5*.

  Independently from the substate of *S4* in which the process actually resides - *S1*, *S2*, or *S3* -, it will immediately change to *S5*, if the event *a* occurs.

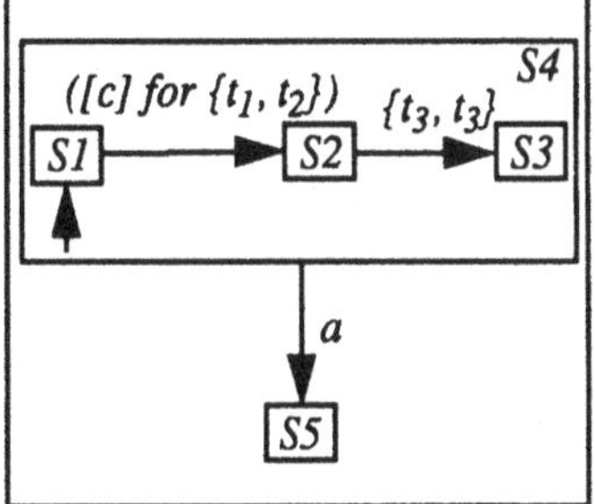

Hence, Timed Statecharts' interleaved way of using timed and untimed transitions suffices for real-time applications and furthermore retains the advantage to define computation sequences (traces) which only contain one transition at any point.

Consumption of Events. We introduce a more flexible way of event consumption which is motivated as follows:

- In Timed Statecharts an event persists until time progresses i.e. until an (arbitrary) timed transition fires. This means that more than one transition can be triggered by the same event.
- An alternative definition exists for (conventional) Statecharts: In every substate of an AND-state an event can be used at most once to trigger a transition, then it is consumed (i.e. no more available).

Since it establishes the most flexible solution, we introduce the following: One can decide for every transition, but fixed for it, whether its triggering events are consumed.[6]

2.2 Prompts

Prompts are control flows with predefined semantics to determine the effect of a control process on data processes. We introduce additional prompt types:

6. The distinction between transitions with/without event consumption is proposed in [28].

- *activate, deactivate*

  Usually [3, 6], only two prompt types to control data processes are provided: *activate* and *deactivate*. If an atomic data process is activated, its mini specification is executed from its very beginning, and if it is deactivated, it stops its execution at once.

- *suspend, resume*

  The ability to suspend an atomic data process, i.e. to stop the execution of its mini specification at the current statement, and to resume it later on, so that the execution continues at this statement, is necessary. Therefore we use further prompts *suspend* and *resume* [29] with the afore-mentioned semantics.

- *interrupt*

  We introduce a third possibility to stop the execution of the mini specification of a data process. Every atomic data process contains a set of interrupt handling routines with the appropriate one being selected when an interrupt occurs.[7] Such an interrupt handling routine cannot be stopped by any event, so once started it will be executed to its very end. If event flows and prompts ending in the data process become active while an interrupt handling routine is executing, they will be ignored. We have taken this decision due to easy modelling: If an analyst wants to specify non interruptible procedures, he simply can use the interrupt prompt.

Prompts may also end in nonatomic data processes. Their semantics are presented in section 4.

3 Functional Modelling

We have enhanced data flows as well: They are additionally characterized by two attributes: *overwrite-property* and *read-property*. Their values are:

- *blocking / non-blocking* (overwrite-property)
- *consuming / non-consuming* (read-property)

A data flow is

- *blocking* if the precondition for writing new data on it is that the old one is already read,
- *non-blocking* if the actual data may be overwritten by new data in any case,
- *consuming* if its data are read destructively, i.e. data disappear from the flow if they are read,
- *non-consuming* if its data are read non-destructively.

7. If the set of interrupt handling routines of an atomic data process is empty, an interrupt has the same effect as a deactivation.

read-property \ overwrite-property	*blocking*	*nonblocking*
nonconsuming	—|→ *	——→ *
consuming	—|→	——→

Table 1: Data flow representation

In contrast to [30] we do not differentiate between synchronous and asynchronous data flows, since loose coupling - asynchronous communication - of data processes is a characteristic property of SA which should be maintained.

4 Semantics

One considerable lack of SA-RT-IM is its imprecise and incomplete semantics definition. Among other things this concerns data processes and control processes.

4.1 Semantics of Data Processes and Control Processes

Although the usage of SA-RT-IM is very widespread, the behaviour of its processes is not defined precisely. Especially the interrelations between a parent data process and its child (control and data) processes have been neglected up to now. Therefore we developed an unambiguous semantics for these processes and furthermore enhanced the syntax of data processes - by defining data-existent tables - in order to provide the possibility that the behaviour of each individual data process can be specified more precisely.

Enhanced Finite Automata for Semantics Specification. We additionally use enhanced finite automata for the description of the semantics of data processes and control processes. To avoid a potential misunderstanding: This usage must not be mixed up with the specification of individual control processes by finite automata (section 2.1, Concurrent Control) or with the specification of individual atomic data processes by mini specifications in the application of SA-RT-IM.

To describe the semantics of processes formally, we define three finite automata: the Nonatomic Data Process Automaton (NDPA) for nonatomic data processes, the Atomic Data Process Automaton (ADPA) for atomic data processes, and the Control Process Automaton (CPA) for control processes. Their representations essentially using the Statecharts notation[8] are given in figures 3, 4, and 5.

---

8. Here we use OR-states and the history-mechanism of this notation. The history-mechanism provides the following facility: The execution of a transition represented by an arrow ending in the history symbol H (see figure 4) lying in an OR-state *S* causes a change to that substate of *S* which has been the last one active.

In order to determine interactions between processes, we need a communication mechanism between NDPAs, ADPAs, and CPAs. For this purpose Statechart's broadcasting is inappropriate, since in our case the receiving automata have to be mentioned explicitly when information is sent. Therefore we have defined the transition labels of the enhanced finite automata accordingly. (Each *effect* in an *action* is associated with a *targetlist*):

transition_label ::= *condition* | *condition '/' actionlist*

condition ::= *prompt* | *event* | *comparison*

prompt ::= *'act'* | *'deact'* | *'suspend'* | *'resume'* | *'interrupt'*

event ::= *'data_existent'* | *'end_of_minispec'* | *'block'* | *'unblock'* | *'end_of_interrupt'* | *'interrupt_ended'*

comparison ::= *'n=0'*

actionlist ::= *action* | *action ';' actionlist*

action ::= *targetlist ':' effect* | *assignment*

targetlist ::= *target* | *target ',' targetlist*

target ::= *'parent'* | *'child'* | *'control'*

effect ::= *prompt* | *'interrupt_ended'*

assignment ::= *'n := # child processes'* | *'n := # data processes'* | *'n := n-1'*

The terminal symbols have the following meaning:

- *act* = *activate*
- *deact* = *deactivate*
- *data_existent* = all necessary input data flows of the data process are active, i.e. the data process is provided with sufficient data; the data-existent table (section 4.1, Data-Existent Table) of the process determines the necessary input data flows
- *end_of_minispec* = execution of the mini specification is finished
- *end_of_interrupt* = execution of an interrupt handling routine is finished
- *interrupt_ended* = the process has left the state *interrupted*
- *block* = execution of the mini specification is stopped, because an output onto a blocking data flow could not be done
- *unblock* = the reason for disabling an output onto a data flow does not exist any more
- *parent* = the parent data process
- *child* = each child data process and the child control process
- *control* = the control process in the same data flow diagram
- *n := # data processes* or *n := # child processes*

  After the execution of one of these two assignments, the (integer) variable *n* contains the number of data processes in the same data flow diagram or the number of all child processes (incl. control process), respectively.

A state transition diagram represents an initial state as usual by an arrow having no source.

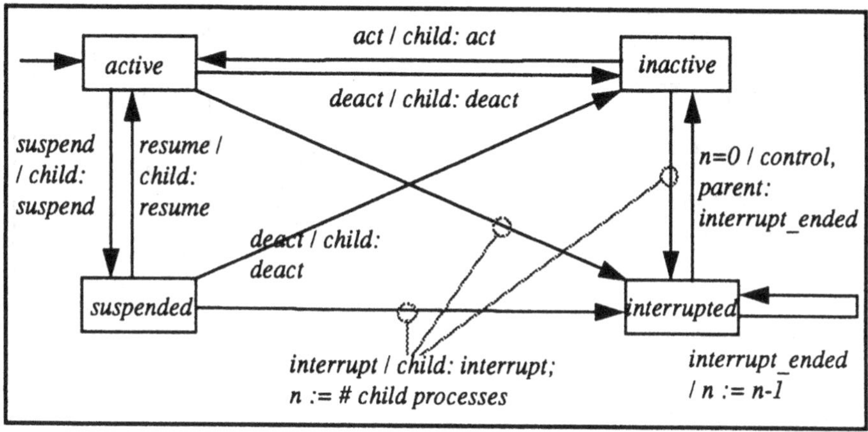

Fig. 3. Nonatomic data process automaton (NDPA)

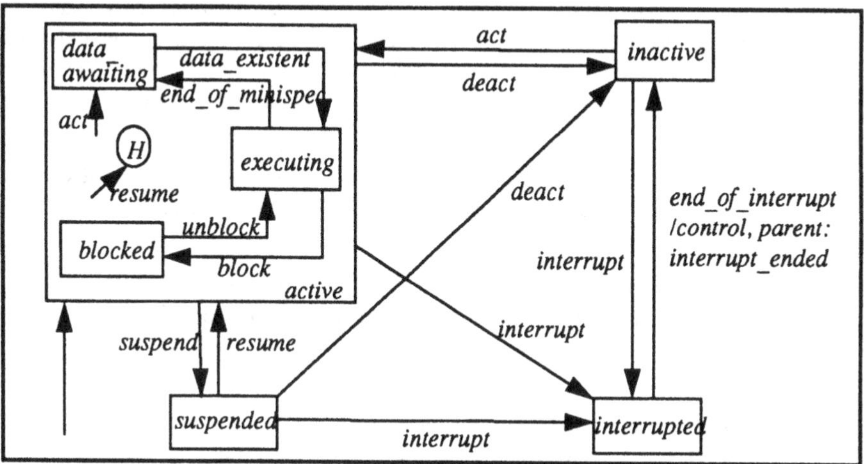

Fig. 4. Atomic data process automaton (ADPA)

Figures 3 and 4 are quite similar: The state *active* of the NDPA is refined into the three substates *data_awaiting*, *executing*, and *blocked* of the ADPA.

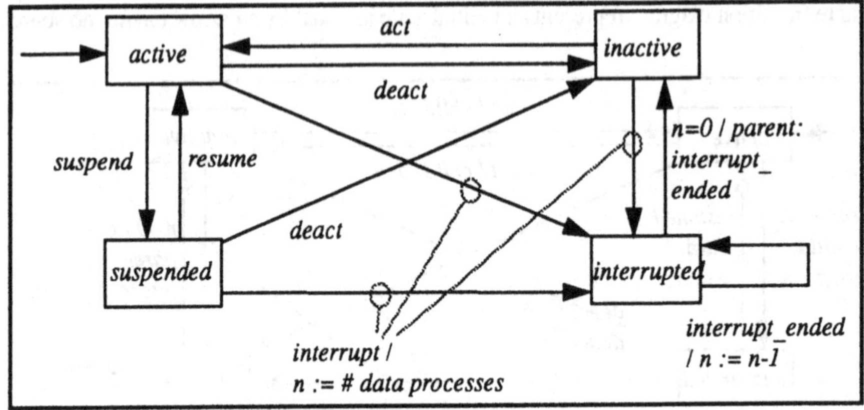

Fig. 5. Control process automaton (CPA)

To explain the CPA, its states are described in more detail:

- *active*
  The "usual" state of a control process is *active*. In this state the control process can react on incoming events, i.e. its finite automaton can perform state changes. This means - assuming zero time state changes - that there is always at least one active state in the control process specification, if the control process is *active*. If a control process gets *active* by an activation, its specifying finite automaton resides in its initial state.

- *inactive*
  If the control process is *inactive*, it cannot react on incoming events, represented by the fact that its specifying finite automaton does not reside in a defined state.

- *suspended*
  If the control process is *suspended*, it cannot react on incoming events. After a resumption the finite automaton specifying the control process will reside in the same state as it has been, before the last suspension occurred.

- *interrupted*
  If the control process is *interrupted*, it cannot react on incoming events. In contrast to the states *inactive* and *suspended*, the state *interrupted* can only be left by the event *interrupt_ended* sent by the last data process which resides in the same data flow diagram as the control process and which changes its state from *interrupted* to *inactive*. (This is represented by the condition *n=0* in the transition label.)

State changes in the CPA occur, when activations, deactivations, suspensions, resumptions, or interruptions occur. Since we do not allow prompts ending in control processes, the corresponding prompts signalling these occurrences end in the parent data process of the control process or even in one of its ancestor processes.

Data-Existent Table. We still have to define, when the *data_existent* condition is fulfilled. Therefore we introduce *data-existent tables* one of which has to be filled for every atomic data process *P*. This table determines exactly, but in a very flexible manner, which input data flows have to be active[9], so that the data_existent condition is fulfilled and *P's* mini specification begins to execute. To describe this with the ADPA (figure 4): If it resides in the state *data_awaiting* and the *data_existent* condition is fulfilled according to *P's* table, then a state change to *executing* is performed.

A data-existent table of an atomic data process *P* contains a set of conditions $\{c_1,..., c_m\}$ with $c_i = \{d_1, d_2,..., d_n\}$, $1 \leq i \leq m$ and d_j = input data flow of *P*, $1 \leq j \leq n$, (*m* depends on *P*, *n* depends on *i*). If there exists at least one c_i, $1 \leq i \leq m$, so that all $d_j \in c_i$, $1 \leq j \leq n$, are active, then the *data_existent* condition is fulfilled for *P*.

4.2 Dependencies between Processes on Different Refinement Levels

Effects of Prompts on Subsequent Data Processes and Control Processes. Prompts need not end in atomic data processes. The semantics of a prompt ending in a nonatomic data process *P* is defined by the semantics of the same type of prompts ending in each of *P's* child processes.

The effect of prompt *pr* (figure 6, left DFD) - ending in the nonatomic data process *P* - on *P's* child processes *C* and P_{child} is equivalent with the entirety of the effects of the prompts *pr1* and *pr2* (figure 6, right DFD) ending in these child processes for all prompt types *pr*=*pr1*=*pr2* ∈ {*activate, deactivate, suspend, resume, interrupt*}. This means e.g. that an *activate* prompt *pr* ending in *P* has the same effect on *C* and P_{child} as two *activate* prompts *pr1* and *pr2* ending in *C* and P_{child}, respectively.

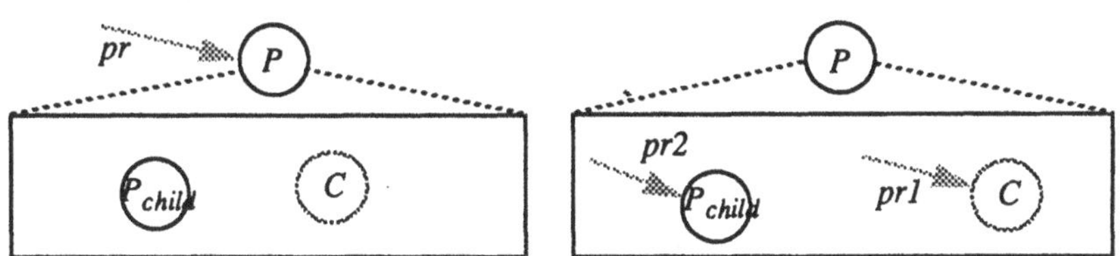

Fig. 6. Effects of prompts on child processes

Relationships between a Parent Data Process and its Child Processes. The afore-mentioned effects imply relationships between a parent data process *P* and its child processes. These are valid for the whole period in which *P* remains in the corresponding state, and not only for the moment when *P* is prompted. The relationships are shown in table 2. Each table row states an implication between the state of a parent data process and the states of its child processes.

9. A data flow is active if there are data on the flow.

parent data process	child data processes	child control process
*active**	*active, inactive, suspended* or *interrupted*	*active*
inactive	*inactive* or *interrupted*	*inactive*
suspended	*suspended, interrupted* or *inactive*	*suspended*
interrupted⁺	*inactive* or *interrupted,* but at least one is *interrupted*	*interrupted*

Table 2: Relationships between parent and child process states

* The situation can arise that the control process is the only active child process of the active parent data process.

⁺ The actual state *interrupted* of a parent data process *P* does not imply that all child data processes are interrupted. According to section 4.2, Effects of Prompts on Subsequent Data Processes and Control Processes, each child data process P_{child} of *P* will get an *interrupt* signal, when *P* becomes *interrupted.* Depending on its current state, P_{child} therefore can become *interrupted,* but after some time it will become *inactive,*

1. if P_{child} is atomic and its interrupt handling routine has been finished, so that the event *end_of_interrupt* is generated (cf. figure 4), or
2. if P_{child} is nonatomic and (recursively) each of its child processes will have changed its state from *interrupted* to *inactive.*

P remains *interrupted* until its last child process becomes *inactive*, then *P* becomes *inactive*, too (cf. figure 3).

5 Related Work

In contrast to the graphical language Timed Statecharts many very abstract textual languages for real-time systems exist. They belong to the classes of real-time temporal logics (e.g. MTL [31], TCTL [32]) or timed process algebras (e.g. TCSP [33], ATP [34]). They all provide formally defined semantics, but they do not offer easy usage. Furthermore, temporal logic specifications are relatively unstructured.

Modechart, an enhancement of Statecharts, is presented in [18] as a mean of expressing timing constraints by a first order logic language called RTL (Real Time Logic) introduced by [35]. The usage of RTL for timing purposes seems to be more difficult than the usage of Timed Statecharts' timed transitions.

In [19] ARGOS, a multi-level transition free restriction of Statecharts, is described. Also some other minor restrictions of Statecharts are introduced. The main disadvantage of ARGOS compared with Timed Statecharts is the nonexistence of timed transitions.

HMS-machines [20] provide a graphical state-based formalism, which is executable, whose transitions have execution or synchronization intervals associated with them, and which provide multi-level specifications with an abstract upper level and a detailed lower level. Though the method of using HMS-machines leads to expressive, hierarchical, and real-time specifications, its intricate usage has to be mentioned.

For a more extensive discussion the reader is advised to consult reference [36].

6 Conclusion and Further Work

We have proposed several changes and enhancements for the requirements analysis method SA-RT-IM. They were motivated from SA-RT-IM's lack of expressing concurrent control and real-time constraints clearly. Moreover, the method's loosely defined semantics gave rise to several semantic considerations.

In detail we enhanced the RT-part of SA-RT-IM by Statecharts' refineable states and transitions which may be simultaneously active, so that concurrent control can be specified clearly.

Furthermore, we provided SA-RT-IM with the ability to specify time information in control processes, so that the method is applicable for real-time systems as well.

Moreover, we introduced

- data flow attributes specifying operational behaviour of data flows,
- new prompt types offering more possibilities of data process control, and
- data-existent tables specifying the activation condition of data processes.

Additionally, we developed a precise semantics for control and data processes.

Data-existent tables should also be introduced for nonatomic data processes. This has to be done in a way that the table of a nonatomic data process *P* is consistent with the data-existent tables of *P's* child data processes.

Since executable specifications are very appropriate for describing requirements - especially for non-experts - we work on an executable version of SA-RT-IM.

References

1. T. DeMarco: *Structured Analysis and System Specification*, Yourdon Press, (1979)

2. S. McMenamin, J. Palmer: *Essential Systems Analysis*, Englewood Cliffs, Prentice Hall, (1984)

3. D. Hatley, I. Pirbhai: *Strategies for Real-Time System Specification*, New York: Dorset House, (1987)

4. M. Keller, K. Shumate: *Software Specification and Design: A Disciplined Approach for Real-Time Systems*, John Wiley & Sons, Inc., (1992)

5. P. Ward, S. Mellor: *Structured Development for Real-Time Systems*, New York, Yourdon Press, (1985)

6. E. Yourdon: *Modern Structured Analysis*, Prentice-Hall, (1989)

7. A. Finkelstein, S. Goldsack: *Requirements engineering for real-time systems*, IEE Software Engineering Journal, May, (1991)

8. E. Brinksma: *Information Processing Systems - Open Systems Interconnection - LOTOS - A Formal Description Technique based upon the Temporal Ordering of Observational Behaviour*, Draft International Standard ISO 8807, (1988)

9. R. Milner: *A Calculus of Communicating Systems*, LNCS 92, Springer-Verlag, (1980)

10. C. Hoare: *Communicating Sequential Processes*, Prentice Hall, (1985)

11. C. Jones: *Systematic Software Development Using VDM*, Series in Computer Science, Prentice Hall, 2. edition, (1990)

12. Y. Kesten, A. Pnueli: *Timed and Hybrid Statecharts and their Textual Representation*, LNCS 571, Springer-Verlag, pp. 591-620, (1992)

13. O. Maler, Z. Manna, A. Pnueli: *From Timed to Hybrid Systems*, LNCS 600, Springer-Verlag, pp. 447-484, (1992)

14. A. Salomaa: *Formal Languages*, ACM Monograph Series, Academic Press, (1973)

15. D. Harel: *Statecharts: A visual formalism for complex systems*, Sci. Comput. Program., vol. 8, pp. 231-274, (1987)

16. D. Harel, H. Lachover, A. Naamad, A. Pnueli, M. Politi, R. Sherman, A. Shtull-Trauring, M. Trakhtenbrot: *STATEMATE: A Working Environment for the Development of Complex Reactive Systems*, IEEE Trans. on Software Eng., vol. 16, pp. 403-414, (1990)

17. A. Pnueli, M. Shalev: *What is in a Step: On the Semantics of Statecharts*, LNCS 526, Springer-Verlag, pp. 244-264, (1991)

18. F. Jahanian, R. Lee, A. Mok: *Semantics of Modechart in Real Time Logic*, Proc. 21st Hawaii Int. Conf. on System Sciences, pp. 479-489, (1988)

19. F. Maraninchi: *Operational and Compositional Semantics of Synchronous Automaton Compositions*, LNCS 630, Springer-Verlag, pp. 550-564, (1992)

20. M. Franklin, A. Gabrielian: *Multi-Level Specification and Verification of Real-Time Software*, Proc.12th Int. Conf. on Software Engineering, pp. 52-62, (1990)

21. D. Harel, A. Pnueli: *On the development of reactive systems* in: Logics and Models of Concurrent Systems, ed. by K. Apt, Springer-Verlag, pp. 477-498, (1985)

22. J. Bergerand, P. Caspi, N. Halbwachs: *Outline of a real-time data flow language*, Proc. IEEE-CS Real-Time Systems Symposium, San Diego, (1985)

23. G. Berry, L. Cosserat: *The ESTEREL Synchronous Programming Language and its Mathematical Semantics*, ENSMP, Centre de Mathématiques Appliquées, Sophia-Antipolis, 06565 Valbonne, France, (1985)

24. B. Melhart, N. Leveson, M. Jaffe: *Analysis Capabilities for Requirements Specified in Statecharts*, Technical Report, University of California, Irvine, (1988)

25. R. Alur, D. Dill: *Automata for modeling real-time systems*, Proc. 17th ICALP, LNCS 443, pp. 322-335, Springer-Verlag, (1990)

26. R. Koymanns, R. Shyamasundar, W. de Roever, R. Gerth, S. Arun-Kumar: *Compositional semantics for real-time distributed computing*, Proc. of Logics of Programs, LNCS 193, Springer-Verlag, pp. 167-190, (1985)

27. T. Henzinger, Z. Manna, A. Pnueli: *Timed Transition Systems*, LNCS 600, Springer-Verlag, pp. 226-251, (1992)

28. A. Classen: *Modulare Statecharts: Ein formaler Rahmen zur hierarchischen Prozeßspezifikation*, Master Thesis, Lehrstuhl für Informatik II, Technical University of Aachen, (1993)

29. W. Bruyn, R. Jensen, D. Keskar, P. Ward: *ESML: An Extended Systems Modelling Language based on the Data Flow Diagram*, Software Engineering Notes, vol.13, no.1, pp. 58-67, (1988)

30. R. France: *Semantically Extended Data Flow Diagrams: A Formal Specification Tool*, IEEE Transact. on SE, vol. 18, no. 4, pp. 329-346, (1992)

31. R. Koymans: *Specifying real-time properties with metric temporal logic*, The Journal of Real-Time Systems, vol. 2, pp. 255-299, (1990)

32. R. Alur: *Techniques for Automatic Verification of Real-Time Systems*, Ph.D. Thesis, Stanford University, Stanford, California, USA, (1991)

33. S. Schneider, J. Davies, D. Jackson, G. Reed, J. Reed, A. Roscoe: *Timed CSP: Theory and Practice*, LNCS 600, Springer-Verlag, pp. 640-675, (1992)

34. X. Nicollin, J. Sifakis: *The algebra of timed processes ATP: theory and application*, Technical Report RT-C26, LGI-IMAG, Grenoble, France, (1990)

35. F. Jahanian, A. Mok: *Safety Analysis of Timing Properties in Real-Time Systems*, IEEE Transactions on Software Engineering, vol. 12, no.9, pp. 890-904, (1986)

36. M. von der Beeck: *Integration of Structured Analysis and Timed Statecharts for Real-Time and Concurrency Specification*, Aachener Informatik-Berichte, AIB Nr. 92-26, Technical Report, Technical University of Aachen, (1992)

Language Constructs for Cooperative Systems Design

Flavio DePaoli

Dipartimento di Elettronica e Informazione
Politecnico di Milano
Piazza L. da Vinci, 32 - 20133 Milano - Italy
depaoli@IPMEL2.ELET.POLIMI.IT

Francesco Tisato

Dipartimento di Scienze dell'Informazione
Università di Milano
Via Comelico, 39 - 20135 Milano - Italy
tisato@HERMES.MC.DSI.UNIMI.IT

Abstract. This paper presents the basic constructs of CSDL, a language designed for both specifying and designing synchronous cooperative systems. It is part of a project that deals with the building of an environment supporting design and execution of computer-based multimedia cooperative systems. CSDL tries to address the difficulties of integrating different aspects of cooperative systems: cooperation control, communication, and system modularization.
CSDL's basic unit is the *coordinator*. It is composed of a *specification*, a *body*, and a *context*. The specification defines the cooperation policy, the body controls the underlying communication channels, and the context defines coordinators' interaction in complex and modular systems.

1. Introduction

Distributed systems consisting of high-powered workstations connected by high-speed networks are becoming prevalent. Current software applications take little or no advantage of networking capabilities. Most of them are still single-user applications, while classical distributed systems exploit distribution for gaining performance, for sharing information or for increasing data availability, but do not provide a sound support for the most significative aspect of human activities: cooperation.
People need to cooperate, and the challenge of the next decade is providing computer-based cooperative environments [1]. Several examples of computer supported cooperation are already present in the every-day life: electronic mail, voice and video teleconferencing systems, electronic classrooms. Many such systems are still in naive version, or they are prototypes. In any case, there is a lack of general models supporting the design of cooperative systems and of *collaboration-aware* applications [12].
With the term cooperative systems we intend systems in which users interact synchronously through a *shared workspace* [11], i.e., a set of tools and facilities accessible by each user. It is based on the concept of *what you see is what I see* [19], i.e., when a user changes the status of a shared tool, that modification is perceived by the other users. It is usually accomplished through a work surface that participants use for creating, displaying, and interacting. Multimedia technology adds audio and video to the traditional graphic screen.
Cooperative systems usually rely on proprietary hardware and software platforms that can be hardly integrated into standard environments [7, 16]. Since heterogeneous environments are the future scenario, integration is a crucial issue in the design of large cooperative systems. It means that workstations with different configurations, devices, operating systems, and

This work has been partially supported by CNR - Progetto Finalizzato "Sistemi Informatici e Calcolo Parallelo", CEFRIEL, and CRAI-Progetto MADE.

networking support must cooperate to let people cooperate. In particular, multimedia workstations and multimedia networking systems are going to be widely available, therefore multimedia applications based on specialized hardware or networks must be integrated into industry standard architecture.
An environment supporting the design and development of cooperative systems should fulfill several basic requirements. First, it must provide the designer with abstractions that model the logical behavior of cooperative activities. Second, it must support a proper system layering by separating logical behavior from system- and media- dependent issues. Third, it must emphasize modularization. Modular systems have the double advantage of encouraging the construction of toolkits, and of supporting the design of open systems.
This paper proposes CSDL (Cooperative Systems Design Language) as specification language that formalizes the architectural model for collaborative applications. The architectural model decomposes a cooperative system in independent modules, each one dealing with a particular task. The language constructs support the design of modules devoted to the cooperation control, and their integration with the rest of the system. The definition of CSDL is part of research activities, which involve Università di Milano, Politecnico di Milano and CEFRIEL, that aim at building a Unix-based environment supporting design and execution of computer-based multimedia cooperative systems.
Section 2 of the paper introduces the architectural model on which the whole project is based. Section 3 discusses how the cooperation rules are modeled and implemented in CSDL. Section 4 presents the basic language constructs. Section 5 describes modularization in CSDL. Section 5 presents related works. Section 6 discusses the state of the project, open issues and future developments.

2. The Architectural Model

A cooperative system has the ultimate goal of granting multiple access to shared tools in a controlled way. For example, it should allow several users to access cooperatively a document, each user with the capability of reading and writing it. Moreover, there should be some access rules to prevent two users from updating concurrently the same part of the document. The system can be designed by separating the shared text editor, which manipulates the document, from the module that controls the access to the editor, and the module implementing the user interface. The access control module can be further decomposed in two modules: a module that defines the access rules, i.e., the cooperation policy, and a module that controls the underlying communication system, i.e., enables and disables the communication channels to users. An architecture that decomposes a system in this way provides a suitable separation of concerns. Since modules are independent entities, each one can be designed and implemented in different ways. It means that the system design has to be independent from the execution environment.
Fig. 1 illustrates a possible configuration for a system in which users share the text editor xedit[1]. (The reader can refer to [6] for a complete discussion of this example.) On site0 there is the xedit process, and the other processes forming the cooperative system. The module CooperationControl defines the cooperation policy, and pilots the module Communication accordingly. The module Communication manages the multiplexing and demultiplexing of data streams between users and the shared editor. For example, when the user on site1 has the grant of writing the document, it enables the input channel from site1 to xedit, and

---

[1] At this stage, for the sake of clarity we consider a process for each module of the system. Actually, the current implementation allows the designer to collect homogeneous modules in a single process, or to replicate a module to support distribution.

disables the others. The decision that user on site1 is the current writer is taken by the CooperationControl module. The separation between communication control and cooperation control issues improves flexibility (it is possible to change the cooperation policy without changing any other part of the system), portability and system reconfiguration (all system and network dependencies are encapsulated into the Communication module).

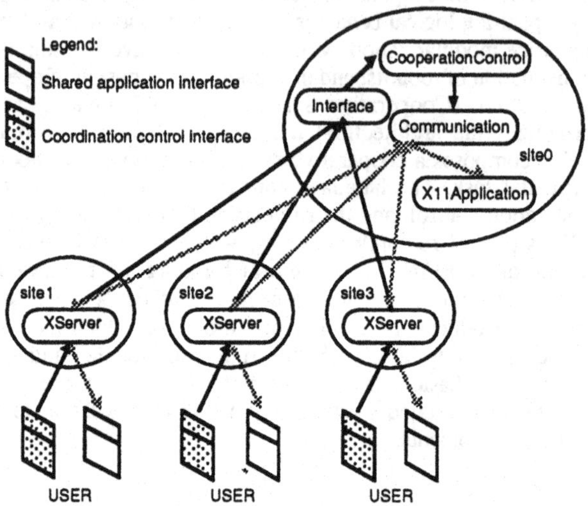

Fig. 1. A cooperative system.

The two user interfaces put in evidence that a user can perform two classes of actions. On the one side, users can control the access to the shared editor. For example, the user on site1 can make himself the current writer, thus preventing other users from modifying the document. On the other side, users interact with the shared tools. For example, they can input data, or issue commands like *save*, *search*, or *format*.

CSDL provides a set of constructs for the definition of the cooperation rules, and primitives for driving the underlying communication network. CSDL enforces layering by separating cooperation policies from data flow control. At an abstract specification level, cooperation strategies can be defined without considering which media are involved. At a more concrete level, cooperation strategies are mapped into the control of *virtual channels* devoted to different media. Virtual channels are controlled through device-independent interfaces. In other terms, at a design stage no assumption is required on communication protocols or device control issues. The hiding of system dependent features permits the integration of heterogeneous hardware and software platforms without affecting the system design.

In the example above, the shared tool is a single-user X11 application. It is shared by duplicating its output and simulating a single user to it. This task is accomplished by the communication module. Its implementation is environment dependent (in this case, it is requested of manipulating XProtocol messages), but it can be controlled through CSDL's primitives. This schema supports the inclusion of any single-user application designed with a client-server model [18], as well as *collaboration aware* applications.

The internal architecture of modules devoted to cooperation control is based on two ideas: cooperating people are characterized by the *role* they play inside a cooperative environment, and cooperation is controlled by *rules* governing role changes [4]. In CSDL a module is called coordinator. It is defined as a set of *groups* of users, each one representing a role, and a set of *requests* it can satisfy.

Let us consider a conferencing environment where persons listen to a speaker talking from a floor. Participants may interact with the speaker by asking questions. The conference rules state that a listener that has a question raises his or her hand, and then waits for the floor. There should be one speaker at a time. Therefore a listener plays temporarily the role of speaker when he or she is allowed to expose the question, while the speaker plays temporarily the role of listener.

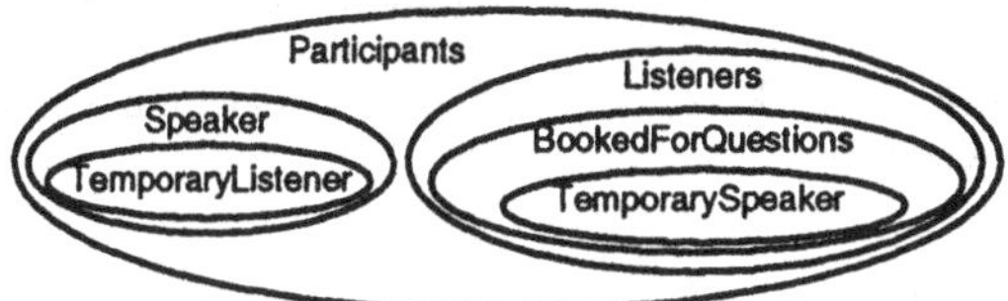

Fig. 2. A coordinator.

Fig. 2 is a graphical representation of that coordinator. Each group corresponds to a role in the conference. For example, Participants are people in the conference room, or users connected to the communication system in a computer supported environment. Listeners listen to the speaker (i.e., they are enabled to receive data through some output channels). They may join the BookedForQuestions group if they wish to put a question. In a computer-based environment they still have the output channels enabled, and are waiting for having the input channel enabled.

Users perceive their group membership through the rights they have, i.e. actions they are allowed to perform. For instance, a Listener may raise his or her hand to become BookedForQuestions, whereas the Speaker (of course) cannot. On the other side, the Speaker's role is characterized by the fact that he or she may send input data to the shared workspace (e.g. by speaking, or by issuing commands to a text editor). Moreover, he or she may select a TemporarySpeaker from the BookedForQuestions group.

Group nesting means that a user may play multiple roles, with the meaning that an inner group represents a role that is a specialization of the role represented by the outer one. Users in a group G2 inherit the rights of the containing group G1, and get also those specifically associated with G2. For instance, BookedForQuestions are also Listeners: they still listen to the speaker. A TemporarySpeaker takes the right of speaking, and inherits the right of listening from Listeners. A right associated with an outer group may be disabled in the inner one: the TemporaryListener is a Speaker, but he or she has temporarily lost the right of speaking and, possibly, of selecting a TemporarySpeaker.

From the example we can argue that the main advantage of considering user roles as a key concept is that the actual identity and location of the users need not be considered. A user is viewed as long as he or she belongs to a *group* of users characterized by the *role* they play. This abstraction is crucial when designing a distributed system with an arbitrary number of users. Another advantage is that the evolution of the system can be described in a simple and clear way. The system status changes if, and only if, one or more users change their role. Suitable *rules* state when a role change is legal. Role changes may be triggered either by external events (i.e. user commands) or by messages generated inside the system, depending on its structure. In both cases, they are *requests* sent to coordinators.

3. CSDL

CSDL unit is the *coordinator* [5]. A coordinator is composed of a *specification*, a *body* and a *context*. A specification defines roles and policies in terms of *groups* and *requests* that groups' members can issue; in turn, a request is defined by the *actions* it triggers. A body defines the implications of group memberships in terms of communication control. A context defines how a coordinator interacts with other coordinators when it is a component of a complex and modular system. Specification and body are presented in this section by referring to the example above. Since context subunit deals with modularization, it will be presented in the next section.

3.1. Coordinator Specification

A coordinator specification consists of an *invariant* and several *group specifications*. The following is the textual specification of the coordinator in Fig. 2.

```
coordinator Conference {
  invariant   #Speaker ≤ 1 and
        ( #TemporaryListener = 1 and
        #TemporarySpeaker = 1 or
        #TemporaryListener = 0 and
        #TemporarySpeaker = 0 )
  group Participants {
    type Set;
    requests ...; }
  group Speaker {
    type Set;
    nestedIn Participants;
    requests ...; }
  group TemporaryListener {
    type Set;
    nestedIn Speakers;
    requests ...; }
  group Listeners {
    type Set;
    nestedIn Participants;
    requests ...; }
  group BookedForQuestions {
    type Queue;
    nestedIn Listeners;
    requests ...; }
  group TemporarySpeaker {
    type Set;
    nestedIn BookedForQuestions;
    requests ...; }
}
```

The **invariant** is a logic expression that allows consistency checks. Since the cooperation model considers groups as anonymous collections of users, invariants are typically expressed in terms of groups' cardinality. In the example, group Speaker and group TemporarySpeaker may have at most one member. Moreover, if there is a TemporarySpeaker, there is also a TemporaryListener (i.e. the Speaker plays the role of TemporaryListener).

A **group** specification includes a *type*, a *nesting*, and a set of enabled *requests*. The **type** of a group defines the strategy for members storing and retrieving. Possible types are Set, Queue, and Stack[2]. The construct **nestedIn** expresses that a member of the nested group is also a member of the nesting one. In the example the TemporaryListener (if any) must be a member of the Speaker group. A group cannot be nested in two disjoint groups.

The section introduced by the keyword **requests** defines which requests can be issued by a member of the group. Since the evolution of a cooperative activity is defined in terms of role changes, and roles correspond to groups, the only requests that can be specified are related to users' movements between groups. They permit to put (remove) a user into (from) a group, and take the form

join *GroupName User* **leave** *GroupName User*

---

[2] We may allow user-defined type, but it is unessential at this stage.

A request involves a group and a user. The user can be formally expressed by the keywords **myself** and **other**, or it can be omitted. **Myself** stands for the sender of the request. **Other** stands for any other but the sender. When nothing is specified a user is selected according to group types and cooperation policies.
A request is composed of two (optional) parts: *pre-conditions* and *effects*. Pre-conditions are introduced by the keyword **requires**, and are expressed in term of group membership and group cardinality. They must be verified in order to accept the request. Effects of an accepted request are specified after the keyword **actions**. A cooperation policy is implemented through these actions. When no action is specified the request execution has no effects. A request is indivisible. At request completion both nesting and invariant rules are checked.
An example of requests specification is included in the following group specification

```
group Speaker {
  type Set;
  nestedIn Participants;
  requests
    join TemporarySpeaker other {
      requires:  other in BookedForQuestions and #TemporarySpeaker = 0;
      actions:   insert TemporarySpeaker other,
                 insert TemporaryListener myself; }
    join TemporarySpeaker {
      requires:  #BookedForQuestions ≥ 1 and #TemporarySpeaker = 0;
      actions:   insert TemporarySpeaker select BookedForQuestions,
                 insert TemporaryListener myself; }
    leave Speaker myself {
      actions:   extract Speaker myself; }
}
```

Actions are expressed by means of *internal operators*:

select *GroupName*
remove *GroupName*
insert *GroupName User*
extract *GroupName User*

Insert and **extract** modify the membership of the mentioned group by inserting and extracting the mentioned user into and from groups. **Select** and **remove** operator returns a member selected according to the type of the group. Remove also extract the user from the group. Select and remove support anonymous manipulation of users. In group Speaker, the anonymous request *join TemporarySpeaker* selects a user from the BookedForQuestions group, and inserts him or her into the TemporarySpeaker group. Since BookedForQuestions has been declared of type Queue, the first member is selected.
Requests define coordinator's interface. Actually a user may issue only requests associated with groups he or she belongs to. When a user is member of two nested groups, the union of the two sets of requests are enabled for him. Note that requests can be redefined in a nested group. In this case the inner definitions hide the outer ones. A request defined in the outer group can be disabled in the inner one by redefining it with an empty **actions** section.

3.2. Coordinator Body

The coordinator specification defines the requests that users may issue, and their effects in terms of memberships change and constraints. The coordinator body defines the implications of group membership in terms of *communication channels control*.
A coordinator body consists of a set of channel specifications and a set of group body

specifications. The ultimate goal of a cooperative system is to exchange data between users and the shared workspace (i.e. application programs) through physical communication channels. By physical channels we mean everything that connects users and applications, e.g. Unix sockets, ISDN connections, high-speed video channels, and the like. The logical management of communication channels is achieved in CSDL by introducing the concept of *virtual channel.* Virtual channels are controlled by *virtual switchers* that model multiplexing and demultiplexing of data streams in terms of connection matrixes, as sketched in Fig. 3.

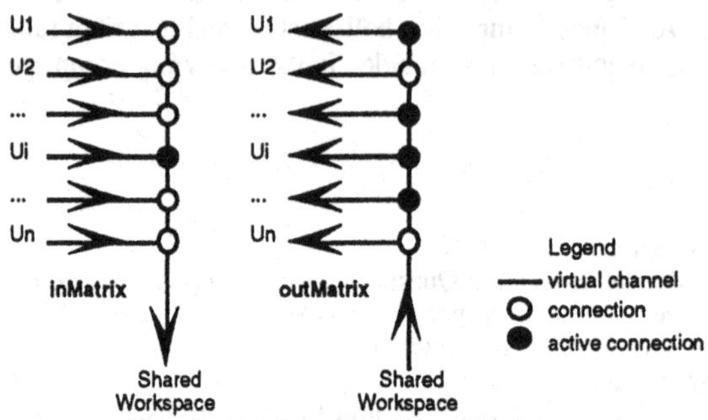

Fig. 3 **InMatrix** and **outMatrix**.

A matrix models a unidirectional flow of data between the shared workspace and the users. Bidirectional data-flows can be modeled by pairs of matrixes. This abstraction allows modeling any kind of physical channels, if bidirectional channels (e.g., sockets) or unidirectional channels. This facility is crucial when dealing with multimedia applications where logical data flows can be realized by multiple physical channels of different nature.
A declaration like

```
switcher inOut AChannel;
```

defines a virtual switcher and its mode. Unidirectional channels are declared **in** (for input channels), or **out** (for output channels). Bidirectional channels are declared **inOut**.
Virtual channels are controlled through a set of *communication clauses* that define the status of a group's member concerning the communication channel(s). The available clauses are:

```
connected           inOff
disconnected        outOn
inOn                outOff
```

The **connected** clause states that the group's members are connected to the channel. The opposite holds for **disconnected**. The **inOn** (**inOff**) clause enables (disables) the group's members to send inputs. **OutOn** and **outOff** are defined for the output channel.
In our example, the coordinator body looks like the following

```
coordinator body Conference {

  switcher inOut  AChannel;

  group Participants {
    connected;
    inOff;
    outOff; }
  group Speaker {
    inOn;
    outOn; }
  group TemporaryListener {
    inOff; }
  group Listeners {
    outOn; }
  group TemporarySpeaker {
    inOn; }
}
```

A nested group inherits the communication clauses defined for the nesting group. The clauses that are redefined in nested groups override those defined in the nesting ones. In the example, the members of Participants are connected to the bidirectional channel, but with inputs and outputs disabled. As soon as a user becomes a Speaker his or her status changes. The corresponding inputs and outputs become enabled, and he or she can exchange data with the shared application. When a speaker gets the role of TemporaryListener, his or her inputs are disabled, while his or her status concerning outputs does not change.
To complete the definition of a communication coordinator, we must ultimately deal with the mapping between virtual and physical channels. To describe physical channels we need to identify the entities of the system, i.e., the users (or, better, the processes associated with them) and the applications in the shared workspace. This is accomplished through a definition of switchers. It defines how users and applications can be reached through system or network addresses. They are identified by Service Access Points (SAP) in the ISO/OSI terminology [20]. Depending on the underlying communication model, SAP may be a process name, a host name, a socket identifier, a telephone number, and the like. If needed, an optional **pragma** specifies system dependent parameters.
An example of switcher declaration is:

```
switcher inOut AChannel {
  connects U1 through SAP1 pragma {...},
        U2 through SAP2 pragma {...},
        ...
        Un through SAPn pragma {...},
  to Application through SAPa pragma {...};
}
```

It specifies that there is a set of users accessible through SAP1, SAP2, ..., SAPn, and a tool accessible through SAPa. Note that a connection is established only when a user joins a group that includes the clause **connected**.
Switcher definition above looks quite static. It has been presented in a declarative form for the sake of readability. An existing prototype version of the environment underlying CSDL supports dynamic connections. The connection of a new user implies the invocation of a daemon that provides information about the SAP to be used.

4. Modularization

It is widely accepted that modularization is the right way for designing and building non-trivial systems [8]. Since coordinators (CSDL modules) define a common interface, it is easy to connect them to build new systems. As already illustrated in the previous section, information hiding has been exploited to separate cooperation control from communication control issues. This helps in reusing potentially every existent application or networking system.
Suppose we need to modify the conferencing system discussed along this paper as follows. We need to model that participants should register themselves at the front desk before entering the conference room. The chairman is designated among those users who are in the room, and he or she becomes implicitly the speaker of the current section.
We may choose to modify the coordinator Conference by adding new groups, and changing requests' actions. CSDL modular design style suggests building a new coordinator FrontDesk with the new features only, and then integrate it into the existing system.
We say that a coordinator A *controls* a coordinator B if membership of groups belonging to A implies membership of groups belonging to B. We call this mechanism *mapping*: if a group G1 of A is mapped into a group G2 of B then G2 has the same members as G1. This

is achieved by means of requests to B issued by A, as by any other client of B. Such requests cannot be rejected. Fig. 4 illustrate how the coordinator FrontDesk controls the coordinator Conference. Arrows represent group mapping.

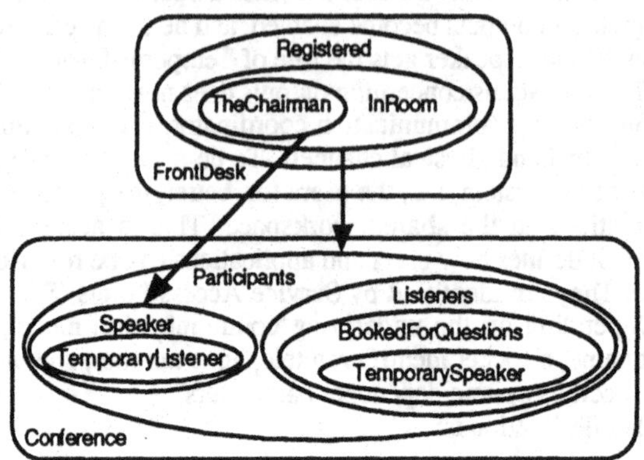

Fig. 4. Coordinators' hierarchy.

In CSDL control hierarchy and group mapping are defined in the optional **context** section of both controlling and controlled coordinators. The FrontDesk coordinator specification is shown below

```
coordinator FrontDesk {
  group Registered {
    type Set;
    requests
      join InRoom myself {
        actions:
          insert InRoom myself;}
      leave Registered myself {
        actions:
          extract Registered myself;}
  }
  group TheChairman {
    type Set;
    nestedIn InRoom;
    invariant #TheChairman ≤ 1;
    requests
      leave TheChairman myself {
        actions:
          extract TheChairman myself;}
  }
  group InRoom {
    type Set;
    nestedIn Registered;
    requests
      join TheChairman myself {
        requires: #TheChairman = 0;
        actions:
          insert TheChairman myself;}
      leave InRoom myself {
        actions:
          extract InRoom myself;}
  }
}
```

To integrate FrontDesk with Conference it must be enriched with a **context** section.

```
coordinator context FrontDesk {

  controls Conference;

  group Registered {
    notControlled; }
  group InRoom {
    notControlled;
    mappedTo Conference.Participants; }
  group TheChairman {
    notControlled;
    mappedTo Conference.Speaker; }
}
```

The declaration **controls** specifies the name of one or more controlled coordinators. The construct **mappedTo** specifies which groups are controlled.

Each group is labeled as **controlled** or **notControlled**. In the former case all requests that affect the membership of the controlled group are disabled for any user, as such requests can be issued by the controlling coordinator only according to the group mapping. This is to guarantee that group memberships cannot be modified at the controlled coordinator without notifying the controller.
In the example, who is InRoom may become TheChairman by issuing a request to the FrontDesk coordinator, while the request to become a Speaker associated with group Participants has been disabled. Groups TemporarySpeaker, BookedForQuestions and TemporaryListener are not controlled, therefore requests affecting these groups are still enabled at the Conference level. This models the fact that, once stated who participate and who the designated speaker is, the FrontDesk delegates the Conference coordinator the discipline of questions asking protocol.
On the Conference side, we need to add labels that specify which groups are controlled[3]

```
coordinator context Conference {
  group Participants {
    controlled }
  group Speaker {
    controlled }
}
```

Requests concerning controlled groups, coming from a controller are defined as follows:

```
join GroupName User {
  actions:  insert GroupName User ; }
leave GroupName User {
  actions:  extract GroupName User ;}
```

As mentioned above a request from a controlling coordinator does not have pre-condition, since it cannot be rejected. Invariants guarantee system consistency.
In the example above the FrontDesk coordinator does not have a **body**. This corresponds to the fact that, in a well-structured hierarchy, higher level coordinators only control the lower level ones without dealing with communication issues. On the other side, coordinators at the bottom level are in charge of managing communication channels. The CSDL design style considers these two behaviors incompatible. In other terms, a coordinator with a non empty **controls** clause in its **context** section should not have a **body** section, and vice versa.
A cooperative system can be defined as a *collection of coordinators connected to form a hierarchical control tree*. Coordinators of leaves have bodies, while coordinators of nodes have a context that specifies the control of the next nodes of the tree. Design style suggests partitioning cooperation policy issues among nodes, while leaves only include communication issues. Following this definition, leaves are also called *communication coordinators*. The simplest example is provided by the two module-coordinator CooperationControl and Communication in Fig. 1.
Applying the suggested design style the best version of the conferencing system becomes the one illustrated by Fig. 5. We suppose that the shared workspace is composed of an audio application and a video application.

---

[3] By default a group is considered **notControlled**.

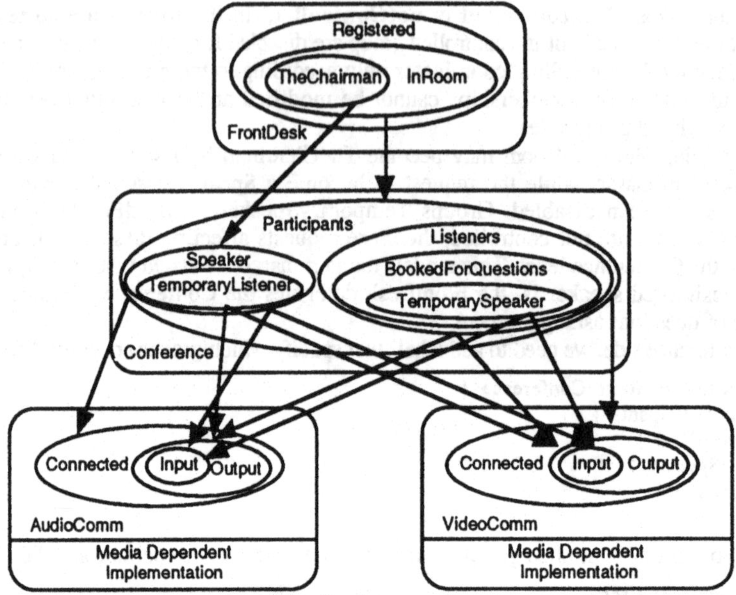

Fig. 5. An example.

Coordinator Conference specification is unmodified from the one presented in section 3.1. Since it controls other coordinators, it does not have a body, and its context defines the mapping to AudioComm, and VideoComm coordinators:

```
coordinator context Conference {

  controls AudioComm, VideoComm;

  group Participants {
    controlled;
    mappedTo AudioComm.Connected;
    mappedTo VideoComm.Connected; }
  group Speaker {
    controlled;
    mappedTo AudioComm.Input;
    mappedTo VideoComm.Input; }
  group TemporaryListener {
    notControlled;
    mappedTo AudioComm.Output;
    mappedTo VideoComm.Output; }
  group Listeners {
    notControlled;
    mappedTo AudioComm.Output;
    mappedTo VideoComm.Output; }
  group TemporarySpeaker {
    notControlled;
    mappedTo AudioComm.Input;
    mappedTo VideoComm.Input; } }
```

The two communication coordinators may have the same definition, but they differ in the definition of the switchers. AudioComm can be defined as follows:

```
coordinator AudioComm {
  group Connected {
    type Set; }
  group Output {
    type Set;
    nestedIn Connected; }
  group Input {
    type Set;
    nestedIn Output; }
}
```

```
coordinator context AudioComm {
  group Connected {
    controlled; }
  group Output {
    controlled; }
  group Input {
    controlled }
}
```

```
coordinator body AudioComm {

  switcher inOut Audio;

  group Connected {
    connected;
    inOff;
    outOff; }
  group Output {
    outOn; }
  group Input {
    inOn; }
}
```

As expected, the coordinator's specification does not define any cooperation policy. This is expressed by the absence of requests' specifications. Requests can only come from a coordinator controller. As a consequence, this coordinator cannot be used in isolation, since members cannot issue any command.

5. Related Work

In recent years many prototypes of collaborative applications have been developed. Most of them have specialized architecture that supports only particular applications. Examples are writing and drawing tools, cooperative agendas and multi-player games. Only a few are based on general architecture. Among environments supporting cooperative applications, we can distinguish Conference Toolkit [2], LIZA [9], MMConf [3], Rendezvous [13], and GroupKit [17].

CSDL also derives from the experience gained with Conference Toolkit, a prototype environment that allows the sharing of X11 applications. The key idea is the insertion of a process between the application, and the X11 server. This process acts as conferencing window server by simulating the X11 server to the application, and multiplexing, and demultiplexing data for multiple-users. This model has been included in CSDL to allow the inclusion of single-user applications.

LIZA is a groupware toolkit focused on multi-user interface design. LIZA proposes an architecture based on *active objects*. A collaborative application consists of an active object (the kernel object), and an active object for each participant (the image objects). Image objects are responsible for the user interface. LIZA supports centralized tools, and cannot include unmodified single-user applications. CSDL model overcomes the LIZA model by introducing modularization and separation of concerns.

MMConf consists of a user interface toolkit and a separate conference manager process. It adopts a replicated architecture since it has significant performance, versatility, and device-independence advantages over a centralized one. MMConf does not support latecomers, imposes a single floor-holder, and cannot support the inclusion of single-user applications.

Rendezvous architecture consists of two parts: a run-time architecture for managing interactions among users and a start-up architecture for managing the network connectivity. The run-time architecture is a centralized process, possibly decomposed into light-weight processes, that includes the shared application and interfaces to remote virtual terminals. The key idea is the separation between the internal data representation and its presentation to the user. Every interface manages the display and the interaction of a user with the shared application without any direct concern for the presence of other users. Rendezvous's implementation is based on a user interface management system that extends Common Lisp. The nature of Rendezvous requires a specific environment, thus reducing its potential use in other contexts. In particular, it cannot include unmodified single-user applications nor support replication.

GroupKit adopts an approach similar to the one underlying CSDL. It proposes a replicated architecture providing process and run-time support, overlays, and open protocols. Overlays are transparent windows placed on top of the main application graphics shown by the conference graphics. They have been implemented for gesturing and annotations. Open protocols provide a mean of implementing flexible policies.

6. Conclusions and Future Work

CSDL and the environment around it intend to provide designers with suitable supports for both specifying and implementing collaborative applications. As specification language, CSDL supports the definition of cooperation policies through the definition of groups and requests. As design language, CSDL provides the virtual switcher abstraction that allows the definition of the status of each user, and the specification of SAPs that defines system configuration and physical connections of system entities.

The proposed design style separates the two aspects in independent coordinators. Therefore, communication coordinators can be designed and implemented as independent drivers. This independence from the context (i.e., from the cooperation policies, and system configurations) allows the inclusion of any application. In particular it is possible to include in a cooperating system multimedia applications, and single-user applications. This property ensures portability, and prevents the environment from becoming obsolete due to new technologies, and new applications.

The possibility of sharing existing single-user software is a crucial property for any successful cooperative system. Technical and human issues support this thesis. From the human point of view, it ensures a quiet transition between individual and shared workspaces [10]. In such a way, users can use the same tools in a stand-alone situation as well as in collaboration. This means that no training nor habit is required for new users. From a technical point of view, the reuse of existing software eliminates the costs of re-implementing applications like word-processors, spreadsheets, etc. For example, we designed and implemented a communication coordinator in which channels are Unix sockets, and the protocol of messages is XProtocol. It permits to share any X11 application without modifications [6].

CSDL architecture supports both centralized and replicated implementations [7, 15, 16]. The centralized solution is much easier to implement since it does not suffer from consistency problems. On the other hand, a replicated solution is much more efficient in terms of network traffic for output-intensive applications (e.g. the graphic ones). In fact, output can have a local effect only, while in a shared implementation they are broadcast through the network.

The choice between the two architectural solutions is a matter of cost-performance trade-off. The experiments have shown that the two solutions can be chosen freely, or may even coexist, without affecting the system design. Only the switcher definitions need to be changed, i.e., the description of physical channels, and possibly part of the implementation of the shared applications. A discussion of this issue can be found in [6]. An example of a replicated architecture is ImageAnnotator developed at CEFRIEL [14].

CSDL supports the design of open systems: each branch of a coordinator tree can be activated dynamically. It allows users to run new tools, or change cooperation policy, without stopping the system. This capability has been included in the prototype environment we are developing around CSDL. The environment provides also run-time supports for systems' configuration, systems' startup and users' connections.

In the near future, we plan to complete the definition of the language with the constructs that allow the dynamic control of the system (startup of new tools, and definition of latecomers). The environment will be integrated with a user interface management system to provide the designers of a suitable user interface development system, and with a toolkit to provide a set of coordinators to be used as building blocks for new systems.

Acknowledgments

The authors wish to thank S. Pozzi and E. Di Nitto from CEFRIEL for helpful discussions and comments on this paper.

References

1. —, Special issue on Collaborative Computing. *Communication of the ACM 34*, 12 (December 1991).

2. Bonfiglio, A., Malatesta, G., and Tisato, F. Conference Toolkit: A Framework for Real-Time Conferencing. In *Proceedings of the First European Conference on Computer-Supported Cooperative Work*, Gatwick, September 13-15 1989, pp. 303-316.

3. Crowley, T., Milazzo, P., Baker, E., Forsdick, H., and Tomlinson, R. MMConf: An Infrastructure for Building Shared Multimedia Application. In *Proceedings of Conference on Computer-Supported Cooperative Work*, ACM SIGCHI &SIGOIS, Los Angeles, October 1990, pp. 329-342.

4. DePaoli, F. and Tisato, F. A Model for Real-Time Co-operation. In *Proceedings of the Second European Conference on Computer-Supported Cooperative Work*, Amsterdam, September 25-27 1991, pp. 203-217.

5. DePaoli, F. and Tisato, F. Coordinator: a Basic Building Block for Multimedia Conferencing Systems. In *Proceedings of GLOBECOM '91*, IEEE, Chicago, December 2-5 1991.

6. DePaoli, F. and Tisato, F. Development of a Collaborative Application in CSDL. In *Proceeding of the International Conference on Distributed Computing Systems*, Pittsburgh, May 25-28 1993.

7. Ellis, C.A., Gibbs, S.J., and Reln, G.L. GROUPWARE. Some Issues and Experiences. *Communication of the ACM 34*, 1 (January 1991), 38-58.

8. Ghezzi, C., Jazayeri, M., and Mandrioli, D. *Fundamentals of Software Engineering*, Prentice Hall, Englewood Cliffs NJ (1991).

9. Gibbs, S.J. LIZA: An Extensible Groupware Toolkit. In *Proceedings of the Conference on Human Factors in Computing Systems (CHI'89)*, ACM SIGCHI, Austin, Texas, April 30 - May 4 1989, pp. 29-35.

10. Ishii, H. TeamWorkstation: Towards a Seamless shared Workspace. In *Proceedings of Conference on Computer Supported Cooperative Work*, ACM SIGCHI&SIGOIS, Los Angeles, October 1990, pp. 13-26.

11. Ishii, H. and Miyake, N. Toward an Open Shared Workspace: Computer and Video Fusion Approach of TeamWorkStation. *Communication of the ACM 34*, 12 (December 1991), 36-50.

12. Lauwers, J.C., Joseph, T.A., Lantz, K.A., and Romanov, A.L. Replicated Architecture for Shared Window Systems: A Critique. In *Proceedings of the Conference on Office Informations Systems*, ACM, Cambridge, Massachusetts, April 25-27 1990, pp. 249-260.

13. Patterson, J.F., Hill, R.D., Rohall, S.L., and Meeks, W.S. Rendezvous: An Architecture for Synchronous Multi-User Applications. In *Proceedings of Conference on Computer-Supported Cooperative Work*, ACM SIGCHI & SIGOIS, Los Angeles, October 1990, pp. 317-328.

14. Pozzi, S., Peterc, D., Concolino, P., DiNitto, E., and Molinaro, A. ImageAnnotator: An Image-Based Cooperative Application. In *Proceedings of the Conference on Image Communication IMACOM '93*, Bordeaux (France), March 1993.

15. Rodden, T. and Blair, G. CSCW and Disstributed Systems: The Problem of Control. In *Proceedings of the Second European Conference on Computer-Supported Cooperative Work*, Amsterdam, September 25-27 1991, pp. 49-64.

16. Rodden, T., Mariani, J.A., and Blair, G. Supporting Cooperative Applications. *Computer-Supported Cooperative Work (CSCW) 1*, 1-2 (1992), 41-67.

17. Roseman, M. and Greenberg, S. GroupKit: A Groupware Toolkit for Building Real-Time Conferencing Applications. In *Proceedings of Conference on Computer-Supported Cooperative Work*, ACM SIGCHI & SIGOIS, Toronto, October 31- November 4 1992, pp. 43-50.

18. Sinha, A. Client-Server Computing. *Communication of the ACM 35*, 7 (July 1992), 77-98.

19. Stefik, M., Bobrow, D.G., Foster, G., Lanning, S., and Tartar, D. WYSIWIS Revised: Early Experiences with Multiuser Interfaces. *ACM Transactions on Office Information Systems 5*, 2 (April 1987), 147-186.

20. Tanenbaum, A.S. *Computer Networks - Second Edition*, Prentice Hall, Englewood Cliffs, New Jersey (1988).

Scrutiny: A Collaborative Inspection and Review System

John Gintell, John Arnold, Michael Houde, Jacek Kruszelnicki, Roland McKenney, and Gérard Memmi

US Applied Research Laboratory
Bull HN Information Systems Inc.
300 Concord Road - MS 821A
Billerica, MA 01821 USA

(email: j.gintell@bull.com)

Abstract. This paper describes a Bull US Applied Research Laboratory project to build a collaborative inspection and review system called Scrutiny using ConversationBuilder from the University of Illinois at Urbana-Champaign. The project has several distinct aspects: technology oriented research, prototype building, experimentation, and tool deployment/ technology transfer. Described are the design of the current operational version of Scrutiny for inspection-only, the evolutionary design of Scrutiny to handle various forms of review, and some initial thoughts on integration with other CASE frameworks and tools. The problem domain selected, the development environment, lessons learned thus far, some ideas from related work, and the problems anticipated are discussed here.

1 Introduction

Scrutiny is a collaborative system for inspection and review of software engineering work products. It is a distributed system that can be used by geographically separated users. Scrutiny uses general purpose mechanisms for integration with tools and CASE frameworks. It is tailorable for different software engineering process models. Scrutiny is intended for widespread use within our company to obtain usage experience with real users. As a starting point we implemented a working prototype restricted to inspection called CIA (Collaborative Inspection Agent) and obtained promising results from initial use. These results confirmed that our problem selection, technology choice, and initial design are sound. The results are guiding us in our next steps.

There have been a number of other efforts for computer assisted inspection and review described recently (see Section 7). Each describes a dimension of inspection that extends beyond the traditional view of what inspection is. Scrutiny differs from the work in these systems because it combines 1) a distributed collaborative environment, 2) integration with other tools using general purpose and standardized mechanisms, and 3) support for multiple process models.

This is a work-in-progress paper. Scrutiny has been underway for more than one year now[1]. We have a working prototype, some experimental users, favorable initial reaction from management as well as users and have obtained a first set of

1 At the time of publication of this paper the project will have been underway for two years.

results. We continue to investigate, build prototypes and get practical experience with some of the prototypes by making them robust and putting them into extensive practice. As a large company that is distributed in a number of locations worldwide, we have an ideal environment to test out some of these ideas in non-research oriented software engineering environments.

The remainder of this section describes the motivation for this project. Section 2 describes the CSCW technology selected as the basis on which to implement Scrutiny. Section 3 describes its design and implementation. Section 4 describes the current status and lessons learned. Sections 5 and 6 describe future work for Scrutiny. Section 7 describes related work in this problem domain. Section 8 contains our conclusions.

1.1 A Perspective on this Project

Inspection was chosen because it is a widely accepted practice within Bull [22] and it is well-defined. We wanted to build a tool that would be used by a variety of users who could give us usage-based feedback to guide future development. Selecting a widely accepted practice was a necessary condition for obtaining acceptance for the tool. Being a well-defined process gave us an excellent model to emulate as a starting point. Scrutiny was constrained to fit the Bull model so that using it would count as an "official" inspection.

Face-to-face inspection of all work products (e.g. documents, code, and tests) has proven to be an effective means for achieving higher product quality. Inspection is a well-defined process first developed by Fagan at IBM [6]. Inspection is usually performed without computerized assistance. It is generally done with a team of people who first prepare independently, and then meet in a room to perform a group inspection with individuals assigned to specific roles. It is a collaborative process because it takes teamwork to properly identify and classify the defects. After the inspection has been completed, defects identified during the meeting and other relevant information including metrics about the inspection itself are manually entered in various databases for later processing.

Uniformity of the inspection process is required so that results can be collected and rolled up for later analysis and process improvement. The motivation for this has been stimulated by the need to obtain ISO 9001 [9] certification and by the Software Engineering Institute sponsored Capability Maturity Model [8] [17].

There is a general desire to automate the inspection and review process, to allow it to be performed by geographically spread teams, and to integrate it with other environments (e.g. configuration management or bug tracking systems). Further, there is a continuum of process sub-models ranging from inspection to review-with-construction. This variety of forms of use led us to produce a tool that is configurable in many modes. We envision a number of advantages to be reaped with a distributed tool used for inspection and review and that is integrated with other tools and environments.

Computer-Supported Cooperative Work (CSCW) is currently a very active field. Many CSCW projects implement some form of shared writing and/or review. Scrutiny augments collaboration technology with controls at those points of people/application interaction governed by the rules of the inspection process.

2 Technology Selected - ConversationBuilder

We require a distributed system environment suitable for rapid application development. It must support collaborative work with simultaneous display of information on multiple users' screens under both application and individual user control. It must support user-role definitions so that the tools generated can comply with process rules and practices. It must be open and extremely flexible with respect to integration with other tools. It must be operational and supported. It should also be under active development so it can keep pace with new technologies and can evolve as requirements are generated by our applications and experiences.

ConversationBuilder (CB) [12] from University of Illinois at Urbana-Champaign was selected because of its architecture and the kind of problems it was designed to solve. CB supports a structured conversation model and was influenced by the Language - Action model by Winograd/Flores [23]; thus it is well suited to handling the discourse that occurs during inspection and review. CB's architecture is suitable for a wide variety of applications, for the linkage between them and for integration with other externally defined tools and environments. It satisfies all our requirements. It is under active development at the University of Illinois; Bull has become one of the sponsors of the work there.

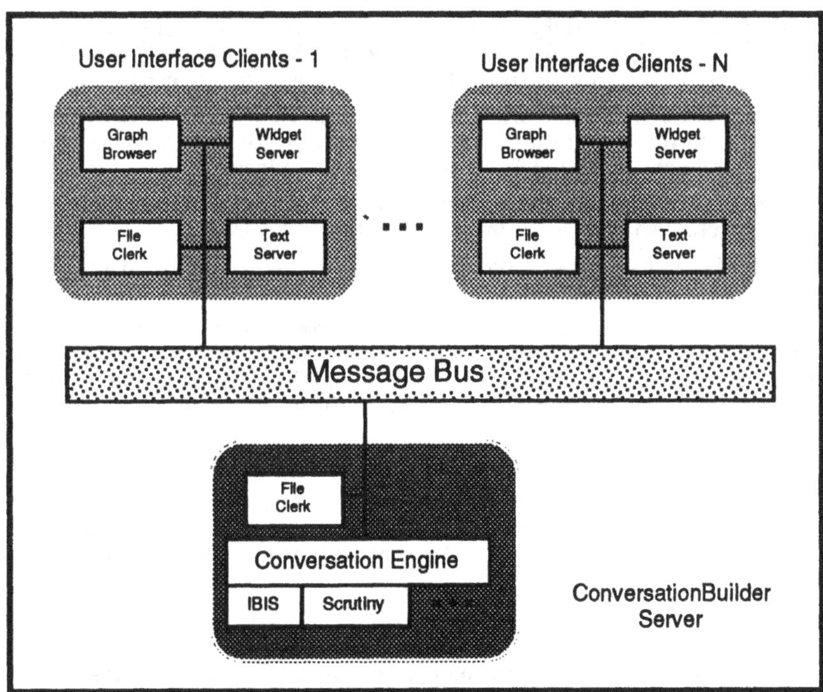

Fig. 1. ConversationBuilder Architecture

ConversationBuilder is a distributed system depicted in Figure 1; its major components are:

- the **Message Bus** - a multi-user control integration mechanism used to interconnect tool components; it acts as the vehicle for multi-cast message passing between all of the other components that comprise CB and its applications. The Message Bus is a FIELD-inspired form of integration [18].
- a **User Interface Suite** for each user that includes a **Motif-based Widget Server** to manage the user interface, a **Graph Browser**, a **Text Server**, and a **File Clerk** to manipulate files and their contents.

- the **Conversation Engine** itself whose job is to support collaboration and to manage the actual application activities. The applications are called protocols. A protocol is a CLOS (Common Lisp Object System) description of a conversation flow that is enacted by the engine.

CB is written in CLOS and C and runs on UNIX™; the applications themselves are also written in CLOS enabling them to inherit the classes defined in CB and thus build upon its mechanisms. In addition to Scrutiny, there are CB protocols either in experimental or operational form for a wide variety of collaborative processes: IBIS[2] [3], Design Rationale, Shared Whiteboard, Shared Editor, WorkFlow, Configuration Management, and Bug Tracking.

3 Description of Scrutiny

3.1 Inspection Roles as implemented by Scrutiny

Based on the Fagan model, the inspection roles are as follows:

- a **Moderator** to control the inspection activities from beginning to end. He or she chooses the inspection team, coordinates the entire process, moderates the group meeting, and ensures that all steps are taken correctly.
- the **Inspectors** to do the work of defect finding. Their work is performed first privately to do preparation and then as part of the group to identify and classify the defects. The Moderator also acts as an Inspector.
- a **Reader** to read (or paraphrase) every line/section to all participants during the inspection so that the entire work product is covered.
- a **Recorder** to classify and record defects. All records of the inspection are made by the Recorder.
- a **Producer** of the work product. The Producer is present to supply additional information about the work product. A second but less important function is to collect non-defect comments gathered during the inspection that would be useful for future revisions to the work product.

Scrutiny does not implement all these roles explicitly. The Inspector and Moderator roles are kept intact. The Producer is not distinguished from other Inspectors. The Moderator performs the Reader role by highlighting the current focus of attention in the work product on each user's screen. The Recorder role is performed by the Moderator in collaboration with the Inspectors and the application itself.

3.2 Inspection Stages in Scrutiny

The inspection has four sequential stages: **Initiation, Preparation, Resolution, and Completion.**

- **Initiation** for the Moderator to set up the inspection by obtaining the work product(s) to be inspected, identify and invite the participants, and do all of the up-front work needed to ensure a successful inspection.
- **Preparation** for the Inspectors to examine the work product and prepare comments and questions (which we call annotations). In this stage each of the Inspectors work independently.

---

2 IBIS is an acronym for Issue Based Information System, a structured method for discourse on issues; it is considered a classical CSCW application.

- **Resolution** for the formal defect processing. The Moderator paces the meeting by stepping through the work product. All Inspectors contribute collectively by reading the results of others' preparation and then creating more annotations (defects, questions, actions for the future, ...). The Recorder classifies the defects based upon the annotations.
- **Completion** for the results of the Inspection to be processed and prepared for transmission to other stages of the software development process. For example, at a later time, the Producer would remove the defects by making a revision of the work product (perhaps requiring a reinspection). This stage is performed by the Moderator and Recorder.

3.3 Artifacts created by Scrutiny

Items entered by Inspectors are called annotations and are initially labeled as a question, potential defect, remark, or reply. They later may be modified, made obsolete or relabeled. Each defect is further classified; they are treated as a separate class of artifacts because of their importance to the process. There is a polling procedure invoked by the Moderator to obtain consensus; the results are preserved as artifacts. At the end of the inspection a variety of reports may be prepared to document the results and actions taken during the inspection. The defects are also formatted in a manner suitable for insertion into defect managing systems.

Figure 2 describes the attributes of the stages of Scrutiny to show the relationship among the artifacts, roles and stages.

	INITIATION	PREPARATION	RESOLUTION	COMPLETION
PARTICIPANTS	• Moderator • Producer	• Inspectors	• Moderator • Inspectors • Producer • Recorder	• Moderator • Recorder
SYNCHRONY		• asynchronous	• synchronous	
ACTIONS	• get work product • select participants • schedule meeting	• study materials • find related info • make annotations	• refine annotations • identify defects • classify defects • resolve issues	• finish defect classification • prepare reports • close meeting
ARTIFACTS CREATED		• annotations	• annotations • defects • polls	• defect list • reports • statistics

Fig. 2. Scrutiny Stages and their Attributes

3.4 Scrutiny User Interface

The Scrutiny user interface attempts to balance two different points of view on collaborative inspection and review: the process and role points of view. The user interface may be affected by either of these points of view. The effect is realized by enabling or disabling menu selections and/or buttons in the appropriate windows.

The process orientation affects the user interface depending on the current state of the inspection/review process. The process, described with Petri nets (see Section 3.5), defines the states a role can reach at a given point in the inspection. This results in a somewhat modal interface, but the modality is necessary to accurately reflect the inspection model we have chosen. For example, an Inspector cannot create a new annotation when a poll is in process because the defined process does not allow it.

The role orientation affects the user interface depending on the role of the individual user. For example, an Inspector can neither convene the meeting (i.e., move it from Preparation stage to Resolution stage) nor change the current focus of the work product; these actions are restricted to Moderator and Reader roles.

Two types of information can be displayed in the windows: private and shared. Private information is seen only by the user who created it. Shared information can be accessed by any participant in the inspection/review. The shared information can be presented in a synchronous or asynchronous manner. Synchronous, shared information is managed such that all changes are immediately reflected in each user's view. Asynchronous, shared information is managed by presenting the information when requested by the user. For instance, the annotations list in the middle of Figure 3 is updated (during Resolution stage) with a new entry whenever any user creates a new annotation; thus, it is asynchronous, shared information. The text of the annotation is shared, synchronous information, however, since it is only presented to the user when he/she acts to display the full annotation.

The Scrutiny Control Window (Figure 3) acts as a control panel for the application. Each participant sees a copy of this window. The Participant Status information at the top is a shared, synchronous pane; each user sees exactly what the other users see. As a user acts, his or her status is updated. For instance, Figure 3 shows user 'gintell' is annotating. The buttons are activated or deactivated depending on their applicability to the particular role and state of the inspection.

The annotation pane contains a list of annotations on the work product that have been made so far. This list can be sorted in a number of ways. The defect pane contains a list of defect reports that have been classified. Finally, the poll pane lists the polls that have been taken during this inspection and their results. Selecting an annotation, defect, or poll will open a window for the object showing it in more detail. The annotation, defect, and poll panes are shared, synchronous panes. As a new object of the given type is created, a new entry appears in the appropriate

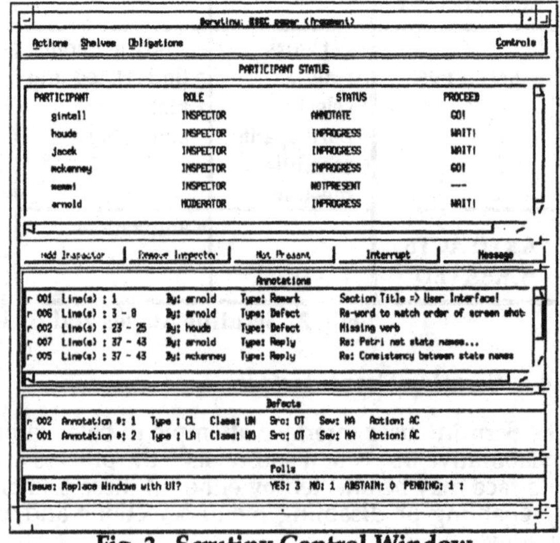

Fig. 3. Scrutiny Control Window

pane. However, accessing the new object is asynchronous since the object itself is only displayed when the user requests it. This allows the users to look at annotations in any order (just as they can leaf through the work product in a face-to-face inspection).

The Scrutiny Work Product Window (Figure 4) presents a shared view of the Work Product being inspected. The top pane shows the pathname of the work product and the line(s) of the current focus in the document. The primary pane displays the work product itself. The bold and underlined region is the current focus. Each user can scroll this pane independently though they are not allowed to modify it. Beneath this, there are two rows of buttons. The navigation buttons (Previous Line, Next Line, Go To Line, and Create Zone) and the Take Poll button are active for the Moderator only. The Annotate button is used to create an annotation about the current focus.

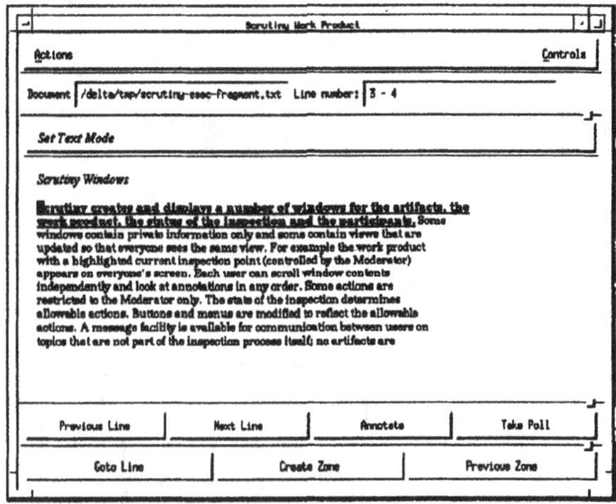

Fig. 4. Scrutiny Work Product Window

The Scrutiny Annotation Window (Figure 5) is used to create or display the details of an annotation. The top panes include information about the annotation such as the focus on which this annotation was made, author, and title. The middle pane is a buffer in which the body of the annotation is typed or displayed. At the bottom, there are radio buttons which categorize the annotation and another set of buttons for frequently used actions on the annotation.

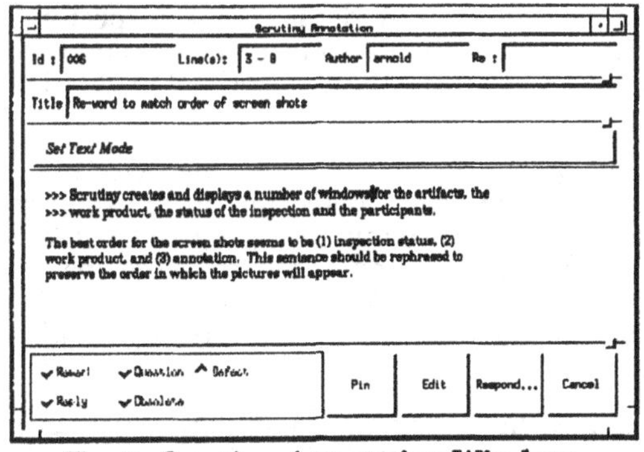

Fig. 5. Scrutiny Annotation Window

3.5 Model of the Resolution stage

The Resolution stage of Scrutiny models face-to-face inspections as closely as possible. Thus the participants are engaged in synchronized collaboration to adhere to the requirements of the inspection process. It is this property of inspection that distinguishes Scrutiny from many of the other cooperative applications where the cooperation is controlled by the users and not the application.

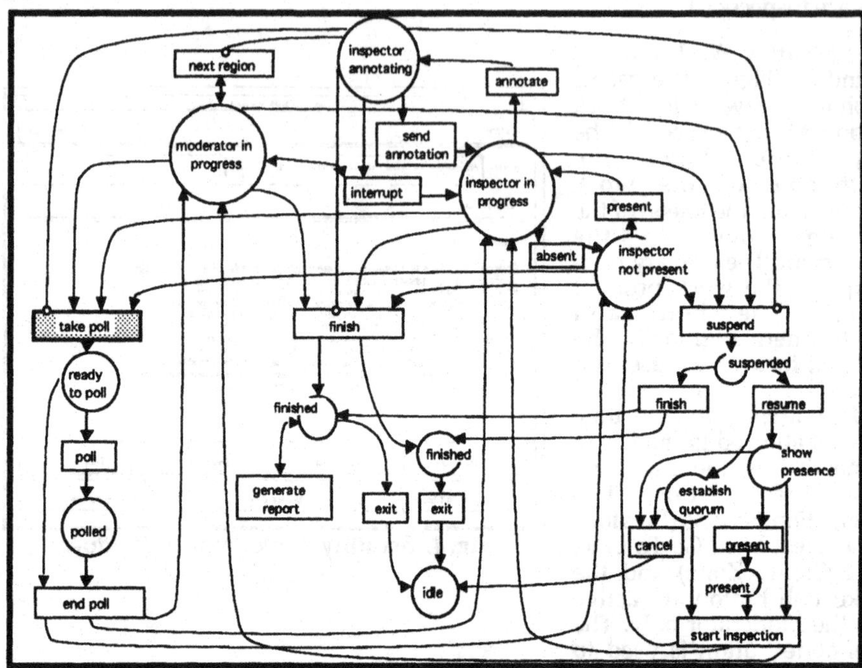

Fig. 6. High level Petri net Diagram for Scrutiny Resolution Stage

This high level Petri net (Figure 6) describes a simplified version of the behavior of the Resolution/Completion stages of Scrutiny. Each place (circle) represents a possible state for a Moderator or an Inspector. Each transition (box) represents a possible action. The intent is to provide an idea of the level of interaction between the two roles during these stages, not to describe a precise design of this stage[3].

As an example, consider the poll sub-process. The *take poll* transition (highlighted in Figure 6) is enabled when no Inspector is annotating and the Moderator is *in progress*. Then, every Inspector (in the state *in progress* or *not present*) and the Moderator all move into the state *ready to poll*. Each respondent may vote or not; however, once having voted the vote may not be changed. The Moderator decides when to enable the transition *end poll*. Whether they responded to the poll or not, each participant then returns to the place occupied prior to the taking of the poll.

Note also the *interrupt* transition, which was not implemented in the early versions of Scrutiny. This transition was added to permit the Moderator to force Inspectors out of *inspector annotating* and into *inspector in progress*. Otherwise, the Moderator was unable to move to the *next region*, *take poll* or even *suspend meeting* if an Inspector should walk away from his or her workstation while in *inspector annotating*.

---

3 The full design requires labeling edges and transitions, giving an interpretation of the entire diagram, and to complete the set of individual actions allowed (most of which do not change the global state of Scrutiny).

4 Current Status and Lessons Learned

At the time of submission of this paper, Scrutiny is used by the Scrutiny team and another project's team to use it to perform inspections and find and classify defects[4]. This paper, some code and a number of other documents have been inspected with Scrutiny. We have been performing demos and working with several other groups within Bull for informal training and evaluation. Scrutiny (named CIA at the time) was demonstrated at the ACM 1992 Conference on Computer-Supported Cooperative Work in Toronto, Canada (November 1992) and at the ACM SIGSOFT 1992 Fifth Symposium on Software Development Environments in McLean, Virginia (December 1992).

We are increasing the volume of experimentation with volunteers from other development groups and will learn more during the next few months. We have already made a number of improvements suggested by these initial users and have a number of ideas for developing a much improved system. The remainder of this section summarizes what we have learned and done.

4.1 Effectiveness of Computer-Supported Inspection

Inspections done with Scrutiny are at least as effective as those performed via face-to-face meetings; they appear to take about the same amount of time and identify defects as effectively as face-to-face inspections. We found that inspection-trained users could start using Scrutiny effectively with less than 2 hours of training, and in several cases they were able to learn "on-the-fly".

Some significant advantages over the face-to-face process have been demonstrated. Because the defects are collected in machine-readable form for subsequent processing by other tools, clerical and administrative work that is performed after an inspection is eliminated. This was one of the first features we added in response to user requests. Because all of the non-defect comments are captured, the Producer doesn't have to waste valuable inspection time recording them or collecting Inspectors' marked up papers or listings. Similarly, the Recorder doesn't have to pause the inspection while doing bookkeeping or manual transcription during the inspection meeting. We have some evidence that Inspectors do a more comprehensive job of preparing because the results of preparation will be seen by others; this might result in more defects being found.

4.2 Stages and Roles

The initial version of Scrutiny did not have the Preparation stage integrated in the tool. Based upon initial experience, this was the highest priority improvement to make to Scrutiny and it is now operational. This allows Inspectors to work independently while doing preparation with the tool and then enables reuse of annotations made during the Preparation stage during the Resolution stage; this reuse enables a noticeable speedup of the Resolution stage.

Our original assumption was that the computer assistance was sufficiently powerful that the Recorder role could be handled by the Moderator. We have discovered that the Recorder role must be explicitly implemented - the inspection is slowed down if the Moderator must always do all of the Recorder's work as well as controlling the meeting and inspecting.

4 The most exciting times have been while using an imperfect version of Scrutiny to inspect design documents about Scrutiny itself since the annotations and comments are all self-referential in real-time.

4.3 Performance

One of our initial assumptions about performance was that the Message Bus would be a potential bottleneck. We obtained considerable data about the performance of the underlying mechanisms (e.g., the Message Bus and the Conversation Engine) while using Scrutiny [21]. The preliminary data showed that the bottleneck was in the Conversation Engine. As a result of this data the CB team redesigned the underlying mechanisms and with some rework on our part we obtained a 3-5 times improvement. We also did some experimentation with CB components distributed over a WAN and found that if the network was at least 50KB/sec Scrutiny performance was essentially the same as our day-to-day use on a LAN. There is considerably more work to do in collecting and analyzing data, but these first experiments done at this early stage of the project have been valuable to us.

4.4 User Interface

As a result of the experimental usage we have made a number of modifications to the number and format of windows to simplify the user interface. We replaced some pull-down menus with buttons for frequently used requests. For example, we added a *respond* button to the annotation window since responding was a frequent use for annotations. We modified Scrutiny to indicate what portions of the work product were already inspected. We added support for the use of the CB graph browser facility to give users an additional means for looking at annotations.

The experience strongly supported our expectations about the influence the user interface will have on the overall usability and acceptance of Scrutiny; a few minor changes have already made a big difference; however, substantial improvement remains to be made.

4.5 ASCII-only Work Products

Work products processed by Scrutiny are restricted to ASCII files only. Documents that are produced by most word processors can have text-only versions created, but diagrams, charts and formatting can not be inspected. Scrutiny has been used to inspect documents where the diagrams (if present) were inspected manually. In the future we will address this through integration with other tools that can process complex documents.

Inspection is usually performed by moving the focus on the work product from beginning to end in sequential order. How to handle complicated diagrams or charts is a problem that requires further study.

For code inspection, ASCII text format is usually sufficient. A different issue arises when the structure of the code itself suggests other possible orderings for the inspection. Integration with code analysis tools will allow "structured" inspections to be performed; this should prove to be an additional advantage of computer-assisted inspections over face-to-face inspections.

4.6 Audio Channel

Face-to-face meetings have the advantage of high bandwidth communication using voice, gestures, and informal and spontaneous hand-written notes or drawings. Such communication has the disadvantage of usually not being preserved. Scrutiny was designed so that it can work with no audio facilities. We took this approach so that the absence of audio support would not preclude use of Scrutiny. In general, such facilities are not readily available particularly between geographically separated locations. Usage thus far shows that effective inspections can be done without audio.

We have done some experimentation using Scrutiny in the same room with people talking, with teleconference, and with audio facilities built into the work stations to see the effect on the inspection. Synchronization and quick question/answering is much easier with audio and speeds up the Resolution stage. As a result of this experimentation we are adding some more easy-to-invoke discussion facilities than that offered by the creation of annotations to reap some of these advantages of audio. Handling mixed capabilities is an open research issue.

5 Generalizing the process

The work to evolve Scrutiny for activities similar to inspection such as reviews and requirements collection is well under way. In essence, this changes the rules concerned with operations performed by the various roles and during the several stages to make Scrutiny's behavior less constrained than required for inspection.

In inspection, the Preparation stage has each Inspector working independently whereas the Resolution stage has all work synchronized by the Moderator. For review, neither independent preparation activity nor synchronized resolution activity is required by the process. Uncontrolled shared preparation can be useful for people to work in an interactive fashion while elaborating on their incompletely formed initial thoughts. On the other hand, moderated inspection-like work is useful to assist in reaching closure on issues. To address this in Scrutiny, we will divide the Preparation stage into two sections where the first is for private work and the second is for collaborative shared preparation. The Resolution stage remains the same although with effective shared preparation it may be very short. Classified defects are not produced during review and thus the artifacts produced by the Resolution stage are different.

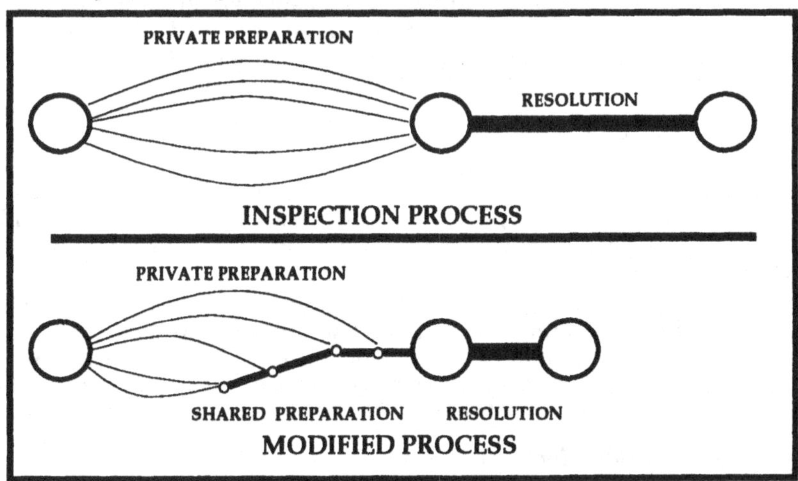

Fig. 7. Modified process

Figure 7 shows a comparison between the inspection process and the process modified for review. The thin lines represent private preparation activities by participants, thick lines represent collaborative preparation, and the very thick lines represent synchronized resolution activities. Large circles represent stage changes and small circles represent the joining of participants for shared preparation. In this process instantiation, each participant switches from private to shared participation at his or her own selected time. As each participant joins this shared participation he or she sees the previously joined participants' annotations and vice-versa. This permits collaboration to begin for some people while others continue private participation, joining later. Scrutiny will permit a variety of policies as to when and how this switching occurs for different review models. This flexibility will also enable experimentation with changes to the Inspection process.

6 Future Work for Integration with Tools and Environments

Inspection and review should be more than isolated processes acting on a fixed set of work products that are "input" to the activity. Scrutiny needs to be integrated with other tools. Some examples include a static analyzer to use in code inspections, the tool used to deposit data in a metrics database, and a document processor for non-ASCII text so compound documents can be managed and displayed by the producing software instead of having to be translated to another form for processing by Scrutiny.

There are a number of significant enhancements that we can make by using data integration, control integration, process integration, and distributed processing services to integrate CB/Scrutiny with other tools, services, and information. In the remainder of this section we briefly describe this aspect of our research. Much of this work is exploratory with unresolved issues that will take considerable time to resolve.

6.1 Data Integration for Tool Access

The introduction of an external OMS (object management system) presents a challenge because CB has its own interim persistent object store. Our initial work with data integration uses the GIE Emeraude implementation [7] of the Portable Common Tools Environment (PCTE) [5]. In an environment where all of the software engineering work products are maintained by an OMS, Scrutiny access to this OMS will enable two significant enhancements to Scrutiny:

- During an inspection, identified defects are associated with regions of the work product. After the inspection, the removal of these defects is managed as part of the standard software engineering process; but not all may be removed at the same time. Traditionally, the defects are managed in a separate defect tracking system. With the use of an OMS that includes versioning of objects, the defect reports can be explicitly associated with the objects themselves.
- Scrutiny should be able to easily find and display up-to-date versions when needed. While inspecting a pre-defined set of work products, it is often desired to examine a related set of work products whose need was not necessarily known at the start of the inspection (e.g., previous versions when inspecting code, or documents in the reference list of a design document).

6.2 Control Integration for Tool Access

The Message Bus of ConversationBuilder is Scrutiny's control integration mechanism. It allows tools to send commands and notifications to the other tools that are connected to the Message Bus. It is influenced by FIELD as shown in its multicast mechanism that connects tools *through* the bus rather than directly to each other. Unlike many other FIELD-inspired messaging systems, the Message

Bus is a multi-user system; this enables messages sent due to one user's actions to be "seen" by other Scrutiny users. We see further use of this aspect of the Message Bus to control each user's interaction with non-Scrutiny tools as well as for the control actions of the Scrutiny protocols. FIELD-like systems have also demonstrated considerable value for the loose integration of existing UNIX tools [1]. Thus the Message Bus is well suited as the basis for interapplication communication between Scrutiny applications and encapsulation of existing tools such as the static analyzer mentioned earlier.

6.3 Process Integration

We are investigating various process modeling and work flow tools. One such tool is the Marvel system, a rule-based software engineering environment developed at Columbia University [11]. Within this system it is possible to encode the rules that describe the Software Development Process and use these rules to control the execution of the tools that perform the process steps. We are investigating integration of Marvel and CB and are experimenting with Scrutiny in this merged environment.

6.4 Distribution and Connection

We want to use Scrutiny for inspections and reviews where not all of the participants are at the same site and in fact may be separated by many network hops and time zones (Figure 8). To support this, we have been studying Scrutiny/CB/Message Bus communication to understand the traffic pattern, simulate various modes of operation, and prepare for revised distribution architectures.

Another issue in this domain is that Scrutiny and CB itself currently assume that all participants must be connected to use the system. CB is sufficiently robust that an unconnected user doesn't prevent the others from continuing and he or she can later reconnect and catch up. The advent of notebook computers and other detachable systems yields the possibility of some work being done on a non-networked system. In fully connected Scrutiny, even though the individual users are not aware of each other's preparation, the system is. The challenge here is to correctly synchronize this independent work with that done by the other participants at a later time.

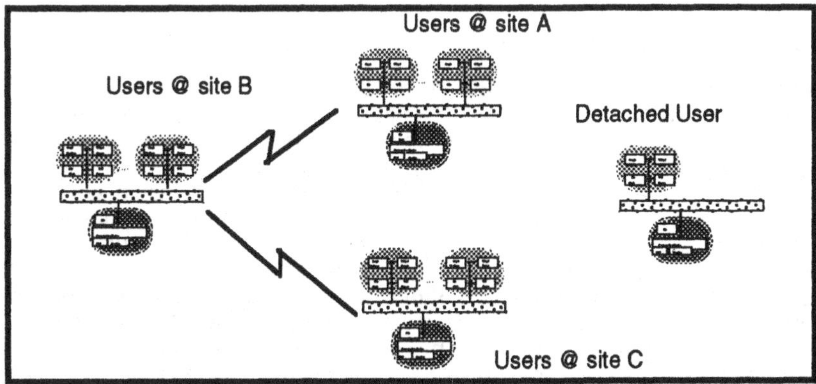

Fig. 8. Scrutiny Distributed and Detached

7 Related Work on Inspection

This section describes some key points we have observed by study of other people's work. We have loosely classified them into ideas that improve comprehensiveness, ideas that decrease the time and effort, and ideas that are related to process change.

7.1 Inspection Comprehensiveness

One of the problems associated with inspections is that it is difficult to even find most of the defects. Various techniques are used with the most common technique involving building checklists and having all inspectors use these checklists. InspeQ by Knight/Myers [13] has the capability of displaying checklists and corresponding standards with cross referencing and examples in specific displays and to guide the Inspectors in their work. This illustrates another advantage of computer assisted inspection by making this form of information readily available to the inspectors and also ensuring that up-to-date information is available.

Martin/Tsai [14] discuss a technique where multiple teams inspect the same requirements document to maximize the likelihood of finding defects. Then a common moderator collates the results to produce a single defects list. They have applied this to mission-critical software, with excellent results. Of course, one can't afford to inspect every item more than once. Applying this technique to the requirements phase is exactly the right place since undetected and thus remaining defects in requirements documents have the most expensive consequences. This technique lends itself to computer assisted inspection in managing and coordinating these inspections, particularly if they are geographically distributed where traditional means of coordination would be slow. This is an example of where a change to improve inspection comprehensiveness introduces a major change to the model of inspection which has significant implications to the design of the system.

As described earlier, there is a desire to give inspectors/reviewers access to related materials that were not identified at the start of the inspection. CSRS by Johnson/Tjahjono [10] implemented a scheme for managing and viewing other related artifacts during the inspection and have obtained good results during reviews.

7.2 Time and effort needed to perform Inspections

Inspecting large work products cannot be done in a single session because people cease to be effective after inspecting for a period of time. The traditional way to solve this problem is to do the first 200 lines in the first session, the second 200 lines in the second, etc. InspeQ (Knight/Myers) describes a Phased Inspection where the division is logical instead of physical and each division is called a Phase. Inspectors are assigned specific topics to cover with some phases being assigned to one person only (e.g. looking for spelling errors) while other phases are done collaboratively. InspeQ itself assists the Moderator in managing the process. It can easily be seen that this allows more parallelism and can consume less total effort than the traditional division. (Imagine going to the seventh 2-hour meeting and trying to remember the context that was set in the first meeting 2 weeks ago.) This is a good example of a major change in the inspection model that is more manageable with an automated tool.

Russell [19] describes results, costs, and cost savings in a very large Bell/Northern Research project performed in 1988. He shows how large the inspection effort is and provides additional motivation for computer assistance to manage it and make inspection more efficient.

7.3 Other Changes to the Inspection Process

Johnson/Tjahjono, in describing CSRS, state that a system allows one to collect considerable empirical data about the inspection process and use that data to test various assumptions for validity. For example, they point out that the effectiveness of the use of checklists can be questioned. Inspection results with and without checklist usage can be compared in a rigorous fashion more readily using a system like CSRS than by ad-hoc or anecdotal methods.

Icicle [2] is an inspection system built at Bellcore to support users who are in the same room. Like Scrutiny, it was done to explore a number of research issues, gain payoff from use, extend it to distributed inspections and reviews, and to try integration into other frameworks. The authors felt that such work would enable process changes to produce higher quality software more cost effectively. Similar issues are presented in [4].

In a separate experiment in our lab [15], a prototype inspection tool modeled after Scrutiny was built in EAST [20], an environment based upon PCTE. In this tool, the work product being inspected is stored in the PCTE Object Management System. When defects are found, they are stored as hyper-links in versions of the work product. This allows the defects to be carried along with the object itself. We will apply the results of this work to Scrutiny.

8 Conclusion

This paper presents an overview of the Scrutiny system, the architecture and description of its main features, and to some extent a view on its future evolution. This presentation should be understood as an example of the benefit that Software Engineering tools can draw from CSCW technology. We deliberately chose to focus on inspection in the software life-cycle both because this process is particularly collaborative and because, to our knowledge, no "off-the-shelf" efficient tools for inspection exist today.

The first experiences have been very encouraging and enriching. In spite of some shortcomings in the current implementation, some individuals prefer inspecting with Scrutiny, citing the advantages of having the results in electronic form. While enhancing Scrutiny, we will continue experimentation by product development teams. Developing iteratively and working with users will guide us in the next improvements. After new experimentation with Scrutiny we expect to be able to share more results in the near future.

The goals of this project include both building an inspection tool and testing the integration technologies. Our relationship with the ConversationBuilder development team lets our experience influence CB evolution and lets us rapidly take advantage of the subsequent improvements.

Finally, we would like to stress the importance of integration with audio, video, and other multimedia facilities. Widespread use of such technology is currently precluded by cost and availability. However, we have no doubt that the appeal of multimedia is extremely strong.

9 Acknowledgments

This paper could not have been written without the work of many people who have worked with us on the design or have been experimental users. Simon Kaplan's ConversationBuilder team and in particular, Doug Bogia and Bill Tolone have been invaluable.

10 References

1. John E. Arnold and Gérard Memmi. Control Integration and its Role in Software Integration. In: Toulouse '92 Fifth International Conference: Software Engineering & its Applications, Proceedings (December 1992)

2. L. Brothers, V. Sembugamoorthy, and M. Muller. ICICLE: Groupware for Code Inspection. In: Proceedings of CSCW '90, ACM Press (October 1990)

3. J. Conklin and M. Begeman. gIBIS: A hypertext tool for exploratory policy discussion. In: Proceedings of CSCW '88 (1988)

4. Janet Drake, Vahid Mashaykhi, John Riedl, and Wei-Tek Tsai. Support for Collaborative Software Inspection in a Distributed Environment: Design, Implementation, and Pilot Study. University of Minnesota Technical Report, TR 92-33 (June 1992)

5. ECMA. Portable Common Tool Environment (PCTE) Abstract Specification. ECMA-149 (December 1990)

6. Michael E. Fagan. Design and Code Inspections to Reduce Errors in Program Development. In: IBM Systems Journal, Vol. 15 - No 3 (1976)

7. The Emeraude Environment, Reference Manual Set, GIE Emeraude (July 1990)

8. W.S. Humphrey. Managing the Software Process. Addison-Wesley, Reading, MA, (1989)

9. Quality Systems - Model for Quality assurance in design/development, production, installation and servicing: ISO 9001. International Organization for Standardization (1987)

10. Philip Johnson and Danu Tjahjono. Improving Software Quality through Computer Supported Collaborative Review. University of Hawaii, ICS-TR 92-04 (1992)

11. Gail E. Kaiser, Peter H. Feiler, and Steven S. Popovich. Intelligent assistance for software development and maintenance. In: IEEE Software, 5(3) - 40-49 (May 1988)

12. Simon M. Kaplan, William J. Tolone, Douglas P. Bogia, and Celsina Bignoli. Flexible, active support for collaborative work with ConversationBuilder. In: Proceedings of CSCW '92, ACM Press (November 1992)

13. John C. Knight and E. Ann Myers. Phased Inspections and their Implementation. In: ACM - Software Engineering Notes, Vol. 16 - No 3, ACM Press (July 1991)

14. Johnny Martin and W.T. Tsai. N-Fold Inspections: A Requirements Analysis Technique. In: Communications of the ACM, Vol. 33 - Number 2, (February 1990)

15. Reza Morakabati. PCTE-based Inspection Tool - Design and Implementation. Bull USARL Research Report, RAD/USARL/93018 (1993)

16. Susanna Opper, Henry Fersko-Weiss. Technology for Teams. Van Nostrand Reinhold (1992)

17. Mark C. Paulk, et.al. Capability Maturity Model for Software. CMU/SEI-91-TR-24, Software Engineering Institute (August 1991)

18. Steve Reiss. Interacting with the FIELD Environment. Brown University Department of Computer Science, Technical Report No CS-89-51 (May 1989)

19. Glen W. Russell. Experience with Inspection in Ultralarge-Scale Developments. In: IEEE Software (January 1991)

20. EAST Environment, Manual set. SFGL (1992)

21. Li-Tao Shen, Pascal Petit, and Patrick Denimal. Performance Evaluation of the Message Bus of ConversationBuilder through the Scrutiny application. Bull USARL Research Report. RAD/USARL/93019 (1993)

22. Edward F. Weller. Lessons Learned from Two Years of Inspection Data. In: Proceedings of The 3rd Annual Applications of Software Management Conference (November 1992)

23. Terry Winograd and Fernando Flores. Understanding Computers and Cognition. Addison-Wesley (1987)

COO: A transaction model to support COOperating software developers COOrdination

C. Godart

CRIN-CNRS, BP 239, F-54506 Vandoeuvre, France
godart@loria.fr

Abstract. A software development is a multi-user process. These users cooperate and compete to execute processes. These processes require consistent concurrent accesses. Unfortunately, their uncertain duration, uncertain development during execution, long interactions with other processes and interactions with the user break traditional transaction atomicity boundaries. The central idea of this paper is that a transaction model based on software process modeling can surpass the limits of traditional transaction models. It describes how a goal oriented software process model connected with a concurrency control protocol can provide active support to consistent cooperation of software developers.

1 Introduction

The COO project has been settled in the continuation of the ALF project with the objective to increase COOperation support between software developers. At this time, two aspects have been especially deepened: human decision support by planning technics taking into account inter-actions between several plans built at the initiative of several agents; consistent inter-action support by encapsulating software processes into long-term and cooperative transaction. This paper is about the second point. The first point is largely described in [4].

A software development is a multi-agent process. These agents cooperate and compete to execute software processes. "These processes require consistent concurrent accesses as traditional database transactions support. Unfortunately, their uncertain duration, uncertain development during execution, long interactions with other processes and interactions with the agent break traditional transaction atomicity boundaries [13]". The central idea of this paper is that a transaction model based on software process modeling can surpass the limits of traditional transaction models. It describes how a goal oriented software process model connected with a concurrency control protocol can provide active support to consistent cooperation of software developers.

Traditional transaction protocols ensure that a result of a current transaction cannot be seen until this transaction commits. This assumption is much too strong for SPs[1]: SPs are not only *competitive* but also *cooperative*. It means that a SP can want to share intermediate results with one or many selected SPs. As an example, the development of a module M1 consisting in an interface I1 and a body B1 can be encapsulated in a SP A1. However, it is clear that in a real software process, as soon

[1] SP: Software Process

as a version of I1 has been produced, it can be used by a SP A2 which develops a module M2 whose interface I2 depends on I1, even if the body B1 corresponding to I1 does not exist, i.e. even if A1 is not ended. However, it is also clear that while A1 is not completed, I1 is subject to modification. Thus A2 is dependent on A1 life and this dependence must be managed: A2 must be aware of I1 evolutions done in A1. *A SP can share intermediate results with other SPs: that implies dependences between SPs and these dependencies must be managed.*

In traditional transaction protocols, recovery is directly supported by atomicity. If a transaction fails, the recovered correct state is the state in which the database was when the transaction was started. This policy is not applicable to SPs which are long uncertain duration processes. Suppose a system or agent failure during a conceptual activity which was initiated two days before: the traditional protocol would imply all the intermediate results to be lost. *SPs are long duration processes: that implies intermediate results of SPs to be saved and more sophisticated recovery procedures to be developed.*

In traditional transaction protocols, a transaction is considered as an *a priori* completely defined and consistent atom. Then, serializabilty assumes consistency of transaction sequences. Unfortunately, that is also not applicable to SPs, especially because of the need of cooperation but also because a SP can generate actions non forecast at the beginning of the activity. Fixing a bug is an example of such a SP whose development is uncertain: depending on the bug nature, this activity can be simple (debug, edit, compile, link) or really complex if the bug reveals a design mistake with a lot of unpredictable consequences. Thus a "fix a bug" activity can cause a lot of non forecast interrelated SPs to execute. *SPs are cooperating uncertain development operations, i.e. it is not possible to assert a priori the consistency of all SPs: SPs consistency control needs to develop a new protocol.*

To surpass the limits of traditional transaction protocols, new transaction models and protocols have been proposed, especially in the domain of CAD/CAM and more generally in the domain of design databases. These proposals have been source of inspiration for the model we propose below. They point out that it will be difficult to provide a general transaction model and an efficient protocol for design applications as existing protocols provide for conventional data-processing applications. For example, in [1], we find: *We rely on intelligent cooperation of designer within the same project for the preservation of integrity constraints to ensure that the database remains consistent.* We go further and assert that *A transaction model for software engineering processes must take into account the semantic of the software development to be controlled* and that *a transaction model for SPs must be based on software process modeling.* That is due to the critical nature of visible intermediate results. These results are consistent enough to be seen by some specific SPs, but not consistent enough to be seen by all: only the software process can indicate which SPs are allowed to see such a result. That is also due to the uncertainty of a software development. It is not possible to *a priori* forecast a set of completely defined and atomic SPs and the corresponding sets of executions: it is only possible to define a gross model of execution and expected qualities of some products at some defined checkpoints.

In this paper, we provide a transaction model based on software process modeling and a protocol to support consistent cooperation and competition of a set of agents executing long duration SPs (to simplify our discourse, we will consider each SP as a transaction). Our experience gained in the ALF project, the transaction model in [1], and [14], gave us the idea that process modeling should be *goal oriented.*

The remainder of the paper is organized as follows: section 2 describes our goal oriented software process model, section 3 defines a cooperative execution, section 4 specifies the idea of an *intermediate result* and section 5 this of workspace. Section 6 describes our concurrency control protocol and finally section 7 concludes, especially with some implementation considerations.

2 Software process type and software process

2.1 Software process type

As aforementioned, it seems difficult to coordinate the agents cooperating to a particular software development without taking into account the specific process governing this development, without knowledge on this process: that is the goal of a software process model to describe such a knowledge.

As in [14], we consider a software process model is a set of high levels goals and a description of how to decompose these goals into sub-goals. Thus, the execution state of a software process is the state of its goal tree and the data produced during the execution.

We also call a software process model a software process type. A software process type description is a 7-uples <*S, V, P, O, I, C, R*>.

1. *S*: a list of <parameter: type> couples called *signature*. When the parameters of a process type are instantiated with actual values, a new process of the type is created,
2. *V*: a set of object types which define the *view* the processes of the process type have on the global object base[2],
3. *P*: a first order logical formula called *precondition* which, for any correct instantiation of the parameters, must be true to allow the corresponding process to start,
4. *O*: a set of *insert a tuple in a relation*, *delete a tuple in a relation* and *update a function* clauses, called *objective*, which describes for each correct instantiation of the parameters the objective of the corresponding process (the process effects when it completes).
5. *I*: a set of process types called *implementation*: to execute a process *p* of type *t*, only processes of types in the *implementation* of *t* can be instantiated by the agents associated to *p*. If its *implementation* is empty, the process type is called an *activity type*, if not it is called a *task* type. In addition, *init()* and *terminate()* activities are in the *implementation* set of all tasks. *init*() executes to start a task and to make initialization. *init*() cannot execute if the precondition of the

[2] We make no choice on the real object model used to structure the objects the processes operate on. In [6], we suppose that this object base can be modeled as an algebraic structure, i.e. by means of relations and functions: we think that most important models enter this class.

task is not validated. *terminate()* activity executes inside a task to terminate this task: it cannot execute if this task has not reached its objective, has not produced the right effect,
6. *C*: a set of first order temporal logical formulas called ***integration constraints***. We go into the details of these constraints in the next subsection,
7. *R*: a set of roles they define the human agent qualities requested to execute a process of the type.

The *objective* of a process describes its goal. The *objectives* of processes in its *implementation* are subgoals of this goals. Thus, we obtain a tree of goals. *Integration constraints* and *preconditions* describe how subgoals synchronize to contribute to the achievement of their father goal. Note that if the description of goals is hierarchically organized, a process generally executes as a network of subgoals.

Integration constraints Integration constraints are used to coordinate, to integrate sub-processes. We distinguish between integrity constraints and transition constraints.

Integrity constraints Integrity constraints are safety constraints. To express them, we use this special kind of temporal formula:

$\forall x_1 : t_1, ..., x_k : t_k,$
$\Box(\alpha \supset \Box(\beta \; \mathcal{B} \; \gamma))$

where

- x_1, x_2, ..., x_n are the variables of type t_1, t_2, ... t_n,
- $\Box$ means "*we have always*",
- $\mathcal{B}$ means *before*,
- α is a non temporal and non disjonctive formula,
- β et γ are non temporal formula.

Intuitively, such a constraint is interpreted by "in all execution of a process of the type being defined, if an execution enters a state (of the object base) in which α is true, it is not possible for this execution to enter a state in which β is false until it enters a state in which γ is true".

Example:
∀ x: module,
□((being_modified(x) = true ∧
responsible_for_modif(x) = z) ⊃
□(responsible_for_modif(x) = z $\mathcal{B}$ being_modified(x) = false))
means that the people responsible for a module cannot change if this module is being modified.

Transition constraints Transition constraints are vivacity constraints. To express transition constraints, we use this special kind of temporal formula:

$\forall x_1 : t_1, ..., x_k : t_k,$
$\Box(\alpha \supset \Diamond(\beta \; \mathcal{B} \; \gamma))$

where x_1, ... , x_k, $\Box$, α, β, γ have the same meaning than in the previous kind of formula and where $\Diamond$ means "*it is inevitable*".

Intuitively, such a constraint is interpreted by "in all execution of a process of the type being defined, if an execution enters a state (of the object base) in which α is true, it is inevitable for this execution to enter a state in which β is false before to enter a state in which γ is true".

Example:
$\forall$ i: interface,
$\Box(new^3(\text{i}) \supset$
$(\Diamond\ new(body(used\_by(\text{i})))\ \mathcal{B}\ terminated(@\text{t})))$

means that each time the interface of a module is modified, the body of all modules which depend on this module need to be revisited before the current process terminates[4].

Semantics To define the semantics of constraints, we arrange the successive states of a process execution in an ascending order.

A state sequence σ satisfies an integrity constraint
$\Omega = \Box(\alpha \supset \Box(\beta \; \mathcal{B} \; \gamma))$, if, for all substitutions δ of the variables in Ω and for all state s_i of σ, i $\geq$ 0

if $s_{i,\delta} \models \alpha$ then
$\forall j, i \leq j < \mu,$
$s_{j,\delta} \models \beta$ with $\mu = min(\{k \mid k \geq i \wedge s_{k,\delta} \models \gamma\} \bigcup \infty)$

A state sequence σ satisfies a transition constraint
$\Omega = \Box(\alpha \supset \Box(\beta \; \mathcal{B} \; \gamma))$, if, for all substitutions δ of the variables in Ω and for all state s_i of σ, i $\geq$ 0

if $s_{i,\delta} \models \alpha$ then
$\exists j, i \leq j < \mu,$

$s_{j,\delta} \models \beta$ with $\mu = min(\{k \mid k \geq i \wedge s_{k,\delta} \models \gamma\} \bigcup \infty)$

Special cases of constraints A special case of integrity or transition constraints exists when the formula α has the special value *init*. The semantic of such a constraint is the same than above, except that i has the value 0: *init* has the value true in the

[3] *new*(x) is a function which return true each time a new value of x is produced

[4] in our framework, processes are represented as objects. Each object of type process has some attributes; especially, a unique identifier and a current state (invoked, active, suspended and terminated) as attribute. These objects can be used in α, β and γ formulas. *@t* is a variable which always contains the identifier of the task in the context of which the constraint is evaluated.

first state and only in the first state of the process execution of the process which defines the constraint.

Justification If the other components of a description are rather classical in the domain, the way we express integration constraints is more unconventional. The decision to express constraints as logical expressions corresponds to the will to use an unified formalism to describe the differents aspects of processes. The choice of our special kind of temporal formula can be easily justified by the interactive and iterative nature of software processes: the properties we want to assert on the software products depend on the context in which we observe them, and especially on past and forecast states. Due to lack of space, we limit our justification to these two considerations, more items can be found in [6].

Some syntactic aspects In this paper, we do not enter in the details of our language to describe process types. We want only to underline that, when the same free variable appears in S, P, C and O, it represents the same object in all the components of the description.

2.2 Software process

A software process of a process type is obtained by progressively instantiating all the components of the description of the type. A process is invoked by replacing parameters with actual values. By means of free variables which act as placeholders for objects, this instantiates also the precondition and, at least partially, the constraints and the objective of the new process. It also defines sub-processes. Actual parameters are also entry points in the network of objects: this limits the view of the process. Finally, assigning human agents to roles terminates the instantiation.

At this point, a process can start to execute, can produce new objects and corollary new constraints in order to progressively reduce the distance to its objective before to reach it.

We denote a process as a 7-uples <s, v, p, o, i, c, r>.

3 Correct and Cooperative execution of a software process

As in [1], we introduce the idea of the *closure* of a task before to define a cooperative execution.

3.1 Closure of a task

The closure of a task t $<s, v, p, o, i, c, r>$ is a task t* $<s, v^*, p, o, i^*, c, r^*>$ where:

- $i^*(t^*) = \{sp \mid (sp \in i(t) \wedge i(sp) = \emptyset) \vee \exists sp_i \in i(t) \wedge sp \in i^*(sp_i))\}$,
  $i^*(t^*)$ is the set of activities types (processes which do not break down) directly or indirectly enclosed in t.

- $v^*(t^*)$ integrates all the views of all the processes in $i^*(t^*)$[5],
- r* is the union of all the agents playing the different roles in the process.

3.2 Cooperative execution

A cooperative execution of a process t is a serializable execution of activities in $i^*(t^*)$.

In a cooperative execution, activities cannot share intermediate results but tasks can.

3.3 Correct cooperative execution

A correct cooperative execution of a task t is a cooperative execution of t which terminates (the objective of t is reached) and in which each sub-process of t terminates in a consistent state (where integrity and transition constraints are satisfied).

3.4 Example

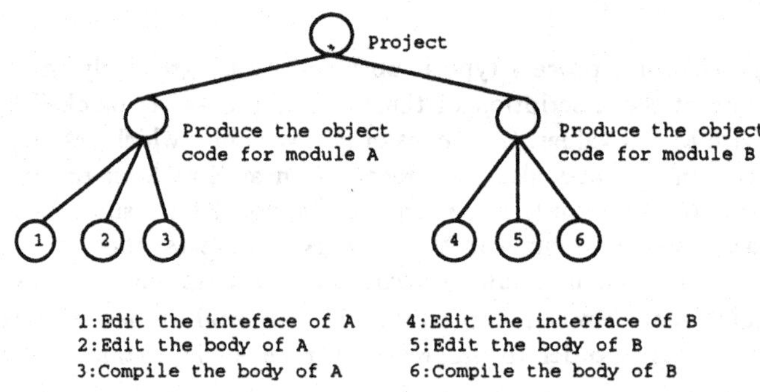

Fig. 1. A simple process description

The objective of the process *Project* in figure 1 is to produce the object code for a *module* A and a *module* B. We suppose that *module* B depends on *module* A: we interpret that by "the interface of *module* A has to be read to edit the body of *module* B" and "it exists a transition constraint: each time the interface of A is modified, the body oy of B must be revisited before the *Project* process terminates". The following schedule is correct in regards to our correctness criteria. However, if we suppose that a *Produce the object code ...* task cannot terminate if a "correct" object code is not produced, it is easy to observe that it is not serializable: in a serializable execution, *produce_the_object_code*(B) cannot read the interface of A while

[5] *view integration* is an open research topic, but not this of this paper: our framework is being developed atop the *Emeraude* system which implements the *PCTE 1.5* interfaces and *integration* has the meaning currently used in this world [3]

produce_the_object_code(A) is active.

init(*Project*());
init(*produce_the_object_code*(A));
edit_the_interface_of_module(A);
init(*produce_the_object_code*(B));
edit_the_interface_of_module(B);
edit_the_body_of_module(B);
compile_the_body_of_module(B);
edit_the_body_of_module(A);
compile_the_body_of_module(A);
edit_the_interface_of_module(A);
edit_the_body_of_module(A);
compile_the_body_of_module(A);
edit_the_interface_of_module(A);
edit_the_body_of_module(B);
edit_the_body_of_module(A);
compile_the_body_of_module(A);
terminate(*produce_the_object_code*(A));
compile_the_body_of_module(B);
terminate(*produce_the_object_code*(B));
terminate(*Project*());

4 Concept of intermediate result

4.1 Intuitive definition

The key idea of a cooperative execution of a software process is *the ability to share intermediate results between processes*: one can want to allow others to see some of its intermediate results and another can want to see them. To refine the idea of intermediate results, we distinguish between three levels of object consistency: stable, semi-stable and non stable objects[6]. Stable objects can be operated by any process. A semi-stable object is considered as consistent enough, by the process which produces it, to be shared with a restricted set of other processes. A non stable object is the property of a process and cannot be operated by another process until the owner makes it semi-stable or stable. *A semi-stable result is what we call an intermediate result.*

4.2 Semantics

We define the semantics of intermediate results through their behavior in regards to integration constraints.

[6] The fact that an object is stable, semi-stable or not stable is completely depending on the semantic of the development process

We think that an intermediate result is of some interest if, by definition, it has some impact(s) on other objects, or in other terms, if the corresponding final result can "produce new constraints", can restrict the set of acceptable following states of the execution.

In addition, as the objective of constraints is to have a better control on the current software development, i.e. to know as soon as possible the constraints on the development, and if when an intermediate result is produced, it is inevitable the corresponding final result to be produced, *we use intermediate results when evaluating α formula in constraints.*

However, in our mind, integration constraints restrict only the values of final results, i.e. not these of intermediate results or more precisely: we do not want integration constraints to restrict values of intermediate results, but only these of final results, i.e results not in a semi-public database and which are not currently being modified. As a consequence, *constraints restrict only final results and intermediate results have not to be used when evaluating β and γ formula.*

5 The concept of workspace

5.1 Workspace management

The way we manage workspaces is inspired of [7], but dataflows between databases are defined differently (when a sub-process want to make visible an intermediate result, it transfers it in the semi-public database of its father process, not its proper semi-public database. We distinguish between three kinds of databases(cf. figure 2)):

- stable objects are stored in a unique public database. Any sub-process can transfer any object (we say *CHECK OUT*) from the public database into its private database, provided it has the visibility on this object,
- semi-stable objects are stored in semi-public databases. Each process has its proper semi-public database. These objects are intermediate results produced by sub-processes. A sub-process can transfer objects from its private database (we say *UPWARD COMMIT*) into the semi-public database of its father process. A sub-process can transfer (we say also *UPWARD COMMIT*) objects from its semi-public database to the semi-public database of its father process. A sub-process can *CHECK OUT* objects from its chain of ancestor semi-public databases into its private database, but only to read it. When a new value of an intermediate result is produced, a sub-process which previously checked it out can *REFRESH* the value of this result with the new value,
- non stable objects are stored in private databases. One private database is associated to each sub-process and only this sub-process can operate on its private database,
- when a process terminates (reach its objective), it CHECKs IN its final results from its private database to the private database of its father process.

The workspace of a process is its private database and the semi-public database of its father process(*read* only).

When a process want to access an object, the object is searched successively in:

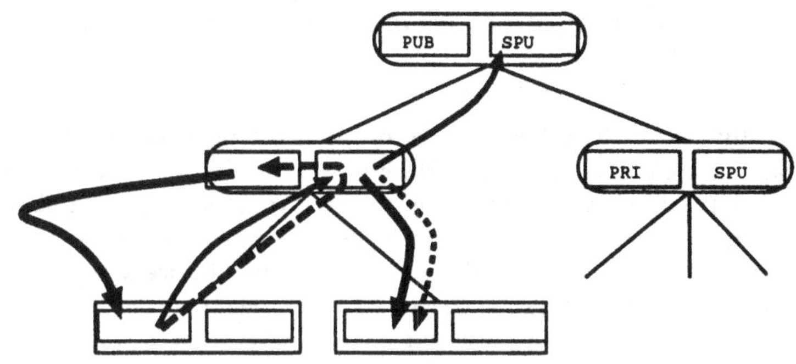

PUB: base d'objets publique
PRI: base d'objets prive'e
SPU: base d'objets semi-publique

Fig. 2. Transferts between databases

- in its private database,
- in the semi-public database of its father process (if *read* mode),
- in the workspace of its father in the same order (first private, then semi-public),
- recursively in the workspaces of its chain of ancestors in the same order (finally in the public database: we consider the public database is the semi-publicd database of the root process).

We say that the search for objects is *in Z* (cf. figure 3).

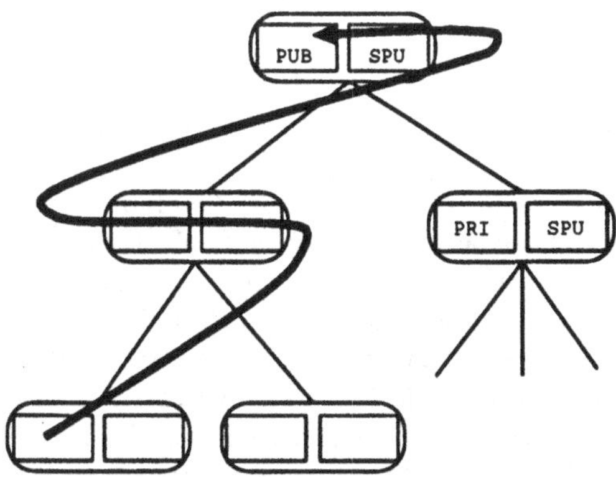

Fig. 3. Search in Z

6 A protocol to support cooperative execution of software processes

As classically defined, a protocol is a set of rules that restricts the set of admissible executions. Less classically, we distinguish between *independent* rules and *semantic* rules: each software process has its proper *semantic* rules (rules depending on some explicit knowledge on the current process) but *independent* rules are the same for all processes. Typically, the *two phase locking protocol* defines a set of independent rules; at the opposite, integration constraints are *semantic rules*. Our protocol will combine these rules to ensure consistent flows of data between workspaces.

We do not require a protocol to capture all possible correct cooperative executions since such a requirement is not feasible in practical systems[7]. We will be satisfied with a protocol which ensures correctness of some cooperative executions (of a subset of all cooperative execution).

6.1 A software process as a nested transaction

We consider that each process executes as a virtually atomic entity: each process is encapsulated in a transaction. We say that a process is atomic in the sense that it has one an only one objective and it cannot terminate before it reaches this objective. However, we say that atomicity is virtual in the sense, that, at the opposite of traditional transactions, the execution of a transaction can exchange intermediate results with other transactions, provided these exchanges verify the protocol rules.

Corresponding to the structure of a software process, a transaction encapsulating a process p_1 which breaks down into sub-processes $p_{1_1}, \dots, p_{1_n}$, will invoke sub-transactions, each sub-transaction encapsulating one p_{1_i}. Thus, a process execute as a nested transaction. At the leaves of the tree, we find database operations (*Read* and *Write*), at the adjacent level, transactions encapsulate activities which do not break down, the root transaction encapsulate the whole project and intermediate node transactions encapsulate sub-processes (cf. figure 4). A transaction can transfer data between databases by means of CHECK OUT, CHECK IN, UPWARD COMMIT and REFRESH activities.

6.2 Independent rules

Detecting and solving conflicts without negotiation Independent rules to manage public and private databases are inspired of these of [12] which are inspired of [9].

Synchronization of concurrent operations on the same resource is ensured by a lock mechanism. A lock is characterized by an *external mode* and an *internal mode*. To simplify, we suppose here a transaction can check out an object either to Read it or to Write it (respectively in mode R or W). The *external mode* of a lock controls synchronization of accesses between a transaction and all transactions which are not enclosing, nor nested (either directly or transitively) to it. The *internal mode*

[7] It was shown in [11] that testing for serializability is an NP-complete problem and in [1] that testing for correctness of a cooperative execution is more complex that testing for serializability

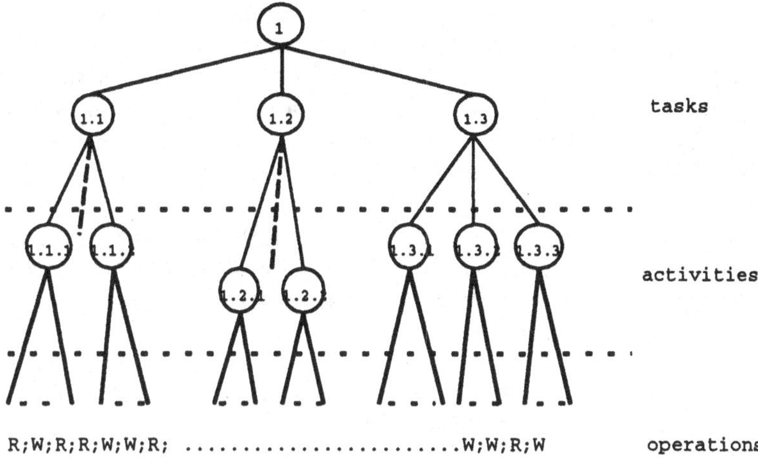

Fig. 4. A software process as a nested transaction

of a lock controls synchronization of accesses between all transactions which are nested (either directly or transitively) to it. The *external mode* of a lock defines the maximum usage[8] a transaction want to do of an object, the *internal mode* of a lock defines its current usage. In addition, note that the *internal mode* is always weaker or equal to the *external mode*.

A transaction which wants to CHECK OUT an object from the public or a private database has to establish a lock on the object. At this time, only the value of the external mode is requested and the transaction can establish the lock on the object if its *external* mode is compatible (cf figure 5):

- with the *external mode* of all locks held on the object by transaction which are not enclosing nor nested to the issuing transaction,
- the *internal mode* of all locks already established by its sibling transactions on the resource

	R	W	free
R	yes	wait	yes
W	wait	wait	yes

Fig. 5. Compatibility of lock modes

When a transaction establishes a lock on an object, the *external mode* of this lock becomes the *internal mode* of the lock in the context of the ancestor transaction

[8] We define the ordre free<read<write (a transaction which can *write* an object can also *read* it. The inverse is false)

which is the owner of the database from which the object is checked out.

When a transaction terminates (the process it encapsulates has reached its objective), its locks are inherited by its directly enclosing transaction for all objects it has not yet another lock. The internal mode of these locks are released to *free*.

In addition, a transaction can promote consistently a lock mode, i.e. can transform it to a stronger one.

Solving conflicts with negotiation The idea here is, rather to impose a process to wait when a *read/write* or *write/write* conflict is detected, to initiate negotiations[9] between the human agents associated with the processes in conflict[10].

The conclusion of a negotiation can be:

- in case of a *Read/Write* conflict to make the object, which creates the conflict, an intermediate result of the process which writes it,
- in case of a *Write* on *Write* conflict to give a copy of the object which creates the conflict to each process and to define a merging procedure[11] to merge the modifications of the two processes when they terminate.

6.3 Semantic rules

Intuitively and in accordance with 4.2, the semantic rules we use are:

1. A process cannot complete if it has not reached its objective,
2. Each time an intermediate result is introduced or modified in a semi-public database of a transaction, its sub-transactions can read this result,
3. A transaction cannot produce a final result (check_in) if it can violate an integration constraint,
4. We also say that:
   (a) a transaction t_1 is a *client* of another transaction t_2 from the point of view of the object O if t_2 has read an intermediate value of O produced by t_1 and t_2 cannot terminate before it has read the final value of O produced by t_1,
   (b) a transaction t_1 is a *controller* of another transaction t_2 from the point of view of the object O if t_2 has read an intermediate value of O produced by t_1 but t_2 can terminate before it has read the final value of O produced by t_1.

If it is easy to understand how rules 1,2 and 4 can be implemented, we feel it is necessary to go into the details of the algorithm we use to support rule 3: the central idea is to transform constraints in terms of pre- and post-conditions for activities, and especially for UPWARD-COMMIT and CHECK-IN activities. Transformation of constraints is inspired of [8].

[9] Negotiations are supported by establishing a communication channel between each father process and each of its child processes: communications are also hierarchically organized.

[10] We demonstrate in [6] that negotiations are requested only between the process which creates the conflict and its brother processes.

[11] defining such a procedure is not in the scope of our work

Evaluating our constraints needs not only the knowledge of the current state of the database, but also this of past states. To memorize these past states, we introduce for each type of constraint an additional predicate whose arguments are the variables appearing in the constraint description. This predicate must be entered as true in the database for a substitution ψ by the activity which validate a condition α if:

- in case of an integrity constraint, the β formula must not be evaluated to true with that substitution in the next states until a state, in which γ is evaluated to true with that substitution, occurs,
- in case of a transition constraint, the β formula remains to be checked with that substitution in the next states before a state, in which γ is evaluated to true with that substitution, occurs.

We call such a predicate a *memo*. The basic idea we use to implement constraints is to extend the precondition and objective of activities to manage *memos* in a consistent way. The typical activities we consider are these which change at least one constraint component: α, β or γ.

Transformation of an integrity constraint: $\Box(\alpha \supset \Box(\beta \mathcal{B} \gamma))$

In a first step, we introduce a predicate named, for the example, *A*lways *B*efore (AB)[12], whose arguments are the variables in β and γ. Then,

1. the objective of all activity types which can validate the α formula is extended to give the value *true* to AB when α becomes *true* (this is implemented by inserting a tuple representing this fact in the database),
2. the objective of all activity types which can validate the γ formula is extended to give the value *false* to AB when γ becomes *true* (this is implemented by deleting the corresponding tuple in the database),
3. the precondition of all activity types which can validate the β formula is augmented to verify that the AB formula has not the value *true* (to test that the corresponding tuple AB does not exist). The effect is to prevent an activity to violate a constraint.

This is depicted in figure 6.

can validate the formula	*precondition*	*objective*
1		*insert* TA$(x_i, \ldots, x_j, x_{k+1}, \ldots, x_{k+n})$ si $\alpha \wedge \neg\gamma$
2	$\neg$TA()	
3		*delete* TA$(x_i, \ldots, x_j, x_{k+1}, \ldots, x_{k+n})$ si γ

Fig. 6. Transformation of integrity constraints

[12] it is clear that more application oriented names can be used in real processes

Transformation of a transition constraint: $\Box(\alpha \supset \Diamond(\beta \mathcal{B} \gamma))$

Transition constraints are transformed in the same way, except that an activity insert a *SB* tuple (*SB* for *S*ometime *B*efore) when it makes α true, delete a *SB* tuple when it makes β *true* and that an activity cannot execute if it can make γ *true* and a tuple *SB* exists. This is depicted in figure 7.

can validate the formula	*precondition*	*objective*
1		*insert* SB($x_i, \ldots, x_j, x_{k+1}, \ldots, x_{k+n}$) si $\alpha \wedge \neg\beta$
2		*delete* SB($x_i, \ldots, x_j, x_{k+1}, \ldots, x_{k+n}$) si β
3	¬SB()	

Fig. 7. Transformation of transition constraints

The aforementioned transformation rules we provide to implement constraints is quite rough. However, we discovered that, if they are not enough refined to produce satisfactory solutions without human interactions, they are really structuring and helpful for designers.

Examples

Transformation of an integrity constraint Transformation of:
∀ x: module[13],
□((being_modified(x) = true ∧
responsible_for_modif(x) = z) ⊃
□(responsible_for_modif(x) = z $\mathcal{B}$ being_modified(x) = false))

In a first time, we introduce a predicate *responsible_cannot_be_modified*(x,z). This predicate can be inserted by the activity *upward_commit*(y:module) if (being_modified(x)) is true. It we suppose an activity *modify_responsible*(y:module, t:personne), the precondition of this activity should be extended with the predicate ¬*responsible_cannot_be_modified*(x,z). Finally, this predicate can be deleted by the activity *check_in*(y:module) if (being_modified(x)) is false.

Transformation of a transition constraint Transformation of:
∀ i: interface,
□(*new*(i) ⊃
(◇ *new*(*body*(*used_by*(i))) $\mathcal{B}$ *terminated*(@t)))

In a first time, we introduce a predicate *has_been_modified*(i). This predicate can be inserted by the activity *upward_commit*(i:interface). If we suppose an activity *produce_a_program*(p) which manages dependencies between its modules, the precondition of the activity *terminate*(@t) should be extended with the predicate ∀ i: interface, ¬*has_been_modified*(i). Finally, this predicate must be deleted by the activity *check_in*(b: body).

[13] We make the hypothesis that our example is enough simple to be intuitively understood.

7 Conclusion

Our framework supports cooperative work in the sense that it allows *consistent visibility of intermediate results*, consistent exchange of information between active tasks. That cannot be achieved by a classical transaction model which do not allow visibility of intermediate results. That can be supported by an environment based only on software process description, but only in the hypothesis that all semantic rules, all integrity constraints are known and encoded in software process descriptions: if not, exchanges can be inconsistent. Unfortunately, as it is pointed out in traditional applications that all integrity constraints cannot be known and that is still more true in complex application like software processes. In this paper we propose a semantic transaction model which takes advantage of both transaction and software process modeling capabilities to allow only consistent exchange of data between tasks. In fact, serializability, the traditional correctness criteria, is assumed only between activities, not between tasks: tasks can exchange intermediate results, but only if these results respect the software process rules, and especially, the integration constraints. As a consequence, our software processes can have the qualities of a strongly constrained (hierarchical organization) and of a weakly constrained (set of activities) organizations: respectively, control of development quality and synergetic effects. Figure 10 describes a short scenario of typical exchange between processes:

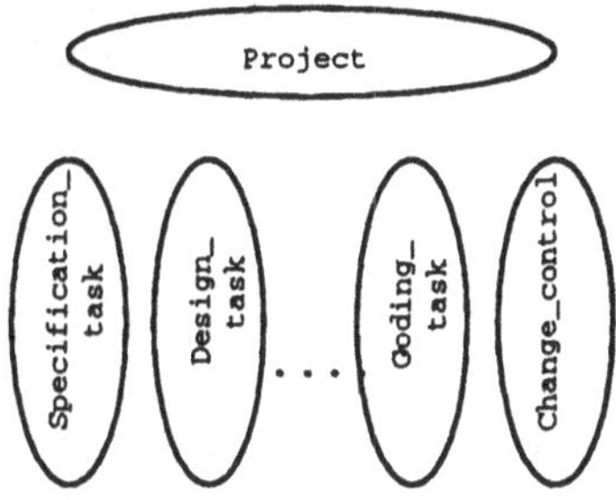

Fig. 8. Gross architecture of a software development

1. *coding_task* reports a bug,
2. *change_control* analyses the bug,
3. *change_control* assigns to *design_task* a fix bug request,
4. *design_task* fixes the bug and
5. deliver a design modification,
6. *control_change* controls the design modification and
7. transfers it for coding modification,
8. *coding_task* fixes the bug in the code.

It is clear that this scenario cannot be supported by a classical transaction model and if it could be supported by an architecture without control specific to concurrency between agents, probably the same architecture could also accept incorrect executions.

All these exchanges take place without transaction creation nor ending. That is another interesting effect of cooperative transactions: it reduces the number of transaction creations and endings which are resource consuming operations: in the extreme, a process will start as a root transaction and then expand and expand until it atomically terminates[14]). That is what figures 9 and 10 illustrate for the process whose gross architecture is depicted in figure 8.

Implementation is not in the scope of this paper. However, we can briefly say that our experimentation is based on mechanisms developed in the ALF project [5] atop the Emeraude environment kernel which implements the PCTE 1.5 interfaces. The main enhancement of ALF requested to support cooperative transaction was on workspace management. Note that cooperative transactions are modeled as persistent PCTE objects: that provides effective support to recovery and re-organization and allow to explicitly program the concurrency control protocol.

The architecture we discussed in this paper do not support all kinds of interactions. In fact, we discussed a lot *read/write* conflicts, but not *write/write* conflicts: we show in [6] that this architecture can be used to organize negotiations between human agents and provide an active support to *write/write* conflicts.

About related works, a first conclusion is that a lot of work on software process enaction do no consider explicitly concurrency control. In other words, Software Development Environment based on such process models request agents to work in isolation.

Our model is distinct of transaction models which explicitly manage configuration of data like [10]. We think that it is in the *Marvel* process-centered Software Development Environment that support to cooperation is the more sophisticated and the more close to our [2].

A first difference between the two approaches is that cooperation is explicitly encoded in Marvel while we deduce such rules by transforming software process descriptions which do not depend on an execution mode (the conceptual level) into descriptions taking into account a specific execution mode (the logical level). A serial, serializable or cooperative execution can be deduced from the same conceptual description: our model is supported by a design framework. A second difference is that, in our framework, no predefined solutions to all potential conflicts need to be explicitly described to be solved: our solution is more general; however, it is clear that for conflicts whose solutions are directly encoded in Marvel, our framework is less effective.

We enter now a phase of validation of our model which requests to prototype typical situation like ISPW6/7 example, group decision support and finer granularity processes integration.

---

[14] We do not consider here re-modeling (however, note that it can supported by intermediate result visibility and persistence of transaction structure as we point out in [6]

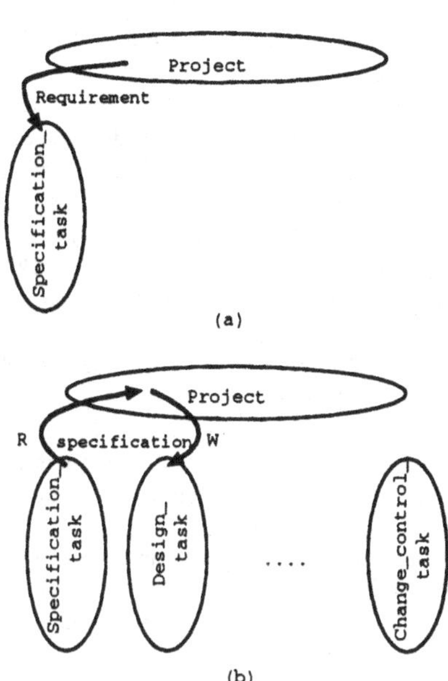

Fig. 9. Software process extension

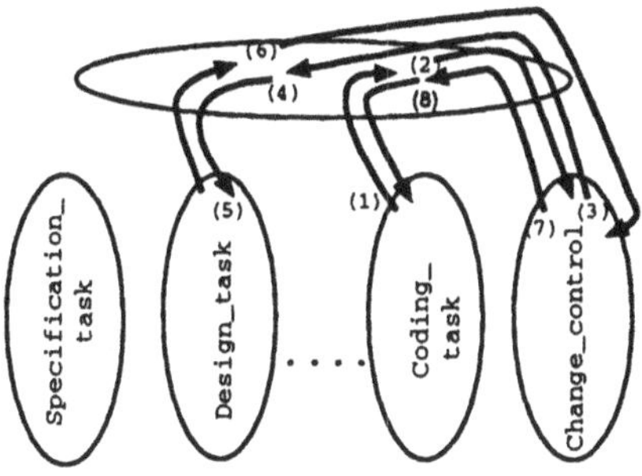

Fig. 10. Taking into account a bug report

References

1. F. Bancilhon, W. Kim, and H. Korth. A Model for CAD Transactions. In *Proceedings of the 11th international conference on VLDB*, pages 25–33, Stockholm, august 1985.
2. N. S. Barghouti. *Concurrency Control in Rule-Based Software Development Environments.* PhD thesis, Columbia University, 1992. Technical Report CUCS-001-92.
3. I. Campbell. Portable Common Tool Environment. *Computer Standard and Interfaces*, 8, 1988.
4. Gérôme Canals. *Des Mécanismes pour l'Assistance aux Utilisateurs dans un Atelier de Génie Logiciel Conduit par des Modèles.* PhD thesis, CRIN – Université de Nancy I, Nancy, octobre 1992.

5. J.C. Derniame, C. Godart, V. Gruhn, and J. Lonchamp. Process Centered Ipses in ALF. In *Proceedings of the 5th International Workshop on Computer-Aided Software engineering*, pages 179–190, Montreal, Canada, july 1992.
6. C. Godart. *Contribution à la modélisation des procédés de fabrication de logiciel: support au travail coopératif.* Thèse d'état, Université de Nancy I, 1993.
7. W. Kim, R. Lorie, D. McNabb, and W. Plouffe. A Transaction Mechanism for Engineering Design Databases. In *Proceedings of the 10th international conference on VLDB*, pages 355–362, Singapore, August 1984.
8. U.W. Lipeck. Stepwise specification of dynamic database behavior. *ACM SIGMOD*, pages 387–397, 1986.
9. J. Elliot Moss. *Nested Transactions: An Approach to Reliable Distributed Computing,*. PhD thesis, MIT, 1981.
10. M.N. Nguyen and Reidar Conradi. Cooperating transactions in a versioned database. Technical report, University of Trondheim, 1992.
11. C.H. Papamitriou. Serialisability of concurrent updates. *Communications of the ACM*, 26(4):631–653, october 1979.
12. PCTE+. C functionnal Specification Issue 2, July 1988.
13. C. Pu, G. Kaiser, and N. Hutchinson. Split Transactions for Open-Ended Activities. In *Proceedings of the 14th international conference on VLDB*, pages 26–37, Los Angeles, September 1988.
14. Ian thomas. The Software Process as a Goal-directed Activity. In *Fifth International Software Process Workshop*, 1989.

An Experiment in Software Retrieval

Rolf Adams

University of Karlsruhe
Institut fuer Programmstrukturen und Datenorganisation
Postfach 6980
W-7500 Karlsruhe (Germany)
Email: adams@ira.uka.de

Abstract

This paper evaluates a knowledge-based approach for software retrieval. It describes a knowledge-based software information system that uses an expressive terminological knowledge representation to represent software and that offers a natural language query interface. The system is used to implement a cross reference tool for C++ and a tool for locating UNIX commands. The retrieval effectiveness is compared to approaches based on automatic indexing. It is shown that the knowledge-based approach is more precise than three different automatic indexing approaches, while providing excellent recall and adequate runtime performance.

Keywords: software libraries, software reuse, software maintenance, information retrieval, knowledge representation, knowledge acquisition, terminological reasoning

1 Introduction

Software information systems are systems that inform about software components and support software development and maintenance. They help in finding reusable software, understanding existing software, locating errors, and performing changes. Typical software information systems are software libraries [40, 31, 30, 8, 7, 13, 20, 18, 19], cross reference tools [38, 37, 9, 16], or systems representing different kinds of information about a given software system [10, 14]. A software information system can improve the productivity of software developers and the quality of developed software.

There are numerous approaches for building software information systems: classical information retrieval methods [20, 18], relational databases [9], hypertext systems [19, 14] and AI-based methods [10, 25, 33]. Characteristics of software information systems are the represented knowledge, the effort for knowledge acquisition, the user interface (graphics, windows, query language), the methods for retrieval and presentation, and finally the knowledge sources. For example, automatic indexing acquires the knowledge automatically from available natural language documentation. The retrieval is based on statistical agreement between terms given by the user and terms present in the documentation. Output is ranked according to the degree of agreement. On the other hand, AI-based approaches require semantic modelling and the effort for knowledge acquisition is much higher. The user interface is based on a formal query language or natural language and the retrieval is according to the semantics of the language. The AI-based approach allows the representation of all kinds of knowledge without the availability of any kind of document [10].

This paper describes the system YAKRSIS, where an AI-based approach has been used for building a software information system. It builds upon the LaSSIE project [10, 35, 11]. Knowledge about software is represented by a terminological knowledge representation system, and the system is coupled with a natural language parser as user interface. Compared to the LaSSIE system, YAKRSIS offers a more expressive knowledge representation language for modelling software and a more sophisticated integration with a natural language parser. We also show that the runtime of YAKRSIS is satisfactory and that YAKRSIS's retrieval performance is superior to three automatic indexing approaches.

The rest of the paper is organized as follows. In the next section, the architecture of the software information system and the knowledge representation system are explained. Section 3 explains the automatic indexing approaches against which YAKRSIS is evaluated. Section 4 contains the evaluation and the last section the conclusions.

2 The software information system YAKRSIS

YAKRSIS is a software information system based on a terminological knowledge representation system with a natural language interface. The overall architecture is shown in figure 1.

The kernel of the system is a tool called YAKR. YAKR consists essentially of three components: a terminological knowledge representation system called YAKS, a natural language parser for German called SARA, and a component for coupling these two subsystems.

The system contains a number of knowledge bases. The parser uses a lexicon for the morphological analysis and a case table for the cases used in caseframes. The caseframes are automatically generated from annotations in the YAKS knowledge bases. The YAKS system uses knowledge bases that either contain generic (terminological) knowledge or specific (assertional) knowledge about a certain domain. For the last form of knowledge, there may exist information abstractors that automatically acquire knowledge out of existing software documents. We have implemented one such information abstractor, CPPREF, that works on C++ source code.

The end user can choose between two kinds of query languages. The user interface of the parser accepts questions in restricted German, while the interface of YAKS accepts queries according to the formal query language of YAKL. More complicat-

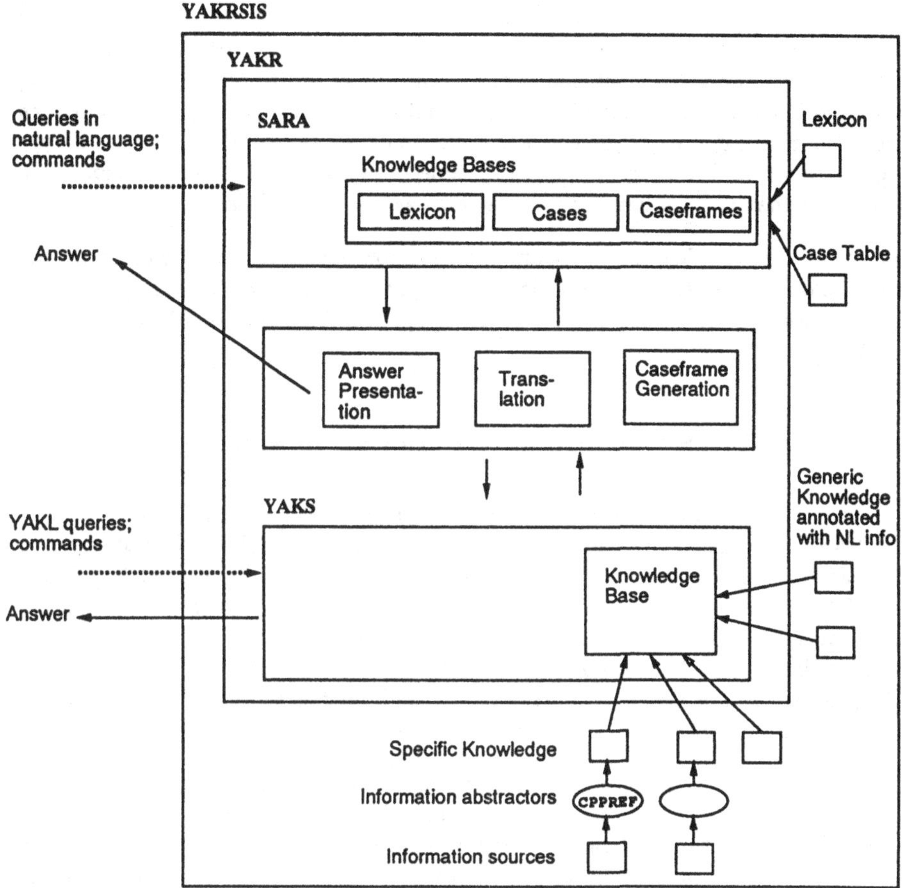

Figure 1: *The YAKRSIS software information system*

ed queries can be given in the formal query language including operators such as negation, disjunction, conjunction, and many others. On the other hand, the user of YAKL has to know the exact names of the knowledge structures, that is, concepts, roles and individuals (see subsection 2.1). Furthermore, long and error prone strings according to the syntax of the query language must be typed in. An automatic typing correction and a query editor could remedy the problem. However, experience has shown that natural language queries are easier to formulate and faster to type.

In the following, the YAKS system and the two knowledge bases already implemented are explained. A detailed description of the parser SARA is found in [28], and a detailed description of the components for coupling YAKS and SARA can be found in [29, 1].

2.1 The YAKS knowledge representation system

The terminological knowledge representation system YAKS is an implementation of the YAKL formalism. This formalism is another one in the KL-ONE tradition and comparable to formalisms such as KANDOR [26], CLASSIC [5, 6], BACK [27, 32], CANDIDE [4], LOOM [23, 24] and KRIS [3, 2]. These formalisms are termed ***hybrid, logic-based*** formalisms or ***terminological logics*** or ***description logics.*** They vary in the subformalisms used for representing ***terminological*** knowledge, ***assertional*** knowledge, and the query language. Furthermore, the implementations of the formalisms differ in the implementation techniques and inference algorithms used.

There are two sublanguages in YAKL for representing terminological knowledge: a ***concept language*** and a ***role language.*** These are used to declare the ***vocabulary*** or ***terminology*** of the application domain. The vocabulary consists of terms that are declared by so-called ***concepts*** and ***roles.*** Concepts are used to declare objects, actions, states, etc. They have so-called ***individuals*** or ***instances*** as members. Roles are binary relations between members of certain concepts and are declared with the concepts that represent the ***domain*** of the role. A concept is interpreted as a set of individuals and a role as a set of pairs of individuals. The individuals that are members of a certain concept and the pairs of individuals that are members of a certain role are also termed the ***extension*** of the concept or role. Individuals in the range of a role are also termed ***fillers*** of the role (for a certain individual in the domain).

Concept names are declared by specifiying a concept expression that represents either a ***necessary,*** a ***necessary*** and ***sufficient,*** or a ***sufficient*** condition for an individual to be a member of the concept. Is the condition only necessary, then the concept is called ***primitive.*** Is the condition necessary and sufficient, then the concept is called ***defined.*** Is the condition ***sufficient,*** then the concept is called ***derived.*** Examples for the declarations of concepts are the following:

```
PRIM-CONCEPT Pointer-Types =
  AND(Datatypes
      EXACTLY-ONE(has-basetype)).
DEF-CONCEPT Comparators =
  AND(Subprograms
      SOME(has-purpose,Compare-Actions)).
```

They can be interpreted as follows:

- **If** an individual X is a pointer type, **then** it is a datatype and has exactly one basetype.
- **If** an individual X is a comparator, **then** X is a subprogram and has as purpose a compare action.
  If an individual X is a subprogram that has as purpose a compare action, **then** X is a comparator.

Only a necessary condition is given for the concept `Pointer-Types`. Therefore, the following conclusion is **not** valid:

- **If** an individual X is a datatype and has exactly one basetype, **then** X is a pointer type.

For example, arrays are also datatypes that have exactly one basetype. Would the conclusion be valid, then the concept `Pointer-Types` should have been declared as a defined concept.

There are three basic relationships between concepts: *subsumption, equivalence*, and *disjointness*. A concept c_1 subsumes a concept c_2, *iff* an individual that is member of c_2 is always a member of c_1, that is, the concept c_1 is a generalization of concept c_2 and c_2 is a specialization of c_1. c_1 is also called a *superconcept* or *subsumer* of c_2 and c_2 a *subconcept* or *subsumee* of c_1. Two concepts are equivalent iff they always have the same extension. Two concepts are disjoint iff their extensions are always disjoint.

The concept declarations form a *hierarchy* or *taxonomy* according to the derived subsumption relationships. This hierarchy is represented as a *directed, acyclic* graph. Nodes represent concept names and there is an arc from concept name c_1 to concept name c_2, iff c_1 is an *immediate* superconcept of c_2, that is, c_1 subsumes c_2 and there is no other concept name c such that c_1 subsumes c and c subsumes c_2. The graph represents a finite partial order and a unique basis for the subsumption relation $\preceq_{\mathcal{T}}$, that is, a minimal relation such that the reflexive and transitive closure is identical with $\preceq_{\mathcal{T}}$. For equivalent concepts, the graph contains one concept as the representative and there is a special arc from the representative to an equivalent concept and back. Derived concepts are not incorporated in the hierarchy. Their definition is only evaluated during query time and only if it is necessary.

YAKL has a number of *predefined* concepts. These are the concepts **anything**, **nothing**, **integers**, **strings** and **specifiers**. The concept **anything** is the root of the concept hierarchy and subsumes every other concept. The concept **nothing** is the only leaf of the concept hierarchy and is subsumed by every other concept. It has as members those individuals whose declarations are inconsistent and is equivalent to those concepts whose declarations are inconsistent. The concepts **integers** and **strings** represent the concrete domains of the integer numbers and the strings. The concept **specifiers** is the superconcept of concepts whose extension is fixed and whose individuals correspond to adverbs and adjectives in natural language. An example is the concept **Function-Specifiers** when modelling C++. Its extension is {**inline**, **static**, **const**}.

Assertions are simply given by indicating that an individual is a member of a concept expression *c*:

```
INSTANCE i = c.
```

The assertions in a loaded knowledge base form a so-called *world description*. The assertional language is identical to the concept language. Furthermore, the query language is identical to the concept and role language. YAKL allows concept queries as well as role queries. In concept queries, all individuals belonging to a derived concept expression are retrieved, while in role queries all pairs of individuals belonging to a role expression are retrieved.

Additional information can be associated with concept declarations, such as the declaration of roles, the declaration of default values for role fillers, and assertions about certain members of the concept that hold in all world descriptions. The declaration of roles is with the concepts that represent the domain of the role. Analogously to concepts YAKL distinguishes between *primitive*, *defined* and *derived* roles.

Furthermore, YAKS implements a number of commands. In particular there are commands for computing the concept hierarchy and determining the most specific concepts of which an individual is a member. The computation of the concept hierarchy is called *classification* and the computation of the most specific concepts of individuals is called *realization*. Classification and realization must be done before queries can be given.

A more detailed description of the YAKL formalism, how to model with YAKL, the implementation techniques used, and the inference algorithms used can be found in [1].

2.2 Implemented knowledge bases

The first software information system that has been implemented using YAKR is a cross reference tool for C++. The basis for this tool is a comprehensive YAKL model of the programming language C++ as described in [12]. The model consists of about

190 concept and 130 role declarations (including inverse roles). The model is much more detailed than the simple model of C++ used in CIA++ [16] and CODE-BASE [35]. In these tools, the model consists essentially of five concepts (entities) and four relations. Hence, our model can answer queries that cannot be answered with the simpler models.

Besides the information explicitly present in source code, other information may be useful for software developers. For example, it is useful to represent the functionality of source code components, especially those of subprograms. Therefore, we developed a classification of subprograms according to there functionality. This model consists of twelve concept declarations.

To support knowledge acquisition, a tool called CPPREF [36] has been developed. This tool scans C++ source code and feeds the C++ model with the corresponding assertions. The first domain included three classes of the NIH class library which is described in [15]. The model consists of 90 concept declarations and 971 individuals and describes cross reference information as well as information about the functionality of subprograms.

The second software information system that has been implemented using YAKR is a software library for 70 UNIX commands. The conceptual model of UNIX is much simpler than the corresponding model of C++. Most concepts are declared as simple, primitive concepts. The model consists of about 280 concept declarations, 168 role declarations and 275 individuals. The effort for creating the model was about one person month.

The UNIX commands can also be classified according to their functionality. But classifying UNIX commands is difficult and there are different classifications possible. For example concepts, such as **E-Mail-Commands**, **Text-Processing-Commands**, **Editor-Commands** are possible. **E-Mail-Commands** is declared as follows:

```
DEF-CONCEPT E-Mail-Commands =
  AND(Commands
      SOME(has-purpose, AND(Works-On-Actions
                            SOME(works-on, E-Mails)))).
```

This declaration can be interpreted as follows:

> **If** an individual X is an email command, **then** it has at least the purpose to work on emails. **If** an individual X is a command that works on emails as one of its purposes, **then** X is an email command.

We declared 28 such functionality concepts. Concepts declaring actions, as for example **Works-On-Actions** are organized into a hierarchy. This classification enables YAKRSIS to answer many different kinds of questions about an individual command by simply categorizing it in one or multiple command concepts.

3 Automatic indexing approaches

Automatic indexing systems extract terms (words) out of existing natural language documentation. Every document is represented by a ***profile*** which consists of a list of terms together with assigned weights. The weight of a term specifies how characteristic the term is for the document. A frequently used function for computing the weight ρ of a term t in document d is:

$$\rho(t,d) = tf(t,d)/df(t)$$

where $tf(t,d)$ is the frequency of occurence of term t in document d and $df(t)$ is the number of documents where term t occurs. This weighting function is usually referred to as a $tf \times idf$ (term frequency $\times$ inverse document frequency) weighting function.

In automatic indexing systems, queries may also be given as natural language text. This text is then taken as a document and indexed using the same methods as described above. The answer to such a query is then determined by computing similarity measures between the profile of the query and the profile of documents. The output are the documents that are similar to the query ranked according to degree of similarity. A simple method for determining the similarity of two documents $d1$ and $d2$ is the ***inner product***:

$$sim(d1,d2) = \sum_{t \in (T(d1) \cap T(d2))} \rho(t,d1) \times \rho(t,d2)$$

$T(d1)$ and $T(d2)$ are the terms of $d1$ and $d2$ respectively and ρ(t,d) the weight of term t in document d. Other measures, which have the advantage that the similarity values are normalized and have only values between 0 and 1, are described in [34].

The two basic measures for measuring the effectiveness of information retrieval methods are ***precision*** and ***recall***. For determining the two measures it is necessary to know the ***relevant*** documents of the queries, that is, those, that should be retrieved as the answer. Precision and recall of a query are measured as follows:

$$Precision = \frac{\text{number of retrieved relevant documents}}{\text{number of retrieved documents}}$$

$$Recall = \frac{\text{number of retrieved relevant documents}}{\text{number of totally relevant documents}}$$

Hence, the precision measures how well the system avoids to retrieve irrelevant documents and the recall measures how well the system retrieves all relevant documents.

Information retrieval systems with high precision usually have low recall and vice versa. One method to increase precision is to use phrases for indexing instead of single words. Such a method is described by Maarek et. al. ([21, 22, 20]). The phrases are termed *lexical relations* and consist of exactly two content words. The lexical relations of a document are determined by the following simple method. Each content word in a sentence is paired with each content word in the following five words to form a lexical relation. Every lexical relation is transformed into normal form by a simple morphological analysis. Nouns are transformed to singular form and verbs to infinitive. Furthermore, the two words are arranged in alphabetical order. The weight ρ of a lexical relation (t_1, t_2) for document d is determined by the following formulas:

$$\rho(t_1, t_2, d) = f(t_1, t_2, d) \times INFO(t_1, t_2)$$
$$INFO(t_1, t_2) = -log_2(P(t_1) \times P(t_2))$$

where $f(t_1, t_2, d)$ is the number of occurences of the lexical relation (t_1, t_2) in d and $P(t)$ is the probability of occurence of term t in all indexed documents. The formulas can be interpreted as follows: The more often a lexical relation appears in a document the higher its weight, and the more often a term occurs in all documents the lower the weight of a lexical relation containing that term.

In order to compare the ρ values of different documents, they are *standardized* resulting in so called ρ_z values:

$$\rho_z = (\rho - \overline{\rho})/\sigma$$

$\overline{\rho}$ is the mean and σ the standard deviation of the ρ values in a document. The sum of the ρ_z values for a document is then zero and therefore the mean also zero. Furthermore, the standard deviation is 1. Finally, only those lexical relations whose weight ρ_z is greater or equal to 1 are incorporated into the profile of a document.

Reference [22] suggests to use the same method as described before for indexing queries. But using the same method results in a problem. There are only a few lexical relations for a query and the standardized ρ_z value is lower than 1 for most lexical relations. It seems appropriate to assimilate all lexical relations of a query in the associated profile. Therefore, the profile of a query is given by the ρ values of all computed lexical relations.

The measure of similarity between the profiles of two documents d_1 and d_2 are computed with the *inner product*:

$$sim(d_1, d_2) = \sum_{t \in (T(d_1) \cap T(d_2))} (\rho(t, d_1) \times \rho(t, d_2))$$

where $T(d)$ is the profile of document d and $\rho(t, d)$ the ρ value of lexical relation t in profile $T(d)$. If this method retrieves no document, the similarity measure can be relaxed by summing over the product of the weights of lexical relations that have only one word in common.

A well known method to improve retrieval effectiveness of an information retrieval system is *relevance feedback*. This method allows the user to indicate relevant documents for an initial query and the system computes a new query profile taking into account this information. For a description of this method see [34].

4 Evaluation

4.1 Retrieval Effectiveness

For evaluating the retrieval effectiveness (precision and recall) an experiment has been performed. The basis of the experiment were 70 UNIX commands and 30 test queries. The 30 test queries were chosen by Maarek to evaluate the effectiveness of the GURU system [20]. The queries and the relevant components are shown in table 1.

The functionality of 70 UNIX commands was modelled with YAKR. The modeller didn't know the test queries nor the relevant components for these. The initial model took about one person month. The model was tested with the 30 test queries and the queries that couldn't be answered were protocolled. These queries were then given to the modeller in order to extend the model (without knowing the relevant components). Finally, the extended model was tested again. The results were as follows (see table 2):

- Initially about one fourth of the queries could be answered successfully and usually YAKR found exactly the relevant components.
- If unprocessable queries were pruned, for example by omitting certain adjectives or a part of a conjunction, the number of successfully processed queries increased from one fourth to about one half, while the system still retrieved exactly the relevant components.
- After extending the model, YAKRSIS achieved precision and recall values of nearly 1.0. The only restriction is that in two queries, due to limitations of the parser, a conjunction and a number had to be omitted.

The automatic indexing of the UNIX manual pages for the 70 commands was performed with three different tools. First the public domain software WAIS (Wide Area Information Server) of Thinking Machines Corporation was used. A detailed description of the weighting function used in WAIS is not available. However, WAIS performed poorly. For half of all the queries, there was no relevant document among the first five documents. The system retrieves on average 36 documents.

The second approach uses a non-normalized $tf \times idf$ weighting function without a threshold value, that is, all terms are used for indexing a document, even if their weights are small. As similarity measure we chose the inner product. The result was much better than for WAIS and can be summarized as follows:

Table 1: Test queries with the relevant documents

	query	relevant documents
1	locate a regular expression in a file	grep, egrep, awk
2	find lines that match a regular expression in a file	grep, egrep, awk
3	look for a pattern in a file	grep, egrep, awk
4	compare two files	diff, cmp, sccs-sccsdiff
5	join columns of two different files into a single file	join
6	delete a file	rm
7	change the permission access to a file	chmod
8	rename a directory	mv
9	overwrite a file	mv, cp
10	put a file in another directory	mv
11	get the name of the current directory	pwd
12	create a new directory	mkdir
13	change the owner of a file	chown
14	become the root user	su
15	get information about the type of a file	file
16	distinguish between ascii and binary files	file
17	change the form of a cursor	- (no relevant document)
18	copy a window under X into a file	xwd
19	make a postscript file out of an X window	xwd, xpr
20	adding a route to a routing table	route
21	turn my system off	shutdown
22	change my password	passwd
23	display when a file was last written to	ls
24	set time and date of the clock	date
25	copy a file from a remote host	rcp
26	format C source code, C programs	cb
27	stop a process	kill
28	split files according to a pattern parameter	csplit
29	send binary files via electronic mail	uuencode
30	source control	SCCS-commands

Table 2: Average precision and recall values for the different approaches

System	Precision (average)	Recall (average)
YAKRSIS (initial model)	0.9	0.3
YAKRSIS with query pruning	0.9	0.5
YAKRSIS (extended model)	1.0	1.0
$tf \times idf$	0.1	1.0
lexical relations	0.5	0.8

- The approach finds all relevant documents, that is, the recall is 1.0. It finds on average 54 documents and the maximum position of a relevant document is 11. Considering the first 11 documents per answer, the precision of the approach is about 0.1.
- For 10 queries, there was no relevant document among the two retrieved documents with the highest degree of agreement.
- No relevant document exists for query 17, but the system retrieves many documents.

The third approach uses *lexical relations* as described in section 3 for indexing. The results are:

- The average precision is 0.5 and the average recall 0.8.
- For five queries the system does not find the relevant documents and in further two cases the relevant documents were retrieved at position 5 or 11. The relaxed similarity measure for the five unsuccesful queries results in varied success. Relevant documents are at positions 1, 2, 3, 6, 7, 15 and 18. In general, many documents are retrieved using the relaxed similarity measure (on average 21) and precision decreases to about 0.06. 13 documents are retrieved for query 17, where no relevant documents exist.

4.2 Runtime Performance

The runtime performance of YAKR was measured on a SUN Sparc 2 computer (4/75 GX) with 32 MByte main memory. First we measured the speed of the main inferences: classification and realization. The user and system time was measured using the UNIX command `time` (see table 3). The average time for classification of a concept was 0.3 sec for the 190 concepts of the C++ model and 0.37 sec for the 270 concepts of the UNIX model. The realization of an individual takes 0.18 sec for the C++ plus NIH model and 0.1 sec for the UNIX model.

Note that the runtime for classification depends on the order in which the concepts are classified, as well as on the complexity of the concept declarations. Furthermore, the average runtime increases with the number of classified concepts. An empirical study of Heinsohn et. al. [17] indicate that the runtime for classification increases at least quadratically with the number of concepts. The study showed that the runtimes for different implemented terminological systems vary considerably. In one case, the runtime of one system was 1000 times slower than that of another system. In comparison to the systems tested in the study, the runtime performance of YAKS seems to be nearly as good as those of the faster ones. However, the programming language and computer plays a major role when measuring runtime, and the runtime for realization and retrieval is much more important than the runtime for classification.

Table 3: Runtime of YAKS in seconds (user time + system time) on a SUN Sparc 2 machine (4/75GX) with 32 MByte main memory

	C++ modelling	additionally NIH modelling	UNIX modelling
	190 concepts and 134 roles and 22 individuals	90 concepts and 0 roles and 971 individuals	283 concepts and 170 roles and 586 individuals
Loading	1.7	14.8	5.3
Classification	56.2	19.7	104.8
Realization	1.4	171.8	56.7

Table 4: Runtime (real time) for answering the test queries on a SUN Sparc 2 machine (4/75GX) with 32 MByte main memory

Query No.	1	2	3	4	5	6	7	8	9	10	11	12	13	14	15
Real time (sec)	7	30	10	5	5	10	43	12	10	13	235	19	55	6	155
Query No.	16	17	18	19	20	21	22	23	24	25	26	27	28	29	30
Real time (sec)	24	1	7	23	6	7	40	12	7	6	20	6	6	12	1

YAKS supports a persistent storage of inferences performed, that is, it allows to save a concept hierarchy together with the concept declarations as well as the most specific concepts of individuals together with the assertions about individuals. The runtime for classification and realization is minimal when the declarations and assertions extended with inference information have been loaded. Classification and realization then needs only about 1 sec per modelling.

The runtime for parsing and retrieval has not been measured separately. It was only measured how long parsing plus retrieval takes when asking the 30 queries given in table 1 for the UNIX model. Table 4.2 shows the results. On average, the retrieval time is about 27 sec. The retrieval time is typically short except that for some queries it is extremely high. This is due to ambiguities in caseframe parsing.

5 Conclusions

We have explored a knowledge-based approach for software information systems. It has been shown that a terminological knowledge representation system with an expressive representation language and a natural language interface is suitable for implementing software information systems:

- It allows an **adequate** description of the functionality and other kinds information about software, for example cross reference information.
- It supports knowledge acquisition through inferences like **classification, realization and inconsistency detection.**
- **Efficient, sufficiently complete** inference algorithms exist.
- Precision and recall are both **higher** than in classical information retrieval systems.

Compared to automatic indexing approaches we have the following differences:

- The effort for knowledge aquisition is much higher for the knowledge based approach although a domain specific lexicon is also necessary for automatic indexing.
- Automatic indexing requires natural language documentation. Retrieval is based on statistical agreement between words occuring in documents and queries. The knowledge based approach, however, does not require the existence of documents.
- The knowledge based approach does not allow full text as queries. However, the example queries have shown that single questions are sufficient to find the corresponding document, and there is no evidence that unlimited text is necessary. The improvement when using relevance feedback is limited since only a single document is relevant in more than two third of the queries.

We have not compared YAKRSIS to *enumerated* or *faceted* classification, such as the classification scheme of Prieto-Diaz [30, 31]. However, such a classification scheme can be easily implemented with YAKRSIS and should have the same retrieval efficiency.

Further knowledge bases and information abstractors for YAKRSIS should be implemented. For example, the domain of software configuration management could be modelled and a tool implemented that automatically extracts information out of an RCS database [39].

Another area of future work is the use of the formalism YAKL as an object-oriented design formalism. YAKL descriptions could then be transformed into C++ class descriptions. For example, the YAKL model of C++ was the basis for the design of a C++ class hierarchy as part of the implementation of CPPREF. This class hierarchy was used to store the information about the source code during processing.

Acknowledgements

Several people have made contributions to the YAKRSIS system. Walter Tichy supervised the development and suggested the experiment. Lutz Prechelt developed and implemented the parser and developed a large lexicon and a case table. The coupling of YAKS and the parser was developed together with Lutz Prechelt and Finn Dag Buo. The C++ model and the classification of subprograms were developed with the help of Matthias Ott. The NIH and UNIX model were developed by Matthias Ott. CPPREF was developed together with Tore Syvertsen.

References

[1] R. Adams. *Knowledge representation and acquisition in a natural language software information system (in German)*. PhD thesis, University of Karlsruhe, Faculty of Computer Science, November 1992.

[2] F. Baader and B. Hollunder. A terminological knowledge representation system with complete inference algorithms. In *International Workshop on Processing Declarative Knowledge*, pages 67–86. Springer-Verlag, 1991.

[3] Franz Baader and Bernhard Hollunder. KRIS: Knowledge representation and inference system. *ACM SIGART Bulletin*, 2(3):8–14, June 1991.

[4] H. Beck, S. Gala, and S. Navathe. Classification as a query processing technique in the CANDIDE semantic data model. In *International Conference on Data Engineering*, pages 572–581, 1989.

[5] A. Borgida, R. Brachman, D. McGuinness, and L. Alperin Resnick. CLASSIC: A structural data model for objects. In *ACM SIGMOD International Conference on Management of Data*, pages 59–67, 1989.

[6] R. Brachman, D. McGuinness, P. Patel-Schneider, and L. Resnick. Living with CLASSIC: When and how to use a KL-ONE like language. In John Sowa, editor, *Principles of Semantic Networks*, pages 401–456. Morgan Kaufmann Publishers, 1991.

[7] J. Browne, T. Lee, and J. Werth. Experimental evaluation of a reusability-oriented parallel programming environment. *IEEE Transactions on Software Engineering*, 16(2):111–120, February 1990.

[8] B. Burton, R. Aragon, S. Bailey, K. Koehler, and L. Mayes. The reusable software library. In *Tutorial: Software Reuse. Editor: W. Tracz.* IEEE Computer Society Press, 1988.

[9] Y.-F. Chen, M. Nishimoto, and C. Ramamoorthy. The C information abstraction system. *Communications of the ACM*, 16(3):325–334, March 1990.

[10] P. Devanbu, R. Brachman, and P. Selfridge. LaSSIE - a knowledge-based software information system. *Communications of the ACM*, 34(5):34–49, May 1991.

[11] P. T. Devanbu and D. J. Litman. Plan-based terminological reasoning. In *International Conference on Principles of Knowledge Representation and Reasoning*, pages 128–138, 1991.

[12] Margaret A. Ellis and Bjarne Stroustrup. *The Annotated C++ Reference Manual.* Addison Wesley, Reading, Mass., 1990.

[13] W. Frakes and B. Nejmeh. An information system for software reuse. In *Tutorial: Software Reuse. Editor: W. Tracz.* IEEE Computer Society Press, 1988.

[14] P. Garg and W. Scacchi. A hypertext system to manage software life-cycle documents. *IEEE Software*, pages 90–98, May 1990.

[15] Keith E. Gorlen, Sanford M. Orlow, and Perry S. Plexico. *Data Abstraction and Object-Oriented Programming in C++.* Wiley, Chichester, 1991.

[16] J. Grass and Y.-F. Chen. The C++ information abstractor. In *Usenix C++ Conference Proceedings*, pages 265–278, 1990.

[17] J. Heinsohn, D. Kudenko, B. Nebel, and H.-J. Profitlich. An empirical analysis of terminological representation systems. In *Conference of the American Association of Artificial Intelligence*, pages 767–773, 1992.

[18] R. Helm and Y. Maarek. Integrating information retrieval and domain specific approaches for browsing and retrieval in object-oriented class libraries. *ACM SIGPLAN Notices*, 26(11):47–61, November 1991.

[19] L. Latour and E. Johnson. Seer: A graphical retrieval system for reusable ada software modules. In *International IEEE Conference on Ada Applications and Environments.* IEEE Computer Society Press, 1988.

[20] Y. Maarek. Software library construction from an IR perspective. *SIGIR Forum*, 25(2):8–18, Fall 1991.

[21] Y. Maarek and F. Smadja. Full text indexing based on lexical relations. An application: Software libraries. In *Proceedings of the ACM SIGIR Conference on Research and Development in Information Retrieval*, pages 198–206, 1989.

[22] Y. S. Maarek, D. M. Berry, and G. E. Kaiser. An information retrieval approach for automatically constructing software libraries. *IEEE Transactions on Software Engineering*, 17(8):800–813, August 1991.

[23] R. MacGregor. A deductive pattern matcher. In *Conference of the American Association of Artificial Intelligence*, pages 403–408, 1988.

[24] Robert MacGregor. Inside the LOOM description classifier. *ACM SIGART Bulletin*, 2(3):88–92, June 1991.

[25] S. Meggendorfer and P. Manhart. A knowledge and deduction based software retrieval tool. In *Knowledge-Based Software Engineering Conference*, pages 127–133. IEEE Computer Society Press, 1991.

[26] P. Patel-Schneider. Small can be beautiful in knowledge representation. In *Proceedings of the IEEE Workshop on Principles of Knowledge-Based Systems*, pages 11–16. IEEE Computer Society Press, 1984.

[27] C. Peltason, A. Schmiedel, C. Kindermann, and J. Quantz. The BACK system revisited. Technical Report 75, Technische Universitaet Berlin, Fachbereich Informatik, Projektgruppe KIT, 1989.

[28] L. Prechelt. The SIS project: Software reuse with a natural language approach. Interner Bericht 2/92, University of Karlsruhe, Department of Informatics, 1992.

[29] L. Prechelt, F. D. Buo, and R. Adams. Transportable natural language interfaces for taxonomic knowledge representation systems. In *International Conference on Artificial Intelligence Applications*, 1993.

[30] R. Prieto-Diaz and G. Jones. Breathing new life into old software. In *Tutorial: Software Reuse. Editor: W. Tracz.* IEEE Computer Society Press, 1988.

[31] Ruben Prieto-Diaz and Peter Freeman. Classifying software for reusability. *IEEE Software*, 4(1):6–16, January 1987.

[32] J. Quantz and C. Kindermann. Implementation of the BACK system version 4. Technical Report 78, Technische Universitaet Berlin, Fachbereich Informatik, Projektgruppe KIT, December 1990.

[33] E. J. Rollins and J. M. Wing. Specifications as search keys for software libraries. In K. Furukawa, editor, *Proceedings of the International Conference on Logic Programming*, pages 173–187, 1991.

[34] G. Salton and M. McGill. *Introduction to Modern Information Retrieval*. McGraw-Hill Book Company, 1983.

[35] P. G. Selfridge. Knowledge representation support for a software information system. In *International Conference on Artificial Intelligence Applications*, pages 134–140. IEEE Computer Society Press, 1991.

[36] T. Syvertsen. CPPREF - an information abstractor for C++. Master's thesis, University of Karlsruhe, April 1992.

[37] W. Teitelman. *The Interlisp Reference Manual*. Xerox Palo Alto Research Center, Palo Alto, California, 1978.

[38] W. Teitelman and L. Masinter. The Interlisp programming environment. *IEEE Computer*, pages 25–33, April 1981.

[39] Walter F. Tichy. RCS — a system for version control. *Software—Practice and Experience*, 15(7):637–654, July 1985.

[40] Murray Wood and Ian Sommerville. An information retrieval system for software components. *Software Engineering Journal*, 3(5):198–207, September 1988.

Using Formal Methods to Construct a Software Component Library*

Jun-Jang Jeng and Betty H.C. Cheng

Department of Computer Science
Michigan State University
East Lansing, MI 48824, USA

Abstract. Reusing software may greatly increase the productivity of software engineers and improve the quality of developed software. Software component libraries have been suggested as a means for facilitating reuse. Using formal specifications to represent software components facilitates the determination of reusable software because they more precisely characterize the functionality of the software, and the well-defined syntax makes processing amenable to automation. This paper presents an approach, based on formal methods, to the classification and organization of reusable software components. From a set of formal specifications, a two-tiered hierarchy of software components is constructed. The formal specifications represent software that has been implemented and verified for correctness. The hierarchical organization of the software component specifications provides a means for storing, browsing, and retrieving reusable components that is amenable to automation. A prototype browser that provides a graphical framework for the classification and retrieval process is also described.

1 Introduction to Software Reuse

Software reuse has been claimed to be a means for overcoming the software crisis [1, 2, 3, 4]. However, current techniques to represent and manage software component libraries are not sufficient. Information retrieval methods based on analyses of natural-language documentation have been proposed for constructing software libraries [5, 6]. Unfortunately, software components represented by natural-language may hinder the retrieval process due to the problems of ambiguity, incompleteness, and inconsistency inherent to natural languages. All of the above mentioned problems can be minimized by using formal specifications to represent software components [7, 8, 9, 10, 11, 12, 13].

The major objective of a reuse system is to classify the reusable components and to retrieve them from an existing library [14]. Formal specifications facilitate the

* The work is supported in part by NSF grant CCR-9209873 and a Michigan State University All University Research Initiation Grant.

above tasks because they provide a precise characterization of the purpose of a piece of software and make it easier to determine the reusability of software. We present a classification scheme and algorithms for automatically constructing a hierarchy of software components that provide a means for representing, storing, browsing, and retrieving reusable components.

The hierarchical relationships of the reuse system are based on a *generality* relationship and similarities between software components. The similarities are calculated with respect to a partition of operators into equivalence classes. In order to combine these two concepts into one framework, the component library is structured as a two-tiered hierarchy in two stages. The resulting library structure consists of lower-level and higher-level hierarchies. The lower-level hierarchy is created by a *subsumption test algorithm* that determines whether one component is more general than another. Based on the *generality* relationship, the most general components are placed at the top of the hierarchy and the more detailed or restrictive components at the bottom. The higher-level hierarchy is generated by a classical *hierarchical clustering algorithm* that groups the most similar components together. The end result is a connected hierarchy of software components organized from the most general to the most specific.

The GURU project [5] automatically assembles large components by using information retrieval techniques. The construction of the library consists of two steps. First, attributes are automatically extracted from natural language documentation by using an indexing scheme. Then a hierarchy is automatically generated using a clustering technique similar to our hierarchical clustering algorithm. Their indexing scheme is based upon analysis of natural-language documentation obtained from manual pages or comments. The assumption is that natural-language documentation is a rich source of conceptual information. However, natural language is not a rigorous language to specify the behavior of software components. A formal specification language can serve as a contract, and a means of communication among a client, a specifier and an implementer [13]. Because of their mathematical basis, formal specifications are more precise and more concise than natural-language documentation.

The MAPS system [10] applies formal specifications termed *case-like expressions* to specify software modules. MAPS exploits the unification capability to search through reusable modules in the library. However, their library is not hierarchically organized, thus the search space could become very large once the number of software modules in the library increases.

The remainder of this paper is organized as follows. Section 2 describes the notation used in the specification of software components. Section 3 describes the subsumption test algorithm. The hierarchical clustering algorithm is described in Section 4. Section 5 describes searching techniques for reusable components in the two-tiered hierarchy. Section 6 describes the implementation of a browser that handles the construction of a two-tiered hierarchy and the search and retrieval of reusable components. Finally, Section 7 summarizes this work and discusses future investigations.

2 Specification of Software Components

In this project, predicate logic is used to specify software components. Most software is made up of procedural and data abstractions, that is, procedures and user-specified and system-defined data structures [15]. Object-oriented analysis can be used to decompose complex software, which involves defining a set of user-specified data abstractions or *abstract data types* (ADTs) [16, 17, 18, 19, 20, 21]. Thus, in order to apply an object-oriented approach to software reuse, this project focuses on data abstraction, where it is assumed that procedural abstractions are implicitly addressed when discussing the operations that are applicable to the data abstractions. The specification for a software component corresponds to the specification of an abstract data type and a set of methods that operate on that abstract data type. Each method is specified by an *interface*, *type declarations*, a *precondition*, and a *postcondition*. The interface of a method describes the syntactic specification of the method. The typing information describes the types of input and output parameters and internal (local) variables. The precondition describes the condition of the variables prior to the execution of the method whose behavior is described by the postcondition [22]. Currently, program *invariants* are not used in the construction and retrieval processes, with the understanding that the software components being handled are simple enough such that the invariants can easily be derived.

Figure 1 gives the grammar of the specification language. In this grammar, symbols expressed in the roman font represent non-terminals, italicized symbols represent terminals, bold-faced symbols denote keywords, the Kleene star (*) denotes zero or more repetitions of the preceding unit, and parentheses ('()') indicate groupings. The symbol '::' separates an identifier from a description of the *value* denoted by the identifier, and the symbol ':' separates identifier declarations from a description of the *type* associated with the identifier. The boolean operators obey the following decreasing precedence order: negation ($\neg$), conjunction ($\wedge$), disjunction ($\vee$), implication ($\Rightarrow$), and if and only if ($\Leftrightarrow$). Primitive types, including *Bool*, *Int*, and *Real*, are pre-defined and can be referenced by the users.

Figure 2 shows an example specification of the abstract data type *Array*, which has been stored as a software component. Three methods are defined on *Array*: *assign_element*, *sort*, and *last_element*. The lines beginning with *in*, *out*, and *local* describe the types of input parameters, output parameters, and internal (local) variables, respectively (comments are delimited by %). In a software component specification, it is possible to give polymorphic definitions [23], that is, an operation may have more than one meaning. For example, the method *last_element* of *Array* is defined as a polymorphic function that returns the last element of an array, where element can be of any type. The bars || || at the beginning of the definition introduce a generically typed variable E, which indicates that the type of variable E is irrelevant.

3 Lower-Level Hierarchy

The objective of this project is to construct a hierarchical organization of reusable components that will provide a fast means for browsing, retrieving, and searching of software components exploiting the automated reasoning techniques applicable to

component = **type** type_name: (*method*)*
method = **method** method_name
sort: (type_name)* → (type_name)* **is**
in((variable: type_name)*)
local((variable: type_name)*)
out((variable: type_name)*)
{ **pre**: *expression* }
{ **post**: *expression* }
expression = true
| false
| (*expression*)
| ¬ *expression*
| *expression* ∧ *expression*
| *expression* ∨ *expression*
| *expression* ⇒ *expression*
| *expression* ⇔ *expression*
| (∀ variable : type :: *expression*)
| (∃ variable : type :: *expression*)
| predicate_name [(*term* (, *term*)*)]
| *term* $\stackrel{\text{def}}{=}$ *expression*

term = variable
| function_name [(*term* (, *term*)*)]

Fig. 1. Grammar for software component specifications

predicate logic specifications. The lower-level hierarchy provides a means for a fine-grained, precise determination of reuse, where logical reasoning can be applied to the specifications. The construction of the lower-level hierarchy serves to classify a set of software components according to the subsumption relationship between reusable components, where, in simple terms, component A is said to subsume component B if A is more *general* than B, denoted by $A \sqsupseteq_{comp} B$. A new resolution rule is described that increases the range of candidates, as compared to the number of exact matches, that can be retrieved using automated reasoning techniques.

Component A is *more general* than component B ($A \sqsupseteq_{comp} B$) if, for every method (operation) f in component A, there exists at least one method f' in component B such that f is more general than f', denoted by $f \sqsupseteq_{method} f'$. Method f is said to be more general than another method f' if $pre(f') \sqsupseteq pre(f)$ and $post(f) \sqsupseteq post(f')$, where $pre(f)$ and $post(f)$ represent the pre- and postconditions of f, respectively. The *subsumption* relationship between clauses ($\sqsupseteq$), methods ($\sqsupseteq_{method}$), and components ($A \sqsupseteq_{comp} B$) is further explained in the following section. If component A is more general than component B, then B is said to be a *child* of A and A is a *parent* of B. The pre- and postconditions for a method of a given component are expressed in *disjunctive normal form* (DNF). Therefore, in order to determine which method is more general is to determine which method contains more

type Array:

method ||E|| assign_element: Array × $E \rightarrow$ Array **is**
in(s: Array, e: E)
local()
out(s': Array)
{ **pre**: true }
{ **post**: $len(s') = len(s) + 1 \wedge s'(len(s')) = e$
% len: index of the last element in array with a value
}

method sort: Array $\rightarrow$ Array **is**
in(s: Array)
local(i, j, min, max: Int)
out(s': Array)
{ **pre**: true }
{ **post**: s' = permutation(s) $\wedge$
$(\forall\ i : \text{min} \leq \text{i} \leq \text{max} :: (\forall\ \text{j} : \text{min} \leq j < i :: s'(j) \leq s'(i)))$
}

method ||E|| last_element: Array $\rightarrow E$ **is**
in(s: Array)
local()
out(e: E)
{ **pre**: $len(s) \neq 0$ }
{ **post**: last_element(s) $\stackrel{\text{def}}{=} s(len(s))$
}

Fig. 2. Specification of software component *Array*

general postconditions, that is, weaker requirements. Section 3.2 gives an algorithm that builds the lower-level hierarchy based on the *generality* relationship between components ($\sqsupseteq_{comp}$).

An abstract data type (ADT), is a behavioral notion and may be implemented by many different classes. A class is a program module that implements an abstract data type. A subtype is also an ADT, each of whose objects behave in a way similar to objects of its supertypes. A subclass is an implementation that is derived by inheritance from its superclass. A subtype represents a behavioral relationship. When a subtype is derived from some supertype, the object's behavior with this subtype can be verified according to the objects with its supertype instead of reverifying this subtype. In contrast, a subclass relationship is a purely implementation relationship. In the C++ language, the subclass relationship is implementation-specific and cannot represent the true supertype-subtype relationship. The *generality* relationship in our system is similar to the *supertype-subtype* relationship.

3.1 Determining generality relationship between two components

Chang and Lee's subsumption test algorithm [24] is used to decide the *subsumption* relationship between clauses, that is, whether clause A subsumes clause B, denoted by $A \sqsupseteq B$. In this algorithm, the traditional resolution strategy [25] (shown in Figure 3) is exploited to compute the resolvents of two clauses, say C_1 and C_2. Atom L is said to be *congruent* to atom L', denoted by $L \simeq L'$, when both L and

$$\frac{\begin{array}{l} C_1\colon L, K_1, ..., K_n \\ C_2\colon \neg L, M_1, ..., M_m \end{array}}{\text{resolvent: } K_1, ..., K_n, M_1, ..., M_m.}$$

Fig. 3. Resolution Rule

L' are in an equivalence class partition *eq_class* that may be defined by the user or the system (see Section 4.1 for further details). Following the approach of the resolution rule, if a *congruity* relationship exists between L and L', then L and $\neg L'$ can be eliminated in order to obtain a *c-resolvent*, a resolvent with respect to the congruity relationship. As a result, a modified resolution rule given in Figure 4 is derived, where σ is a *substitution* that maps variables to terms.

$$\frac{\begin{array}{ll} C_1\colon L, K_1, ..., K_n & \\ C_2\colon \neg L', M_1, ..., M_m & L\sigma \simeq L'\sigma \end{array}}{\text{resolvent: } K_1\sigma, ..., K_n\sigma, M_1\sigma, ..., M_m\sigma.}$$

Fig. 4. Modified Resolution Rule

Using the modified resolution rule, the subsumption test algorithm [24] is modified to find the *c-resolvent* of two clauses C_1 and C_2 rather than their resolvent. The modified subsumption test (MST) algorithm can be applied to every pair of methods of the two components being compared in order to determine the *generality* relationship between two components. The MST algorithm between two sets of methods is shown in Figure 5, where $methods_A$ ($methods_B$) is the set containing the methods of the component $Comp_A$ ($Comp_B$). The cardinality of $methods_A$ ($methods_B$) is m (n).

3.2 Algorithms for Building the Lower-level Hierarchy

Based on Algorithm 1, the *generality* relationship can be determined between any pair of components in order to build the lower-level hierarchy. The straightforward approach is to construct the lower-level hierarchy by performing a pair-wise comparison between all components. The pair-wise comparison algorithm is shown in

Algorithm 1 *More_General_Component*

Input: *Two sets* $methods_A = \{A_1, A_2, ..., A_m\}$ *and* $methods_B = \{B_1, B_2, ..., B_n\}$.
Output: *The* generality *relationship between components* $Comp_A$ *and* $Comp_B$.
Procedure:

```
begin
  find ← true;
  while methods_A ≠ {} and find = true do
        select some A_i ∈ methods_A;
        methods_A ← methods_A \ A_i;
        set_B ← methods_B;
        find ← false;
        while set_B ≠ {} and find = false do
              select some B_j ∈ set_B:
              set_B ← set_B \ B_j;
              if A_i ⊒_method B_j
              then find ← true;
        endwhile;
  endwhile;
  if find = false
  then return("¬(Comp_A ⊒_comp Comp_B)");
  else return("Comp_A ⊒_comp Comp_B");
end.
```

Fig. 5. Using MST to decide the *generality* relationship between components $Comp_A$ and $Comp_B$.

Figure 6. However, the transitivity property of the *generality* relationship can be exploited in order to reduce the computational complexity of building the lower-level hierarchy. If $A \sqsupseteq B$ and $B \sqsupseteq C$ then the relation $A \sqsupseteq C$ is automatically established without having to compare components A and C. A few definitions are given before presenting the improved algorithm. For some *set of lattices* (SOL) Ψ, the set of top nodes in Ψ is denoted by $Top(\Psi)$ and the set of bottom nodes by $Bottom(\Psi)$. If node α has no parent nodes in the SOL Ψ, then $\alpha \in Top(\Psi)$. Similarly, if α has no children nodes in the SOL Ψ, then $\alpha \in Bottom(\Psi)$. The internal nodes in Ψ are defined as $Internal(\Psi) = \Psi \setminus (Top(\Psi) \cup Bottom(\Psi))$, where '\' represents set subtraction. For some node $\alpha \in \Psi$, the set of parent nodes of α is denoted by $parent(\alpha)$ and the set of children nodes by $child(\alpha)$. The set of the descendants of α, denoted by $descendant(\alpha)$, is defined as follows:

$$\beta \in descendant(\alpha) \Leftrightarrow ((\beta \in child(\alpha)) \vee (\exists\gamma : \gamma \in child(\alpha) : \beta \in descendant(\gamma))$$

The set of the ancestors of α, denoted by $ancestor(\alpha)$, has a similar definition. A parallel algorithm to build the lower-level hierarchy based on recursive comparisons and the generality relationship is given in Figure 7. A pictorial representation of an example construction of the lower-level hierarchy by procedure *Recursive_Comparison* is shown in Figure 8, where dashed lines represent the application of the procedure

Algorithm 2 *Pairwise_Comparison*

Input: *A set of components* $SET = \{C_1, C_2, ..., C_n\}$.
Output: *A hierarchy of components based on the generality relationship.*
Procedure:

```
begin
  while SET ≠ {}
        select some component C_i ∈ SET;
        SET ← SET \ C_i;
        set ← SET;
        while set ≠ {}
              select some C_j ∈ set;
              set ← set \ C_j;
              if C_i ⊒_comp C_j
              /* More_General_Component algorithm will be used to compare C_i and C_j */
              then make C_i a parent of C_j
              else if C_j ⊒_comp C_i
                   then make C_j a parent of C_i
                   endif
              endif
        endwhile;
  endwhile;
end.
```

Fig. 6. Building the lower-level hierarchy by pair-wise comparison.

Recursive_Comparison, solid lines represent the *generality* relationship, and the dotted lines encapsulate SOLs. Initially, the example contains eight SOLs and each SOL contains only one component. These eight SOLs are merged into one SOL after applying the two procedures *Compare* and *Merge*.

$Compare(\Psi_i, \Psi_j)$ determines the generality relationship between nodes in SOLs Ψ_i and Ψ_j by using a recursive approach. For example, if some node α is more general than some top node β of Ψ, then it is not necessary to compare α with the descendants of β. However, if some top node β is more general than α then the comparison between α and the descendants of β is required. The same reasoning can be applied to the comparison between α and the bottom nodes of the SOL Ψ. The procedure $Merge(\Psi_i, \Psi_j)$ "connects" the newly generated *generality* relationship between SOLs Ψ_i and Ψ_j to form a new SOL. *Recursive_Comparison* can be implemented as a parallel algorithm since the comparisons between the SOLs are independent of each other. Only the nodes in *Top* and *Bottom* sets are compared in the procedure *Compare*.

Applying algorithm $Compare(SOL_A, SOL_B)$ to two SOLs SOL_A and SOL_B is illustrated in Figure 9. For discussion purposes, attention is focused on the top node E in SOL_A and the bottom node F in SOL_B. If $F \sqsupseteq E$, then make node F a parent of node E since all nodes in $ancestor(F) \cup \{F\}$ must subsume the nodes in $descendant(E) \cup \{E\}$. However, if $E \sqsupseteq F$, then node E needs to be compared

Algorithm 3 *Recursive_Comparison*

Input: *A set* $\{\Psi_0, \Psi_1, ..., \Psi_{n-1}\}$, *where* Ψ_i *represents a set of lattices and assume* $n = 2^m$. *Initially,* $\Psi_i = \{C_i\}$ *where* C_i *is a component.*

Output: Ψ_0 *contains a hierarchy of components based on the generality relationship.*

Procedure:

```
begin
  for i := 0 to m-1 do
      d ← 2^i;
      do all Ψ_k where 0 ≤ k ≤ 2^m − 1     /* Parallel execution of all iterations */
          if k mod 2^(i+1) = 0
          then
              Compare(Ψ_k, Ψ_(k+d));
              Ψ_k ← Merge(Ψ_k, Ψ_(k+d));
          endif;
      end_do_all;
  endfor;
end.
```

Fig. 7. Building lower-level hierarchy by recursive comparison.

with the nodes in *ancestor*(F) and node F needs to be compared with the nodes in *descendant*(E) in order to obtain complete *generality* relationships. Using the recursive method to build the lower-level hierarchy may reduce the computational time of construction since the comparisons of the internal nodes in the SOL can be eliminated.

4 Higher-Level Hierarchy

After applying the MST, the software components may be grouped into disjoint clusters in a set of graphs (ASG). In order to form a connected hierarchy of software components, a conventional clustering algorithm [26] is applied to the most general components obtained from the MST, that is, the roots of trees and the top elements of the lattices in ASG.

Classification by clustering techniques has been used in many areas of research, including information retrieval and image processing [27]. Typically, the objective of clustering is to form a set of clusters such that the intercluster similarity is low, and the intracluster similarity is high. Applying a clustering algorithm to the most general components of the lower-level hierarchy leads to the generation of the higher-level hierarchy of the component library. The similarity between two components X and X', denoted by $s(X, X')$, is used as the basic criterion to determine clusters. In general, the criterion used to evaluate similarity determines the shape of the resultant clusters.

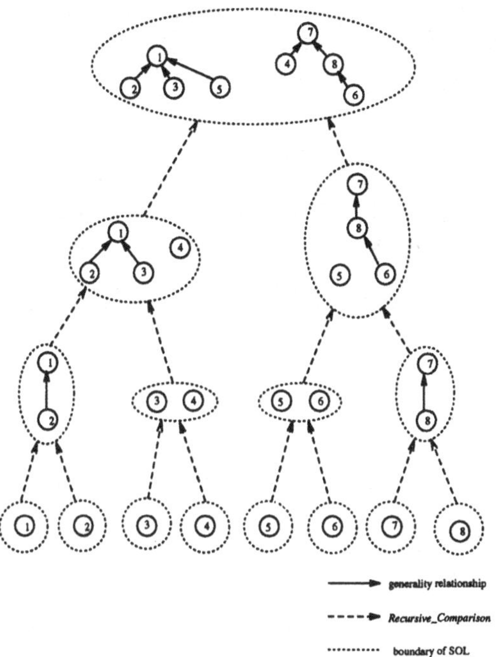

Fig. 8. Example of building hierarchy by recursive comparison.

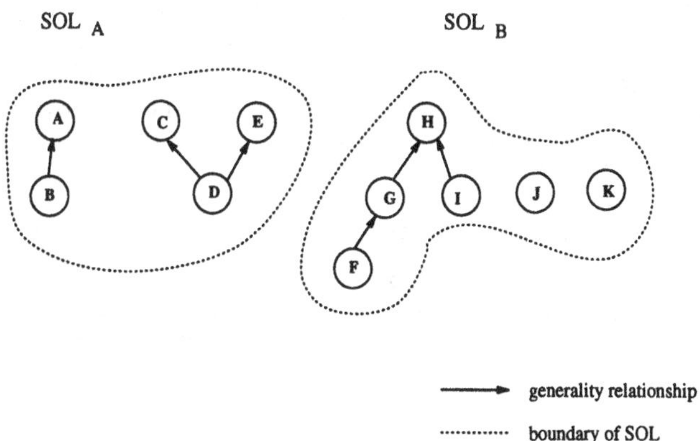

Fig. 9. Example of comparing two SOLs.

4.1 Measure of Similarity between Components

In this section, a simple evaluation method for computing similarity is given. The similarity between a pair of components, X and Y, is denoted by $s(X,Y)$. Similarity is symmetric, thus for any two components, X and Y:

$$s(X,Y) = s(Y,X).$$

In addition, similarity s is said to be normalized if $0 \leq s(X,Y) \leq 1$. Each predicate formula in the library expressed in DNF represents a software component and is regarded as one of the input objects that are to be classified by the hierarchical clustering algorithm.

If $s(X,Y)$ represents the similarity between two software components X and Y, then it is assumed that X and Y are of the following forms.

$$X = x_1 \vee x_2 \vee \ldots \vee x_m \text{ and}$$
$$Y = y_1 \vee y_2 \vee \ldots \vee y_n.$$

The disjuncts x_i and y_i are defined in terms of conjuncts, that is,

$$x_i = p_{i_1} \wedge p_{i_2} \wedge \ldots \wedge p_{i_{u_i}}, \quad 1 \leq i \leq m \quad \text{and}$$
$$y_i = q_{i_1} \wedge q_{i_2} \wedge \ldots \wedge q_{i_{v_i}}, \quad 1 \leq i \leq n,$$

where u_i and v_i are the number of conjuncts within disjunct x_i and y_i, respectively.

The disjuncts of each object are ordered from left to right in a nondecreasing order according to the number of conjuncts in each disjunct. Given that u_i and v_i represent the number of conjuncts for disjuncts x_i and y_i, respectively, the following inequalities are *true*: $u_{i-1} \leq u_i$ and $v_{i-1} \leq v_i$, for all i. Moreover, each conjunct p_{i_k} is associated with an equivalence class **eq_class**. For example, if $p_{i_k} = greater(a,b)$ and *greater* is in the equivalence class for *comparison*, then $\textbf{eq\_class}(p_{i_k}) = comparison$. The equivalence classes may be specified by the users or be system-defined.

The number of equivalence classes in a software component library is assumed to be a known value, say T. Using the above definitions, a matrix $X_{m\times(T+1)}$ is constructed for every component X. The matrix $X_{m\times(T+1)}$ derived from component X has m rows and T+1 columns. $X(i,j)$ represents the entry in row i and column j. Row i represents the ith disjunct of X as follows, where there are u_i conjuncts in disjunct x_i.

$$X(i,0) = u_i, \quad 0 \leq i \leq m-1 \text{ and}$$
$$X(i,j) = l, \quad x_i \textit{ has } l \textit{ terms in eq\_class } j.$$

Similarly, for component Y containing v_i conjuncts in disjunct y_i, the corresponding matrix is defined by

$$Y(i,0) = v_i, \quad 0 \leq i \leq n-1 \text{ and}$$
$$Y(i,j) = l, \quad y_i \textit{ has } l \textit{ terms in eq\_class } j.$$

From the derived matrices $X_{m\times(T+1)}$ and $Y_{n\times(T+1)}$, the *similarity matrix* $s'_{m\times n}$ is constructed. The following expression defines $s'_{m\times n}$.

$$\begin{aligned} &for\ all\ i,j\quad if\quad X(i,0)=Y(j,0)\\ &\qquad then\quad s'(i,j)=\frac{\sum_{t=1}^{T}2*min(X(i,t),Y(j,t))}{\sum_{t=1}^{T}(X(i,t)+Y(j,t))}\\ &\qquad else\quad s'(i,j)=0 \end{aligned} \tag{1}$$

where $s'(i,j)$ is the similarity of the ith disjunct of X and the jth disjunct of Y. The similarity between two conjunctive expressions from two software components is calculated according to the minimum number of common occurrences of a given equivalence class. Since the results from the clustering process are purely based on syntactic similarities, only the disjuncts with the same number of conjuncts are selected for comparison. The semantic similarities are used in the construction of the lower-level hierarchy. Assume N is the number of nonzero entries in $s'_{m\times n}$. The similarity between software components X and Y is calculated as follows:

$$s(X,Y)=\frac{\sum_{i=1}^{m}\sum_{j=1}^{n}s'(i,j)}{N}. \tag{2}$$

Here, $s(X,Y)$ is a normalized similarity since $0\leq s(X,Y)\leq 1$. The following example is presented for clarification purposes.

Example 1. Suppose the similarity of two components X and Y is to be computed, where both specifications are in DNF. Let $X=(C_1\wedge C_2)\vee(C_2\wedge C_3\wedge C_3)\vee(C_3\wedge C_4\wedge C_5)$ and $Y=(C_3)\vee(C_2\wedge C_3)\vee(C_3\wedge C_3\wedge C_5)\vee(C_2\wedge C_5\wedge C_5)$, where C_i refers to the term that corresponds to the ith equivalence class. There are 5 equivalence classes in this case, so $T=5$. X has 3 disjuncts and Y has 4 disjuncts. The corresponding matrices for X and Y are shown in Figures 10a and 10b, where the vertical axis represents the disjuncts in each component and the horizontal axis refers to the equivalence classes. From Formula (1), the similarity matrix $s'(X,Y)$ can be computed yielding results shown in Figure 10c, where the vertical axis represents the disjuncts in component X and the horizontal axis refers to the disjuncts in the Y component. From Formula (2), the similarity $s(X,Y)=\frac{2/4+4/6+2/6+4/6+2/6}{5}=\frac{1}{2}$ is obtained. This value is used as input to the clustering algorithm when determining which software components should be merged into one cluster.

4.2 Hierarchical Clustering

Input to a clustering algorithm is a set of components and the similarity values between each pair of components. A finite set of components is denoted by $X=\{x_1,x_2,...,x_n\}$. Output from the clustering algorithm is a partition $\Gamma=\{G_1,G_2,...,G_N\}$, where $G_k, k=1,...,N$ is a subset of X such that

$$G_1\cup G_2\cup\ldots\cup G_N=X,\qquad \forall\, l,k,l\neq k,\ G_l\cap G_k=\emptyset, \tag{3}$$

and $G_1,G_2,...,G_N$ are the clusters of Γ.

(a) Matrix for X

	0	1	2	3	4	5
1	2	1	1	0	0	0
2	3	0	1	2	0	0
3	3	0	0	1	1	1

(b) Matrix for Y

	0	1	2	3	4	5
1	1	0	0	1	0	0
2	2	0	1	1	0	0
3	3	0	0	2	0	1
4	3	0	1	0	0	2

(c) $s'(X,Y)$

	1	2	3	4
1	0	2/4	0	0
2	0	0	4/6	2/6
3	0	0	4/6	3/6

Fig. 10. Matrices for components X, Y, and $s'(X,Y)$, respectively

The relationship between the partition of clusters generated from the intermediate stages of refinement, denoted by Γ^i, $i = 1, ..., K$, is expressed as follows:

$$\Gamma^i = \{G_1^i, ..., G_{N_i}^i\}, \quad \Gamma^j = \{G_1^j, ..., G_{N_j}^j\}, \qquad i = 1, ...K, \; i < j < K+1, \qquad (4)$$

where for all l, $N_l \geq N$, and N is the final number of partitions. Γ^j is a refinement of Γ^i, $i < j$, that is, for any member subset $G_k^i \in \Gamma^i$, there exists $G_l^j \in \Gamma^j$ such that $G_k^i \subseteq G_l^j$. Such groups formed by intermediate partitions yield a hierarchy of clusters. A method for generating such a hierarchy is termed *hierarchical clustering* [26].

In general, hierarchical clustering algorithms are divided into two categories: *divisive* algorithms and *agglomerative* algorithms. A divisive algorithm starts with the set X and divides it into a partition $\Gamma^K = \{G_1^K, ..., G_{N_K}^K\}$, then each cluster G_i^K is subdivided to form a finer partition Γ^{K-1}, and so on. An agglomerative algorithm initially regards each component as a single cluster: $\Gamma^1 = \{\{x_1\}, \{x_2\}, ..., \{x_n\}\}$. The clusters are merged into a coarser partition Γ^2, and the merging process continues until the trivial partition $\Gamma^K = \{X\}$ is obtained. Thus an agglomerative clustering algorithm generates a sequence of partitions $\Gamma^1 \rightarrow \Gamma^2 \rightarrow ...\Gamma^K$ that is ordered from a finer partition to a coarser one. This algorithm can be stopped at any partition $\Gamma^l, 1 \leq l \leq K$, if the maximum value of computed similarities is below a specified threshold or if the number of clusters generated for a partition is equal to a user-specified or system-defined value.

In most agglomerative algorithms, only one pair of clusters is merged at a time. Hence if $\Gamma^i = \{G_1^i, ..., G_{N_i}^i\}$ and $\Gamma^{i+1} = \{G_1^{i+1}, ..., G_{N_{i+1}}^{i+1}\}$, then $N_{i+1} = N_i - 1$. That is, $N_i = n - i + 1, i = 1, ..., n$ and $\Gamma^1 = \{\{x_1\}, \{x_2\}, ..., \{x_n\}\}, \Gamma^N = \{X\}$. Figure 11 gives a pictorial representation of the refinement process. Similarity between clusters is used as the criterion for the selection of a pair of clusters in Γ^i that are to be merged. A pair of clusters (G_p, G_q) is selected to be merged if it has the maximum value of similarity among all pairs of clusters. Let the current partition be $\Gamma = \{G_1, ..., G_N\}$. The similarity value between two clusters is the maximum value of all similarities calculated between disjuncts from the respective components.

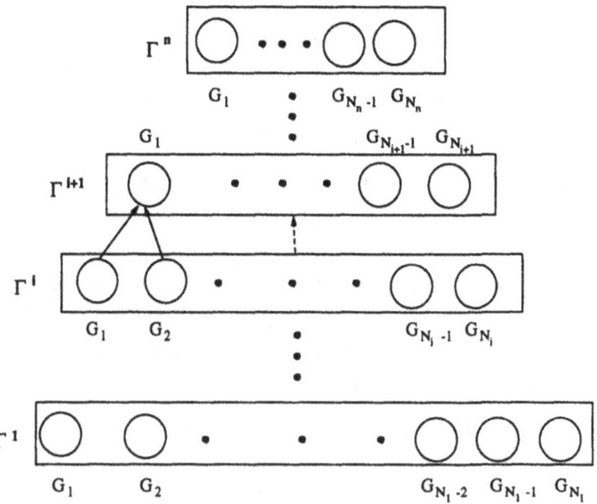

Fig. 11. Refinement of partitions in an agglomerative clustering algorithm

Formally, the *sim* relationship is expressed as

$$sim(G_p, G_q) = \max_{G_p, G_q \in \Gamma_{n-N}} \left(\max_{X \in G_p, Y \in G_q} s(X, Y) \right).$$

An agglomerative procedure is given in Figure 12. The similarities between the

Algorithm 4 *Agglomerative Clustering*

Input: *A set of disjoint lattices.*
Output: *A unified cluster.*
Procedure:

1. *Let each root of a tree or the top element of a lattice of the* ASG *be an initial cluster consisting of the single element.*
2. *Find the pair of clusters that has the maximum value of similarity among all pairs of clusters.*
3. *Merge the pair of clusters found in step 2 into a new cluster.*
4. *If there is only one cluster remaining, then stop. Otherwise, update similarity values between clusters; go back to step 2.*

Fig. 12. Agglomerative Hierarchical Clustering Algorithm

new cluster and other clusters are computed as follows: if G_p and G_q are merged into a new cluster G_r, then

$$\forall i,\ sim(G_r, G_i) = min(sim(G_p, G_i), sim(G_q, G_i)).$$

4.3 Hierarchical Clustering Algorithm

The hierarchical clustering algorithm used is similar to Kruskal's algorithm for finding a minimal spanning tree [28], which always chooses an edge with the least weight in the construction of the spanning tree. In this case, weights are replaced by similarity values for software components and the maximal weight rather than the least weight is sought. After applying the algorithm, a tree-like hierarchical clustering is obtained. Figure 13 contains the detailed description of the hierarchical clustering algorithm where X is the set of predicate

components, $s(X_i, X_j)$ is the similarity between components X_i and X_j, and $sim(G_k, G_l)$ is the similarity between clusters G_k and G_l. The algorithm begins by creating a cluster for each software component to be classified, that is, the most general components found in the lower-level hierarchy, and the first partition contains all of the initial clusters. Next, a pairwise calculation of similarity between the clusters is made. Based on the similarity values, two clusters yielding the greatest value are selected to be merged. After the two clusters are merged, the similarity values between clusters is updated, thus defining the partition for the next iteration of the clustering algorithm. The user may specify an upper bound on the number of iterations (refinements) or stop the clustering algorithm while viewing the clustering process. This flexibility allows the user to incorporate background experience in order to determine when further refinements will fail to yield substantial changes between partitions. The final hierarchically organized library could be of the form given in Figure 14, where filled nodes, termed *real nodes*, represent software components and unfilled nodes are newly generated nodes created by the hierarchical clustering algorithm, called *meta-nodes*. A meta-node acts as a container for the software components from it which it was derived. Dashed lines represent relationships formed by the MST algorithm and the solid lines are formed by the hierarchical clustering algorithm representing similarity relationships.

5 Search for Reusable Candidates

The construction of the hierarchy is performed in two stages, beginning with the lower-level, the results of which are used in the construction of the higher-level. In contrast, the search and retrieval process proceeds from the higher-level hierarchy to the lower-level one, that is, from a coarse-grained search to a fine-grained one for reusable candidates. At the higher-level hierarchy, a query is mapped to some index that indicates the starting nodes within the hierarchy at which the searching algorithm is to begin. After performing the coarse-grained search, the search space may be greatly reduced. The remaining portion of the higher-level hierarchy and the corresponding lower-level is searched using formal reasoning techniques, thus providing an exact determination method. Three possible classes of existing specifications may be retrieved using logic reasoning techniques: an exact match to the new specification, a component more general than the current specification, or a

Algorithm 5 *Hierarchical Agglomerative Algorithm*

Input: *The set* $X = \{x_1, x_2, ..., x_n\}$ *and the similarities* $s(x_i, x_j)$, $1 \leq i, j \leq n$.
Output: *one or more clusters.*
Procedure:

```
begin
        N = n;
        for i = 1,...,N do
                G_i = {x_i}
        endfor;
        Γ_1 = {G_1, G_2, ..., G_N};
        Limit = 1;
        for 1 ≤ i,j ≤ N, i ≠ j do
                sim(G_i, G_j) = s(x_i, x_j)
        endfor; /* Initialization */

        /* If there is more than one cluster then iterate, otherwise stop. */
        while (N > Limit) do
                N = N − 1;
                /* Select the pair of clusters to be merged */
                find a pair of clusters G_p and G_q such that
                        sim(G_p, G_q) = max_{G_i,G_j ∈ Γ_{n−N}, i≠j} sim(G_i, G_j)
                                      = max_{G_i,G_j ∈ Γ_{n−N}, i≠j} max_{x∈G_i, y∈G_j} s(x, y);
                G_r = G_p ∪ G_q;
                Γ_{n−N+1} = (Γ_{n−N} − {G_p, G_q}) ∪ {G_r}
                /* Update the similarity values */
                for all G_i ∈ Γ_{n−N+1}, G_i ≠ G_r, do
                        calculate sim(G_r, G_i) = max_{x∈G_r, y∈G_i} s(x, y)
                endfor;
                Limit = query_user_for_number_of_clusters;
                /* Query user for a limit on the number of generated clusters*/
        endwhile;
        return Γ_{n−N+1}
end.
```

Fig. 13. Hierarchical Clustering Algorithm

component more specific than the current specification. At any time, the user may opt to manually browse through the hierarchically organized specifications applying domain-specific knowledge to further the search process. Further search mechanisms in the hierarchy are currently under investigation.

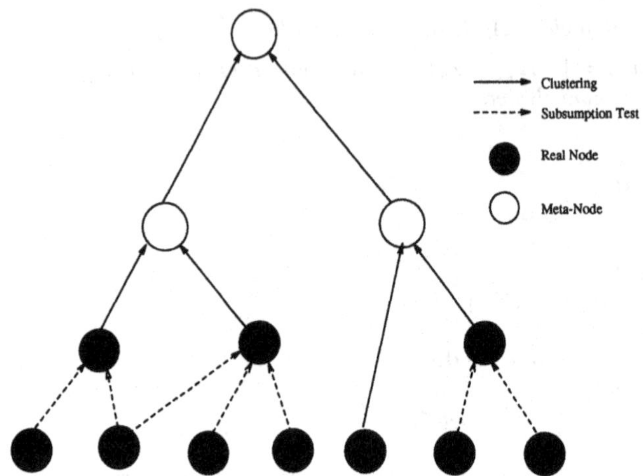

Fig. 14. Two-tiered hierarchy formed by the subsumption test and the clustering algorithms

6 Graphical Browser

A prototype browser that provides a graphical framework for the algorithms has been developed in the Quintus ProWindows language[2] a dialect of Prolog that supports the object-oriented organization of graphical elements [29]. The browser enables a user to graphically traverse the hierarchically organized specifications of software components. By making information about class hierarchies and method specifications more accessible, the browser facilitates the iterative process of developing and accessing reusable specifications.

Figure 15 contains an example application of the *Subsumption* option, where the original set of fifteen components in the library have been organized into four clusters shown in the four subwindows, respectively. The arrows indicate specific-to-general relationships. Figure 16 shows the results of the clustering algorithm, where the components *class1*, *class2*, and *class3* represent newly-created *meta-nodes*. Upon completion of the construction process, the user may choose to rename meta-nodes (e.g. *class1* and *class2*) to more descriptive names.

In searching for a reusable candidate, the user may select the node to begin the search, or the system will select the root node based on the syntactical components of the query. Figure 19a shows the state of the hierarchy before the search, where the user requests the search to begin at node *class2* as shown by the position of the doubly-nested menus containing the search option. Figure 19b shows the result of a search for an exact match among the software components, where the path of the

[2] A product of Quintus Computer Systems, Inc.

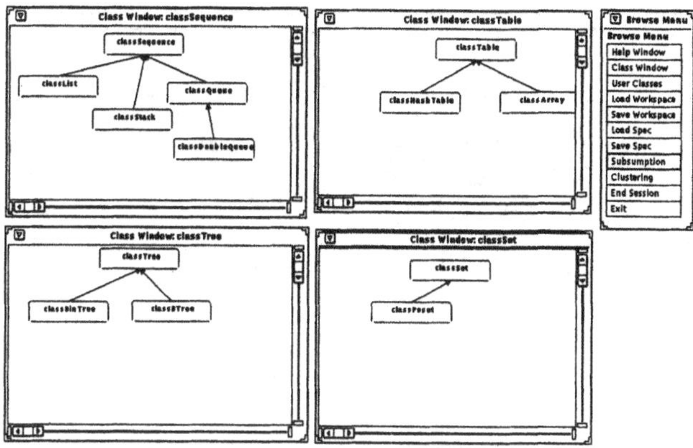

Fig. 15. Sample application of subsumption test algorithm

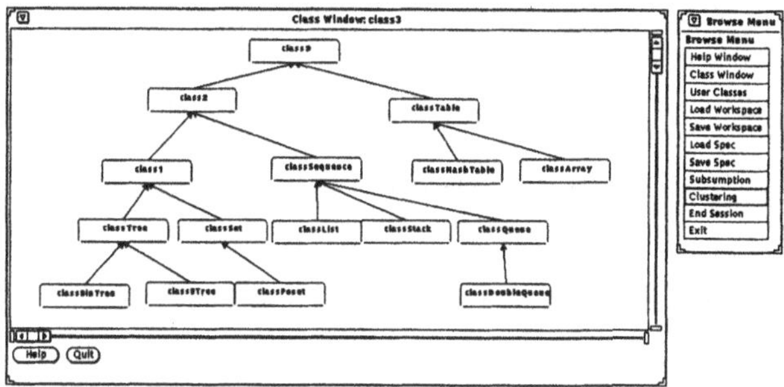

Fig. 16. Sample application of clustering algorithm

search is indicated by the highlighted nodes. In addition, the respective specifications of operations of the highlighted nodes may be displayed.

7 Conclusion

A classification scheme of software components expressed in first-order logic specifications has been presented in this paper. We have also described algorithms for implementing this scheme. The algorithms, implemented in Prolog, are able to construct a two-tiered hierarchical library from formal specifications. Thus, the hierarchy

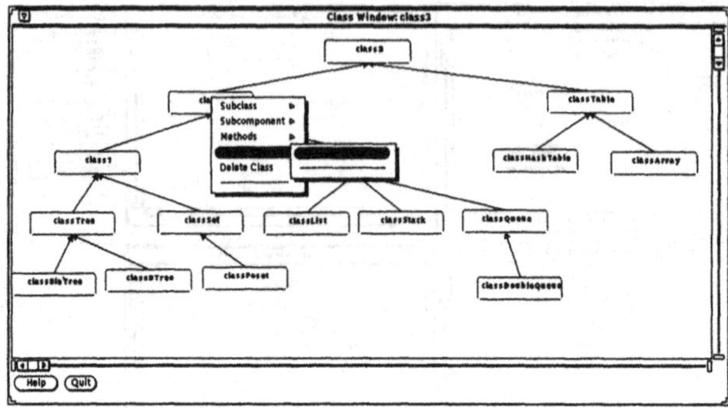

Fig. 19a. Hierarchy of components before invoking search routine

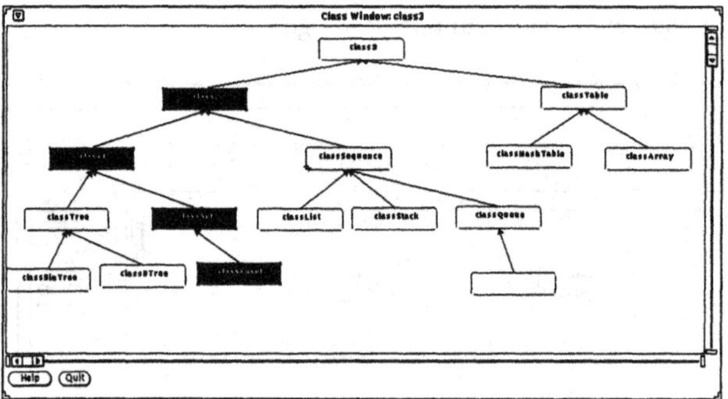

Fig. 19b. Sample search for an exact match among the software components

can help users store, browse, and retrieve existing reusable components. This work, although in its preliminary state of development, is a new approach to reusability, especially for reusing software components based upon formal specifications.

Given the framework that we have built, the system will be extended in several aspects. Efficient techniques are being developed to determine functional similarity between two software components. The abstraction scheme to form *meta-nodes* of software components will also be further investigated. An efficient searching algorithm that includes hashing and reasoning schemes will be developed. Specifications representing the inheritance relationship and the genericity of software components needs to be studied in order to exploit the properties of object-oriented development techniques. Our work provides a framework for a software reuse and retrieval system and we are investigating the integration of this system into a software development environment comprising tools for formal specification editing [30, 31], program visualization from formal specifications [32], and a tool that abstracts formal specifications from program code [33, 34].

References

1. Ted J. Biggerstaff. An Assessment and Analysis of Software Reuse. In Marshall C. Yovits, editor, *Advances in Computers*, volume 34, pages 1–57. 1992.
2. Ted J. Biggerstaff, editor. *Software Reusability Vol. 1: Concepts and Models.* ACM Press, New York, 1989.
3. Ted J. Biggerstaff, editor. *Software Reusability Vol. 2: Applications and Experience.* ACM Press, New York, 1989.
4. Charles W. Krueger. Software Reuse. *ACM Computing Surveys*, 24(2):131–183, June 1992.
5. Y.S. Maarek, D.M. Berry, and G.E. Kaiser. An Information Retrieval Approach for Automatic Constructing Software Libraries. *IEEE Trans. Software Engineering*, 17(8):800–813, August 1991.
6. R. Helm and Y.S. Maarek. Integrating Information Retrieval and Domain Specific Approaches for Browsing and Retrieval in Object-Oriented Class Libraries. In *Proceedings of OOPSLA'91*, pages 47–61, 1991.
7. Betty H.C. Cheng and Jun-Jang Jeng. Formal methods applied to reuse. In *Proceedings of the Fifth Workshop in Software Reuse*, 1992.
8. Jun-Jang Jeng and Betty H.C. Cheng. Using Automated Reasoning to Determine Software Reuse. *International Journal of Software Engineering and Knowledge Engineering*, 2(4):523–546, December 1992.
9. R.L. London. Specifying Reusable Components Using Z: Realistic Sets and Dictionaries. *ACM SIGSOFT Software Engineering Notes*, 14(3):120–127, May 1989.
10. F. Nishida, S. Takamatsu, Y. Fujita, and T. Tani. Semi-Automatic Program Construction from Specification Using Library Modules. *IEEE Transaction on Software Engineering*, 17(9):853–870, 1991.
11. C. Rich and R.C. Waters. Formalizing Reusable Software Components. In *Proc. Workshop on Reusability in Programming*, pages 152–158, Newport, RI, September 1983.
12. B.W. Weide, W.F. Ogden, and S.H. Zweben. Reusable Software Components. *Advances in Computers*, 33:1–65, 1991.
13. Jeannette M. Wing. A Specifier's Introduction to Formal Methods. *IEEE Computer*, 23(9):8–24, September 1990.
14. G. Caldiera and V. Basili. Identifying and Qualifying Reusable Software Components. *IEEE Computer*, 24(2):61–70, Febrary 1991.
15. Barbara Liskov and John Guttag. *Abstraction and Specification in Program Development.* MIT Press and McGraw-Hill, Cambridge, 1986.
16. Rebecca Wirfs-Brock, Brian Wilkerson, and Lauren Wiener. *Designing Object-Oriented Software.* Prentice Hall, Englewood, New Jersey, 1990.
17. James Rumbaugh, Michael Blaha, William Premerlani, Frederick Eddy, and William Lorensen. *Object-Oriented Modeling and Design.* Prentice Hall, Englewood Cliffs, New Jersey, 1991.
18. Peter Coad and Edward Yourdon. *Object-Oriented Analysis.* Yourdon Press, Prentice Hall, Englewood, New Jersey, 1990.
19. Bertrand Meyer. *Object-Oriented Software Construction.* Prentice Hall, Englewood, New Jersey, 1988.
20. Keith E. Gorlen, Sanford M. Orlow, and Perry S. Plexico. *Data Abstraction and Object-oriented Programming in C++.* John Wiley & Sons, 1990.
21. Ann L. Winblad, Samuel D. Edwards, and David R. King. *Object-Oriented Software.* Addison-Wesley, Publishing Company Inc., 1990.

22. Betty Hsiao-Chih Cheng. *Synthesis of Procedural and Data Abstractions.* PhD thesis, University of Illinois at Urbana-Champaign, 1304 West Springfield, Urbana, Illinois 61801, August 1990. Tech Report UIUCDCS-R-90-1631.
23. Stephen Bear. An Overview of HP-SL. Technical report, Hewlett Packard Laboratories, March 1991.
24. Chin-Liang Chang and Richard Char-Tung Lee. *Symbolic Logic and Mechanical Theorem Proving.* Academic Press, 1973.
25. J.A. Robinson. A Machine Oriented Logic Based on Resolution Principle. *Journal of ACM*, 12(1):227–234, 1965.
26. S. Miyamoto. *Fuzzy Sets in Informational Retrieval and Cluster Analysis.* Kluwer Academai Publishers, 1990.
27. D.H. Ballard and C.M. Brown. *Computer Vision.* Prentice-Hall, Englewood Cliffs, New Jersey, 1982.
28. J.B. Kruskal. On the shortest spanning subtree of a graph and the traveling salesman problem. In *Proc. of the American Mathematical Society*, 1956.
29. Douglas K. Pierce and Betty H.C. Cheng. Intelligent Browser for Formal Specifications of Software Components. Technical Report MSU-CPS-91-14, Department of Computer Science, Michigan State University, 1991.
30. Robert H. Bourdeau and Betty H.C. Cheng. An object-oriented toolkit for constructing specification editors. In *Proceedings of COMPSAC'92: Computer Software and Applications Conference*, pages 239–244, September 1992.
31. Michael R. Laux, Robert H. Bourdeau, and Betty H.C. Cheng. An integrated development environment for formal specifications. In *Proc. of IEEE International Conference on Software Engineering and Knowledge Engineering*, San Francisco, California, July 1993.
32. M. V. LaPolla, J. L. Sharnowski, B. H. C. Cheng, and K. Anderson. Data parallel program visualizations from formal specifications. *Journal of Parallel and Distributed Computing*, May 1993.
33. Betty H.C. Cheng and Gerald C. Gannod. Constructing formal specifications from program code. In *Proc. of Third International Conference on Tools in Artificial Intelligence*, pages 125–128, November 1991.
34. Gerald C. Gannod and Betty H.C. Cheng. A two-phase approach to reverse engineering using formal methods. In *Proc. of Formal Methods in Programming and Their Applications Conference*, June 1993.

Capsule Oriented Reverse Engineering for Software Reuse

Harald Gall and René Klösch

Vienna University of Technology

Institute of Information Systems, Department of Distributed Systems

Argentinierstrasse 8, A-1040 Vienna, Austria, Europe.

e-mail kloesch@infosys.tuwien.ac.at

Abstract

Much research effort concerning the reuse of software components has been invested on questions such as classification, attribution and organization of modules in software components libraries. Further problems like the obtaining of reusable components and their interconnection to form new software systems have been discovered. Reverse engineering can be used for different purposes, like maintenance effort reduction, documentation improvement, etc., but also for software reuse. In the process of software reuse, reverse engineering can be used to extract reusable components from existing software systems.

In this paper we provide insights into a reverse engineering method called capsule oriented reverse engineering method (COREM) that realizes the extraction of object similar capsules from existing systems implemented in a procedural language. For this, COREM transforms the original procedural system to an object based system (consisting of capsules). These capsules can then be used for further object-oriented system development. By using object-oriented system development methods the problem of module interconnection can be skillfully solved.

The paper points out the three main steps of the COREM process and describes the framework of COREM for the production of software from capsules.

Index Terms - software reuse, reverse engineering, object-oriented programming, *Reuse Engineering*, module interconnection, reusable components, capsules.

1 Introduction

Software reuse has shown to be a very important factor to improve productivity as well as quality during software development. Research on software reuse has uncovered different problems which have been examined in literature:

Which are the parts to be reused? Most of recent research projects use the term "software component" or "module" for the reusable parts. In most cases a component is defined in the terms of the used programming language (e.g. modules in Modula-2). [6], [19], [20]

How can reusable components be obtained? Should these components be extracted from existing software or created from scratch? Which criteria and rules are necessary for this process of extraction? The most common and promising way is to extract reusable components from existing software systems using reverse engineering methods. Reverse engineering is mostly seen in connection with software maintenance, but can also be used for software reuse [2]. Reverse engineering is well suited for a revision of existing programs in order to achieve a better-structured system, which can be used for the extraction of reusable components.

In which way can reusable components be organized in order to guarantee feasible access for further reuse? Many projects deal with questions like organization of modules and realization of software components libraries [16], [17]. Some approaches do not only store the software component itself, but also additional information (e.g. the development documentation). Using an appropriate development documentation the reuse engineer will be able to understand and modify a specific component and therefore reuse it.

How can new systems be constructed by reusing existing software components? Even if you find some appropriate components in a software components library, the problem of interconnecting them will still be waiting for a solution. Forming new software systems by interconnecting existing components through "module interconnection languages" (MIL) was investigated by [12], [15], [21].

As shown above there exists a variety of problems concerning the reuse of software. Our approach, called *Reuse Engineering*, tries to handle these problems and offers a complete software development cycle (based on the conventional software life-cycle). Some parts of this software development cycle use approved methods (like the organization of reusable modules in software components libraries or the development of new systems using object-oriented development methods). In this paper we describe our method for extracting reusable components from existing software systems by using reverse engineering.

In the next section we want provide a brief overview on the area of reverse engineering in general as well as related work.

2 Reverse Engineering

2.1 Objectives and Benefits

Reverse engineering includes the identification and extraction of software components from an existing system and their interrelationships, but it doesn't involve the modification of the target system or the generation of new systems. The following objectives are pursued by applying reverse engineering to an existing software system [10]:

1. Software Reuse
2. Documentation Improvement
3. Information Recovery
4. Maintenance Reduction
5. Platform Migration
6. Migration to CASE Environment

These six objectives form a basis to which a reverse engineering process can be applied. This means that suitable candidates for reverse engineering may have one or more of the following characteristics:

- The code is poorly structured
- The system requires corrective maintenance
- Coping with increasing complexity
- Migration to a new software or hardware platform is performed

Considering all these aspects leads to the question: "What are the benefits of applying a reverse engineering process to a given software system?" The benefits can be derived from the above given objectives, so that cost savings in the maintenance phase, improvement of the software quality and enhancement of the applicability of software reuse form the central benefits of reverse engineering.

Therefore it is possible to look at reverse engineering from completely different viewpoints: The maintenance staff is enabled to reduce their effort in analyzing and understanding a given software system by means of automated assistance, the software developers get some feedback about the quality of the produced software and, last but not least, potential candidates of software components can be selected to act as input for further software development.

The origin of reverse engineering is obviously the maintenance of given software. Nowadays reverse engineering is no more limited to that field of application but moreover bridging the gap to a very powerful *Reuse Engineering.*[1]

[1]In section 3 the term *Reuse Engineering* will be discribed in more detail.

2.2 Current and Related Work

For a more detailed discussion it is necessary to classify the set of existing reverse engineering tools into different categories:

- Software Resource Analyzers (e.g. cross reference tools, metric analyzers, etc.)
- Code Translators
- Code improvement tools
- Test case generators
- Re-engineering[2] tools

It should be mentioned here that most tools cover only some activities of the reverse engineering process in the way it was defined by Chikofsky and Cross [7].

Many of the available (commercial) reverse engineering tools support the maintenance of COBOL programs. The *Catalyst Tools Set* for example consists of a static analysis tool (*path score*), which produces two metrics, a complexity metric and a special independent structuredness metric. Sneed and Jandrasics [23] have developed a special source-to-source translator, which translates COBOL-74 into COBOL-85 programs: A static analysis is performed to identify the modules within the source code in order to restructure them as well as to optimize their performance. This tool can also be seen as a kind of re-engineering tool.

There are many more tools but all of them operate on code of procedures/functions or the code description of data. Performance optimizations (like the Sneed and Jandrasics system does) are not the central theme in reverse engineering, since the focus is on understanding but not re-engineering the given software system.

In contrast to commercial reverse engineering tools most projects funded by or in association with the European ESPRIT programme (e.g. REDO [24]) try to use formal methods to move from the source-code level up to formal specifications. The system of Martin Ward [25] transforms source code to Z specifications using an intermediate language representation. A similar system was developed by Breuer and Lano [5]. Haughton and Lano [13] describe a process for deriving Z++ objects from code and specifications to enhance understandability, modularity and maintainability of code.

The *capsule oriented reverse engineering method* (COREM) is a special kind of reverse engineering method for extracting reusable components from existing programs applied within reuse engineering. COREM therefore pursues some of the mentioned objectives of reverse engineering (i.e. software reuse and maintenance).

[2]Re-engineering means that the requirements definition as well as the whole system is generated by this kind of process.[7]

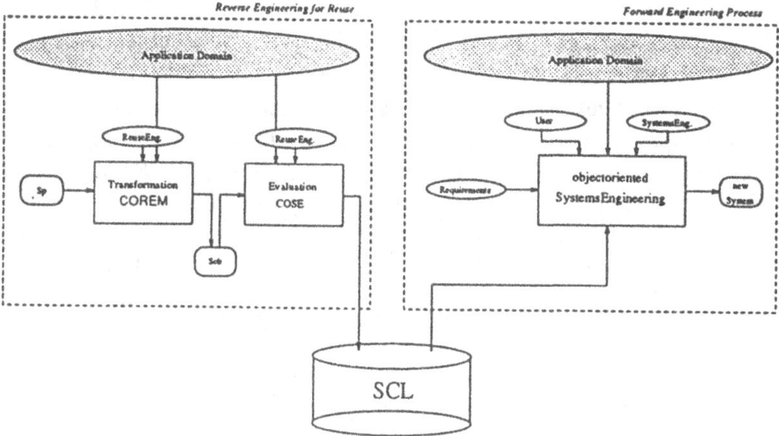

Figure 1: The *Reuse Engineering* approach

The *Reuse Engineering* approach and the role of the COREM process within this development cycle is explained in more detail in section 3.

The COREM process transforms an initial procedural software system to an object based system, which consists of capsules similar to objects.[3] By changing the paradigm (from the procedural paradigm of the initial system to the object-oriented paradigm of the resulting system) COREM is a powerful step for bridging the gap between module retrieval and module interconnection. Especially the problem of producing new systems from existing components through module interconnection can be solved by using conventional object-oriented system development methods.

3 Reuse Engineering

In this section we briefly describe the *Reuse Engineering* approach, which acts as a framework for the COREM process. It describes a complete software development process that produces new software by reusing already existing software components. The *Reuse Engineering* approach was developed by the *Reuse Engineering* research group at the Vienna University of Technology and is described in detail in [11].

The *Reuse Engineering* approach consists of two major phases, connected through a software components library (see Figure 1). Phase one (*Reverse Engineering for Reuse*) deals with the extraction of modules from existing software systems in order to obtain reusable components (i.e. capsules). Phase one is subdivided into two steps: The first step - called *capsule oriented reverse engineering method*

[3]As we will show in section 4, there exist some differences between objects and capsules, but capsules have the main important features of objects.

(COREM) - transforms a procedural software system S_p, implemented in a conventional procedural language (like Pascal, C, Modula, etc.) to an object based system consisting of object similar capsules (we therefore call the resulting system capsule based system S_{cb}). This capsule based system is used as an input for the second step - called *capsule oriented system evaluation* (COSE) - concerning the evaluation of reusable components (i.e. capsules) obtained through COREM. The results of the COSE process (i.e. reusable capsules) are stored in a software components library (SCL) for later reuse using approved methods for attribution, classification and organization of modules in a software components library ([19],[14], [3]).

The second phase of the *Reuse Engineering* approach (*Forward Engineering Process*) covers the actual software production process. New software systems are constructed through object-oriented system development methods using reusable components (i.e. capsules) from the software components library ([4], [26], [22]).

As mentioned above, the COREM process incorporates the first step in phase one of the *Reuse Engineering* approach. Starting from a given software system S_p the COREM process forms a new system, which is functional equivalent to the original one but consists of capsules. These capsules are similar to objects, but are on a higher level of abstraction than the original system S_p.

The capsules obtained by the COREM process are easier to extract than the procedures or functions from the original procedural system. The reasons are:

- Capsules realize the concept of data encapsulation in an object oriented sense. That means that data structures and their manipulating procedures (functions) are put together into the same capsule and it is therefore easier to use them more independently.
- Each kind of indirect communication (e.g. through common global data) is resolved by the COREM process.
- Communication between capsules is only realized through their interfaces (*message passing*).

Through the transformation process of COREM we are able to store object similar capsules in a software components library, which can be reused for object oriented software development in phase two of the *Reuse Engineering* approach. Therefore the module interconnection problem of procedural components (extensively discussed in the area of Module Interconnection Languages [21],[12],[15]) can be solved using capsules for object-oriented system development.

In the next section the COREM process will be described in more detail.

4 The Capsule Oriented Reverse Engineering Method (COREM)

4.1 The Encapsulation Process

It seems obvious that only some of the data structures of a software system are of really high importance for the whole system. We call this kind of data structures "application-semantic". Most of the data structures of a system are used for local purposes and are not relevant for a system wide view. They are not application-semantic in our sense.

The capsule oriented reverse engineering method tries to form capsules around the application semantic data structures of a given software system, putting those procedures into one capsule that directly operate on them.

The encapsulation process of COREM consists of three main steps, as they are:

1. Identification of application-semantic data structures and their corresponding operations (i.e. procedures and functions). Here we examine those data structures that are not basic in the sense of a `real` or `integer` or `character`. Type constructors like `array`, `record`, `set`, `file`, etc., which are provided by procedural programming languages like Pascal, are a central point of examination.
2. Examination of the interrelationships and dependencies of the procedures and functions. In this process we have to distinguish between procedures that directly operate on application-semantic data structures and those that are indirectly coupled to these procedures.
3. Encapsulation of application-semantic data structures with their directly corresponding procedures and functions in an object-oriented sense.

The usual method for realizing the data flow between the procedures of the system is by passing parameters via the interface of the procedure. We have to distinguish between two kinds of parameter passing: *call-by-value* and *call-by-reference*.

The later described algorithm for the reduction of procedure interfaces is mainly influenced by those two kinds of parameters. *Call-by-value* parameters simply act as input parameters whereas *call-by-reference* parameters are the subject of manipulation of a procedure (result parameter).

4.2 Identification of application-semantic Data Structures

The identification of application-semantic data structures (asDS) cannot only be performed on the source-code level, but needs some higher level information (design as well as application domain information). This information is mainly given by the corresponding software development documentation and the programmer himself.

So this process of identification of asDS has to make this acquisition of knowledge to one of its tasks: This can be performed by examining the existing documentation or by developing an application domain model. Conventional application domain modelling techniques mainly make use of structured analysis methods [1], [18]. In our COREM approach we suggest forming a new application domain model by using object-oriented methods, e.g. OOA [8], OSA [9], or OMT [22].

The identification process maps the objects defined in the application domain model to the data structures found in the software system. The mapping of application-domain objects (resulting from the object-oriented application domain model) to the recovered data structures leads to a set of asDS, with which capsules can be formed in a further step. The difficult problem of deciding in which asDS (resp. capsule) a procedure or function should be encapsulated can only be solved by applying the mapping of the domain objects to the source-code data structures.

The set of asDS form a basis for the next step in the COREM process: finding and restructuring the interrelationships between those procedures that directly operate on these application-semantic data structures and those that are indirectly needed for performing the specified action.

In the sense of data encapsulation the process of COREM puts together all procedures and functions that operate on the same data structures to form new capsules.

4.3 The Input System for COREM

The objective of the encapsulation process is to put each of the previously found asDS together with those procedures that directly operate on them into one capsule. Some additional facts have to be considered before forming the capsules in the described way:

- the scope of each application-semantic data structure can be extended to several modules or units of the program.
- procedures can operate on more than one application-semantic data structure, so that it would belong to more than one capsule
- procedures directly operating on an application-semantic data structure can call other procedures to perform their action (*coupling*). So these called procedures operate indirectly on the examined application-semantic data structure.

The procedural input system of the COREM process can be represented in a directed acyclic graph (DAG), in which the dependencies and relations between procedures and their application-semantic data structures are shown (figure 2).

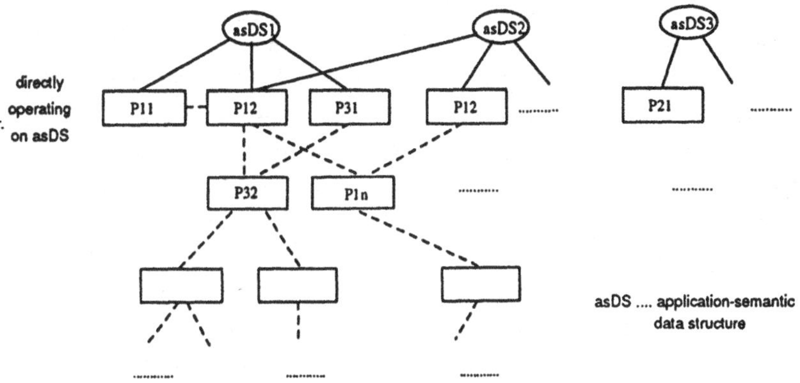

Figure 2: Input System for COREM

On the first level are the procedures which directly operate on the corresponding application-semantic data structure. On the levels below there are the procedures that are called from procedures of the first level and are therefore indirectly coupled with the application-semantic data structures (this is shown in figure 2 by dotted lines). Furthermore you can see in this DAG that procedures can belong to more than one application-semantic data structure (and therefore to more than one capsule, e.g. P_{12} belongs to $asDS_1$ and $asDS_2$) and the degree of coupling of procedures on lower levels. Consider that the procedures of the first level (connected with a application-semantic data structure) may belong to different modules of the original procedural system (e.g. P_{11} and P_{12} of $asDS_1$ belong to module 1 and P_{31} belongs to module 3).

The coupling-problem of different procedures can be solved by well-known means of decoupling [27] (e.g. localization of common environment, standardization of connections, etc.). Considering the scope of each application-semantic data structure leads to the splitting of the concerned modules of the procedural system into more than one capsule. It is important to put together all those procedures that manipulate the same data independently of the module structure of the procedural input system.

Procedures that directly operate on more than one application-semantic data structure have to be examined in a further step of COREM: One practical solution is to put such a procedure into each possible capsule, thereby increasing the redundancy of the software system. A more skilled solution examines the relationships of those application-semantic data structures that are manipulated by more than one procedure in a direct way. The object-oriented application domain model is taken as a basis for forming the capsules.

Figure 2 shows an example of the above mentioned problem: On the source-code level it cannot be automatically decided in which capsule ($asDS_1$ or $asDS_2$) the procedure P_{12} has to be encapsulated. Referring to the application domain objects this difficulty can be solved and a useful encapsulation can be performed.

The problem of procedure interdependencies (below the first level) can be solved by forming so-called management capsules, where procedures that do not directly operate on application-semantic data structures are put together because of their functional similarities. Typical management capsules are those of i/o operations, file management, etc.

In order to explain our COREM process we want to show a brief example of a simple program that manipulates rectangles in the way of initializing it, copying it to another rectangle, moving and growing it, computing its area and checking if a point is part of it. Let us assume now that `Point` and `Rectangle` are two application-semantic data structures.

```
TYPE Point = RECORD
       x,y : integer;
             END;
    Rectangle = RECORD
       a,b,c,d : Point;
             END;
```

```
Rectangle = CAPSULE
       Point = RECORD
          x,y : integer;
             END;
    /* Procedures and Functions */
    /* for Rectangle            */
            END;
```

Constructing capsules from a given procedural program is not just a process of copying procedures that operate on the same data into a new representation with a kindly redefinition of the term "object". It consists of a sophisticated interface transformation step, which examines each procedure interface to transform it for object-oriented usability. It must be noted here that objects have an internal state whereas procedures are completely state-less. So this transformation step considers especially those data types that are commonly shared within a capsule (respectively object) and adapts the interfaces of all directly connected procedures of this capsule. The reason for this reduction of the interface parameters is that after the encapsulation of the application-semantic data structure and its manipulating procedures the application-semantic data structure is known within the capsule and doesn' t need to appear as a parameter in the interfaces of the procedures.

This interface transformation algorithm is described in more detail now:

1. Examine each procedure interface and search for the existence of any of the given application-semantic data structures[4] (obtained from the previous process step). Σ_P is noted to be the set of those asDS that were found in the interface of procedure P. If $|\Sigma_P| = 1$ then perform step 2, else if $|\Sigma_P| > 1$ then perform step 3.

[4]Application-semantic data structures are from now on abbreviated to 'asDS'

2. The interface contains a single asDS and any other parameters that are not application-semantic in our sense. Consider that the asDS of the interface can appear as call-by-value and/or call-by-reference parameter. So we have to distinguish between two cases in the encapsulation process:

   (a) If the asDS $\sigma \in \Sigma_P$ is a call-by-value parameter (σ =*valp*) as well as a call-by-reference parameter (σ =*refp*) then the call-by-value parameter is deleted from the interface and the procedure is added to the capsule formed around the asDS σ.

   Example: σ = `Rectangle`
   ```
   PROCEDURE Copy (var rnew:Rectangle; r:Rectangle);
   ⇓
   PROCEDURE Copy (var rnew:Rectangle);
   ```

   (b) If the asDS σ is only a call-by-reference parameter (σ =*refp*) then σ is deleted from the interface and the procedure is added to the capsule formed around the examined asDS σ.

   Example:
   ```
   PROCEDURE Move (var r:Rectangle;dx,dy:integer);
   ⇓
   PROCEDURE Move (dx,dy:integer);
   ```

   (c) If the asDS σ is only a call-by-value parameter (σ =*valp*) then σ is deleted from the interface and the procedure is added like in the above mentioned cases to the actual capsule.

   Example:
   ```
   FUNCTION AreaOf (r:Rectangle):REAL;
   ⇓
   FUNCTION AreaOf ():REAL;
   ```

3. The interface contains more than one asDS and like step 2 other non-application-semantic parameters. This step has in addition to step 2 to decide to which asDS the examined procedure or function belongs to.

   (a) The simplest case is that of only one asDS $\sigma_i \in \Sigma_P$ occuring as a call-by-reference parameter and all the other asDS σ_j occuring as call-by-value parameters. The procedure then belongs to the capsule of σ_i and their interface is reduced in the way that σ_i is treated as the only "real" asDS (neglecting all the other asDS σ_j) and the reduction can be performed as described in step 2.

   (b) In every other case, that includes

      i. two or more asDS of the examined procedure interface are call-by-reference parameters and the rest of the asDS are call-by-value parameters, or

      ii. all asDS are call-by-reference parameters, or

      iii. all asDS are call-by-value parameters,

the decision, to which capsule the actual procedure belongs to, has to be made by taking into account the mapping of the asDS and their manipulating procedures to the application domain objects. That means that the procedure is encapsulated in the capsule that represents an application domain object and includes a similar object method.

The results of the encapsulation process are capsules that consist of procedures and functions that operate on a common data structure. This application-semantic data structure is offered (in connection with its operations) to other capsules in an object similar way.

The differences between capsules and objects result from their different origins: capsules are extracted from already existing procedural programs. These programs were designed in a different paradigm, regardless of public, private or shared data. Furthermore capsules do not distinguish explicitly between private and public procedures (methods) like objects do.

4.4 The Results of the COREM process

The resulting capsule structure obtained by COREM consists of capsules formed on the basis of application-semantic data structures and remaining components that are put together to capsules on account of functional similarities in order to guarantee the consistency of the resulting system. Consider that these capsules are not of interest for further system development in the *Reuse Engineering* approach but are necessary to keep the original system working. Capsules obtained on account of application-semantic data structures will be selected for storage in a software components library and later reuse (see figure 1). These COREM capsules have the following characteristics:

- encapsulation
- direct communication only
- clear interfaces

Because of these properties the capsules generated by COREM are well suited to be reused in an object based way of system design. For that the original objective to reuse procedural programs in an object-oriented environment is achieved by this reverse engineering process. In order to clarify our COREM approach we would like to show a brief example of a simple program that manipulates rectangles in the way of initializing, copying to another rectangle, moving and growing it, computing its area and checking if a point is part of it. This example program is shown both as procedural input program for COREM and as capsule-based program as result of the COREM process.

The following example shows the program in its original procedural form:

```
TYPE Point = RECORD
     x,y : integer;
     END;

     Rectangle = RECORD
     a,b,c,d : Point;
     END;

PROCEDURE Init (VAR R : Rectangle; xa,ya,xb,yb : Point);
PROCEDURE Copy (VAR RN : Rectangle; R : Rectangle);
PROCEDURE Move (VAR R : Rectangle; dx,dy : integer);
PROCEDURE Grow (VAR R : Rectangle; dx,dy : integer);
FUNCTION Contains (R : Rectangle; P : Point) : BOOLEAN;
FUNCTION AreaOf (R : Rectangle) : REAL;
```

After the identification of Point and Rectangle as application-semantic data structures the whole program is changed in the way that all procedures that directly operate on Rectangle are put together into one capsule. Since the data structure Rectangle maps to an application domain object only one capsule is created:

```
Rectangle = CAPSULE

     TYPE Point = RECORD
            x,y : integer;
          END;
     VAR a,b,c,d : Point;
     /* Procedures and functions operating on rectangle */
     PROCEDURE Init (xa,ya,xb,yb : Point);
     PROCEDURE Copy (VAR RN : Rectangle);
     PROCEDURE Move (dx,dy : integer);
     PROCEDURE Grow (dx,dy : integer);
     FUNCTION Contains (P : Point) : BOOLEAN;
     FUNCTION AreaOf () : REAL;
             END;
```

Consider that the interfaces of the procedures have been changed by the COREM process, because the components of Rectangle (a,b,c,d:Point) are known in all procedures of this capsule. Therefore the parameter Rectangle was deleted from most interfaces of the procedures of the capsule.

The COREM process can be seen in connection with many categories of existing reverse engineering tools: It acts as a software resource analyzer by examining the given procedural source code to find out the application-semantic data structures and their corresponding operations (procedures and functions). COREM can also be seen as a kind of code translator respectively code improvement tool in the way that procedural programs (written in Pascal, Modula or C) can be transformed to object-oriented programs in the same programming language (with its object-oriented extension), e.g. C++, object-oriented Pascal. So COREM offers the opportunity to work as a source-code transformer that generates object-oriented programs from procedural programs, thereby using additional high-level knowledge.

5 Conclusion and Future Work

This paper introduced a reverse engineering method that uses the principles of object oriented programming. The capsule oriented reverse engineering method (COREM) acts as a special data oriented reverse engineering process: Capsules are generated out of procedural programs by forming capsules around their application-semantic data structures and the procedures that directly operate on them. These capsules have properties that are very similar to those of objects. With these properties it is possible to build new software systems by using object-oriented methods. Using object-oriented system development methods enables to solve the module interconnection problem when constructing new systems from existing components (capsules).

The *Reuse Engineering* approach described above is part of research work which is in progress and has reached different stages of progress. As shown in section 3 the framework for the COREM process is well-defined. Some parts are conceptually modelled and subject to critical theoretical evaluation.

Current work of our research group deals with the application of the COREM process to different commercial software systems. The small example above should only increase the understandability of the COREM process and is not representative for the size of the examined software systems. The domain of commercial applications offers a great number of large software systems and is well-suited for applying reverse engineering methods and demonstrating object-oriented methods.

Furthermore, the necessity of integrating the experience of a reuse engineer into the COREM process is examined. The development of a tool depends on this integration of "human experience".

Acknowledgements

We are grateful to Prof. Helmut Kerner from the Vienna University of Technology and Prof. Roland Mittermeir from the University of Klagenfurt for many interesting discussions on this topic.

References

[1] G.F. Arango. *Domain Engineering for Software Reuse.* PhD thesis, University of California, Irvine, 1988.

[2] V.R. Basili. Viewing maintenance as reuse-oriented software development. *IEEE Software*, 7(1):19–25, September 1990.

[3] E. Bertino and L. Martino. Object-oriented database management systems: Concepts and issues. *IEEE Computer*, 24(4):33–47, April 1991.

[4] G. Booch. Object-oriented development. *IEEE Transactions on Software Engineering*, 12(2):211-221, February 1986.

[5] P.T. Breuer and K. Lano. *From Programs to Z Specifications.* Z User's Meeting, 1989.

[6] B.A. Burton, R.W. Aragon, S.A. Bailey, K.D. Koehler, and L.A. Mayes. The reusable software library. *IEEE Software*, 4(4):25–33, July 1987.

[7] E.J. Chikofsky and J.H. Cross. Reverse engineering and design recovery: A taxonomy. *IEEE Software*, 7(1):13–17, January 1990.

[8] P. Coad and E. Yourdon. *Object Oriented Analysis.* Yourdon Press Computing Series. Prentice Hall, Inc., Englewood Cliffs, 1991.

[9] D. Embley, K. Kurtz, and W. Woodfield. *Object-Oriented Systems Analysis.* Prentice Hall, Inc., Englewood Cliffs, 1992.

[10] A. Frazer. Reverse engineering - hype, hope or here? In P.A.V. Hall, editor, *Software Reuse and Reverse Engineering in Practice*, volume 12 of *UNICOM Applied Information Technology*, pages 209–243. Chapman & Hall, 1992.

[11] H. Gall and R. Klösch. Reuse engineering: Software construction from reusable components. *Proceedings of COMPSAC '92, Chicago, USA*, pages 79–86, Sept. 1992.

[12] J.A. Goguen. Reusing and interconnecting software components. *IEEE Computer*, 19(2):16–28, February 1986.

[13] H.P. Haughton and K. Lano. Objects revisited. *IEEE Conf. on Software Maintenance, Sorento, Italy*, pages 152–161, October 1991.

[14] L. Hsian-Chou and W. Feng-Jian. Software reuse based on large object-oriented library. *ACM SIGSOFT Software Engineering Notes*, 18(1):74–80, January 1993.

[15] G.E. Kaiser and D. Garlan. Melding software systems from reusable building blocks. *IEEE Software*, 4(4):17–24, July 1987.

[16] Y.S. Maarek, D.M. Berry, and G.E. Kaiser. An information retrieval approach for automatically constructing software libraries. *IEEE Trans. on Software Engineering*, SE-17(8):800–813, August 1991.

[17] R.T. Mittermeir and M. Oppitz. Software bases for the flexible composition of application systems. *IEEE Trans. on Software Engineering*, SE-13(4):440–460, April 1987.

[18] R. Prieto-Diaz. Domain analysis for reusability. *Proceedings of COMPSAC '87*, pages 23–29, October 1987.

[19] R. Prieto-Diaz. Classification of reusable modules. *ACM Press Software Reusability*, 1:99–122, 1989.

[20] R. Prieto-Diaz. Implementing faceted classification for software reuse. *Communications of the ACM*, 34(5):88–97, May 1991.

[21] R. Prieto-Diaz and J.M. Neighbors. Module interconnection languages. *The Journal of Systems and Software*, 11(6):307–334, June 1986.

[22] J. Rumbaugh, M. Blaha, W. Premerlani, F. Eddy, and W. Lorensen. *Object-Oriented Modeling and Design*. Prentice Hall, Inc., Englewood Cliffs, 1991.

[23] H.M. Sneed and G. Jandrasics. Inverse transformation of software from code to specification. *Conf. on Software Maintenance*, pages 102–109, 1988.

[24] H.J. van Zuylen, editor. *The REDO Compendium - Reverse Engineering for Software Maintenance*. John Wiley & Sons, Ltd., Chicester, 1993.

[25] M. Ward. Transforming a program into a specification. Computer Science Technical Report 88/1, University of Durham, 1988.

[26] A.I. Wasserman, P.A. Pircher, and R.J. Muller. An object-oriented structured design method for code generation. *ACM SIGSOFT Software Engineering Notes*, 14(1):32–55, January 1989.

[27] E. Yourdon and L.L. Constantine. *Structured Design: Fundamentals of a Discipline of Computer Program and Systems Design*. Prentice Hall, Inc., Englewood Cliffs, 1979.

Automatic Replanning of Task Networks for Process Model Evolution in EPOS

Chunnian Liu*, Reidar Conradi**

Beijing Polytechnic University, Beijing, China
Norwegian Institute of Technology, Trondheim, Norway

Abstract. Evolution is crucial in Software Process Modeling (PM) and its support systems. EPOS is a PM support system, using the same Configuration Management (CM) techniques for the Process Schema (types and meta-types) as for instances of these (tasks with related products and tools etc.).
Further, EPOS merges CM and PM with AI, applying AI planning to an important area of Software Engineering. Given a goal, the EPOS Planner instantiates a hierarchical task network based on the available task types and the current Product Structure. When the Product Structure or task types change, the network may have to be partially reconstructed.
This paper presents a general, incremental replanning algorithm, which readjusts the existing task network to reflect the changes in the Product Structure and/or in task types. The mechanism to automatically initiate replanning upon changes is also discussed.

1 Introduction

A remark on terminology: We will use *process model* to denote the *internal* computer representation of an *external* process to be supported, e.g. software production or banking applications. However, several authors use "process model" only about a *Process Schema* (types, templates, rules).

Software Processes and their Process Modeling (PM) support systems are intended to operate in human-oriented systems [CFFS92]. Their overall control and planning facilities should therefore serve as an intelligent and cooperative assistant, not as a strait-jacketing controller. During the process life-cycle, evolution (both customisation and refinement) of the Process Schema and its instances is crucial. Such a schema provides a common, often typed description of a class of software *artifacts*, i.e. activities and their related products, application tools, human roles, and organisation.

We can very coarsely identify the following life-cycle phases of PM meta-processes, that must be supported by methods, formalisms and tools:

* Dept. of Computer Science, Beijing Polytechnic University (BPU), Beijing 100022, P.R. China. Phone: +86 1 771-1177 ext. 470, Fax: +86 1 771-4088

** Div. of Computer Systems and Telematics, Norwegian Institute of Technology (NTH), N-7034 Trondheim, Norway. Phone: +47 7 593444, Fax: +47 7 594466, Email: conradi@idt.unit.no.

PM0. Provide PM Support: process modeling language, process tools.
PM1. Elicit requirements for process model.
PM2. Analyse/design a *template* model ("symbolic program").
PM3. Implement an *enactable* model ("load image").
PM4. Executing[3] an *enacting* model ("running image").
PM5. Assess external process performance.

There is no assumption that the phases PM1–PM5 should be done in a strict "waterfall" sequence for all parts of the model. And in PM support systems with late / dynamic binding, the distinction between the above template, enactable (instantiated) and enacting models is blurred. That is, definition and evolution of process models is an incremental and never-ending meta-process.

The focus of this paper is to support incremental (re-)planning of meta-process PM3 (generation of task networks in EPOS), based on changes both in PM2 (concerning types) or in PM3 (concerning instances of products). We will completely ignore the problems of having the internal process model to be kept in synchrony with the modeled entities in a changing, external process.

The rest of this paper is organised as follows: Section 2 gives an overview of related work. Section 3 gives an overview of EPOS including the techniques to customise and refine Process Schemas in EPOS, and the impacts on the Planner. Section 4 briefly describes the over-all meta-process in EPOS. Section 5 then presents a general incremental replanning algorithm dealing with changes in product structure and/or types. A non-trivial example of the application of the algorithm is given in Section 6. Section 7 discusses using triggers to automatically initiate replanning upon changes, and Section 8 gives a conclusion.

2 Related Work

2.1 Related Work on PM Evolution

We should support evolution in the meta-process phases PM0–PM5 above. What is then the **process variables**, when and how can they be changed, for what reason, and by whom? A variety of mechanisms have been suggested and implemented; usually employing late / dynamic binding combined with reflection. Note the analogy with schema evolution in databases.

In the following, some PM systems will be commented upon according to their support for evolution in meta-process PM3 (task networks), caused by changes in PM2 (types) and PM3 (products). Obviously, the process activity formalism – Task Net, Rule-Based / Triggers, or Process Programming – strongly influences the possibilities for such evolution. E.g. with a Rule-Based / Trigger formalism, the task network is implicit and the above evolution problem does not arise. But then also the functionality is rather low-level: e.g. there are problems to distinguish a task derivation graph from a product dependency graph, and

[3] *Enact* has often been used to cover both automatic and manual interpretation and execution.

to express and reason about decomposed and delayed/long-term activities; see [CLJ91] for a discussion.

In **MELMAC**, process models are expressed as refinable FUNSOFT nets. Some transition nodes can represent *modification points*, to be be manually expanded before executing it. The network can only evolve vertically, not horizontally, and redoing a network dynamically is probably not possible.

SPADE, employing an extended Petri net formalism, has recently introduced reflection to manage process evolution [BF93]. Here, a meta Petri net will dynamically and incrementally be invoked to produce an enactable Petri net, based on existing product structures and type information. However, network generation is rather low-level and not goal-oriented, and remaking the network upon later changes is problematic.

APPL/A [JHO90] extends Ada with persistent relations, triggers, predicates, and transaction statements. Some support for task network evolution is reported, but the compiled nature of Ada is an inconvenience.

IPSE 2.5 [Sno92] enables to express Process Schemas in terms of *Roles* and *Interactions* that are described by object-oriented classes. Executing roles may be evolved also by changing the network topology of interacting instances.

Grapple [Huf89] adopts a state-based hierarchical planning approach. Processes are defined by special planning operators. An operator consists of a precondition, effects, goal (post-condition), and a constraint clause. Plans are constructed dynamically by instantiating operators. Only products, not operators or plans are stored in the database.

Process WEAVER [Fer93] from Cap Gemini Innovation allows dynamic growth of enacted tasks. A task network (process model) is modeled as a set of inter-linked Petri nets that execute C++ programs, but the links cannot be dynamically restructured.

That is, many PM systems resort to manual or semi-automatic building of task networks, which also are hard to evolve later. We could also mention systems for project management, PERT diagrams or office workflow, usually with automatic planning (allocation and scheduling) of activities. However, they only cover partly the functionality of a full-fledged PM system.

2.2 Related Work on AI Planning

Typical domain-independent, non-linear planning algorithms can be found in IPEM [AIS88] and TWEAK [Cha87]. TWEAK gives a formal treatment to the subject of non-linear planning. IPEM tries to integrate planning, execution and monitoring in fine granularity, mainly for exception handling. Both TWEAK and IPEM address the non-linear planning problem in a domain-independent way, with examples mainly from the Block World domain (robot applications).

Most AI planning rules have no formal Input/Output specifications, which are essential for software development tasks. Project customisation can be done by simple rule grouping and substitution, even if the rule space is rather flat. Process evolution can generally be supported by replanning and re-execution.

3 An Overview of EPOS

EPOS [COWL91] is a multi-user, kernel software engineering environment, covering both Configuration Management (CM), PM and Process Management. In the next subsections we will present the EPOSDB, the SPELL language, some examples using SPELL, and the three basic EPOS PM tools: Schema Manager, Execution Manager, and Planner. The emphasis is on the Planner and on the demands for replanning. A Project Manager and a Cooperation Manager is sketched in Section 4 on the EPOS meta-process.

3.1 The EPOSDB

All process artifacts are represented by model entities (objects) with mutual relationships. A process model in EPOS consists of the relevant model entities and relationships, and their Process Schema with types and meta-types.

The entire process model is persistently stored in a versioned software engineering database, **EPOSDB**. Thus, conventional CM technology can, at least partially, be used to manage the model, guided by an explicitly modeled *meta-process*. However, changing a "process program" during its execution is never easy, cf. dynamic reconfiguration in telecommunication and distributed systems.

EPOSDB is a client-server database with nested and cooperative transactions [CM91] against checked-out workspaces containing files. It implements a *Change Oriented Versioning* model (COV) [LCD+89]. A transaction is executed on the current database *version*, i.e. the visible sub-database.

3.2 The SPELL process specification language

EPOSDB supports a DDL for a structurally object-oriented data model to describe entity and relationship types with simple inheritance. The client DML interface is expressed in Prolog. The **SPELL** [CJM+92] process specification language unifies the DDL and DML of the underlying EPOSDB, and offers extensions in two levels.

The lower SPELL layer supports **behavioural** and **reflexive object-orientation** in Prolog: schema types and meta-types stored as `TypeDescrs`, type-level attributes, type- and instance-level procedures, and triggers for these. Meta-types are defined inside types. The set of declared procedures and triggers in a type is open-ended, and with dynamic binding as in Smalltalk. Attributes and procedures can be `Private` or `Public`, giving some degree of modularisation. This SPELL layer is implemented by a SPELL Interpreter. In addition comes a Schema Manager (Section 3.4).

The upper SPELL layer adds **tasking**[4], by making *task objects* concurrently active. It is implemented by a Execution Manager (Section 3.5) cooperating closely with a Planner (Section 3.6). A task type expresses an **activation rule** by the type-level attributes PRE_DYNAMIC, CODE, and POST_DYNAMIC.

[4] Neither of the available Concurrent Prologs were judged suitable for EPOS.

Tasks are connected in a typed *task network* with chaining and decomposition. The "horizontal" part of the network resembles a Petri net, where transition nodes (tasks) are connected with places (products in EPOS).

The type-level attributes serve as shared *process parameters*, and can be redefined by subtyping and versioned between projects. Most of the type-level procedures and attributes are used to instrument the PM tools, and similar for some of the instance-level procedures.

A **Process Schema** is a set of SPELL types and meta-types. For example, the `TaskEntity` type and its subtypes describe activities, called tasks in EPOS. `DataEntity` and its subtypes mainly describe *products* and their parts. `Entity` is the common root entity type.

3.3 Sample Types in EPOS

Below is shown the main `TaskEntity` type, and a `Build` task type to describe building (derivation) of executable code from a family of C source programs:

```
ENTITY_TYPE TaskEntity : Entity        |ENTITY_TYPE Interactor:TaskEntity{...}
{INSTANCE_LEVEL                        |
   PROCEDURES                          |ENTITY_TYPE Deriver   :TaskEntity{...}
     i_convert: %Convert instance      |
                %to sub/supertype      |ENTITY_TYPE Build : Deriver
   ATTRIBUTES                          |{TYPE_LEVEL
     String TaskState:='created';      |   ATTRIBUTES
 TYPE_LEVEL                            |     PRE_STATIC:  Input is 'coded'
     %% See type-attributes below.     |     PRE_DYNAMIC: % Start condition
   PROCEDURES                          |     CODE:        ... <empty> ...
     t_create:  %Create new subtype    |     POST_STATIC: Output is 'created'
     t_change:  %Change type           |     POST_DYNAMIC:% Exception handling
     t_delete:  %Delete type           |     FORMALS:     Family -> Executable
     i_create:  %Create new instance   |     DECOMP:      {Ccompile, Link}
} % of TaskEntity-type                 |} % of Build-type
```

This is a composite task type, so *subtasking* (see below) is needed to carry out its job. In the following we show also parts of several other task types which have some connections with the `Build` type:

```
ENTITY_TYPE Implement : Interactor     |ENTITY_TYPE Ccompile : Deriver
{    ...                               |{    ...
     PRE_STATIC: Input is 'designed'   |     PRE_STATIC:  Input is 'coded'
     CODE:        ... <empty> ...      |     CODE:        call CC
     POST_STATIC:Output is 'created'   |     POST_STATIC: Output is 'created'
     FORMALS:     Family -> Executable |     FORMALS:     Csource + $Cinclude
                                       |                    -> ObjectCode
                                       |                  %% '$' means list-of
     DECOMP:    {SystemCoding, Build}  |     DECOMP: {}
} % of Implement-type                  |} % of Ccompile-type
                                       |
                                       |
```

```
ENTITY_TYPE SystemCoding:Interactor    |ENTITY_TYPE SourceCoding : Interactor
{    ...                               |{    ...
     PRE_STATIC: Input is 'designed'   |     PRE_STATIC:  Input is 'coded'
     CODE:         ... <empty> ...     |     CODE:        call emacs
     POST_STATIC:Output is 'coded'     |     POST_STATIC: Output is 'coded'
     FORMALS:    Family -> Family      |     FORMALS:     CSource -> CSource
     DECOMP:     {SystemCoding,        |     DECOMP: {}
                  SourceCoding}        |
} % of SystemCoding-type               |} % of SourceCoding-type
                                       |
ENTITY_TYPE Link : Deriver             |
{    ...                               |
     PRE_STATIC: Input is 'created'    |
     CODE:         call linker         |
     POST_STATIC:Output is 'created'   |
     FORMALS:  $ObjectCode + $Library  |
                 -> Executable         |
} % of Link-type                       |
```

The following `DataEntity` subtypes are mentioned above or used later:

```
Family,  a subsystem of program units| ObjectCode, a relocatable program
Csource, a source program            | Library,     a aggregate of above
Cinclude,a C header program          | Executable, a run-able program
```

Some relevant relationship types are explained in comments for Figure 1 in Section 6. The type-level attributes FORMALS, PRE_STATIC, POST_STATIC, and DECOMP express legality constraints on the structure of the task network, cf. *graph grammars*. The Planner uses this information (Section 3.6).

Given the above types, our task network must look as follows: A local root task of type `Implementation`, composed of one `SystemCoding` subtask followed by one `Build` subtask. The `SystemCoding` subtask can be recursively decomposed for sub-families until we reach a set of `SourceCoding` leaf tasks. The `Build` subtask is decomposed of a set of `Ccompile` subtasks, feeding into one `Link` subtask.

As an extension of the above model, there might be a `Develop` parent task (Section 4). This could be decomposed into a `Design` task, feeding into the above `Implemented` task.

3.4 Schema Manager

The **Schema Manager** [JLC92] is responsible to browse, edit, and generally manage the set of types. The type-level procedures **t_create**, **t_change**, and **t_delete** are used to manipulate the Process Schema. This happens during the PM2-Design when customising the Schema, and later during PM4-Enactment for corrections and supplements. These procedures are often subtyped, and initially defined in the `Entity` type.

Type changes can have a profound effect on its instances, and on instances of related types (subtypes, role types of relationship types, types in FORMALS and DECOMP specifications). The feasibility of a requested type change must be evaluated against its possible *impact* on the whole Process Schema and its instances. A list of consistency *constraints* will be consulted. If the impact is too big, a new subtype might be defined, so that only a *subset* of the extent of the old type will be affected.

Type changes are termed **hard** (but simple!), if they involve changes in definitions of instance-level attributes or "type surgery" on the type hierarchy. Hard type changes are allowed to some degree in EPOS, using the i_convert procedure to convert some of the old instances. This usually involves delicate human intervention, see [JLC92] on aspects of this.

Type changes can also be **soft** or behavioural (and complex!). These involve changing procedures/triggers or type-level attributes. Although such type changes easily can be implemented in SPELL, they may have big consequences for the Execution Manager and Planner. E.g. the Execution Manager should not allow changing the CODE script of active tasks ("pulling the rug"). On the other hand, the PRE_DYNAMIC condition could be allowed to change, if the affected tasks are `Waiting` or perhaps `Active`. For the impact of soft type changes on existing task networks – the main issue here – see Section 3.6 on the Planner.

3.5 Execution Manager

Tasking is realised by the **Execution Manager**, interpreting the upper SPELL layer (in meta-process PM4). It utilises three type-level attributes:

- **PRE_DYNAMIC**, specifying the condition on when to execute an instance of the given task type. The condition is combined with local task information about task state (see below) and goal-directed vs. opportunistic execution (lazy vs. busy). This condition is (re)evaluated using polling, and can be optimised using triggers activated from preceding tasks (not explained here). The evaluation can have *side-effects*, e.g. by reading a mailbox.

- **CODE**, being a sequential program to perform the intended job of the given task type. Thus, executing a task means interpretation of its CODE.
  For an *atomic* task type like `Ccompile`, the CODE contains all the relevant actions. For a *composite* or high-level task type like `Build`, the middle part of CODE is empty, causing the Planner to be invoked to prepare subtasking (see Section 3.6).

- **POST_DYNAMIC**, e.g. to treat errors, not mentioned here for simplicity.

The Execution Manager also maintains the instance-level attribute `TaskState`, whose value domain is: `Initiated` during Planner instantiation, `Waiting` on its PRE_DYNAMIC, `Active` while executing CODE, or `Terminated` in case of successful goal-oriented execution.

3.6 Planner

The AI **Planner** is technically a procedure (in meta-process PM3). It is implicitly and incrementally invoked by the Execution Manager to detail composite tasks, as indicated above. That is, the Planner will automatically generate a new subtask network for such tasks – and so on in due time. This corresponds to *hierarchical planning* in AI.

In practise, the Planner is mostly used to generate the subtasks of Develop and the Cooperation Manager (Section 4). See examples later, using the task and product types explained above.

The Planner starts with a composable Task and its desired Output, being the *goal*. It applies backward chaining and hierarchical decomposition, combined with domain-specific knowledge, to build a proper subtask network (a plan in AI terms). The planning is based on the Process Schema as a Knowledge Base (KB), and a representation/model of the Product Structure (PS) as a World State Description (WSD) [Liu91]. The paper addresses replanning of task networks, in case of evolving Process Schema and PS.

There are two layers in the Planner. The *inner layer* or *core* of the Planner is a **domain-independent, AI non-linear planning** algorithm, resembling that in TWEAK and IPEM. The integration of planning, execution and monitoring is at a coarse granularity through hierarchical planning. The generated plan (a task network) satisfies the basic requirement: *Every pre-condition of every node (task) in the plan is matched by a post-condition of another node.* Otherwise, the plan is not completed, and the planning process continues.

The *outer layer* of the Planner is **domain-specific** to PM. It transforms certain type-level attributes of task types (PRE/POST_STATIC and FORMALS) into AI pre/post-conditions of nodes, so the core layer can work. This transformation also considers the PS, as we can see in the following small examples. We first explain the four relevant type-level attributes:

- **PRE_STATIC** and **POST_STATIC** express necessary conditions that must hold, respectively, before and after execution of a task of the given task type.
- **FORMALS**, divided in **FORMALS_IN** and **FORMALS_OUT** by the `'->'` delimiter, specifies the legal "product" types of actual parameter instances (Inputs/Outputs) of the given task type.
- **DECOMP** (decomposition) specifies an unordered pool of candidate task types for subtasks of the given composite task.
  Note: An empty middle part in CODE assumes a non-empty DECOMP.

None of the above attributes are supposed to have any side-effects upon (re)evaluation, thus facilitating goal-oriented reasoning.

We classify the possible changes in the Process Schema or PS, and their impact on the Planner, in four points:

- **AI PRE-conditions**[5]:
  These consist of three pieces of information for a given task node **A**: PRE_STATIC, FORMALS_IN, and the current PS.
  For instance, atomic `Ccompile` task node **A** (Section 3.3) will be introduced

[5] In this paper we use "pre/post-conditions" in the context of AI, while "PRE/POST_" are name prefixes of SPELL attributes.

into the plan, if its post-condition (see next point) matches the pre-condition of an already established **Link** task.
The first two pieces of information in the pre-conditions (called *subgoals* in AI) of this node **A** are now: "**Csource** object is **coded** and **Cinclude** objects are is **coded**". We then derive that some **Csource** object (named **m.c**) must be part of **A**'s Inputs. Therefore, the **Cinclude** headers (named ***.h**) included in this object, are searched for in PS – and so on transitively. However, we must also add domain knowledge that the possible **Csource** bodies (named ***.c**) of such headers, can be Inputs to even more **Ccompile** tasks. These will all feed into one, succeeding **Link** task. Such domain knowledge is expressed by instance-level procedures in **Ccompile**, see below point on PS.
Changes in the above information imply some changes in the corresponding pre-conditions of node **A**, making some of them unsupported. So, replanning on its **A_parent** task is needed.

- **AI POST-conditions:**
  These consist of three pieces of information for a given task node **A**: POST_-STATIC, FORMALS_OUT, and the current PS.
  The first two pieces of information in the post-conditions of the above **A** may simply be "**ObjectCode** object is **created**", where the object is deduced to be named **M.o**.
  Changes in the above information imply changes in the corresponding post-conditions of node **A**, turning some of these unsupported. So, replanning on task **A_parent** is again needed.

- **AI goals for hierarchical planning:**
  If node **A** is a composite task, the above three pieces of information are also used to form a set of AI goals for the planning process on **A**. In addition, the DECOMP attribute and the PS is considered.
  Suppose that family **f** in the current PS contains a sub-family **fb**, and two source programs **m.h** and **m.c**. Then the set of AI goals for the **SystemCoding** task **A** will be "there is a **coded Cinclude** object named **m.h**, and a **coded Csource** object named **m.c**, and a **coded family** object named **fb**".
  A change in the DECOMP of the type of **A** implies replanning on **A**. For instance, new types in the type pool of DECOMP will be used as additional knowledge rules for the replanning process. Likewise, nodes whose types disappear in the new/modified DECOMP should be removed from the (sub)task network. As a consequence, some pre-conditions of succeeding nodes become unsupported, and some post-conditions of preceding nodes become useless.

- **More about the PS:**
  As we see from the above, the current PS gives inputs to the translations from the type information of task node **A** into the internal AI goals of **A**. However, there are two more points in connection with PS:

  1. The transformation procedures are type-specific, using domain knowledge. A part of this is defined as two instance-level procedures **subgoals** and **make_goal** in certain task types (not shown).

2. The affected scope of PS changes, i.e. which part of the existing task network is effected, is more difficult to determine than for changes in type definitions. If the PS changes are systematic and well-informing, as e.g. the result of a (re) `Design` task (not modeled), then replanning should start with the existing `Implement` task which will (re)implement the (re)designed software system. But even when the PS changes are more undisciplined, we deduce the relationship between the PS (the data dependency graph) and the affected task network (the derivation graph).

We have above identified various aspects of evolution of Process Schema and PS that demand replanning. We know in each case which part of the task network that needs to be replanned, and so on recursively if needed. See the replanning algorithm in the next section.

The easiest solution is to drop (part of) the old task network, and replan from scratch, based on the new KB (types) and/or the new WSD (the PS). Rather, we want an incremental replanning mechanism, that readjusts the existing task network to comply with the changes (which are usually local and small), rather than replanning from scratch. In the next section we propose a general incremental replanning algorithm dealing with all kinds of changes listed above.

4 The EPOS Meta-process and Project Context

Although meta-processes are not the main theme of this paper, we add a short description to show the overall infrastructure of the EPOS PM support tasks.

A long EPOSDB transaction is associated to a `Project` task. Its most important subtasks are the **Schema Manager** (meta-process PM2), a **Project Manager** (in PM3) to start and finish child projects/transactions, a **Cooperation Manager** (mostly in PM3–PM4) with a Workspace Manager to coordinate with possibly overlapping sibling tasks [CM91], and a **Develop** task (PM4) that contains the real production subtasks.

We get started by manually generating a transaction, that defines a database version of the entire process model, and a local `Project` governing this. This may require negotiation and delegation from a parent project, e.g. according to an incoming change-request. Under our local `Project` task, the Planner will generate the above infrastructure of subtasks.

First, we use the Schema Manager to refine and adapt the "inherited" Process Schema of the parent project into a more specific one. This meta-activity results in appropriate type descriptions of local activities, products, production tools, and roles. Facilities for impact analysis of changes may be modeled by procedures in special task types. Such schema evolution can also be done incrementally later, if the meta-model in the Schema Manager allows this.

We then use the Cooperation Manager to establish cooperation protocols (negotiation and propagation rules and patterns) against possible overlapping neighbour projects/transactions. Thereafter we install (or check-out) the relevant workspace files from database "long fields".

Then Develop can start, and its subtasks can be gradually (re)planned and (re)executed – respectively in meta-process PM3 and PM4. This process depends on the actual production activities (PS changes) and meta-process activities (type changes). In parallel, we may have communication with neighbour projects, and we can start and finish new subprojects *manually* via the Project Manager.

Finally, the local **Project** task will check-in the modified workspace files to the database, and close itself after committing the database transaction. The Project Manager of the parent project is notified about all this.

NB: We have purposefully left out roles and access rights (locking).

5 A General, Incremental Replanning Algorithm

We summarise all possible changes which demand replanning as follows.

1. **Systematic and Well-informing PS Changes**: as part of the (re)design activity.
2. **Opportunistic PS changes**: e.g. when the programmer changes `#include` statements in a C source file.
3. **Systematic Changes in the Process Schemas**: e.g. when new task subtypes are introduced during the process customisation phase.
4. **Dynamic Process Schema Evolution**: e.g. changes in task types during enactment of a Process Schema.
5. **Changes in the Schema's product types, either Systematic or Opportunistic**. The latter ones represent more arbitrary changes.
6. **Changes in Nested Transactions**: upon new sub-transactions.

We claim that the big variety of possible changes does not mean that we need a separate replanning algorithm for each kind of changes.

All possible changes listed in Section 3.6 can disturb an existing plan only in the following ways:

- Some new pre-conditions come in;
- Some old pre-conditions become unsupported;
- Some post-conditions become obsolete;
- Some nodes should be removed, e.g. due to changes in DECOMP or the PS, causing problems similar to the last two items above.

All these disturbances will turn the existing plan into an uncompleted one, and the planning steps will be re-started automatically. Such a replanning process differs from the original planning process only in that it does not start from scratch.

In light of the above observations, we have designed and prototyped a general, incremental replanning algorithm dealing with changes in the Process Schema and PS, which cover the case 1, 3, 4, 5, and (partly) 2 of the list given at the beginning of this section. We are working on the extension of the mechanism to cover case 6 as well. We first recite the original planning algorithm of [Liu91]:

```
ALGORITHM1: Non-Linear Planning
INPUT:  I1. Composite task A.
        I2. Current PS.
OUTPUT: Plan of A, i.e. a (sub)task network carrying out A's job.
PLANNING METHOD:
1. Create AI goals G for A from its POST_STATIC/FORMALS_OUT, and PS;
2. Build a germinal plan P0 with two special nodes:
   BEGIN with PS as its post-conditions
   END with G as its pre-conditions, all unsupported initially;
3. Inspect the current partial plan Pi, for each flaw (e.g. unsupported
   pre-condition P), we have a meta-rule to fix it up (e.g. introducing
   a new task to support P). Pairs of [flaw, fix] are ordered in
   an agenda AG based on heuristics about their priorities;
4. IF   AG is empty, % Pi is flaw-free
   THEN Stop.       % Pi is the OUTPUT
5. Fix the flaw in AG[top] to transform Pi into a new partial plan Pi+1;
6. Pop AG and readjust it by inspecting the new Pi+1;
7. GOTO step 4.
```

We now present our general, incremental replanning algorithm:

```
ALGORITHM2: Incremental Replanning
INPUT: I1. Composite task A and its plan = the (sub)task network of A.
       I2. Any changes in Process Schema or PS which require
           replanning of A (as listed in Section 3.6).
OUTPUT: Readjusted plan of A, coping with the changes.
PLANNING METHOD:
1. IF   there is any change in PS, or in FORMALS_OUT/POST_STATIC of A,
   THEN re-create the AI goals G' for A;
2. IF   there is a change in DECOMP of A,
   THEN delete those nodes whose types disappear in new DECOMP of A;
        %% New types in DECOMP will be added to the KB in step 6 below
3. FOR each node Ai in the old plan:
   IF   there is any change in PS, or in FORMALS_OUT/POST_STATIC of Ai,
   THEN readjust the post-conditions of Ai based on new/modified info.
        (specially, BEGIN has new PS as its post-conditions);
4. FOR each node Ai in the old plan:
   IF   there is any change in PS, or in FORMALS_IN/PRE_STATIC of Ai,
   THEN readjust the pre-conditions of Ai based on new/modified info.
        (specially, END has new goals G' as its pre-conditions);
5. Delete 'dead' tasks from the plan; (a task supporting
   no pre-conditions of other nodes became 'dead');
6. %% Now we have changed the old flaw-free plan of A
   %% in various ways, and introduced some new flaws.)
   Invoke Planner to resume its work at step 3 of Algorithm1 to find
   and fix up the flaws introduced in step 1--4 of this Algorithm2.
7. FOR each composite subtask Ai in the new plan of A,
   IF   Ai is newly introduced, or Ai was in the old
```

```
     plan but had not been expanded (planned)
THEN do nothing (planning on Ai will be done later
     when Execution Manager tries to execute Ai);
ELSE %% Ai, and its own (sub)task network, was in the old plan
     Apply this Algorithm recursively to Ai
     (it may need replanning as well as its parent A).
```

The above is a general mechanism taking all possible changes into consideration. If the PS or some type attribute (DECOMP, FORMALS etc.) has not changed, the corresponding steps in the algorithm may be skipped, of course.

6 An Example

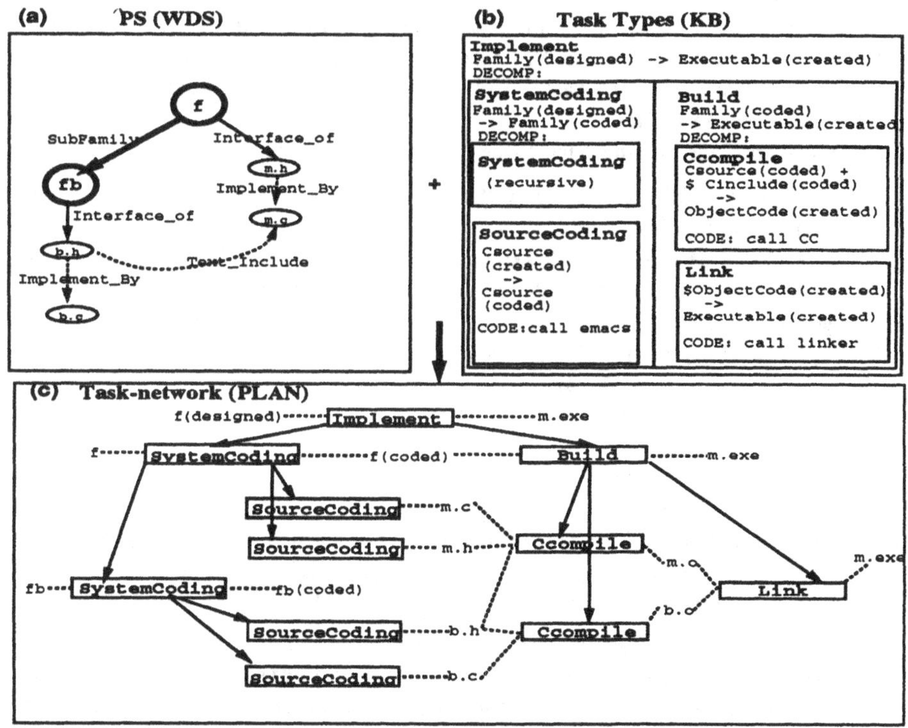

Fig. 1. PS + Types ==> Task Network, or WSD + KB ==> Plan.

Now we present a non-trivial example of changes both in a Process Schema and in a PS, and the corresponding readjustment of the existing task network. Figure 1 shows a configuration which is the starting point of the example.

Part (a) is a sample PS. This PS describes the data dependency in the software product on which our PM is currently working. PS is also the WSD for our AI Planner.

The indicated relationships are as follows: `SubFamily` describes family decomposition, and `Interface_of` links a family to its interfaces (e.g. C headers), again linked with `Implement_By` to its bodies (e.g. C bodies). `Text_Include` describes normal file inclusion dependencies.

Part (b) is a part of the Process Schema, containing definitions of relevant task types. These types are the KB of our AI Planner. Here we use short notations to save space: For example, in the `Implement` task type `Family(designed) -> Executable(created)` is a combination of FORMALS and PRE/POST_-STATIC of the type. It means that the Input should be a `designed` family, and the Output should a `created` executable code. DECOMP is depicted by nested boxes of types.

Part (c) is the result of the planning process from (a) and (b): the plan (in AI terms) or task network (in PM terms) with explicit Input/Output for each task node. This is also the task derivation graph, generated from the product dependency graph in (a).

Our example is dealing with three combined changes:

1. **FORMALS_IN** of `Link` type is expanded from `$ObjectCode -> ...` to `$ObjectCode + $Library -> ....`
2. **DECOMP** of `Build` type is expanded from {`Ccompile, Link`} to {`Ccompile, Link, Toolar`}. This reflects that a new task type `Toolar` is added:

```
ENTITY_TYPE Toolar : Deriver
{... PRE_STATIC:  Input is 'created'
     CODE:        call ar
     POST_STATIC: Output is 'created'
     FORMALS:     $ObjectCode -> Library
     DECOMP:      {}
} % of Toolar-type
```

3. The PS is changed by a (re)`Design` task (not shown) as follows: sub-family `fb` now has two new C source programs `b1.c` and `b2.c` instead of the original `b.c`; and there is a new library `b.a` in `fb` to hold all object code in `fb`.

The replanning process is invoked explicitly by the Execution Manager, when the above changes have been approved by, say, a `Review` task (not modeled here). The replanning Algorithm2 starts with the `Implement` task, and performs recursively on the `SystemCoding` and `Build` tasks. Figure 2 shows the resulting new configuration: modified PS, modified type definitions, and the readjusted task network. In the modified task network, two dead tasks (`SourceCoding` for `b.c` and `Ccompile` for `b.c`) have been removed, while three new tasks (two `Ccompile` for `b1.c` and `b2.c`, and one `Toolar` to build the library `b.a`) have been introduced. Note also that the `Link` task now has `m.o` and `b.a` as Inputs (previously the latter was `b.o`).

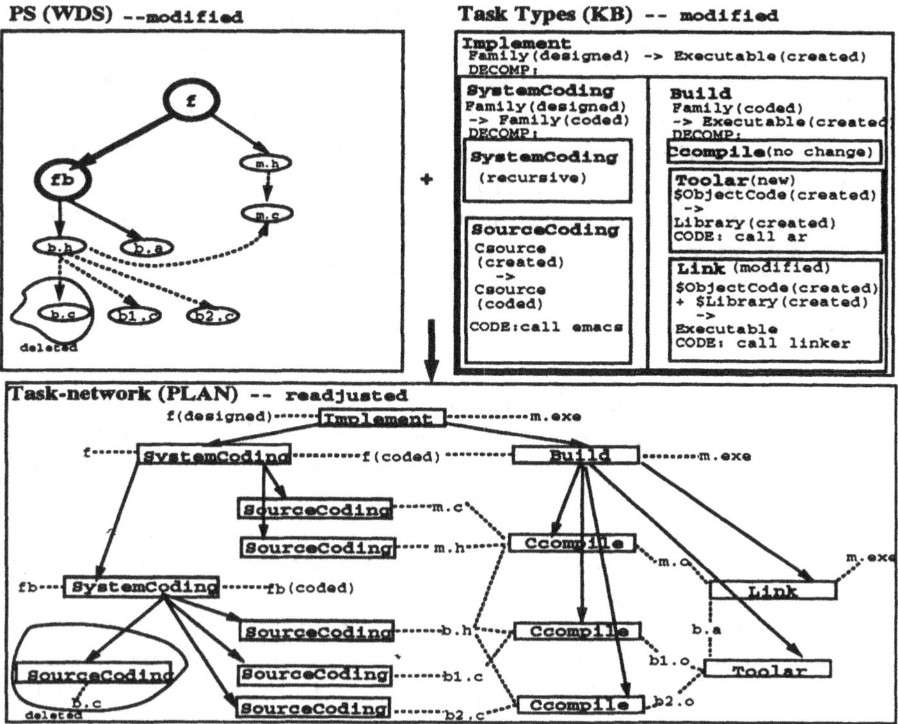

Fig. 2. Readjusted Task Network According to Changes in PS and Types.

7 How to Initiate Replanning upon Changes

If some of the affected tasks are `Active`, the replanning must be delayed (not dealt with here). Another interesting problem is how to automatically initiate the replanning process upon changes. In the example in Section 6, replanning is invoked explicitly by the Execution Manager at some appropriate point. A better way is to exploit the new *trigger* feature in SPELL. We may specify the replanning process as an instance-level procedure in task types as follows:

```
ENTITY_TYPE T : TaskEntity
{INSTANCE_LEVEL
   PROCEDURES replanning: ...
 TYPE_LEVEL
   PROCEDURES t_change: ...
   TRIGGERS PROC = t_change, WHEN = after,
            ACTION = invoke replanning;
} of T-type
```

That is, when the type-level procedure `t_change` is invoked to perform changes in the definition of task type `T`, the ACTION of the trigger will be executed automatically. This will in turn invoke the instance-level procedure `replanning` to deal with the changes introduced by the `t_change` call. The instance-level procedure `replanning` can be originally defined in `TaskEntity`, and refined in each task type which is a subtype of `TaskEntity`.

Similarly, automatic triggering of replanning caused by PS changes can be formalised by triggers in product types.

8 Conclusion

EPOS uses an AI Planner to incrementally instantiate the task network. Close cooperation between the Execution Manager and the Planner is achieved by our hierarchical planning mechanism. The non-linear, core planning layer works efficiently, and actually faster than IPEM when we execute it on the Block World examples cited in [AIS88]. The Planner has also been customised by a PM-specific outer layer, offering the PM user with intelligent assistance on both the product and project level.

As demonstrated in this paper, most of this planning functionality can survive in dynamically evolving Process Schemas and product structures. The replanning algorithm given in Section 5 covers a large portion of all possible changes. Initial experiments on the ISPW'7 example and the one presented in Section 6 (a subset of a real case) have shown that it works properly.

It may be objected that the "back-end" task networks might have been easily generated by available *make-generators*. However, we wanted a task network (re)builder that is applicable over a broader domain.

In the future, we will seek to utilise some of the (re)planning functionality to assist *impact analysis* upon type changes in our Schema Manager.

Acknowledgments go to all members of the EPOS team at NTH.

References

[AIS88] José A. Ambros-Ingerson and Sam Steel. Integrating planning, execution and monitoring. In *Proc. of AAAI'88*, pages 83–88, 1988.

[BF93] Sergio Bandinelli and Alfonso Fuggetta. Computational Reflection in Software Process Modeling: the SLANG Approach. In *Proc. ICSE'15, Baltimore, USA, IEEE-CS Press (forthcoming)*, May 1993.

[CFFS92] Reidar Conradi, Christer Fernström, Alfonso Fuggetta, and Robert Snowdon. Towards a Reference Framework for Process Concepts. In *J.-C. Derniame (ed.): Proc. from EWSPT'92, Sept. 7–8, Trondheim, Norway, Springer Verlag LNCS 635*, pages 3–17, September 1992.

[Cha87] David Chapman. Planning for conjunctive goals. *Artificial Intelligence*, 32:333–377, 1987.

[CJM+92] Reidar Conradi, M. Letizia Jaccheri, Cristina Mazzi, Amund Aarsten, and Minh Ngoc Nguyen. Design, use, and implementation of SPELL, a language for software process modeling and evolution. In *J.-C. Derniame (ed.): Proc. from EWSPT'92, Sept. 7–8, Trondheim, Norway, Springer Verlag LNCS 635*, pages 167–177, September 1992.

[CLJ91] Reidar Conradi, Chunnian Liu, and M. Letizia Jaccheri. Process Modeling Paradigms. In *7th International Software Process Workshop – ISPW'7, Yountville (Napa Valley), CA, USA, 16–18 Oct. 1991. Proceedings forthcoming on IEEE Press*, page 3 p., 1991.

[CM91] Reidar Conradi and Carl Chr. Malm. Cooperating Transactions and Workspaces in EPOS: Design and Preliminary Implementation. In Rudolf Andersen, Janis A. Bubenko jr., and Arne Sølvberg, editors, *Proc. of CAiSE'91, the 3rd International Conference on Advanced Information Systems, Trondheim, Norway, 13–15 May 1991*, pages 375–392. LNCS 498, Springer Verlag, 578 p., 1991.

[COWL91] Reidar Conradi, Espen Osjord, Per H. Westby, and Chunnian Liu. Initial Software Process Management in EPOS. *Software Engineering Journal (Special Issue on Software process and its support)*, 6(5):275–284, September 1991.

[Fer93] Christer Fernström. Process WEAVER: Adding Process Support to UNIX. In *Leon Osterweil (ed.): Proc. from 2nd Int'l Conference on Software Process (ICSP'2), Berlin. IEEE-CS Press*, pages 12–26, March 1993.

[Huf89] Karen E. Huff. *Plan-Based Intelligent Assistance: An Approach to Supporting the Software Development Process.* PhD thesis, University of Massachusetts, September 1989.

[JHO90] Stanley M. Sutton Jr., Dennis Heimbigner, and Leon Osterweil. Language Constructs for Managing Change in Process-Centered Environments. In *Proc. of the 4th ACM SIGSOFT Symposium on Software Development Environments, Irvine, California. In ACM SIGPLAN Notices, Dec. 1990*, pages 206–217, December 1990.

[JLC92] M. Letizia Jaccheri, Jens-Otto Larsen, and Reidar Conradi. Software Process Modeling and Evolution in EPOS. In *Proc. IEEE 4th International Conference on Software Engineering and Knowledge Engineering, Capri, Italy*, June 1992. 13 p.

[LCD+89] Anund Lie, Reidar Conradi, Tor M. Didriksen, Even-André Karlsson, Svein O. Hallsteinsen, and Per Holager. Change Oriented Versioning in a Software Engineering Database. In *Walter F. Tichy (Ed.): Proc. of the 2nd International Workshop on Software Configuration Management, Princeton, USA, 25-27 Oct. 1989, 178 p. In ACM SIGSOFT Software Engineering Notes, 14 (7)*, pages 56–65, November 1989.

[Liu91] Chunnian Liu. Software Process Planning and Execution: Coupling vs. Integration. In Rudolf Andersen, Janis A. Bubenko jr., and Arne Sølvberg, editors, *Proc. of CAiSE'91, the 3rd International Conference on Advanced Information Systems, Trondheim, Norway, 13–15 May 1991*, pages 356–374. LNCS 498, Springer Verlag, 578 p., 1991.

[Sno92] Robert Snowdon. An example of process change. In *J.-C. Derniame (ed.): Proc. from EWSPT'92, Sept. 7–8, Trondheim, Norway, Springer Verlag LNCS 635*, pages 178–195, September 1992.

Provence: A Process Visualization and Enactment Environment

Balachander Krishnamurthy and Naser S. Barghouti

AT&T Bell Laboratories, 600 Mountain Avenue, Murray Hill, NJ 07974 USA

Abstract. A process-centered software development environment must be open and as non-intrusive as possible. Openness is important because the nature of software process work is experimental, making it difficult to determine the forms of assistance that are needed. An extensible architecture that can incorporate new tools is more appropriate than one that fixes its components and functionality. Providing process support in a non-intrusive manner relieves organizations adopting process technology from having to change their working environment significantly. We present *Provence*, an architecture that inculcates these criteria and realizes them by integrating existing software components. Supporting cooperation is equally important, but we do not address this issue yet. Provence monitors developers' activities, maps them to process steps, and maintains process and product data. Further, it provides a dynamic visual representation of changes to process and data throughout the lifetime of a project.

1 Introduction and Motivation

Efforts to improve programmer productivity and software quality have recently focused on supporting the software process. Process-centered software development environments (PSDEs) assist in modeling and enacting software processes. The forms of assistance include: (1) monitoring actual development in order to verify that developers are following a particular process; (2) planning future development activities; (3) automating parts of the process; and (4) enforcing a specific process. These forms of assistance, if provided in a non-intrusive manner, are particularly useful in software engineering environments. Several PSDEs were proposed and some have been built in the past few years [10, 9].

Most existing PSDEs, however, have a closed environment in which the developers work entirely within the PSDEs; i.e., all interaction between the developers and the project's components is done via the PSDE. This approach, which we call the *monolithic environment approach*, assumes that organizations adopting process technology will alter their working environment significantly.

Message-passing environments, such as Forest [3] and Field [8], remove the restriction that all development has to be done from within the environment. However, they still require that all tools must be enveloped to permit interaction via the message server in the environment; i.e., the developers cannot use a new tool without enveloping it.

Both of these approaches suffer from major drawbacks. First, it is very difficult to convince software developers to move to a completely new family of SDEs (process-centered SDEs), especially when the advantages of process-centered environments over more traditional SDEs have not yet been demonstrated. Second, they cannot readily integrate existing technology or use new technology, e.g., software tools, but must instead provide alternatives.

In this paper, we outline the architecture and functionality of Provence, a process-centered SDE architecture that overcomes both of these shortcomings. With respect to the first shortcoming, the architecture makes it possible to introduce features of process-centered environments incrementally, in order to convince developers that there is an added value to using them. Secondly, Provence is component-based, where software tools that are already being used by developers serve as most of the components; new tools can be integrated through a well-defined interface among the components.

There have been a few proposals to move towards a component-based process-centered architecture [10]. These proposals define a set of *services* needed to provide process-centered assistance [4]. However, the proposals do not identify the components that would implement these services, clarify whether or not the services will be provided in a non-intrusive manner, or state how the component interfaces will be designed or implemented.

1.1 Overview of Provence

We have analyzed the requirements for effective process-centered assistance, and have identified five necessary components: (1) a *process server* that assists in process transitions, based on definition of a software process; (2) a *data management system* that stores process and product data in one or more databases and permits querying of the databases; (3) a *smart file system* that detects and announces tool invocations and events related to changes to files; (4) an *event engine* that matches arbitrary event patterns, detects announcements and notifies the process server; and (5) a *visualizer* that displays an up-to-date view of both the process and project data. Figure 1 depicts how these five components are integrated in Provence.

The process model is supplied as input to the process server, which generates specifications expressing interest in low level file system events. These specifications are registered with the event-action engine. The smart file system notifies the event-action engine about file system related activities. The event-action engine filters events of interest and passes them onto the process server. The process server interacts with the data manager to store and retrieve the project's data. The data manager manipulates the data according to the data model supplied to it by the process administrator.

Forest [3] provides a mechanism for achieving some of the same objectives of Provence, namely integration of independent tools into an integrated environment. Field provides a framework based on selective broadcasting, where tools register the message patterns they are interested in and receive messages that match these patterns.

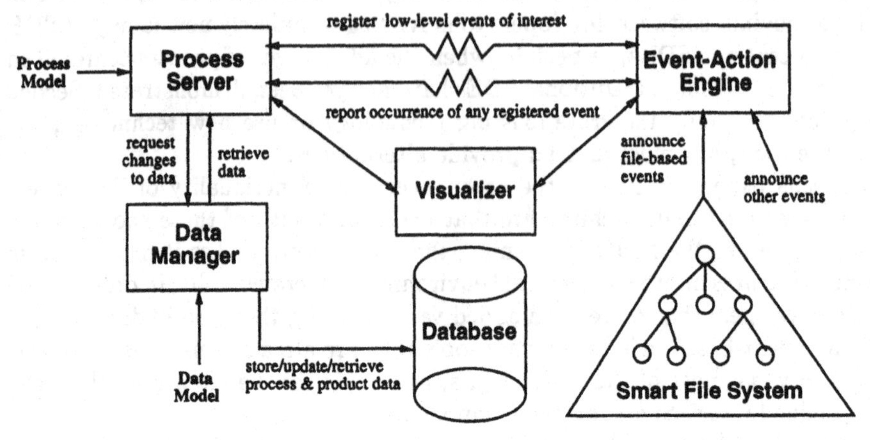

Fig. 1. The components of Provence

1.2 Assumptions

Provence makes several assumptions about the projects that might benefit from it:

- The project has a clear development process. This implies that the process can be modeled in a process modeling language.
- Product data (source code, documentation, executables, etc.) are stored on the file system.
- The project has a well-understood data model (e.g., it is divided into a set of subsystems, each of which can be subdivided into modules.).
- There are two kinds of activities involved in the project: on-line activities (e.g., software tool invocations, accessing files) and manual activities (e.g., attending meetings, making decisions).
- There is a mechanism to announce the occurrence of manual activities to a software tool through a very simple interface (e.g., command line-oriented).

Given a project that meets these expectations, Provence: (1) monitors the development process of a project without forcing developers to change their working environment; (2) maintains data about the process and the end product of a project; (3) answers queries about the status of the software process and the various components of the project, based on the information it collected during the life cycle; and (4) dynamically visualizes transitions in the process. A further step would be to let Provence automate certain parts of the process in as non-intrusive a manner as possible. Eventually, Provence will have the capability to enforce a specific process. The level of intrusion can be calibrated depending upon the strictness of enforcement.

The rest of the paper is organized as follows. We first present a high-level example that gives a flavor of how Provence would assist in carrying out a specific development process. Next, we describe briefly the tools that we are using to realize the architecture shown in Fig. 1; all of these tools are available. We then explain how we are connecting the various tools to provide an open and non-intrusive process enactment. We revisit the example and expand on the details of the various pieces. Finally, we conclude with a summary and a discussion of possible applications of Provence and future directions.

2 A High Level Example

We illustrate the functionality of Provence by a simple example. The development process of a software project typically consists of several phases. We consider here the initial phase, which involves business planning and requirements engineering. Business planning ensures that the end product makes business sense, and requirements engineering involves drafting a document that specifies the technical and functional requirements that the end product must meet. The business planning step is carried out by a the BP (business planning) team headed by a manager, Andrea. The requirements engineering step is done by the architecture team composed of Bala and Naser.

Assume the following process: the requirements engineering step cannot be started except after the business planning team has created a draft of the business information. The architecture team uses the business information to draft a set of requirements for the project. Further steps, such as design, coding, and documentation, cannot start until a draft of the requirements document is created. Both the business planning document and the requirements document are stored as files; the two documents are modified in the "working" area of the project and moved to the "released" area upon finalization.

The following scenario illustrates the kind of assistance that Provence would provide. Say that after the business planning team has worked on the business document for some time, the team's manager Andrea approves a draft of the document, which she moves to the "released area". The smart file system component automatically detects that a draft has been created and notifies the process server via the event-action engine. The process server, through its automation, in turn notifies Naser and Bala that they can start working on the requirements document. In addition, the process server updates the project database, to indicate that the business planning step has been completed and that the requirements engineering step can be started. Bala and Naser create the requirements document and work on it for some time in the "working area". Finally, they both agree on a draft of the document and move that draft to the "released area". Again this is automatically detected and the design team is notified that they can start working on the design document.

The project manager can inquire about the status of various project components or the state of the process. Since the developers' activities have been tracked, these queries can be answered accurately. In addition Provence can visualize all changes to the project components and the process.

3 A Realization of Provence Using Existing Tools

Provence is composed of the five components shown in Figure 1. These components provide most of the services discussed in the ECMA report [4]. In addition to identifying these components and defining their functionality, we have mapped four existing software tools to these components: Marvel [1] (maps to both the process server and the database manager), the 3D File System [5], Yeast [7], and Dotty. The different technologies of these four tools complement each other, and they can be combined to provide assistance in modeling and managing the development process.

Whereas Marvel's rule language can be used to model the software process at a high level, Yeast can serve as a low-level monitor of process-related events. Yeast accepts notification of file-based events, which are automatically generated by the 3D File System. Dotty can visualize the information in the process and project database maintained by Marvel and update the display whenever the database changes. Further, the user can interact directly with Dotty, providing another interface to the process server.

All four tools, which provide most of the functionality of the components, are fully implemented and currently available. The 3D File System, Yeast and Dotty were designed to be open tools in the sense that they can interact with other tools at the operating system level (e.g., via inter-process communication, files, etc.). The connection between the 3D File System and Yeast has been implemented; the connection between Marvel and Yeast, which is done via another tool called the Enactor (explained in the next section) has been partially implemented.

We now describe the four tools briefly and then explain how we connect them.

3.1 Yeast

Yeast (Yet another Event-Action Specification Tool) is a general-purpose platform for constructing distributed event-action applications using high-level specifications. Yeast is based on a client-server architecture where the server is a persistent, network wide daemon. Transient Yeast clients from any machine on the local area network interact with the daemon to register, manipulate and query event-action specifications. A Yeast client program can be executed directly from the computer system's command interpreter.

A Yeast specification consists of an *event pattern* and an associated *action*. When Yeast detects that the event pattern has occurred, the corresponding action is triggered. An event pattern is formed by combining simple events. Yeast supports three combinators: *and* (matched when both components of the pattern are simultaneously true), *or* (matched when either components are true), *then* (right hand component matched only after left hand component has been matched). The patterns can be combined to arbitrary depths and disambiguated via parenthesis.

Simple events are those that occur in the environment of the system, such as temporal events, changes to file system objects, change of state of processes. Most of these events can be detected automatically. Other events of interests, such as a requirements document being approved, is not detectable by the operating system. Thus, Yeast supports three categories of simple events: *temporal events*, *object events*, and *announced events*.

Temporal events are either absolute time events (to be matched at a specific time in the future), or relative time events (that will be matched after the specified time interval has elapsed from the time of specification). Absolute time events can be expressed fully; i.e. it is possible to specify day, date, month, year, hour, minute and seconds. Further, the Yeast language permits the keywords *daily, weekly, monthly, yearly.* Relative time events can be used to express relative time intervals in well understood temporal units. In addition, it is possible to specify both the earliest time at which matching should commence as well as the latest time at which matching should cease.

Object events consist of changes to the values of attributes of objects belonging to a variety of pre-defined object classes, such as files, directories, machines, users. These object classes have a number of pre-defined attributes of varying types. The file object class, for example, has the last modification and access times, size, owner, and permissions as its set of pre-defined attributes. The process object class has among its attributes its status (running, stopped etc.), size, and amount of time used.

Rather than using disparate programs written specifically to watch for the occurrence of operating system events, Yeast unifies the detection of such events in a single daemon.

Apart from pre-defined object classes and their attributes, Yeast permits users to define new object classes and attributes. New attributes can be added to existing object classes as well. However, since the value of such attributes cannot be automatically determined by Yeast, it must be told about them; this is done via explicit notification, known as *announcements*. Announcement is a Yeast client command that sets the value of the user defined attribute of an object.

Given the three types of simple events and the combinators, a complex set of events that require combinations of temporal events, changes in operating system entities etc. can be succinctly expressed in the Yeast specification language and an action can be triggered upon the successful matching of the complex pattern.

As an illustration, consider a requirements document, which is an instance of the *file* object class. The *file* object class already has a pre-defined attribute *mtime* (last modification time). In addition to being notified about file modifications, the development team might be interested in knowing when a document attains the "Draft" status. Yeast provides a way for defining new attributes and specifying their types. This is done via the *defattr* client command:

```
defattr file status string
```

which defines a string valued attribute called *status* to the *file* object class. While only the user who defines an attribute has authorization to generate announcements on it, such authorization can be shared with others.

The following compound specification watches for the occurrence of two events: a change in the *mtime* attribute of the file reqdoc and its *status* attribute becoming "Draft".

```
addspec file reqdoc mtime changed and
        file reqdoc status == Draft
do      tell_enactor draft reqdoc
```

The *and* connector indicates that the specification will match only when the file has been changed *and* its status has become "Draft". The fact that the file reqdoc was changed can be detected automatically. The *status* attribute's value has to be set via an announcement. This is done as follows by any user who has authorization on that attribute:

```
announce file reqdoc status = Draft
```

Once the specification is matched, the action portion of the specification (following the keyword do) is triggered. In this case, the action is tell_enactor, a command script that notifies the Enactor tool, which liaises between Marvel and Yeast (explained later), about the change in status of the file reqdoc.

3.2 The 3D File System

The 3D File System provides a mechanism that allows users to create dynamic views of the software and make changes relative to this view, without affecting the underlying software base. The 3D File System traps a series of system calls that deal with file and naming operations. It is provided as a user level library enabling all programs to run transparently above it.

A slight modification to the 3D File System enabled it to notify the Yeast daemon of changes in the file system. Once a change in the file system has been detected, a user level process (in this case, the Yeast daemon) could be notified. Thus, every time a file is created, deleted, modified, etc. the 3D File System notifies Yeast via an announcement. The Yeast daemon matches this announcement with any specification made by users who had expressed interest in the creation, deletion, modification, etc. of such files.

The singular advantage of using the 3D File System is the transparency it provides to the users while still generating appropriate notifications to Yeast [6]. Users in various projects can use any of their regular tools that do *not* have to be enveloped or otherwise modified. Further the generation of announcement can be customized at various granularities, such as per-session, per-process, or per directory hierarchy. Early measurements have indicated that the load on the file system is not significant due to the overhead of announcement generation.

3.3 Marvel

Marvel is based on three main ideas: (1) providing a PSDE kernel, where the process model is defined in terms of rules; (2) facilitating the integration of conventional Unix tools into the tailored PSDE rather than building specialized tools; and (3) supporting cooperation and coordination among multiple developers within a single software process.

The project's data is modeled in terms of object classes. Each class defines a set of typed *attributes* that can be inherited from multiple superclasses. Loading the data model into Marvel instantiates a project-specific environment. Developers create the actual project components as instances of the classes; Marvel stores all objects in a project database, which is controlled by a centralized server. The project's development process is modeled in terms of condition-action-effects rules. Each rule defines the condition for initiating a process step, the action (e.g., invoking a tool) involved in the step, and the possible effects of the step on the objects in the database.

When a developer requests a command from Marvel's menu, Marvel automatically fires a rule that implements the command by manipulating the attributes of the objects in the database. If the effect of a rule changes the values of objects' attributes in such a way that the conditions of other rules become satisfied, all of those other rules are fired automatically, in a forward chaining manner. Alternatively, if the condition of a rule is not satisfied, backward chaining is performed to attempt to make it satisfied. If that fails and the condition remains unsatisfied, then the rule cannot be executed at that time.

The interaction between Marvel and its users is closed in the sense that developers must request all development activities via Marvel. In the graphical interface, this is done by clicking on a command from either the built-in command menu or the project-specific command menu that corresponds to the loaded rules. All project components must be stored in the project database, which is controlled by Marvel. Furthermore, all the tools used by a project must be enveloped in order to be integrated into the Marvel environment.

We use Marvel's database to store process data and only an image of the product data. The actual code, documentation, etc. of the project is expected to be stored in the file system and manipulated by the same set of tools that developers currently use. The job of the Enactor, as will be explained in detail in the next section, is to translate developers' activities on the file system into Marvel-specific commands.

3.4 Dotty

Dotty is a programmable graph editor that may be used as a standalone tool or as a front end for applications that use graphs. Dotty allows the user to view and manipulate graphs interactively in multiple windows. Users or applications can insert or delete nodes and edges, and change drawing attributes such as color, font names and font sizes. The graph layout is computed automatically via Dot [2]. The Dot tool reads and writes graphs in an attributed graph description language.

4 Connecting the Component Tools

Figure 2 depicts how Marvel, Yeast, the 3D File System and Dotty are connected.

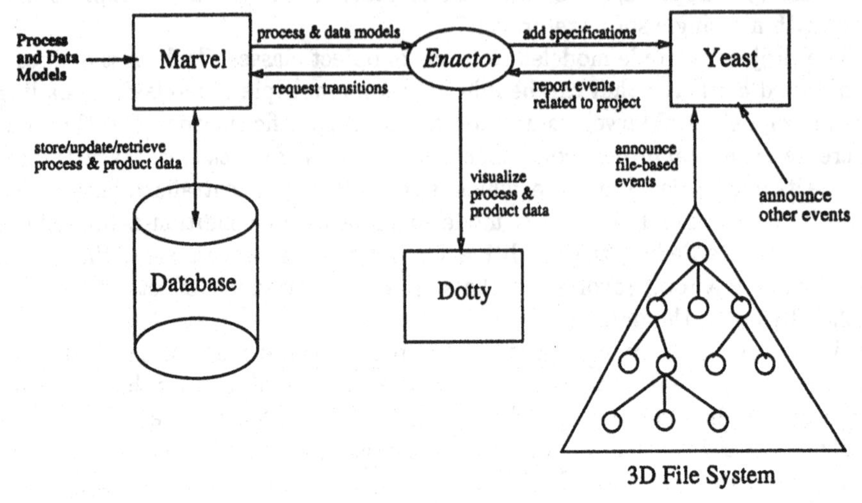

Fig. 2. A realization of Provence

While this is one realization of the Provence architecture, other realizations that use a different set of tools can be achieved with roughly the same amount of effort. We now discuss exactly how the component tools are connected in a realization of Provence.

The information needed for process monitoring that can be supplied by the 3D File System includes the full pathname of the file whose status has changed, the process that caused the change, the owner of the process, and the process identifier. With these bits of information it is possible to keep track of which tool (editor, compiler etc.) changed the file, who executed the tool etc. It is now upto the higher levels of the process environment to express interest for the appropriate file events via specifications and have Yeast match the events (announcements) generated by the file system. The mechanism is thus non-intrusive and general. The sole drawback is the large number of announcements that may be generated but that is easily controlled by masking out announcements when not needed.

Given that Yeast can monitor low level file system events, these need to be translated into high level process transitions. We need a tool that liaises between Marvel and Yeast to generate a set of Yeast specifications based on Marvel's high-level process and data models and to translate the matching of events in Yeast to actions that Marvel can understand. The Enactor is a software tool that performs this role.

Both Marvel and Yeast have client/server models. Marvel on the other hand, supports interactive long-lived clients. The Marvel server controls access to a single database, where all process and product data belonging to a project are stored. The Enactor first establishes a connection with Marvel and then opens another channel for submitting Yeast specifications and accepting Yeast updates.

The Enactor obtains from the Marvel server the set of rule definitions and database objects belonging to the project, and generates appropriate Yeast specifications, accordingly. These specifications are registered with Yeast. The action portion of the specifications require a simple notification to be sent to the Enactor upon matching of the specification. The Enactor maintains a translation table that map Marvel rule names to Yeast specifications generated by the Enactor. The Enactor makes the following assumptions:

1. Marvel must have information about all the pathnames of files that are part of the project. This will be done, for the time being, by having a pathname attribute of every Marvel object that includes a file.
2. Marvel must know which tools can be executed on which objects. This is already part of the standard process modeling in Marvel, where each rule is treated as a method of some object class. The rule's activity indicates which tool in actually invoked when the rule is fired.

For every object that includes a file in Marvel's database, the Enactor generates Yeast specifications that monitor if the status of the file corresponding to the object has changed. Whenever the status of the file changes, Yeast (via the 3D File System) tells the Enactor the user id of the developer who made the change and the pathname of the tool used to change the file. The Enactor maps these pieces of information to the name of a rule and the actual parameter of that rule. Finally, the Enactor instructs Marvel to fire the rule, causing Marvel to make all necessary transition and updates in its database.

In the present model, Marvel ensures that the events generated in the system are only the ones that can be mapped to the process model. This ensures that there can be no inconsistency between the events generated within Marvel and those that are sent to Marvel from the enactor.

In addition to acting as a liaison between Marvel and Yeast, the Enactor also drives the visualization of the process. The programmable aspect of Dotty allows it to establish two-way communication with other processes. In order to visualize the process, the Enactor starts a Dotty process and establishes a two-way connection with it. Initially the Enactor translates the process-related information that Marvel stores in its database into a specification in the Dot language. This specification is sent as input to Dotty. The display generated by Dotty at this stage represents the process model, which shows all the possible transitions.

Whenever a process transition occurs, the Enactor sends a message to Dotty to update the visual representation of the process, showing the transition graphically. Dotty might use color coding to indicate the initiation, progress and completion of process steps. Similarly, color coding and size of nodes may be used to indicate the completion status of a project component.

```
PROJECT :: superclass ENTITY;
    business_info: DOC;          # business planning document
    requirements: DOC;           # the requirements document
    global_proc: PROCESS;        # global process information
    ...
end

DOC :: superclass ENTITY;
    status: (Empty,Initial,Draft,Baselined) = Empty; # Default is Empty
    owner: user;                 # The user id of the document's owner
    ...
end

PROCESS :: superclass ENTITY;
    status: (Initial, BP, RA) = Initial; # Default is Initial
    BP: SUBPROCESS;              # business planning subprocess info
    RA: SUBPROCESS;              # requirements eng. subprocess info
end

SUBPROCESS :: superclass ENTITY;
    status: (NotBegun, Active, Completed) = NotBegun;
    current_step: string;
    team: link TEAM;             # Pointer to team responsible for process
end
```

Fig. 3. Data model of example in Marvel

5 Revisiting the Example

To illustrate the realization of Provence depicted above, we revisit the example discussed in Section 2, and present the details of how the various tools assist in carrying out the process. The example postulated a business planning team creating a business plan. When the plan becomes a draft, the requirements architects need to be notified about it so that they can proceed with their editing of the requirements document.

The first step is defining the data model described in section 2. This includes the organization and structure of project data and the data the needs to be maintained about the process. Figure 3 shows the Marvel classes that specify most of the data model:

Next, we define the process model of Sec. 2 in terms of the two Marvel rules shown in Fig. 4. The first rule specifies that a draft of the business planning document can be created at any time by the owner of the business planning object. As a result of the creation of this draft, the status of the business planning object is changed to "Draft" and the status of the business planning subprocess is

```
draft_bp_info [?bp_info: DOC]:
      (and (exists PROJECT ?proj suchthat (member[?proj.business_info ?bp_info]))
           (exists PROCESS ?proc suchthat (member[?proj.global_proc ?proc]))
           (exists SUBPROCESS ?bp suchthat (member[?proc.BP ?bp])))
      :
      # condition: only the owner can create a final draft
      (?bp_info.owner = CurrentUser)

      { } # no activity

      # effects:
      (and (?bp_info.status = Draft)    # draft of bp info is available
           (?bp.status = Completed)); # BP subprocess is completed


begin_req_doc [?proj:PROJECT]:
      # get all the relevant objects from the database
      (and (exists DOC ?bp_info suchthat (member[?proj.business_info ?bp_info]))
           (exists DOC ?req suchthat (member[?proj.requirements ?req]))
           (exists PROCESS ?proc suchthat (member[?proj.global_proc ?proc]))
           (exists SUBPROCESS ?ra suchthat (member[?proc.RA ?ra]))
           (exists TEAM ?team suchthat (linkto [?ra.team ?team])))
      :
      # condition: The business information must be in draft form
      (?bp_info.status = Draft)

      {MAIL send_mail ?team "draft of BP info available"}

      (and (?req.status = Initial)   # requirements doc. is initialized
           (?proc.status = RA)       # update status of global process
           (?ra.status = Active));   # RA subprocess is now active
```

Fig. 4. Process model rules in Marvel

changed to "Completed". Once the first rule is completed, Marvel automatically initiates the second rule. The second rule states that whenever the status of the business planning object becomes "Draft", then the members of the architecture team are notified of this via electronic mail. In addition, the rule's effect updates the status of the requirements document, and makes transitions in both the global process and the requirements architecture subprocess.

Given the two rules and the data model, the Enactor generates Yeast specifications to watch for the events that are relevant to the process. The set of Yeast specifications for the example are the following:

```
addspec file /proj/release/bplan created == true and
        file /proj/release/bplan status == Draft
do      tell_enactor draft_bp_info bplan
```

```
addspec file /proj/working/reqdoc mtime changed
do      tell_enactor edit_req_doc reqdoc
```

The first specification requires that the business plan must be created in the release area *and* its status must be "Draft" before it can be matched. When the business plan file is created in the release area, the 3D File System detects it and notifies Yeast. This matches the first half of the first specification. When the person responsible for completing business plans decides it is done, he/she generates an announcement setting the status attribute of the business plan file to be "Draft". The specification is fully matched now and Yeast triggers the action that notifies the Enactor that the business plan information has been drafted.

The Enactor in turn maps this information to the draft_bp_info rule shown above. The Enactor sends a message to Marvel instructing it to fire the rule, and passes to it the object representing `bplan` as an actual parameter. Marvel fires the rule, which causes forward chaining to the begin_req_doc rule. The net effect will be that Marvel will send a notification to the members of the architecture team and update information in its database, reflecting the process transitions that have taken place.

Likewise, when a member of the architecture team changes the working version of the requirements document (the file working/reqdoc changes), the second Yeast specification is matched. As a result of this the Enactor is notified, which in turn, instructs Marvel to fire the edit_req_doc rule (not shown here). Marvel notifies the other members of the architecture team of these changes.

Note that the members of the business planning and architecture teams work without unnecessary intrusions by Provence since they do not have to inform Provence manually about automatically detectable activities. Moreover, they can use any tools (editors, formatters, etc.) to perform their activities. The advantages of non-intrusiveness through automatic data capture, and open environments are reflected in the simple example above.

6 Conclusions and Future Work

We presented Provence, a component-based architecture for modeling, enacting and visualizing the software process. Provence departs from recent work on process-centered SDEs in two main respects:

1. The main components of a process-centered SDE have been identified and separated with clear interfaces, making them more easily replaceable. This contrasts the monolithic architectures where these components are tightly coupled and made to work only with each other.
2. The realization of Provence we presented is based on existing tools, which together can be used to provide the needed assistance in modeling and managing software processes. It is possible to replace any of the tools or to extend the set of tools. However, each of the tools must conform to the set of interface requirements for the component to which it is mapped to guarantee

openness. For example, the smart file system component must provide information about file-related events and operating system process invocations in a format that is accepted by the event engine.

We believe that the open architecture of Provence is more appropriate to the experimental nature of software process work. This is very important because it is difficult to determine the forms of process-related assistance that are needed by development organizations. Consequently, an architecture that can be easily extended or changed to incorporate different tools is more appropriate than one that fixes its components and functionality.

Currently, all the tools discussed in Section 4 as well as the interfaces between them have been implemented. The pending portion of the implementation is the automatic generation of specifications for the Enactor, as well as the link between the Enactor and the visualization component. After implementing a prototype realization of Provence, we shall conduct several experiments involving projects in development organizations. Our aim is to model the processes of these projects within our system, employ the system in a manner similar to what we have described in this paper, and measure the effects of employing the system on the software process. We hope that these experiments will help us achieve the following goals:

1. identify the appropriate form(s) of process-centered assistance that development organizations need to increase their productivity. Expected forms of assistance include:
   - monitoring of the process for the purpose of analyzing it both dynamically and statically
   - automating parts of the process so as to relieve developers from menial chores
   - measuring the actual duration of each step in a process for the purpose of planning future processes or the remaining parts of the process.
2. detect shortcomings and inefficiencies in existing processes.
3. determine the effectiveness and feasibility of our approach.

One of the applications of Provence is dynamic project management. A project manager can be notified by Provence about changes to the state of the development process and the project components, as soon as these changes occur. Early notification about specific milestones help managers avoid situations where they find out about a potential disaster (e.g., a two-week delay in delivering a major component) too late to be able to replan around it. The information produced by Provence can also be used to generate various project-related reports and charts.

Acknowledgements

David Rosenblum and Alex Wolf provided input in the earlier phase of our project. We thank Dewayne E. Perry for reviewing earlier drafts of this paper. We would also like to thank the anonymous referees for their comments.

References

1. Naser S. Barghouti and Gail E. Kaiser. Scaling Up Rule-Based Development Environments. In *Third European Software Engineering Conference, ESEC '91*, pages 380–395, Milan Italy, October 1991. Springer-Verlag. Published as *Lecture Notes in Computer Science* no. 550.
2. Emden Gansner, Eleftherios Koutsofios, Stephen C. North, and Kiem-Phong Vo. A method for drawing directed graphs. *IEEE Transactions on Software Engineering*. To appear.
3. David Garlan and Ehsan Ilias. Low-cost, adaptable tool integration policies for integrated environments. In R. N. Taylor, editor, *Fourth ACM SIGSOFT Symposium on Software Development Environments*, pages 1–10, Irvine CA, December 1990. ACM Press. Special issue of *Software Engineering Notes*, 15(6), December 1990.
4. NIST ISEE Working Group. A Reference Model for Frameworks of Computer Assisted Software Engineering Environments, Draft version 1.3. In *Reprints of the Seventh International Software Process Workshop*, Yountville, CA, October 1991.
5. David G. Korn and Eduardo Krell. 'A New Dimension for the UNIX File System'. *Software Practice and Experience*, 20(S1):19–34, June 1990.
6. Eduardo Krell and Balachander Krishnamurthy. COLA: Customized overlaying. In *Proceedings of the USENIX Winter 1992 Conference*, pages 3–7, 1992.
7. Balachander Krishnamurthy and David S. Rosenblum. An event-action model of computer-supported cooperative work: Design and implementation. In K. Gorling and C. Sattler, editors, *International Workshop on Computer Supported Cooperative Work*, pages 132–145. IFIP TC 6/WG C.5, 1991.
8. Steven P. Reiss. Connecting tools using message passing in the field environment. *IEEE Software*, 7(4):57–66, July 1990.
9. Wilhelm Shaefer, editor. *Proceedings of the Eighth International Software Process Workshop*, Schloss Dagstuhl GERMANY, March 1993. In press.
10. Ian Thomas, editor. *Reprints of the Seventh International Software Process Workshop*, Yountville CA, October 1991.

Process Programming with Active and Passive Components

Christian J. Breiteneder
Centre Universitaire d'Informatique
Université de Genève
CH-1204, Genève, Switzerland
chris@cui.unige.ch

and

Thomas A. Mueck
Department of Information Systems
University of Vienna
A-1010, Vienna, Austria
mueck@ifs.univie.ac.at

Abstract. *Software process programming languages*, i.e., languages designed to support the development of executable software process models, represent a recent and rapidly growing research topic in software engineering. *Process programming environments* and *process run time environments* are also on the research agenda, as large CASE workbenches have to be controlled and even driven in a project specific fashion by process programs to be written and executed in an appropriate environment. A certain need for specialized process programming languages emerges from the fact that software process programs have to be based on very heterogeneous modeling constructs. In particular, each process program is defined upon distinct object categories like projects, persons, equipment or documents, it contains different control constructs like place transition nets, first order predicates, predicates stated in temporal or fuzzy logic calculi and it has to allow for different initiative policies like program *controlled* policies, program *driven* policies or mixtures of both.

The PROMOLA process programming language, as proposed in this paper, supports a place transition net used for object behavior modeling together with entity-relationship based data modeling constructs. Active event propagation is supported by trigger specifications which allow for complex activity threads. The process programming environment shares meta-data with the run time environment. In particular, all process program information is stored in a repository by the process programming environment components and subsequently used as decision meta-data by the run time environment.

1. Introduction

The term *software process program* (or just *process program*; see [11]) refers to an executable software process model which can be constructed, validated and executed using well-established software engineering techniques adapted for this purpose. Similar to any conventional program, a process program is based on the support components of an appropriate process programming environment as well as on the program enforcing control components of a process run-time environment [4]. Prominent examples of process program based environments (or process centered environments) in this sense are the Arcadia environment [17], the MELMAC approach [5], the IPSE2.5 approach [18], the Oikos project [1] and the MARVEL environment [7]. Extending the analogy to conventional programming, formal notations which have been designed to yield process programs instead of descriptive, but not immediately executable process models, are called *software process programming languages* ([15] and [16] on APPL/A; [13] on MVP).

Applying well-known engineering considerations for software projects, a rigorous methodological backbone and, above all, an integrated set of supporting software tools is needed to put theoretical process programming concepts to practical work. Considering, for example, the set of different process programs for a software factory working on different classes of development projects gives us a description of partially concurrent sub-processes which have to cooperate in order to obtain high quality results (i.e., software systems) in minimal time. The sub-processes operate on a common set of objects belonging to different semantic categories like persons, documents, code fragments, tools, hardware facilities and so on. However, the formalization of concurrently executing processes operating on a common object set is already known to be a complex problem (various software engineering disciplines are confronted with this kind of complexity).

As far as the evaluation of a new approach is concerned, several publications cover different aspects and requirements with regard to language notation and interfacing techniques, language constructs and language tool support. For example, [15] contains a list of basic requirements which includes

- an explicit representation of object and object relationship structures, in other words a data model for the set of objects participating in a process,
- an explicit representation of constraint structures with regard to object change, i.e., explicit object behavior specifications with object state change constraints,
- means for process automation in the context of object state change propagation, consistency constraint enforcement and tool invocation and
- means for process abstraction using multi-level process models.

Using similar (and in any case quite heterogeneous) requirement specifications for SPPLs, recent publications [4] advocate some sort of multi-paradigm representation framework, i.e., the use of different language paradigms for different modeling subtasks. Reacting to this proposal, we present an SPPL approach focusing on a clear distinction between language constructs used for process *specification* (passive components) and language constructs used for process *execution* (active components). The former include augmented place-transition nets for behavioral and ER diagrams for structural specifications, the latter event templates and trigger executions in the context of activity modeling.

Previous SPPL proposals (see [3] for a short overview and [4] for a more detailed study) have been used as a starting point for an integrated process programming approach. The main language design problem is characterized by some sort of trade-off between expressive power on the one hand and executability on the other hand. Traditional process modeling approaches demonstrate impressive modeling capabilities but fail to provide executable models whereas recent process programming approaches yield executable models but reveal several modeling weaknesses. Consequently, any new SPPL has to bridge that gap between expressive power and executability.

PROMOLA, the SPPL proposed in this paper, is based on an event-driven program interface. External agents (humans, tools, calendar daemons) supply event streams, i.e., streams of atomic actions used to drive processes and to change process object states. In particular, any external application program written in a conventional programming language may communicate with process programs using a standard call interface and a

standard message interchange protocol. In the following, external agents are called *process program clients* and the process program run-time system is called the *process program server*, since it is responsible for event processing. Potential process steps are represented by event requests launched by process program clients. The process program server checks all requests against the model constraints and decides to process or reject each request. Accepted requests cause events and therefore process steps. A brief comparison of related work can be found in [3].
The remainder of this paper has the following structure. Section 2 contains a short outline of the PROMOLA language together with a number of small examples. Additional details concerning the specification of PROMOLA can be found in [3]. The design of the PROMOLA software environment is described in Sections 3 and 4. The former describes the programming environment, the latter a possible run-time environment structure.

2. An Outline of the PROMOLA Language

Following the structure of the language, Section 2 contains three subsections. Subsection 2.1 contains a very brief description of the basic ER formalism used as the data model specification language. Expecting the reader to be familiar with this well-known formalism, a detailed description is omitted. Subsection 2.2 describes a modification of a place transition net formalism presented in [10]. This formalism was created for the specification and enforcement of object behavior constraints (see [9] on constraint enforcement) and subsequently adapted for the needs of object behavior specifications in the context of process programming (a similar place transition net oriented approach can be found in [2]). Subsection 2.3 deals with event trigger specifications put on top of the static data model and the object behavior model. Executable trigger units are used to produce event request sequences which are able to cause numerous object state changes as a consequence of one single event.
Each PROMOLA program is based on process data stemming from a few distinct semantic categories. In particular, there are object types containing state attributes (called *aspects*). This term is used to stress the difference between ordinary object attributes not relevant to the process program and state attributes which represent the basic data structures for the process program. Each attribute value of an aspect represents a particular object state. Actually, one object type may contain more than one aspect. For example, an object type PERSON may contain aspects *FamilyState*, *EducationalState* and *WorkState*. An update of an aspect value which corresponds to an object state change may be achieved only by executing an event request corresponding to a certain event type. From the viewpoint of the process model and the corresponding active system component it is irrelevant whether the event request is issued by an external tool, by an external application program or by a human agent. In this context, the term external should be read as external to the process program run-time environment. In each case the process program defines whether or not the event request is semantically legal with respect to the object behavior model and the current process state. With respect to these concepts, the fundamental semantic categories used in PROMOLA process programs can be given as:

- A set of *object types* containing some *aspects* which are part of a particular process model. Each aspect belongs to exactly one object type and is defined over one finite domain, i.e., a finite nonempty set of aspect values to be interpreted as object states.

- A set of *objects*, in which each object is identified by exactly one object surrogate value. Each object belongs to at least one object type.
- A set of *event types*, in which each event type contains a formal parameter list representing a list of participating object types and therefore a list of slots for participating objects in actual event requests.
- A sequence of *events requests*, in which each event request is an extension of a certain event type. In contrast to objects which may be assigned to various object types (generalization hierarchies based on EER diagrams), each event request corresponds to exactly one event type. Consequently, each event request *actual parameter list* has to be object type compatible to the corresponding formal parameter list of the event type. In other words, an event request actual parameter list represents the objects participating in the event request. An event request which is considered legal by the run-time system is executed and is therefore resulting in an *event*.

Due to the fact that place transition nets are the fundamental constructs used as a starting point for the MODYN methodology described in Subsection 2.2, some standard definitions are used which are originating from this field. In [12], a detailed survey on the subject is given.

Usually, *transitions* represent activities, whereas *places* are used to model passive information stores marked by zero or more *tokens*. A set of *arcs* is used to connect transitions and places. If an arc is going from a place p (from a transition t) to a transition t (to a place p), p is called input place (output place) of t. If a transition *fires* (which means in the context of this paper that an event takes place), the token distribution, i.e. the *marking*, changes according to the set of arcs connected to the transition. A transition t may fire, if and only if each input place p_i of t contains at least as many tokens as there are arcs going from p_i to t (this is called the *enabling rule*). Firing a transition t removes from each input place p_i exactly as many tokens as there are arcs from p_i to t and inserts into each output place p_j exactly as many tokens as there are arcs from t to p_j. Any place p may be input place as well as output place for any transition t.

2.1 Data model specification language

A PROMOLA process program is based on a conceptual database schema containing the object type and aspect specifications together with all relationships between object types. This subdivision of a process program corresponds to the type declaration and variable definition subdivision of a conventional program. The underlying data structures are of prime importance for program specification as well as for execution. For example, an event type formal parameter has to match an entity type name contained in the underlying data model. The latter refers to the fact that the process program server relies on object, aspect and relationship data retrieved from the information base at event request execution time. However, the conceptual schema and the information base have to contain additional data not related to process model ortho-data, e.g. the process program itself. Consequently, this kind of non-ortho-data is called process program meta-data.

The overall structure of the process program database, i.e., the "coarse-grained" conceptual schema, is formulated in a simple entity-relationship diagram language which is restricted to relationship types of degree 2. After the specification of an entity relationship diagram describing the coarse-grained conceptual schema needed for a particular process program, the object types (trivially mapped to ER "entity types") are

refined by means of a linear notation. Those two subtasks are briefly considered in the sequel.
The coarse-grained conceptual schema represented by an ER-diagram has to contain all entity types relevant for a particular process program. The detailed attribute structure of those entity types is described by an entity type refinement specification also belonging to the data model specification. The structure of such an entity type refinement specification is shown in the following example.

Example 1: coarse-grained conceptual schema and its entity type refinement

A particular project database contains object types PERSON, PROJECT, DESIGN-DOC and TEAM. Identifying attributes are *PersId*, *ProjId*, *DesDocId* and *TeamId*. Various persons are assigned to one team which is assigned to exactly one project. Each person may be assigned to one or zero teams. Each team has one leader, one supervisor and a number of team members. The leader of a team as well as the supervisor are also considered team members. Each project team produces and maintains various design documents for the corresponding project. Each design document belongs to exactly one project.

ER-Model: `project-db`

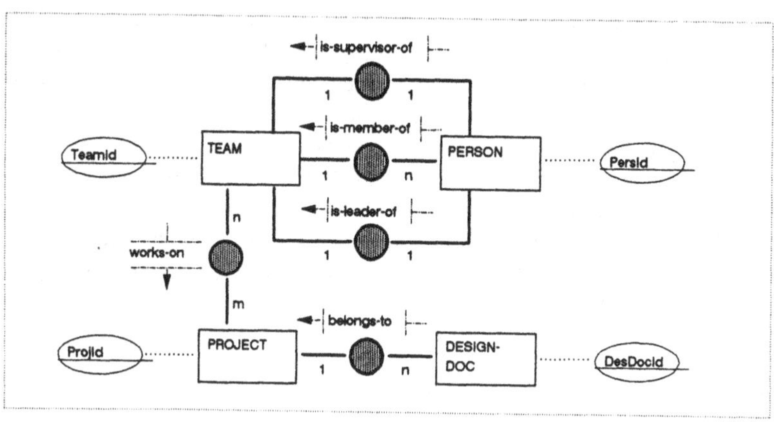

Figure 1: Coarse-grained conceptual schema

```
REFINEMENT SPECIFICATION project-db
  TYPE Person IDENTIFIED BY PersId
  ATTRIBUTES
    PersName: CHAR(30); Address: CHAR(40)
  ASPECTS
    WorkState: (assigned, unassigned, on-vacation, on-training)
    Qualification: (novice, experienced, expert)
  TYPE Project IDENTIFIED BY ProjId
  ATTRIBUTES
    ProjName: CHAR(20); Manager: IDENTIFIER
  ASPECTS
    Progress: (started, collecting-requirements,
    elaborating-specification, designing-overall-structure,
    designing-modules, coding-modules, testing-modules,
    integrating-modules, finished)
```

```
TYPE Design-Doc IDENTIFIED BY DesDocId
ATTRIBUTES
  DocNumber: INTEGER(8); Folder: CHAR(40)
ASPECTS
  ReviewState: (unapproved, in-work, in-review, approved)
TYPE Team IDENTIFIED BY TeamId
ATTRIBUTES
  InfName: CHAR(20); Location: CHAR(40)
ASPECTS
  SetUpState: (leader-assignment-possible,
  supervisor-assignment-possible, working, released)
```

Parts of this example are used throughout the paper to produce a familiar application context as a guide line for all new modeling constructs introduced in the next subsections[1)]. At this point, we are able to focus the language description on the net component of PROMOLA.

2.2 Object Behavior Specification Language

MODYN is based on an augmented place transition net formalism initially designed for the specification and enforcement of dynamic constraints in database management systems. Consequently, the original MODYN design was already focused on computable specifications. MODYN specifications serve as meta-data input for components used as constraint enforcement monitors in database management systems. In this paper, the original MODYN formalism is transformed to a slightly different place transition net based notation which is better suited for the formulation of executable process models. In this subsection, the description contains basically two steps. In the first step, traditional place transition nets have to be interpreted in terms of the underlying data modeling categories as given above. In the second step, place transition nets are augmented to provide all modeling constructs necessary for object behavior modeling in the context of process models.

2.2.1 Interpretation of Places and Transitions

The first step is straightforward and well-known from previous research work in conceptual modeling (see [6] or [14] for examples). Actually, the set of event types is mapped to the set of transitions and the union of all aspect domains is mapped to the set of places.

Domain elements have to be qualified by the corresponding aspect identifier in order to obtain unique place identifiers. This kind of qualification is visualized by *attribute borders* in the following graphical representations. Starting from a basic place transition net inscribed by aspect domain elements (places) and event type names (transitions), several add-on constructs are used to meet the needs of process specification and control. In particular, the following extensions are needed:

---

1) It has to be stressed that all examples are only meant to illustrate the application of PROMOLA constructs, which means that the merits of the resulting particular process program are not considered. Actually, this paper deals with process programming languages and not with the quality of particular process programs.

I) *colored tokens* used to identify process objects

Tokens are marked by object surrogates in order to represent objects. All object surrogates (token colors) are denoted by $\omega_1, .. \omega_n$ in the sequel. Consequently, a particular object participating in a process is represented in a net by a number of identically colored tokens, one for each aspect of the underlying object type. In particular, the current state of an object, say ω_k, is represented by the current positions of the ω_k-colored tokens in the net.

II) *transition inscriptions* representing event type semantics

Each transition *t* has to be inscribed by the corresponding list of formal parameters (p_1:o_1, .. p_v:o_w). Optionally, some guarded actions can be added (see below). Considering an event request for transition *t*, the actual parameters are bound to the formal parameters according to their position. Of course, the run-time system has to check the object types of the actual parameters.

As already mentioned, a distinction has to be made between *event request* and *event*. Event requests may be launched concurrently by several process program clients. Subsequently, they are passed to the active system component, namely the process program server, which is used as an integrity enforcement monitor. The process program server determines whether or not the event request is semantically legal with respect to the process program and the process state. If the event request is semantically legal, it will be executed thus producing an event. If the event request is semantically illegal, it will be rejected by the process program server. In those cases, adequate information concerning the negative decision will be passed to the launching component.

III) Modified *enabling* and *firing* rules

Unfortunately, the final problem of modified enabling conditions and token flows for colored tokens (enabling rule and firing rule) requires more considerations. However, the semantic interpretation of the terms *enabling rule* and *firing rule* is almost trivial, namely:

- *enabling rule*
  Is a particular event request semantically legal with regard to the states of the objects used as event request formal parameters?
- *firing rule*
  To what extent does the execution of a semantically legal event request change the states of the participating objects and therefore the state of the process?

The enabling rule has to decide whether or not a particular event request belonging to event type *t* is legal according to the specification of the net and its current marking which means according to the process program and the current process state. To come to a decision, the constraint enforcement monitor has to inspect the current marking of all input places of transition *t* (see description above) with respect to the bag of object surrogates used as actual parameters in the event request. In particular, the bag of input places can be divided into subbags according to the aspect structure of the net. Example 2 is illustrating this partitioning. A transition *t* is said to be enabled for an event request if and only if all aspects are active for that particular event request and an optional GUARD-predicate evaluates to true. Consequently, an aspect *s* is said to be active for an event request, if there is at least one enabling set of properly colored tokens placed in those incoming places of *t* which belong to *s*. An enabling set for an aspect *s* is a set of tokens with the following properties:

- there is one token for each arc going from a place *p* of *s* to *t* (of course, the particular token has to be located in the place belonging to the arc, namely *p*)

- all tokens in the set are marked with object surrogates being actual parameters of the event request in question

There are situations in which a number of different enabling sets exist. Generally it is not determined which token has to be in which place to activate an aspect. This property turns out to be useful for the representation of constraints like "*n* objects out of *m* have to be in state *s*". However, it is possible to override this property using an arc inscription, i.e., an identifier from the event type formal parameter list. Such an inscription enforces the presence of one particular token in one distinct place. The following example is based on the data structure definition given in Example 1.

Example 2: legal/illegal event request

Assigning a supervisor to a team requires the team being in state *supervisor-assignment-possible* for aspect *SetUpState*. Any supervisor assignment is achieved by an event of type assign-supervisor (T: TEAM; P1,P2: PERSON). The person to be assigned as supervisor should be passed as the first person (parameter P1), the team leader has to be supplied as the second participating person (parameter P2). A supervisor has to be either in state *expert* or in state *experienced* for aspect *Qualification* and must be in state *unassigned* for aspect *WorkState*. The execution of a legal event request has to cause a state change of the object supplied as P1 to *assigned* for aspect *WorkState* and has to cause the insertion of relationship is-supervisor-of (P1, T) into relationship type is-supervisor-of. The corresponding team has to make a state change from *supervisor-assignment-possible* to *working* for aspect *SetUpState*.

Resulting sub-net (with an assumed marking representing a particular process state):

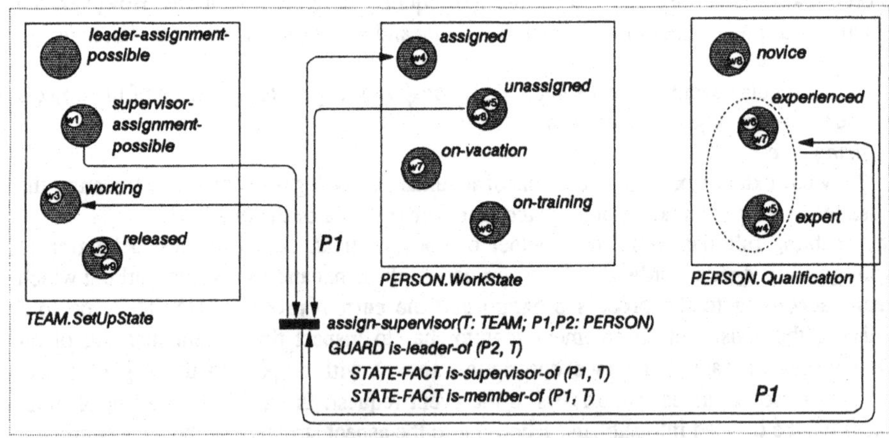

Figure 2: Assign-supervisor (T:TEAM; P1,P2:PERSON)

The subnet in Figure 2 reflects the requirements given above, since the three aspects TEAM.*SetUpState*, PERSON.*Qualification* and PERSON.*WorkState* are connected with the transition inscribed by assign-supervisor in the appropriate way. Also, the arc inscriptions with P1 indicate that the object surrogate bound to P1 is to be interpreted as the person which should be assigned as supervisor. This may be seen from the state change of P1 for aspect PERSON.*WorkState*, whereas the object surrogate bound to P2 is to be used in the GUARD-predicate of the transition. The guarded STATE-FACT statements are meant to establish the relationship between the team and the supervisor and the team membership of the supervisor in case of event request execution.

Considering the marked net of Figure 2 and assuming that the relationship is-leader-of is currently containing the tuples { .. (ω_2, ω_7), (ω_1, ω_6), (ω_3, ω_4) .. }, different event requests might be checked. In particular, an event request assign-supervisor (ω_1, ω_4, ω_6) would be rejected, since ω_4 is not in state *unassigned* for aspect *WorkState*. An event request assign-supervisor (ω_1, ω_5, ω_8) would be rejected since ω_8 is not the leader of team ω_1. On the contrary, an event request assign-supervisor (ω_1, ω_5, ω_6) would be accepted, since ω_1 is in state *supervisor-assignment-possible* for aspect *SetUpState* and ω_5 is in state *unassigned* for aspect *WorkState* and ω_5 is in state *expert* for aspect *Qualification* and ω_6 is-leader-of team ω_1.

One final feature not yet described has already been used in Example 2, namely OR'd input places (also referred to as *place aggregations*) as a modeling construct for sets of alternative object states. Place aggregations are transparent with regard to the enabling rule since they are handled like simple places. The integrity enforcement monitor substitutes the place aggregation by the actual place of the token, i.e., if a particular token with a requested color is in one place participating in the aggregation, the token may be member of an enabling set. If the token is chosen as member of the actual enabling set, the current place of the token replaces the aggregation. Consequently, all place aggregations are resolved during any enabling rule evaluation.

After the enabling rule, the *firing rule* has to be considered; i.e., the *token flow* in case of event request execution has to be defined. From the process engineering point of view, the token flow represents the state change behavior of participating process objects. Similar to the token flow in basic place transition nets, firing transition t causes the removal of one token per input arc from the set of input places and the insertion of one token per output arc into the set of output places. Basically, a transition in a MODYN net has to be conservative unless it is a creating transition, i.e., a transition which represents an event type responsible for token generation in the context of object creation. However, the MODYN firing rule has to cope with token colors (object surrogates). Consequently, the corresponding token flow with respect to token colors and to the domain and object type semantics has to be described in greater detail. Omitting special cases not relevant in the context of this paper, such a description can be given informally by two rules:

(1) If possible, a token returns to the place it came from. This kind of token flow represents a state precondition which remains true after the event.

(2) If possible, a token returns to the aspect it came from. This means a state precondition and a state change for the object denoted by the token.

At first, rule (1) is evaluated. For tokens remaining unassigned after the evaluation of rule (1), rule (2) is evaluated. Unassigned tokens after executing both rules indicate an inter-aspect token flow or a token flow representing an object type change. Neither case is covered in this paper (see [10] for a discussion of object type change specifications). The following example demonstrates the token flow caused by an event request execution.

Example 3: Token flow

Reconsidering Example 2, the execution of the legal event request *assign-supervisor* (ω_1, ω_5, ω_6) yields the marked net depicted in Figure 3. Resulting sub-net (with an assumed marking representing a particular process state):

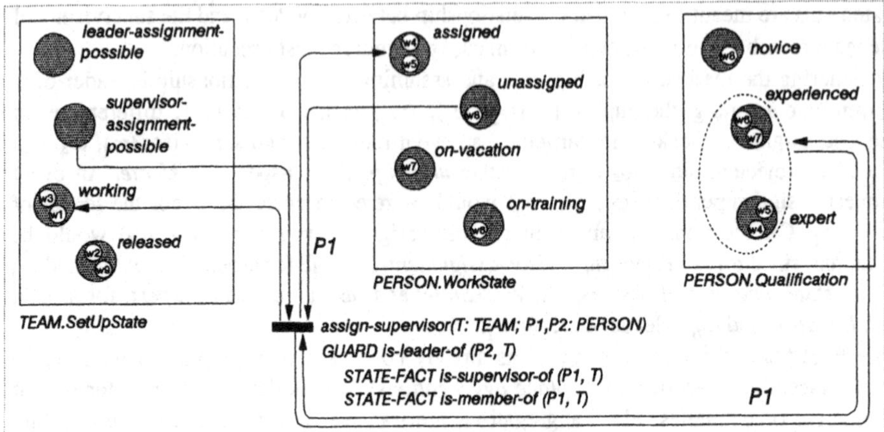

Figure 3: New marking (event request execution)

Similar to the possible existence of more than one enabling set for an event request, a net specification may yield a set of legal token flow variants for some or all transitions. The specification of ambiguous token flows may be used to model state transitions taking place with certain probabilities, which means that a process engineer has to be fully aware of the semantics of ambiguous token flow specifications. On the contrary, avoiding such specifications is not difficult as the APTN graph editor (see Section 3) can be configured to reject this type of token flow specifications. In this case, ambiguities can be resolved using arc inscriptions (similar to those used in the enabling rule). Again, the corresponding modification of the token flow rule is straightforward and corresponds to the modification of the enabling rule given above.

2.3 Trigger Specification Language

In an augmented place transition net, the execution of an event request of a certain type may only result in state changes of participating objects. This means that the execution of an event request may affect only those objects which are passed as actual parameters to the formal parameter slots specified in the event type template. However, there are several situations for which this type of state change concept is not sufficient. Very often, the firing of a transition should also be used as a signal to trigger other event types, i.e. to launch other event requests related to different aspects. Consequently, an event request execution must be able to initiate some sort of *event chain* given by interconnected trigger specifications used to set up activity threads.

To fulfill those requirements as well, an event trigger specification language has to be introduced. As usual, the corresponding evaluation schema for event trigger specifications has to be discussed in order to get a first grasp of the trigger semantics. Informally, an event request execution may trigger subsequent event types if its event type specification is used in a trigger unit as *initiating event type*. Executing such an event causes the evaluation of all trigger units in which the corresponding event type is used as initiating event type.

Each trigger unit consists of three parts: a *repository specification*, a *symbol specification* and a *statement specification*. Since a trigger unit most likely refers to process objects described in the object type specification (Subsection 2.1), a connection to the data model has to exist. The repository specification contains declarations for these data sets related to the object type specifications which are subsequently used in the symbol specification and in the statement specification of the trigger unit. The symbol specification is used to define variables (single valued or set valued). Attribute names which have been supplied in the repository specification might be already used in the symbol specification. The statement specification may contain constructs like simple assignment statements, assignment statements with relational select clauses on data sets from the repository specification, conditional event request triggers and for each loops for object set processing. The syntactic structure of a trigger unit, as well as the operational semantics, are illustrated by Example 4 which relies on the entity types of Example 1. All formal definitions can be looked up in [3].

Example 4: Trigger unit

The termination of a project (indicated by an event of type delivery (P: PROJECT)) has to cause a state change for the project as well as the deallocation of the corresponding project team. Resulting sub-net (with an assumed marking representing a particular process state):

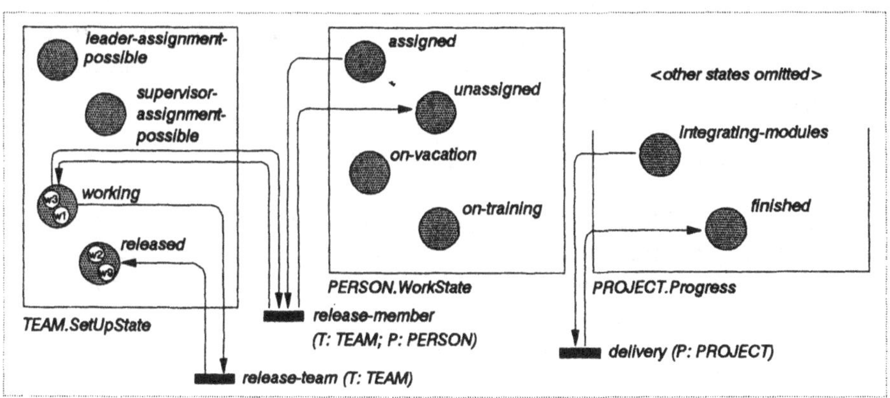

Figure 4: Net parts connected by trigger unit

Resulting trigger unit:

```
TRIGGER UNIT free-project-team ON delivery
    REPOSITORY
      works-on ( TeamId, ProjId )
      is-member-of ( PersId, TeamId )
    SYMBOL
      ProjectFinished: 1 OF delivery ( P: PROJECT )
      SetOfPersons: SET OF PersId
      TeamToRelease: TeamId
      PersonToUnassign: ELEMENT OF SetOfPersons
    STATEMENT
      TeamToRelease :=
        SELECT TeamId FROM works-on
          WHERE ProjectFinished = works-on.ProjId
      SetOfPersons :=
        SELECT PersId FROM is-member-of
```

```
            WHERE TeamToRelease = is-member-of.TeamId
        FOR EACH PersonToUnassign DO
          FIRE release-member ( TeamToRelease, PersonToUnassign )
        END
        FIRE release-team ( TeamToRelease )
  END free-project-team
```

The evaluation of the trigger unit given above follows a straightforward thread of control. Initially, the execution of an event request of type *delivery* (P: PROJECT) invokes the trigger unit and binds an object surrogate to the variable `ProjectFinished`, since *delivery* is the initiating event type of the trigger unit. Subsequently, the surrogate of the corresponding project team is selected and stored in the variable `TeamToRelease`. Further on, all surrogates of team members are selected and stored in the set valued variable `SetOfPersons`. The following for-each loop uses `PersonToUnassign` as control variable which has been defined to process the members of `SetOfPersons`. The body of the for-each loop consists only of one statement used to launch one event request of type release-member (T: TEAM; P: PERSON) per member of `SetOfPersons` in order to unassign the team members. Finally, an event request of type release-team (T: TEAM) is issued in order to transfer the corresponding object of type TEAM to the final state, namely *released*.

It should be noted that the required effect can not be achieved by any single event type specification because there is a set of subsequent event requests related to one initiating event request.

3. The PROMOLA Programming Environment

The structure of the PROMOLA programming environment PROMOLA/D is closely related to the language structure as described in Section 2. For each of the three language components, an appropriate software tool with an interactive user interface has been designed. In particular,

- the data model specification language (Subsection 2.1) is supported by an ER graph editor together with a syntax directed object type editor (for the refinement information) and a DDL compiler for final translation.
- the object behavior specification language (Subsection 2.2) is supported by a net editor accepting net specifications according to the previously defined object type structures.
- the event trigger specification language (Subsection 2.3) is supported by a syntax directed trigger unit editor which provides a friendly user interface for event trigger programming.

These tools, together with a database management system and a library management system, form the PROMOLA/D programming environment. Basically, the programming environment and the run-time environment are designed to use the PROMOLA meta-database as a common repository containing process program information produced by the various components of the programming environment.

The process program information is used in turn by the run-time environment at process execution time to determine whether or not a particular process step (event request) is semantically legal with respect to the stored process program.

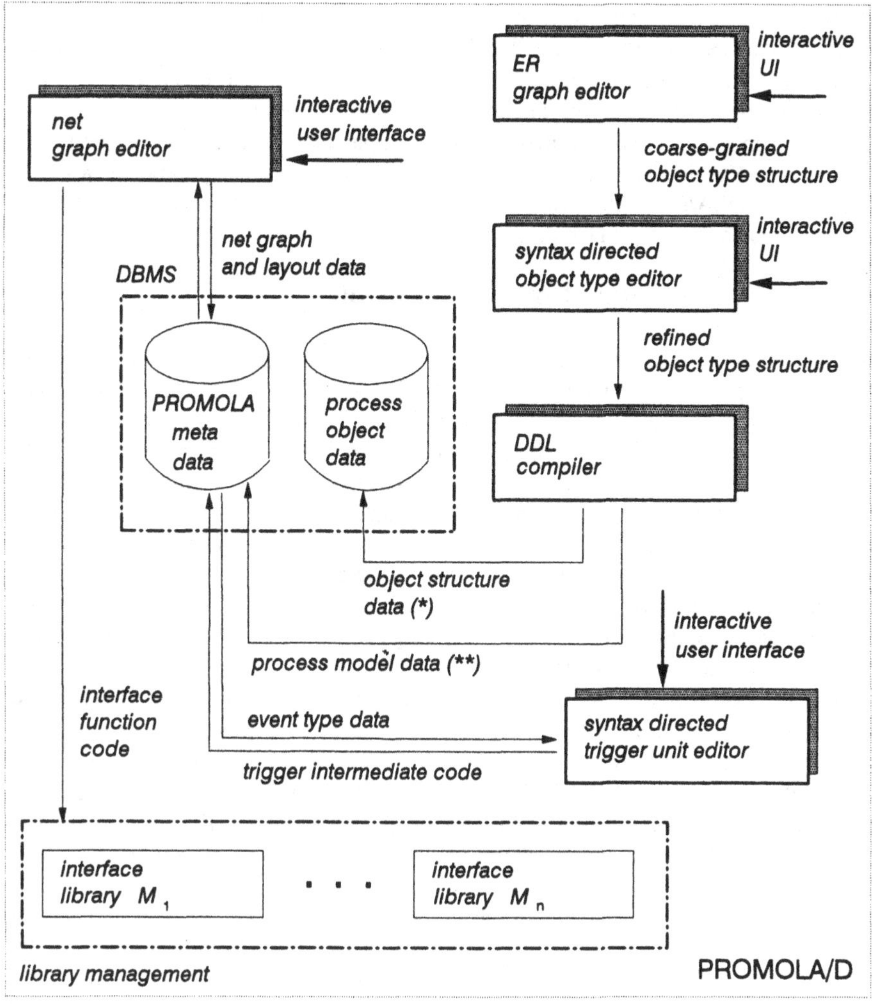


```
(*) e.g. CREATE TABLE Design-Doc (Doc# INTEGER, Folder CHAR(40) ..)
(**) e.g. INSERT INTO OType VALUES (<model>,<otype>,"Design-Doc")
```

Figure 5: PROMOLA/D system structure

The term *process object data* refers to the data corresponding to real world objects participating in a real world process, i.e., people, projects, design documents, source code modules and so on. Modifications of the process object data caused by application programs, tools or human agents launching event requests are restricted by the process program since the process program has to match the requirements of the real world process specification.

The term *PROMOLA program data* refers to all types of information concerning the process program itself (i.e., object structure data, augmented place transition net data and trigger unit data) and all kinds of run-time execution information used to store particular

process states (net markings and event request queues). Regarding the process object data as application domain "ortho"-data, the PROMOLA program data is called PROMOLA "meta"-data to emphasize the different levels of abstraction. The interplay of the five components, as well as the corresponding data flow, is depicted in Figure 5.
After a sequence of component invocations, a complete PROMOLA process program is stored in the PROMOLA meta-database. Consequently, the process program data is used by the PROMOLA/R run-time environment to determine whether a particular thread of event requests conforms with the process program.

4. The PROMOLA Run-Time Environment

The description of PROMOLA/R deals with those software components designed to guide or even drive process executions based on PROMOLA process models. During process execution, event requests (possible process steps) might be issued by application programs, tools like document editors, language translators and so on, or even human agents using an appropriate interactive interface. However, the PROMOLA/R system components must process the event requests without regard to their source as long as all event requests are syntactically in conformance with the underlying process program.
Additionally, all event requests have to be passed to the run-time system in the correct manner, i.e., the PROMOLA/R interprocess communication protocol has to be executed. Since the whole software environment is designed for System V platforms, the IPC protocol is based on System V message queues.
Consequently, one interface function library per process model is created during model development in order to provide all clients with an easily accessible interface to the run-time system. From a different point of view, the run-time system structure can be considered as a front-end / back-end structure. One front-end library per process model (essentially the interface function library) has to be linked to each client of the particular process model (i.e., to each process which plans to launch event requests for the particular process at run time).
Calls to front-end library functions result in event requests passed to the back-end (i.e., the core run-time system). This front-end / back-end architecture allows hiding of the details of the PROMOLA/R communication protocol from run-time system clients. Nevertheless, the possibility exists to pass event requests directly to the back-end. In particular, the back-end components have to

- accept event requests from front-end components or directly from clients via the IPC protocol; queue up those event requests in the event request queue and pass scheduled requests (i.e., timed requests which launch time has finally arrived) to the request driver.
- decide upon the semantic legality of event requests with respect to the underlying process program and the current process state and to execute those event requests which are considered legal in the current process state.
- execute trigger units, i.e., evaluate trigger unit code if an event request is accepted which belongs to an initiating event type used in one or more trigger units.
- execute non-aspect updates which are bound to event requests executed by the event request driver.

According to these four main tasks, the back-end consists of four processes:

- the *event request queue handler*,

- the *event request driver*,
- the *trigger unit interpreter* and
- the *non-aspect update driver*.

Using a process of its own for the non-aspect update driver is a result of basic integrity considerations. It has to be ensured that a non-aspect update may never affect aspect values (i.e., object states). A straightforward solution to this is a separate process lacking any update privileges for aspect values in the underlying database. Figure 6 illustrates the data flow between the processes.

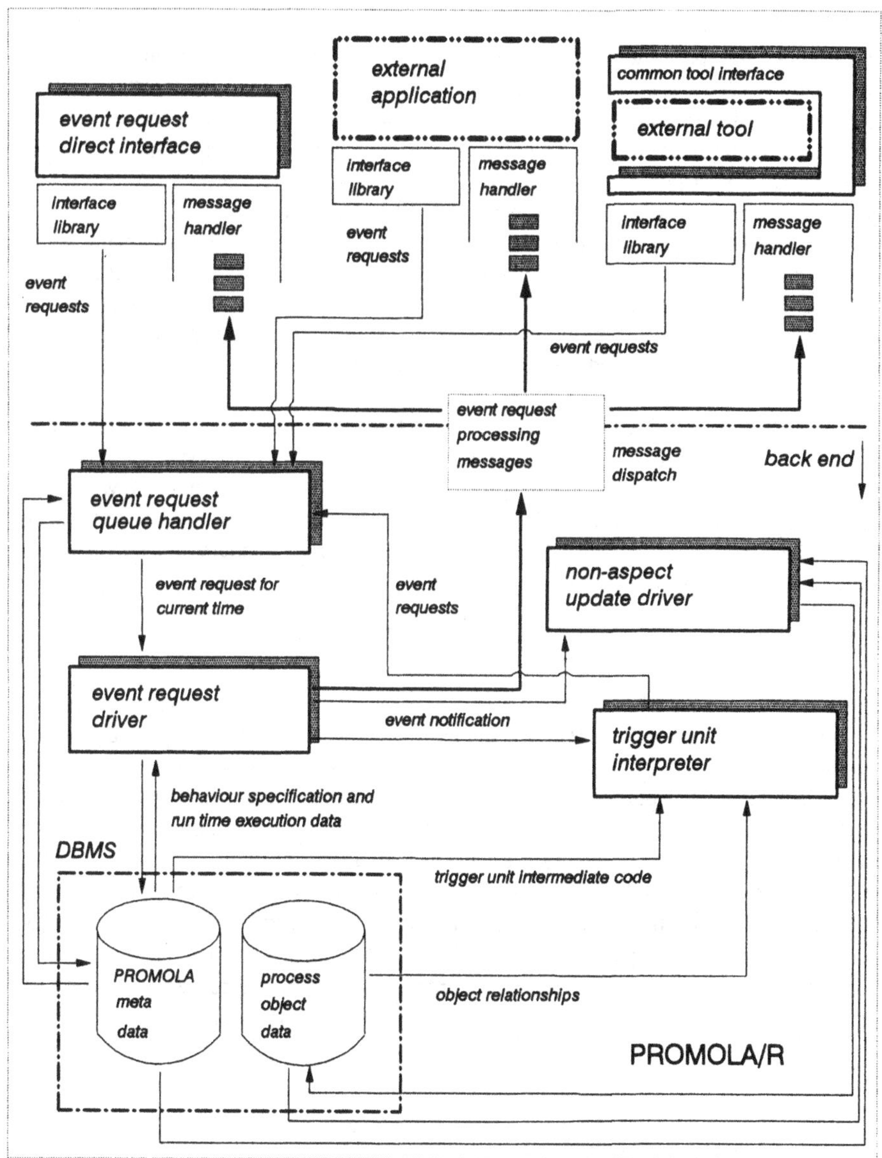

Figure 6: PROMOLA/R system structure

A particular client process calls the corresponding interface function of the front-end library. The interface function produces an appropriate IPC message and passes the message to the *event request queue handler*. The queue handler checks the time information coming with the event request and inserts the request into the *event request queue*. Additionally, the event request queue handler uses the system clock device to locate queued event requests which have to be passed to the event request driver, i.e., event requests for which the launch time has finally arrived. These event requests are processed by the *event request driver*, which determines whether or not the event request is semantically legal at the current point of time. The event request driver informs the client about the decision.

Basically, an appropriate message is put into the client's message queue which has to be accessed by the front-end message handling functions coming with the interface library. Any interface library call may be launched in a blocking or non-blocking fashion, therefore the client is able to decide whether it wants to wait for the corresponding event request processing message or not. Additionally, in case of event request execution, the trigger unit interpreter and the non-aspect update driver are notified.

The *trigger unit interpreter* uses the event request to determine if the corresponding event type is used as initiating event type in one or more stored trigger units. If so, it retrieves the trigger unit intermediate code from the meta-database and executes the trigger units. On that occasion, new event requests may emerge. These requests are passed to the event request handler to be processed like event requests stemming from run-time system client processes.

The *non-aspect update driver* determines if an optional attribute (i.e., non-aspect) update was issued in the context of the executed event request. Possibly existing non-aspect updates are retrieved from the meta-database, preprocessed for the DBMS query processor and finally passed to the query processor. In other words, updates for aspects are passed to the query processor by the event request driver, updates for attributes are handled by the non-aspect update driver.

5. Conclusions

Referring to a number of challenging requirements stated in previous publications (see [15] and [4] for example), a new combination of process programming language and supporting software environment is presented. With regard to the previous sections, we are convinced that our approach fulfills these requirements to a great extent. PROMOLA contains object behavior modeling constructs (based on place transition net derivates), data modeling constructs (textually refined entity-relationship diagrams) and constructs for trigger specifications. The software environment consists of a process programming environment and a run-time environment which is able to control and/or drive processes. The process programming environment and the run-time environment use a common repository in which all process program information is stored. The run-time environment uses the program meta-data from the repository as input to all decision tasks.

6. References

[1] Ambriola V., Ciancarini P., Montangero C.: Software Process Enactment in Oikos; Proc. of the 4th ACM SIGSOFT Symposium on Software Development Environments; in: SIGSOFT Software Eng. Notes Vol.15/#6, ACM Press, 1990

[2] Bandinelli S., Fuggetta A., Ghezzi C., Grigolli S.: Process Enactment in SPADE; Proc. of EWSPT'92, LNCS 635, Springer 1992

[3] Breiteneder C.J., Mueck T.A.: Yet Another Language for Process Programming; TR-ISI/InfoSys-114, Dep. of Information Systems, University of Vienna, 1991

[4] Curtis B., Kellner M.I., Over J.: Process Modeling; CACM 35/#9, ACM Press 1992

[5] Deiters W., Gruhn V.: Managing Software Processes in the Environment MELMAC; Proc. of the 4th ACM SIGSOFT Symposium on Software Development Environments; in: SIGSOFT Software Eng. Notes Vol.15/#6, ACM Press, 1990

[6] De Antonellis V., Zonta B.: Modeling Events in Database Applications Design; Proc. of the 7th Int'l Conf. on Very Large Databases, Cannes, 1981

[7] Kaiser G.E., Barghouti N.S., Sokolsky M.H.: Preliminary experience with process modeling in the Marvel software development environment kernel; Proc. of the 23rd Annual Hawaii Int'l Conf. on System Sciences, IEEE Computer Society, 1990

[8] Kellner M.I.: Representation Formalisms for Software Process Modeling; Proc. of the 4th Int'l Software Process Workshop: Representing and Enacting the Software Process; in: ACM Software Engineering Notes 14/#4, ACM Press, 1989

[9] Mueck T.A., Polaschek M.: CASE Support for Specification and Enforcement of Transitional Constraints; Proc. of the 2nd Int'l Work. Conf. on Dynamic Modeling of Information Systems, North-Holland 1991

[10] Mueck T.A., Vinek G.: Modeling Dynamic Constraints Using Augmented Place Transition Nets; Information Systems 14/#4, Pergamon Press, 1989

[11] Osterweil L.J.: Software processes are software too; Proc. of the 9th Int'l Conference on Software Engineering, IEEE Computer Society Press, 1987

[12] Peterson J.L.: Petri Net Theory and the Modeling of Systems, Prentice-Hall, 1981

[13] Rombach H.D.: An experimental process modeling language: Lessons learned from modeling a maintenance environment; Proc. of the Conf. on Software Maintenance; IEEE Computer Society, 1989

[14] Solvberg A., Kung C.H.: On Structural and Behavioral Modeling of Reality; in: Steel T.B., Meersman R. (eds.): Database Semantics, North-Holland 1986

[15] Sutton S.M. Jr., Heimbigner D., Osterweil L.J.: Language Constructs for Managing Change in Process Centered Environments; Proc. of the 4th ACM SIGSOFT Symposium on Software Development Environments; published in: SIGSOFT Software Eng. Notes Vol.15/#6, ACM Press, 1990

[16] Sutton, S.M. Jr.,: APPL/A: A Prototype Language for Software-Process Programming; PhD Thesis, University of Colorado, 1990

[17] Taylor R.N., et al.: Foundations for the Arcadia environment architecture; Proc. of the ACM SIGSOFT/SIGPLAN Software Engineering Symposium on Practical Software Development Environments; ACM Press, 1988

[18] Warboys B.: The IPSE2.5 Project: Process Modeling as the basis for a Support Environment; Proc. of the 1st Int'l Conference on System Development Environments and Factories, Pitman Publishing, 1989

A Formal Framework for ASTRAL Intra-Level Proof Obligations

Alberto Coen-Porisini[§]
Richard A. Kemmerer[‡¤]
Reliable Software Group - Department of Computer Science
University of California, Santa Barbara, CA 93106
Dino Mandrioli[‡¤]
Dipartimento di Elettronica e Informazione
Politecnico di Milano, Milano 20133, Italia

Abstract. ASTRAL is a formal specification language for realtime systems. It is intended to support formal software development, and therefore has been formally defined. This paper focuses on formally proving the mathematical correctness of ASTRAL specifications. ASTRAL is provided with structuring mechanisms that allow one to build modularized specifications of complex systems with layering. In this paper further details of the ASTRAL environment components and the critical requirements components, which were not fully developed in previous papers, are presented. Formal proofs in ASTRAL can be divided into two categories: *inter-level* proofs and *intra-level* proofs. The former deal with proving that the specification of level i+1 is consistent with the specification of level i, while the latter deal with proving that the specification of level i is consistent and satisfies the stated critical requirements. This paper concentrates on intra-level proofs.

1 Introduction

ASTRAL is a formal specification language for realtime systems. It is intended to support formal software development, and therefore has been formally defined. [GK 91a] discusses the rational of ASTRAL's design and demonstrates how the language builds on previous language experiments. [GK 91b] discusses how ASTRAL's semantics are specified in the TRIO formal realtime logic. It also outlines how ASTRAL specifications can be formally analyzed by translating them into TRIO and then using the TRIO validation theory.

Recently, a number of approaches have been proposed to build formal proofs for realtime systems [Ost 89, ACD 90, CHS 90, Suz 90, FMM 91, GF 91]. Many of these exploit the so called "dual language approach" [Pnu 77, Ost 89] where a system is modeled as an abstract machine (e.g., a finite state machine or a Petri net) and its properties are described through some assertion language (e.g., a logic or an algebraic language). However, they are based on low level formalisms, i.e., abstract machines

§ Alberto Coen-Porisini is supported by Consiglio Nazionale delle Ricerche- Comitato Nazionale per la Scienza e le Tecnologie dell'Informazione

‡ This research was partially funded by the National Science Foundation under grant CCR-9204249

¤ This research was partially supported by the Loral Western Development Laboratories and the University of California through a MICRO grant and/or assertion languages that are not provided with modularization and abstraction mechanisms. As a consequence, the proofs lack structure, which makes them unsuitable for dealing with complex real-life systems.

On the contrary, ASTRAL is provided with structuring mechanisms that allow one to build modularized specifications of complex systems with layering [GK 91a, GK 91b]. In this paper further details of the ASTRAL environment components and the critical requirements components, which were not fully developed in previous papers, are presented.

Formal proofs in ASTRAL can be divided into two categories: *inter-level* proofs and *intra-level* proofs. The former deal with proving that the specification of level i+1 is consistent with the specification of level i, while the latter deal with proving that the specification of level i is consistent and satisfies the stated critical requirements. This paper concentrates on intra-level proofs.

In the next section a brief overview of ASTRAL is presented along with an example system, which will be used throughout the remainder of the paper for illustrating specific features of ASTRAL. Section 3 discusses how to represent assumptions about the environment as well as the representation of critical requirements for the system. Section 4 presents a formal framework for generating proof obligations in ASTRAL, and section 5 presents an example proof. Finally, in section 6 some conclusions from this research are presented and possible future directions are proposed.

2 Overview of ASTRAL

ASTRAL uses a state machine process model and has types, variables, constants, transitions, and invariants. A realtime system is modeled by a collection of state machine specifications and a single global specification. Each state machine specification represents a process type of which there may be multiple instances in the system. The process being specified is thought of as being in various *states* with one state differentiated from another by the values of the *state variables*. The values of these variables evolve only via well defined *state transitions*, which are specified with Entry and Exit assertions and have an explicit nonnull duration. State variables and transitions may be explicitly exported by a process. This makes the variable values readable by other processes and the transitions callable by the external environment; exported transitions cannot be called by another process. Interprocess communication is via the exported variables, and is accomplished by inquiring about the value of an exported variable for a particular instance of the process. A process can inquire about the value of any exported variable of a process type or about the start or end time of an exported transition.

The ASTRAL computation model views the values of all variables being modified by a transition as being changed by the transition in a single atomic action that occurs when the transition completes execution. Thus, if a process is inquiring about the value of an exported variable while a transition is being executed by the process being queried, the value obtained is the value the variable had when the transition commenced. Start(Op_i, t) is a predicate that is true if and only if transition Op_i starts at time t and there is no other time after t and before the current time when Op_i starts (i.e., t is the time of the last occurrence of Op_i). For simplicity, the functional notation Start(Op_i) is adopted as a shorthand for "time t such that Start(Op_i, t)", whenever the quantification of the variable t (whether existential or universal) is clear from the context. Start-k(Op_i) is used to give the start time of the kth previous occurrence of Op_i. Inquiries about the end time of a transition Op_i may be specified similarly using End(Op_i) and End-k(Op_i).

In ASTRAL a special variable called Now is used to denote the current time. The value of Now is zero at system initialization time. ASTRAL specifications can refer to the current time ("Now") or to an absolute value for time that must be less than or equal to the current time. That is, in ASTRAL one cannot express values of time that are to occur in the future. To specify the value that an exported variable var had at time t, ASTRAL provides a past(var,t) function. The past function can also be used with the Start and End predicates. For example the expression "past(Start(Op),t) = t" is used to specify that transition Op started at time t.

The type ID is one of the primitive types of ASTRAL. Every instance of a process type has a unique id. An instance can refer to its own id by using "Self". For inquiries where there is more than one instance of that process type, the inquiry is preceded by the unique id of the desired instance followed by a period. For example, i.Start(Op) gives the last start time that transition Op was executed by the process instance whose unique id is i. However, when the process instance performing the inquiry is the same as the instance being queried the preceding id and period may be dropped.

An ASTRAL global specification contains declarations for all of the process instances that comprise the system and for any constants or nonprimitive types that are shared by more than one process type. Globally declared types and constants must be explicitly imported by a process type specification that requires them.

The computation model for ASTRAL is based on nondeterministic state machines and assumes maximal parallelism, noninterruptable and nonoverlapping transitions in a single process instance, and implicit one-to-many (multicast) message passing communication, which is instantaneous.

A detailed description of ASTRAL and of its underlying motivations is provided in [GK 91a], which also contains a complete specification of a phone system example. In this paper only the concepts of ASTRAL that are needed to present the proof theory are discussed in detail. These concepts are illustrated via a simple example that is a variation of the packet assembler described in [Zav 87].

> "The system contains an object which assembles data items (in the order in which it receives them) into fixed-size packets, and sends these packets to the environment. It also contains a fixed number of other objects, each of which receives data items from the environment on a particular channel and sends those items to the packet maker. The packet maker sends a packet to the environment as soon as it is full of data items.
>
> Each data receiver attaches a channel identifier to each incoming data item; these channel identifiers are included with the data items in the outgoing packets.
>
> If a data receiver does not receive a new data item within a fixed time since the last item arrived, its channel is considered closed until the next data item arrives. Notifications of channel closings are put into the outgoing packets as well as data items. If all channels are closed then the packet maker should send an incomplete packet to the environment rather than wait for data to complete it."

In the remainder of this paper this system is referred to as the CCITT system.

[CKM 92] contains a complete ASTRAL specification of the CCITT system. It consists of a packet maker process specification, an input process specification (of which there are N instances), and the global specification. The input process specification, which corresponds to the data receiver in Zave's system description, contains two transitions: New_Info and Notify_Timeout[1].

New_Info is an exported transition, with no Entry conditions, that models the receipt of data items from the environment. It has duration N_I_Dur.

```
TRANSITION New_Info(x:Info)  N_I_Dur
  EXIT
      Msg[Data_Part] = x
  &   Msg[Count] = Msg[Count]' + 1
  &   Msg[ID_Part] = Self
  &   ~Channel_Closed
```

In ASTRAL Exit assertions, variable names followed by a ' indicate the value that the variable had when the transition fired.

Notify_Timeout is used to notify the packet maker process that an input process has not received any input from the environment within some fixed time (constant Input_Tout in the specification). It has duration N_T_Dur.

```
TRANSITION Notify_Timeout  N_T_Dur
  ENTRY
        EXISTS t1: Time (Start(New_Info,t1) & Now - t1 ≥ Input_Tout)
  &   ~Channel_Closed
  EXIT
      Msg[Data_Part] = Closed
  &   Msg[Count] = Msg[Count]' + 1
  &   Msg[ID_Part] = Self
  &   Channel_Closed
```

The packet maker specification also has two transitions: Process_Msg and Deliver, which correspond to processing a message from an input channel and delivering a packet, respectively.

```
TRANSITION Process_Msg(R_id:Receiver_ID)  P_M_Dur
  ENTRY
      LIST_LEN(Packet) < Maximum
  &   ( EXISTS t1: Time (Receiver[R_id].End(New_Info) = t1 & t1 > Previous(R_id))
      | (    Receiver[R_id].Msg[Data_Part]=Closed
        &   past(Receiver[R_id].Msg[Data_Part],Previous(R_id)) ≠ Closed ))
  EXIT
      Packet = Packet' CONCAT LIST(Receiver[R_id].Msg)
  &   Previous(R_id) BECOMES Now
```

---

[1]An earlier version of this specification that did not take into account the environment and with different invariants and schedules was presented in [GK 91b].

```
TRANSITION Deliver Del_Dur
  ENTRY
    LIST_LEN(Packet) = Maximum
  | (  LIST_LEN(Packet) > 0
    & ( EXISTS t:Time (Start(Deliver, t) & Now - t ≥ Del_Tout)
        | Now = Del_Tout - Del_Dur + N_I_Dur))
  EXIT
      Output = Packet'
    & Packet = EMPTY
```

3 Environmental Assumptions and Critical Requirements

In addition to specifying system *state* (through process variables and constants) and system *evolution* (through transitions), an ASTRAL specification also defines desired system *properties* and *assumptions* on the behavior of the environment that interacts with the system. Assumptions about the behavior of the environment are expressed in environment clauses and imported variable clauses, and desired system properties are expressed through invariants and schedules. Because these components are critical to the ASTRAL proof theory and were not fully developed in previous papers, they are discussed in more detail in this section.

3.1 Environment Clauses

An *environment clause* formalizes the assumptions that must always hold on the behavior of the environment to guarantee some desired system properties. They are expressed as first-order formulas involving the calls of the exported transitions, which are denoted Call(Op_i) (with the same syntactic conventions as Start(Op_i)). For each process p there is a local environment clause, Env_p, which expresses the assumptions about calls to the exported transitions of process p. There is also a global environment clause, Env_G, which is a formula that may refer to all exported transitions in the system.

In the CCITT example there is a local environment clause for the input process and a global clause. The local clause states that for each input process, the time between two consecutive calls to transition New_Info is not less than the duration of New_Info, and that there will always be a call to New_Info before the timeout expires:

```
     (EXISTS t:Time (Call-2 (New_Info, t))                          [Env_in]
        → Call (New_Info) - Call-2 (New_Info) ≥ N_I_Dur)
  &  (Now ≥ Input_Tout
        → EXISTS t:Time (Call (New_Info, t))
        & Now - Call(New_Info) < Input_Tout)
```

The global environment clause states that exactly N/L calls to transition New_Info are cyclically produced, with time period N/L*P_M_Dur + Del_Dur (where P_M_Dur is the duration of transition Process_Message, Del_Dur is the duration of Deliver, and L denotes a constant that is used to specify that N/L processes are producing messages)[2]:

---

[2]For simplicity, the traditional cardinality operator, | |, is adopted even though it is not an ASTRAL operator.

```
    FORALL t:Time (t MOD (N/L*P_M_Dur + Del_Dur) = 0                    [EnvG]
    → EXISTS S: Set_Of_Receiver_ID
        (   |S| = N/L
        &  FORALL i:Receiver_ID (i ISIN S ↔ Receiver[i].Call(New_Info) = t)))
&   FORALL t:Time (t MOD (N/L*P_M_Dur + Del_Dur) ≠ 0
      → FORALL i:Receiver_ID  (~Receiver[i].Call(New_Info, t)))
```

3.2 Imported Variable Clauses

Each process p may also have an *imported variable clause*, IV_p. This clause formalizes assumptions that process p makes about the context provided by the other processes in the system. For example IV_p contains assumptions about the timing of transitions exported by other processes that p uses to synchronize the timing of its transitions. It also contains assumptions about when variables exported by other processes change value. For instance, p might assume that some imported variable changes no more frequently than every 10 time units.

In the CCITT example only the Packet_Maker process has an imported variable clause. It states that the ends of transition New_Info executed by input processes follow the same periodic behavior as the corresponding calls. The clause is similar to the global environment clause.

3.3 Invariant Clauses

Invariants state properties that must initially be true and must be guaranteed during system evolution, according to the traditional meaning of the term. Invariants can be either local to some process, I_p, or global, I_G. These properties must be true regardless of the environment or the context in which the process or system is running. Invariants are formulas that express properties about process variables and transition timing according to some natural scope rules, which are not detailed here due to space limitations.

In the CCITT example the global invariant consists of two clauses. The first clause states that every input data will be output within H1 time units after it is input, but not sooner than H2 time units:

```
  FORALL i:Receiver_ID, t1:Time, x:Info                                  [IG]
      (t1≤Now - H1 & past(Receiver[i].End(New_Info(x)),t1) = t1
  →   EXISTS t2:Time, k:Integer
      ( t2 ≥ t1 + H2 & t2 ≤ Now & Change(Output,t2)
      &  0 < k & k ≤ LIST_LEN(past(Output,t2))
      &  past(Output[k][Data_Part],t2)=x
      &  past(Output[k][Count],t2) = past(Receiver[i].Msg[Count],t1)
      &  past(Output[k][ID_part],t2) = Receiver[i].Id))
```

The other global clause states that no message is output other than those produced by the input processes.

The Input process local invariant states that after Input_Tout time units have elapsed without receiving any new message a timeout occurs, and that the last message received is kept until a Deliver timeout occurs.

The Packet_Maker's local invariant states that changes in the exported variable Output occur at, and only at, the end of a Deliver and that no new messages are generated by the packet assembler. It also states that the order that messages appear in an output packet is the order in which they were processed from a channel, this order is preserved across output packets, and every message in Output was previously in Packet and if Output changes Now, then each of the elements of Packet are unchanged from when they were put into the packet. Due to space limitations all of the invariants could not be presented here; they can be found in [CKM 92].

3.4 Schedule Clauses

Schedules are additional system properties that are required to hold under more restrictive hypotheses than invariants. Unlike invariants, the validity of a schedule may be proved using the assumptions expressed in the associated environment and/or imported variable clauses .

Like invariants, schedules may be either local, Sc_P, or global, Sc_G, and obey suitable scope rules in the same style as invariants. Unlike invariants, however, they may refer to calls to exported transitions. Typically, a schedule clause states properties about the reaction time of the system to external stimuli and on the number of requests that can be "served" by the system. This motivates the term "schedule".

Because there may be several ways to assure that a schedule is satisfied, such as giving one transition priority over another or making additional assumptions about the environment, and because this kind of decision should often be postponed until a more detailed design phase, in ASTRAL the schedules are not required to be proved. It is important, however, to know that the schedule is feasible. That is, it is important to know that if further restrictions are placed on the specification and/or if further assumptions are made about the environment, then the schedule can be met. For this reason, a further assumptions and restrictions clause may be included as part of a process specification. Unlike other components of the ASTRAL specification this clause is only used as guidance to the implementer; it is not a hard requirement. The details of this clause are given in the next subsection.

In the CCITT example the global schedule states that the time that elapses between the call of a New_Info transition and the delivery of the message it produced is equal to N/L*P_M_Dur + N_I_Dur + Del_Dur.

The local schedule for the Input process states that there is no delay between a call of New_Info and the start of its execution. The Packet_Maker's schedule states that the transition Deliver is executed cyclically and that a packet is always delivered with N/L elements.

```
    (EXISTS t:Time (End-2(Deliver,t))                                    [Scpm]
          → End(Deliver) - End-2(Deliver) = N/L*P_M_Dur + Del_Dur)
  & FORALL t: Time (past(End(Deliver), t) = t → LIST_LEN(past(Output, t)) = N/L)
```

A proof of the Packet_Maker's schedule is presented in section 5.

3.5 Further Assumptions and Restrictions Clause

As mentioned before, schedules can be guaranteed by exploiting further assumptions about the environment or restrictions on the system behavior. These assumptions constitute a separate part of the process specification, the *further assumptions and restrictions clause,* FAR_p. It consists of two parts: a further environment assumptions section and a further process assumptions section.

The *further environment assumptions* section, $FEnv_p$, obeys the same syntactic rules as Env_p. It simply states further hypotheses on the admissible behaviors of the environment interacting with the system. Of course, it cannot contradict previous general assumptions on the environment expressed in Env_p and Env_G.

A *further process assumptions* section, FPA_p, restricts the possible system implementations by specifying suitable selection policies in the case of nondeterministic choice between several enabled transitions, TS_p, or by further restricting constants, CR_p. In general, FPA_p reduces the level of nondeterminism of the system specification.

The *transition selection* part, TS_p, consists of a sequence of clauses of the following type:

{OpSet$_i$} <Boolean Condition$_i$> {ROpSet$_i$}

where

- {OpSet$_i$} defines a set of transitions.
- {ROpSet$_i$} defines a restricted but nonempty set of transitions that must be included in the set defined by {OpSet$_i$}.
- <Boolean Condition$_i$> is a boolean condition on the state of process p.

The operational semantics of the transition selection part is defined as follows.

1. At any given time the set of enabled transitions, {ET}, is evaluated by the process abstract machine.
2. Let {OpSet$_i$}, <Boolean Condition$_i$> be a pair such that ET is {OpSet$_i$} and <Boolean Condition$_i$> holds. Notice that such a pair does not necessarily exist.
3. If there are pairs that satisfy condition 2, then the set of transitions that actually are eligible for firing is the union of all {ROpSet$_i$} corresponding to the above pairs {OpSet$_i$}, <Boolean Condition$_i$> that are satisfied.
4. If no such pair exists, the set of transitions eligible for firing is {ET}.

The *constant refinement* part, CR_p, is a sequence of clauses that may restrict the values that system constants can assume w.r.t. what is stated in the remaining part of the system specification. For example, one can further restrict a constant T1 that is bounded between 0 and 100, by stating that T1's value is actually between 10 and 50, or that it is exactly 5.

Notice that the further assumptions and restrictions section can only restrict the set of possible behaviors. That is, if {B} denotes the set of system behaviors that are compatible with the system specification without the FAR clause and {RB} denotes the set of behaviors that are compatible with the system specification including the FAR clause, then it is easy to verify that {RB} is contained in {B}.

For the CCITT system two different further assumptions clauses were used with the Packet_Maker process. The first contains both a constant refinement part and a transition selection part. The CR part states that the timeout of transition Deliver is 0 and that the packet length is equal to N/L.

Del_Tout = 0 & Maximum = N/L

The TS part states that the Process_Message transition has higher priority than Deliver.

{Process_Message, Deliver} TRUE {Process_Message}

The second further assumptions clause contains only a constant refinement part, which states that Deliver's timeout is N/L*P_M_Dur + Del_Dur and that Maximum = N.

Either of these further assumptions clauses is sufficient to prove that the schedules are met.

4 Intra-Level Proof Obligations in ASTRAL

In this section the ASTRAL intra-level proof obligations are presented. However, it is first necessary to present some notation.

Let S denote a top level ASTRAL specification. S is composed of a set of process specifications P_p and a global specification G. Each P_p, in turn, is composed of a set of transitions $Op_{p1},\ldots,Op_{pn}$, a local invariant I_p, a local schedule Sc_p a local environment Env_p, imported variable assumptions IV_p, a further local environment $FEnv_p$, a further process assumption FPA_p and an initial clause $Init\_State_p$. Moreover, every transition Op_{pj} is described by entry and exit clauses denoted EN_{pj} and EX_{pj}, respectively. The global specification G is made up of a global invariant I_G, a global schedule Sc_G and a global environment Env_G clause.

Proving that S satisfies its critical requirements can be partitioned into the following proof obligations:

1) Every process specification P_p guarantees its local invariant I_p;
2) Every process specification P_p guarantees its local schedule Sc_p;
3) The specification S guarantees the global invariant I_G;
4) The specification S guarantees the global Sc_G.

For soundness the following proof obligations are also needed:

5) The imported variable assumptions IV_p are guaranteed by the specification S.
6) All the assumptions about the environment (Env_G, Env_p and $FEnv_p$) are consistent.

In what follows a formal framework for these proof obligations is presented.

4.1 ASTRAL Abstract Machine

An informal description of the ASTRAL computational model is given in [GK91a, GK91b]. However, a formal description of the ASTRAL abstract machine is needed to carry out the ASTRAL proofs.

The semantics of the ASTRAL abstract machine is defined by three axioms. The first axiom states that the time interval spanning from the starting to the ending of a given transition is equal to the specified duration of the transition.

FORALL t: Time, Op: Trans_of_p [A1]
(Now - t $\geq T_{Op} \rightarrow$ (past(Start(Op),t) = t $\leftrightarrow$ past(End(Op),t+T_{Op}) = t +T_{Op})),

where T_{Op} represents the duration of transition Op.

The second axiom states that if a processor is idle and some transitions are enabled then one transition will fire. Let S_T denote the set of transitions of process p.

FORALL t: Time (EXISTS d: Time, S'_T: SET OF Trans_of_p [A2]
(FORALL t_1: Time, Op: Trans_of_p
($t_1 \geq t - d$ & $t_1 < t$ & Op ISIN S_T & past(Start(Op),t_1) < past(End(Op),t)
& $S'_T \subseteq S_T$ & $S'_T \neq$ EMPTY
& FORALL Op':Trans_of_p (Op' ISIN $S'_T \rightarrow$ Eval_Entry(Op',t))
& FORALL Op':Trans_of_p (Op' ~ISIN $S'_T \rightarrow$ ~Eval_Entry(Op',t))
$\rightarrow$ UNIQUE Op':Trans_of_p (Op' ISIN S'_T & past(Start(Op'),t)=t)))),

where Eval_Entry(Op, t) is a function that given a transition Op and a time instant t evaluates the entry condition EN_{Op} of transition Op at time t.

Because the ASTRAL model implies that the starting time of a transition equals the time in which its entry condition was evaluated, the Eval_Entry function is introduced to prevent the occurrence of a contradiction. More specifically, when the entry condition of transition Op refers to the last start (2nd last, etc) of itself, the evaluation at time t of Start(Op) in the entry condition should refer to the value of Start immediately before the execution of Op at time t. Since Op has a nonnull duration this can be expressed by evaluating Start(Op) at a time t' which is prior to t and such that transition Op has not fired in the interval [t', t).

Finally, the third axiom states that for each processor the transitions are nonoverlapping.

FORALL t1, t2: Time, Op: Trans_of_p [A3]
(Start(Op)=t_1 & End(Op)=t_2 & $t_1 < t_2$
$\rightarrow$ FORALL t_3: Time, Op': Trans_of_p
($t_3 \geq t_1$ & $t_3 < t_2$ & Start(Op')= $t_3 \rightarrow$ Op = Op' & $t_3 = t_1$)
& FORALL t_3: Time, Op': Trans_of_p
($t_3 > t_1$ & $t_3 \leq t_2$ & End(Op')= $t_3 \rightarrow$ Op = Op' & $t_3 = t_2$))

4.2 Local Invariant Proof Obligations

The local invariant I_p represents a property that must hold for every reachable state of process p. Furthermore, the invariant describes properties that are independent from the environment. Therefore, the proof of the invariant I_p may not make use of any assumption about the environment, imported variables or the system behavior as described by Env_p, $FEnv_p$, IV_p and FPA_p.

To prove that the specification of process p guarantees the local invariant one needs to show that:

1) I_p holds in the initial state of process p, and
2) If p is in a state in which I_p holds, then for every possible evolution of p, I_p will hold.

The first proof consists of showing that the following implication is valid:

$Init\_State_p \ \& \ Now = 0 \rightarrow I_p$

To carry out the second proof one assumes that the invariant I_p holds until a given time t_0 and proves that I_p will hold for every time $t > t_0$. Without loss of generality, one can assume that t is equal to $t_0 + \Delta$, for some fixed Δ greater than zero, and show that the invariant holds until $t_0 + \Delta$.

In order to prove that I_p holds until time $t_0 + \Delta$ it may be necessary to make assumptions on the possible sequences of events that occurred within the interval $[t_0 - H, t_0 + \Delta]$, where H is a constant *a priori* unbounded, and where by event is meant the *starting* or *ending* of some transition Op_{pj} of process p.

Let σ denote one such sequence of events. A formula F_σ composed of the sequence of events that belong to σ can be algorithmically associated with σ. For each event occurring at time t one has:

$Eval\_Entry(Op_{pj}, t) \ \& \ past(Start(Op_{pj}, t), t)$ if the event is the start of Op_{pj} or

$past(EX_{pj}, t) \ \& \ past(End(Op_{pj}, t), t)$ if the event is the end of Op_{pj}.

Then the prover's job is to show that for any σ:

$A1 \ \& \ A2 \ \& \ A3 \vdash F_\sigma \ \& \ FORALL \ t{:}Time \ (t \leq t0 \rightarrow past(I_p,t)) \rightarrow$ $FORALL \ t_1{:}Time \ (t_1 > t_0 \ \& \ t_1 \leq t_0 + \Delta \rightarrow past(I_p, t_1))$

Notice that, as a particular case, the implication is trivially true if F_σ is contradictory, since this would mean that σ is not feasible.

4.3 Local Schedule Proof Obligations

The local schedule Sc_p of a process p describes some further properties that p must satisfy when the assumptions on the behavior of both the environment and p hold (i.e., Env_p, IV_p, $FEnv_p$ and FPA_p).

To prove that the specification of process p guarantees the local schedule Sc_p it is necessary to show that:

1) Sc_p holds in the initial state of process p, and
2) If p is in a state in which Sc_p holds, then for every possible evolution of p compatible with FPA_p, when the environment behavior is described by Env_p and $FEnv_p$, and the imported variables behavior is described by IV_p, Sc_p will hold.

Note that one can also assume that the local invariant I_p holds; i.e., I_p can be used as a lemma. The initial state proof obligation is similar to the proof obligation for the local invariant case; however the further hypothesis on the values of some constants expressed by CR_p can be used:

$Init\_State_p \ \& \ Now = 0 \ \& \ CR_p \rightarrow Sc_p$

The second proof obligation is also similar to the local invariant proof. However, in this case events may be external calls of exported transitions Op_{pj} in addition to the starting and ending of all transitions of p. If the event is the call of Op_{pj} from the external environment, then "past(Call(Op_{pj}), t) = t" can be used to represent that transition Op_{pj} was called at time t.

The prover's job is to show that for any σ:

> A1 & A2' & A3 & A4 & Env_p & $FEnv_p$ & $IV_p \vdash$
> CR_p & F_σ & FORALL t:Time ($t \leq t_0 \rightarrow$ past(Sc_p, t) $\rightarrow$
> FORALL t_1:Time ($t_1 > t_0$ & $t_1 \leq t_0 + \Delta \rightarrow$ past(Sc_p, t_1))

where A2' and A4 are defined in what follows.

A2' is an axiom derived from A2 by taking into account the TS_p section which restricts the non-determinism of the machine and that the exported transitions can fire only if they are called by the environment.

The TS_p section can be viewed as the definition of a function TS: $2^{\{Op1,\ldots,Opn\}} \rightarrow 2^{\{Op1,\ldots,Opn\}}$, having as domain and range the powerset of the transitions of process p. Its semantics is the following: denoting with ET the set of enabled transitions then TS(ET) returns a restricted set of enabled transitions, ET', where ET' $\subseteq$ ET. The processor will non-deterministically select which transition to fire from the transitions in ET'.

Let ST denote the set of transition of process p:

```
FORALL t: Time (EXISTS d: Time, S'T: SET OF Trans_of_p                    [A2']
  ( FORALL t1: Time, Op: Trans_of_p
     (  t1 ≥ t - d & t1 < t & Op ISIN ST & past(Start(Op),t1) < past(End(Op),t)
     &  S'T ⊆ ST & S'T ≠ EMPTY
     &  FORALL Op':Trans_of_p (Op' ISIN S'T → Eval_Entry'(Op',t))
     &  FORALL Op':Trans_of_p (Op' ~ISIN S'T → ~Eval_Entry'(Op',t))
     → UNIQUE Op':Trans_of_p (Op' ISIN TS(S'T) & past(Start(Op'),t)=t)))),
```

where Eval_Entry'(Op',t) = Eval_Entry(Op',t) & Issued_call(Op') iff Op' is exported, and Eval_Entry'(Op',t) = Eval_Entry(Op',t) iff Op' is not exported.

A4 states that Issued_call(Op) is true iff the environment has called transition Op and transition Op has not fired since then:

```
FORALL Op: Trans_of_p                                                     [A4]
  ( EXISTS t1: Time
     (  t1 ≤ Now & Call(Op, t1)
     &  FORALL t: Time
         (t ≥ t1 & t ≤ Now & ~Start(Op,t) →  past(Issued_call(Op),t)))
  & EXISTS t1: Time
     (  t1 ≤ Now & Start(Op, t1)
     &  FORALL t: Time
         (t > t1 & t ≤ Now & ~Call(Op,t) →  ~past(Issued_call(Op),t))))
```

4.4 Global Invariant Proof Obligations

Given an ASTRAL specification S composed of n processes, the state of S can be defined as the tuple $<s_1,...,s_n>$, where s_p represents the state of process p. The global invariant I_G of S describes the properties that must hold in every state of S.

To Prove that I_G is guaranteed by S it is necessary to prove that:

1) I_G holds in the initial state of S, and
2) If S is in a state in which I_G holds, then for every possible evolution of S, I_G will hold.

Since the initial state of S is the tuple $<Init\_State_1,...,Init\_State_n>$, where each $Init\_State_p$ represents the initial state of process p, to prove point 1 one needs to prove the validity of the following logical implication:

$$\bigwedge_{p=1}^{n} (Init\_State_p) \ \& \ Now = 0 \rightarrow I_G$$

Point 2 can be proved in a manner very similar to the local invariant case. However in this case the sequences of events σ will contain starting and ending events for exported transitions belonging to any process of S. Moreover, the local invariant of each process p composing S can be used to prove that every σ preserves the global invariant.

The prover's job is to show that for any σ:

$$A1 \ \& \ A2 \ \& \ A3 \vdash F_\sigma \ \& \ FORALL\ t{:}Time\ (t \le t_0 \rightarrow past(I_G, t)) \rightarrow$$
$$FORALL\ t_1{:}Time\ (t_1 > t_0 \ \& \ t_1 \le t_0 + \Delta \rightarrow past(I_G, t_1))$$

4.5 Global Schedule Proof Obligations

The global schedule Sc_G of the specification S describes some further properties that S must satisfy, when all its processes satisfy their own schedules and the assumptions on the behavior of the global environment hold.

Thus, to prove that Sc_G is consistent with S one has to show that:

1) Sc_G holds in the initial state of S, and
2) If S is in a state in which Sc_G holds, then for every possible evolution of S, Sc_G will hold.

In both proofs one can assume that the global invariant I_G and every local invariant I_p and local schedule Sc_p holds as well as the global environment assumptions Env_G. Note that none of the local environment assumption (Env_p and $FEnv_p$) may be used to prove the validity of the global schedule.

The first proof requires the validity of the formula:

$$\bigwedge_{p=1}^{n} (Init\_State_p) \ \& \ Now = 0 \ \& \ Env_G \rightarrow Sc_G$$

The second proof requires the construction of the sequences of events σ. Each σ will contain calling, starting and ending of exported transitions belonging to any process p of S. The prover's job is to show that for any σ:

$$\begin{array}{l} A1 \ \& \ A2'' \ \& \ A3 \ \& \ A4 \ \& \ Env_G \vdash F_\sigma \ \& \\ \quad \text{FORALL } t{:}\text{Time } (t \leq t_0 \rightarrow past(Sc_G, t)) \rightarrow \\ \quad\quad \text{FORALL } t_1{:}\text{Time } (t_1 > t_0 \ \& \ t_1 \leq t_0 + \Delta \rightarrow past(Sc_G, t_1)) \end{array}$$

where A2" is an axiom derived from A2 by taking into account that the exported transitions can fire only if they are called by the environment.

FORALL t: Time (EXISTS d: Time, S'_T: SET OF Trans_of_p [A2"]
(FORALL t_1: Time, Op: Trans_of_p
($t_1 \geq t - d$ & $t_1 < t$ & Op ISIN S_T & past(Start(Op),t_1) < past(End(Op),t)
& $S'_T \subseteq S_T$ & $S'_T \neq$ EMPTY
& FORALL Op':Trans_of_p(Op' ISIN $S'_T \rightarrow$ Eval_Entry'(Op',t))
& FORALL Op':Trans_of_p (Op' ~ISIN $S'_T \rightarrow$ ~Eval_Entry'(Op',t))
$\rightarrow$ UNIQUE Op':Trans_of_p (Op' ISIN S'_T & past(Start(Op'),t)=t)))),

where Eval_Entry'(Op',t) = Eval_Entry(Op',t) & Issued_call(Op'), iff Op' is exported and Eval_Entry'(Op',t) = Eval_Entry(Op',t), iff Op' is not exported.

4.6 Imported Variable Proof Obligation

When proving the local schedule of a process p one can use the assumptions about the imported variables expressed by IV_p. Therefore, these assumptions must be checked against the behavior of the processes from which they are imported.

The proof obligation guarantees that the local environment, local schedule and local invariant of every process of S (except p), and the global environment, invariant and schedule imply the assumptions on the imported variables of process p:

$$A1 \ \& \ A2 \ \& \ A3 \ \& \bigwedge_{i \neq p} Env_i \bigwedge_{i \neq p} I_i \ \& \bigwedge_{i \neq p} Sc_i \ \& \ Env_G \ \& \ I_G \ \& \ Sc_G \rightarrow IV_p$$

4.7 Environment Consistency Proof Obligation

Every process p of S may contain two clauses describing assumptions on the behavior of the external environment, Env_p and $FEnv_p$. These clauses are used to prove the local schedule of p. The global specification also contains a clause describing assumptions on the system environment behavior Env_G.

For soundness, it is necessary to verify that none of the environmental assumptions contradict each other, i.e., that a behavior satisfying the global as well as the local assumptions can exist. This requires proving that the following formula is satisfiable:

$$\bigwedge_{i=1}^{n} Env_i \ \& \bigwedge_{i=1}^{n} FEnv_i \ \& \ Env_G$$

5 An Example Correctness Proof in ASTRAL

In this section the proof of the local schedule of process Packet_Maker is considered:

Sc_{pm}:

EXISTS t:Time (End-2(Deliver, t))
→ End(Deliver) - End-2(Deliver) = N/L*P_M_Dur + Del_Dur
& FORALL t:Time (past(End(Deliver),t) = t → LIST_LEN(past(Output,t)) = N/L)

To prove Sc_{pm} the imported variables assumptions IV_{pm} and the second further process assumptions FPA_{pm} of process Packet Maker are used:

IV_{pm}:

FORALL t:Time ((t - N_I_Dur) MOD (N/L*P_M_Dur + Del_Dur) = 0
→ EXISTS S:Set_of_Receiver_ID (|S| = N/L
& FORALL i:Receiver_ID (i ISIN S ↔ Receiver[i].End(New_Info) = t)))
& FORALL t:Time ((t - N_I_Dur) MOD (N/L*P_M_Dur + Del_Dur) ≠ 0
→ FORALL i:Receiver_ID (~Receiver[i].End(New_Info) = t))
& FORALL i:Receiver_ID (Receiver[i].Msg[Data_Part] ≠ Closed)

FPA_{pm}:

Del_Tout = N/L*P_M_Dur + Del_Dur & Maximum = N

Consider a time instant p_0 such that Sc_{pm} holds until p_0; it is necessary to prove that Sc_{pm} holds until $p_0 + \Delta$, where Δ is big enough to require an End(Deliver) to occur within $(p_0, p_0 + \Delta]$. Without loss of generality, assume that:

1) at time p_0 transition Deliver ends and
2) Δ = N/L*P_M_Dur + Del_Dur.

Now, by [A1] one can deduce that at time p_0 - Del_Dur a Start(Deliver) occurred. Figure 1 shows the relevant events for the discussion that follows on a time line.

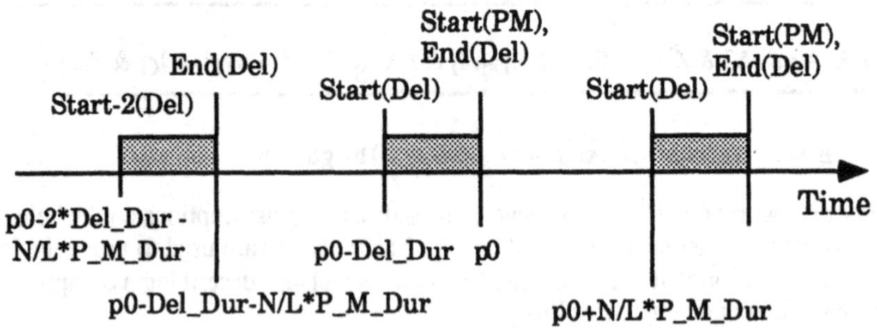

Figure 1

The Entry assertion of Deliver states that Deliver fires either when the buffer is full or when the timeout expires and at least one message has been processed.

EnDel:
LIST_LEN(Packet) = Maximum
| (LIST_LEN(Packet)>0
& EXISTS t: Time (Start(Deliver,t) & Now - t ≥ Del_Tout)
| Now = Del_Tout + N_I_Dur - Del_Dur))

Because Sc_{pm} holds until p_0 and from the Exit assertion for Deliver it is known that:

1) For all t less than or equal to p_0 and such that an end of transition Deliver occurred, Output contains N/L messages at time t (Sc_{pm}), and
2) The content of Output at the end of Deliver is equal to the content of Packet at the beginning of Deliver (Exit assertion of Deliver).

From this one can conclude that at time t - Del_Dur Packet contained N/L messages, i.e., it was not full. As a consequence <u>transition Deliver has fired because the timeout has expired</u>.

Furthermore, assume as lemma L1 that Process_Message is disabled every time Deliver fires (this lemma will be proved later).

The Entry condition of Process_Message is:

LIST_LEN(Packet) < Maximum
& (EXISTS t1: Time (Receiver[R_id].End(New_Info) = t1 & t1 > Previous(R_id))
| (Receiver[R_id].Msg[Data_Part] = Closed
& past(Receiver[R_id].Msg[Data_Part], Previous(R_id)) ≠ Closed))

and since

1) the buffer is not full (Sc_{pm}), and
2) no notification of closed channel can arrive (IV_{pm})

one can conclude that <u>no new message is available when Deliver fires</u> (L1).

IV_{pm} states that N/L messages are received every N/L*P_M_Dur + Del_Dur time units. As a consequence:

1) the N/L messages output at time p_0 have been received before time p_0 - Del_Dur - N/L*P_M_Dur, in order to allow Process_Message to process each of them, and
2) they have been received after the second last occurrence of Delivery prior to p_0 (because of L1).

Thus, one can conclude that the N/L messages output at time p_0 have been received in the interval:

(Start-2(Deliver), p_0 - Del_Dur - N/L*P_M_Dur],

i.e., (p_0 - 2*Del_Dur - N/L*P_M_Dur, p_0 - Del_Dur - N/L*P_M_Dur]

because of Sc_{pm}.

As a consequence of IV_{pm}, N/L new messages will arrive after N/L*P_M_Dur + Del_Dur time units from the last arrival, i.e., in the interval (p_0 - Del_Dur, p_0].

Thus, at time p_0 Process_Message will become enabled and the N/L messages will be processed within time p_0 + N/L*P_M_Dur, since Deliver is disabled until that time.

Moreover, at time p_0 + N/L*P_M_Dur Process_Message will be disabled, since there are exactly N/L messages to process.

Thus, at time p_0 + N/L*P_M_Dur the buffer contains N/L messages and Deliver fires because the timeout has expired. Also, at time p_0 + N/L*P_M_Dur + Del_Dur Deliver ends and the length of the Output buffer will be equal to N/L (Exit clause of Deliver).

Therefore, the schedule will hold until time p_0 + N/L*P_M_Dur + Del_Dur.

To complete the proof it is necessary to give an inductive proof of lemma L1, which states that Process_Message is disabled every time Deliver fires.

Initially, the first time that Deliver fires, Process_Message is disabled. In fact, the first N/L End(New_Info) occur at time N_I_Dur (IV_{pm}). Transition Process_Message will finish processing these messages at time N_I_Dur + N/L*P_M_Dur, and at that time Deliver will become enabled.

Since no End(New_Info) can occur in (N_I_Dur, N_I_Dur + N/L*P_M_Dur + Del_Dur) (by IV_{pm}), then at time N_I_Dur + N/L*P_M_Dur transition Process_Message is disabled and Deliver fires.

Now suppose that when Deliver fires Process_Message is disabled; it is necessary to prove that Process_Message is again disabled the next time Deliver fires.

Let q_0 be the time when Deliver starts; by hypothesis at time q_0 Process_Message is disabled. As a consequence the messages in Packet at time q_0 have been received in the interval (q_0 - Del_Dur - N/L*P_M_Dur, q_0 - N/L*P_M_Dur] (Sc_{pm}).

Thus, by IV_{pm} the next N/L messages will arrive in the interval (q_0, q_0 + Del_Dur]. Furthermore, the timeout for Deliver will expire at time q_0 + N/L*P_M_Dur + Del_Dur. Therefore, Deliver cannot fire before that time unless the buffer is full.

At time q_0 + Del_Dur Process_Message will become enabled, and it will fire until either all messages have been processed or the buffer becomes full. At time q_0 + Del_Dur + N/L*P_M_Dur the N/L messages that arrived in the interval (q_0, q_0 + Del_Dur] will be processed and since no new message can arrive before q_0 + Del_Dur + N/L*P_M_Dur at that time Process_Message will be disabled. Similarly, at that time Deliver will be enabled and thus will fire.

This completes the proof of lemma L1 and thus the proof of Sc_{pm}.

6 Conclusions and Future Directions

In this paper the environment and critical requirements clauses, which were only briefly sketched in previous papers, were presented in detail. The intra-level proof obligations were also presented and an example proof was demonstrated.

All of the proofs for the CCITT specification have been completed. In addition, the proofs of five different schedules that can be guaranteed by using different further assumptions clauses have also been completed. The proofs of these schedules did not require any new or changed invariants.

Future work will concentrate on defining the necessary inter-level proof obligations for ASTRAL.

References

[ACD 90] Alur, R., C. Courcoubetis and D. Dill, "Model-Checking for Realtime Systems," *5th IEEE LICS 90*, IEEE, pp. 414-425, 1990.

[CHS 90] Chang, C., H. Huang and C. Song, "An Approach to Verifying Concurrency Behavior of Realtime Systems Based On Time Petri Net and Temporal Logic," *InfoJapan 90*, IPSJ, pp. 307-314, 1990.

[CKM 92] Coen-Porisini, A., R. Kemmerer and D. Mandrioli, "Formal Verification of Realtime Systems in ASTRAL", Report no. TRCS 92-22, Department of Computer Science, University of California, Santa Barbara, California, September 1992.

[FMM 91] Felder, M., D. Mandrioli and A. Morzenti, "Proving Properties of Realtime Systems through Logical Specifications and Petri Net Models," Tech. Rept. 91-72, Dip. di Elettronica-Politecnico di Milano, December 1991.

[GF 91] Gabrielian, A. and M. Franklin, "Multilevel Specification of Realtime Systems," *CACM 34*, 5, pp. 51-60, May 1991.

[GK 91a] Ghezzi, C. and R. Kemmerer, "ASTRAL: An Assertion Language for Specifying Realtime Systems," *Proceedings of the Third European Software Engineering Conference*, Milano, Italy, pp. 122-146, October 1991.

[GK 91b] Ghezzi, C. and R. Kemmerer, "Executing Formal Specifications: the ASTRAL to TRIO Translation Approach,"*Proceedings of TAV4: the Symposium on Testing, Analysis, and Verification*, Victoria, B.C., Canada, pp. 112-119, October 1991.

[Ost 89] Ostroff, J., *Temporal Logic For Realtime Systems*, Research Studies Press LTD., Taunton, Somerset, England , Advanced Software Development Series, 1, 1989.

[Pnu 77] Pnueli, A., "The Temporal Logic of Programs," *Proceedings of the 18th Annual Symposium on Foundations of Computer Science*, pp. 46-57, 1977.

[Suz 90] Suzuki, I., "Formal Analysis of Alternating Bit Protocol by Temporal Petri Nets," *IEEE-TSE 16*, 11, pp. 1273-1281, November 1990.

[Zav 87] Zave, P., PAISLey User Documentation Volume 3: Case Studies, Computer Technology Research Laboratory Report, AT&T Bell Laboratories, Murray Hill, New Jersey, 1987.

Assertion-based debugging of imperative programs by abstract interpretation

François Bourdoncle

DIGITAL Paris Research Laboratory
85, avenue Victor Hugo
92500 Rueil-Malmaison — France
Tel: +33 (1) 47 14 28 22

Centre de Mathématiques Appliquées
Ecole des Mines de Paris, BP 207
06560 Sophia-Antipolis Cedex
France

bourdoncle@prl.dec.com

Abstract. Abstract interpretation is a formal method that enables the static determination (i.e. at compile-time) of the dynamic properties (i.e. at run-time) of programs. So far, this method has mainly been used to build sophisticated, optimizing compilers. In this paper, we show how abstract interpretation techniques can be used to perform, prior to their execution, a *static* and *automatic* debugging of imperative programs. This novel approach, which we call *abstract debugging*, lets programmers use assertions to express *invariance properties* as well as *inevitable properties* of programs, such as termination. We show how such assertions can be used to find the origin of bugs, rather than their occurrences, and determine *necessary conditions of program correctness*, that is, necessary conditions for programs to be bug-free and correct with respect to the programmer's assertions. We also show that assertions can be used to restrict the control-flow of a program and examine its behavior along specific execution paths and find necessary conditions for the program to reach a particular point in a given state. Finally, we present the *Syntox* system that enables the abstract debugging of *Pascal* programs by the determination of the range of scalar variables, and discuss implementation, algorithmic and complexity issues.

1 Introduction

Since most, if not all, programmers are unable to write bug-free programs, debugging has always been an important part of software engineering. The most common approach for debugging a program is to run this program on a well chosen set of examples and check that each run is bug-free, that is, that the program "behaves as expected". However, this approach has several severe shortcomings.

For instance, even with an extensive and carefully chosen set of examples, the method offers absolutely no guaranty that every part of the program's code has been tested under all possible conditions, which is unacceptable for mission-critical systems. Moreover, it is sometimes very difficult, with "post-mortem" debuggers such as *adb* or *dbx*, to find the *origin* of a bug just by looking at the current memory state right after the bug has occured.

Methods have been proposed to help programmers at this stage by allowing the reverse execution of programs, but these methods require that every assignment encountered during the execution of the program be memorized, which makes them only applicable to functional programs with few side-effects [21]. It would thus be desirable to have a framework allowing the *static*, *formal* and *automatic* debugging of programs. Even though this might seem impossible at first glance, since the general problem of finding all the bugs in a program is undecidable, we introduce in this paper an assertion-based framework that enables the static and automatic discovery of certain categories of bugs.

This framework is based on abstract interpretation, which is a formal method, pioneered by Patrick and Radhia Cousot [7, 10, 12], that enables the static and automatic determination of *safe* and *approximate* run-time properties of programs. So far, abstract interpretation has mainly been used in compilers to optimize, vectorize, determine the lifetime of dynamically allocated data structures (compile-time garbage collection), etc. The emphasis has thus been put on the efficient determination of general properties of correct executions of programs rather than on the determination of correctness conditions, and abstract interpretation has always been considered as a batch, optimization-oriented method, that should not be made accessible to the programmer.

In this paper, we propose a method where the programmer is allowed to insert assertions in the source-code of the program being debugged, and where violations of these assertions are treated as run-time errors. Two kinds of assertions can be used. *Invariant assertions* are properties which must *always hold* at a given control point, and are similar to the classical `assert` statement in *C* programs. *Intermittent assertions* are properties which must *eventually hold* at a given control point. Differently stated, intermittent assertions are *inevitable properties* of programs, that is, properties such that every execution of the program inevitably leads to the specified control point with a memory state satisfying the intermittent property.

For instance, the *invariant* assertion *false* can be used to specify that a particular control point *should not* be reached, whereas the intermittent assertion *true* can be used to specify that a particular control point *should* be reached. In particular, the termination of a program can be specified by inserting the intermittent assertion *true* at the end of the program. Invariant and intermittent assertions can be freely mixed, which gives the programmer a great flexibility to express correctness conditions of a program and test its behavior along certain execution paths.

This paper is organized as follows. In section 2, we give several examples of the categories of bugs that can be automatically discovered by abstract debugging and describe how a programmer can interact with an abstract debugger to locate these bugs. Then, in section 3 we give an intuitive presentation of the basic ideas and techniques of abstract debugging, and explain why and how they can be used to debug programs. Finally, in section 4, we present the prototype *Syntox* system that enables the abstract debugging of *Pascal* programs without procedure parameters by the determination of the range of scalar variables. We discuss implementation, algorithmic and complexity issues, show that even very simple properties such as the range of variables enable the determination of non-trivial bugs, and show that this system can be used to safely suppress most array bound checks during the execution of *Pascal* programs.

2 Examples

In this section, we exemplify the concept of abstract debugging on a few erroneous programs. A very common programming error consists in using out-of-bounds array indices in loops. For instance, the "For" program of figure 1 will obviously exit on a run-time error when accessing T[0], unless $n < 0$ at point ①. Moreover, if the index i ranges from 1 to n instead of 0 to n, then the program will abort when accessing T[101] unless $n \leq 100$ at point ①. Similarly, program "While" will loop unless b is *false* at point ①, and program "Fact" will loop unless $x \geq 0$ at point ①.

It might seem quite difficult to discover these bugs automatically. However, an abstract debugger such a *Syntox*, described in section 4, will automatically discover and report the above necessary conditions of correctness. A compiler could use these conditions to issue a warning or generate a call to a specific error handler to do some clean-up and exit safely, or else could enter a special debugging mode to do a step-by-step execution of the program until the bug actually occurs.

The interesting fact about abstract debugging is that it predicts bugs *before* they actually happen, which permits a safe handling of these bugs. Further more, an abstract debugger always attempts to find the *origin* of bugs, rather than their occurrences, and *back-propagates* necessary conditions of correctness as far as possible in order to minimize the amount of information delivered to the programmer. Consequently, this feature makes abstract debugging much more useful than traditional methods and global flow analyzers such as *Lint* for instance, which is well known for the large number of warnings it generates.

For example, it is much more interesting to know that variable n of program "For" must be lower than 100 at point ① than to know that i must be less than 100 at point ② since the former test can be done once and for all after n has been read, whereas the latter must be done for every access to T. Moreover, if $n > 100$ at point ①, then it is *certain* that the program will either loop or exit on a run-time error in the future.

As we shall see in the next section, abstract debugging is a combination of *forward* and *backward* analyses of programs. Forward analyses mimic the forward (i.e. regular) execution of programs, whereas backward analyses mimic the *reverse* execution of programs and are responsible for the "discovery" and the "factorization" of the correctness conditions of programs.

As an example, consider program "BackwardAnalysis" of figure 1. Starting from the beginning of the program, a forward analysis will find 1) that $j \leq 3$ at point ③ and that unless $j \geq -1$, a run-time error will occur when reading $T[j+2]$, and 2) that $j \geq 4$ at point ④ and that unless $j \leq 100$, a run-time error will occur when reading $T[j]$. A forward analysis thus determines potential occurrences of bugs in a program. However, a backward analysis of the same program will successively show that in order for the program not to abort on a run-time error, the following properties must hold: $j \in [4, 100]$ at point ④, $j \in [-1, 3]$ at point ③, $j \in [-1, 100]$ at point ②, and finally $i \in [-1, 49]$ at point ①.

This last information can then be combined with the forward data flow, which shows that the post-condition $i \in \mathbf{Z}$ of the "read" procedure call does not imply the pre-condition $i \in [-1, 49]$ determined by the backward analysis. Hence, a warning can be issued to inform the programmer that if $i \notin [-1, 49]$ at point ①, then his program

```
program While;
var i : integer;
    b : boolean;
begin
    i := 0; read(b);  ①
    while b and (i ≤ 100) do
     ② i := i − 1
end.
```

```
program For;
var i, n : integer;
    T : array [1..100] of integer;
begin
    read(n);  ①
    for i := 0 to n do
     ② read(T[i])
end.
```

```
program Intermittent;
var i : integer;
begin
    read(i);  ①
    while (i ≤ 100) do
     ② i := i + 1  ③
 ④
end.
```

```
program Select;
    var n, s : integer;
    function Select(n : integer) : integer;
    begin
        if (n > 10) then
            Select := Select(n + 1)
        else if (n > −10) then
            Select := Select(n − 1)
        else if (n = −10) then
         ③ Select := 1
        else
            Select := −1
        end;
    begin
        read(n);  ①
        s := Select(n);
        writeln(s);  ②
    end.
```

```
program Shuttle;
    label 1;
    const N=100;
    var i, j, tmp : integer;
        T : array [1..N] of integer;
begin
    for i := 1 to N − 1 do
    begin
        for j := i downto 1 do
            if (T[j] > T[j+1]) then begin
                tmp := T[j];
                T[j] := T[j + 1];
                T[j + 1] := tmp
            end else
                goto 1;
    1:
    end
end.
```

```
program Fact;
    var x, y : integer;
    function F(n : integer) : integer;
    begin
        if (n = 0) then
            F := 1
        else F := n * F(n − 1)
    end;
begin
    read(x);  ① y := F(x)  ②
end.
```

```
program BackwardAnalysis;
    var i, j : integer;
        T : array [1..100] of integer;
begin
    read(i, b);  ① j := 2 * i + 1;
 ② if (j <= 3) then
     ③ read(T[j + 2])
    else
     ④ read(T[j])
 ⑤
end.
```

Figure 1: Examples

will *certainly* fail later on. Hence the *origin* of the bugs, i.e. the fact that the program does not test variable i after reading it, has been found, and a necessary condition of correctness, which is also sufficient in this particular case, has thus been discovered. Also, note that a further forward analysis would show that $j \in [4,99]$ holds at point ④ for any correct execution of this program, which refines the property $j \in [4,100]$ determined by the backward analysis.

As stated in the introduction, an important feature of abstract debugging is that programmers can freely insert *invariant assertions* and *intermittent assertions* in their programs to either statically check that important invariance properties are satisfied or check under which conditions a program eventually reaches a control point while satisfying a given property.

Intermittent assertions allow for a very powerful form of debugging. As an example, if the intermittent assertion $i = 10$ is inserted at point ② of program "Intermittent" of figure 1, then *Syntox* shows that a necessary condition for the program to *eventually* reach control point ② with $i = 10$ is that $i \leq 10$ at point ①.

The way intermittent assertions are handled *bottom-up* is easy to understand. In this particular case, an abstract debugger would start from the set $\{\langle ②, 10\rangle\}$ representing the program state $i = 10$ at point ②, and compute all the possible ancestors, namely $\langle ①, 10\rangle$, $\langle ③, 9\rangle$, $\langle ①, 9\rangle$, $\langle ③, 8\rangle$, $\langle ①, 8\rangle \ldots$, adding them one by one to the set of "correct states".

It is thus possible to determine the set of program states (and, in particular, of input states) from which a program eventually reaches a given control point, by simply inserting the intermittent assertion *true*, representing all the possible states, at this point. So for instance, if the intermittent assertion *true* is inserted at point ② of program "Select" of figure 1, *Syntox* shows that a necessary condition for the program to terminate is that $n \leq 10$ at point ①. Differently stated, if $n > 10$, then the program will certainly loop or exit on a run-time error.

Further more, if the invariant assertion *false* is inserted at point ③, *Syntox* shows that $n < -10$ at point ① is a necessary condition for the program to terminate without control ever reaching point ③. And finally, if the intermittent assertion $s = 1$ is inserted at point ②, *Syntox* shows that a necessary condition for this assertion to eventually hold is that $n \in [-10, 10]$ at point ①.

Invariant assertions can therefore be used to restrict the control flow and examine the behavior of a program along specific execution paths, and contrary to intermittent assertions, invariant assertions are handled *top-down*, that is, states which violate the invariants assertions, as well as all their ancestors, are removed, rather than added, from the set of correct states.

3 Abstract debugging

As stated in the introduction, abstract interpretation aims at computing safe approximations of *flow-insensitive* run-time properties of programs, that is, properties which hold at a given control point independently of the path followed to reach it. These properties, which are not limited to boolean properties, can be for instance the range or congruence properties [15] of integer variables, or relational properties such as linear inequalities of the form $i \leq 2 * j + 1$ between the variables of a program.

The method is based on a characterization of program properties as *fixed points* of monotonic functions over complete lattices. For instance, if τ is a *predicate transformer* describing the operational semantics of a program, then for every program property ψ, $\tau(\psi)$ is a property characterizing the set of states reached after one program step executed from states satisfying ψ, and the *program invariant*, which characterizes the set of descendants of a set of input states satisfying a property ψ_0 is known to be the *least fixed point*, with respect to implication, of the function:

$$\psi \longmapsto \psi_0 \vee \tau(\psi)$$

or, equivalently, the least solution of the equation:

$$\psi = \psi_0 \vee \tau(\psi)$$

This equation simply states that program states reached during executions of the program started from an input state satisfying ψ_0 are either input states satisfying ψ_0 or descendants of other reachable states.

The previous equation reflects the forward execution of the program. However, forward execution is not sufficient for the purpose of abstract debugging. To see why, let us consider an *invariant assertion* Π_a and an *intermittent assertion* Π_e that one wishes to prove about the program. Two properties are of interest:

- The property **always**(Π_a) which characterizes the set of states whose descendants satisfy Π_a.
- The property **eventually**(Π_e) which characterizes the set of states for which there exists at least one descendant satisfying Π_e.

For instance, if there are input states which do not satisfy **always**(Π_a) or, worse, if no input state satisfy **always**(Π_a), then it is sure that the program is not correct with respect to Π_a, that is, every execution starting from an input state which does not satisfy **always**(Π_a) will certainly lead to a state which does not satisfy Π_a.

Similarly, if there are input states which do not satisfy **eventually**(Π_e), then every execution starting from an input state which does not satisfy **eventually**(Π_e) will never reach a state satisfying Π_e.

So for instance, let Π_{out} and Π_{err} respectively characterize the sets of output states and the set of error states, and let $\overline{\Pi}$ denote the negation of property Π. Then **eventually**(Π_{out}) characterizes the set of states for which the program terminates, **eventually**(Π_{err}) characterizes the set of states leading to a run-time error, **always**$(\overline{\Pi_{out}})$ characterizes the set of states which either cause the program to loop or to exit on a run-time error, and **always**$(\overline{\Pi_{err}})$ characterizes the set of states which do not lead to a run-time error.

It can be shown [12] that if the program is deterministic, as it is the case for imperative languages, then **always**(Π_a) is the *greatest* solution (w.r.t. implication) of the equation:

$$\psi = \Pi_a \wedge \tau^{-1}(\psi)$$

and **eventually**(Π_e) is the *least* solution of the equation:

$$\psi = \Pi_e \vee \tau^{-1}(\psi)$$

where τ^{-1} is the predicate transformer describing the *backward semantics* of the program, that is, if ψ is a program property, then $\tau^{-1}(\psi)$ is the property which characterizes the set of direct *ancestors* of the states satisfying ψ. Note that, for technical reasons, we make the assumption that output states are fixed points of the transition relation defining the operational semantics of the program. We can see that the two properties of interest are defined in terms of the *backward* semantics of the program. The abstract debugging of a program can then be performed as follows.

a) Compute the *program invariant* **I** which represents the set of program states that can be reached during program executions which are correct with respect to the programmer's specifications Π_a and Π_e (see below).

b) Signal to the programmer every *input* state which does not satisfy **I** and every state satisfying **I** whose direct descendant does *not* satisfy **I**.

Step *b* thus determines a minimum set of "frontier" states that certainly lead to an incorrect execution of the program. These states are produced by the forward data flow but their descendants are not part of the backward flow. As illustrated in section 2, frontier states typically correspond to "read" statements or to entry points of loops. Hence, step *b* determines, as expected, the *origin* of bugs, rather than their occurrences.

As shown with program "BackwardAnalysis" in section 2, the program invariant **I** can be computed as the *limit* of the decreasing chain $(\mathrm{I}_k)_{k\geq 0}$ (w.r.t. implication) defined by $\mathrm{I}_0 = \mathit{true}$ and iteratively computed by applying the following steps in sequence:

1) Compute the characterization I_{k+1} of the set of descendants of input states satisfying I_k as the *least* solution of the forward equation:

$$\psi = \mathrm{I}_k \wedge (\psi_0 \vee \tau(\psi))$$

2) Compute the characterization I_{k+2} of the set of states satisfying I_{k+1} whose descendants satisfy Π_a as the *greatest* solution of the backward equation:

$$\psi = \mathrm{I}_{k+1} \wedge (\Pi_a \wedge \tau^{-1}(\psi))$$

3) Compute the characterization I_{k+3} of the set of states satisfying I_{k+2} for which there exists at least one descendant satisfying Π_e as the *least* solution of the backward equation:

$$\psi = \mathrm{I}_{k+2} \wedge (\Pi_e \vee \tau^{-1}(\psi))$$

Note that if the programmer only specifies one of the two assertions Π_a or Π_e, then only one of the two steps 2 or 3 has to be applied. Also, note that in practice, it is often sufficient to apply steps 1-2-3-1, although, in general, the chain $(\mathrm{I}_k)_{k\geq 0}$ can be infinitely strictly decreasing, i.e. $I_0 \Leftarrow I_1 \Leftarrow I_2 \cdots$, since each step can refine the previous one. For instance, if a backward propagation "removes" several erroneous input states, then the next forward propagation will eliminate the descendants of these input states, etc.

For example, if the *intermittent* assertion $y \leq 0$ is inserted at point ② of program "Fact", to determine if it is possible for the program to terminate with $y \leq 0$, *Syntox* shows after steps 1-3-1 that a necessary condition for this property to hold is that $x \geq 1$ at point ①. But if step 3 is applied once more, then *Syntox* shows that no correct program execution can satisfy this property. Therefore, it is proven that the *invariant* assertion $y \geq 1$ holds at point ②, that is, if control ever reaches point ②, then $y \geq 1$.

So far, we have assumed that programs are deterministic, but most programs are not deterministic. For instance, programs with "read" statements or logic programs are not deterministic, and program states can have several descendants. However, it can be shown that the above method remains valid, that is, that the condition stating that frontier states are incorrect is still a *necessary* condition of correctness, but is not sufficient in general.

For instance, if the statement "i := i + 1" of program "Intermittent" is replaced by "read(i)" then the conditions $i \leq 200$ at points ① and ③ and the condition $i = 200$ at point ④ are necessary conditions for property $i = 200$ to *eventually* hold at the end of the program, but these conditions are not sufficient, since the program might loop forever if the values read for variable i are always less than 100.

Of course, the method we have described is interesting from a mathematical point of view, but is not directly implementable, since fixed points over infinite domains are not computable in general. This is why abstract interpretation defines standard methods [3, 4, 5, 6, 7, 10, 11, 12] for *finitely* and *iteratively* computing *safe approximations* of **I**. These approximate invariants $\mathbf{I}^\#$ describe true properties about the run-time behavior of the program, that is $\mathbf{I} \Rightarrow \mathbf{I}^\#$, but are not necessarily optimal.

Note that if the approximation of the program invariant **I** is necessary for the approach to be tractable, this approximation implies that the correctness conditions determined by an abstract debugger are *necessary* but not always sufficient, even for deterministic programs. For example, if a necessary and sufficient condition of correctness is that an integer variable x be such that $x \in \{1,3,5\}$, and the interval lattice is used to represent approximate properties, then $x \in [1,5]$ is only a necessary condition for the program to be correct.

4 The Syntox system

The *Syntox* system is a prototype interprocedural abstract debugger that implements the ideas of section 3 for a subset of *Pascal*. This debugger can be used to find bugs that are related to the range of scalar variables, such as array indexing, range sub-types, etc. The interval lattice used to represent program properties is thus non-relational, but we have shown [4] that any relational lattice can be chosen, and that the results can be arbitrarily precise, even in the presence of aliasing, local procedures passed as parameters, non-local gotos and exceptions (which do not exist in *Pascal*).

Even though the interval lattice is quite simple, we shall see in section 4.5 that it allows to determine non-trivial bugs and program properties.

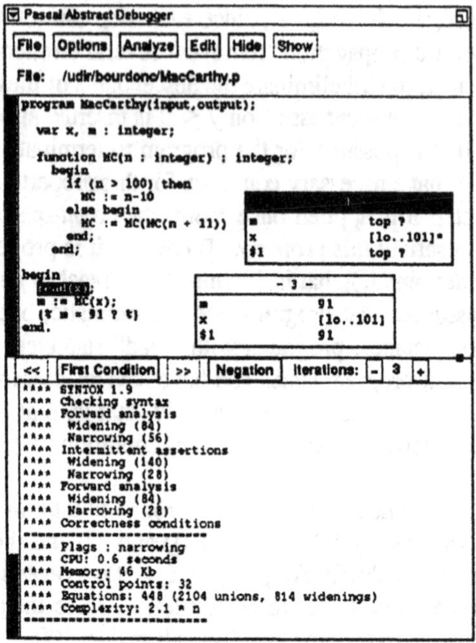

Figure 2: The *Syntox* system

4.1 Semantic issues

A problem that has to be solved to allow the abstract interpretation of *Pascal*-like languages is the *aliasing* induced by the formal reference parameters of procedures and functions, which create different variables with the same actual address. In order to increase the precision and reduce the complexity of the analysis, *Syntox* uses a non-standard, copy-in/copy-out semantics of first-order *Pascal* programs (i.e. programs without procedures passed as parameters) with jumps to local and non-local labels. This semantics, which is described in Bourdoncle [2, 4], determines the exact aliasing of programs, and is very well suited to abstract interpretation. We have shown that it is equivalent to the standard, stack-based semantics of *Pascal* [1]. We have also designed a version of this semantics for higher-order imperative languages that can be found in Bourdoncle [4], and shown that it is also equivalent to the standard semantics of the following classes of higher-order imperative programs with jumps to local and non-local labels:

- Second-order programs, i.e. programs where procedures which are passed as parameters to other procedures have non-procedural parameters only. Every *Wirth-Pascal* program [22] is second-order, but *ISO-Pascal* programs [18] can be higher-order.
- Higher-order programs with exceptions but without local procedures.

These classes can be shown to be sufficiently general to allow the abstract debugging of *C* programs with `setjmp` and `longjmp` statements (not considering the pointer-induced aliasing problems). As a matter of fact, exception handlers can be emulated by local procedure passed as parameter, and a `longjmp` statement is no more than a call to the exception handler which restores the `setjmp` context and branches to a local label of its enclosing procedure.

4.2 Language restrictions

Although the above theoretical results show that this could be done without any major problem, *Syntox* does not yet allow procedures to be passed as parameters to other procedures. Variant records and the "with" construct are not allowed in programs. Only the most standard *Pascal* library functions are predefined. Programs with pointers to heap-allocated objects are accepted, but are not always handled safely with respect to aliasing; other works on the abstract interpretation of heap-allocated data structures such as Deutsch [13, 14] could be used to handle pointer-induced aliasing. Records are accepted, but no information is given on their fields. This decision was made to simplify the design of the debugger, but records can be handled without much trouble. Jumps to local and non-local labels are fully supported. It should be emphasized that although this system is efficient, it is only a research prototype and a test-bed for new ideas.

4.3 Implementation

Syntox consists of approximately 20.000 lines of *C*, 4.000 of which implement a user-friendly interface under the *X Window* system, with its own integrated editor. Once a program has been analyzed, the user can click on any statement and the debugger pops up a window displaying run-time properties holding after the execution of the selected statement (fig. 2). If needed, the window can be dragged to a permanent position on the screen. When a procedure has reference parameters, *Syntox* gives a description of all the possible "alias sets" of this procedure [2], that is, all the subsets of variables having the same address in each procedure activation. Intermittent and invariant assertions can be inserted before every statement.

The analysis of a program is done in several steps. The first step consists in writing the *intraprocedural semantic equations* associated with each procedure of the program. The forward system of equations directly follows from the syntax of the program, and the backward equations are built by a trivial inversion of the forward system [4, 6].

The debugger then repeatedly performs a forward analysis and two backward analyses (one for each kind of assertion) and stops after a user-selectable number of passes. The default is to perform a forward analysis, two backward analyses and a final forward analysis, which is sufficient, in practice, to find most interesting bugs. However, the example given at the end of section 3 shows that this is not always the case, and it is sometimes necessary to continue the analysis one or several steps further.

Each analysis consists of a fixed point computation (either a least fixed point or a greatest fixed point) with a *widening* phase and a *narrowing* phase. Widening and narrowing [3, 4, 7, 10, 12] are standard *speed-up techniques* of abstract interpretation that can be used to compute safe approximations of fixed points when the height of the lattice of program properties is infinite or very large, as for the interval lattice. These techniques transform possibly infinite, but exact, iterative computations of least or greatest fixed points into finite, but approximated ones. For instance, the computation of a fixed point over the lattice of intervals, which can require up to 2^n iterations when integers are coded on n bits, is reduced to at most four iterations, which makes an entire analysis only sixteen times more complex than constant propagation.

Note that when the program has recursive procedures, the interprocedural call graph is dynamically unfolded during the analysis, and each procedure activation is "duplicated" according to the value of its *token* [2, 3, 4, 19] which consists of the static calling site of the activation and the set of all its aliases. For instance, the analysis of program "Fact" would create two instances of function "F".

The duplication of procedures according to their calling sites has proven to be very useful since calling sites tend to be associated to well-defined contexts and analysing the behavior of a procedure for each context separately leads to very precise results. Of course, when this duplication is too costly in terms of time and memory, it is possible to avoid it, at the cost of a loss of precision.

4.4 Algorithms and complexity

Two fixed point computation algorithms are used by *Syntox*. Each algorithm is based on a hierarchical decomposition of the control flow-graph into strongly connected components and sub-components, described in Bourdoncle [4, 5], which defines two chaotic iteration strategies [5, 8] as well as admissible sets of widening points, that is, control points were "generalizations" take place to avoid infinite computations when working with lattices of infinite height [6, 12].

The first algorithm is used for intraprocedural analysis, for which the control flow graph is known in advance, and attempts to "stabilize" sub-components each time a component is stabilized. When the graph is acyclic, the complexity of this algorithm is linear, and when the graph is strongly connected, its worst-case complexity is the product of the height h of the abstract lattice by the sum of the individual depths of the n nodes in the decomposition of the graph, which is always bounded by:

$$\frac{h \cdot n \cdot (n+1)}{2}$$

Note that the use of widening and narrowing techniques over the lattice of intervals leads to the same complexity with $h = 4 \cdot v$, where v is the number of variables of the program. The second algorithm is used for interprocedural analysis and is based on a depth-first visit of the (dynamically unfolded) interprocedural control flow graph. Its worst-case complexity for a program with n control points, c procedure calls, p procedures and l intraprocedural loops is at most:

$$h \cdot n \cdot (c+p+l) \quad = \quad \rho \cdot h \cdot n^2$$

where $\rho \leq 1$ is the sum $l/n + c/n$ of the densities of intraprocedural loops and procedure calls in the program, and of the inverse of the average size n/p of procedures. However, practice shows that this quadratic bound is rarely reached, except for programs which

```
program BinarySearch;
    type index = 1..100;
    var  n : index;  key : integer;
         T : array [index] of integer;
    function Find(key : integer) : boolean;
         var m, left, right : integer;
    begin
         left := 1;
         right := n;
         repeat
          ① m := (left + right) div 2;
             if  (key < T[m])  then
                   right := m − 1
             else
                   left := m + 1
         until (key = T[m]) or  (left > right);
         Find := (key = T[m])
    end;
begin
    read(n, key);
    writeln("Found  =  ", Find(key))
end.
```

```
program QuickSort;
    var  n : integer;
         T : array [1..100] of integer;
    procedure QSort(l, r : integer);
         var i, m, v, x : integer;
    begin
         if  l < r  then begin
              v := T[l]; m := l;
              for i := l + 1 to r do
                   if  T[i] < v  then
                   begin
                    ② m := m + 1; x := T[m];
                       T[m] := T[i]; T[i] := x
                   end;
              x := T[m]; T[m] := T[l]; T[l] := x;
              QSort(l, m − 1);
              QSort(m + 1, r)
         end
    end;
begin
    readln(n);  ① QSort(1, n);
end.
```

Figure 3: Examples

consist of tightly coupled mutually recursive procedures. The average complexity of interprocedural analyses of real-life imperative programs should thus be almost linear, since large programs are generally linear programs with local loops and relatively small groups of mutually recursive procedures.

4.5 Results

Apart from abstract debugging, another interesting use of *Syntox* is to prove that array accesses in a program are statically correct, so that a compiler need not generate the code to check that array indices are correct at run-time.

Classical methods used to perform compile-time array bound checking are always based on forward data-flow analyses [16, 17]. Indeed, it is not be obvious that backward propagation is interesting in this context. However, it is easy to see that every reference T[i] to the i-th element of an array T of n elements in a program is an implicit invariant assertion $i \in [1, n]$. Therefore, when the program is incorrect, the back-propagation of these assertions gathers the correctness conditions on a few program points and gives better results everywhere else.

For instance, *Syntox* automatically shows that every array access is statically correct in an implementation of HeapSort and that most accesses (i.e., all but one or two) are also correct in other implementations of various sorting algorithms. In particular, *Syntox* shows that if the conditions $n \leq 100$ at point ① and $m \leq 99$ at point ② are satisfied at run-time, then every array access in program "QuickSort" of figure 3 is guaranteed to

Program	Size	Memory	Time
BinarySearch	17	44 kB	0.5 sec
Fact	24	44 kB	0.5 sec
Select	61	64 kB	0.9 sec
Ackermann	72	99 kB	1.9 sec
QuickSort	92	98 kB	2.1 sec
HeapSort	96	108 kB	2.4 sec

Figure 4: Statistics

be correct. Without back-propagation, six tests instead of two must be done at run-time. Finally, if the main call to procedure "QSort" is replaced by the erroneous call "QSort(0, n)", *Syntox* shows that a necessary condition of correctness is that $n \leq 0$ at point ①.

Similarly, every array access is statically proven correct in program "Shuttle" of figure 1, which is taken from Markstein et al. [17], and in program "BinarySearch" of figure 3. Although this last program is fairly simple, the result is non-trivial since the test of the "repeat" loop does not make an explicit reference to the bounds 1 and 100.

It is important to remark that there is absolutely no magic behind this and the above results, and the properties $m, right, left \in [1..100]$ at point ① of program "BinarySearch" have been automatically inferred by the abstract debugger during the fixed point computation. These properties are thus the *results* of the fixed point computation, and definitely not "guessed" properties proven by a theorem prover. Also, remark that *Syntox* is not based on symbolic execution, since this method does not allow the automatic, i.e. non-interactive, determination of program invariants. The beauty of abstract interpretation is that program invariants are *synthesized* rather than simply proven [3].

The experimental comparison between the above programs compiled with and without run-time array bound checking shows a speed-up ranging from 30% to 40%.

Finally, note that the time and memory requirements for the abstract debugging of programs are reasonable. Figure 4 shows the size of differents examples (i.e. the total number of control points after having unfolded the interprocedural call graph), the allocated memory in kbytes, and the analysis time in seconds for a DEC 5000/200 Ultrix workstation. These results show that, in practice, the amount of time and memory required is almost linear in the size of the program, and therefore invalidate a common belief according to which static analysis of programs would be exponential.

5 Conclusions and future work

We have presented a new static, semantic-based approach to the debugging of programs that allows programmers to use invariant and intermittent assertions to statically and formally check the validity of a program, test its behavior along certain execution paths, and find the origin of bugs rather than their occurrences. We have shown that this method can be efficiently implemented with a worst-case quadratic complexity, and shown that non-trivial bugs can be automatically discovered even when the lattice of abstract properties is fairly simple. Finally, we have presented the prototype abstract debugger *Syntox* which can be used to debug a subset of first-order *Pascal* programs.

The techniques we have developed can be directly applied to most "safe" imperative languages such as *Modula-2*, safe subsets of *Modula-3* or *C++*, but they are also easily applicable to functional or logic programming languages.

Although we have not tried to debug large, real-life programs with *Syntox*, all experiments done to date indicate that the time and space complexity of abstract debugging lies somewhere between linear and quadratic, and that only intrinsically complex programs tend to be complex to analyze. We are therefore confident that this technique can be effectively applied to reasonably sized programs, but only experiments on the abstract debugging of real-life programs and languages will demonstrate the effectiveness of the approach.

Future work will be to implement abstract debugging in a real-world programming environment and give the programmer the ability to determine different categories of "standard" program properties (e.g. *nil* pointers, parity of integer variables, congruence relations [15], intervals, linear inequalities between variables [9], etc).

References

[1] Alfred V. Aho, Ravi Sethi and Jeffrey D. Ullman: "Compilers — Principles, Techniques and Tools", Addison-Wesley Publishing Company (1986)

[2] François Bourdoncle: "Interprocedural Abstract Interpretation of Block Structured Languages with Nested Procedures, Aliasing and Recursivity", *Proc. of the International Workshop PLILP'90*, Lecture Notes in Computer Science 456, Springer-Verlag (1990)

[3] François Bourdoncle: "Abstract Interpretation By Dynamic Partitioning", *Journal of Functional Programming*, Vol. 2, No. 4 (1992)

[4] François Bourdoncle: "Sémantiques des langages impératifs d'ordre supérieur et interprétation abstraite", *Ph. D. dissertation*, Ecole Polytechnique (1992)

[5] François Bourdoncle: "Efficient Chaotic Iteration Strategies with Widenings", *Proc. of the International Conf. on Formal Methods in Programming and their Applications*, Lecture Notes in Computer Science, Springer-Verlag (1993) *to appear*

[6] François Bourdoncle: "Abstract Debugging of Higher-Order Imperative Languages", *Proc. of SIGPLAN '93 Conference on Programming Language Design and Implementation* (1993)

[7] Patrick and Radhia Cousot: "Abstract Interpretation: a unified lattice model for static analysis of programs by construction or approximation of fixpoints", *Proc. of the 4th ACM Symp. on POPL* (1977) 238–252

[8] Patrick Cousot: "Asynchronous iterative methods for solving a fixpoint system of monotone equations", Research Report IMAG-RR-88, Université Scientifique et Médicale de Grenoble (1977)

[9] Patrick Cousot and Nicolas Halbwachs: "Automatic discovery of linear constraints among variables of a program", *Proc. of the 5th ACM Symp. on POPL* (1978) 84–97

[10] Patrick Cousot: "Méthodes itératives de construction et d'approximation de points fixes d'opérateurs monotones sur un treillis. Analyse sémantique de programmes", *Ph. D. dissertation*, Université Scientifique et Médicale de Grenoble (1978)

[11] Patrick and Radhia Cousot: "Static determination of dynamic properties of recursive procedures", *Formal Description of Programming Concepts*, North Holland Publishing Company (1978) 237–277

[12] Patrick Cousot: "Semantic foundations of program analysis", in Muchnick and Jones Eds., *Program Flow Analysis, Theory and Applications*, Prentice-Hall (1981) 303–343

[13] Alain Deutsch: "On determining lifetime and aliasing of dynamically allocated data in higher-order functional specifications", *Proc. of the 17th ACM Symp. on POPL* (1990)

[14] Alain Deutsch: "A Storeless Model of Aliasing and its Abstractions using Finite Representations of Right-Regular Equivalence Relations", *Proc. of the IEEE'92 International Conference on Computer Languages*, IEEE Press (1992)

[15] Philippe Granger: "Static analysis of arithmetical congruences", *International Journal of Computer Mathematics* (1989) 165–190

[16] Rajiv Gupta: "A Fresh Look at Optimizing Array Bound Checking", *Proc. of SIGPLAN '90 Conf. on Programming Language Design and Implementation* (1990) 272–282

[17] Victoria Markstein, John Cocke and Peter Markstein: "Optimization of Range Checking", *Proc. of the SIGPLAN'82 Symp. on Compiler Construction* (1982) 114–119

[18] ISO/IEC 7185: "Information technology — Programming languages — Pascal", Revised 1983, Second edition (1990)

[19] Micha Sharir and Amir Pnueli: "Two Approaches to Interprocedural Data Flow Analysis" in Muchnick and Jones Eds., *Program Flow Analysis, Theory and Applications*, Prentice-Hall (1981) 189–233

[20] R.E. Tarjan: "Depth-first search and linear graph algorithms", *SIAM J. Comput.*, 1 (1972) 146–160

[21] Andrew P. Tolmach and Andrew W. Appel: "Debugging Standard ML Without Reverse Engineering", *Proc. 1990 ACM Conf. on Lisp and Functional Programming*, ACM Press (1990) 1–12

[22] Niklaus Wirth and Kathleen Jensen: "Pascal user manual and report" (Second Ed.), Springer-Verlag (1978)

Springer-Verlag and the Environment

Lecture Notes in Computer Science

For information about Vols. 1–639
please contact your bookseller or Springer-Verlag

Vol. 640: C. Sledge (Ed.), Software Engineering Education. Proceedings, 1992. X, 451 pages. 1992.

Vol. 641: U. Kastens, P. Pfahler (Eds.), Compiler Construction. Proceedings, 1992. VIII, 320 pages. 1992.

Vol. 642: K. P. Jantke (Ed.), Analogical and Inductive Inference. Proceedings, 1992. VIII, 319 pages. 1992. (Subseries LNAI).

Vol. 643: A. Habel, Hyperedge Replacement: Grammars and Languages. X, 214 pages. 1992.

Vol. 644: A. Apostolico, M. Crochemore, Z. Galil, U. Manber (Eds.), Combinatorial Pattern Matching. Proceedings, 1992. X, 287 pages. 1992.

Vol. 645: G. Pernul, A M. Tjoa (Eds.), Entity-Relationship Approach – ER '92. Proceedings, 1992. XI, 439 pages, 1992.

Vol. 646: J. Biskup, R. Hull (Eds.), Database Theory – ICDT '92. Proceedings, 1992. IX, 449 pages. 1992.

Vol. 647: A. Segall, S. Zaks (Eds.), Distributed Algorithms. X, 380 pages. 1992.

Vol. 648: Y. Deswarte, G. Eizenberg, J.-J. Quisquater (Eds.), Computer Security – ESORICS 92. Proceedings. XI, 451 pages. 1992.

Vol. 649: A. Pettorossi (Ed.), Meta-Programming in Logic. Proceedings, 1992. XII, 535 pages. 1992.

Vol. 650: T. Ibaraki, Y. Inagaki, K. Iwama, T. Nishizeki, M. Yamashita (Eds.), Algorithms and Computation. Proceedings, 1992. XI, 510 pages. 1992.

Vol. 651: R. Koymans, Specifying Message Passing and Time-Critical Systems with Temporal Logic. IX, 164 pages. 1992.

Vol. 652: R. Shyamasundar (Ed.), Foundations of Software Technology and Theoretical Computer Science. Proceedings, 1992. XIII, 405 pages. 1992.

Vol. 653: A. Bensoussan, J.-P. Verjus (Eds.), Future Tendencies in Computer Science, Control and Applied Mathematics. Proceedings, 1992. XV, 371 pages. 1992.

Vol. 654: A. Nakamura, M. Nivat, A. Saoudi, P. S. P. Wang, K. Inoue (Eds.), Parallel Image Analysis. Proceedings, 1992. VIII, 312 pages. 1992.

Vol. 655: M. Bidoit, C. Choppy (Eds.), Recent Trends in Data Type Specification. X, 344 pages. 1993.

Vol. 656: M. Rusinowitch, J. L. Rémy (Eds.), Conditional Term Rewriting Systems. Proceedings, 1992. XI, 501 pages. 1993.

Vol. 657: E. W. Mayr (Ed.), Graph-Theoretic Concepts in Computer Science. Proceedings, 1992. VIII, 350 pages. 1993.

Vol. 658: R. A. Rueppel (Ed.), Advances in Cryptology – EUROCRYPT '92. Proceedings, 1992. X, 493 pages. 1993.

Vol. 659: G. Brewka, K. P. Jantke, P. H. Schmitt (Eds.), Nonmonotonic and Inductive Logic. Proceedings, 1991. VIII, 332 pages. 1993. (Subseries LNAI).

Vol. 660: E. Lamma, P. Mello (Eds.), Extensions of Logic Programming. Proceedings, 1992. VIII, 417 pages. 1993. (Subseries LNAI).

Vol. 661: S. J. Hanson, W. Remmele, R. L. Rivest (Eds.), Machine Learning: From Theory to Applications. VIII, 271 pages. 1993.

Vol. 662: M. Nitzberg, D. Mumford, T. Shiota, Filtering, Segmentation and Depth. VIII, 143 pages. 1993.

Vol. 663: G. v. Bochmann, D. K. Probst (Eds.), Computer Aided Verification. Proceedings, 1992. IX, 422 pages. 1993.

Vol. 664: M. Bezem, J. F. Groote (Eds.), Typed Lambda Calculi and Applications. Proceedings, 1993. VIII, 433 pages. 1993.

Vol. 665: P. Enjalbert, A. Finkel, K. W. Wagner (Eds.), STACS 93. Proceedings, 1993. XIV, 724 pages. 1993.

Vol. 666: J. W. de Bakker, W.-P. de Roever, G. Rozenberg (Eds.), Semantics: Foundations and Applications. Proceedings, 1992. VIII, 659 pages. 1993.

Vol. 667: P. B. Brazdil (Ed.), Machine Learning: ECML – 93. Proceedings, 1993. XII, 471 pages. 1993. (Subseries LNAI).

Vol. 668: M.-C. Gaudel, J.-P. Jouannaud (Eds.), TAPSOFT '93: Theory and Practice of Software Development. Proceedings, 1993. XII, 762 pages. 1993.

Vol. 669: R. S. Bird, C. C. Morgan, J. C. P. Woodcock (Eds.), Mathematics of Program Construction. Proceedings, 1992. VIII, 378 pages. 1993.

Vol. 670: J. C. P. Woodcock, P. G. Larsen (Eds.), FME '93: Industrial-Strength Formal Methods. Proceedings, 1993. XI, 689 pages. 1993.

Vol. 671: H. J. Ohlbach (Ed.), GWAI-92: Advances in Artificial Intelligence. Proceedings, 1992. XI, 397 pages. 1993. (Subseries LNAI).

Vol. 672: A. Barak, S. Guday, R. G. Wheeler, The MOSIX Distributed Operating System. X, 221 pages. 1993.

Vol. 673: G. Cohen, T. Mora, O. Moreno (Eds.), Applied Algebra, Algebraic Algorithms and Error-Correcting Codes. Proceedings, 1993. X, 355 pages 1993.

Vol. 674: G. Rozenberg (Ed.), Advances in Petri Nets 1993. VII, 457 pages. 1993.

Vol. 675: A. Mulkers, Live Data Structures in Logic Programs. VIII, 220 pages. 1993.

Vol. 676: Th. H. Reiss, Recognizing Planar Objects Using Invariant Image Features. X, 180 pages. 1993.

Vol. 677: H. Abdulrab, J.-P. Pécuchet (Eds.), Word Equations and Related Topics. Proceedings, 1991. VII, 214 pages. 1993.

Vol. 678: F. Meyer auf der Heide, B. Monien, A. L. Rosenberg (Eds.), Parallel Architectures and Their Efficient Use. Proceedings, 1992. XII, 227 pages. 1993.

Vol. 679: C. Fermüller, A. Leitsch, T. Tammet, N. Zamov, Resolution Methods for the Decision Problem. VIII, 205 pages. 1993. (Subseries LNAI).

Vol. 680: B. Hoffmann, B. Krieg-Brückner (Eds.), Program Development by Specification and Transformation. XV, 623 pages. 1993.

Vol. 681: H. Wansing, The Logic of Information Structures. IX, 163 pages. 1993. (Subseries LNAI).

Vol. 682: B. Bouchon-Meunier, L. Valverde, R. R. Yager (Eds.), IPMU '92 – Advanced Methods in Artificial Intelligence. Proceedings, 1992. IX, 367 pages. 1993.

Vol. 683: G.J. Milne, L. Pierre (Eds.), Correct Hardware Design and Verification Methods. Proceedings, 1993. VIII, 270 Pages. 1993.

Vol. 684: A. Apostolico, M. Crochemore, Z. Galil, U. Manber (Eds.), Combinatorial Pattern Matching. Proceedings, 1993. VIII, 265 pages. 1993.

Vol. 685: C. Rolland, F. Bodart, C. Cauvet (Eds.), Advanced Information Systems Engineering. Proceedings, 1993. XI, 650 pages. 1993.

Vol. 686: J. Mira, J. Cabestany, A. Prieto (Eds.), New Trends in Neural Computation. Proceedings, 1993. XVII, 746 pages. 1993.

Vol. 687: H. H. Barrett, A. F. Gmitro (Eds.), Information Processing in Medical Imaging. Proceedings, 1993. XVI, 567 pages. 1993.

Vol. 688: M. Gauthier (Ed.), Ada-Europe '93. Proceedings, 1993. VIII, 353 pages. 1993.

Vol. 689: J. Komorowski, Z. W. Ras (Eds.), Methodologies for Intelligent Systems. Proceedings, 1993. XI, 653 pages. 1993. (Subseries LNAI).

Vol. 690: C. Kirchner (Ed.), Rewriting Techniques and Applications. Proceedings, 1993. XI, 488 pages. 1993.

Vol. 691: M. Ajmone Marsan (Ed.), Application and Theory of Petri Nets 1993. Proceedings, 1993. IX, 591 pages. 1993.

Vol. 692: D. Abel, B.C. Ooi (Eds.), Advances in Spatial Databases. Proceedings, 1993. XIII, 529 pages. 1993.

Vol. 693: P. E. Lauer (Ed.), Functional Programming, Concurrency, Simulation and Automated Reasoning. Proceedings, 1991/1992. XI, 398 pages. 1993.

Vol. 694: A. Bode, M. Reeve, G. Wolf (Eds.), PARLE '93. Parallel Architectures and Languages Europe. Proceedings, 1993. XVII, 770 pages. 1993.

Vol. 695: E. P. Klement, W. Slany (Eds.), Fuzzy Logic in Artificial Intelligence. Proceedings, 1993. VIII, 192 pages. 1993. (Subseries LNAI).

Vol. 696: M. Worboys, A. F. Grundy (Eds.), Advances in Databases. Proceedings, 1993. X, 276 pages. 1993.

Vol. 697: C. Courcoubetis (Ed.), Computer Aided Verification. Proceedings, 1993. IX, 504 pages. 1993.

Vol. 698: A. Voronkov (Ed.), Logic Programming and Automated Reasoning. Proceedings, 1993. XIII, 386 pages. 1993. (Subseries LNAI).

Vol. 699: G. W. Mineau, B. Moulin, J. F. Sowa (Eds.), Conceptual Graphs for Knowledge Representation. Proceedings, 1993. IX, 451 pages. 1993. (Subseries LNAI).

Vol. 700: A. Lingas, R. Karlsson, S. Carlsson (Eds.), Automata, Languages and Programming. Proceedings, 1993. XII, 697 pages. 1993.

Vol. 701: P. Atzeni (Ed.), LOGIDATA+: Deductive Databases with Complex Objects. VIII, 273 pages. 1993.

Vol. 702: E. Börger, G. Jäger, H. Kleine Büning, S. Martini, M. M. Richter (Eds.), Computer Science Logic. Proceedings, 1992. VIII, 439 pages. 1993.

Vol. 703: M. de Berg, Ray Shooting, Depth Orders and Hidden Surface Removal. X, 201 pages. 1993.

Vol. 704: F. N. Paulisch, The Design of an Extendible Graph Editor. XV, 184 pages. 1993.

Vol. 705: H. Grünbacher, R. W. Hartenstein (Eds.), Field-Programmable Gate Arrays. Proceedings, 1992. VIII, 218 pages. 1993.

Vol. 706: H. D. Rombach, V. R. Basili, R. W. Selby (Eds.), Experimental Software Engineering Issues. Proceedings, 1992. XVIII, 261 pages. 1993.

Vol. 707: O. M. Nierstrasz (Ed.), ECOOP '93 – Object-Oriented Programming. Proceedings, 1993. XI, 531 pages. 1993.

Vol. 708: C. Laugier (Ed.), Geometric Reasoning for Perception and Action. Proceedings, 1991. VIII, 281 pages. 1993.

Vol. 709: F. Dehne, J.-R. Sack, N. Santoro, S. Whitesides (Eds.), Algorithms and Data Structures. Proceedings, 1993. XII, 634 pages. 1993.

Vol. 710: Z. Ésik (Ed.), Fundamentals of Computation Theory. Proceedings, 1993. IX, 471 pages. 1993.

Vol. 711: A. M. Borzyszkowski, S. Sokołowski (Eds.), Mathematical Foundations of Computer Science 1993. Proceedings, 1993. XIII, 782 pages. 1993.

Vol. 712: P. V. Rangan (Ed.), Network and Operating System Support for Digital Audio and Video. Proceedings, 1992. X, 416 pages. 1993.

Vol. 713: G. Gottlob, A. Leitsch, D. Mundici (Eds.), Computational Logic and Proof Theory. Proceedings, 1993. XI, 348 pages. 1993.

Vol. 714: M. Bruynooghe, J. Penjam (Eds.), Programming Language Implementation and Logic Programming. Proceedings, 1993. XI, 421 pages. 1993.

Vol. 715: E. Best (Ed.), CONCUR'93. Proceedings, 1993. IX, 541 pages. 1993.

Vol. 716: A. U. Frank, I. Campari (Eds.), Spatial Information Theory. Proceedings, 1993. XI, 478 pages. 1993.

Vol. 717: I. Sommerville, M. Paul (Eds.), Software Engineering – ESEC '93. Proceedings, 1993. XII, 516 pages. 1993.

Vol. 718: J. Seberry, Y. Zheng (Eds.), Advances in Cryptology – AUSCRYPT '92. Proceedings, 1992. XIII, 543 pages. 1993.